The Fiscal Revolution
in America

THE GRADUATE SCHOOL OF BUSINESS
UNIVERSITY OF CHICAGO

FIRST SERIES (1916–1938)
Materials for the Study of Business
Edited by DEAN LEON CARROLL MARSHALL and
DEAN WILLIAM HOMER SPENCER

SECOND SERIES (1938–1956)
Business and Economic Publications
Edited by DEAN WILLIAM HOMER SPENCER

THIRD SERIES (1959–   )
Studies in Business and Society
Edited by DEAN W. ALLEN WALLIS
and DEAN GEORGE P. SHULTZ

The Fiscal Revolution

in America

HERBERT STEIN

The University of Chicago Press

CHICAGO AND LONDON

LIBRARY OF CONGRESS CATALOG CARD NUMBER 69-14828

THE UNIVERSITY OF CHICAGO PRESS, CHICAGO 60637
THE UNIVERSITY OF CHICAGO PRESS, LTD., LONDON W.C.1

For my wife Mildred

Acknowledgments

Chapter 2 is reprinted with permission from *The Journal of Law and Economics* where it first appeared.

The following have granted permission to quote from their publications:

Alfred A. Knopf, Inc., for Marriner S. Eccles, *Beckoning Frontiers*

Doubleday & Company, Inc., and Wm. Heinemann Ltd., for Dwight D. Eisenhower, *The White House Years: Waging Peace 1956-1961*. Copyright © 1965 by Dwight D. Eisenhower

Harcourt, Brace & World, Inc., for J. M. Keynes, *A Treatise on Money;* J. M. Keynes, *The General Theory of Employment, Interest and Money;* J. M. Keynes, *The Economic Consequences of the Peace;* J. M. Keynes, *Essays in Persuasion;* and James MacGregor Burns, *Roosevelt: The Lion and the Fox*

Harper & Row, Publishers, Incorporated, for Theodore C. Sorensen, *Kennedy*

Harvard University Press, for Walter W. Heller, *New Dimensions of Political Economy*

Herbert Hoover Foundation, for Herbert C. Hoover, *The State Papers and other Public Writings of Herbert Hoover*

Houghton Mifflin Company, for John Morton Blum, *From the Morgenthau Diaries, vol. 1, Years of Crisis,* and Arthur M. Schlesinger, Jr., *A Thousand Days*

Macmillan & Co. Ltd., St. Martin's Press Inc., and The Macmillan Company of Canada Ltd., for Roy F. Harrod, *The Life of John Maynard Keynes*

Macmillan & Co. Ltd. and The Trustees of the late Lord Keynes, for J. M. Keynes, *The Means to Prosperity* and J. M. Keynes, *A Tract on Monetary Reform*

Simon & Schuster, Inc., for Harold L. Ickes, *The Secret Diary of Harold L. Ickes*

U. S. News & World Report for a copyrighted interview with George M. Humphrey published in the *U. S. News & World Report* of June 12, 1953

Contents

Foreword

I TAKE great pleasure in welcoming
this distinguished work to our series.

The subject developed by Herbert Stein has enormous implications for
the operations of national economies here and elsewhere. The management of
the Government's gross flows of expenditures and taxes, of the relations between these large sums, and of their interaction with monetary and other
variables is a critical element in economic policy. In studying the revolution
in thought and action on the issues involved, Dr. Stein has developed and
used a concept that is unique and powerful. His basic theme portrays current
views as the results of a long process of interaction among changes in economic analysis, the emerging factual circumstances of the economy, and the
political opportunities and constraints faced by successive Presidents. Thus,
theory plus factual developments plus politics equals revolution.

Success in this ambitious effort has demanded the high order of scholarship on display throughout the work. This professional competence is
matched by the lucidity of style and general skill in exposition for which
Dr. Stein has long been known.

Scholars and professionals should be able to draw on the ideas, insights,
and methods put forward by Dr. Stein in their own studies of fiscal and other
areas of public policy. As a fiscal dividend, so to speak, this book will provide
returns to those who, without any special interest in economic policy as such,
wish to understand better the general problems and processes of public policy.

The Graduate School of Business of The University of Chicago has always
considered the encouragement and nurture of research to be a fundamental
part of its mission and has long sponsored the publication of important works
of scholarship. More than half a century ago the School inaugurated a significant publications program. The series, *Materials for the Study of Business*,
was initiated in 1916 under the editorship of Dean Leon Carroll Marshall;

it was continued by Dean William Homer Spencer. Fifty titles were published; many became classics in their fields. In 1938 the series was renamed *Business and Economic Publications;* under the editorship of Dean Spencer, 13 titles were published. Also, in the two decades prior to 1948, the School published some 70 monographs under the general title *Studies in Business Administration.*

The current series, *Studies in Business and Society* (formerly *Studies in Business*), was initiated in 1959 under Dean W. Allen Wallis, who edited the first six volumes. Dr. Stein's work is the 14th in the series.

Dr. Herbert Stein holds his professional degree from the University of Chicago, and it is a pleasure and honor to continue the association through publication of a book that should be as influential as it is professional and profound.

GEORGE P. SHULTZ, Dean
October 15, 1968   Graduate School of Business
University of Chicago

Preface

T<small>HIS</small> book tells the story of a major change in national policy that occurred between the times of Herbert Hoover and Lyndon Johnson. It describes how the evolution of conditions, goals, and ideas influenced the responses of policy-makers to their problems and how the responses in turn influenced subsequent conditions, goals, and ideas. The particular policy which is the subject of this book—fiscal policy—is important for the prosperity and freedom of Americans. There has been incessant and well-publicized controversy about it during the four decades covered by this story. The main characters in the narrative are men about whom we know much and about whom we are curious to know more. But even if this were not true the story would deserve attention as an account of human minds in action.

I could not have written this book without the experience of twenty-two years as an economist with the Committee for Economic Development in Washington. This gave me an unusual opportunity to observe the making of fiscal policy in the government. It also permitted me to observe closely the development of the thinking of a group of intelligent and concerned national leaders, the businessmen who constitute the Committee for Economic Development. In 1965–66 I was able to spend a year at the Center for Advanced Study in the Behavioral Sciences, with the generous support of the CED and the center, and this book was begun there. I owe much to Dr. Ralph Tyler, who was then the director of the center, to his staff, and to the extraordinary group of social scientists who were there that year. I am also indebted to the Brookings Institution for its generosity with my time during the year 1967–68, when the book was finished.

I have been assisted by discussions of the subject of this book with Messrs. Arthur F. Burns, William M. Capron, Samuel M. Cohn, Edward F. Denison, Marriner S. Eccles, Kermit Gordon, James W. Knowles, David Lusher,

xiii

Woodlief Thomas, Lawrence Woodworth, and Ralph A. Young and with Mrs. Rachel Epstein. I received valuable suggestions from Messrs. Emile Despres, Walter S. Salant, Eli Shapiro, Allan Sproul, and Benjamin Stein, who read parts of the manuscript, and from Mr. Joseph A. Pechman and Mr. Norman Ture who read it all. Mrs. Anna J. Schwartz read the entire manuscript with great care and gave me the benefit of her close study of the economic history of the period. Dr. Lauchlin Currie permitted me to use his illuminating unpublished memoir of the New Deal days and Dr. Gabriel Hauge allowed me to quote an important letter from him to President Eisenhower. I have been helped by librarians at the Library of Congress, Stanford University, the Hoover Institution of War, Peace and Revolution, the Franklin D. Roosevelt Library at Hyde Park, the University of Chicago, Columbia University and The Brookings Institution. Mrs. Laura Hamilton typed the manuscript, more than once, beautifully. Mrs. Erna Tracy provided secretarial help. The index was prepared by Mr. Paul Courant.

To all of the foregoing I am grateful.

My main indebtedness and gratitude are to my wife, who served as research assistant, bibliographer, and copyreader and who read several drafts, constructively and appreciatively.

For errors and inadequacies I am solely responsible.

HERBERT STEIN

The Brookings Institution

December 10, 1968

The Fiscal Revolution
in America

1

Introduction

HERBERT HOOVER recommended a big tax *increase* in 1931 when unemployment was extremely high and a large budget deficit was in prospect.

John F. Kennedy recommended a big tax *reduction* in 1962 when unemployment was again a problem, although a much less serious one, and a large budget deficit was again in prospect.

The contrast between these two Presidential decisions symbolizes the revolution in fiscal policy that occurred in the intervening thirty-one years. This revolution was the main ingredient in the transition to the "new economics," the installation of which was widely hailed in the early 1960's as the basis for confidence that full employment and steady growth would be maintained in the future.

There is a common mythology about what the fiscal revolution was and how it came about. One part of this mythology is the belief that President Hoover raised taxes because he cared about balancing the budget but not about unemployment, whereas President Kennedy cut taxes because he cared about unemployment but not about balancing the budget. Another is that before a certain date—the publication of a certain book or the election of a certain President—all was darkness and we did not know what to do, while after that date all was clear. A third is that the fiscal revolution was won against the dogged opposition of conservatives, businessmen, and classical economists by liberals and Keynesian economists who, as Heroes of the Revolution, have a unique claim to confidence in their further prescriptions.

The truth is more complex. Hoover proposed a tax increase *both* to raise employment and to balance the budget. Kennedy proposed a tax cut *both* to balance the budget and to raise employment. The "revolution" has really

3

been an evolution, with several critical points and gradual movement between them. The evolution has not been in a straight line, steadily moving
toward truer analysis and better policy. It has had on occasion to retrace
its steps and synthesize with new ideas some that had first been discarded.
And no political party, economic sector, or school of thought had a monopoly
of wisdom or good intentions in bringing the revolution about.

The fiscal revolution is not over. Despite celebrations after the 1964
tax reduction, subsequent discussion of fiscal policy, including the debate
over the 1968 tax increase, has reminded us of that. It is important to look
at the revolution to this point, to see how far we have come in order to see
how far we still have to go. Moreover the fiscal revolution is a leading case
of a radical transformation of American policy in our lifetime. Its history
can tell us something about how such changes occur.

John F. Kennedy once said that he had difficulty remembering the difference between fiscal policy and monetary policy but was helped by the
fact that William McChesney Martin was head of the Federal Reserve and
that "Martin" started with an "M", as did "monetary," so he knew that
monetary policy was what the Federal Reserve did. (Apparently he was not
bothered by the fact that "fiscal" and "Federal Reserve" both start with
an "F.") One can sympathize with Kennedy in this problem. Fiscal policy
has no precise boundaries, and was once thought of as comprising all governmental financial policy, including monetary policy and the management of
the debt. However "fiscal" in the "fiscal revolution" refers to policy about
the large aggregates in the budget—total expenditures and total receipts
and the difference between them—as directed toward affecting certain overall characteristics of the economy, such as employment and unemployment,
price levels, and the total share of government activity in the economy.

It is the change in policy about such matters that constitutes the revolution. The policy changed because the view of the economic and political
world changed, and the view changed partly because the facts changed and
partly because the interpretation of the facts changed. For example, in 1929
the federal budget was about 2 percent of the gross national product whereas
in 1965 it was about 20 percent. This enormous increase was not the result of
the change in fiscal policy, except perhaps to a very limited degree, but it
inevitably influenced fiscal policy and would have done so even if there had
been no prior change in thinking. The budget became much too big a cannon
to be allowed to run loose on the deck of the economy; its economic effects
had to be taken into account.

Changes in the facts of the economy are a large part of the story of the
fiscal revolution, but not all of it. The way we thought about the facts also

changed. This was partly the result of experience. The fact that the depression lasted so long after 1929 demonstrated to many people that a depression *could* last a long time, and recognition of this undoubtedly changed fiscal policy. But changes in the factual situation and accumulating experience seldom lead unequivocally to particular changes of policy. The facts and the experience have to be interpreted in some way. In part the fiscal revolution was propelled by the development of new ideas with which to understand the facts, new or unchanged, and the experience. The story of the fiscal revolution is the story of the combined action of changing facts, experience, and ideas upon the image which makers of fiscal policy had of the world in which they operated.

2

Pre-revolutionary Fiscal Policy:
The Regime of Herbert Hoover

Tourists in Leningrad are shown the cruiser "Aurora," moored in the Neva at the spot from which it fired the shell into the Winter Palace in October, 1917, opening the Revolution. But the guide neglects to say that the Winter Palace was occupied at the time not by the Czar but by Alexander Kerensky, a Social Revolutionary. This does not make the shot any less revolutionary, but it does change the character of the October revolution and the factors which must be called up to explain it.

Just so the story of the "Keynesian" or "Keynes-Kennedy" revolution in fiscal policy of the past thirty-five years is likely to be vague about the nature of the regime against which that revolution was made. A generation of political oratory has left us with the impression that the revolution was really against the "Czar"—against a fiscal policy that disregarded the welfare of the people, served the moneyed classes, and kowtowed to "laissez-faire" and the "balanced budget." Government is imagined to have been either passive and ignorant or, if aware of any economics, aware only of "classical" economics as Keynes later described it, believing in wage reduction as the sovereign remedy for unemployment.

If this picture were correct, explaining the fiscal revolution would be easier than it is. The revolution could be ascribed to the inevitable triumph of truth over error and of humanitarianism over callousness. But the situation was not exactly like that. There was a great depression, and the government did fail to discharge its responsibilities, in fiscal policy and other ways. However, the sins and errors of the old regime were more complicated and so was the process of their correction.

6

THE "NEW" ECONOMICS—OF THE 1920'S

Americans who thought about such things in the 1920's did not regard themselves as the accidental beneficiaries of the workings of the invisible hand in a system of laissez-faire. They believed that theirs was an era of deliberate social engineering. It was a period of research and rationalization, in government as well as in industry.

Reviewing the decade in 1929, Wesley C. Mitchell said:

> From the use of abstruse researches in pure science to the use of broad economic conceptions and the use of common sense, the method of American progress in 1922–28 has been the old method of taking thought.
>
> If the prime factor making for prosperity has been the application of intelligence to the day's work, then Government agencies must be credited with an indispensable, though indirect, part in what has been accomplished.[1]

These were not just the remarks of an American economist who happened to be somewhat out of the mainstream of academic economic orthodoxy. They were the remarks of the economist chosen by Herbert Hoover, when Secretary of Commerce, to write the key section of a report on recent economic changes and chosen again by Hoover, when President, to chair his Research Committee on Social Trends.

Hoover was the most important representative of belief in the deliberate application of thought to social problems. He entered the cabinet in 1921 with a reputation as a liberal and a planner. When President Harding proposed to name him Secretary of Commerce, the conservative Republican leadership of the Senate threatened not to confirm him, but was subdued by Harding's threat not to name Andrew Mellon Secretary of the Treasury if Hoover were not accepted.

Even before he became Secretary of Commerce, Hoover believed the era of laissez-faire to be long gone.[2]

Years later, on July 26, 1933, he was to complain to his friend and economic adviser, Arch W. Shaw:

> I notice that the Brain Trust and their superiors are now announcing to the world that the social thesis of laissez-faire died on March 4. I wish they would add a professor of history to the Brain Trust. The 18th century thesis of laissez-faire passed in the United States half a century ago. The visible proof of it was the enactment of the Sherman Act for the regulation of all business, the transportation and public utility regulation, the Federal Reserve System, the Eighteenth Amendment, the establishment of the Farm Loan Banks, the Home Loan Banks, the Reconstruction Finance Corporation. All are but part of the items marking the

total abandonment of that social thesis. However, there are many other subjects upon which I could comment which are not news to you.[3]

Unemployment was high on the list of problems which Hoover regarded, years before it became his personal cross, as requiring thought and social action. In 1921 at his suggestion President Harding convened a conference of leading citizens both to consider how to take care of the unemployed over the winter of 1921–22 and to initiate a long-range study of the problems of unemployment and business cycles. The work of the conference continued in several committees for the next eight years, and Hoover was the guiding spirit in its activities throughout. Hoover's relation to the conference is shown by this excerpt from a report of the 1921 session in the *International Labor Review:*

> For the first time intelligence of a very high order has been brought to bear upon the problems of unemployment in the United States. . . . In the midst of a season called reactionary [Secretary Hoover's] alone among the oustanding national leaders has been the spirit which perceived the dreadful human consequences of involuntary unemployment.[4]

In many speeches Hoover decried the idea that depressions were "acts of God" against which mortals could do nothing. He certainly considered himself to be in the "Do Something" camp. Speaking of the advice he got after the 1929 stock market crash he said:

> Mr. Mellon had only one formula: "Liquidate labor, liquidate stocks, liquidate the farmers, liquidate real estate." . . . Secretary Mellon was not hard-hearted. In fact he was generous and sympathetic with all suffering. He felt there would be less suffering if his course were pursued. . . . But other members of the Administration, also having economic responsibilities—Under Secretary of the Treasury Mills, Governor Young of the Reserve Board, Secretary of Commerce Lamont, and Secretary of Agriculture Hyde—believed with me that we should use the powers of government to cushion the situation.[5]

Perhaps Hoover was drawing a sympathetic picture of himself. But in May, 1932, by which time Hoover's qualities had been tested, Walter Lippmann concluded:

> For whatever else may be said about Mr. Hoover, however much one may disagree with his policies, it cannot be said that he has overlooked the need of restoring employment. Mr. Hoover's concern with the problem has been quite as sincere and his efforts to deal with it quite as persistent as those of any man living.[6]

Hoover did not believe that the economy would manage itself, but thought the deliberate social application of knowledge was necessary. He particularly recognized the need for purposeful action to deal with unemployment. Moreover, he had a set of ideas about how the economy worked which provided him with the basis for a policy to deal with unemployment. These ideas were not "classical" in the sense later described by Keynes.

Hoover viewed the problem as one of keeping the flow of expenditures and income going. This has already been suggested by his disagreement with the "liquidation" view of Secretary Mellon, and it underlies every approach he made to the Depression, or at least every explanation he gave of what he was doing, even when he was using means that would now be regarded as deflationary. One of his simplest statements was made in a message to the Elks on April 18, 1930, asking them to cooperate in measures to accelerate building construction:

> These measures will provide employment, enlarge buying power, increase the circulation of money, create markets for farms and factories, and assure prosperity and contented homes.[7]

Such statements do not suggest any very sophisticated theory of income determination, but for many practical purposes even a naive theory may be sufficient. Explaining J. M. Keynes' insights before 1936, Lawrence Klein said: "Economists can sometimes go very far in the advocacy of proper, sound policy measures based on an inadequate formal theory."[8] This may be true of Presidents as well as of economists.

Hoover believed that the maintenance of wage rates would contribute to sustaining economic activity and employment. This belief was simply the application to the Depression of the general American high-wage philosophy that became popular in the 1920's. One of Hoover's first acts after the 1929 stock market crash was to summon industrial leaders to the White House and ask them to pledge not to cut wage rates. They agreed, and there was at the time little argument over the wisdom of this policy. Later, of course, wage rates were cut, and by 1932 there emerged some public argument in favor of wage reduction as a cure for unemployment. However, Hoover did not change his position.

More important for the subject of this book are two fiscal policy ideas of the 1920's, shared by Hoover and his contemporaries. One idea was that reduction of tax rates would raise the revenue. The other was that an increase of spending for public works could reduce unemployment in a depression.

In order to yield its beneficial effect upon the revenue, a tax reduction had to be of the right kind. It had to be a cut of the higher income tax rates, which would induce the saving classes to invest in productive United States enterprises rather than put their money in tax-exempt securities or foreign bonds or hoard it or consume it. The additional investment would raise the national income, and therefore the tax base, enough to yield enlarged revenues even at the lower tax rates. No explicit, comprehensive theory of national income determination went with this idea about revenue-raising tax reductions, which is not to deny that one could be constructed. But reductions of federal income taxes in 1924, 1926, and 1928 were each followed by an increase of federal revenues. To some, this seemed proof enough that a tax cut would or could raise the national income and thereby raise the revenue.

The idea of the revenue-raising tax cut was later to be associated with the name of Andrew Mellon, but Mellon himself was cautious in advancing the proposition. His usual statement was that because of the rise of taxable income resulting from tax rate reductions, the revenue loss would be less than otherwise expected.[9] However the important point is the recognition that a tax reduction, at lease of a certain kind, could raise the national income.

That increased expenditure on public works could be a powerful instrument against depression unemployment was part of the conventional wisdom of the 1920's, shared by public officials, businessmen, labor leaders, economists and other leaders of public opinion. The 1921 Unemployment Conference, which Hoover inspired, placed great weight on public works as a remedy and did much to establish the acceptability of the policy. The continuing work of the Conference during the 1920's, including the 1923 report on business cycles and the 1929 report on public works, drew further attention to the value of this instrument, but with cautious recognition of the limits set by the availability of useful projects and the difficulty of adapting the timing of the work. These reports were signed by such leaders of the business community as Owen D. Young and John J. Raskob, as well as by William Green of the American Federation of Labor and other people well qualified to reflect and transmit the established doctrine of the 1920's.

As Secretary of Commerce, Hoover was instrumental after the recovery of 1922 in getting several hundred millions of dollars in funds that had been appropriated for federal construction set aside for use later when the economy might need more stimulation. In 1928 he endorsed Senator Jones' Prosperity Reserve Bill, which provided for automatic doubling of federal public works appropriations whenever total construction contract awards fell by a specified percentage below the 1926–27 level. Later in 1928, after the election, came—on paper—Hoover's most daring venture in the use of public works as an anti-depression device. Governor Brewster of Maine announced Hoover's "$3 billion reserve fund" program to the national Conference of State Governors "at the request of Herbert Hoover as an authorized exposition of a portion of his program for stabilizing prosperity." The plan "proposed that federal, state and local governments, in addition to appropriating money the expenditure of which cannot be hastened or postponed, shall make certain credits available, in connection with public works planned well in advance, which credits shall be used only when specified, official indexes of economic conditions show that business appears to be headed for a depression."[10] The total credits to be provided in advance were $3 billion, or about 3 per cent of the gross national product of 1929, which in relation to the gross national product of 1968 would be about $25 billion.

Popular discussion of the expansion of public works during depressions was often vague or silent about how this expansion was to be financed. However, no one demanded, or as a practical matter expected, that it would be financed out of current taxation. Summing up his study of thinking about public works during the 1920's, E. Jay Howenstine, Jr. said:

> Fifth, significant proposals were made on budgetary and financial policy. Cash reserves as a means of financing emergency public works were definitely frowned upon, but the building up of credit reserves or borrowing power, and the authorization in advance of contingency bond issues, so that funds could be readily available in time of need, received widespread approval."[11]

Whether the effectiveness of the emergency public works program was thought to depend upon its being financed by borrowing, or whether borrowing was simply an expedient way of paying in the short run, is not clear. The difference between bond finance and tax finance seems not to have been regarded as *per se* critical for the short run effects of the expenditures. In the long run, expansion of public works in depression would be balanced by restraint in prosperity, and over some appropriate period the total expenditures would be balanced by taxes.

There had been some controversy among economists about whether public works expenditures would bring about a net increase of employment. The answer was seen to hinge upon the effects of the means used to finance the expenditures. The distinction between tax finance and bond finance was not regarded as conclusive, but something more had to be specified about the nature of the taxes and the borrowing and the surrounding monetary conditions before the question could be answered. The upshot of this controversy as it stood at the beginning of the Depression is fairly summarized by Douglas and Director, who said:

> We can conclude therefore that it is possible for government to increase the demand for labor without a corresponding contraction of private demand, and that this is particularly the case when fresh monetary purchasing power is created to finance the construction work.[12]

Hoover and the country confronted the Depression with a package of attitudes and ideas which even today sound modern. They did not believe that they had or wanted laissez-faire. They accepted the need for social action to prevent or correct unemployment. This action was to sustain the flow of expenditures, not to try to put the economy through a salutary liquidation. Wage rates were to be maintained. Public works expenditures were to be expanded, and financed by borrowing if necessary. Even the income-stimulating effect of tax reduction was recognized, although this idea had not been specifically applied to the depression problem.

But obviously this package was not enough. There were other conditions and ideas present which explain the inadequacies and errors of the policies that were actually to be followed.

The President as Leader

Acceptance of the passing of laissez-faire and recognition of the need for social control did not mean elevation of the central government to the role of manager of the economy. The alternative to the automatic, atomistic system was the cooperative system, in which the elements of the society— state and local governments as well as the federal, businesses and associations of businesses, and individuals—worked together consciously and voluntarily to achieve the objectives of the society. This cooperative system required leadership—someone to point the way that the parties should take—and this function might be performed by the President, directly or by assembling the best and most influential minds. But this "indicative" role did not give the central government responsibilities that were otherwise different from those of other elements in the society.

This view of how the system could and should work was at the core of Hoover's outlook. As Food Administrator during the war one of his main activities had been calling upon the American people to eat less meat and make jelly without sugar. As head of Belgian and other European relief programs he had called upon the American people for voluntary support. These were the performances that had made him an American hero. The Unemployment Conference called at his suggestion in 1921 was not called to discuss what the federal government should do, but to discuss what everybody should do. In his remarks opening the conference, Hoover made that clear and warned against excessive reliance upon the federal government. Under his direction, branches were set up in every state where there was serious unemployment, and the state branches set up subcommittees in cities or counties. As he described the program later, *they* (state branches and subcommittees) had responsibility to look after the destitute, while *we* (federal government) undertook national and local drives for money for their use. "We developed cooperation between the federal, state, and municipal governments to increase public works."[13] The subsequent reports which grew out of the Unemployment Conference, down through 1930, distributed their advice impartially to businesses, banks, states and localities.

As Secretary of Commerce, Hoover was the leader of the movement to organize businesses in trade associations for better cooperation with each other and with the government to reduce waste, including the waste resulting from unemployment. Secretary Hoover's emphasis on the collection and dissemination of economic statistics was also based on the belief that with better information more constructive social action might be voluntarily forthcoming.

It is worth noting, as symptomatic of contemporary thinking about how to organize an economy, that the monetary authority was highly decentralized, the twelve Federal Reserve Banks having great independence of the Federal Reserve Board in Washington, which in turn had real independence of the government.

Hoover's inaugural address in March, 1929, had voluntary cooperation for the solution of national problems as one of its main themes. He called a special session of Congress to meet in the next month to do something about the farm problem (and tariffs) and said in his opening message:

> I have long held that the multiplicity of causes of agricultural depression could only be met by the creation of a great instrumentality clothed with sufficient authority and resources to assist our farmers to meet these problems, each upon its merits.[14]

He thereupon proposed creation of a Federal Farm Board to assist *organizations of farmers* to hold their product off the market. The *government* was to provide no subsidy or support. This was not reliance upon the workings of free markets, but neither was it reliance upon the power of the central government.

In someone else the call for cooperation might have been an excuse for inactivity, but not in the case of Hoover. He did more than call for cooperation. He was indefatigable in creating organizations to promote cooperation, and in nagging, wheedling and threatening in an effort to get it.[15]

A similar, but not identical, point was made about Hoover by Lippmann in October, 1931:

> Thus in meeting the depression he has in respect to those elements which are governmental and require his leadership—like tariffs, debts, reparations, political

stabilization—been extremely disinclined to act and greatly bewildered by political opposition and public criticism. He does not seem to know how the political funtions of the President are exercised effectively, and to be rather dismayed at not knowing. On the other hand, he has had the utmost confidence and boldness in attempting to guide and oversee the industrial life of the country, initiating major policies as to wages, purchases of raw materials, capital investment and what not. Scarcely a week passes but some new story comes out of Washington as to how Mr. Hoover has had somebody on the telephone and is attempting to fix this situation or that.

Thus he spends his energies lavishly in fields where under our political system the President has no powers and no responsibility; he is unable to use his energy successfully on the major political tasks where he alone has the power of leadership and the consequent responsibility. This is the reason why he has fallen under the double criticism that he is both inactive and meddlesome, and that is the reason why his advisers are alarmed at the lack of confidence now so commonly felt about him in high Republican circles.[16]

A generation later Lippmann's list of subjects on which Hoover failed to act seems archaic; indeed, Hoover's preoccupation with international debts and reparations is hard for us to understand. But Lippmann's picture of Hoover trying to manage the economy by talking to its vital forces on the telephone is important.

The attempt to summon up the cooperation of state and local governments and of businesses and banks is better understood if the relatively small size of the federal government at the beginning of the Depression is appreciated. In 1929 total federal expenditures were about 2.5 per cent of the gross national product, federal purchases of goods and services about 1.3 per cent, and federal construction less than .2 per cent. In 1965, for comparison, these figures were 18 per cent, 10 per cent, and 1 per cent. There was a little more room for action on the revenue side. Receipts were about 3.7 per cent of the GNP in 1929, but by 1931 they had fallen 50 per cent in dollar amount to 2.7 per cent of the diminished GNP. A very large percentage change in the revenue or expenditure side of such small budgets would have been required to make a significant dent in the national economy. Moreover, during the 1920's the size of the federal budget had been fairly constant. The federal government was not then, as it later became, a machine constantly generating new programs and expansions of old ones so that in order to get an emergency increase of expenditures it was only necessary to advance the implementation of plans already in the pipelines. It was perhaps natural in those circumstances that a President should think the most valuable application of his leadership would be in affecting the expenditures of state and local governments and of private businesses rather than in manipulating the expenditures of the federal government.

Several other features of the economic and political scene at the onset of the Depression may be noted here as factors to be encountered later in the story of the fiscal policies and actions of the Hoover administration:

1. Hoover and the other decision-makers of his time were deficient in tools for appraising the economic situation in which they found themselves. At no time did they have even reasonably reliable and current information on the amount of unemployment. Perhaps more important, estimates of the national income, of investment expenditures, and of state and local expenditures were available only long after the event, so that the administration was always in the dark about the quantitative effect of its efforts to sustain the economy by stimulating those categories of expenditures. Morever, such information as was currently available was interpreted in the light of three recent recessions in 1919, 1924, and 1927, only the first of which had been deep, and none of which had been long. In only one year of the twentieth century had unemployment exceeded 10 per cent of the labor force. That was 1921 when the figure was 11.9 per cent. America was not prepared to visualize a decade in which unemployment never fell below 14 per cent. The only long depression with which anyone in 1930 had any experience had been in the 1890's. Hoover remembered graduating from Stanford in the middle of that depression with $40 in his pocket and beginning to make his fortune, so it probably did not leave a searing impression on him. Also, the 1929 depression began in the heyday of "business cycle theory," when economists accepted the idea of recurring, regular fluctuations in economic activity, with built-in forces making for declines and recoveries. Thus both recent experience and economic "science" (in an age devoted to science) led to the expectation that strong natural forces would intervene to bring about recovery, and the currently available data were not adequate to show promptly that the expectation was not being fulfilled.

2. The government, if it pursued an anti-depression fiscal policy, or wished to do so, could not assuredly count on the cooperation of the monetary authority—the Federal Reserve System. The Federal Reserve Board's legal independence of the government did not necessarily mean that the Federal Reserve would not cooperate, for example, by helping to finance a government deficit. But the government could not compel cooperation, and cooperation might not be forthcoming, either because the Federal Reserve had a different idea of proper policy or because of legal limits on the Federal Reserve's own capacities.

3. The United States was on a form of gold standard and the leaders of American thinking and policy were committed to maintaining the convertibility of dollars, whether held by foreigners or by Americans, into gold

at a fixed price. This required that care be taken to avoid policies which might give rise to a demand for such conversions on a large scale.

4. The idea that government budgets should be balanced had a great deal of force in popular thinking and in the thinking of leaders of government, business, and finance. As has been suggested in the discussion of public works above, and as we shall see in the story of Hoover's fiscal policy, the budget balancing principle left considerable room for maneuvering, but that it was an inhibition to some degree is undeniable.

1930—Anti-Depression Plan A

Hoover's initial response to the stock market crash in October, 1929, was prompt, active, and strictly according to the book. He held a number of conferences with business leaders and public officials and announced his preliminary conclusions in a public statement on November 15. He pointed out that during the period of speculation through which the nation had passed, capital had been diverted to the security markets, leaving a large backlog of investment, including federal, state, and local public works, to be done. "The magnificent working of the Federal Reserve System and the inherently sound conditions of the banks have already brought about a decrease in interest rates and an assurance of abundant capital—the first time such a result has been so speedily achieved under similar circumstances."[17] As a consequence, private and public investment expenditures might be expected to go forward rapidly.

The President said that any lack of confidence was "foolish," but he took a dim view of trying to sustain the economy by talk.

> My own experience has been, however, that words are not of any great importance in times of economic disturbance. It is action that counts. The establishment of credit stability and ample capital through the Federal Reserve System and the demonstration of the confidence of the Administration by undertaking tax reduction with the cooperation of both political parties, speak louder than words.[18]

The reference to tax reduction is to a decision to cut taxes on 1929 incomes, payable in calendar year 1930, by about $160 million—or about 4 per cent of annual federal revenues. This decision was to be spelled out on December 4, 1929, in the budget message. Meanwhile, between November 19 and November 23 the President conferred with railroad executives, other businessmen, and labor leaders and communicated with the governors of the 48 states. His objective was to obtain agreements for the maintenance of wage rates and industrial peace and for the enlargement of private investment and public works expenditures.

In his state of the Union message to Congress on December 3, the President reported on these conferences with satisfaction:

> I have, therefore, instituted systematic, voluntary measures of cooperation with the business institutions and with state and municipal authorities to make certain that fundamental businesses of the country shall continue as usual, that wages and therefore consuming power shall not be reduced, and that a special effort shall be made to expand construction work in order to assist in equalizing other deficits in employment. Due to the enlarged sense of cooperation and responsibility which has grown in the business world during the past few years the response has been remarkable and satisfactory. We have canvassed the Federal Government and instituted measures of prudent expansion in such work that would be helpful, and upon which the different departments will make some early recommendations to Congress.
>
> I am convinced that through these measures we have reestablished confidence. Wages should remain stable. A very large degree of industrial unemployment and suffering which would otherwise have occurred has been prevented. Agricultural prices have reflected the returning of confidence. The measures taken must be vigorously pursued until normal conditions are restored.[19]

Of the twenty-eight pages in President Hoover's state of the Union message only one and a half were devoted to the general economic situation, and these came near the middle of the message, between "Alien Enemy Property" and "Agriculture," without any special emphasis. Hoover said later that he did not want to alarm the public. Reports of his meetings with businessmen indicate that he viewed the situation with considerable gravity.[20] Nevertheless he could believe that he had moved with unprecedented speed, energy and sophistication to deal with the situation. Like a good general, the President had estimated his problem and given orders for Plan A to deal with it.[21] That the estimate was inaccurate, and that the orders would not be carried out, because they could not be, he did not know.

The December, 1929, budget message[22] did not mention the business decline except for one use of the phrase "under the present circumstances" which probably refers to it. This phrase occurs in the discussion of the tax reduction, which had been announced on November 15 as part of the program to sustain the economy. The message said, on this score:

> With an estimated surplus of over $225,000,000 this year [fiscal year 1930, from July 1, 1929 to June 30, 1930] and $122,000,000 next year it is felt that some measure of reduction in taxes is justified. Since the fiscal year 1921 four reductions in taxes have been made. Experience has shown that each reduction in taxes has

resulted in revenue in excess of the mathematically computed return under the reduced rates. Undoubtedly an increase in the prosperity of business brought forth by tax reduction is partly responsible for this experience. Such reduction gives the taxpayer correspondingly more for his own use and thus increases the capital available for general business. Under the present circumstances I am in favor of a reduction in income taxes to be effective on returns for the calendar year 1929, which will be due March 15, 1930. . . . Our effort will be to conduct our financial requirements so as to continue the benefits of reduced taxation for succeeding calendar years. It would not, however, at this time be safe to extend the period of the reduction. A year hence we will know more definitely whether the condition of our finances justifies a continuation or extension of the reduction.[23]

This is a paradoxical statement. On the one hand the tax reduction seems to be recommended as a step to bring about "an increase in the prosperity of business." On the other hand the tax reduction is justified by the prospect of budget surpluses in the fiscal years 1930 and 1931. But the prospective budget surpluses, especially that for fiscal 1931, depended on the continuation of prosperity.

The most striking feature of the budget, in retrospect, is that it estimated that income tax receipts would be exactly the same in fiscal year 1931 as in fiscal year 1930, before allowing for the recommended tax cut. This implied little or no economic decline between 1929 and 1930.[24] Whether the administration believed these receipts estimates to be probable, whether it put them forward to demonstrate and inspire confidence, or whether it had some other reason for calculating the revenues as they would be under conditions of high employment, the record does not show. In any case, the administration recommended a tax cut, claiming that it would have beneficial effects upon the general economy, while it was consistent with a balanced budget only on the assumption that there would be little or no recession in 1930.

On the expenditure side of the budget, there is no visible sign of the President's intention to increase federal public works in order to increase employment. There is some reference to proceeding "expeditiously" in the federal building program, but this is related to having overcome some previously encountered delays rather than to any current need for urgency. The budget estimates are not classified in a way that permits identification of any total for public works or construction.

Total expenditures for all purposes, excluding debt reduction, were to increase as follows:

Fiscal year 1929, actual	$3,298 million
1930, estimate	3,394 million
1931, estimate	3,468 million

These increases were almost entirely due to rising expenditures of the Federal Farm Board, and were not the result of policies adopted to deal with the business decline.

The budget message does not explain what surely looks like a major discrepancy between the President's talk about pushing forward public works and his financial plan. In fact, the budget messages of the time explain very little.[25]

The budget presented for fiscal year 1931 called for slight change in the budget position. If economic conditions were fairly prosperous throughout 1930, so that the estimated revenues were actually achieved, the budget surplus would be a little smaller in fiscal 1931 than in 1929 or 1930. The excess of receipts over expenditures, excluding expenditures for debt reduction,[26] was estimated as follows:

Fiscal year, 1929, actual	$735 million
1930, estimated	775 million
1931, estimated	678 million

Of course if, as turned out to be the case, 1930 was not a year of prosperity, receipts would be below the estimate and there would be a deficit for fiscal 1931.

Having set its course during November and early December, the administration then entered a period of consolidation. The President went about explaining the new policy of cooperative, responsible application of intelligence to the problem of the day and counting its results. He explained to the press at the Gridiron Club on December 15, that the President not only was the "Chief Executive of the greatest business in the world," but also "must, within his capacities, give leadership to the development of moral, social, and economic forces outside of government which make for betterment of our country." The subjects with which the President was concerned "cover the whole range of human thought, and I do not arrogate to myself the combined knowledge or judgment of the technologists, the philosophers, the scientists, the social thinkers, the economists, and the thousand callings of our people."[27] Therefore he would have to call upon the knowledge of expert citizens. Carrying out this principle, he announced four days later the establishment of a Committee on Social Trends to make a three-year study. Wesley Mitchell, Chairman of the Committee, and the other members, Charles E. Merriam, W. F. Ogburn, H. W. Odum and S. M. Harrison, were all distinguished and modern social scientists of their time.

On January 3, 1930, Hoover announced that "Our drive for increase in construction and improvement work to take up unemployment is showing most encouraging results, and it looks as if the work undertaken will be larger for 1930 than for 1929."[28] He reported responses from states, localities, railroads and public utilities to his appeal for expansion of capital expenditures, but significantly did not refer to expenditures by the federal government itself. In the middle of the year the President addressed the annual Conference of State Governors on the radio, and thanked them for their cooperation in speeding up public works. He estimated that in the first six months of 1930 the amount spent or contracted for in federal, state, and local public works had been at least $1.7 billion, exceeding the figure for the same period of 1929 by over $200 million.[29] By this time the federal government was beginning to participate in the President's program for the nation. On April 22, 1930, the administration had sent to Congress a supplemental request for appropriations for public buildings for the fiscal year 1931 amounting to about $140 million, not all of which was for expenditure in that year. The request noted that "Submission at this time of these additional projects for specific authorization and appropriation will afford employment for many thousands of men engaged in the building trades and allied industries."[30] When the fiscal year 1931 opened, expenditure estimates for that year had been revised upward, by about $100 million over the estimates for fiscal 1931 submitted in the December, 1929, budget message and about $200 million over actual expenditures in fiscal year 1930. The increase was largely due to the speeding up of public works "in order to assist in unemployment together with the increased relief of veterans." Because of these increased expenditures and "possible reduction of revenue arising from slack times" the Cabinet would make an effort to prune the budget. However, this would have to be done "without interfering in the program of aid to unemployment."[31]

In the fall the President announced that investment expenditures of railroads and public utilities in the first eight months of 1930 had been $4.5 billion, compared with $4.0 billion in the same period of 1929. He cited this as evidence of the effectiveness of the new instrument of social policy—voluntary responsible behavior.

The President believed throughout 1930 that his policy was working and would work. He later denied that he ever said that prosperity was just around the corner. However, on May 1, 1930, he told the Chamber of Commerce of the United States, "I am convinced we have passed the worst." When he came to write his memoirs in 1952 he explained this optimism on the ground that Presidents must be encouraging. However, even in 1952 he described the latter part of 1930 as a period in which "the country was steadily and successfully readjusting itself despite some adversities and much licking of wounds."[32]

In June, 1930, a delegation from the National Unemployment League, consisting of several clergymen and other concerned citizens, called on the President in the White House to recommend a $3 billion public works program. The President rejected this idea.

Hoover also turned down a more moderate suggestion for federal spending from a group in whom he might have been expected to have more confidence. On October 17, 1930, the President had established a Cabinet Committee to consider a program for dealing with unemployment during the winter of 1930–31 within the framework of the general philosophy he had already laid down. The appointment of this committee did not result from any belief that the situation was deteriorating, but rather from the thought that improvement of economic conditions would still leave a problem of unemployment relief during the winter. The President named Colonel Arthur Woods, an old associate from the 1921 Conference on Unemployment, to develop suggestions for consideration by the Cabinet Committee. Woods in turn named a committee to work with him.

Shortly after it was appointed, in the fall of 1930, "the Committee in a confidential memorandum recommended that he ask Congress, when it assembled in December, for authorizations and appropriations in the sum of $840,000,000."[33] The committee thought that even if, as was hoped, business turned up in the summer, the amount of unemployment remaining would be large enough to justify the expanded public works program in the second half of 1931. However, the President rejected this advice. While he went along with the idea that the economy needed some immediate stimulation in the form of increased federal expenditures, he would not commit the government to enlarged public expenditures beyond the middle of 1931, by which time recovery was expected to be under way.

For Hoover, at least, this optimism was based in part on the belief that his policy was working. In December he was estimating that the construction work of governments, railroads, public utilities and large business organizations would be $7 billion in 1930 as against $6.3 billion in 1929. For others, things just seemed so bad that they had to get better. Thus, the *Commercial and Financial Chronicle* said in October, 1930:

> No change of any great moment is to be noted in the general situation. The industries of the country still remain in a state of great depression, and he would be a bold man who would undertake to predict, with any great degree of assurance, when the country is to emerge from this unfortunate situation. The most that can be said is that the slump has continued so long and has proceeded so far that it seems hardly tenable to believe that the end is still far off. It is on this idea . . . that a spirit of optimism is growing up in business circles. . . .[34]

Confidence in an imminent upturn was not confined to the naive and the wishful. Reviewing a long career as an economist at the Department of Agriculture, much of it devoted to forecasting, Louis Bean said, "Like most economists we misjudged the information at the end of 1930 and expected that the low point would come in the summer of 1931, and it didn't come until the summer of 1932."[35]

But the Hoover policy was not working. True, public works expenditures had increased, the federal, state, and local total rising from $2,468 million in 1929 to $2,858 million in 1930.[36] Federal spending increased by a third —from $155 million to $209 million—but accounted for a small part of the total rise. However the public works increase was swamped by the decline in private construction, despite the President's appeals and meetings. Private nonresidential construction fell from $5.0 billion to $4.0 billion and residential construction from $4.0 billion to $2.3 billion.

The administration's optimism was clear in the revenue estimates in the December budget message. Receipts for the fiscal year that would end on June 30, 1931, were estimated to be only about 8 per cent below receipts for the year that had ended on June 30, 1930. Receipts for the fiscal year 1932 were estimated to be higher than for fiscal year 1931 and even a little higher than for the fiscal year 1930. These estimates implied in the first place that calendar year 1930 individual and corporate incomes were much better than they actually had been, and in the second place that calendar year 1931 would be much better than calendar year 1930. The level of the national income at the beginning of 1931 was substantially below the average for 1930 so that the estimates implied a very sharp rise during the calendar year 1931.

With these assumptions about the economic prospect the administration's position was that need remained for increasing federal public works expenditures during the remainder of fiscal 1931 (January to June, 1931) but that extraordinary expenditures to support employment should be tapered off after that. The President asked for a supplementary appropriation of $150 million for emergency public works in the fiscal year 1931, saying, "The test of the value of such relief is the ability to pay wages between now and the end of the fiscal year."[37] He estimated that the normal rate of federal expenditures for public works, including loans for shipbuilding, naval vessel construction, and military aviation, had increased from $250 million in fiscal 1928 to $500 million in fiscal 1931, and would continue at the higher rate or more, in the future. His emergency program would raise that to $650 million during the calendar year 1931.

Because of the higher expenditures, both normal and emergency, and the deficiency of the revenues as compared with previous estimates, the President decided that the tax relief given a year earlier could not be continued. Even with the restoration of the one percentage point that had been cut off income tax rates on 1929 incomes and the optimistic assumptions underlying the revenue estimates, the net budget position would shift from a surplus of $180 million in fiscal 1930 to a deficit of the same size in fiscal 1931. The budget for fiscal 1932 would be almost exactly in balance, showing a surplus of $30 million on a total of about $4 billion.[38]

Until the end of 1930, President Hoover had maintained his position as the leader of the activists in dealing with the Depression. After that time his position was increasingly challenged. This challenge came especially from advocates of what were always called "vast" public works programs, the same adjective being used in the press whether the amount involved was $1 billion, $3 billion, or $5 billion—these being the favorite figures. The following list of proposals, certainly incomplete, gives some idea of their frequency, size and sponsorship:

December, 1930	Emergency Committee for Federal Public Works	$1.0 billion
January 5, 1931	90 economists endorse above proposal	
May 1, 1931	National Unemployment League proposal to U. S. Chamber of Commerce	$3.0 billion
June 1, 1931	28 mayors of large cities	$5.0 billion
September 4, 1931	Congressman W. M. White	$8.5 billion
September 5, 1931	Engineering News-Record	$7.0 billion
September, 1931	Petition of 1200 publicists, economists and clergymen	$3.5 billion
September 7, 1931	League for Independent Political Action	$3.0 billion
September 8, 1931	Senator Wagner	$2.0 billion
September 21, 1931	William Randolph Hearst (later endorsed by 31 economists)	$5.0 billion
September 26, 1931	Dr. John O'Grady	$6.0 billion

As proposals of amounts of money to be spent for federal construction in a short period, perhaps a year or two, these suggestions could not be taken seriously. The federal government could simply not raise its construction expenditures quickly by one or two billion dollars a year, for instance, and have any structures to show for it. Federal construction expenditures were only $210 million in 1930—a small base on which to erect a program of several billion dollars. The larger proposals were intended to finance expansion of state and local public works expenditures, in addition to federal, as were the later $3.3 billion and $4.8 billion programs of the New Deal. But even combined federal, state, and local construction expenditures in 1930 were less than $3 billion. It is significant that the New Deal did not succeed until 1939 in raising the annual amount of public construction by $1.5 billion over the 1930 rate, in 1930 prices.

The impracticability of the "vast" programs appearing almost daily in 1931 did not mean that everything was done, then or later, that could have been done. Probably a reasonable appraisal of the possibilities was contained in a letter from James S. Taylor, Chief of the Division of Public Construction of the Department of Commerce, to Wesley Mitchell on June 3, 1931: "When one gets to very high figures, physical impracticability alone can be used as an argument, but in the field of state highways alone I dare say the State Highway Departments could have spent several hundred millions additional of Federal Funds."[39]

The "vast" public works programs of 1931 probably served to push Hoover a little in 1931 and in 1932 and helped to lay the groundwork for the New Deal efforts. The programs were a training ground for the discussion of Depression fiscal policies. On the other hand, this discussion of $3 billion, $5 billion, and even $7 billion spending programs helped to create in Hoover's mind the idea that he was fighting a war on two fronts. He had to defend the country against the Depression. At the same time he had to defend the country against the wild men, especially dangerous since the Democratic gains in the 1930 Congressional elections, who were prepared to spend any amount of money.

1931 — Fiscal Stimulation by Inadvertence

However, neither the big fiscal action of 1931 nor the big fiscal issue, as a practical matter, lay in the field of public works. The big fiscal action was the payment on the veterans' adjusted service certificates, and the big fiscal issue was whether to raise taxes for 1932.

While the administration was slowly raising federal public works expenditures by $60 million, enactment of a law providing for advance payment on the veterans' adjusted service certificates put one billion dollars into the hands of the public at one swoop. True, the money was already theirs—the veterans'. Congress had passed a bonus bill in 1924, promising to pay the veterans of World War I certain amounts in about 1945. A veteran's dependents would immediately receive the full amount to which he was ultimately entitled if he died before 1945. Also, the veteran could borrow a percentage—in 1930 the percentage was 22 1/2—of the "face value" ultimately due. The government was preparing for payment of the total benefit in 1945 by depositing each year in a trust fund an amount which, with interest, would accumulate to the required amount. These annual deposits, out of the general revenue, ran around $110 million.

In the early part of 1931, when many veterans were unemployed and needy, nothing seemed more natural than that the government should pay them what it had promised to pay later anyway. Proposals to this end were introduced in Congress and, after a debate in which the President's opposition was made known, the House passed a compromise suggested by Owen D. Young, conservative industrialist and possible Democratic Presidential candidate. The Young Plan allowed each veteran to borrow at a low rate of interest up to 50 per cent of the amount to which he would finally be entitled. This proposal passed the House of Representatives, whereupon the President sent a letter to Senator Smoot, chairman of the Senate Finance Committee, objecting chiefly on the grounds that most of the payments under the bill would go to persons who were not in need, whereas the Treasury's borrowing to finance the payments would absorb credit that might have been used by private business to employ the needy. This argument did not prevent the Senate from passing the bill, nor did it prevent the Congress from repassing the bill over the President's veto.

Payment of the veterans' certificates, although the biggest single fiscal action of the Hoover period, was not a "pure" act of anti-depression fiscal policy. For one thing, the immediate beneficiaries, the veterans, had an exceptional amount of political power in the Congress and sympathy in the country. Moreover, the nature of the transaction was such as to put relatively little demand upon the budget. All but about $100 million of the billion paid to veterans under the act came out of a trust fund, and trust funds were not then considered part of the budget when people talked of balancing the budget. This did not at all relieve the Treasury of the necessity to find the money to make the payments, and probably did not affect the economic consequences of the payments, but it surely made the bill easier to swallow.

As for President Hoover's veto of the bill, perhaps one can say of that what Arthur Schlesinger, Jr., said in explaining and forgiving President Roosevelt's veto of a similar bill four years later: "Opposition to the bonus was one of the virtuous issues of the day; it was considered to show both an enlightened concern for the public welfare as against selfish special interests and a true dedication to economy in government."[40]

The Hoover administration's anti-depression fiscal actions in 1931 were inhibited by the recurrent belief that the corner had been turned and recovery was in sight, and by the small size of the budget with which it worked and the difficulty of increasing expenditures rapidly. Nevertheless, as a result of the automatic decline of revenues with falling incomes, and the payment on the veterans' certificates, the changes in the budget between 1929 and 1931 were very large relative to the size of the budget, and even of quite substantial size relative to the size of the economy in 1929. Receipts declined by almost 50 per cent and expenditures rose by almost 60 percent. The swing from surplus to deficit was over 3 percent of the 1929 gross national product, or about equivalent to a swing of $25 billion from surplus to deficit relative to the 1968 GNP. E. Cary Brown has made a sophisticated attempt to measure the stimulating effect of fiscal policy on the total demand for goods and services during the 1930's. The method need not be described here, except to say that it applies the common sense of "modern" theories of the impact of fiscal policy and usual judgments about the magnitudes of certain key factors. The conclusion of the Brown study is that the net stimulating effect of federal fiscal policy was larger in 1931 than in any other year of the 1930's except 1934, 1935, and 1936—of which only 1936 (when another bonus payment was enacted over a President's veto) was much larger than 1931. The increase in the stimulating effect of the federal budget from 1929 to 1931 was larger than in any other two-year period. The stimulating effect of the fiscal policy of all governments —federal, state, and local—was larger in 1931 than in any other year of the 1930's.[41]

The Decision to Raise Taxes

The fiscal actions of 1930 and 1931 may be explained, at least in part, by factors which from the standpoint of policy were accidental. The decision to recommend a large tax increase at the end of 1931 was a different matter. Unlike failure to increase expenditures more rapidly, it cannot be explained by technical, administrative, or forecasting limitations. Nothing would have been administratively simpler than *not* to raise taxes. The proposed tax increase was to expire on June 30, 1934—two and a half years later—in the expectation that by then recovery would have proceeded far enough to balance the budget without the higher taxes. Subjecting the economy to the restrictive effect of higher taxes in 1932 and 1933 was not based on an optimistic forecast for those years.

Budget Balance as an Elastic Limit

The decision taken by the President at the end of 1931 to raise taxes was obviously based on the felt necessity to balance the budget. But this does not explain the decision. The administration knew that "balancing the budget" is an elastic concept, although they did not appreciate the range of its elasticity as well as we do today. They knew in the first place that balancing the budget did not mean balancing it every year. Surpluses in some years could make room for deficits in other years. In his budget message of December, 1930, which forecast a deficit for the fiscal year 1930–31, President Hoover said:

> I do not look with favor on any attempts to meet this deficit by reduction of the statutory redemption of the public debt, which now amounts to about $440,000,000 per annum. Nor do I look with great concern upon this moderate deficit for the current fiscal year, which, in fact, amounts to less than five percent of the total Government expenditure. The adverse balance can be met by reducing the general fund balance from the amount in it at the beginning of the year, supplemented, if necessary, by temporary borrowing by the Treasury. When we recollect that our Budget has yielded large surpluses for the last 11 years, which have enabled us to retire the public debt, in addition to retirements required by law, to the extent of nearly $3,500,000,000, we can confidently look forward to the restoration of such surpluses with the general recovery of the economic situation, and thus the absorption of any temporary borrowing that may be necessary.
>
> It will probably be necessary for Congress to appropriate additional money for expenditure within the present fiscal year in order to increase employment and to provide for the drought situation. I have presented this matter in my annual message on the state of the Union. While this will operate to increase the amount of the deficit as above estimated, I believe such increase can be accommodated by the methods indicated. On the other hand, no appropriations should be made for such purposes which look beyond such action as will ameliorate the immediate situation during the next six months.[42]

The administration knew in the second place that it had some leeway in the definition of the budget, some room to decide whether to declare a given condition of the budget "balance" or "unbalance." There are several examples of this:

1. As already noted, little of the payment to veterans in the spring of 1931 appeared in the budget, and not because of the inevitable nature of things but because of a decision about accounting procedures made in 1930.

2. Throughout the Hoover administration the budget expenditure totals included a substantial sum, about $500 million a year, for debt retirement required by statute. The administration recognized that it could plausibly regard the budget as balanced if receipts covered expenditures without that amount. In fact, the tax increase proposed at the end of 1931 was calculated to "balance" the 1932–33 budget in this sense. In January, 1931, the Chicago

banker Melvin Traylor suggested that payments on the sinking fund should be reduced or halted, in order to avoid the need for a tax increase. But the administration rejected this easy way to make the 1931 and 1932 picture look better.

3. In December, 1931, when it was proposing the tax increase, the Administration also proposed creation of the Reconstruction Finance Corporation with authority to lend for a large variety of purposes. The Treasury was to buy the capital stock of the corporation, which amounted to $500 million, and the corporation was authorized to borrow up to $3.3 billion in addition, either from the Treasury or elsewhere. During the fiscal years 1932 and 1933 the corporation borrowed $1,585 million, all from the Treasury. However only the $500 million subscription to the capital appeared as a budget expenditure—until the Roosevelt administration revised the books retroactively. The decision to include the $500 million but not the $1,585 million was arbitrary, in terms of the "real" condition of the Treasury.

4. There were frequent suggestions in 1931 and 1932 that the budget could be regarded as balanced even though part of the expenses were met by borrowing if one or both of two conditions were met: (a) that the borrowing should finance capital expenditures and (b) that provision should be made for paying interest and principal on the borrowing out of future revenues. Quite respectable financial experts—Owen D. Young, Bernard Baruch, and Winthrop Aldrich, to name a few—could be lined up in support of this idea, as could numerous congressmen, both Republican and Democratic. However, the administration in the end rejected all such suggestions.

Acceptance of budget balancing as a principle did not *require* the administration to recommend a tax increase in December, 1931. According to the estimates the administration presented at that time, the debt increase resulting from deficits in the three fiscal years 1931, 1932, and 1933 would be, without the tax increase, $3,247 million. This would be less than the amount by which debt reduction had *exceeded sinking fund requirements* during the preceding eleven years. The administration could have said that while the budget does have to be balanced, and the debt reduced in the long run, taking good times with bad, this did not require balancing the budget in fiscal years 1932 and 1933—especially in view of the large surpluses of the 1920's. It could have reduced the apparent deficit for fiscal 1932 by excluding the capital subscriptions to the RFC and the Federal Land Banks from the expenditure side of the budget. It could have segregated other "emergency" expenditures. It could have shown that the existing tax rates would be sufficient to yield a surplus when recovery came.

There would have been complaints, of course. But a charge of fiscal irresponsibility could not have been made to stick against Hoover, Mellon, and Mills to a degree that would have compromised their ability to carry out the policy—or been a net disadvantage in the 1932 election. In fact, the *New York Times*, perhaps tauntingly, predicted in 1931 that Hoover would not ask for a tax increase before the November, 1932, election because a tax increase would hurt him at the polls.[43]

If neither his own nor other peoples' devotion to the simple principle of balancing the budget required Hoover to recommend a tax increase in December, 1931, why did he do it? The answer must be found not in the formal but malleable notion of balancing the budget but in what were believed to be the real consequences of certain real conditions.

LIVING WITH A DEFICIT

During the spring and summer of 1931 the President's decision was uncertain, even though reports of tax collections showed that the deficit was running much higher than had been forecast and that a large deficit for fiscal 1932 would be inevitable. Attention was first focused on the problem in the second half of March, after the March 15 income tax payments had been counted and found to be much below expectations. The estimate of the deficit for fiscal 1931, which had been put at $180 million in the December 1930 Budget message, was raised to $700 million or more. The *New York Times* reported on March 29, 1931, that Treasury officials and Congressional leaders feared the effect of the deficit on Republican party chances in the 1932 election but at the same time were against a quick increase of federal tax rates. Some Congressional leaders, including Congressman Longworth and Senator Watson, the Republican floor leaders, suggested temporary suspension or limitation of sinking fund appropriations for debt reduction, in order to avoid a tax increase. The President and the Treasury, on the other hand, were said to oppose this and to be willing to accept deficits in fiscal 1931 and 1932 as temporary phenomena caused by the Depression and destined to disappear with it.[44]

This difference between the Congressional leaders and the administration seems now to be entirely a matter of words. There is more substance in the following view, also reported in the *Times*: "Confronted with the choice of increasing taxes or borrowing money to meet current expenses, administration officials have favored the latter method on the ground that a tax increase at a time when business is quickly responsive to any unfavorable developments would be a blunder."[45] And three days later the *Times* reported:

"At the Treasury it was pointed out that during a period when business is slack it would appear to be better policy to increase the public debt than to raise taxes."[46]

On May 21, Treasury Undersecretary Ogden Mills made a speech which was reported by the *New York Times* as strengthening the belief that there would be no tax increase. He said, among other things:

> We should so adjust our tax system that year in and year out there will be no great variation between receipts and expenditures and that a comparatively small deficit one year will be offset by a comparatively small surplus the next.
>
> The second essential step is to ascertain whether our present tax system, once business conditions have returned to normal, will be adequate to furnish the necessary receipts.[47]

Referring to the latter point, which sounds like a lost hint of the idea of setting tax rates to balance the budget at high employment, Mills said that the present year (1931) itself was an inadequate criterion for judging the ability of the revenue system to meet normal requirements.

On June 2, 1931, the President's announcement that the deficit for fiscal 1931 would be in excess of $900 million—counting statutory debt reduction as an expenditure—set off another flurry of talk about a possible tax increase. Nonetheless, the "inside dope" from Washington was that Hoover thought the budget could be "balanced" by borrowing until the Depression was over and that the Treasury's discussion of the inadequacies of the existing tax system was intended only to start a long-range educational campaign, not to get taxes raised in the next session of Congress.[48] Senator Smoot of Utah, chairman of the Senate Finance Committee, said on June 30 that there might be a tax increase in the next session, but only if business is "measurably improved." "It would appear to me impossible to increase taxes during the present depressed conditions." If conditions did not improve, bond issues would be used to meet government costs.[49]

The mounting actual and prospective deficits during the spring and summer of 1931 caused no crisis of confidence in the financial community or, as far as can be seen, elsewhere. On March 25, Senator Fess had said that Treasury certificates would be taken up "like hotcakes" because of confidence in Secretary Mellon. The inflow of gold and the excess reserves of the banking system may have been more important than confidence in Secretary Mellon, but in any case the certificates did go like hotcakes. Treasury certificates of indebtedness sold on September 15, 1931 bore the rate of 1 1/8 per cent, the lowest at which such certificates had ever been issued. Bonds were sold on the same date at an interest rate of 3 per cent, the lowest in twenty years. Yields on Treasury bills were about one-half of one per cent during the summer.

RESPONSE TO FINANCIAL CRISIS

The financial conditions facing the Treasury changed drastically after Britain went off the gold standard on September 21, 1931, and was followed by about 25 other countries. Three things happened very shortly:

1. Gold began to flow out of the United States in large quantities, beginning the week before September 21 when the British action was expected, in speculation that the United States might also go off the gold standard.

2. Interest rates rose sharply in the United States, on U.S. government securities as well as on other securities, as bank reserves declined.

3. Both bank failures and the withdrawal of currency from banks by depositors soared.

The decision to raise taxes was made against the background of these facts.

Hoover had two great concerns in the weeks after the British went off gold. One was to keep the dollar from going the way of the pound. The other was to assure the availability of credit to business borrowers in the United States, which he regarded as the necessary condition for recovery. Both of these concerns pointed him in the direction of "balancing the budget," or of demonstrating that the budget was under control. His first visible response to the British move was an attempt to defend the budget. While he had known for some time that the British might go off gold, it was only on September 19 that he was informed that it would happen on September 21. September 21 was the day on which Hoover was scheduled to address the annual convention of the American Legion, in Detroit. His initial reaction in view of the international financial crisis was to cancel his speech. However at dinner on the 19th with Secretaries Stimson, Mellon and Lamont that plan was revised. A demand for a new bonus payment was the main item of the Legion's agenda. The world financial situation made it imperative to try to prevent this "raid on the Treasury." Hoover made a dramatically rapid trip, spending only one hour in Detroit, and delivered a forceful appeal, warning against the "grave risks" of increasing government expenditures. The Legion was persuaded to withdraw its demand, at least for the time.

The British departure from gold caused the President to speed up a move he had been planning for some time to strengthen the credit situation.[50] He called a meeting, held on October 4, with the heads of leading banks, insurance companies, and other financial institutions. The purpose of the meeting was to ask them to set up an institution with a capital of $500 million and borrowing authority of $1 billion "to help banks in need and to loan against the assets of closed banks, so as to melt large amounts of frozen deposits and generally stiffen public confidence."

Two days later the President met with the Congressional leaders and explained in dramatic terms that "we are now faced with the problem, not of saving Germany or Britain, but of saving ourselves." To this Mills "added further explanations, including our impending deficit." Hoover told the leaders that if the private cooperative effort did not suffice he would recommend establishment of a finance corporation (subsequently the RFC) "with available funds sufficient for any legitimate call in support of credit."[51] He also announced then, or took within a few weeks, a number of other measures to strengthen the supply of farm and real estate credit.

These steps were part of an effort by the administration to liquefy the financial system and stimulate the flow of credit in the face of a Federal Reserve System that was reluctant to expand the reserves of the banks. The decision taken in late 1931 to raise taxes should also be regarded as part of this effort, as a way to prevent federal government borrowing from drawing off some of the pool of funds available for private investment and from depressing the asset values of the financial institutions. It was a kind of bond support program, to be carried out with tax receipts rather than with newly created money. It must be understood in the light of the unwillingness, or inability, of the Federal Reserve to support bonds by creating more new money in the fall of 1931.

The President's decision to raise taxes was made sometime in the five weeks after the British left gold on September 21. The form of the tax increase to be recommended was not decided for a few weeks more and not announced until the state of the Union and budget messages of early December. The increase proposed was a big one—estimated to yield over $900 million in fiscal 1933, or about one-third as much as all existing taxes. Most of the additional revenues would come from selective excises, but individual and corporate income taxes were also to be raised—about twenty per cent in the aggregate. The amount of the tax increase was calculated to balance the fiscal 1933 budget exactly—without provision for the sinking fund debt reduction.

There is no need here to trace the Revenue Act of 1932 through the Congress. There was a long and bitter fight, but the fight was over the nature of the tax increase, not over the wisdom of raising taxes by such a staggering amount at a time of massive unemployment. Once the President and his financial experts had said that balancing the budget was imperative, there were few, in the Congress or in the country, who would take the responsibility for denying it. Some congressmen did rise to say that the tax increase was unnecessary, that the Treasury was having no difficulty in borrowing, that the debt was smaller than it had been ten years earlier, that the citizens would be better able to pay $10 after the Depression than $1 during it, and so on. But these were backbenchers or mavericks. For the Democratic leadership in the Congress the President's tax proposal was an invitation either to take responsibility for a big deficit or to share responsibility for a big tax increase. Their riposte was to support the idea of a tax increase, thus aligning themsleves with "sound finance," but to attack the particular tax increase the President proposed as a "rich man's tax bill," thus escaping the wrath of the majority of tax payers. This tactic dragged out the debate over the tax bill, which was not enacted until June 6, 1932, but it provided no confrontation on the budget-balancing question.

The key decision was the President's, made in October and November of 1931. If he had not asked for the tax increase there would have been no other leadership to demand it, and once he did ask for it there was no leadership to deny it.

The administration explained the need mainly in terms of the effects of government borrowing on the credit situation. Thus, in his December 8, 1931, state of the Union message, President Hoover said:

> Whatever the causes may be, the vast liquidation and readjustments which have taken place have left us with a large degree of credit paralysis, which together with the situation in our railroads and the conditions abroad, are now the outstanding obstacles to recovery. . . . Many of our bankers, in order to prepare themselves to meet possible withdrawals, have felt compelled to call in loans, to refuse new credits, and to realize upon securities, which in turn has demoralized the markets. The paralysis has been further augmented by the steady increase in recent years of the proportion of bank assets invested in long-term securities, such as mortgages and bonds. These securities tend to lose their liquidity in depression or temporarily to fall in value so that the ability of the banks to meet the shock of sudden withdrawal is greatly lessened and the restriction of all kinds of credit is thereby increased. The continuing credit paralysis has operated to accentuate the deflation and liquidation of commodities, real estate, and securities below any reasonable basis of values.
>
> Our first step toward recovery is to reestablish confidence and thus restore the flow of credit which is the very basis of our economic life.
>
> The first requirement of confidence and of economic recovery is financial stability of the United States Government.
>
> Even with increased taxation, the Government will reach the utmost safe limit of its borrowing capacity by the expenditures for which we are already obligated

and the recommendations here proposed. To go further than these limits in either expenditures, taxes, or borrowing will destroy confidence, denude commerce and industry of their resources, jeopardize the financial system, and actually extend unemployment and demoralize agriculture rather than relieve it.[52]

Undersecretary Mills was more explicit on some points in a speech to the Economic Club of New York a few days later on December 14, 1931:

> I do not mean to suggest that the addition of $3,000,000,000 or even $4,000,-000,000 to our national debt could conceivably impair the national credit. That debt stood at $25,000,000,000 a decade ago, and the national credit was unimpaired, but I do say, with all the force at my command, that any temporizing with the situation, any failure to take the steps necessary to bring our budget into balance within a reasonable time, any misuse of the public credit, would furnish evidence of lack of sound financial principles as might well result in shaken confidence and in apprehension lest these conditions prevail long enough to result in real damage. Our long-term bonds are selling today at a discount, even those bearing as high an interest rate as $3\frac{3}{4}$ percent. Allowing for tightened money conditions, and for all the unusual circumstances which surround us, there is no doubt but that some of the weakness manifested reflects the response of the investing public to the possibility that we may be confronted with a rapid increase in the public debt, and in the volume of Government securities outstanding.[53]

Why Did He Do It?

Conventional talk about the need to balance the budget had always emphasized the importance of preserving confidence in the credit of the government and in the currency, and of not absorbing to finance the deficit funds that would otherwise be used to finance private investment. As long as interest rates were low and gold was flowing into the country, this concern about confidence could be dismissed as merely ritualistic. But in the fall of 1931 it began to look very real. Money was tight, interest rates were high, confidence in the dollar—as against gold or foreign currencies—and in bank deposits—as against currency—was low. Continued government borrowing to finance deficits, or even the prospect of it, held several dangers. It would depress security prices and raise interest rates further, increasing the difficulty of private businesses in borrowing, reducing the value of bank assets, and further straining confidence in the banks. Moreover, expectation of continued deficits might give rise to fears of inflation in the United States and accelerate the outflow of gold.[54]

Milton Friedman and Anna J. Schwartz have argued with great force that the monetary contraction was not inevitable in the United States in the months after Great Britain went off gold, but was the result of erroneous policy followed by the Federal Reserve.[55] In the debates over policy within the Federal Reserve during this period, the administration—as represented by Ogden Mills—was on the side of monetary expansion. However, the necessity or wisdom of the monetary policy followed in the United States after September, 1931, is not the subject at issue here. The important point is that the decision to raise taxes was made in a condition of rising interest rates, falling bond prices, increasing bank suspensions, and large gold outflow. A more relaxed attitude toward balancing the budget did not appear in government policy until the Roosevelt administration when all of these conditions were radically changed.

Whether taxes would have been raised in 1932 if there had not been the gold outflow of 1931, the monetary contraction, and concomitant developments is impossible to tell today. Certainly Hoover believed in balancing the budget. Possibly he would have recommended a tax increase rather than project a budget deficit for three fiscal years in a row. But Hoover also believed in recovery and in his own reelection and, as we have argued above, the idea of budget-balancing did not compel him to raise taxes when he did.

Probably President Hoover and his close advisers had prejudices in favor of balancing the budget which made them exceptionally sensitive to the dangers of continuing budget deficits in the conditions they faced. However, economically sophisticated observers, who did not share the budget-balancing prejudice, did share the belief that in the domestic and international monetary conditions of the United States after September, 1931, and possibly continuing to the bank holiday of 1933, budget deficits might be harmful rather than helpful.

The reply of Professor J. M. Clark to a query from Senator Wagner in the spring of 1932, when monetary conditions were much more favorable than they had been in the preceding fall, is illustrative. He agreed that a policy of financing government expenditures by borrowing during a depression was ordinarily sound. Yet he found the problem "puzzling" at that particular time, the answer depending in part on certain conditions that he was not in a good position to judge. He was concerned about the danger that additional government borrowing, with a credit system abnormally contracted and apparently unable to expand, would lower security values and undermine the shaky collateral on which bank credit rests.[56]

In a lecture on February 20, 1933, Professor Jacob Viner pointed out the advantages of a deliberate policy of inflation and said that the "simplest and least objectionable" procedure for carrying it out would be a government deficit financed by monetary expansion. But he went on:

I cannot see any justification for confidence that an aggressive inflationary policy of this sort would not immediately result in a flight from the dollar, in panicky anticipation of the effects in business circles of a grossly unbalanced government budget, and therefore in more injury than good, at least as long as we remained on the gold standard.[57]

Viner was "firmly convinced" that the United States could not consider deliberate abandonment of the gold standard. He concluded:

If we are to have inflation, therefore, we must have it within the gold standard and without resort to budgets badly enough unbalanced to terrify Wall Street. These two conditions suffice to make impossible any policy of deliberate inflation on a large scale through unilateral action on our part.[58]

At the beginning of 1933, Viner could blame the Hoover administration for the fear of deficits which made a sophisticated budgetary policy impossible or unworkable.

For the federal government, the campaign for balancing the budget had made it dangerous to increase the debt substantially because of the adverse effect it would have on the morale of a proud public taught to measure the stability of government by the financial record for a single year or short period of years.[59]

However, in the fall of 1931 when the Hoover administration was deciding to raise taxes, it was the administration itself that was frightened. Moreover, its fright does not seem to have been entirely self-induced, but arose from some objective facts—the gold outflow, the rise of interest rates and decline of bond prices, and the run on the banks.[60] It is true that thereafter administration warnings about the dangers of deficits became more and more terrifying, partly to push the tax increase through an uncooperative Congress and partly for the purposes of the 1932 election.

The relevance of the facts which troubled the administration in 1931 is neatly shown in this quotation from J. M. Keynes, the father of the "new" or "non-Hoover" economics:

If, for example, a Government employs 100,000 additional men on public works, and if the multiplier (as defined above) is 4, it is not safe to assume that aggregate employment will increase by 400,000. For the new policy may have adverse reactions on investment in other directions.

It would seem (following Mr. Kahn) that the following are likely in a modern community to be the factors which it is most important not to overlook (though the first two will not be fully intelligible until after Book IV has been reached):

(i) The method of financing the policy and the increased working cash, required by the increased employment and the associated rise of prices, may have the effect of increasing the rate of interest and so retarding investment in other directions, unless the monetary authorities take steps to the contrary; whilst, at the same time, the increased cost of capital goods will reduce their marginal efficiency to the private investor, and this will require an actual *fall* in the rate of interest to offset it.

(ii) With the confused psychology which often prevails, the Government programme may through its effects on "confidence," increase liquidity-preference or diminish the marginal efficiency of capital, which, again, may retard other investments unless measures are taken to offset it.

(iii) In an open system with foreign-trade relations, some part of the multiplier of the increased investment will accrue to the benefit of employment in foreign countries, since a proportion of the increased consumption will diminish our own country's favorable balance; so that, if we consider only the effect on domestic employment as distinct from world employment, we must diminish the full figure of the multiplier.[61]

This means, for our present purposes, that in the Keynesian universe, there is a possible constellation of monetary conditions, "confidence," and international economic relations that will make the stimulative effects of a budget deficit small, or zero, or if the speculative reactions are sufficiently adverse, even negative. These were just the three factors that the Hoover Administration seems to have regarded as necessitating an attempt to balance the budget, although the aspect of the international balance that concerned them was not trade but a speculative flight from the dollar, with its domestic monetary consequences. To explain how fiscal policy subsequently changed, it is not sufficient to rely upon the emergence of a new, Keynesian, model of the economic system, because even the new model would give the old answers if applied to the old facts. What was necessary, before a new fiscal policy could be adopted, was a change in the basic facts. There had to be a coordinated or permissive monetary policy, so that government deficits would not force up interest rates to an undesired degree. There had to be either international economic independence or international economic cooperation, so that domestic expansionary policy would not be hamstrung by adverse international trade reactions or flight from the currency. It would also be desirable, although if the first two conditions are given perhaps not absolutely necessary, that business and public reaction to deficits should not be "bearish."

The government's fiscal policy did not begin to change markedly until after these facts had changed. Of course they did not just happen to change. They were made to change, and partly in an effort to liberate fiscal policy. Other things changed as well. There was the experience of many more years of depression and also the experience of war finance and war boom.

There was a revolution in the way economists thought about fiscal policy and another revolution in the way governments thought about economists. But neither the policy of 1931—what surely seems now the desperate folly of raising taxes in a deep depression—nor the subsequent departure from that policy can be understood without taking account of the limitations set by domestic and international monetary conditions and by the state of confidence.

·§ 3 ℰ·

Roosevelt Liberates Fiscal Policy

ON April 5, 1933, Franklin Roosevelt wrote to his old friend, President Wilson's former confidant, Colonel House:

> While things look superficially rosy, I realize well that thus far we have actually given more of deflation than of inflation. . . . It is simply inevitable that we must inflate and though my banker friends may be horrified, I still am seeking an inflation which will not wholly be based on additional government debt.[1]

The President was too modest. It was true that many of the steps he had taken in the previous month were deflationary. But however muddled they seemed and may actually have been at the time, in retrospect they look like a brilliant strategy to make possible inflationary or, as we might now say, expansionary action. Also, by April 5, plans were well under way for several actions at least intended to be expansionary.

CLEARING THE DECKS FOR EXPANSION

President Roosevelt had found, on the day of his inauguration, conditions similar in several respects to those which had confronted President Hoover in the fall of 1931. Bank runs had reached epidemic proportions, and holidays limiting withdrawals from banks had been declared in about half the states. Gold was again flowing out of the country. Interest rates had risen sharply, government security prices were depressed, the Federal Reserve System had raised rediscount rates.

These were not conditions favorable to the execution of expansionary policy, especially a policy of increasing budgetary deficits which might depress security prices and further impair confidence in the banks and in the dollar. Both President Hoover and President Roosevelt had the problem of either changing these limiting conditions or operating within them. Both tried to do some of each, but the proportions were quite different. Hoover mainly tried to operate within the limits facing him by working hard to balance the budget, thus reducing the government's drain on the supply of savings and indirectly bolstering the banking system and the dollar. But he did also try to change the financial limits upon his policy. He obtained creation of the RFC to put the government's credit behind that of weak financial institutions, his administration initiated the Glass-Steagall Act of 1932,[2] which loosened the dependence of Federal Reserve credit on the supply of gold and commercial paper, and his Secretary of the Treasury urged the Federal Reserve to adopt a less restrictive policy, as it finally did in the spring of 1932.[3] These measures helped the country get through 1932 without collapse, and if there was an upturn in the middle of 1932, a point still disputed between Republicans and Democrats, they probably contributed to it.[4] But they did not definitely liberate federal fiscal policy, primarily because the vulnerability to gold drain remained and because the RFC operation was too slow, small, and selective to deal with the contagion of bank runs.

The reaction to the financial crisis of March, 1933, largely but not entirely President Roosevelt's reaction, was more direct and more drastic. Instead of trying to demonstrate the advantage of keeping money in the country and in the banks, he closed the doors and windows so the money couldn't get out.

1. He suspended the convertibility of dollars into gold for domestic citizens. This suspension has been permanent.

2. He suspended the export of gold. This suspension was later, in January, 1934, lifted for monetary transactions between the U.S. and foreign treasuries or central banks, but only after the value of the dollar in gold had been reduced about 40%.

3. He closed all the banks temporarily and then reopened those whose solvency and liquidity the government was prepared to endorse and maintain.

4. He obtained passage of legislation (Emergency Banking Act of 1933) authorizing the Federal Reserve to lend to member banks without limitation on the character of the security accepted.

All of these actions were taken by March 9, 1933—within five days of the inauguration. The picture may be rounded out with these developments of the next few months:

5. He accepted the Thomas Amendment to the Agricultural Adjustment Act, authorizing the President to issue unsecured currency—greenbacks— up to the amount of $3 billion. Roosevelt is sometimes described as accepting

this authority reluctantly, in order to avoid Congressional enactment of a mandate to issue greenbacks. In fact, while Roosevelt did not want to be under a mandate, and did not seek the authority, he seemed pleased with the deal that gave it to him.[5]

6. Congress enacted in the Banking Act of 1933 a temporary program of deposit insurance, beginning January 1, 1934, which was subsequently made permanent.

7. The President obtained legislation setting up in the Treasury a fund of $2 billion from the profit on the revaluation of gold to be available for the purchase of gold, foreign exchange, or government securities.

These steps freed the government from monetary restraints, foreign or domestic, upon the execution of inflationary or expansionist policies, whether through the budget or otherwise. Fear of a gold drain into domestic circulation was gone, probably forever. Fear of a gold loss abroad was gone for 25 years. Fear that "unorthodox" government policy might lead to runs on banks was gone, apparently forever. And fear that government deficit finance in a depression might cause interest rates to rise and security prices to fall to a degree in conflict with the government's wishes was also removed by the increase of the monetary powers of the Treasury and the Federal Reserve and by the Federal Reserve's acceptance of increased responsibility toward government financing. The President had said that the nation had nothing to fear but fear itself, and his first steps had been to free his financial policy from the restraint of fear.

There can be no doubt that obtaining domestic and international monetary freedom was a deliberate, high-priority, Rooseveltian objective. In several discussions between the November, 1932, election and the March, 1933, inauguration, Hoover had tried to persuade Roosevelt to declare some commitment to the gold standard and to international economic cooperation. Moley describes Roosevelt's refusal approvingly as deliberate selection of a course of national economic independence. In June of 1933, Roosevelt sent his famous "bombshell" message—which earned the praise of J. M. Keynes as "magnificently right"—to the London Economic Conference, declaring that for the United States, domestic recovery and reflation must take priority over stabilization of international exchange rates.

In his 1933 inaugural address the President promised an "adequate and sound currency." He always refused to be drawn into any precise definition of what this meant. On April 7, 1933, he told the press: "I am not going to write a book on it."[6] However, on several occasions in 1933 he described the monetary situation resulting from his actions as a "managed currency," using this term with apparent pride. The distinction between using newly printed currency to pay the current deficit of government and using it to buy already outstanding government debt was important to him. The former was "greenbackism" and unsound, whereas the latter exchanged one government debt for another and was not unsound.

The following remarks from Roosevelt's press conference of January 15, 1934, explaining the gold devaluation message of that date, have the ring of straight-from-the-heart Rooseveltian monetary philosophy:

> PRESIDENT: Now, in a nutshell, the first portion of this, down to the first line, might be called philosophical. In other words, it merely goes into the general theory that the issuance of money or currency or any medium of exchange is solely a Government prerogative and always has been since the days of Babylon or the time they used sea shells or coral beads in the South Sea Islands. In theory, coral beads are a perfectly good medium of exchange, perfectly good money as such, provided there is control over them. It becomes a question of control. Throughout history it has always been advisable, for the sake of stability, to have some basis behind the currency which, as a matter of practical fact through the ages, has been the precious metals, gold and silver.
>
> QUESTION: Might we assume that that is an argument against greenbacks—what you have just stated?
>
> PRESIDENT: It certainly is an argument against starting of the printing presses. On the other hand, of course, as you know, there has been a very great difference of opinion as to what is a greenback and what is not a greenback. This is the easiest illustration—if we were to start tomorrow to pay off the deficit of this year just by printing greenbacks, they really would be greenbacks; there is no question about that.
>
> On the other hand, a limited amount of non-interest-bearing five- and ten-dollar bonds to retire an outstanding debt and with provision for retirement of those new non-interest-bearing bonds would not be greenbacks.
>
> What people fear about greenbacks is, of course, that some future Congress may take off the limit—take off the lid.[7]

One thing Roosevelt obviously meant by a managed money system was that the government was going to manage the market for its own securities. Whether the government's money manager was going to be the President or the Federal Reserve was not a question that seems to have concerned him. The monetary powers of the Thomas Amendment and the January, 1934, Gold Act were powers of the President. The relations between Roosevelt and Marriner Eccles, who was the chairman of the Federal Reserve during most of his administration, seemed to include freedom for Mr. Eccles to advise and argue on all kinds of matters and ultimate authority for the President on everything.

CONFIDENCE AND THE BALANCED BUDGET

The monetary measures taken in the early days of the Roosevelt administration gave relief, of course, only from monetary restraints. There were other possible restraints in the way of a policy of Federal spending and deficits. These restraints were psychological, political and ideological. One of these was the need to preserve confidence. Loss of confidence could no longer cause a flight into gold and was unlikely to cause a run on the banks or a decline in government bond prices. But it could cause a slowdown in private spending, especially private business investment, which would impede recovery. Action of a budget-balancing and economizing character was considered helpful for the preservation of confidence.

Moreover, in a campaign speech, Candidate Roosevelt had strongly denounced Hoover for failure to balance the budget, and had promised to perform that feat himself if elected. This created some obligation, perhaps small but not zero, to behavior that could be reconciled with the promise.

Finally there was Roosevelt's own belief in budget balancing. Roosevelt's biographers are agreed on the strength of this belief. Schlesinger refers to "one of the few economic doctrines which Roosevelt held in a clear way— that an unbalanced budget was bad."[8] And Burns, describing Roosevelt's position as revealed up to 1938, says:

> On one economic matter, however, Roosevelt had shown a dogged tenacity and consistency. This was balancing the budget. Not, of course, that he had balanced the budget—but it remained a central objective of his fiscal policies. Again and again during the first term he had returned to the point until it had become a refrain.[9]

But Roosevelt's own belief in budget balancing was not to stand in the way of a policy of deficits. The belief was probably real enough, but it was not so high in Roosevelt's scale of values that he was prepared to sacrifice much for it. Also, his conception of what budget balancing meant was elastic enough to accommodate the fiscal policy he wanted. Budget-balancing did not necessarily mean that all expenditures had to be covered by taxes.

This elastic view of budget-balancing was general in the Roosevelt entourage of 1932–33. Thus, Schlesinger says of Hugh Johnson: "In his basic diagnosis, Johnson had many points of agreement with the brain trust. Where he conspicuously differed lay in his deep commitment to budget-balancing."[10] It is true that in June, 1932, Johnson had written a memorandum to himself and friends in which he stressed the importance of balancing the budget. But he did not regard this as inconsistent with recommending in the same memorandum a $2 billion-a-year bond issue for self-liquidating public works, service of the debt to be guaranteed by new taxes to yield $80 million a year.[11] Johnson's mentor, Bernard Baruch, had similar ideas about what budget-balancing meant.[12]

Tugwell also regarded budget-balancing as consistent with borrowing to pay for some government expenditures. He reports that before the inauguration he did not believe that "budgetary deficits would need to be resorted to." But in January, 1933, he gave an interview to the *New York World-Telegram* recommending a program which "included $5 billion for public works, with direct federal relief and an expansion of RFC activities: it also envisaged sound currency and *a balanced budget*, to be achieved through drastic increase of income taxes and *through borrowing*."[13]

Roosevelt's own desire for a balanced budget was not exacting and was easily satisfied. He was more concerned with the desire of the public for a "sound" financial policy, and with the possible economic and political consequences of the belief that his policy was not sound. But these would be the consequences of the public image of his policy, and could be averted by presenting the proper image, without changing the policy.

This attitude is seen in an exchange of letters before the inauguration with his friend, Pierre Jay, chairman of the Fiduciary Trust Company of New York. Jay wrote urging him to "bare his teeth" and balance the budget. He recognized that this would increase unemployment and reduce purchasing power "in the first instance, but this is a valley we have got to go through." On February 1, 1933, FDR replied that "I go along with you wholly in the thought that budget balancing will have a marked effect upon confidence," but here is a "conundrum." Suppose the "regular budget" can be balanced. What will be the effect on public confidence if the President still has to borrow for unemployment relief, RFC, etc.?[14]

Roosevelt's strategy was to place himself at the head of the economizing, budget-balancing forces, and to present his program as the surest route to their objectives. He began on this course in a powerful message to Congress on March 10, 1933, six days after inauguration. Much of what he said then was later to be quoted against him, but for the time being he laid fears of unsound finance to rest. The message contains the memorable statement: "Too often in recent history liberal governments have been wrecked on the rocks of loose fiscal policy." He estimated that the budget deficit would probably amount to $5 billion for the four fiscal years 1931–34 inclusive. Then he went on:

> With the utmost seriousness I point out to the Congress the profound effect of this fact upon our national economy. It has contributed to the recent collapse

of our banking structure. It has accentuated the stagnation of the economic life of our people. Our Government's house is not in order and for many reasons no effective action has been taken to restore it to order.[15]

On this basis he asked Congress for emergency powers to cut expenditures, especially government payrolls and veterans' benefits for non–service-connected disabilities. He assured Congress that "if this is done there is a reasonable prospect that within a year the income of the Government will be sufficient to cover the expenditures of the Government."[16]

The message was effective. Congress passed the requested legislation, the Economy Act of 1933, on the same day. More important, a glow of fiscal soundness was cast over the whole New Deal. The National City Bank *Monthly Letter* said that the monetary expansion which would have to accompany the reopening of the banks made a balanced budget doubly imperative, in order to avoid inflation. "For this reason, the grant to the President, upon his own demand, of authority to enforce economies necessary to balance the Federal budget, comes at a time when it is of incalculable value. Complementing the banking program, it has renewed confidence in the integrity of the dollar."[17]

Even people close to the situation could be confused about where Roosevelt was going. In March, 1933, Marriner Eccles, still a Utah banker but already a champion of compensatory fiscal policy, wrote to friends warning of the deflationary effect of Roosevelt's economy program. Senator LaFollette agreed. However, Secretary of War Dern, Eccles' friend from Utah, said that the administration was committed to "the sound economic policy of a balanced budget." There was visible evidence of this. According to Eccles, although the Economy Act of March 10 seemed to call for cuts in the normal administrative functions of government, "Roosevelt also ordered a halt to the public-works program begun by Hoover. The naked, rusting girders of the Department of Commerce Building in Washington stood for months as a token of Roosevelt's resolve to balance the budget."[18]

But Roosevelt did not have a resolve to balance the budget.[19] By the time he submitted his economy message it was already determined that he would have a spending program, and only its size was in doubt. However, he was resolved that his program would not have the look of loose fiscal policy, with consequent adverse economic and political reactions. When he sent his $3.3 billion spending program to Congress, on May 17, it was clothed in the language and trappings of "sound finance." Sternly he declared: "In carrying out this program it is imperative that the credit of the United States Government be protected and preserved." Therefore he proposed that new taxes be raised to pay *interest and amortization* on the cost of the program. "Careful estimates" indicated that at least $220 million of additional revenue would be required for this purpose.[20] This provision of the 1933 spending program was as close as the Roosevelt administration ever came to a "dual budget" as a guide to policy, in the sense that taxes were raised to service the debt created to finance the expenditures that were not paid for immediately out of revenues.

A special tax levy to service the debt for extraordinary depression spending had been recommended by Baruch and Johnson in 1932. The most ardent budget-balancer in the administration, the Budget Director Lewis Douglas, who had opposed the whole spending program, strongly advocated this method of finance once the President had decided to go ahead with the spending. Possibly the provision for servicing the debt satisfied Roosevelt's own desire to balance the budget. Certainly it satisfied his need to be able to explain that he had followed a sound fiscal course.

Perhaps this financing plan convinced people that the budget was balanced. Perhaps they did not really care. In any case there was little opposition to the $3.3 billion spending program to be financed by borrowing or to the $220 million of new taxes to service the resulting debt. Congress accepted the soundness of this with as little question as it had accepted the soundness of Hoover's last-ditch program to balance the budget a year earlier—and they were largely the same Congressmen. As a year earlier, the big argument in Congress was over the form of the tax increase.

In his fireside chat of July 24, 1933, reviewing the recovery program to that date, the President explained his fiscal policy:

> For years [before FDR's inauguration] the Government had not lived within its income. The immediate task was to bring our regular expenses within our revenues. That has been done.
>
> It may seem inconsistent for a government to cut down its regular expenses and at the same time to borrow and to spend billions for an emergency. But it is not inconsistent because a large portion of the emergency money has been paid out in the form of sound loans which will be repaid to the Treasury over a period of years; and to cover the rest of the emergency money we have imposed taxes to pay the interest and the installments on that part of the debt.
>
> So you can see that we have kept our credit good. We have built a granite foundation in a period of confusion. That foundation of the Federal credit stands there broad and sure. It is the base of the whole recovery plan.[21]

Roosevelt's strategy of 1933 would not permanently insulate him against the charge of loose finance. He would have to contend with that charge through most of his first two terms. But for 1933 at least, he had freed himself of restraints arising from the fear that an expansionist budget policy would weaken business confidence and alienate the affection of the voters. He had done something more than that. He had shown how small an obstacle the budget-balancing ideology was to a pragmatic fiscal policy, if the policy was described in a way that met the formal requirements of the ideology and did not raise opposition on other grounds.

THE ROUTES TO EXPANSION

The monetary measures of March and April, and Roosevelt's manner of presenting his budgetary plans, opened the way for an expansive fiscal policy. However, they were permissive only. They did not assure that the administration's program would include an expansive fiscal policy. In fact fiscal policy was only one of several routes to expansion which seemed to be available, and the President had no commitment to this particular route.

> There is one final objective of my policy which is more vital and basic than all else. I seek to restore the purchasing power of the American people. The return of that purchasing power, and only that, will put America back to work.[22]

This idea, quoted from his speech in Boston on October 31, 1932, ran through all of Mr. Roosevelt's utterances on the economic situation during 1932 and early 1933. But up to the time of his inauguration, and indeed for several weeks thereafter, he had not committed himself to a choice among the possible ways of restoring purchasing power. The air was filled with new ideas and new versions of old ideas for getting the economy moving. Most of these fell into one or another of five categories:

1. Direct action to raise wages and prices, and to "control" and "plan" production and employment. While this idea of course had an old history, it regained vigor in the early 1930's, mainly with support from the business community. The central point was that businesses should agree, without interference by the anti-trust laws, on minimum prices and maximum production, thus putting an end to "unfair competition," "chiselling," "over-production" and other such "evils" from which the economy was thought to be suffering. In some versions the program was to be under the control, or at least review, of a national economic council or other supreme body, and the whole idea enjoyed the appearance of being simultaneously planned and voluntary. A somewhat different version of this idea grew up on the labor side. The objective was to bring about by voluntary cooperative action or by government regulation a reduction of weekly hours of work and an increase of hourly wage rates. Both the business and the labor version of the idea of direct action had support in the Congress.

2. A change in the price of gold, either a once-for-all increase or a continuous manipulation of the price. This idea, especially in its manipulative version, was important because Roosevelt's Dutchess County neighbor, Henry Morgenthau, Jr., who was to become Secretary of the Treasury, had been persuaded of its value by friends at Cornell University. Some Congressmen from gold-mining states were interested in it also.

3. Monetary expansion through unorthodox means—"greenbacks" and "printing presses." Support for this had been growing throughout 1932, especially in the Congress.

4. Monetary expansion by orthodox means, that is by the use of the instruments of the Federal Reserve System to increase the lending power of the banks, with the expectation that they in turn would increase their loans and investments and thereby bring about an increase in bank deposits, the largest element of the money supply.

5. Increased federal spending, especially for unemployment relief and public works. This, as we have seen in the previous chapter, had much support in many quarters.

The Roosevelt administration in 1933 chose, or got without choosing, some of each of these five policies in one form or another. The National Recovery Administration provided for a reduction of working hours and increase of wage rates and in addition encouraged labor to organize and get more of both on their own. In "exchange," businesses were given immunity from the anti-trust laws to get together and "rationalize" their own behavior. The Agricultural Adjustment Administration did for agriculture what businesses were being organized to do for themselves. The price of gold was raised in a series of steps from $20.67 an ounce until it was stabilized at $35.00 in January, 1934. The President accepted the Thomas Amendment, authorizing him to issue up to $3 billion of paper money, and there is some question whether Congress might not have given him this authority even if he had not agreed to accept it. Federal Reserve policy brought about some expansion of bank reserves during 1933, and expansion of reserves continued in succeeding years as a result of gold inflow.[23] The federal government embarked upon a program of increased spending for public works and relief almost as soon as the Economy Act was out of the way.

The administration never provided any comprehensive rationale for this combination of measures. It was willing to try various things and see what worked. But certain general inferences can be reasonably drawn from what the administration said and did. The NRA and the AAA, at least for their more enthusiastic supporters and probably also for the President, were both means to recovery and permanent structural reforms for keeping the economy at a high level once recovery was achieved. Underlying these reforms was the thought that in the twenties too small a share of the national income had gone to workers and farmers—the consuming classes—and too large a share had gone to savers. As a result investment had run for a time at a rate which could not be sustained by the rate of consumption, and had then collapsed, causing the Depression. The NRA and the AAA were to raise and sustain the share of workers and farmers and thereby raise and sustain the share of consumption in the total national income. The new programs were not, however, expected to work to the disadvantage of profits, because a high and sustained national income would mean high and sustained *total* profits, even though the proportionate *share* of profits would be smaller than it had been during the twenties.

Raising the price of gold was probably intended as a transitional step. It was expected, primarily by reducing the price of the dollar relative to other currencies, to bring about an increase in the dollar price of internationally traded goods, especially raw materials. This would raise the purchasing power of farmers and miners. Also, raising the price of gold would permit other, domestic, reflationary steps to be taken without fear that they would cause an outflow of gold. The goal was to achieve a certain higher level of U.S. prices, at which both commodity prices and gold prices could be stabilized. The administration probably did not contemplate continued manipulation of the price of gold, although it did propose to retain a high degree of freedom for domestic economic policy against international restraints.

The authority to issue greenbacks was a weapon to be kept in reserve, a club in the closet to guarantee the independence of the government in its chosen policies. The administration visualized the possibility that the bankers might strike, refusing to buy government securities. In that case resort might be had to greenbacks. The government might also have to meet a drain of currency from the banks. But direct issue of paper money did not have a positive role in the program of recovery. The role of montary expansion by the orthodox mechanics of the Federal Reserve was only slightly greater. After the bank holiday, easy money was to be restored, so that the financing of private investment could proceed. But beyond some point at which credit was considered "easy," monetary expansion would not be pushed as an active force for recovery.

THE ROLE OF SPENDING POLICY

In this package of recovery measures, Roosevelt was not inclined to give a major role to government spending. In his "Forgotten Man" speech, on April 7, 1932, he had belittled the idea:

It is the habit of the unthinking to turn in times like this to the illusions of economic magic. People suggest that a huge expenditure of public funds by the Federal Government and by State and local governments will completely solve the unemployment problem. But it is clear that even if we could raise many billions of dollars and find definitely useful public works to spend these billions on, even all that money would not give employment to the seven million or ten million people who are out of work. Let us admit frankly that it would be only a stop-gap.[24]

Moley describes Roosevelt as "frankly leery" of the arguments for public works in 1932 and early 1933:

Again and again, when we were formulating the plans for the campaign in 1932, Roosevelt had been urged by Tugwell and others to come out for a $5,000,000,000 public-works program. He repeatedly shied away from the proposal. This seems to have been partly because, as Roosevelt explained, Hoover, despite all his preparations, had not been able to find over $900,000,000 worth of "good" and "useful" projects. But it was also because Roosevelt certainly did not, at that time, subscribe to the pump-priming theory.[25]

These statements reveal two elements in Roosevelt's thinking on the subject which were to appear repeatedly in 1933 and later. First, he thought the amount of useful work on which the government could spend money was small. Second, and more important, he was skeptical about any indirect effects from spending. He did not believe that spending could stimulate the economy to a point where prosperity would be sustained without continuation of the spending. He conceived of the economy as having some critical structural defect, related to the planning of production and the distribution of income, which prevented full employment from being sustained. Without correction of that defect stable prosperity could not be achieved. Government spending would not correct the defect, although it might provide a certain number of jobs in the interim. This is the meaning of calling public works a "stop-gap" and of not subscribing to "pump-priming theory." Roosevelt was doubtful that public-works spending would provide jobs beyond the number actually employed at the construction site, plus possibly those employed in producing the materials for the project. He was skeptical of arguments about jobs that would be created as a result of the consumption expenditures of the construction workers.

Despite these reservations, Roosevelt was willing from the beginning to try public-works spending as far as it would go. At the end of February, 1933, he talked to Frances Perkins about becoming Secretary of Labor, and she outlined the policy she would propose, including an extensive program of public works. "The program received Roosevelt's hearty endorsement . . ."[26] Miss Perkins also received approval for the general idea of expanding public works at the first Cabinet meeting of the new administration. But the size of the program remained unsettled.

Many of the people around Roosevelt in early 1933 were for a "big" program, which then meant something like $4 or $5 billion. This included Senators Wagner, LaFollette, and Costigan, as well as Miss Perkins, Tugwell, Ickes, and Hugh Johnson. In general, their support of a spending program did not rest on the "pump-priming" idea that temporary spending would lead to sustained prosperity, or on a "multiplier" idea that public spending would generate private spending which would also create jobs. They wanted simply to increase employment for the government and for its contractors and suppliers.

In terms of the later history of fiscal thinking, it is Hugh Johnson's advocacy of a large public-works program that is most interesting, because he came closest to seeing the program as an integral part of the recovery effort and not just as a temporary bandage. (This judgment stands even if Johnson's account of his views in *The Blue Eagle* is assumed to benefit from considerable hindsight.) Johnson was then engaged in formulating what became the NRA with the assistance of Alexander Sachs, economist of Lehman Brothers and soon to be the first chief of NRA's Research and Planning Division. As Johnson described their reasoning:

> The most obvious, immediate way to erase the effect of the depression on wages and hours was the NRA project to decrease hours, to spread work and to increase wages to maintain purchasing power. The whole idea of shortening hours and raising wages has been attacked on this argument:
> "The principal element of cost in any article is the labor cost. Increases in that cost by higher payments to those benefited simply increases price to the whole people whose capacity to buy is already so limited, that it may be assumed that they are buying all they can. The result can only be reduction in the tonnage of consumption and hence of manufacture and hence of net employment."
> There is no doubt in the world that there is much here to give us pause. Dr. Sachs and I considered it prayerfully when we blocked out the NRA program. We relied, however, on PWA [the public works program] to activate the heavy industries at once and thus increase the *total number of available purchasers*. We relied on AAA to increase farm purchasing power immediately and thus still further add to the *number of purchasers*. These added to NRA additions would so far increase *volume* that we thought (and I still think) the increased labor cost could be absorbed without much increase in price.[27]

Johnson and Sachs relied upon the public-works spending to release them from the circular character of the argument in favor of NRA. The

NRA was supposed to increase employment and production by increasing the purchasing power of workers—by increasing wage rates more than prices. But in order to get this result—higher real wage rates—without a depressing effect on profits it was necessary to have an increase in volume of production. So achieving higher production and employment depended upon having higher production and employment. The increase of public-works spending was a way to assure the increase of production which would permit higher real wage rates without smaller total profits and thereby permit an increase of production. This argument, in effect, was recognition that even with the assistance of the NRA the economy could not lift itself by its bootstraps, but required an outside stimulus—which the public-works program would provide. Some obvious questions follow from this. If the economy could not rise without external assistance, could it stay up without continued outside assistance? In the combination of NRA and public works it seems to be the public works component that is doing all the lifting. In that case why is the NRA needed? However, what interests us here is not the argument for or against NRA but the attempt to trace the effects of public works spending through the economic system.

We can see in Johnson's writing an early version of an investment multiplier, which was presumably much clearer in the mind of Sachs.[28] Johnson thought that the NRA could raise production and employment in consumers' goods industries, by raising workers' purchasing power, but that this increase would not be enough and would certainly fail unless it were balanced by an increase in the heavy or capital goods industries. He and Sachs calculated that a $3 to $4 billion federal program of spending and lending for heavy goods "would do the trick," and by fall would increase heavy industries' employment by 1,000,000 alongside an expected increase of 3,000,000 in consumers' industries employment.[29]

However, such sophisticated argument was rare in Washington in the spring of 1933. It is true that legislation authorizing the public-works program was included in the same act that set up the NRA, but this was apparently not because of Johnson's analysis of the economic relation between the two programs. Moley reports that he suggested early in March the idea of combining the public works and NRA legislation as a strategy for getting the public works approved by the President. Another account reports that the President on May 10 made a typically spontaneous decision which resulted in the combination of the two programs.[30]

During much of April and May a debate went on within the administration about the amount to be spent on public works. In this debate Roosevelt himself was the chief opponent of a big program, with Budget Director

Douglas his main supporter. Unlike the President, Douglas based his opposition to public-works spending on the importance of balancing the buget. Douglas became one of the leading proponents of the industry-codes approach to recovery, because that did not involve spending government money and unbalancing the Federal budget.

Roosevelt's own views were revealed in a press conference on April 19, 1933:

> QUESTION: The public works program will fit in this general campaign sooner or later, will it not?
>
> PRESIDENT: Oh yes, and, by the way, entirely off the record, do not write stories about five or six billion dollars of public works. That is wild. In other words, the public works program will be as much as we can usefully use between now and next spring. There is no use attempting to go ahead with a program of projects which will require all kinds of engineering in the first instance and with the actual employment unable to start for a whole year. What we want is the type of public works that will put people to work immediately—get them to work as soon as possible.
>
> QUESTION: Is that off the record?
>
> PRESIDENT: I think you can use that.
>
> QUESTION: That won't be so much then?
>
> PRESIDENT: It won't be five or six billion dollars. I have no idea, but it will not be anything like that.
>
> QUESTION: It won't be much more than a billion?
>
> PRESIDENT: We are looking over the field and seeing how many public works there are that are practical, useful, self-sustaining as far as possible, and that can be started quickly. There is a limit to that.[31]

Ten days later there was discussion at a Cabinet meeting of an appropriation of $5 billion for public works. Roosevelt asked what projects could call for such money. Miss Perkins gave him a list of projects, arranged by states, which had been prepared for her by an association of contractors and architects. Roosevelt looked at the section for New York State, and "proceeded to rip that list to pieces," showing that to his own knowledge many of the projects were impractical or useless.[32]

Two weeks later the Budget Bureau came up with a figure of $3.3 billion of public-works funds for two years as the amount that could be used and financed. Douglas, according to Miss Perkins, was still trying to keep public works out of the recovery program entirely. Ickes still preferred $5 billion, but thought $3.3 billion was better than Roosevelt's suggestion of $1 to $1.5 billion. Moley later said, "The interesting figure of $3,300,000,000 for public works, to which Roosevelt finally agreed early in May, 1933 always seemed to me to represent a compromise between the $5,000,000,000 program that had been urged on him and the $900,000,000 Hoover figure that Roosevelt personally regarded as the probable outside limit of useful plans and projects."[33]

The President requested the $3.3 billion in a message to Congress on May 17, saying: "A careful survey convinces me that approximately $3,300,000,000 can be invested in useful and necessary public construction and at the same time put the largest possible number of people to work."[34] This amount was provided by Congress on June 13 in Title II of the National Industrial Recovery Act, Title I of which established the NRA.

Spending was the ugly duckling of Roosevelt's 1933 barnyard, not to become the swan for several years, and then mainly by default. The NRA was first found to be unworkable and then found to be unconstitutional. The gold policy did not produce the results its original proponents had claimed for it, and probably could not be carried further without reprisals from abroad. Money has been made "easy." And still the conditions which had been visualized as permitting the termination of extraordinary spending had not been achieved. Unemployment remained high. Something had to be done, and more spending was left as the only thing that could be done. Whether for this reason or independently, new theories emerged to explain why more spending was the best thing to do.

The elevation of spending to the front rank of recovery measures was to come later. But this does not diminish the significance of the milestone that was passed in 1933. Never again would there be a serious effort, like Hoover's of 1932, to balance the budget in a depression or offset the revenue loss caused by the depression itself. Neither would the government be deterred from providing relief and jobs to those most critically in need during a depression for fear that the budget could not stand it. The main reason for the change was that such self-denial was seen to be unnecessary. With a strong financial system and a cooperative monetary policy, both of which dated from 1933, there was no danger that a large deficit would cause a financial crisis, domestic or international, and so make the depression worse. And while there was still ideological attachment in the country to budget-balancing, this was seen to be neither so strong nor so precise in its requirements as to prevent substantial adjustment of budget policy to the clear demands of the economic situation. These developments greatly widened the range for choice of fiscal policies. What the principles of fiscal policy should be within that widened range, and how those principles should be carried out, was not decided in 1933 and has not been decided yet. But a large part of the distance between 1932 and 1964 had been traveled by 1933.

4

Fiscal Drift

1933–1936

By the time Congress adjourned in July, 1933, the President was in a position to proceed with a spending program. He had abundant legislative authority. His reputation as an economizer —as a champion of sound finance—had been established. Financial conditions were favorable because interest rates were low and credit was abundant. The business and banking communities were at least reconciled to a temporary surge of extraordinary spending.

But the President was in no hurry. He did not accept the thesis of Hugh Johnson that the NRA and the public-works program had to go hand-in-hand, the public-works spending to offset at the beginning the restrictive effects of the cost-raising features of the NRA. If Roosevelt had accepted this idea he probably would not have decided to split the administration of the two titles of the NIRA, with Johnson confined to the code provisions and Ickes in charge of the public works. This decision, coming without prior notice, surprised, angered, and dismayed Johnson. He wanted to quit, and there is a sad story of his driving around Washington with Miss Perkins while she persuaded him to stay.[1]

It has been said that the whole course of the recovery would have been different if the dynamic Johnson had been given the public-works job and careful "Honest Harold" entrusted with the codes. But this leaves out the influence of the President. Certainly Ickes had no feeling during the summer of 1933 or later that the President was pushing him. FDR was approving public-works projects one by one, which was no way to get a $3.3 billion program going.[2] According to Ickes, the President thought that recovery might come quickly and did not want to be stuck with huge commitments for public-works spending stretched out into the future.[3] The course of events provided some basis for the expectation of quick recovery. Industrial production nearly doubled from March to July as earlier fears vanished and businesses hurried to accumulate inventories before the NRA raised costs and prices.

The 1933 recovery was short-lived, however, and by fall the first "Roosevelt recession" made spending again an acute issue in the administration. A little "spending" group formed in Washington. Around the first of November, Marriner Eccles had dinner at the Shoreham Hotel with Tugwell, Ezekiel, Wallace, Hopkins, Jerome Frank, Dern, and others. "They needed arguments on how a planned policy of adequate deficit financing could serve the humanitarian objective with which they were most directly concerned; and second, how the increased production and employment that the policy would create was the only way a depression could be ended and a budget balanced."[4] The other side of the issue was led, as in the spring, by Lewis Douglas.

The immediate decision did not rest on any sophisticated arguments, whether supplied by Eccles or others. Unemployment was rising, winter was coming, and Roosevelt, like Hoover, was especially sensitive to the problem of how the unemployed would get through the winter. So he accepted the proposal urged upon him by Hopkins to start an emergency program of light work that could quickly give jobs to four million people during the winter. The program was to be managed by the Civil Works Administration, with Hopkins at its head, and to be provided with funds from the relief and public-works appropriations and from the RFC. About $800 million would be spent on this program between December, 1933, and April, 1934.

The President did not regard this decision as permanently settling the future of the administration's fiscal policy. In announcing the plan for the CWA he acknowledged that it was a relatively costly way to provide assistance and said that he would revert to the more economical method of direct relief when the existing crisis had been passed. The spending argument continued within the administration.

Still, the decision to launch the CWA in the fall of 1933 revealed what was to be the administration's policy for the first Roosevelt term. Expenditure decisions would be made in terms of the needs and direct benefits of particular programs—among which work relief was the most important—rather than in terms of the indirect contribution of spending to total employment and prosperity. Also, the CWA program raised total spending sharply to a level which would be continued unchanged for the next three years. If expenditures for veterans are excluded, expenditures in the fiscal years 1934, 1935, and 1936 were almost exactly constant and rose about 15 percent in 1937, largely because of the social security program which had its own special financing. Veterans' expenditures followed a course of their own, independent of and contrary to administration policy. In fact, one could say that the spending policy of the administration was to keep spending constant during 1934, 1935, and 1936. But this was not because of any principle that expenditures should be constant. It was rather because there were conflicting objectives, and continuing to spend what had been spent avoided the appearance of choosing among them.

FOCUS ON THE DIRECT RESULTS OF SPENDING

President Roosevelt did not "intend to write a book" about fiscal policy, any more than he "intended to write a book" about monetary policy. At various times he and other members of his administration said various things, but they never produced any general theory of the fiscal policy under which they were working. On occasion Roosevelt would invoke a theory that spending had indirect benefits in raising income and employment. As time went on and continued spending needed more defense, and other aspects of the New Deal disappeared or lost their appeal, he claimed more and more for the indirect benefits of spending in promoting recovery.

However, what Ickes noted in his diary on September 13, 1935, seems to be the basic Rooseveltian attitude during the first term. "No one has been able to mention indirect employment to the President for a long time. He simply has no patience with the thought."[5] It was around this time that the President instructed Ickes not to make the indirect employment argument in testimony before Congressional committees. Roosevelt's unwillingness to count the indirect results made Ickes the usual loser in his unending competition with Harry Hopkins. Ickes' public-works program had the advantage, in the President's opinion, that its projects were of greater long-range value, per dollar of expenditure, than the work performed by Hopkins' WPA. The WPA projects were the object of much criticism as wasteful, if not useless. Moreover, there was some hope that the federal government would be repaid by states and localities for part of its public works expenditures. But the President could not get over the fact that, per dollar, the WPA program put about four times as many men to work *directly* as did the public-works program. The comparison would have been less unfavorable to the public-works program if indirect effects had been considered.

The issue of spending as a means of providing general support for the economy was raised in 1935 when the Congress passed a bill to pay a bonus to the veterans. Here was an opportunity to put a large amount of money into the hands of consumers quickly, and without the administration having to take the responsibility for extravagence. There was a group in the Treasury —Oliphant, Gaston, Haas, and McReynolds—who argued for approving the bonus on the grounds that it would stimulate consumption expenditures and thereby contribute to recovery.

> They also argued that the appropriate time for the Treasury to borrow to pay the bonus was during a depression. The bonus was due in any case in 1945, they pointed out, and if the country then happened to be on the crest of a boom, payment might precipitate runaway inflation. In 1935 or 1936, on the other hand, the bonus would lift the lagging economy by giving a large group of consumers funds to spend. The bonus, moreover, would go out to veterans at a rate much more rapid than that at which the $4.8 billion [recovery and relief appropriation] could be expended. It would immediately expand consumption on a nation-wide basis, a condition which Morgenthau's advisers considered so important that they recommended the Secretary consider paying the bonus out of the work relief appropriation.[6]

The idea of using the work-relief appropriation to finance the bonus did not appeal to Secretary Morgenthau. Work relief funds were to provide jobs for those on relief, not to provide generalized stimulation for the economy. Roosevelt agreed with him.

The message vetoing the 1935 bonus bill, which Roosevelt himself dictated with suggestions from Morganthau, is probably the clearest statement available of the administration's attitude toward spending in the years before 1938. It specifically denied the efficacy or propriety of "mere spending" for the sake of recovery. Analyzing the claim that the bonus payment would increase consumers' purchasing power, the President said:

> First, the spending of this sum, it cannot be denied, would result in some expansion of retail trade. But it must be noted that retail trade has already expanded to a condition that compares favorably with conditions before the depression. However, to resort to the kind of financial practice provided in this bill would not improve the conditions necessary to expand those industries in which we have the greatest unemployment. The Treasury notes issued under the terms of this bill we know from past experience would return quickly to the banks. We know, too, that the banks have at this moment more than ample credit with which to expand the activities of business and industry generally. The ultimate effect of this bill will not, in the long run, justify the expectations that have been raised by those who argue for it.[7]

Later in the message he said:

> The final "whereas" clause [of the bonus bill], stating that spending the money is the most effective means of hastening recovery is so ill considered that little comment is necessary. Every authorization of expenditure by the 73rd Congress in its session of 1933 and 1934, and every appropriation by the 74th Congress to date, for recovery purposes, has been predicated not on the mere spending of money to hasten recovery, but on the sounder principle of preventing the loss of homes and farms, of saving industry from bankruptcy, of safeguarding bank deposits, and most important of all—of giving relief and jobs through public work to individuals and families faced with starvation. These greater and broader concerns of the American people have a prior claim for our consideration at this time. They have the right of way.[8]

It should not be concluded that the Congressional majority which had passed the bonus bill was a majority for a more expansionist fiscal and monetary policy. Congressman Wright Patman, who was the leader of the bonus forces in the Congress, undoubtedly placed great weight on the generation of more purchasing power and more income, as his long consistent record on that side of economic issues shows, and there were other proponents of the bonus, in and out of Congress, including Father Coughlin, who shared his attitude. The largest number of the bill's supporters probably only wanted to do something for the veterans. In fact, subsequent revision of the bill to assure that enough votes could be mustered in 1936 to override a veto dropped what was considered the most inflationary aspect of the 1935 bill, the provision that payment be made in newly issued Treasury notes—"greenbacks."

When Congress convened in January, 1936, with national elections on the horizon, passage of the bill was inevitable. Roosevelt went through the motions of a one-page veto message, referring to his 1935 message, but the veto was overridden. However there is no reason to think that Roosevelt had changed his mind about "mere spending" for recovery or that Congress had espoused that idea.

Only a few months after the veto of the first bonus bill Roosevelt took a more enthusiastic view of the indirect benefits of spending. In a speech on September 30, 1935, dedicating the Boulder Dam, he said of the public works program:

> In a little over two years, this great national work has accomplished much. We have helped mankind by the works themselves and, at the same time, we have created the necessary purchasing power to throw in the clutch to start the wheels of what we call private industry. Such expenditures on all of these works, great and small, flow out to many beneficiaries; they revive other and more

remote industries and businesses. Money is put in circulation. Credit is expanded and the financial and industrial mechanism of America is stimulated to more and more activity.[9]

The January, 1936, budget message was even more exultant about the pump-priming consequences of spending.

> Our policy is succeeding. The figures prove it. Secure in the knowledge that steadily decreasing deficits will turn in time into steadily increasing surpluses, and that *it is the deficit of today which is making possible the surplus of tomorrow*, let us pursue the course we have mapped.[10]

There was to be more in this vein in the 1936 Presidential campaign. While the willingness of the President to use these ideas was a step toward later policy, especially the policy of 1938, during the first term these ideas were not the basis on which decisions were made. They were part of the basis for justifying a policy chosen on other grounds. Spending remained for Roosevelt what it had been in 1932—a "stop-gap." It was a way of meeting certain emergency needs, especially for work relief, until his other reforms— NRA, AAA, "cleaning up" the financial system, tax revision, etc.—would produce recovery. The spending question was how much was needed to meet the relief rolls, or to sustain the price of cotton, or to satisfy other specific objectives, not how much was needed to produce recovery or reduce unemployment by some target amount.

How Much Spending?

Others have said, as we suggest here, that government spending, at least before 1938, was not regarded as a means to bring about recovery, or as we would now say "full employment," but was rather thought of as a way to provide "relief." It is sometimes implied that this view of its function necessarily results in a rate of expenditure that is inadequate or in any case less than if the broader objective were recognized. For example, John H. Williams, writing in 1941, made this observation on the pre-1938 period:

> Government spending was primarily for relief and was regarded mainly as the unavoidable accompaniment of unemployment until recovery could be achieved by other means. I have been inclined to agree with those who held that relief expenditures do not reach down far enough into the economic process to afford much leverage.[11]

However, the effects of the spending depend much more on its scale than on how the spending is regarded, and regarding the objective as relief does not prevent the scale from being very large. In fact, a government intending to provide work relief with prevailing wage standards for all the existing unemployed might plan to spend much more than a government calculating that its expenditures would have large indirect, multiplier, effects upon employment. The limitations of the spending program did not result from failure to conceive of it as a "recovery" program rather than a "relief" program, but from the decision to confine relief to the neediest cases and to provide it on a minimum scale.

In January, 1935, the President, asking for a $4 billion appropriation for relief and recovery, explained that it was intended to provide work-relief jobs for the estimated 3.5 million employables then on relief. He was questioned at a subsequent press conference about why the program provided jobs only for persons who were on relief. His answer had two parts. First, he said that estimates of unemployment as high as 18 or 20 million, then current, were grossly exaggerated. (Later estimates would support him on that. The number is now believed to have been around 10 or 11 million in early 1935.) Second, he said "Conservative estimates indicated" that the direct employment of 3.5 million on work relief would provide employment for another 3.5 million as a result of expenditures for materials and equipment. (In subsequent news stories, the *New York Times* referred to the $4 billion program as one "designed to create 7,000,000 jobs.")[12]

This statement is interesting as an early, and at that time rare, use of the indirect-employment argument by the President. However, as an explanation of the expenditure program it is not credible. The size of the expected indirect effect is puzzlingly large. One of the major features of the work-relief program was that expenditures for supplies and equipment were kept as low as possible—to about 20 percent of total expenditures—in order to maximize direct employment. It is hardly likely that the spending of 20 percent of the total could yield 3.5 million private jobs at private wage rates if the spending of 80 percent of the total yielded only 3.5 million jobs at much lower work-relief wage rates. The argument might have been more plausible if the President had said that 3.5 million private jobs would be created by the consumption expenditures of the work-relief employees as well as by the expenditures for supplies and equipment, but the President did not say that. Anyway, the work-relief wages were almost entirely a substitute for direct relief payments, so the additional consumption expenditures could not be very large. In fact, since the budget in January, 1935, proposed not an increase but a decrease in total relief and recovery expenditures, in total Federal expenditures, and in the deficit, it is hard to see from what source an increase in private employment was to be expected.

However, aside from its merits, the argument does not explain the decision not to spend more. Before the $4 million figure was arrived at, there had been a considerable debate within the administration. The proponents of a bigger figure were precisely those who assigned the most weight to indirect effects—Hopkins, Ickes, and Eccles. The main opposition had come from Morgenthau, the administration's voice of "sound finance."

Even after the decision was made to provide jobs for the 3.5 million employables on relief, determination of the total amount of expenditures required determination of the expenditure per person. The President later explained this to a meeting of WPA administrators by doing the arithmetic in reverse:

> We have to divide three and a half million men into four billion dollars. Almost anybody can understand that. In other words, Congress has given us four billion dollars. The objective is to put three and a half million men to work during the coming fiscal year.[13]

And so he demonstrated that the money must be spent "on the average, at the rate of somewhere between eleven hundred dollars and twelve hundred dollars per man. This must of necessity include everything—not only the amount we pay the men themselves but also the amount we pay for the materials as well as the overhead." This, of course, was artificial. The $4 billion had not just been given to the President by the Congress at their own volition. It was precisely the amount he had asked for. Presumably he had calculated the eleven to twelve hundred dollars per man before he asked for the $4 billion.

Part of the explanation for the size of Roosevelt's spending program is that for him the urgency of spending fell off sharply after minimum provision had been made for people on relief. He was quite sensitive to the needs of the people on relief. He sharply distinguished that problem from the problem of the unemployed who were not on relief. As we have just seen, he was skeptical of the unemployment estimates. Even later, in 1940, when the government had its own official estimates of unemployment he thought they overstated the real problem because they included people who were not seriously seeking work or who didn't have to work.

Of course Roosevelt thought that unemployment was a problem; but it was a problem to be solved in the course of general recovery, not something requiring an emergency solution in the form of massive government spending, as relief did. Unemployment was a statistic about which it was important to show progress, whereas relief was people in immediate need.

Still, this by itself does not explain the level of spending. The other side of the equation is that the President always felt that his expenditures were constrained by the requirements of sound finance. Early in his administration (December, 1933) the President personified the tension in describing the role of his budget director, Lewis Douglas. "Douglas' job is to prevent the government from spending just as hard as he possibly can. That is his job. Somewhere between his effort to spend nothing . . . and the point of view of the people who want to spend ten billions additional on public works, we will get somewhere, and we are trying to work out a program."[14] Douglas was a symbol for the requirements of sound finance, and while Douglas would last in the administration only until August, 1934, the requirements would remain a constraint on spending.

THE MEANING OF "SOUND FINANCE"

Roosevelt did not think that sound finance, or avoiding "the rocks of loose finance" on which so many liberal governments had been wrecked, required that the budget be balanced "this year" or "next year." He never had a balanced budget in his twelve years in office, and only once—in 1937 —did he recommend a budget that would be balanced in the next year. But sound finance did have something to do with budget-balancing. In Roosevelt's thinking it had three ingredients:

1. There should be an expectation that when normal business activity was regained the budget would be balanced. Related to this was the idea that even during a depression current revenues should exceed regular expenditures, with the implication that the deficit was entirely due to the depression and would disappear with the depression.

2. There should be an expectation that the balanced budget would be achieved sometime "soon"—soon enough to seem real but not so soon as to be immediately embarrassing.

3. Expenditures and the deficit should decline as recovery progressed.

These three ideas appeared in every budget message of the first Roosevelt term. The budget message submitted in January, 1934, forecast a large reduction of expenditures between the fiscal year ending June 30, 1934, and the year ending June 30, 1935. It then went on to say that the government should "plan" to balance the budget in the next fiscal year. In this same budget message the administration introduced the distinction between "general" and "emergency" expenditures, showing that even then the revenues exceeded the "general" expenditures. Budget Director Douglas had opposed this division, pointing out that on such a standard Hoover had a balanced budget, but the President had ignored his protest.

After its first budget message the administration was more cautious in setting the date when the budget would be balanced. In August, 1934, Morgenthau showed Roosevelt a draft of a speech in which he proposed to say that the administration looked forward to a balanced budget. "The President tried to rewrite the statement, but finally said he did not see how Morgenthau could make it because the budget could not be balanced even in the fiscal year 1936, the period July 1, 1935–June 30, 1936. There had been nothing provided for unemployment or for public works. 'Well,' Morgenthau replied, 'cross it out.' "[15]

Roosevelt's search for a way of promising a balanced budget that was real enough to be attractive but not so binding that it could bother him later is illustrated by the drafting of a speech to be given on October 1, 1936, during the Presidential campaign. The subject was especially sensitive because the speech was to be made at Pittsburgh, site of Roosevelt's famous 1932 speech castigating Hoover for failure to balance the budget. In fact, Roosevelt was concerned about what reference he ought to make to his 1932 speech, and Samuel Rosenman, his General Counsel, advised him to deny he had ever said it. However, referring to his own budget policy, Roosevelt wanted to say, "we will balance the budget sooner than we expect." Then he tried saying, "The Treasury advises me that the budget can be balanced" and promising to leave "no stone unturned to balance the federal budget for the fiscal year of 1938." Finally, following a suggestion of Budget Director Bell, he decided on, "If it [the national income] keeps on rising at the present rate, as I am confident that it will, the receipts of the Government, without imposing any additional taxes, will, within a year or two, be sufficient to care for all ordinary and relief expenses of the Government—in other words, to balance the budget."[16]

This was campaign semantics, and while political significance was not missing from any Roosevelt statement on the budget, the following language from his January, 1936, budget message, repeated in his March, 1936, tax message, gives a better picture of what he believed, and wanted the country to believe, about his policy:

> On the part of the Federal Government . . . the many legislative Acts creating the machinery for recovery were all predicated on two interdependent beliefs. First, the measures would immediately cause a great increase in the annual expenditures of the Government—many of these expenditures, however, in the form of loans which would ultimately return to the Treasury. Second, as a result of the simultaneous attack on the many fronts I have indicated, the receipts of the Government would rise definitely and sharply during the following few years, while greatly increased expenditure for the purposes stated, coupled with rising values and the stopping of losses, would, over a period of years, diminish

the need for work relief and thereby reduce Federal expenditures. The increase in revenues would ultimately meet and pass the declining cost of relief.[17]

These various formulations were all part of an effort to find a version of the budget-balancing idea sufficiently elastic for the administration to live with it. They were intended to provide assurance that despite the current deficits the budget was really under control. The deficits were temporary results of the economic emergency; they would disappear with the emergency, and were in fact declining. The regular expenditures of government were being held within the current revenues, and total expenditures were also declining.

Only the third of the three ingredients of the Rooseveltian version of sound finance—the requirement that the deficit and especially total expenditures should decline—was a serious limitation on policy during the first term. The requirement to behave so that the budget would come into balance when the economy regained normal prosperity did not put the administration to any visible test because the economy was so far below prosperity. But if the test had been made it would have been easily met. A rise of the economy to prosperous levels would have surely raised the revenues from the existing taxes by a substantial amount—at least 25 percent. While all of the expenditures officially labelled as "emergency" would not have disappeared with recovery—some, such as the farm program, still continue at a high level—the total would have shrunk enough to balance the budget. Of course, the administration could not have passed a test on balancing the budget soon, but it usually stated that objective with sufficient evasiveness so that the test could not be clearly applied. The time for balancing the budget was always some time off beyond the next budget year.

However the promise that expenditures would be declining was different. It was not a promise of something to occur at a later date or in different circumstances. It was a description of what would be happening to the budget continuously as the economy recovered, and the administration had no wish to deny that the economy was recovering. The administration always had to show that from "then" on, whenever "then" was, expenditures would decline. The budget messages of January, 1934, 1935, 1936, and 1937 all estimated that expenditures would be lower in the next year than in the present year. Expenditures were not actually declining, but the budget plans had to be made as if they were. While the effects of this could be eased by various subterfuges, and were, it still created pressure to hold down spending.

The expectation that expenditures would decline as the economy recovered was natural and would have been satisfied in time—aside from the war—after the economy regained full employment. But to bring about a decline of spending while the economy was in the first stage of partial recovery from a deep depression was difficult. One problem was that the big extraordinary expenditures, which were supposed to decline, were mainly tied to providing jobs for employables who would otherwise have been on relief. The need for this kind of spending would begin to decline only after a substantial measure of recovery had occurred. The initial increases in production would cause relatively small increases in employment, as output per man increased with higher rates of utilization of overhead. Even when people were drawn into private employment they would generally not come from the work-relief rolls, because employers tended to regard the reliefers as less desirable employees—which in many cases they were, either as a result of having been on relief or for other reasons. Moreover, as long as total unemployment was high, even though its amount was declining, the number of employables seeking relief would be likely to rise as unemployed workers exhausted savings or pride.

Therefore, the decline of emergency expenditures would be slow in the early stages of the recovery. But the recovery was not the only influence on the course of spending in the first term. We were also going through a New Deal, a consequence of which was an increase in the permanent programs and expenditures of government. As evidence of this, the January, 1936, budget transferred expenditures for the AAA, Civilian Conservation Corps, and part of the public works program from the "recovery and relief" category to the "regular" category, indicating that they were no longer expected to vanish with recovery. Other "permanent" programs were constantly being added. This would probably not have prevented a decline of total spending after the economy reached high levels of employment, output, and income, but it did exert a force for an increase in total spending as long as the recovery was at a low level.

The Case for Sound Finance

The rule of sound finance which was operative in restraining expenditures during the first Roosevelt term was that expenditures should decline as the economy recovered. Roosevelt tried to adhere to this rule because it expressed his own belief that a balanced budget was a good thing, from which there should be departures only when there was an emergency requiring extraordinary expenditure, and to which the government should return as the emergency abated. But more important, he tried to adhere to the rule because it was as close as he could practically conform to the budget-balancing ideas that were common in the country.

The prevailing ideas about sound finance and budget balancing were significant to Roosevelt for two reasons. First, he believed that they created a potential political danger for him. Second, he believed, or from time to time believed, that lack of confidence in his fiscal policy on the part of the business community could retard the recovery.

Roosevelt took seriously the possibility that the charge of fiscal irresponsibility would cost him support for his program in the Congress as well as votes in the next election. In August, 1934, Budget Director Douglas resigned on the budget-balancing issue. In the course of an emotional interview the President told Douglas that if he resigned there would be "men marching and blood in the streets."[18] By this he presumably meant that fiscal policy could become an extremely divisive political issue.

There was every reason to think that budget-balancing was a strong political issue. In September, 1935, a poll was taken of public opinion on the question of "the most vital issue before the American people today." The largest percentage of replies, 27 percent, named unemployment, but the second largest percentage, 16 percent, said "balance the budget; reduce the national debt," and the third largest, 6 percent, said "reduce taxes."[19] In December, 1935, a poll showed that 70 percent of the American people believed it was then necessary to balance the budget and start reducing the national debt. Of these 70 percent, 80 percent thought the balancing and reduction should be accomplished by economies in government spending, only 2 percent favored tax increases alone, and 18 percent wanted some of each.[20]

In view of the overwhelming political victory Roosevelt won in 1936 it may be questioned whether the budget issue really carried much weight with the voters. The campaign oratory did not change the opinions of the voters about the desirability of budget-balancing. On November 13, 1936, ten days after the election, 70 percent of those polled said that it was "necessary for the new administration to balance the budget." But the voters had not considered it a crucial issue against Roosevelt. Perhaps some significance should be given to the fact that in the same November, 1936, poll, 62 percent of those with opinions thought that Congress had a greater responsibility than the President for balancing the budget.[21] Whether this reflected a belief that nothing could be hoped from Roosevelt on that score, or Roosevelt's success in projecting a "sound finance" image of himself, is impossible to tell.

Whether or not budget policy was a real political danger for him, Roosevelt thought it was, and thought it important on that account to assume a budget-balancing attitude. The political danger was one of the two arguments Secretary Morgenthau regularly used with Roosevelt in urging more conservative fiscal policy. The other was the "confidence" argument.

The hostility of business to the Roosevelt fiscal policy became more and more pronounced as the years of the first term passed. The reasons for the hostility, its "genuineness," and its implications will be discussed in the next chapter. It is sufficient to say here that the possibility that business reactions against the policy of spending and deficits would depress investment and so retard recovery was a consideration always present in administration thinking. Sometimes Roosevelt was skeptical of the whole idea; sometimes he regarded it as a form of blackmail to which he must not yield; but on the whole it increased the desire of the administration to retain some aspects of orthodoxy in its budget policy.

The Look of Progress

Insofar as the administration's concern with sound finance was a concern with the way it would look to the public and to the business community, that concern could be satisfied as well by doing something about the looks of the policy as by doing something about the policy. The administration was aware of this.

The budget submitted in January, 1934, established an excellent base from which to show progress. Since the Democrats had been in office only a short time, the expenditure needs of the current fiscal year, 1934, could be attributed to the inadequacies of their predecessors' policies. Therefore, the administration felt no shame in submitting an expenditure estimate of $10.5 billion for fiscal 1934, compared to actual expenditures of $4.7 billion in fiscal 1933. Starting from that estimate for fiscal 1934, there was no place to go but down. The budget estimated expenditures for the next year, fiscal 1935, at slightly under $6 billion.[22]

The $10.5 billion estimate for fiscal 1934 was the biggest expenditure estimate Roosevelt was to present until World War II. But this estimate provoked less criticism than many later and smaller estimates. The standard reaction was that at last we were facing the facts, which were not of Mr. Roosevelt's making, and that at last we had a plan for bringing the budget into balance. The *New York Times* wrote a characteristic editorial on the budget under the heading "Stern Realities." But the news columns were already reporting that the realities might not be as stern as the President had pictured them, and that all of the $10.5 billion might not and probably could not be spent. Actual expenditures for the year were only about $6.7 billion, as it turned out. The Administration got credit, not blame, for having over-estimated fiscal 1934 expenditures so grossly. In fact, it got credit twice—first in January, 1934, for planning to spend less in 1935 than it had estimated would be spent in 1934, and again in July, 1934, for spending less in 1934 than it had estimated.

At the end of December, 1934, when preparing his January, 1935, budget message, the President faced the problem of making it appear that expenditures were declining so that fiscal 1936 expenditures would be below those of fiscal 1935. Again the picture was to be created, at least in part, by giving a high estimate of the current year's spending. Morgenthau supplies the following picture of budget-making on December 26, 1934:

> Roosevelt, pencil and paper in hand, tried to figure out from every angle how the Administration could make it appear that the peak of expenditures would fall in 1935, the current fiscal year. After calculating for a long time, he decided to use the estimates submitted by the departments rather than the less dramatic figures which Bell [director of the Bureau of the Budget] felt were closer to being accurate. Bell considered this procedure "just . . . faking," but Morgenthau was pleased because he thought that at last he was making real headway in getting the President to face the basic issues.[23]

The President estimated that fiscal 1935 expenditures would be $8 billion, which enabled him to show that fiscal 1936 expenditures would be a little lower.[24] In fact, fiscal 1935 expenditures were less than $7 billion, which was much less than the initial estimate for fiscal 1936, and slightly less than actual 1936 expenditures aside from the veterans' bonus. But the choice of a high estimate for the current year enabled the President in early 1935 to maintain the position that both spending and the deficit were declining from then on.

Preparation of the budget to be submitted in January, 1936, was complicated by the fact that 1936 was a Presidential election year. The administration wanted to be able to claim that the economy was recovering and that with the recovery its forecast of a declining deficit had been validated. Therefore it wanted to show that the fiscal 1936 deficit was smaller than the fiscal 1935 deficit, and this limited its ability to inflate the 1936 expenditure figures. At the same time, it wanted to show that fiscal 1937 spending would be less than fiscal 1936. And the administration could not risk holding down its relief estimates for fiscal 1937 and possibly being forced by financial limitations to reduce WPA employment during the fall election season.

The President's decision, as far as the January, 1936, budget message was concerned, was to defer the issue and share the responsibility with "business." In December the LaFollette brothers had suggested to the President that he immediately stop all relief and recovery projects with "the announcement that this was what the businessmen of the country were demanding and that he was giving them what they wanted." Roosevelt did not think much of this idea, but he gave more attention to another one with similar intent. This was to send to Congress two budgets. One would be balanced but include nothing for recovery or relief. The other would provide for recovery and relief but would not balance. With these budgets would go a message "calling attention to the fact that there is a good deal of demand, especially in business circles, for a balanced budget, and that if the Congress wanted to adopt a balanced budget, here was one."[25]

However, the budget message actually submitted on January 3, 1936, was more subtle than either of these ideas. It did not force the Congress or the public to choose between Roosevelt and the balanced budget, because the President knew that the idea that the budget should be balanced did not belong exclusively to conservative businessmen but was shared by a large part of the public, including his own Secretary of the Treasury and, at least from time to time, himself. So he aligned himself with the objective of the balanced budget and claimed that his policies were moving in that direction. At the same time he placed on business and Congress the responsibility for deciding how fast that goal should be approached. And for the time being he withheld his own judgment on that question.

The message did not estimate what the deficit for fiscal 1937 would be. That would depend in the first instance on what Congress decided to appropriate for relief, a subject on which the President would submit a recommendation later. In the end, of course, success of the budget-balancing program would depend "on the strength of the efforts put forth by the employers of the United States greatly to increase the number of persons employed by them. . . . The average of the business men of the Nation stand ready to do their share. It is to be hoped that motives and attacks which spring only from the desire for political or financial power on the part of a few will not retard the steady progress we are making."[26]

The figures presented in the January, 1936 budget message may be summarized as follows:[27]

	Fiscal Years (Millions of Dollars)			
	1934	1935	1936	1937
	actual	actual	estimated	estimated
Total receipts (including processing taxes)	3,116	3,800	4,411	5,654
Total expenditures (excluding debt retirement)	6,745	6,802	7,093	6,172*
Regular†	3,084	3,733	4,224	5,069
Recovery & relief†	3,661	3,069	2,869	1,103*
Net deficit	3,629	3,002	2,682	518*

*Includes recovery and relief expenditures from existing appropriations only; additional appropriation requests were to be submitted later.

†The division of expenditures between "regular" and "relief and recovery" cannot be compared with that shown in footnote 23 because of a change in classification between January 1935 and January 1936.

Thus it can be seen that if the additional relief and recovery expenditures to be requested later were less than $2,164 million there would be an uninterrupted decline in the deficit, and if they were less than $1,766 million there would be an uninterrupted decline in the expenditures for relief and recovery. Additional relief and recovery expenditures would have to be held below $921 million to keep total spending from rising, and this was unlikely. But for the time being the decline in the deficit was considered the crucial objective.

While a recommendation on relief expenditures for fiscal 1937 could be kept out of the January, 1936, budget message it could not be deferred for more than a few months. The questions which had not been settled in the budget message remained. Hopkins and Morgenthau thought they could get by with $2 billion for relief, in addition to about $1 billion that would be left over from prior appropriations. This was nearly the maximum amount that would leave the deficit smaller in 1937 than in 1936. Roosevelt had to be persuaded that this would not "take bread away from starving people." On the other hand, he wanted to ask for only $1.5 billion in order to show a significant decline in the deficit. He was prepared to come back for more money later, after the election, if necessary. Morgenthau objected to this as a rather transparent trick unless the President would tell how much money he might have to request later.[28] Roosevelt made a concession to Morgenthau's sensibilities on this point. In his relief message of March 18, 1936, he built up to the figure of $2 billion, pointing out that this would keep relief expenditures going at their current rate and would also permit a reduction in the deficit. He then announced that he was not asking this Congress for $2 billion, but for only $1.5 billion, which would be enough "on condition, however, that private employers hire many of those now on relief rolls."[29]

The challenge to private business was made even more pointed by the statement that, "Frankly, there is little evidence that large and small employers by individual and uncoordinated action can absorb large numbers of new employees. A vigorous effort on a national scale is necessary by voluntary, concerted action of private industry."[30] The NRA had provided the machinery for this vigorous concerted action, the President stated; that was now gone—a dig at the court and at the businessmen who had turned against the NRA. Still, businesses could get together to provide employment, and the President hoped they would do so—indeed, his appropriation request assumed they would.

Thus Roosevelt entered the campaign season able to say that the deficit had declined during his first term and was still declining. He did say that, over and over again, and he did his best to make the statement plausible.

Ickes reports a discussion on August 16, 1936, in which Roosevelt explained that he planned to approve an average of $5 million of public works a week, "in the meantime keeping his eye on his budget for the year."

Ickes notes in his diary:

> For the first time today I understood what all of this public works pulling and hauling is about. The President wants to be in a position to say until election day that his deficit last year was less than the year before and that it will be less this year than last year. He is running on a very slender margin and if he overreaches himself on public works projects, he won't be able to maintain this position. If he had only explained this to me in the first instance, I would have been understanding and sympathetic.[31]

Two weeks after election day the President announced that although reemployment had been increasing rapidly "industry had not yet increased its employment sufficiently to permit the Government to withdraw its aid from the unemployed,"[32] so it would be necessary to ask for more relief funds when the Congress reconvened. In January he asked for an additional $790 million for relief. Between March, 1936, when the original request was submitted, and January, 1937, when the additional funds were requested, the index of industrial production rose by 22 percent. It seems unlikely that the original request had assumed a more rapid recovery than that. In his January, 1937, message Roosevelt explained the size of his supplementary appropriation request as due both to the 1936 drought and to the failure of unemployment to fall in proportion to the recovery of production because of the increase in weekly hours and in the labor force.[33] Probably two other factors were also important. One was that the recovery was raising receipts above the earlier estimates. The other was that the election was over.

THE CAMPAIGN AS PRESIDENTIAL EDUCATION

The administration's explanation and defense of its fiscal policy during the 1936 campaign rested largely on the ideas we have already discussed. First, the President stressed the direct benefits of the spending programs. He gave innumerable speeches dedicating dams or bridges or office buildings in which his local audience had a great interest, each time saying, "And this is what they call boondoggling." Second, he showed that the deficit was declining. Third, he held out the expectation that the budget would be balanced "within a year or two." This was an earlier deadline than his opponent, Governor Landon, would commit himself to; Mr. Landon only said, "We must persevere until we have balanced our budget."

However, in some respects the 1936 explanations of fiscal policy represent a change from the administration's earlier ways of thinking and talking. During the campaign the fiscal policy was given much more credit than previously as a source of the general recovery, and not just as the source of certain specific benefits to farmers, home-owners, people on relief, etc. There were probably several reasons for this. There was more recovery to claim credit for and fewer programs outside the budget to give the credit to —now that NRA was unconstitutional and the gold price manipulation over. Perhaps also, the spending program had to be given the credit because it was most in need of defense. But whatever the reason, his aides were writing and the President was delivering an explanation of his fiscal program which placed more weight on indirect effects. These effects usually related to the circular flow of income and expenditures in a homespun version of multiplier theory. Roosevelt's speech at Detroit, October 15, 1936, illustrates the content and the style:

> The dollars that we spent in relief, in work relief, in C.C.C. camps, in drought relief, in cattle and hog buying and processing, each of these dollars went to work. They were spent in the shops of the city and in the stores of the small towns and villages. They were spent again by the retailers who bought from wholesalers. They were spent again by wholesalers who bought from manufacturers and processors. They were spent again in wages to those who worked and in purchases from those who produced the raw materials back in the mines and on the farms. And once again they were spent in the stores of the cities and the shops of the small towns and villages. You know how many of these dollars have finally come to the City of Detroit in the purchase of automobiles.
>
> I am reminded of a popular song. Literally the music went round and round and round and a lot of it came out right here in Detroit.[34]

During the campaign for the first time the administration seemed to be taking the position that the deficit itself, rather than the expenditures, was the force boosting the economy. Roosevelt asked his audiences this question in a variety of ways: "If you, by borrowing $800, could increase your annual income $2,200 every year, would you do it?" The point was that under his administration the federal debt (net of assets acquired by the government) had risen by $8 billion while the national income had risen by $22 billion. It was clearly implied that the deficit was the price that had to be paid for the increase in the national income and, somewhat less clearly, that the deficit was the cause of the increase in the national income. As we shall see later, Roosevelt was not committed to either of these implications when it came to making future policy, but his willingness to say such things shows an opening up of his thinking as compared, for example, with the message vetoing the bonus in 1935.

⤳ 5 ⤶

Deficits, Taxes, and Business Opposition

Dᴜʀɪɴɢ Roosevelt's first term business opposition to the policy of deficit spending limited the vigor with which that policy was pursued. During the administration of John F. Kennedy business acceptance of a policy of tax reduction in the presence of a deficit helped to make that policy possible. This changed attitude of the business community is an important part of the story of the revolution in fiscal policy from the 1930's to the 1960's. The change had two parts. One was a change in the attitude of businessmen towards deficits in general. The other was a change in the content of the deficit policy. The policy to which business objected in the 1930's was a *spending* policy, which carried with it both the fear and the fact of higher taxes. The policy of the 1960's was a *tax reduction* policy, coupled with the promise of expenditure restraint which would permit more tax reduction later. The opposition of conservatives, and particularly of businessmen, to tax increases and their support for tax reduction has been one of the reliable constants. The revolution was as much a switch of policy to conform to this constant of conservative thinking as it was a change of conservative thinking.

Early Criticism

Roosevelt's first steps to increase federal spending in 1933 provoked little opposition from the business community or elsewhere. As we have seen, the President had first established himself, by word and deed, as a champion of sound finance who could be trusted not to carry spending too far. Also, in the spring of 1933 there were more immediate things to worry about than the size of the budget or the deficit. Roosevelt later told a story of the great bankers flocking to Washington that spring asking for the help of the govern-

74

to save them from insolvency and insisting that it was well worth the price in the form of a bigger federal debt to do that. The President had asked the bankers how big a debt the federal government could stand without serious danger to the national credit. Their answers ranged between 35 and 70 billion dollars.[1] The lower of these numbers was not reached until the end of 1935, and the higher one until the United States was already in World War II. Apparently in 1933 the government was still quite a way from the edge of bankruptcy.

Even the January, 1934, budget, with its estimate of $10.5 billion of expenditures and $7.3 billion of deficit for fiscal 1934, was taken calmly. Wall Street was reported as "staggered," but as believing that the deficit could be financed. There were warnings expressed about the need to balance the budget at an early date, but these were generally tolerant and conciliatory and assumed that the President was in agreement. The *Survey* of the Guaranty Trust Company said: ". . . the President's message is interpreted in many quarters as definitely fixing the cost of the recovery program according to the estimates of the Administration. In this respect the budget, enormous as it is, is considered constructive. And many observers feel that, if the major objectives of the Government's program can be obtained at that price, the results will justify the cost."[2] A true panjandrum of conservatism, Russell Leffingwell of J. P. Morgan and Co. said that while the budget must be balanced, it was premature yet to count on it, and the President's determination to balance the budget at an early date should have popular support.

By the fall of 1934 the continuation of large spending figures made it clear that Roosevelt's "plan" to balance the budget in fiscal 1936 did not exist. The resignation of Budget Director Douglas on August 30 was a dramatic signal not to count on a conservative fiscal policy from the administration. These facts, and the Republican need for issues in the Congressional campaign, served to heat up the spending controversy. Roosevelt's friend, Grenville Clark, wrote to him: "However, one thing is clear: That a great revolt and reaction in which the good as well as the bad would go by the board would be bad for the country. Such a revolt I believe to be in prospect unless the fiscal problem is taken firmly in hand."[3] But the prediction of revolt, like Roosevelt's prediction of "blood in the streets" if Douglas resigned, was wide of the mark. There were resolutions by the U.S. Chamber of Commerce and the Advisory Council of the Federal Reserve, and many speeches calling for a balanced budget, but the country was willing to be reconciled.

Roosevelt and the business community were suspicious of each other but still recognized that they needed each other. The meetings of the American Bankers Association in October, 1934, revealed both attitudes. Mr. Jackson Reynolds, president of the First National Bank of New York, was friendlier in introducing the President than many members of the ABA would have liked. He urged the bankers to consider that they might be in error in expecting early balancing of the budget and the precise setting of a date. The President in his speech was friendlier to the bankers than Hopkins and Morgenthau had desired. The press was uncertain whether the exchange had been conciliatory or not. But the ABA adopted a resolution calling for a balanced budget without setting a date, and their resolution recognized the demands upon the budget created by emergency needs.[4]

The President seems to have been angered by the opposition to his programs in business circles. Ickes reports his saying on November 1 that business was sabotaging his efforts and planting agents in the government for that purpose. What the agents were supposed to be doing is not revealed. Also Roosevelt told Daniel Roper, Secretary of Commerce, that business had until January 3, 1935, when Congress would return, to cooperate. At the same time Roosevelt felt the need not only for speeches but for some action to gain business confidence. Ickes thought that the President wanted to reassure the country by promising a continuing public-works program so that business would have a basis for investment, but this observation may have been Ickes' wishful thinking.[5] There is more evidence that Roosevelt was impressed with Morgenthau's argument about the importance of showing that the deficit and expenditures would be declining, even though a balanced budget was not in sight.

BUSINESS REVOLTS

In his January, 1935, budget message the President did manage to give the picture of declining expenditures and deficits. However the level of both the expenditures and the deficits was much higher than had been forecast a year earlier. The initial reaction to this program in conservative circles—the press, the business community, the Congressional Republicans—was not enthusiastic, but ranged from favorable through relieved to resigned. The *New York Times* editorial was especially pleased with those sentences of the budget message which assured the country that thereafter deficits would be due entirely to relief and recovery expenditures. These sentences had been written by Mr. Charles Merz of the editorial staff of the *Times* whom Secretary Morgenthau had asked to help in drafting the budget message. Others also found comfort in these sentences as partial substitute for the preceding year's "plan" to balance the budget in fiscal 1936. At this news conference after the budget message the President said that a balanced budget might come quickly, but in view of failure to meet the hopes expressed a year earlier he did not want to make a prediction.[6] The President's statement that, "The Federal government must and shall quit this business of relief," even though it only meant that the federal government was going more heavily into the business of work relief, was generally welcomed. The bond market was undisturbed by the large continuing deficits and even rose after the budget message. Moley explained that the President's request for $4 billion for recovery and relief was not "disquieting, businesswise. For, both in his budget message and annual message of 1935, he made it plain that he wasn't committing himself to the policy of purposeless public spending and that he intended to bring the budget into balance as rapidly as possible."[7] Walter Lippmann, writing on January 8, 1935, had a somewhat different view of the conservative philosophy but also agreed that the program comported with that philosophy:

> On the other hand, the new program has been applauded as conservative except by those who distrust all public enterprise and prefer to rely upon a struggle for survival. It *is* conservative. For it presents no threat to personal liberty, and preserves private property, private initiative, and private profit as the dominant characteristics of the social order. It is the only known positive alternative to fascism or communism which can hope to create personal security without regimentation.[8]

Conservative acceptance of Roosevelt's program was fortified by awareness of greater dangers on the horizon. The Democratic victory in the 1934 elections had confirmed a political dominance which might have seemed accidental and temporary when first acquired in the darkness of 1932. What the Democrats would now do with that power was uncertain. One possibility was "greenbackism" as represented by Congressman Patman's popular and populist proposal for a veterans' bonus to be paid in paper money. Another was Huey Long's share-the-wealth tax ideas which also had considerable support in the Congress. By contrast, the President's conventional, if large, program and his call for a period of "good-feeling" were a great relief. According to Moley, the President regarded his moderation at this point as a positive policy for getting the country moving. A generation later, Arthur Schlesinger, Jr., with a different bench mark of neutrality in mind, was to say, "Nevertheless, perhaps because he had no better ideas of his own, Roosevelt still seemed early in 1935 to be drifting back into a pro-business policy."[9]

Although the year opened in a mood of acceptance between the administration and the conservatives, 1935 was to be, as Moley said, "a period of growing bitterness."[10] In April, Walter Lippmann observed that, "At no time since Mr. Roosevelt took office has it been truer than it is today that the progress of recovery is better than the sentiment in business."[11] Schlesinger notes that, "the authorization of a $4.8 billion relief program, at a time when the budgetary deficit was approaching what to businessmen of 1935 was the appalling point of $3.5 billion, sharpened discontent on the right."[12]

This generally observed rise in conservative opposition, including that of business, to the administration's program is important for our story for several reasons. It raises the question whether, or to what extent, the administration's pursuit of an expansive fiscal policy at this time was limited by the opposition or mistrust of business. This opposition or mistrust might have influenced the administration's policy in two ways: through the political reaction that the administration might expect and through the economic reaction it might expect, especially in business investment. It also raises the question whether the opposition of business was an inevitable result of an expansive fiscal policy, in the state of understanding then common, or whether the opposition could have been avoided without abandonment of the policy.

What stands out when the period is reviewed is that the administration's spending and deficit program was only a part, and probably only a relatively small part, of the total picture which aroused conservative anger during 1935. As we have seen, the initial presentation of the spending and deficit plans was received without much heat. The administration did not increase its expenditure programs or deficit estimates during the year. While there was some opposition to the work-relief bill from people who preferred direct relief because it was cheaper, this was not the main source of opposition or of delay in passing the bill. More powerful objection came from organized labor, and its Congressional supporters, who wanted prevailing wages to be paid on work-relief projects. The President defended the more economical side of this issue, and won. The President also won points with the advocates of sound finance by going to Congress in person to deliver his veto of the bonus bill—a veto which stuck for a year.

Roosevelt was not losing ground on the spending and deficit fronts, but he was stirring up opposition by action in a number of other fields. These included the recommendations for the Social Security program, the Public Utilities Holding Company Act, the Banking Act of 1935, and the extension of NRA. The most public eruption of conflict between business and the administration came at the annual meeting of the Chamber of Commerce of the U.S. in Washington at the beginning of May. After the overwhelming Democratic victory in the 1934 Congressional elections, the chamber leadership had decided on a policy of getting along with the administration. They had called for cooperation between business and the government in the promotion of recovery. But business as an organized group had nothing to offer in this cooperation and organized business could not deliver helpful behavior by individual businesses. The National Association of Manufacturers never accepted the conciliatory policy and accused the chamber of "pussyfooting and kowtowing." In early 1935, at a meeting of several business organizations dominated by the NAM, a number of resolutions critical of the administration's program were adopted. Owen D. Young had urged moderation in the drafting of the resolutions, and apparently the meeting thought its action was within the spirit of the President's recent statement welcoming "constructive" criticism. However this was not the way the President looked at it. When a representative of the business organizations called at the White House to present their resolutions, the President refused to see him. Subsequently, Ickes, Hopkins, and other administration officials attacked the resolutions.

As the chamber prepared for its May meeting in Washington, it was clear that the resolutions and speeches would be highly critical of the administration, partly because of the administration's emerging program, partly because the crisis days were being left behind, and partly because of resentment over the administration's attitude toward the earlier resolutions. The lineup of speakers assured strong attacks on the public utilities bill, the banking bill, the continuation of NRA, the Social Security program, and the Reciprocal Trade Agreements plan. Because of the circumstances, the President declined an invitation to address the session. Some question remained whether he would send a message. On May 1, the chamber's committees were drafting resolutions, and the White House was considering what to do about a message. Word of the bitterness of the resolutions determined the White House to send no message, and failure of a message to arrive as the day passed served to steel the resolutions committees. "The permanent staff of the chamber as well as outstanding leaders on important committees, it developed, were in the minority and were unable to muster sufficient influence to sway those who were intent on jamming through the derogatory sections embodied in the resolutions."[13]

During the most tempestuous session in the chamber's history, the resolutions submitted were further strengthened, i.e. made more critical, by amendment from the floor. A true grass-roots movement seemed to be under way. Mr. Harper Sibley, the new president of the chamber, tried to take some of the sting out of what happened by attributing it to emotionalism and confusion. He said that he would seek an interview with the President, but also added that he would be guided by the resolutions adopted by the chamber.

It is significant from our standpoint that the resolutions adopted did not attack the general fiscal policy of the administration. They were against Social Security legislation at the 1935 session of Congress, against renewal of the NRA except on a temporary and limited basis, against the holding company bill, against government's taking over the role of trade associations, against the Wagner labor relations bill, against the thirty-hour bill, against Title II of the Banking Act, against the proposed broadening of the powers of the Agricultural Adjustment Administration; and they were for modification of the Securities Act and for anti-subversives legislation. But they did not "demand" balancing of the budget, they did not attack the work-relief program, and they referred the question of public-works policy back to a committee for consideration. This did not mean that the chamber was supporting the government's fiscal policy. One of its committees had earlier made the traditional call for a balanced budget. But the heat at the May meeting was generated by resentment against "excessive government control," rather than by concern for sound finance.

As Arthur Krock said at the time:

> The rather incongruous partnership between certain conservative business and banking groups and the New Deal was publicly dissolved this week, the mists of fear in which it was formed having been absorbed by the sunlight of recovery. A majority of the delegates of the Chamber of Commerce of the United States decided to go back to their economic home.[14]

The administration took the chamber's action seriously. One administration countermove was an attempt to belittle the representativeness of the chamber. On the same day on which the chamber passed its resolutions, the Business Advisory Council met with the President and submitted a statement endorsing the Social Security Program and supporting the extension of the NRA, with modifications, but opposing certain other pending legislation. This meeting was, of course, no coincidence. The appointment for the BAC to see the President was hastily arranged after the chamber had passed its resolution in the morning. The council included many of the leaders of American business, including Henry I. Harriman, outgoing president of the chamber, as well as Winthrop W. Aldrich, Pierre S. du Pont, Walter Gifford, Gerard Swope, Myron Taylor, and R. E. Wood. Their discussion with the President was amicable and was reported in the press as an endorsement of the objectives of the New Deal. This enabled the President at his news conference the next day to give a lecture, with historical illustrations, on the failure of business associations to represent the business community at large. The speakers at the Chamber of Commerce meeting did not understand the problem of the country, he asserted. "However, the business men who were in here yesterday, I think they understand it pretty well just as I think the overwhelming majority of business men in this country, the individual men, the higher executives and the middle-sized executives and the lower executives, they understand pretty well what it is all about and I go along with them. . . ."[15]

On the other hand, the administration did not act as if it believed that it and "the overwhelming majority of business men" were in agreement. On May 14, the President held a discussion of the political and legislative situation with Senators Johnson, Norris, LaFollette, Wheeler, and Costigan; Secretaries Ickes and Wallace; and Felix Frankfurter and David Niles. "LaFollette said that the attack on the President by the United States Chamber of Commerce was a most fortunate happening. It was the opinion of all that big business in no circumstances will support the President, and I [Ickes] made the observation that this opposition should be capitalized. . . . I left with a distinct impression that it is the President's intention to take a firm stand on his progressive policies and to force the fighting along that line."[16] The reference to the opposition of big business is interesting, because if anything can be deduced from the difference of attitudes between the chamber and the BAC, it is that big business was being more cooperative, and that the sharpest opposition came from smaller businesses. However, the New Dealers always preferred to believe that it was "big" business that opposed them.

More Taxes in Depression

The next big step in the escalation of conflict between the administration and business came with the President's tax message on June 19, which after much debate led to the Revenue Act of 1935. The message called for higher rates of tax on large individual incomes—raising the top tax rate to 75 percent from 59 percent—higher tax rates on large corporations, a federal tax on inheritances on top of the existing federal-state tax on estates, and some less significant changes. The President's message presented no estimate of the revenue to be obtained from his proposals, which were not primarily offered as revenue-raising measures. The amount involved in the act when it was finally passed was around $250 million a year.

One can ask about the Revenue Act of 1935 the same astonished question that is asked about Hoover's Revenue Act of 1932. How can a government facing massive unemployment and spending large amounts of federal money to provide jobs for the unemployed justify raising taxes and draining more funds from the private income stream? This question was, indeed, raised within the administration, by Eccles and others, before the tax program was adopted. The answer given was that these particular tax increases would not be deflationary because they would only draw from incomes and fortunes that were already very large and presumably not "dynamic," to use the word of the President's message. This was a reflection in tax policy of the President's long-standing ideas about purchasing power which had been embodied in the NRA, now about to pass from the scene with the Supreme Court's decision on its unconstitutionality. The income of workers and farmers had a special value as purchasing power to get the economy going and keep it going, a value not shared by the incomes of entrepreneurs and capitalists, which could be taxed with impunity. This was the counterpart, with signs reversed, of Mellon's statement ten years earlier that reducing the tax rates on the poor would not stimulate the economy because the poor had no opportunity to choose between putting capital into productive or unproductive uses.[17]

The purchasing-power argument may explain why the tax increase would not hurt very much. It does not explain why the President wanted to raise taxes. Apparently it was not to make a small step in the direction of balancing the budget. Roosevelt resisted suggestions from Morgenthau that he refer to budget-balancing in the tax message.[18] The reason for recommending a tax increase lay partly in the ambivalence that characterized the Roosevelt policy—the combination or confusion of recovery and reform. The tax program was a reform measure to help create a society in which incomes and power would be less concentrated, and it was to be pushed through when it could be pushed through, even at some risk to immediate recovery. How far Roosevelt was influenced by the desire to outflank Huey Long, or steal his thunder, is uncertain. In retrospect there seems to have been little likelihood that Long could get any part of his "every man a king" tax ideas enacted, since even Roosevelt's much milder proposals were watered down in Congress before they were enacted. But FDR apparently did not want to find himself in the position of dragging his heels against Long's initiatives.[19] Also Roosevelt had a big, restless, liberal majority in the Congress which needed to be led somewhere, so he finally picked up the Treasury proposals which had been lying on his desk for months.

RECOVERY, CONFIDENCE, AND TAX REFORM

The business reaction to the tax proposal was strong. "Roosevelt's tax proposal, the first which reached directly into the pockets of the wealthy, raised an outcry from business and the press such as had greeted none of the President's previous recommendations."[20] The official line had been that the existing taxes were adequate to cover the regular expenses of government and, when recovery came, would be adequate to permit reduction of the emergency-created debt. As recently as January the President had said that he foresaw no need for additional taxes. But now the taxpayers were facing the fifth tax increase in five years. It was no wonder that businessmen felt confirmed in their traditional view that, despite sophisticated budget theories, higher spending and deficits inevitably meant higher taxes. Moreover, the particular tax increases proposed were obnoxious to the business community, not only because they "reached into the pockets of the wealthy," but also because they reflected a denial of all the moral and economic arguments by which large fortunes and large corporations were typically justified. If the President had said that the government needed the money, the conservatives would have understood and might have accepted the tax increases better. But he refused to say that. He would only say that the society needed more equality.

The tax increase of 1935 greatly intensified the opposition of businessmen and other conservatives to the administration's fiscal policy, and the tax increase of 1936 was to aggravate it further. The policy of the 1930's was not just a policy of big spending and big deficits; it was also a policy of tax increases, in a form most distasteful to the business community. The opposition to high taxes and the desire for lower taxes have been much more consistent features of the business position on fiscal policy than opposition to spending and deficits.[21] In fact, the opposition to spending and deficits has been largely derived from the opposition to taxes, and while it might be shown that high spending and big deficits did not lead to higher taxes by any logical necessity, the experience of the thirties was certainly not comforting to those who opposed more taxation. After all, the slogan of the New Deal was believed by its critics to be "Spend and Spend, Tax and Tax, and Elect and Elect." The "Tax and Tax" part was the most worrisome to businessmen.

The businessmen were no more willing or able to distinguish between a spending program and a taxing program than was the administration. When representatives of the U.S. Chamber of Commerce and of the National Association of Manufacturers testified before the Ways and Means Committee in opposition to the tax increase, they did not say that higher taxes were unnecessary or even more dangerous than the deficit.[22] On the contrary, they took the position that they yielded to no one in their desire for a balanced budget, and certainly valued the balanced budget more than the President did, but insisted that the budget should be balanced by cutting expenditures. In fact, they argued that the budget could be balanced *only* by cutting expenditures, because tax increases would reduce the revenue by reducing the national income. The motivating force in the business opposition to Roosevelt's fiscal policy may have been fear of and resentment against tax increases, but the spending and the deficits and the taxes were all wrapped together in one package and condemned without discrimination.

The President tried to reassure business on taxes in a number of statements, but he could never entirely resist a little twist of the knife. In August and September, 1935, he had a widely-publicized exchange of letters with publisher Roy W. Howard on the subject of business confidence. Howard's letter reflects how large the administration's tax policy loomed in business thinking. He said:

> . . . any experienced reporter will tell you that throughout the country many business men who once gave you sincere support are now, not merely hostile, they are frightened. Many of these men whose patriotism and sense of public service will compare with that of any men in political life, have become convinced and sincerely believe:
>
> That you fathered a tax bill that aims at revenge rather than revenue—revenge on business;
>
> That the Administration has side-stepped broadening the tax base to the extent necessary to approximate the needs of the situation;
>
> That there can be no real recovery until the fears of business have been allayed through the granting of a breathing spell to industry, and a recess from further experimentation until the country can recover its losses.

The President replied, in part:

> The tax program of which you speak is based upon a broad and just social and economic purpose. Such a purpose, it goes without saying, is not to destroy wealth, but to create broader range of opportunity, to restrain the growth of unwholesome and sterile accumulations and to lay the burdens of Government where they can best be carried. This law affects only those individual people who have incomes over $50,000 a year, and individual estates of decedents who leave over $40,000.

Of course, those who complained about the 1935 tax law knew very well that it imposed new burdens only on the rich, which was one of their main complaints about it. However, the President did say what many were waiting to hear:

> It seemed to the Congress and to me better to achieve these objectives as expeditiously as possible in order that not only business but the public generally might know those modifications in the conditions and rules of economic enter-

prise which were involved in our program. This basic program, however, has now reached substantial completion and the "breathing spell" of which you speak is here—very decidedly so.[23]

A couple of weeks later the President gave more specific meaning to the "breathing spell" as far as taxes were concerned. In a review of the budget he showed that the fiscal year 1935 deficit had actually been about $1.3 billion below the estimate made in January, 1935, and he now estimated that the fiscal 1936 deficit would be about $1.1 billion below the earlier estimate for that year and also below 1935. Then:

> It may be pointed out in this connection that erroneous and gloomy predictions have frequently been voiced in some quarters to the effect that heavy increases in taxation will be required to balance the Budget and retire our public debt. The underlying tax structure of the Government is now stronger than ever before in our history, and as normal business returns will produce revenues adequate for all essential purposes. The prevailing rate of recovery points to the speedy decline of Federal expenditures for emergency activities. The 1937 Budget is now being prepared with a view to sharply decreasing the spread between income and outgo. Thus it is clear to me that the Federal Government under provisions of present tax schedules will not need new taxes or increased rates in existing taxes to meet the expense of its necessary annual operations and to retire its public debt.[24]

At the same time, the message contained a warning the significance of which few could appreciate until six months later. The President pointed out that the estimates of receipts assumed continued collections of the processing taxes on agricultural products to finance the agricultural adjustment program. The Agricultural Adjustment Act was under attack in the courts, and if the attack succeeded, the President said, "we will have to face the problem of financing existing contracts for benefit payments out of some form of new taxes." This was to be one justification, in the spring of 1936, for the recommendation of an undistributed profits tax, which raised an even greater furore than the "share the wealth" Revenue Act of 1935.

RAISING TAXES AS A FISCAL STIMULUS

The Supreme Court's invalidation of the AAA and the associated processing taxes, followed three weeks later by the enactment of the bonus, immediately raised the question of tax increases. According to Morgenthau "neither the White House nor the Treasury was willing to tolerate the impending deficit."[25] The situation this time was different than it had been in 1935. Then Roosevelt had proposed increases in certain taxes because he

wanted to reduce concentration of wealth, income, and power, not because
he wanted to raise the revenue and reduce the deficit. He had declined to
use the revenue-raising, budget-balancing arguments in his 1935 tax message. But in 1936, while the selection of the particular tax increase to recommend reflected certain other economic and social goals, the decision to raise
taxes was predicated on the need for revenue.

The decision to recommend a tax increase was undoubtedly based as
much on political as on economic considerations. The administration found
itself in the position of being able to show devotion to the idea of reducing
the deficit while placing the blame for the need to increase taxes on others.
It was the Supreme Court, by invalidating the AAA, and the Congress, by
enacting the bonus, that had upset the administration's plans and made a tax
increase necessary. As Eccles remembered the situation, "In an election year
the administration felt the need to make some sort of show at closing the
gap between federal income and outgo."[26] And in the circumstances, the
administration could escape responsibility for the pain that would accompany
this show of virtue.

The administration's decision to recommend a tax increase was made
easier by its belief that it had available a new form of taxation with many
positive advantages. At the outset the President, with support from Henry
Wallace, leaned towards new legislation restoring the processing taxes. Both
Morgenthau and Eccles objected to this, with a characteristic difference of
reasoning. Morgenthau was concerned about hardship to low income groups,
whereas Eccles was worried about the reduction of consumers' purchasing
power. Also, there was doubt about the constitutionality of a processing tax.
An increase in income taxes seemed to be politically unacceptable. Herman
Oliphant, General Counsel of the Treasury, then revived the idea of an undistributed profits tax, an idea that he had first raised in December, 1934.
The proposal was to eliminate the existing tax on corporate profits and
impose a tax only on the profits not distributed to stockholders at a rate of
tax to be graduated with the proportion of profits not distributed. This was
expected to serve a number of purposes, in addition to yielding more revenue.
It would correct the inequity of taxing distributed profits twice—once when
earned by the corporation and once when received by the stockholder—
while undistributed profits were taxed only once at the corporate profits
rate, which was less than the individual income tax rate of many stockholders. It would force or induce the payment of more dividends, which
would presumably increase consumers' expenditures. It would reduce the
advantage of well-established businesses, which could raise capital from their
own earnings, over new enterprises which had to go to the capital markets.

It would also permit stockholders to make their own decisions about how to use their own income, rather than having the decisions made for them by corporate managers.

Discussion of the merits of the undistributed profits tax is not necessary for our story of the evolution of fiscal policy. Yet the recommendation of the tax, whatever its merits, illustrates two important points. First, the administration was operating with a complex and sophisticated model of fiscal policy. The administration knew that some kinds of tax increases might retard recovery, but it believed that there were also some that would stimulate recovery. Whether its judgment about the effects of the tax on undistributed profits was correct would require further analysis.

Second, the choice of the undistributed profits tax shows that the administration, at least in 1936, was not guided in its show of budget-balancing policy by the wish or hope of winning the favor or confidence of business. Few things the administration did were so calculated to rouse business antagonism. The situation was rather that the administration and business each wanted to appeal to the budget-balancing sentiments in the country and show that it, rather than the other, was the true champion of the balanced budget.

The expected opposition to the undistributed profits tax was forthcoming. Business organizations, Republican congressmen, some Democrats, and a large part of the press joined in denouncing the proposal as a harebrained or malicious interference with the processes that had made America rich. Estimating the yield of the tax was difficult because it differed so much from what was then in force, and the Treasury was in continuous trouble over the estimates—which cast doubt on the accuracy of everything else the Treasury said. Moreover, the proposal was too complex to permit easy marshaling of popular sentiment against the wealthy or the powerful. All of Mr. Roosevelt's political force had to be utilized to enact the proposal even in substantially diluted form. The tax continued to be one of the outstanding grievances against the New Deal and became one of the few New Deal innovations ever retracted by subsequent legislation.

BUSINESS AGAINST TAXES, AND VICE VERSA

Like Roosevelt, the typical businessman of the 1930's was in favor of a balanced budget. Roosevelt was able to "rise above" this belief to do what he considered necessary—increase spending. The businessmen might also have been able to "rise above" their belief in budget-balancing in order to achieve what they wanted—lower taxes or at least no higher taxes. But as they saw it, the deficit spending policy which was convenient to the President promised and delivered what was inconvenient for them—higher taxes.

The administration could probably have carried on an expansionary fiscal policy with much less objection from the business community if it had excluded tax increases from its program, and even included some tax reduction. The idea of generating expansion through tax reductions, as well as or instead of expenditure increases, was not beyond the intellectual capacity of 1935 or 1936. For example, the Report on Economic Reconstruction by the Columbia University Commission, in January, 1934, had carried an addendum by the distinguished Professor Joseph A. Schumpeter of Harvard which said, among other things: "I also wish to add that taxation itself may be made a useful instrument of remedial policy if taxes which are in any way proportional to business success are systematically lowered in depression and increased in prosperity, in which case they would act in a way similar to that of the variations of the rate of interest."[27] A more pointed statement was made in November, 1934, by a commission of which Robert Maynard Hutchins was chairman.

> There appears to be no substantial basis for the alarm with which our unbalanced budget is viewed in certain quarters in finance and industry. The maintenance of a large deficit, as an emergency measure, is nowise dangerous to our financial structure; indeed, this policy is probably the only one which will permit that financial structure to be held together at all. If there are dangers, they are less great than those of any alternative program. Indeed, it may be true that serious effort to balance the budget at present would actually make the real deficit larger and more enduring—simply because of effects on business earnings, production and employment.
>
> The widespread criticism of the various expenditure programs is not entirely unjustified, *for the administration has given perhaps too little attention to temporary tax reduction as a means toward the desired deficit. In general, a deficit achieved by tax reduction is as reflationary as one obtained by extraordinary outlays.*[28]

However, the administration was not inclined to follow such suggestions of a more conciliatory route to deficit finance via tax reductions, or at least without tax increases, for several reasons. The President did not think of himself as having a "desired deficit," which he could obtain by tax reduction. Rather he had certain desired expenditures, which unfortunately left him with an undesired deficit. Also he liked the particular tax increases he recommended, considering them not only the prices to be paid for the expenditures but also positive steps toward reform of the American society and economy. The tax program was one of several places where even sympathetic observers like Keynes and Lippmann had warned Roosevelt that his reforms were interfering with his recovery measures. Roosevelt recognized this criticism and tried on several occasions to answer it by saying that the country needed both recovery and reform, as if this removed the necessity to make a choice.

The opposition of business was a factor continuously present in the administration's consideration of budget policy. Business confidence was important to the achievement of the administration's economic objectives, and this confidence was believed to be influenced by the government's fiscal policy. An outstanding feature of the limited recovery of the 1930's was the small recovery of private investment. By 1937 total real output had regained the 1929 level, but private investment, excluding the accumulation of inventories, was still one-third below 1929. And, of course, to regain 1929 output in 1937, when the labor force and productivity had risen, was still to be far short of high employment. There was common recognition that to get up to high employment, or at least to get there without continued emergency expenditure by government, would require a revival of private investment. Several theories were in circulation to explain the low level of private investment. One which came up from time to time in Roosevelt's thinking was that business was sabotaging the administration. Others who were less dramatic cited the failure of the economy to "digest" the big investments made in the twenties, or the changed technological or demographic conditions, or the low rate of profits. But possibly the most widely held idea was that private investment remained depressed because of lack of confidence resulting from New Deal policies. Morgenthau, although loyally devoted to most of the New Deal, especially in its humanitarian aspects, was a constant representative of the view that loose fiscal policy, with big expenditures and big deficits, weakened business confidence and retarded recovery. Roosevelt was intermittently receptive to this argument, and while he felt the compulsion of emergency spending needs, and while he was moved to "anti-business" policies by many economic and political considerations, his desire to strengthen confidence was a force tending to hold expenditures down.

How much, if at all, private investment during 1933–1940 was held back by lack of confidence resulting from the New Deal, and how much responsibility should be assigned to budget policy as compared with other New Deal measures, is impossible to say. However what does seem likely is that the government's expenditure and deficit policies were inhibited by *fear* of weakening confidence, that this fear resulted largely from the expressed opposition of business to the budget policy, and that the opposition, in turn, was much greater than it would otherwise have been because the spending and borrowing were accompanied by tax increases particularly annoying to business. The raising of taxes, a step certainly not required by an expansive fiscal policy, made expansive policy more dangerous and less effective and probably limited the extent to which it was followed.

The opposition of business and of conservatives generally to high taxes was to be more real and continuous in the ensuing years than was their opposition to deficit financing. Thus the tax cut of 1964, commonly viewed as the final defeat of budget-balancing, was also the great victory of conservative fiscal policy.

6

The Struggle for the Soul of FDR, 1937–1939

By the end of 1936, after the election, the administration could look forward with confidence to coming out of the fiscal woods into the clearing. The President's various explanations of his four years of deficits, plus the promised of balanced budgets to come, had defused fiscal policy as an election issue. Moreover, the promise looked as if it could be easily kept in the normal course of events. Recovery was proceeding; some said that it was already here. Revenues were rising rapidly and were forecast to rise further with the rise of national income. At last there was the prospect of a decline in work-relief spending requirements. Only a moderate grip on expenditures seemed necessary to achieve the promised balance.

ROOSEVELT AND RECOVERY

For the first time, the Roosevelt administration confronted an economic situation that was in some degree ambiguous, and in which the immediate need for stimulating and expansive action was not obvious. Production had regained the 1929 levels, which was what many people, sometimes including the President, meant by recovery. Prices were beginning to rise, and this was leading to speculative accumulation of inventories. Worries were being expressed about the possible recurrence of a 1929-type crash.[1]

True, unemployment was still high—probably around 15 percent of the labor force in the winter of 1936–37. (There are no official monthly figures on unemployment for this period but the 1936 rate was 16.9 percent and the 1937 rate 14.3 percent, according to estimates made subsequently.) But the administration did not feel committed to continue extraordinary expenditures and deficits until full employment was reached. We have already seen that the President usually thought of his extraordinary expenditures as needed for certain specific purposes, especially for relief, and that he regarded the deficits as an unfortunate by-product. But even when, during the 1936 campaign, he began to put more weight on the general employment-stimulating effects of the spending and the deficits, he did not imply that this stimulus was to be continued to the point of full employment. He seemed to think of his budget policy as a means to recovery which might still leave a large amount of unemployment to be handled in other ways.

In April, 1936, Roosevelt had pointed out that while production had about regained its pre-Depression peak, employment was almost 20 percent lower than before the Depression. Then he went on to say:

> Some people tell you that even with a completely restored prosperity there will be a vast permanent army of unemployed. I do not accept that. No man who is sensitive to human values dares to accept it. That is why we are not content merely to restore what is sometimes called prosperity. We propose to attack the problem from every conceivable angle.
>
> We readily admit that a greater purchasing power, far more widely distributed, will mean the consumption of more goods—industrial products and farm products. We know that the production of more goods will mean more employment. Most business men, the great majority of them, believe with us that a greater purchasing power on the part of more people will help; they know that their own businesses will be helped thereby.
>
> To work in unity toward that end constitutes one form of attack, an important one; but there are others which we must not overlook.[2]

The other forms of attack on the unemployment problem which he had in mind were retention of more young people in school, retirement of the majority of workers at 65, reduction of the work week, payment of adequate minimum wages, and "the stabilization of employment on an annual basis." What this suggests is that beyond some point the expansion of purchasing power, which we would now call the expansion of aggregate demand, could not be relied upon to push the economy to full employment and that "structural" measures, essentially the reduction of the labor supply, would have to be used in addition.

Harry Hopkins also had the idea that recovery by itself did not necessarily mean the restoration of full employment. Looking ahead in 1936 he said:

> Until the time comes, if it ever does, when industry and business can absorb all able-bodied workers—and that time seems to grow more distant with improvements in management and technology—we shall have with us large numbers of unemployed. Intelligent people have long since left behind them the notion

that under fullest recovery, and even with improved purchasing power, the unemployed will disappear as dramatically as they made their appearance after 1929.[3]

Hopkins' remedy for this situation was different from Roosevelt's. He foresaw the need for continuing public-works and work-relief programs. The point, however, is that both visualized the possible end of the emergency and the Depression with substantial numbers still unemployed. Because he thought the deficit was appropriate only for the depression, which would end before full employment was regained, Roosevelt welcomed the near approach of a balanced budget, and even took some moderate steps to hasten its arrival despite the continued high rate of unemployment at the end of 1936.

There were some dissenting voices in the administration, notably that of Marriner Eccles. In December, 1936, Eccles sent Roosevelt a memorandum which Morgenthau described as follows:

> Eccles' December memorandum on the budget advanced, in his own words and in his own spirit, the ideas which had been given their classic statement by John Maynard Keynes. An attempt to balance the budget, Eccles argued, would put the country into an economic tailspin. The popular analogy between the debt of an individual and the debt of a nation was utterly false. The crucial consideration was not the size of the deficit but the level of national income. It would be unsafe to slash federal expenditures until the expansion of private enterprise took up the whole slack of employment. Meanwhile deficit expenditures were a necessary, compensatory form of investment which gave life to an economy operating below capacity. Ultimately they would lead to restored business activity and increased national income. An attempt to balance the budget for the fiscal year 1938, Eccles maintained, would be dangerously premature, would lead to a new wave of deflation and reverse the processes of recovery thus far set in motion. This would spell doom for the Democratic party, perhaps even pave the way for totalitarianism.[4]

This memorandum, coming as he was about to write his budget message, impressed and disturbed the President. He turned it over to Morgenthau, who of course disagreed with every bit of it. However, what persuaded Roosevelt to reject the Eccles line was not Morgenthau's argument. He rejected Eccles' reasoning because he didn't need it. Revised budget estimates showed that the recovery would bring the 1938 budget into balance naturally, with only a little restraint on expenditures. If it had really been necessary to "slash" expenditures in order to balance the 1938 budget, Roosevelt might have resorted to Eccles' arguments against doing so. But if it was easy to balance the budget, he welcomed the balance with relief.

The revised estimates of the Bureau of the Budget seemed to him [Budget Director Bell] and to the Secretary [Morgenthau] to constitute an overwhelming rejoinder to Eccles. The new figures, they agreed, demonstrated that recovery was well along, that the annual deficit was shrinking, that a balanced budget was in sight. "Golly," Morgenthau said on December 29, "I think we all got every reason to face the new year with the greatest of complacence and comfort. . . ."

Surprised by the improved figures, the President teased Bell, who, he said, had been holding out on him. . . . Without argument, he subscribed to the long-run fiscal program which Morgenthau and Bell advocated.[5]

Most of the movement from the $2.2 billion deficit estimated for fiscal 1937 to the balanced budget for fiscal 1938 would come from the increase of receipts which the Treasury figured at over $1.4 billion. This in turn came largely from the increase of individual and corporate incomes and sales of goods subject to excises as the economy recovered, although about $450 million was the result of the newly imposed Social Security taxes. Balancing the budget thus required a reduction of expenditures by $800 million. But since final payments on the bonus amounted to $564 million in 1937, and this did not have to be repeated in 1938, other expenditures had to decline by only about $250 million, or around 3 percent. Given the recovery under way and forecast, this did not seem an unreasonable expectation. In fact the administration estimated that recovery and relief expenditures would decline by $1 billion, which left considerable room for an increase in regular expenditures, including those for the new Social Security program, within the confines of a balanced 1938 budget.

As usual the budget presented in January was incomplete, containing no estimate for work relief. The President only said that if work-relief expenditures were held below $1,537 million for fiscal 1938 the budget would be in balance for that year, and he expressed confidence that this figure would not have to be exceeded if business did its part in providing employment. On April 20 the President submitted a request for $1.5 billion of relief expenditures for 1938. If this is added to the estimates presented in January, the following fiscal plan emerges:

Budget Plan, as of January, 1937[6]

	Fiscal Years (Millions of Dollars)		
	1936	1937	1938
Receipts	4,116	5,828	7,294
Social Security Taxes	—	325	775
Other	4,116	5,503	6,519

Budget Plan, as of January, 1937–(*Continued*)

	Fiscal Years (Millions of Dollars)		
	1936	1937	1938
Expenditures (excluding debt retirement)	8,477	8,076	7,256
Veterans' Bonus	1,673	564	—
Other	6,804	7,512	7,256
Recovery and Relief	2,777	2,816	1,816
Regular	4,027	4,696	5,440
Social Security	28	400	836
Other regular	3,999	4,296	4,604
Deficit	4,361	2,248	–38 (surplus)

The administration did not describe its achievement of a balanced budget as the result of enforced economies. Rather it was reaping the benefits, in both higher revenues and lower expenditures, of the recovery it had brought about, just as it had always promised.

DEFICITS AND THE BOND MARKET

Early in 1937 the "complacence and comfort" about balancing the budget with which Morgenthau had felt entitled to face the new year began to evaporate. Attainment of the goal appeared both more urgent and more difficult. The urgency arose from two related factors—mounting signs of inflation and a decline in the government bond market. For the President, and for the administration as a whole, the connection between inflation and the budget was a somewhat complicated one. Morgenthau was concerned that continued deficits would impair the government's credit and force it to report to "the printing press," which in turn would cause inflation. The impairment of the government's credit would show up in a decline of the government bond market.

The President at a press conference in April unveiled a more elaborate idea about the state of the economy, prices, and the budget. He said that the production of durable goods was rising more rapidly than the production of consumer goods, which "almost all economists" agreed was a danger sign that we might run into a decline in the production of both kinds of goods in the next twelve to eighteen months. One sign and consequence of this was the rapid rise of the prices of durable materials, such as copper. Therefore, we needed to discourage expenditures for durable goods and encourage expenditures for consumer goods. "We need more expenditures at the bottom and less at the top, because of the fact that expenditures of funds

at the bottom go primarily to people, millions of people, who are the consumers of consumer goods rather than consumers of durable goods." To
accomplish this the government should hold back on its large public-works
expenditures and on defense expenditures while pushing ahead with relief
and light public works, "like dredging channels and building dirt dams."
"I think this policy of the government in regard to its own expenditure is
in line with what we have been talking about in regard to planning." But
the President drew no conclusion that a reduction in total expenditures or
in the deficit was required.[7]

This analysis derived from the thinking of economists in the government,
but it was obviously congenial to the President. Durable goods were produced by big businesses for other big businesses and rich people, whereas consumer goods were bought by the masses. The cold economic analysis was
warmed by sympathy for the poor. Moreover, it was an argument for
achieving balance by planning, which Roosevelt always regarded as more
positive and creative that doing something overall by general financial
measures.

Concern about the bond market was probably more important than
inflation in administration thinking about the budget in early 1937, and also
significant as a recurrence of some of the ideas of 1931 and 1932. To understand this, a brief review of monetary events and policies is needed.[8] After
the middle of 1933 the reserves of the banking system rose very rapidly,
mainly as a consequence of the inflow of gold from abroad, and were increasingly in excess of the reserves the banks were required to hold. The
banks were able to make large increases in their loans and investments, including government securities, without experiencing any shortage of reserves
relative either to the legal requirements or to their own desires. In this
situation interest rates fell to, and remained at, low levels—which was what
the government meant when it talked, as it frequently did, about the strength
of the government's credit despite its continuous deficits.

In the middle of 1936 the Federal Reserve decided to raise the reserve
requirements of the member banks by 50 percent, which would substantially
reduce their excess reserves—those over legal requirements—but still leave
them large by any pre-1933 standards. The motives for this increase were
mixed: partly to restrain the growth in bank loans and investments then
under way and partly to put the Federal Reserve in a position to exercise
restraint later, if that should become necessary, without having to make too
drastic a move. This latter, precautionary intent was emphasized in the
board's public statement on the increase. Before the decision was taken there
was concern in the administration about its possible effect on the prices of

government securities. However, Eccles told the President: "I would not favor action under any circumstances unless assured of authority through the Open Market Executive Committee to counteract any recession of a point or more in the price of governments [securities]."[9] Securities markets responded to the increase of reserve requirements ordered in July, 1936, with only a small decline which was quickly recovered, so that the question of Federal Reserve action to support the markets did not arise.

In January, 1937, the Federal Reserve considered another increase in reserve requirements, with more intention this time of checking an ongoing expansion with inflationary features. Dr. E. A. Goldenweiser, economic adviser to the Federal Reserve, supported the reserve increase but pointed out that the risks were greater than they had been six months earlier when excess reserves were much larger. In his view the continued high rate of unemployment called for caution in the imposition of any restrictive measures. John H. Williams, economist of the New York Federal Reserve Bank, was more emphatic in endorsing the reserve requirement increase. He thought that "the business and economic situation in the United States had reached what might be regarded in a general way as normal and that there were some indications in certain respects it was going beyond a normal state." It was time to "reconsider attitudes formed during the depression."[10]

The Federal Reserve decided to raise reserve requirement by one-third, effective in two steps: on March 1, 1937, and on May 1, 1937. At the same time it authorized the Open Market Committee to buy up to $500 million of government securities if necessary to stabilize securities markets after the increase of reserve requirements. In fact the prices of government bonds did decline after the March 1 increase of requirements went into effect, and the New York Federal Reserve Bank did buy bonds to moderate the drop, but not enough to prevent it entirely. Morgenthau became alarmed and insisted on knowing what the Federal Reserve was going to do about it. The Federal Reserve, with the New York Bank taking the most adamant positions, was unwilling to commit itself to pegging the prices of government bonds at any specified levels. In a meeting with Morgenthau, "Chairman Eccles stated that it continued to be his view that the policy of the Board of Governors and the Federal Open Market Committee should be to maintain easy money conditions, pointing out in this connection, however, that in his opinion *it was imperative that assurance be given that the budget would be balanced in 1938*, that any expenditures that would increase indebtedness should be covered by taxation, and that steps should be taken to reduce the outstanding debt as fast as commercial credit expands." Morgenthau kept pressing and the Federal Reserve agreed to assist the bond market, at least for the time being, if possible by selling short-term bills while buying bonds. However, Eccles told Morgenthau, *"If the Government would balance the budget* and deal effectively with labor and armament problems which result in abnormal price increases, there was no question that the price of Government securities would increase instead of decline."[11]

This incident is interesting for the temporary conversion to budget-balancing of Marriner Eccles, the administration's leading advocate of planned deficits. It shows how much weight was given to stability of the government securities markets in thinking about budget policy, even when what was in question was a much smaller decline in prices of government bonds than President Hoover had faced. It also shows the perennial tendency of the monetary authorities to call for fiscal policies that will make it easier for them to pursue their chosen course, while Treasury Secretaries want the support of monetary policy to make their lives easier.[12]

The possible effects of continued deficits on the market for government securities was something the President understood. Even in the fall of 1936 he had given a lecture to Congressional leaders, with a gleeful Morgenthau in the corner of the room, warning that if the budget was not balanced the government would be unable to sell its bonds. In the spring of 1937 there was another factor present reinforcing Roosevelt's determination to balance the 1938 budget, or at least make a strong show of trying to do so. He had opened his campaign to reorganize the Supreme Court, and by doing that had aroused the antagonism of the conservatives, Democratic as well as Republican, in the Congress. Roosevelt wanted to mollify them in other ways if he could, and the budget was one arena in which he could demonstrate his soundness. He told Garner, whose loyalty on the Court issue was in doubt, "I have said fifty times that the budget will be balanced for the fiscal year 1938. If you want me to say it again, I will say it either once or fifty times more. That is my intention."[13]

SHIFTS IN THE BUDGET

But while the President's determination was growing it was becoming clear that the balance could no longer be simply predicted and harvested; it would have to be won by firm action. Revenues were falling behind the estimates. On April 20, 1937, the President announced that income tax collections for fiscal 1937 would probably be $267 million below the figure contained in the budget message of January and other revenues $337 million less, "which is due in large part to the obstruction of collections by numerous law suits against the Government."[14] For the fiscal year 1938 the revenue estimates were down by $387 million. With allowance for minor expenditure revisions, instead of a balanced budget for 1938 a deficit of $418 million was in prospect unless offsetting action was taken. The bond market declined slightly on this news.

The President directed the heads of the various government agencies to hold down expenditures in 1937 and said that he would "use every means at his command" to eliminate the deficit during 1938 by withholding appropriated funds from expenditures and by liquidating certain assets.[15] These efforts were unsuccessful. Expenditures for 1937 were only about one percent below the January estimate, and the deficit for that year was about $2700 million, as against the $2250 million estimate. When the President submitted new figures for 1938 in October, 1937, before the recession of that fall had affected the estimates, expenditures were put slightly higher than had been estimated in April and receipts significantly lower, so that the prospective deficit was almost $700 million.

Budget for Fiscal 1938[16]

| | Estimates (Millions of Dollars) | | |
	January 1937	April 1937	October 1937
Receipts	$7,294	$6,906	$6,650
Expenditures	7,256	7,324	7,345
Surplus	38	–418	–695

Despite the President's failure to carry out his promise to balance the budget for fical 1938, there was a radical change in the budget position between calendar 1936 and calendar 1937, and especially between the first halves of those two years. Receipts rose sharply and expenditures declined. This shift was only in small part the result of the recovery of national income, or of policy intended to bring the shift about. It resulted largely from the conclusion of the veterans' bonus payment and from the coming of the new Social Security taxes into full effect on January 1, 1937. The size and sources of the swing in the fiscal position can be seen from the comprehensive calendar year figures in the national income accounts, which were not then available. (See table, p. 100).

Recognition of what was going on was obscured by the tendency to look at fiscal year figures. More important was the failure to distinguish between ordinary government expenditures for purchases of goods and services or other payments to the public on the one hand, and expenditures for the purchase of government securities on the other. Under the Social Security program the government made such investments to the extent of $1.6

billion in calendar 1937, as compared with a small net sale of investments in 1936. These investments are, in terms of their economic effects, like payments for the retirement of public debt because they are a use of the proceeds of taxes—Social Security taxes—to reduce the amount of federal debt held by private investors. This was later—as early as 1938—to be noted by the administration, but during the year in which it was first to be important it was not recognized.

Federal Government Receipts and Expenditures[17]
National Income Accounts
(Millions of Dollars)

	Calendar 1936	Calendar 1937
Total Receipts	5,024	7,039
Social Insurance Funds	391	1,573
Other	4,633	5,466
Total Expenditures	8,653	7,397
Veterans Benefits*	1,430	134
Social Insurance Funds	95	142
Other	7,128	7,121
Deficit	3,629	358

*Excludes military pension, disability and retirement payments

However, even if the extent of the fiscal shift had been fully recognized in 1937, it is doubtful whether it would have caused any concern or led to any difference of policy.[18] The movement toward a balanced budget was a cause for self-congratulation from which there were at the time no public dissents. Although concern about a possible recession was beginning to appear, this concern was not based on the decline in the federal deficit that had occurred and was continuing. Rather it was based on the fact that the country was undergoing a considerable boom with some inflation and accumulation of inventories. Such developments in the past had been followed by business declines. People were asking whether we had reached another 1929. The progress toward a balanced budget was regarded as a factor tending to moderate the boom and prolong the recovery.

No Plan for Recession

When the recession began in August, 1937, with the sharpest decline of industrial production on record, the administration and the country seemed, as far as previous statements and actions could show, unprepared with any philosophy or policy for meeting it. As long as he was concerned with an incomplete recovery, the President understandably gave little attention to what he would do in the event of another recession. In his Baltimore speech to the Young Democrats, April 13, 1936, he had shown some concern with the problem:

> We do not yet know enough in a changing economic order to guarantee any Nation permanently or completely against times of depression. We believe, however, that steps like these which we have taken and are taking will at least greatly cushion depressions—will prevent the up-curve from rushing to a violent, mad peak of false prosperity and prevent another violent, mad descent into another slough of suffering and disillusionment like the one from which for the last three and a half years we have been surely emerging.[19]

But he was vague about what the steps were that would cushion recessions.

A sign of more specific preparation was given in February, 1937, when Roosevelt submitted to the Congress a long-range program of public works that had been prepared by the National Resources Committee. The President said: "Now it is time to develop a long-range plan and policy for construction—to provide the best use of our resources and to prepare in advance against any other emergency."[20] By "emergency" he clearly meant "depression." But the President did not push this idea and was not committed to acting on it.

The President couldn't prepare a plan for a recession without admitting that his recovery measures might stop working. His critics, on the other hand, could not propose measures to deal with a possible recession without admitting that the administration's measures were working. Their position was that the New Deal was impeding the recovery, which was proceeding more rapidly in other countries. Their program for recovery was to dismantle the New Deal, or much of it. They had no need for a different program in the event of recession.

Even after the recession started, its extent was only slowly recognized. At a meeting in September the Federal Open Market Committee agreed that there would not be much of a recession, although some decline was foreseen as a result of probable failure of private investment to rise enough to offset the decline in net federal budget stimulus to the economy. At that time the Federal Reserve announced that it had decided to offset the seasonal tightening of credit that would otherwise occur in the last months of the year, although its action was more expansive than this implied. Also in September, Secretary Perkins reported to the Cabinet that her Department of Labor statisticians expected an early upturn in business.

A sharp decline in the stock market on October 19, 1937, was taken as a sign of a real depression and precipitated a "policy crisis in Washington" in Morgenthau's words. Now Roosevelt had his own depression.[21] He was flooded with advice. At a press conference on October 29 he plaintively told of letters received from "two economic experts of the first water."

> One says the entire question is one of the velocity of capital turnover credit, so do not pay any attention to purchasing power. The other one says: forget all this algebraic formula about the velocity of capital turnover credit; the whole question is purchasing power on the part of one hundred and thirty million people. It is a fascinating study.[22]

Anti-Recession Possibilities

The proposals advanced for stopping the recession and resuming recovery were varied and in many respects contradictory:

1. Press firmly on with government economy to give assurances of a balanced budget in fiscal 1939 and thus encourage private investment. This was the key idea of Henry Morgenthau and James Farley, in which they had the support of Morgenthau's distinguished economist, Jacob Viner.

2. Remove the "anti-business" aspects of the New Deal, notably the undistributed profits tax, and thereby stimulate private investment. This naturally was the demand of the business organizations.

3. Restore the planning features of the NRA, insofar as could be done constitutionally, probably by voluntary cooperation by business, and thereby sustain wages and stimulate investment. This was an idea always attractive to the President and it had some support in business circles.

4. Attack the "private concentration of economic power" by trust-busting and regulation, on the hypothesis that monopolies caused the recession either by following their normal economic practices of raising prices and restraining production or by a politically-motivated act of sabotage. Assistant Attorney General Robert Jackson was a leading promoter of this idea, with support from Harold Ickes, Leon Henderson, Benjamin Cohen, and Thomas Corcoran.

5. Resume spending and give up, at least for the present, the idea of balancing the budget. Hopkins and Eccles were the chief proponents of this course, which had the support of numerous economists in the administration, Lauchlin Currie, Mordecai Ezekial, Louis Bean, Isadore Lubin, Harry White, and Leon Henderson being the most prominent.

One proposal of great prophetic significance was made at this time but probably did not reach the President. In October, 1937, Beardsley Ruml asked Leon Henderson what he would think of the idea of forgiving the installment of income tax payments due in December. Ruml, trained as a psychologist, had been a member of the Hutchins Commission mentioned earlier which in 1934 had pointed out the merits of tax reduction, as compared with exclusive reliance upon higher government spending, as a means of stimulating the economy. At that time he had been dean of social sciences at the University of Chicago. In 1937 he was treasurer of Macy's, adviser to the National Resources Committee, and a close friend of Henderson and other economists of the New Deal. The idea of a general, temporary tax reduction was premature in 1937. Not only were the President and the Congress unready for it, but even the leading proponents of an active fiscal policy had not yet passed beyond deficit *spending* as a program. Ruml later was to be a leading figure in the elevation of tax policy to a major position in a stabilizing fiscal program, especially through his influence as a member of the Committee for Economic Development.

All of the other ideas, except undoing the New Deal, the President seriously considered. He could not be expected to adopt a course that would amount to a confession of error for his basic policies of the past five years. Especially he could not make concessions to the business community which he regarded as his enemy and the cause of his embarrassment. He was willing to give them conciliatory language, as he did in the message opening the special session of Congress convened in November to deal with the recession, but he would not do more except with respect to balancing the budget, which he could reasonably say had always been part of his policy.

He did consult with a few businessmen about the idea of resuming some kind of planning, à la NRA, but voluntary this time, government only helping to provide guidelines. He had been looking for a way to do this ever since the NRA had been declared unconstitutional, and even before the recession began he was considering antitrust revision to permit voluntary coordination of business action. He was convinced that the instability of the economy resulted in large part from the inability of competing enterprises to foresee their demands accurately and plan a steady rate of production to meet them. In a press conference on January 4, 1938, he gave several parables to illustrate the problem and then said:

> Don't write the story that I am advocating the immediate reenactment of NRA. But the fact remains that in quite a number of the code industries under NRA it was perfectly legal for the heads of all the companies in a given industry to sit down around a table with the Government, and, from their own statistics and the statistics of their own trade associations and the statistics given them by the Government, figure out much more clearly than they ever had before, as an industry, what the probable demand of the country would be for a period of six months or a year ahead. In other words, they could make a more intelligent

group estimate as to the purchasing power of the country and the inventories of the particular article necessary for the immediate future.

Now, done that way, it is a perfectly legitimate thing for them to do—sitting there, with the Government, and trying honestly to find out what the needs are going to be for the next six months or a year, so that they won't overproduce. It is legitimate just so long as it is done without any attempts at price-fixing or driving competitors out of business or things like that as a result of the conference.

There is a question today whether a meeting of that kind, around a table, is legal under the anti-trust laws. A lot of people are afraid of it. I would very much favor making it a completely legal thing to do: to meet around a table to find out, with the help of the Government, what the demands are, what the purchasing power of the country is, what the inventories are.

QUESTION: How would the estimated annual production be allocated among the units of the industry?

FDR: Don't do that—keep competition. . . .[23]

This reversion to Hoover's rationalization through voluntary association, and precursor of French indicative planning, did not get anywhere in 1938. There had been considerable enthusiasm for this kind of thing in business circles in 1933, but with more experience businessmen thought they knew who would be sitting at the head of the table, and they didn't think it would be a businessman. At the same time many of the President's advisers, even the "planners" among them, were afraid of giving so much control to the businessmen. The prevailing view of this subject within the administration ran in the opposite direction—to take steps to curb the "concentration of economic power." Roosevelt went along with this to the extent of sending Congress a special message on the subject in April, 1938. Congress responded by setting up the Temporary National Economic Committee which, after voluminous hearings and studies, submitted a preliminary report in July, 1939, and a final report with recommendations in March, 1941.

Whichever way Roosevelt turned on the structural issue—towards planning or towards competition—the results were not likely to come rapidly as far as the recession was concerned. And while Roosevelt had been able to afford experimenting with a number of reforms which did not promise immediate recovery from Hoover's depression, he had to get out of his own depression quickly. The arena in which he could take quick action with the hope of quick results was the budget.

More Budget-Balancing

Roosevelt's initial reaction was to push on with an attempt to continue reducing the deficit. The recession insured that the 1938 deficit would be much larger than estimated even in October, and balancing the budget in fiscal 1939 was extremely unlikely. Still, the 1938 deficit would be below that for 1937, and the 1939 deficit could be a little lower than 1938. Except for the effects of the veterans' bonus, he would be able to show continuous annual decline in the size of the deficit beginning in 1934. To stick to this line was the easiest thing for the President to do, because it required no change that might seem an admission of previous error.

The President was much impressed with an analysis by Isadore Lubin which showed that the government's contribution to purchasing power had declined substantially from 1936 to 1937. He reported on this to the press on October 29, 1937, saying that the government's action had reduced the national income $2.5 billion in one year, as a result of declines in payments to veterans and relief workers and increased collections of Social Security taxes.[24] But this did not lead him to the conclusion that Lubin and other administration economists reached—that the government should undo what it had done by raising its expenditures. As Currie later reflected on Roosevelt's thinking in the fall of 1937:

> The President's faith in the basic New Deal policy of deliberately increasing a deficit to increase consumer buying power was obviously shaken. In any case, I always suspected that Roosevelt's adherence to that policy was based more on humanitarian than on economic grounds, despite his statements to the contrary that could be quoted. He was glad to use economic arguments for something he wanted to do on other grounds.[25]

The President believed that business was supposed to take up the effects of the government's contraction, and he was still counting on business to do so. He accepted Morgenthau's argument for balancing the budget as one way to encourage business. In response to urging from Morgenthau and Farley, he agreed to "play the old record," as he described it, about balancing the budget. And he did play it, in his message of November, 1937, to the special session of Congress and in his January, 1938, budget message, and he permitted Morgenthau to play it in a major address to the Academy of Political Science in New York on November 10, 1937.

It was almost like 1932–33, with the national economy declining and Roosevelt talking about balancing the budget. But it was even less likely in 1937–38 than in 1932–33 that balancing the budget would be an immediate determinant of policy. In fact, despite the apparent multitude of choices and diversity of advice, spending was the inevitable policy of 1938. For this there were several reasons:

1. The idea of stimulating business investment by promising to balance

the budget was a chimera. For one thing, business did not take the promise seriously. When Morgenthau made a heartfelt statement about the importance of balancing the budget in his Academy of Political Science speech, there was cynical laughter. But more than that, balancing the budget was not high on the list of the things business considered necessary to create an atmosphere in which investment could go forward. Repealing the undistributed profits tax was probably at the head of the list, followed by some moderation in labor policy. If they could not get what they wanted from Roosevelt they would try getting it from Congress, and in this they were partly successful. Continued declines of business and the stock market showed how futile playing the old record was.

2. Unlike the situation in 1933, there were now influential people in the administration whose power and status depended on the scale of the spending programs they managed. This included Wallace in Agriculture, Hopkins in WPA, Ickes in PWA, and Jesse Jones in the RFC. The case of Jones is particularly interesting, because Jones was generally regarded as a conservative. He had protested vigorously when Roosevelt in his frugal mood of 1937 had called a halt to new loan commitments by the RFC, saying scornfully that the President and Morgenthau did not understand the difference between spending and lending. He was the first to get his spending authority unleashed after the recession started.[26]

3. Machinery existed in the government for bringing about a large increase in spending. Roosevelt's skepticism about spending as a policy in 1933 derived partly from his belief that it was impossible to do much in that direction quickly. He now had programs and agencies that could get the money out rapidly.

4. The spending programs had built up a politically important clientele in the Congress, in the party machinery, in state and local governments, and among the direct beneficiaries. Many of these supporters of bigger expenditures for agriculture, for relief, for loans to small business and housing, and for the development of the West were also of course conservatives in fiscal policy, but that came second, not first.

5. Concern about the federal debt had diminished. The size of the debt had doubled between the end of 1932 and the end of 1937 without visible ill effects. Yields on federal bonds were about 2.7 percent at the end of 1937, compared with about 3.4 percent at the end of 1932. The ability of the Federal Reserve and the Treasury to keep the interest rates on government borrowing low was unquestioned.

6. Some of the policy possibilities that had seemed alternatives to spending in 1933 were no longer in the picture. There was no inclination to resort

to competitive devaluation of the dollar, and perhaps no possibility with gold flowing into the country. "Planning" did not seem possible because of the constitutional and political objections and mistrust between business and the administration. In any case, it did not promise quick results.

7. Expert economic advice within the administration was much more concentrated in the spending school that it had been earlier. Moley, Tugwell, Warren, and others had passed from influence as their ideas had failed or been exhausted. The expert opposition to spending within the administration was mainly in the Treasury, and even the Treasury had its experts on the spending side. The theorists of spending did not rise in influence only by default. They had acquired a new confidence and cohesion as a result of the work of J. M. Keynes (to be discussed in the next chapter) and found an advocate in Harry Hopkins who was very influential with the President.

8. In the course of the 1936 campaign the President had been educated about spending and had educated the public. To defend a fiscal policy into which he had fallen pragmatically and even reluctantly he had used arguments about the general, multiplier effects of deficit spending which had previously been strange and disagreeable to him. These became part, but not all, of his own thinking and of the public's. They would not be so new when urged as a guide to policy, rather than as rationalization of policy, in 1938.

Hopkins arranged for Currie, Henderson, and Lubin, plus Paul Mazur of Lehman Brothers, representing "the Wall Street point of view," to see the President on November 8. The three government economists submitted a memorandum which attributed the recession to the upsurge of costs and prices. Given the rise in costs and prices, prosperity could not be maintained unless purchasing power rose rapidly, which hadn't happened, partly because of the decline in the government's net expenditures. The prescription they offered was an immediate increase in spending, coupled with measures to reduce building costs. Beyond that, Currie said later: "I retained the objective of a balanced budget for 1939, since the fiscal year did not begin until the middle of 1938 and I had various ideas how the budget could be technically balanced while continuing a cash deficit."[27]

There was little tangible result from the meeting, although Currie thought it was part of the long-range process of educating FDR. The only part of the memo the President went along with was balancing the 1939 budget. Opening the special session of Congress on November 15, 1937, he said: "The proposed Federal budget for the coming fiscal year also will shortly be ready for submission to the Congress—a budget which I expect can be brought within a definite balance."[28] He warned Congress that if it enacted a farm program which increased federal costs it should also enact additional taxes to pay for it. In January he submitted a budget which called for expenditures in fiscal 1938 to be about $800 million below those of fiscal 1937, and fiscal 1939 expenditures to be about $750 million lower still.[29] This permitted him to show a declining deficit despite a substantial fall in estimated revenues resulting from the recession. He also, for the first time in a budget message, discussed the significance of the trust accounts for federal finance. He showed that in both fiscal 1938 and fiscal 1939 the investments of the trust accounts, resulting from an excess of their receipts over their outpayments and expenses, would exceed the budget deficit. Therefore, although the total federal debt would rise as a result of the deficit, the debt held outside the government trust accounts would decline in each of those years. (The main trust accounts involved were the old age reserve account and the unemployment insurance trust fund.) The government was actually paying less to the public than it was taking in. As would now be said, although the President did not then use this terminology, the cash budget was in balance.

RELUCTANT TRANSITION

Throughout January, February, and March the President resisted suggestions from many quarters for a change in policy. One of these quarters was J. M. Keynes, who wrote the President an unsolicited letter of advice on February 1. Keynes urged a step-up in spending, especially for public works, and a more conciliatory policy towards business in order to encourage private investment.[30] The President turned the letter over to Morgenthau to draft a reply, which was itself evidence that he was not going to think seriously about the spending argument. Roosevelt remarked to Ickes that he had received this letter from Keynes urging more spending, and went on to comment that "this was the proper thing to do in 1933 when the water had receded to the bottom of the well, but he doubted whether it was the thing to do now with the water within twenty-five or thirty per cent of the top."[31] According to Morgenthau's biographer, the task of answering Keynes' letter was agreeable. "It gave the Secretary the chance to speak for the Administration, and by a calculated silence to reject advice he disliked. . . . The emphasis Keynes put upon government spending Morgenthau simply ignored."[32]

Keynes sent Roosevelt another warning on March 25. "Further experience since I wrote does seem to show that you are treading a very dangerous middle path. You must either give more encouragement to business or take over more of their functions yourself. If public opinion is not ready for the latter, then it is necessary to wait until public opinion is educated. Your present policies seem to presume that you possess more power than you actually have."[33]

However nothing was less likely to impress Roosevelt than the argument that he had to do one thing or another and not some of both.

While still unwilling to adopt more spending as a policy, the President was being forced to accept it as a fact step by step. Relief needs rose with mounting unemployment, and on February 10 he asked for a supplementary appropriation for relief. On February 16 he signed, with commendation, an Agricultural Adjustment Act which failed to meet his requirement that additional revenues be provided for additional expenditures. On February 18 he directed Jesse Jones at the RFC to "make credit available to all deserving borrowers to which you are authorized to lend, especially loans that will maintain or increase employment."[34] On March 18 he directed the Secretary of Agriculture to proceed with the allotment of federal highway funds to the states, which he had been trying to hold back in the interest of economy.

THE CRITICAL DECISION

However the critical decision to turn to spending "for its own sake" as the main road out of the recession did not come until the President spent some days with Harry Hopkins at Warm Springs. Hopkins had been out of circulation after major surgery during most of the winter when the argument about recovery policy was raging in Washington. When Roosevelt went to Warm Springs on March 22, Hopkins was in Florida recuperating. He joined the President about the time—March 25—the stock market took "another sickening dip," in the words of Morgenthau's diary. Hopkins called Leon Henderson and Aubrey Williams, deputy WPA administrator, to station themselves at Pine Mountain Valley, near Warm Springs, where they would be available to assist Hopkins in his campaign for Roosevelt's approval of a spending program. On the train south, Henderson and Williams met Beardsley Ruml, who was on his way to visit Macy's Atlanta store. They persuaded him to join them at Pine Mountain Valley. There the three wrote a number of memoranda which they shuttled over to Hopkins who took them up with Roosevelt.

Exactly what arguments were successful in convincing Roosevelt is not known. Perhaps the continuing decline of business, employment, and the stock market, despite serious efforts to hold a sound fiscal posture, and the nearness of Congressional elections were the key to the successful persuasion.

However, a memorandum of April 1, written by Ruml with the help of Henderson and given to Hopkins, survives as a sample of the kind of intellectual argument employed.

The memorandum begins:

> Within recent months and particularly within recent weeks, a number of observers in reflecting on the present crisis in production have drawn together certain lines of thought which have not ordinarily been associated. As a result there appears in broad outline an appreciation of the system which, if correct in the main, should have a profound effect on current public policy.
>
> The problem centers on the role of national government in economic stabilization or economic advancement.[35]

The memo then proceeded to spell out the arithmetic of the current crisis. A national income of $88 billion was needed for reasonably full employment. The national income was then $56 billion. "If money invested or spent turns over two or three times a year, it would require between 7 and 10 billion dollars per year of *additional* investment or spending, public or private, to get reasonable full employment." That $4 billion of this would come from private investment was an optimistic estimate. To obtain $6 billion more from government spending was out of the question, but $3 billion could, with difficulty, be provided.

The problem was then put in historical perspective. According to the memo, the whole course of American economic advancement had been accompanied and permitted by the alienation of the national domain to create purchasing power for the growing national product. First the gold under the ground had been turned into money—national domain into purchasing power in one step. Then the public lands had been alienated, given to railroads and homesteaders, who borrowed on the lands from the banks and in the process created money—national domain into purchasing power in two steps. Then franchises, public grants of right to engage in certain kinds of business, had been given to corporations, which established enterprises, which borrowed on the strength of their prospective earnings and thus generated money—national domain into purchasing power in three steps.

The gold, land, and franchises had never been in the federal government balance sheet. Their alienation had not appeared as a diminution of a federal asset or increase in a federal liability. Now it was necessary to continue the process one step more. It was necessary to use a small part of the government's tax claim upon the future national income as a basis for borrowing to create purchasing power which would stimulate the national economy.

The government had two choices. It could try to push private production, hoping thereby to generate purchasing power, or it could push consumption, thereby generating production. The latter was the democratic method.

This was a line of thought well calculated to impress the President. It made the whole thing seem very elemental, rather than a complicated financial or economic technicality. It put the President in the picture as an agent of a long historic process, and appealed to his pleasure in the role of prudent manager of the national domain—a role which he himself had said he enjoyed. Also, it was a democratic solution, not a surrender to business.

By April 2 the President had made his decision for a spending program. How much to spend, and for what, still had to be decided. Also, Morgenthau had to be brought into line. The Secretary of the Treasury was hurt and worried. A major fiscal decision had been made without consulting him and in a direction which had to be interpreted as repudiating him. He feared that the capital markets would not absorb the additional borrowing required to finance the new spending. His fear on that score was somewhat relieved by the decision, made after the President's return from Warm Springs, to include in the program steps to increase bank reserves, which would assure the continuation of low interest rates. Still, basically he regarded business confidence as the key to revival, and budget-balancing as the key to business confidence.

The Secretary made no dent on the President, even though he went farther than he had ever gone before in opposition. At a meeting with Congressional leaders where the President unveiled his spending program, Morgenthau emphasized the size of the deficit that would result, an action that infuriated the President. Morgenthau said that he was seriously thinking of resigning, to which the President replied, as he had to Douglas in 1934, that his resignation would destroy the Democratic party. In the end Morgenthau went along.[36]

The President submitted his program to Congress on April 14 and explained it to the public in a radio fireside chat that evening.[37] He divided his program into three parts:

a. Additional appropriations of $1,550 million for fiscal year 1939 for WPA, the Farm Security Administration, the National Youth Administration, and the Civilian Conservation Corps. This part of the program was described as simply continuing the current rate of expenditure and preventing people then receiving assistance from the federal government from being thrown out of work on July 1.

b. Steps to expand the supply of credit, by desterilizing $1.4 billion of gold held by the Treasury and reducing bank reserve requirements by about three-quarters of a billion dollars.

c. "Definite additions to the purchasing power of the Nation by providing new work" by federal expenditures and loans of $1,162 million for
public works and $300 million for housing.

It is clear from the message and from the fireside chat as well that the
President felt the need particularly to justify the third step. This he regarded
as something new, going beyond the continued provision of relief and
relaxation of credit, which he and the country had accepted, to public expenditures primarily for the purpose of generating purchasing power. Aside
from saying that the expenditures would be for "well thought out, needed
and permanent public improvements" he laid no stress on the value of the
work that would be done. This was spending "for its own sake."

There was no explanation of the mechanism by which these expenditures
would stimulate the economy—no "money going round and round," no
"priming the pump" or "letting in the clutch." It was taken as well understood that increasing public spending would raise the national income. An
interim goal of raising the national income—then $56 billion—to $80 billion
was set forth, but no attempt was made to relate the proposed amount of
expenditure to this goal or to explain the amount of expenditure in any
other way. (The federal loans and expenditures proposed came to $3,012
million, close to the $3 billion described in Ruml's April 1 memo as possible
with difficulty.) Surprisingly, in contrast to his past practice, no revised estimates of the budget or the deficit for 1939 were presented, and the deficit
and the debt were barely mentioned. It was as if Roosevelt wanted to get
the whole subject out of that financial framework, as when, two years later,
he wanted to get the Lend-Lease policy freed of the "silly, fool old dollar
sign."

In reviewing the course of events leading up to the recession, the President said:

> At the end of 1936 the efforts of the Government to aid in increasing the
> Nation's purchasing power and in stimulating business had become so well
> recognized that both the business community and the Government felt that a
> large measure of the Government's spending activities could be materially re-
> duced.[38]

However he did not say then, as he was to say later, that the reduction
of expenditures had come too fast. Rather the cause of the recession was
largely in "certain highly undesirable practices" of business—speculation,
overproduction, and price raising. Also, he was at pains to show that since
January 1, 1937, he had recommended only four important measures affecting business, so it was unreasonable to blame the recession, as some critics
did, on his harassment of business.

The President invoked part of the Ruml argument to show that his proposal was not radical in American history:

> In the first century of our republic we were short of capital, short of workers and short of industrial production; but we were rich in free land, free timber and free mineral wealth. The Federal Government rightly assumed the duty of promoting business and relieving depression by giving subsidies of land and other resources.
>
> Thus, from our earliest days we have had a tradition of substantial government help to our system of private enterprise. But today the government no longer has vast tracts of rich land to give away and we have discovered that we must spend large sums to conserve our land from further erosion and our forests from further depletion. The situation is also very different from the old days, because now we have plenty of capital, banks and insurance companies loaded with idle money: plenty of industrial productive capacity and several millions of workers looking for jobs. It is following tradition as well as necessity, if Government strives to put idle money and idle men to work, to increase our public wealth and to build up the health and strength of the people—and to help our system of private enterprise to function.[39]

There was, of course, a great deal of immediate criticism of the program, in the Congress, in the press, and in the financial and business community. But the *New York Times* regarded the initial reaction as generally favorable and reported that the Republicans gave more support than expected. The nature of the criticism is important. Little was heard about the country being ruined, about the government's credit being undermined, or about the inevitability of inflation as a consequence of the deficit spending. Neither was much doubt expressed about the ability of the government to stimulate the economy to some extent and for some time by increasing its expenditures. The general line of the opposition was that spending *alone* would not produce adequate and durable recovery, but had to be accompanied by policies to encourage private investment which the President refused to adopt. This line is well expressed in the *New York Times* summary of the reaction of "the financial community." "The pump-priming expenditures, if sanctioned by Congress, may be expected to give a spurt to business activity when the money starts to move; but it was the prevailing view that, unless other measures were taken to revive the interest of private capital, this spurt could last only as long as the government continued to pour out the money."[40]

The opposition to the President's spending program must be understood against the background of the fight over taxes which had been going on for several months. Business leaders and spokesmen had seen in the recession confirmation of their view that adverse tax treatment, especially the undistributed profits tax enacted in 1936 and the longer-standing taxation of capital gains, was interfering with investment and preventing full recovery. They made the recession an occasion for a campaign to eliminate the undistributed profits tax and reduce the capital gains tax. This campaign won a great deal of support in the Congress. In fact, the Senate passed a bill eliminating the undistributed profits tax and reducing the capital gains tax. However, the President was immovable on the subject. On April 13, the day before he sent up his spending message, he wrote to the chairmen of the House Ways and Means Committee and the Senate Finance Committee, criticizing the Senate bill and supporting the House version which was more to his liking. This letter itself produced a furore in the Senate. The spending program submitted one day later was further proof that the President rejected the conservative route to recovery and would push hard on spending to produce recovery without concessions or conciliation for business.

The President's spending program aroused criticism and bitterness less for what he proposed to do—spend—than for what he proposed not to do—cut taxes on profits and otherwise encourage business directly. Just as the tax increases of 1935 and 1936 had been the main point of business opposition to the President's fiscal program of those years, so the failure to include reduction of certain taxes was the main point of business and conservative objection to the President's recovery program of 1938. This foreshadows the willingness of business to support programs of deficit finance in the postwar period when those programs included substantial reductions in the taxes to which business was most sensitive.

Despite the President's objection, the Congress passed in May a Revenue Act which reduced the capital gains tax and the undistributed profits tax and provided for the latter to expire at the end of 1939. The President criticized this action severely but, in a move unprecedented for him, allowed it to become law without his signature. In June, 1938, Congress enacted the appropriations for the spending program.

June was also the bottom of the recession. Thereafter the economy rose gradually but visibly. However, in August, 1939, just before the economic effects of the European War began to be felt, production and employment were still a few percentage points below their mid-1937 peaks.

LESSONS OF THE RECESSION

The experience of 1937 and 1938 was critical for the development of American fiscal policy. It demonstrated to many people the powerful effect of changes in the budget position upon the economy. Between the first part of 1936 and the middle of 1937 federal expenditures declined and revenues rose significantly, if Social Security contributions are included. Thereafter the economy fell sharply. In the spring of 1938 an enlarged spending and lending program was initiated; the economy began to rise soon thereafter. These variations were not, of course, the only possible explanation of the recession and recovery. The upswing of business that had gone on since early 1933, even though with unusually frequent interruptions, was already 50 months old in mid-1937. It was then twice as long as the average American cyclical expansion. The latter part of the expansion has been marked by price rises, which generated inventory accumulation, and by exceptional uncertainty about the policy of the administration towards business, which depressed investment. By the spring of 1938 substantial liquidation of inventories had been achieved, and favorable action of Congress on taxes had reassured business that it was not helpless before Roosevelt. An explanation of the 1937–38 decline and rise of business can be constructed in such terms. Also, an alternative or supplementary explanation can be constructed out of monetary policy and changes in the money supply. The excess reserves of banks were reduced beginning in mid-1936, after which the supply of money grew less rapidly and then declined before the recession started. In the fall of 1937 the Federal Reserve reversed its policy, and growth of the money supply was resumed around the beginning of 1938, about six months before the upturn of business.[41]

We still do not know with confidence what was the relative influence of the various factors that might have explained the decline of 1937 and recovery of 1938. But this has not prevented the widespread acceptance of the view that fiscal policy was extremely important. Even the National Association of Manufacturers in 1938 listed as one of the immediate causes of the 1937–38 depression, "Drastic instead of gradual reduction in federal cash deficit expenditures."[42]

NATIONAL FISCAL POLICY IN 1938

Roosevelt's efforts of November and December, 1937, and January, 1938, were the last an American President would make to cut expenditures in the midst of a recession. Probably by the spring of 1938 one could say that it was national policy, no matter who the President might be, not to try that. In fact, FDR's efforts were at the time viewed with disbelief by many, who thought that he was not serious about economizing but wanted to occupy the posture of an economizer while the expenditures were forced upon him. But in any case, the policy of cutting expenditures was not practical because of the strong political pressures bound to arise in such circumstances from

the direct beneficiaries of particular expenditure programs. It was also ineffective as a device for stimulating recovery by strengthening business confidence because too many other factors had higher rank as influences on business confidence.

It was probably also national policy by the spring of 1938 that in the
event of a severe recession the government would take strong expansionary
budget measures. The factors listed on pages 105–7 as making it inevitable
that Roosevelt would turn to a spending policy in 1938 have continued to
operate and have grown in force.

It was not, in 1938 or 1939, national policy to use fiscal means—deficit
spending—to whatever degree might be necessary or thought to be necessary
to achieve prosperity and full employment. Fiscal policy did not have the
unlimited, residual role of doing whatever all other means in combination
failed to do. The idea of a national goal to achieve some level of national
income at which there would be prosperity and full employment became
more and more common in these years. Roosevelt spoke frequently about
the goal of an $80 billion national income when the actual figure was around
$60 billion, and this provoked no quarrel either about the particular number
or about the general idea of setting such a target. Also the idea that government spending of $X billion would have the effect at least temporarily of
raising the national income by some multiple of that amount had acquired
common currency. The President could use this concept in press conferences
without having to explain it. But he never went to the point of recommending an increase of federal expenditure of a size calculated to raise the national
income to $80 billion.

There were several reasons for his failure to make this step, which with
hindsight now seems so natural. In 1938 he probably did not have available
the programs and machinery that would have permitted so large an expansion of federal spending. It will be recalled that Ruml's Georgia memorandum had set $3 billion as probably the maximum increase in federal spending
that could be achieved in a year. But this was a limit that could have been
surmounted in time, if effort had been devoted to doing so. During the
spring of 1939, when there had been some recovery from the recession of
1938 but of disappointing scale, the administration did busy itself to devise
another increase of spending. But even this when finally presented to Congress involved additional expenditures of less than one billion dollars for
fiscal 1940.

While the President was willing to set forth the $80 billion national in-
come, corresponding to full employment, as a national goal, he did not
regard its attainment at any near date as imperative for him. It was essential

to show progress toward that goal and to maintain his own position as the best hope of further progress. He had to get the economy moving again after the 1937–38 recession, and to give it another prod when it lagged in the spring of 1939. He also had to demonstrate that the opposition had no program that would generate economic recovery, and this he did very skillfully. But he did not have to produce full employment.

Moreover Roosevelt still did not believe that spending was his only route to full employment. Whenever he talked about the goal of full employment he recited a list of measures to get there, of which spending was only one and not usually the first. By 1938 and 1939 the list had become pretty thin, consisting largely of things already done or things not likely to be done soon. He and his advisers seemed to be out of ideas, or at least out of ideas which could be exposed to the cool political climate of the time. But Roosevelt probably never got over his belief in a possible structural reform of the economy, compounded of planning, competition, and income redistribution, which would give high employment without deficits except for occasional fluctuations. This was, indeed, the standard view of the older liberals of the time as represented, for example, by *The Nation* and *The New Republic*. They accepted deficit spending only as a second-best and temporary policy.

Rexford Tugwell believes that by the end of his first term Roosevelt had gotten over his feeling of guilt about budget deficits. However, they still apparently aroused some feeling of remorse or sorrow. Morgenthau describes Roosevelt as "quite disturbed and shocked" at the end of 1938 when he saw how big the expenditure figures for fiscal 1940 were. He was presenting his sixth budget message and his deficits were bigger than ever, excepting only the year of the veterans' bonus. This must have embarrassed him. In any case he took great pains in the January, 1939, budget message to soften the psychological effect of the deficit. He revived the distinction between the ordinary and extraordinary expenditures, which he had ignored for some years, he balanced the addition to federal assets against the increase in the federal debt, and he showed how much of the increase in the federal debt would be borrowed from the federal trust accounts rather than from the public. This was also the first budget message to use the new treatment of the RFC and other lending agencies which included as budget expenditures only their losses, not their net investments.[43]

How much this continuing sensitiveness on the subject of the deficit reflects Roosevelt's own opinion, and how much it reflects his view of public opinion, is unknown. Public opinion seems to have been in 1939 what it always had been. A survey in March, 1939,[44] asked, "If you were a member of the incoming Congress, would you vote yes or no on a bill to reduce federal spending to the point where the national budget is balanced?" The replies were:

	Yes	No	Don't know
National Total	61.3%	17.4%	21.3%
By Economic Status			
Prosperous	76.3	11.1	12.6
Upper Middle	67.1	17.8	15.1
Lower Middle	62.2	17.8	20.0
Poor	54.8	18.3	26.9
Negroes	40.2	19.5	40.3
Unemployed	57.5	20.0	22.5
By Attitude Toward Roosevelt			
Roosevelt essential	45.6	22.3	32.1
Good outweighs bad	54.5	21.8	23.8
Usefulness over	77.5	12.3	10.2
Roosevelt a calamity	84.6	7.4	8.0

The voters, or at least the great majority of them, had not held his deficits against Roosevelt in 1936. But then the economy was rising vigorously and deficits were declining. He was on less secure ground in 1939 and did not like to violate this common belief in budget-balancing as long as he did not think that he had to do so.

Whatever the people thought, Roosevelt faced a stronger opposition in Congress, on spending as on many other issues, in 1939 than he had ever faced before. It is extremely doubtful whether he could have gotten through Congress in 1939 a much larger spending program than he actually did. In 1939, probably for the first time in our story, national fiscal policy has to be described as what the President and the Congress could agree on, rather than as what the President wanted. Up to this point, except for the two veterans' bonus payments, Hoover and Roosevelt had obtained from the Congress almost all of what they asked for. The defeat of Roosevelt's spending-lending bill in 1939 was the first defeat of a Presidential proposal that went to the heart of fiscal policy.

DEFICITS FOREVER?

By 1939 the issue in fiscal policy was much different than it had been between 1933 and 1937. In the earlier period the New Deal's deficit spending was presented to the country as a temporary expedient. It was either to take care of urgent needs until recovery came, or it was a "pump-priming" device to raise the economy to a level at which it would run by itself without further deficits. Until 1937 the administration could claim that this policy was working. Roosevelt could look at the recovery and say, "We planned it that way." But this position could not be maintained after the 1937–38 recession. The pump was not running; prosperity generated by deficits had not survived the withdrawal of the stimulus.

So the issue now seemed to be whether we should embrace a program of deficit spending "forever." There were some people who did accept this idea, including some associated with the administration. But in general, the idea of perpetual deficits was much harder to accept than the idea of temporary or occasional deficits. It seemed natural to believe that there must be something wrong if the economic system could not operate at high employment without permanent deficits, and that more fundamental reforms were needed to make high employment possible with balanced budgets. This had been the position of Roosevelt and many of the New Dealers in the years after they came to power, when the system to be reformed was the laissez-faire, Hoover, big-business system. It became the position of conservatives in 1938 and later, when the system to be reformed was the New Deal itself and the reforms needed were moderation of New Deal taxes and other policies that hurt business.

Proponents of an active fiscal policy for full employment have often expressed surprise at the failure of businessmen and conservatives generally to recognize that such a policy is really the salvation of free, private enterprise. How could the free enterprisers be so blind as not to see that without a policy of deficit finance there would be massive unemployment, causing deep popular resentment against the system and radical changes in it? But by 1939, after six years of New Deal policy, there were still about ten million persons unemployed, over one-sixth of the labor force. The policy had not demonstrated its ability to save the system by protecting it from massive unemployment. To some extent the deficits may have reduced unemployment, but also to some extent the deficit policy helped to create the need for deficits, because some of the expenditures financed by the deficit were competitive with private investment, and because the deficit generated fears of higher taxes—fears which experience showed were not unfounded. And even if the deficits were propping up the system, the system they were propping up was not free enterprise but the New Deal. The fiscal policy concealed what conservatives regarded as the need for reforms to stimulate private investment. Moreover, in the political situation of 1938 and 1939 it could be reasonably thought that the alternative to deficit spending was not a further extension of the New Deal or more radical measures but rather a turn in the opposite direction. With a conservative coalition in control of the Congress, a drive to get the country moving again by means other than spending might get rid of some of the New Deal measures, as in fact happened with the undistributed profits tax.

Thus opposition to deficit spending was fortified by the belief that deficit spending now meant permanent deficits, as well as by the belief that the alternative to such a policy was at least the partial unwinding of the New Deal. The strength of this opposition, together with Mr. Roosevelt's own reasons for caution outlined above, meant that the country in 1939 was certainly not committed to a policy of using fiscal means continuously and in the degree required to regain and keep full employment. When we were "at the bottom of the well," in Roosevelt's phrase, we would take emergency fiscal measures as Roosevelt had recommended and Congress had approved in the spring of 1938. But aside from that, in less drastic situations we would "float," avoiding a sudden dash for a balanced budget out of respect for the lesson of 1937, but not pushing aggressively to lift the economy to full employment. Undoubtedly policy would have developed in one direction or another if the war had not intervened, but the direction could not be confidently foreseen in 1939.

THE LAST SPENDING EFFORT

The state of policy before the outbreak of the European War is well represented by the experience of the 1939 spending-lending bill. After a vigorous recovery in the second half of 1938 the economy had levelled off. The administration felt the need to do something to get the economy moving again, although there was some speculation that a major effort in this direction would be deferred until 1940 to make sure that its impact was not lost before the Presidential election of that year. It was generally expected that the program would focus on increased spending. The administration had not been generating any new ideas for structural reform of the system. In fact, the year 1939 had opened with assurances from the administration that it was to be a time for consolidation and digestion of the New Deal reforms—for smoothing off their rough edges—and for general peace and quiet in the relations between government and business. The Temporary National Economic Committee's investigation of "Concentration of Economic Power" was getting under way, but whatever that might yield in proposals for economic reform was still in the future.

The administration in the spring of 1939 decided to propose a further stimulus to the economy through spending. In a letter to Senator Byrnes the President proposed that the RFC should be authorized to borrow about $3.8 billion which it would spend or lend, or make available to other government agencies to spend or lend, for purposes which would yield income and repayments to service and retire the debt. The whole operation would be "outside the budget," at least until later when net losses might be encountered.[45] The $3.8 billion was not to be spent at once. It was to constitute a revolving fund out of which expenditures would be made from time to time as economic conditions required. For fiscal 1940 expenditures out of the fund were estimated at around $800 million,

The proposal ran into heavy weather from the beginning. Secretary Morgenthau, testifying for the plan, emphasized that it would not add either to taxes or to the federal debt; indeed, it was reported that this was the reason for his endorsement of the plan. Critics greeted this claim with skepticism. The debt of the RFC would be guaranteed by the federal government, and the distinction between such debt and federal debt seemed a subterfuge. Similar doubts surrounded the idea that the loans or expenditures would be "self-liquidating." Who was going to decide, when the money went out, whether it would be paid back? The administration had counted on the good name of Jesse Jones, longtime head of the RFC and a symbol of sound finance to the Congress. But Mr. Jones maintained an attitude of cool reserve toward the plan, and it was pointed out that while he would raise the money he would have little to do with spending most of it.

A more fundamental question was why the government needed to be in the picture at all, if the projects to be financed were so sure to pay off. Wasn't there plenty of money in the banks, insurance companies, and elsewhere? The administration's answer was that the projects would be self-liquidating at interest rates that the government could charge but not at the higher rates that private lenders would demand. A. A. Berle, one of the original Brain Trusters, advanced a substantial theory in support of this proposition. Since 1900, he said, we had been capable of producing much more than we could consume, and had a lot of savings left over. There was no need to charge interest to draw forth savings or to ration them. We only had to decide which capital investments we wanted or needed and set interest rates at the level that the chosen investments would yield. This argument seemed to frighten more people than it persuaded, because it suggested no limits to either the direction or the amount of the federally-stimulated investments.

The character of the projects included in the spending-lending program supported, and added to, the fears that what was proposed was a vast new incursion of the federal government into the economy. A key item was that the RFC would buy railroad equipment and lease it to the railroads. The RFC, which was already a big lender to railroads, would enter the equipment business. Railroad people thought that the RFC as lender was already exercising too much influence over the management of the railroads and feared the extension of that influence. Another item was the construction of toll roads, bridges, and tunnels by the federal government. This drew opposition both because tolls were to be charged, and because, at least as initially drafted, it seemed to impinge on the functions of the states. The section of the plan providing for foreign loans aroused isolationist furore and was the first to be compromised. Also, the revolving fund idea looked like a way of avoiding annual Congressional scrutiny and so raised suspicions in the Congress.

If the proposal had been different, if it had been inside the budget, if it had not claimed to be "self-liquidating," if the objects of expenditure had been more conventional, the criticism would have been different. Whether the objection would have been less than it was is impossible to say. Probably it would not have been enough less to get the plan adopted. As it was, even after many humiliating concessions to get approval in the Senate, the leadership could not get it through the House.

The basic fact was that in 1939 the country was unwilling to commit itself to spending as the way to prosperity, especially when the commitment seemed to be permanent. To get out of "the bottom of the well," as in April 1938, the government would spend as an emergency measure, but it was not prepared to regularize and perpetuate the process. Even Roosevelt's devotion to the idea was less than enthusiastic. He had not launched the 1939 spending program with a special message to Congress and a radio talk to the nation, as he had in 1938, but had taken the occasion of a letter to Senator Byrnes on another subject to make the suggestion. It was not easy to generate excitement about the fourth big spending program in six years when the need for the fourth cast doubt on the effectiveness of the first three. The President took the defeat of the program calmly, only pointing out that those who had voted against it would have to assume responsibility for any future weakness of the recovery. Morgenthau's diary, admittedly not the most objective of witnesses, still reports Roosevelt in 1939 as not really reconciled to an unbalanced budget.[46]

While Mr. Roosevelt's support was uncertain, the opposition was not. Being free of the necessity to find merit in the policies of the preceding six years, the opposition could and did say not only that the spending program had failed to produce recovery, but also that the New Deal as a whole, including the spending but primarily the tax, labor, and business regulation aspects, had retarded recovery. The spending program to them was futile as a way of achieving lasting prosperity and displaced the measures that would be successful. This opposition was not confined to people who did not understand the mechanism by which government spending could generate income or who had a selfish economic or political interest in defeating and undoing the New Deal. Many sophisticated students, such as Jacob Viner, who had supported spending and deficits as temporary and cyclical remedies, objected when they were proposed as permanent features of economic policy.

So it is fair to say that in 1939, before the economy became dominated by the war, the role of fiscal policy was uncertain. Relief of great distress would be provided in a depression, even at the cost of budget deficits. In extreme situations we would increase spending for the sake of its general effect upon the level of income and employment. We would be tolerant of the deficits that would automatically result from the decline of revenues in a depression. But we were not prepared to go beyond that in 1939, and whether we would have gone farther in 1940 or 1941 if the war had not brought rapid recovery, no one can tell.

While the experience of 1937–39 left the future course of fiscal policy uncertain, the decision to raise expenditures aggressively in the spring of 1938 was a major confirmation of the change in national fiscal policy that had occurred since 1931 and 1932. There were also several other respects in which the experience of that period contributed to the subsequent evolution of fiscal policy.

The Definition of the Budget

The failure of the ordinary budget accounts to reveal the economic impact of federal finance became obvious in 1937, chiefly as a result of the operation of the Social Security program. Beginning in 1936, and increasingly in 1937, the taxes on employers and employees for the old age and unemployment insurance programs yielded large amounts of revenue in excess of the benefit payments made under the programs, but this excess of receipts over payments did not have the effect of tending to reduce the deficit shown in the budget. The excess of receipts over payments was invested in Treasury securities, and this investment was shown as an expenditure in the budget, so that receipts and expenditures for the Social Security accounts were always equal in the budget, despite the actual large excess of receipts over payments to beneficiaries and administrative expenses.[47] This invisible surplus went from zero in fiscal 1936 to $600 million in fiscal 1937 and $1 billion in fiscal 1938, so it was not insignificant with respect to the reported deficits of those years.

The concealment of the Social Security surpluses in the budget accounts contributed to the slowness with which the government and others recognized the extent to which the budget had shifted in a deflationary direction by early 1937. After the 1937 economic decline began, the administration became quite conscious of the effects of Social Security finance and pointed them out on several occasions. Budget messages beginning with that of January, 1938, showed how much of the increased federal debt resulting from the deficits would be acquired by the Social Security trust funds and would not have to be sold to the public. This was roughly the same as showing how much of the reported deficit was not actually a current deficit of the government in its relations with the public. The administration never published in these prewar years any consolidated statement of accounts, including the trust accounts, which would have shown the total flow of receipts and payments between the federal government and the public.[48] This logical next step would be made near the end of the war with the publication of the statement of receipts from and payments to the public, which came to be known as the cash budget.

Instead of following up the idea of consolidating all the federal transactions so that the net financial relation with the public could be seen, the administration became diverted in 1938 and 1939 by a conflicting idea, or rather with a confusion of two conflicting ideas.

The President revived in the January, 1939, budget message the distinction between ordinary and extraordinary expenditures which, with shifting nomenclature, he had used in several earlier budgets. There were, however, two differences between the extraordinary category as used in 1939 and the corresponding categories presented earlier. The extraordinary category was to be a permanent feature of the budget, not something that would disappear with prosperity. Moreover, the items included in the extraordinary category were a mixed bag, some being there because they were for capital purposes, like public works and loans, others qualifying because they were for relief, and others simply being large and nonrecurrent, like the new national defense program. The distinction between ordinary and extraordinary expenditures was not the distinction between current and capital expenditures. The President described the extraordinary expenditures as "those which relate to the nonoperating or unusual costs of government and involve extraordinary expenditures that deal more particularly with the relationship between fiscal policy and the economic welfare of the country. These questions concern government loans, capital outlays, and relief of need. Expenditures made under these heads are of such a flexible character as to provide, through their contraction and expansion, a partial offset for the rise and fall in the national income."[49]

This discussion, and the classification of the figures which accompanied it, had the usual purpose of explaining or justifying the deficit by showing that it was all due to extraordinary expenditures. But it also seems to have had another purpose, namely to establish and regularize the flexible determination of the size and financing of some part of the budget expenditures for the purpose of economic stabilization. The President said:

> May I say emphatically that I am not suggesting an ordinary budget which is always balanced and an extraordinary budget which is always unbalanced. The ordinary expenses of government should continue to be met out of current revenues. But I also hope that those revenues in times of prosperity will provide a surplus which can be applied against the public debt that the Government must incur in lean years because of extraordinary demands upon it.[50]

This carries some implication of an ordinary budget which is constantly in balance and a total budget which is balanced over the business cycle. However, the selection of items for inclusion in the extraordinary budget bears no logical relation to this purpose, and more important the effectiveness of the whole scheme depends upon the amount of the expenditures made under the "extraordinary" heading and the manner of their financing, which is not discussed. But at any rate we see here some early groping for a way of legitimizing the continuous use of fiscal policy as a stabilizing instrument.

Related to and mixed up with this was a groping for a "true" capital budget, with capital expenditures segregated and losses or depreciation related to them shown in a current budget. There was much interest within the administration in Swedish and Danish procedures of this kind. In 1938 one step in this direction had been taken with respect to the Commodity Credit Corporation, which purchased agricultural products or made loans secured by them as part of the farm price support program. It was provided that the expenditures made by the CCC for purchases or loans would not be included in the budget, but only estimated losses from these transactions would be shown as budget expenditures. Also the accounting for the RFC had reverted to the practice of the Hoover days, with RFC expenditures financed by the corporation's own borrowing being completely excluded from the budget. Thus for the category of expenditures made by corporations having their own source of financing and expecting receipts from sales, repayments of loans, and earnings which would eventually liquidate their borrowing, the government was moving toward exclusion from the budget.

The idea of a capital budget seems to have an irresistible fascination, especially for people who want on the one hand to be modern and unconventional about budget policy and on the other hand to be, or seem to be, businesslike. There have been numerous studies of the subject, usually ending with the recommendation that the capital nature of certain federal expenditures should be taken into account in some unspecified way. Basically this idea runs counter to the main trend of modern thinking about the budget. The "capital budget" idea suggests that the government financial plan—for example the size of the deficit or surplus—should be determined by the character of the government's expenditures, whereas the "compensatory" idea is that the financial plan should be determined by the overall needs of the economy. The evolution of fiscal policy in recent years has been dominated by the effort to make practical application of the compensatory idea, and this has left little room for any reflection of the capital budgeting idea in policy. Probably its main significance has been that governments could have recourse to it, as to other fuzziness in the definition of the budget, to conceal contradictions between the policy the government finds economically or politically necessary and the public's preference for balanced budgets.

The question of the definition of the budget was opened up for discussion in the years 1937–39. Attention to the effects of Social Security pointed in the direction which later developments were to take, whereas the "capital-budgeting" fad turned out to be transitory. Another step in this period towards what was to become postwar fiscal policy was the estimation of the effect on the budget of changes in the level of the national income. Of course it had been recognized for a long time, as was indeed obvious, that the receipts which would be collected from a given schedule of tax rates would depend upon the size of the national income and the accompanying sales and employment. In fact, during the 1930's the business press used to read backwards from the budget estimates of receipts to deduce what economic conditions the Treasury was forecasting. However, the relationship between the revenues, and by implication the deficit, and the level of national income was never more precisely stated than in the January, 1939, budget message:

> Revenue from taxes depends mainly on two factors: The rate of taxation and the total of the national income. This holds true not only of direct taxes on personal and corporate income but also of what are known as ad valorem taxes or other forms of indirect taxes, for the very good reason that the volume and value of goods produced or articles imported vary with the rise or fall of the Nation's total income.
>
> We can and do fix the rate of taxation definitely by law. We cannot by a simple legislative act raise the level of national income, but our experience in the last few years has amply demonstrated that through wise fiscal policies and other acts of government we can do much to stimulate it.
>
> In order that you may know the amount of revenue which the Government

may expect under the existing tax structure as the national income rises, the following table is submitted. It shows the estimated revenues which may be derived when national income reaches certain levels between 70 billion and 90 billion dollars.[51]

Estimated federal receipts* by principal sources, at certain assumed
levels of national income based on December 1938 tax rates
(Billions of Dollars)

National income	70	80	90
Income taxes	2.5	3.9	5.7
Miscellaneous internal revenue	2.2	2.6	3.1
Customs	.4	.5	.7
Miscellaneous receipts	.2	.2	.2
Payroll taxes	.7	.8	.9
Total	6.0	8.0	10.6

*Tax liabilities excluding trust accounts. Payroll taxes at calendar year 1938 rates.

The basic fact shown here was later to be an important ingredient in thinking about fiscal policy. Not only did the revenues to be expected from the given tax rates depend upon the level of national income, but the variability was large. The increase in receipts was 20 percent of the increase of national income from $70 billion to $80 billion and 26 percent of the increase of national income from $80 billion to $90 billion. One could not say whether the budget for any future year was balanced without specifying the level of national income for that year. This fact led to a question about the meaning of balancing the budget. Did it mean that the government should so order its affairs that when the national income was at some "normal" or "high" level the budget would be in balance? If so, unless other steps were taken, there would be a deficit when the national income was below the specified level. To keep the budget constantly in balance would require tax increases or expenditure reductions, or both, when the economy declined. This reversed much of the argument about depression deficits. Against a policy of deliberately creating deficits in depressions it could be argued that such a policy would require reliable forecasts as well as expenditure changes that were administratively difficult and wasteful, and tax changes that were inconvenient to the taxpayer. Now it appeared that to keep the budget in balance would require all these things. Recognition of this led to acceptance of depression deficits on practical grounds by people who were not convinced of the value of such deficits in themselves.

Elaboration of the implications of these ideas led to three concepts of fiscal policy which entered the stream of discussion around 1943. One was that the restrictiveness or expansiveness of fiscal policies needed to be mea-

sured at some standardized conditions of national income, just as the speed
of airplanes needs to be measured at some standarized conditions of atmo-
spheric pressure. From this came the idea of the high-employment, or full-
employment, surplus—that the thing to consider in evaluating the impact of
a budget policy is the surplus or deficit it would yield at high employment,
not the surplus or deficit it actually does yield. A second related but not
identical idea is that in ordinary conditions this full-employment surplus
should be constant so that variations in the impact of the budget are not
themselves an independent source of economic fluctuations. A third idea,
related to the second but not necessarily implied by it, is that in general this
constant surplus should be positive or at least zero—that is, not a deficit. We
shall see the emergence of these ideas and their influence upon policy in
subsequent chapters. Here we are only pointing out the explicit recognition,
in 1939, of the facts that made these ideas significant.

   Three changes in the organization of the government made in 1938 and
1939 pointed in the direction of a continuous responsibility of the government for the maintenance of economic stability, the central role of fiscal
policy in carrying out that responsibility, and the increased reliance upon
professional economists for the development of national economic policies.
Early in 1937 a special committee established to suggest improvements in
the administrative management of the government recommended, among
many other things, that the Bureau of the Budget should be transferred from
the Treasury to the Executive Office of the President, that the size of its staff
should be increased, and that it should be given expanded functions of program development and review. It also recommended that the President
should have up to six administrative assistants to help him in maintaining
contact with the proliferating fields and agencies under his charge. After repeated refusals and delays in Congress, the necessary legislation was passed
in April, 1939. The Budget Bureau was transferred to the Executive Office
in September, 1939, and at the same time three of the six administrative
assistants were named. One of the assistants, with responsibility for economic
affairs, was Lauchlin Currie, who had been at the Federal Reserve with
Eccles.[52] The transfer of the Budget Bureau to the Executive Office, where
it was in direct and constant touch with the President, insured that the fiscal
approach to national economic problems got a great deal of attention. It
gave the President a source of financial advice that did not share the Treasury's preoccupation with debt management and international economic
relations—both concerns which predispose one to a conservative view of
financial problems. While the initial statement of the bureau's function in
the White House did not refer to the use of fiscal policy for economic ex-

pansion and stabilization, one of the early steps in the staff expansion of the bureau was the establishment of a group to deal with this question.

The appointment of a professional economist, and particularly of Lauchlin Currie, as administrative assistant to the President, was also an event of significance as a precedent for things to come. The public thought of Roosevelt as always having many intellectuals and Brain Trusters around him, and tended to identify all of them as "economists." In fact, of those close to Roosevelt, only one, Tugwell, was an economist, and he was quite outside of the main stream of economists' thinking. Currie was a professional economist and in touch with the leading currents of economic thought of the time. Moreover his main competence and interest was in overall financial policy—originally monetary policy but increasingly fiscal policy. That the President should see many economic problems for the first time through the eyes of Lauchlin Currie increased the likelihood that weight would be given to the use of the budget as the lever with which to manage the economy.

However, Currie's role in domestic financial affairs was actually quite limited. "I quickly found that the President did not feel any pressing need for an economic assistant and the job would be what I could make of it on my own initiative." Roosevelt used to pass Currie's memoranda on to Morgenthau, which annoyed Currie. An accommodation was reached under which Currie would work with the Treasury on Treasury matters but would not make suggestions on them directly to the President. Currie also felt that Budget Director Smith was cutting him off rather completely from Budget Bureau matters. Soon Currie found himself largely involved in international questions, especially the problem of China, which reflected the President's own preoccupation. However, occasional memoranda from Currie to FDR on economic problems, particularly relating to the postwar economy, continued FDR's education.[53] Moreover the position of a professional economist in the White House, which would blossom later into the Council of Economic Advisers, had been established.

In November, 1938, the President established a temporary Monetary and Fiscal Advisory Board with the Secretary of the Treasury as chairman and the chairman of the Federal Reserve, the director of the Budget Bureau, and the chairman of the Advisory Committee of the National Resources Committee as members. He told his press conference: "The duties of this board will consist of canvassing, systematically, the broader problems of fiscal and monetary policies in relation to national production and the national income. In other words, they will study the whole range of a great many problems that relate to fiscal and monetary policies in respect to sound and orderly recovery, and conditions essential to avoiding the peaks and valleys of booms and de-pressions."[54]

The President said when he set it up that the public should not expect to hear much from this board, and not much was heard from it. The board considered and approved the 1939 Spending-Lending Bill, and Eccles testi-fied for the bill as a member of the board, rather than as chairman of the Federal Reserve. The board was later swallowed up in the machinery for the management of the war.

These moves are significant as precursors of the economy policy-making machinery that would be established after the war—the Council of Economic Advisers in the Executive Office and the various "troikas" and "quadriads" fashioned out of the chairman of the Council, the Secretary of the Treasury, the director of the Budget Bureau, and the chairman of the Federal Reserve. They are even more significant as an indicator of the elevation of fiscal policy to the top rank of economic strategy. Fiscal management was no longer a temporary device to hold the fort until some grand reform of the system could be accomplished which would solve fundamentally the basic problems that financial "gimmicks" could only palliate. Fiscal policy was now estab-lished as *the* solution in Washington thinking.

7

The Fiscal Revolution and the
Keynesian Revolution to 1940

W<small>E</small> have told the story of the fiscal revolution up to this point with only passing reference to the man who is most commonly thought of as the author of that revolution or to the book which is usually considered its blue print. The man, of course, is John Maynard Keynes, and the book is his *General Theory of Employment, Interest and Money*, published in 1936. It is not only economists who regard Keynes as the central figure of the fiscal revolution. In January, 1966, when *Time* magazine wrote a long story celebrating "the new economics," which is mainly the new fiscal policy, it decorated the issue with a cover portrait of J. M. Keynes. For thirty years modern economic policy has been identified by its friends and enemies as Keynesian.

Keynes was a great and important man. But it is possible to describe the evolution of fiscal policy in America up to 1940 without reference to him. And yet, by the outbreak of the war a large part of the fiscal revolution had already occurred. It was accepted policy that we would run deficits in depressions, that we would not raise taxes in depressions in an attempt to balance the budget, and that in severe depressions we would raise expenditures, at least for relief and probably for recovery. We no longer believed that depressions were necessarily short and self-terminating, and we did not think that depression deficits, even if fairly large and prolonged, would lead to national bankruptcy. Keynes helped this policy and these attitudes to emerge, as we shall see, but he was not indispensable for their emergence.

The fiscal revolution was not over at the beginning of the war, and neither was Keynes' influence on it, although most of his writing on the subject had been done by 1940. His ideas had not yet been fully digested. In

1935 he had written to George Bernard Shaw that, "I believe myself to be writing a book on economic theory which will largely revolutionize—not, I suppose, at once but in the course of the next ten years—the way the world thinks about economic problems."[1] The ten years were not up until the war was over. Of course the prophecy was not literally fulfilled. "The world" before Keynes did not think about economic problems in the "classical" manner against which Keynes was revolting and after him did not think in "Keynesian" terms. Both the old ideas and the new were too sophisticated for "the world." But it was true that the people whose ideas mattered came to think in the Keynesian way, largely by 1945 and even more thereafter.

Certainly it is not possible to tell the story of the fiscal revolution efficiently after about 1940 without stopping to absorb some of the Keynesian way of thought. So much of the important discussion of fiscal policy was carried out in Keynesian terms and concepts that it would be extremely wasteful to try to translate it all into some other language rather than learning his. Morever the language he devised is an effective language for talking about fiscal policy. Which does not mean that everyone who talks "Keynesian" language is a Keynesian in outlook or policy, any more than that everyone who talks Russian is a Communist.

Keynes' contribution was more than a language for thinking and talking about fiscal policy. It was also a set of ideas to believe and policies to follow. These ideas and policy prescriptions were to be important in the years after 1940. However they never received as complete acceptance, even among economists, as the manner of thinking that he introduced. The evolution of fiscal policy, even in the period of his influence, is not a straight-line movement towards more and more acceptance of Keynesian ideas. What happened is better described as a convergence between the ideas of "Keynesian" economists on the one hand, and national fiscal policy on the other hand, in which both sides moved. Policy developed in the direction of economists' thinking, but the thinking of economists also came a long way from the first American understanding of Keynesianism. Many of the ideas which seemed most distinctly Keynesian in 1938 and 1939 have been abandoned, and many of the ideas which Keynes seemed most intent on expelling from the body of economics have returned. The Keynesianism to which policy approached is not the Keynesianism of 1936 and even less the position of his American disciples of 1937–40. So we have had not only a Keynesian revolution, but also a revolution within Keynesianism. This second revolution was as necessary as the first to the accomplishment of the fiscal revolution. Some domestication of Keynes—some adaptation to traditional values as well as greater recognition of the facts of the economic and political system—was necessary before Keynesianism could become national policy. Certainly this was true in the United States.

In addition to a language for thinking about fiscal policy and a set of ideas to think, Keynes contributed to the development of fiscal policy in America a corps of devoted followers to carry the word. As Joseph Schumpeter, a leading historian of economic thought, observed, more than any other group of economists except the Physiocrats of the 18th century and the Marxists, the Keynesians constituted a "school."[2] They had a sacred text, with its authorized interpreters, and they believed that they had the key to understanding and solving the economic problems of the time. This school was an independent force in the history of fiscal policy, in addition to the spread of Keynesian ideas themselves. That is, their influence was not just the result and reflection of the ideas they carried but derived to an important degree from their vigor, self-confidence, and cohesion. Moreover their existence and qualities were not a mere reflection of Keynesian ideas but were equally due to Keynes' personality and style and to the historical situation in which they found themselves.

Keynesian language, Keynesian ideas, and Keynesians will be integral parts of the story to be told in the following chapters about developments during and since World War II. In this chapter we consider the two decades from 1920 to 1940. These were years in which Keynes was exceedingly active and prolific. They were also years in which American fiscal policy changed radically. But the relation between Keynes and this change of policy is at most uncertain and probably marginal.

KEYNES BEFORE KEYNES

Keynes burst into the consciousness of intellectuals and politicians around the world with the publication of *The Economic Consequences of the Peace* in December, 1919. He had been the representative of the British Treasury at the Versailles Peace Conference, and while serving in this capacity came to the conclusion that the economic terms being imposed upon Germany were not only a violation of the armistice agreement but also unworkable, and that they would lead inevitably to economic breakdown in Europe and political crisis. Despairing of his ability to effect any substantial improvement while working within the delegation, he resigned in June, 1919, and returned to England, where by September he had completed the book that was to make him famous. The work was a sensation, partly because of its sharp attack upon the policies of the "great" leaders of the great powers and perhaps even more because of the candid portraits of these leaders that Keynes presented.[3]

One of the few people at the Versailles conference for whom Keynes had a good word was Herbert Hoover:

> Mr. Hoover was the only man who emerged from the ordeal of Paris with an enhanced reputation. This complex personality with his habitual air of weary Titan (or, as others might put it, of exhausted prize-fighter), his eyes steadily fixed on the true and essential facts of the European situation, imported into the councils of Paris, when he took part in them, precisely that atmosphere of reality, knowledge, magnanimity, and disinterestedness which, if they had been found in other quarters also, would have given us the Good Peace.[4]

Hoover did not return the compliment. Keynes struck him as one of the most conceited men he had ever met.

Keynes' view of the treaty was not, of course, universally accepted, either in 1919 or later. At the time there were many who thought he was not only wrong about what Germany could pay but also dishonorable in using his inside knowledge to attack agreements reached by his own country's delegation, of which he was a member. Much later he was to be critiziced for having participated in building up a sense of guilt about the treatment of Germany which weakened the resolve of the Allied powers when first confronted by Hitler. But certainly his argument was convincing to many at the time and seemed prophetic later.

What is more important for our purposes than the validity of his analysis in 1919 is the fact that the book established him as a person to listen to. He was looked upon as a person who moved in circles of knowledge and influence and who was yet willing to take independent and dissenting positions, who knew exactly what he thought about a wide range of subjects and who could express himself on these subjects with a power and wit that assured him a large audience. He had won a claim upon the attention of thinking and influential people which was to be useful when he later turned to questions of fiscal and monetary policy.

While *The Economic Consequences of the Peace* is an iconoclastic book with respect to the political leaders of the time, it is not in any sense unorthodox economics. Some have found in it a foreshadowing of the later doctrine of secular stagnation.[5] It is true that in 1919, as later, Keynes' writing was tinged with forebodings about the future of capitalist economies. This was, indeed, part of his appeal, especially to intellectuals. He always saw the society run by bankers, businessmen, and politicians to be in great danger, but he also always saw the possibility of saving the society by listening to the intellectuals. However, what is interesting about the pessimism of 1919 is that its basis was so different from that of 1936 and later. In 1919 Keynes foresaw the slowing down of the rate of growth of capitalist economies as resulting from a slowing down of the rate of saving. After 1936 Keynes, and even more his American disciples, foresaw stagnation as coming from an excessive rate of saving. Moreover, the Keynes of 1919 was worried about the consequences of a high rate of population growth; his followers two decades later were worried about the slowing down of population growth which they thought had occurred.[6]

For some time after the publication of *The Economic Consequences of the Peace* Keynes was concerned with journalistic writing on that subject and with the production of a second book, *A Revision of the Treaty*, which appeared in 1922. By that year, however, his attention was increasingly occupied by questions of monetary and fiscal policy for high employment and stability which were thereafter to be his main concern. Within two years, in a number of newspaper and magazine articles and in *A Tract on Monetary Reform* (November, 1923) he had, according to Roy Harrod, his student, friend, and biographer:

> . . . completed the outline of the public policy which has since been specifically associated with his name—credit control to eliminate the credit cycle, State-sponsored capital development and, for a country in Britain's position, some check upon the outward flow of capital. The main framework was there in 1924. If Keynes put forward these proposals before being in a position to give a full theoretical justification of them, that was, no doubt, because he deemed it urgently needful for Britain to act with speed. It must not be inferred that they were thrown out at random.[7]

Britain's needs may explain why "this patriotic English intellectual," as Schumpeter called him, put forward proposals for meeting them. However, this does not explain how Keynes arrived at this particular set of policies, or how he concluded that they could be safely prescribed for Britain before he had a "full theoretical justification" of them. The fact is that the theoretical framework Keynes was later to construct was not necessary to the policies he was recommending, which later came to be known as Keynesian policies. The old theory—the standard Cambridge (England), "classical" economics—was sufficient to support these policies.

Keynes' economic policy views of the 1920's were unorthodox with respect to what was being done, but not with respect to British academic economics of the time. Orthodox British monetary theory, which Keynes lucidly explained but did not revise in *A Tract on Monetary Reform*, held that the money value of output was determined by the quantity of money and by the value, in purchasing power, of the money that individuals and businesses wanted to hold.[8] According to this theory, anything that affected the quantity of money would probably affect prices or output or both, and it was a proper responsibility of the Central Bank and the government to use their influence over the quantity of money to stabilize the price level and indirectly the economy. The recommendations Keynes was making in the 1920's were applications of this general principle.

While basing himself on the conventional academic monetary doctrine of his time, Keynes was most ingenious and original in applying that doctrine to the situation of Britain in the 1920's. In *A Tract on Monetary Reform* Keynes had argued that domestic economic stability depended largely upon stability of the price level[9] and that stability of the price level could be provided by monetary policy if monetary policy were free to devote itself to that end. However, as things stood, monetary policy could not be directed to internal stabilization but had to be devoted to the maintenance or, in the British case, restoration of the gold standard and stable exchange rates. For example, when domestic stabilization might call for monetary expansion, external financial requirements might call for monetary restriction to raise interest rates and keep capital from flowing out of the country. The monetary reform advocated in *A Tract on Monetary Reform* was abandonment of the commitment to the gold standard and stable exchange rates and concentration of monetary policy on the goal of domestic economic stability.

In a section entitled "Stability of Prices versus Stability of Exchange," Keynes said:

> The right choice is not necessarily the same for all countries. It must partly depend on the relative importance of foreign trade in the economic life of the country. Nevertheless, there does seem to be in almost every case a presumption in favor of the stability of prices, if only it can be achieved. Stability of exchanges is in the nature of a convenience which adds to the efficiency and prosperity of those who are engaged in foreign trade. Stability of prices, on the other hand, is profoundly important for the avoidance of the various evils [unemployment and inequities] described in Chapter 1.[10]

During the 1920's Keynes remained faithful to his belief that a country free of foreign economic restraints could maintain internal stability by the use of monetary, or credit, policy. However, Britain at this time, in spite of Keynes' advice, did not choose to abandon its commitment to restore and then maintain the gold standard. The problem with which Keynes was working was how, given this fact, to correct the excessive unemployment in Britain. It was the international considerations that led Keynes to summon fiscal policy to the aid of monetary policy, rather than relying entirely on monetary policy as he apparently still would have done in the absence of the international restraints.[11]

Keynes' first significant writing on fiscal policy came as a sequel to a letter by Lloyd George to the *Nation and Athenaeum* on April 12, 1924 in which Lloyd George suggested a program of public spending during the slump.[12] Lloyd George's suggestion was so cryptic that without the subsequent discussion a reader in the 1960's would be uncertain of what was intended or expected. He said:

> A far-seeing manufacturer utilizes periods of slackness to repair his machinery, to reequip his workshop, and generally to put his factory in order, so that when prosperity comes he will be in as good a position as his keenest competitor to take advantage of the boom. I suggest that the nation ought to follow that wise example, and that this is the time to do so. Let us overhaul our national equipment in all directions—men and material—so as to be ready, when the moment arrives, to meet any rivals on equal or better terms in the markets of the world.[13]

Lloyd George's letter provoked a considerable correspondence in the *Nation and Athenaeum*. Most of it was favorable, but Walter Layton warned that an expansionist fiscal program would retard needed adjustments in wage rates, and R. H. Brand feared that an increase of government expenditures would reduce business confidence. Keynes joined the discussion on May 24, 1924, with a signed article entitled "Does Unemployment Need a Drastic Remedy?"

> No one has a firmer belief than I in the relation between unemployment and monetary policy, and when, two years ago, the figures were nearly double what they are now, this disastrous situation was, I am sure, largely attributable to the slump provoked by a misguided inflation and prolonged by a misguided deflation. But the evil effects of these policies have been working themselves out. Perhaps this cause is not yet eliminated entirely,—but a monetary policy which aimed at reducing the unemployed by more than (say) a further 100,000 would run dangerously near another inflation.
>
> In the light of such reflections, we can indicate the next steps. The Chancellor of the Exchequer should devote his sinking fund and his surplus resources, not to redeeming old debt with the result of driving the national savings to find a foreign outlet, but to replacing unproductive debt by productive debt. The Treasury should not shrink from promoting expenditure up to (say) £100,000,000 a year on the construction of capital work at home, enlisting in various ways the aid of private genius, temperament and skill.

I look, then, for the ultimate cure of unemployment and for the stimulus which shall initiate a cumulative prosperity, to monetary reform—which will remove fear—and to the diversion of the national savings from relatively barren foreign investment into State-encouraged constructive enterprises at home—which will inspire confidence.[14]

The purpose of the government investment, or government-financed investment, was not to increase total investment but to divert some of the national savings from foreign investment to domestic investment. The trouble with foreign investment, from Keynes' standpoint, was that it did not generate as much demand for British production and employment, per million pounds, as did domestic investment. British funds invested abroad would not all be immediately spent on British goods. Foreigners would then hold more British pounds, and this would tend to cause a decline in the exchange value of the pound unless there was a decline in British prices which increased British export earnings. In the long run the British economy would become adjusted to the rate of foreign investment through a decline in the value of the pound or in the British price level. But in the long run, as Keynes had already said, we are all dead. Explaining his aversion to foreign investment in the *Nation and Athenaeum* of June 7, 1924, he recognized that "sooner or later" there would be an adjustment to such investment, but:

> Our economic structure is far from elastic, and much time may elapse and indirect loss result from the strains set up and the breakages incurred. Meanwhile, resources may lie idle and labour be out of employment.[15]

At this time Keynes' interest in public investment as a way of stimulating employment was related to a combination of conditions which, if not peculiarly British, did not seem highly relevant to the United States. One was a tendency for a large part of British savings to be invested abroad. In 1924 Keynes estimated that one-third to one-half of British savings was going abroad.[16] The other was a small gold reserve, so that an outflow of funds was likely to cause either a decline in the exchange value of the currency or pressure on the internal price level.

Keynes relied upon the foreign repercussions of domestic policy for the answer to the two main kinds of criticisms that proposals for government deficit spending encountered in Britain in the 1920's. The first, and politically most important, was the "Treasury view," which Keynes always identified by that name and which he obviously regarded as the mortal error which he was challenged to set right. This was the position that the amount of savings available at any time was given and in use, so that an increase in government borrowing to pay for public works would only displace private investment and would not add to total employment.[17] On the basis of this argument, the Chancellor of the Exchequer, Winston Churchill, said, as quoted by Keynes: "It is the orthodox Treasury dogma, steadfastly held, that whatever might be the political or social advantages, very little additional employment and no permanent additional employment can, in fact, and as a general rule, be created by State borrowing and State expenditure."[18]

Keynes gave his clearest answer to this objection in a series of articles he wrote in support of another Lloyd George proposal for a public works program in 1929. In opposition to the Treasury view that government deficit spending must be at the expense of private investment, Keynes said that there were three resources which would enable new government investment to create a net increase in employment. They were:

> 1. Savings which we are now disbursing to pay the unemployed. [In other words, the public works expenditures would not be a net increase in government expenditure but would in part replace the dole.]
> 2. Savings which now run to waste for lack of credit.
> 3. Reduction in the net amount of foreign lending.[19]

The second of these points was the link with the other, mainly academic, criticism of Keynes' position on public works. Keynes was saying that part of the total national saving was not put to work because the Bank of England was not providing enough credit. This part of saving could be invested in financing expanded public works without draining funds from private investment, if the bank would permit adequate credit expansion. Some critics, accepting this point, then went on to say that if the bank would permit or generate enough credit expansion, an increase in private domestic investment would follow, and the public works program would be unnecessary.

Keynes did not deny that an expansion of bank credit would bring about an increase in private domestic investment, but he did maintain that under the existing circumstances, an expansion of credit would cause an unbearable outflow of funds and of gold.

> The real difficulty hitherto in the way of an easier credit policy by the Bank of England has been the fear that an expansion of credit might lead to a loss of gold which the Bank could not afford.
>
> Now, if the Bank were to try to increase the volume of credit at a time when, on account of the depression of home enterprise, no reliance could be placed on the additional credit being absorbed at home at the existing rate of interest, this might quite well be true. Since market rates of interest would fall, a considerable part of the new credit might find its way to *foreign* borrowers, with the result of a drain of gold out of the Bank. Thus it is not safe for the Bank to expand credit

unless it is certain beforehand that there are *home* borrowers standing ready to absorb it at the existing rates of interest.

This is the reason why the Liberal plan is exactly suited to the fundamentals of the present position. It provides the necessary condition for an expansion of credit to be safe.

It is, of course, essential that the Bank of England should loyally cooperate with the Government's programme of capital development, and do its best to make it a success. For, unfortunately, it would lie within the powers of the Bank, provided it were to pursue a deflationary policy aimed at preventing any expansion of bank-credit, to defeat the best-laid plans and to ensure that the expenditure financed by the Treasury *was* at the expense of other business enterprise.

We conclude, therefore, that, whilst an increased volume of bank-credit is probably a *sine qua non* of increased employment, a programme of home investment which will absorb this increase is a *sine qua non* of the safe expansion of credit.[20]

How exceptional Keynes thought were the circumstances in which fiscal policy would be needed for economic stabilization is shown by his treatment of the subject in his major work *A Treatise on Money*, date September, 1930. This is a two-volume book bringing up to date and synthesizing all of his thought about monetary theory and the practice of monetary policy. His general position is the one we have already seen, that, international complications aside, a satisfactory degree of economic stability could be maintained by the use of monetary and credit policy. He devotes only one of his 771 pages to fiscal policy, and what he has to say about it is precisely what his previous writings have led us to expect. He introduces fiscal policy in the discussion of international complications that may limit the effective use of monetary policy by a single country, and after suggesting international cooperation as the preferred solution for this problem, says:

Finally, there remains in reserve a weapon by which a country can partially rescue itself when its international disequilibrium is involving it in severe unemployment. In such an event open-market operations by the Central Bank intended to bring down the market-rate of interest and stimulate investment may, by misadventure, stimulate foreign lending instead and so provoke an outward flow of gold on a larger scale than it can afford. In such a case it is not sufficient for the Central Authority to stand ready to lend—for the money may flow into the wrong hands; it must also stand ready to borrow. In other words, the Government must itself promote a programme of domestic investment. It may be a choice between employing labour to create capital wealth, which will yield less than the market-rate of interest, or not employing it at all. If this is the position, the national interest, both immediate and prospective, will be promoted by choosing the first alternative. But if foreign borrowers are ready and eager, it will be impossible in a competitive open market to bring the rate down to the level appropriate to domestic investment. Thus the desired result can only be obtained through some method by which, in effect, the Government subsidizes approved types of domestic investment or itself directs domestic schemes of capital development.[21]

Keynes in *A Treatise on Money* did leave the way open for a later move to a somewhat different position. He pointed out that monetary policy to bring about expansion might be difficult, slow to take effect, and require operations on a massive scale "as a result of some previous mistake which has prevented the slumping tendency from being remedied at an earlier stage before so complete a lack of confidence has sapped the spirits and the energies of enterprise."[22] And after expressing his confidence that the slump of 1930, which was going on as he wrote, could be reversed by a cooperative expansive policy of the Bank of England and the Federal Reserve, pursued *a outrance*, he said:

> Not until deliberate and vigorous action has been taken along such lines as these and has failed, need we, in the light of the argument of this Treatise, admit that the Banking System can *not*, on this occasion, control the rate of investment and, therefore, the level of prices.[23]

KEYNES IN AMERICA

Keynes loved to call himself a "Cassandra." For example, in the preface to *Essays in Persuasion*, November 8, 1931, he says: "Here are collected the croakings of twelve years—the croakings of a Cassandra who could never influence the course of events in time." On the main subjects of his writing the course of events had been influenced, but not in time and not, apparently, by him. "Scarcely anyone in England now believes in the Treaty of Versailles or in the pre-war Gold Standard or in the Policy of Deflation. These battles have been won—mainly by the irresistible pressure of events and only secondarily by the slow undermining of old prejudices."[24]

It is tempting to apply to Keynes, since he took on the role of prophet, the old saw about the prophet not being without honor save in his own country. But, in fact, Keynes was honored in his own country, even in the 1920's; he was widely read, he was in great demand as a speaker, he was editor of the leading professional economic journal, chairman of the board of a high-prestige magazine, advisor to the Liberal Party, and member of important government committees. He was honored, but his advice was not taken.[25]

However, our concern here is with the influence of the prophet outside his own country, specifically in the United States. *The Economic Consequences of the Peace* had been a sensation here, as elsewhere, and won him both an assured audience and severe critics. Many wrote him off as pro-German. There was particular resentment over his acid portrait of President Wilson.

Keynes' chief message for the United States during the 1920's was that it should maintain its economic independence—i.e., not become enslaved to the gold standard—and should maintain economic stability internally by use of credit policy. He did not think that the United States really needed to learn this lesson from him. In *A Tract on Monetary Reform* (1923) he said that United States policy was already very much along the lines he was advocating. Also:

> Out of convention and conservatism it [the U.S. Federal Reserve Board] accepts gold. Out of prudence and understanding it buries it. Indeed the theory and investigation of the credit cycle have been taken up so much more enthusiastically and pushed so much further by the economists of the United States than by those of Great Britain, that it would be even more difficult for the Federal Reserve Board than for the Bank of England to ignore such ideas or to avoid being, half-consciously at least, influenced by them.[26]

During the 1920's there was in the United States an active group of supporters of the idea of stabilizing the American economy by monetary policy, which would involve freeing the United States of the restraints imposed by the international gold standard. The leader of this group was Professor Irving Fisher of Yale, one of the world's great economists. Fisher had been crusading for a monetary policy to stabilize the price level and thereby the economy since he published *The Purchasing Power of Money* in 1911.[27] On his initiative a Stable Money League had been established, and the movement had the support of many economists, businessmen, and politicians. At various times in the 1920's and early 1930's, Congressional committees considered legislation which would have directed the Federal Reserve to use its powers to stabilize the domestic price level, although no such legislation was passed.

As we noted earlier, Keynes differed in detail from Fisher's manner of describing the relation between money and the price level.[28] Moreover, he thought that Fisher's policy program was too automatic and mechanical. Yet, both Keynes and Fisher regarded Keynes as a follower and supporter in a movement which Fisher had pioneered.

Probably few Americans were prepared to go as far as Irving Fisher and his Stable Money League in believing that a fairly simple and objective rule of monetary policy could be laid down which would assure stability of the general price-level and attendant benefits. The Federal Reserve rejected the idea of a simple rule.[29] Nevertheless, there was a good deal of confidence in what a wise, discretionary monetary policy could do to moderate severe economic fluctuations.

These American monetary ideas of the 1920's, which Keynes found congenial, were indigenous; at least they were not learned from Keynes. Unfortunately, Keynes for once was too optimistic. The Americans had not learned their monetary lessons nearly as well as he thought, which was to be revealed at great expense in the Depression. Keynes might have obtained a warning about the state of monetary thinking in America if he had paid attention to the editorials about him in the *New York Times*. For example, in August, 1923, the *Times* commented on an article by Keynes recommending that the Bank of England adopt a policy of regulating its credits to stabilize the price level. The *Times* was contemptuous. "The protection of the banking system is the banker's first duty," it said. "The regulation of prices is the work of those interested in prices—that is, the producers and traders."[30] A year later the *Times* wrote an editorial to explain that the failure of the recent reduction of Federal Reserve discount rates to cause an increase of credit and prices showed the error of Mr. Keynes' theories.[31] In January, 1926, the *Times* raked Keynes over the coals for what they regarded as a rude and presumptuous open letter he had written to "The French Minister of Finance, Whoever He May Be." Keynes suggested that the French should inflate further to reduce the burden of their internal debt. But, said the *Times*, "The French perceive that the way to stabilize the franc is not to depreciate it but to strengthen it. They propose to follow the example of Czechoslovakia, Rumania and other European countries which have easily stabilized their currency after first having stabilized their budget."[32] Having located financial wisdom and virtue in Eastern Europe, the *Times* proceeded a few months later to criticize Keynes for persevering in the belief that the return to gold was a bad thing, even after it had been so successfully accomplished by most of the world.[33]

The United States also had its native pre-Keynesian movement for the use of public works to reduce unemployment. We have described in Chapter 2 the work of the President's Conference on Unemployment in 1921 and thereafter, emphasizing the role of public works in economic stabilization. The public works movement in this country did not find its origin or support mainly in the community of academic economics, but the "standard" American economics of the 1920's accepted the idea, without apparently considering it very important or very controversial.[34]

Probably because of the prevailing prosperity, there was not much debate over proposals that public works should be used in the event of unemployment to provide jobs. There was no need to defend or deny an American counterpart of the British Treasury view with which Keynes was so continuously at war. This was the view, it will be recalled, that the nation's savings would always flow into investment, which provided jobs, so that an increase in government expenditure financed by borrowing, which would have to come out of the nation's savings, would necessarily cut down on private investment by an equal amount and cause no net increase of employment. That this view was not prominent in the U.S. Treasury or other American financial circles is not necessarily a sign of greater sophistication as compared with their counterparts in Britain. The common sense of the matter, to which Keynes frequently appealed, is that if the government spends more and hires more people there will be an increase of total spending and total employment. A fairly sophisticated argument is required to deny this proposition. And then it takes a more sophisticated argument still to show the error in the denial.[35]

Even later, in the second half of 1931 and the first half of 1932, when the Hoover administration was struggling to get a tax increase and fend off Congressional spending programs, it did not resort, except incidentally, to any argument as theoretical and general as the British Treasury view. Instead, it based its position on the specific financial conditions it faced, conditions whose relevance Keynes would have recognized. The Hoover administration could not make a case in general and in principle against deficit spending in a depression. They were much in the position of Churchill who said in 1929, "Our own practice does not entitle me to do so," but in the case of Mr. Hoover it was his prior statements even more than his practice that inhibited him.[36]

KEYNES AND THE DEPRESSION COME TO AMERICA

With the Depression beginning in 1929, public works as a cure for unemployment became a hot issue in the United States. We have seen in Chapter 2 the growing demand for a massive public works program, a demand mainly originating from politicians, publishers, and engineers, but having support from economists. The Depression also changed Keynes' mind about fiscal policy generally and about its application to America.

As late as 1930, in *A Treatise on Money*, Keynes was still talking about deficit spending as a recourse to supplement credit policy for countries in the British position, unable to afford the loss of gold that would result from an expansive credit policy alone. But also in 1930 Keynes was giving another reason for deficit spending. This was that the course of a depression itself would so shake business confidence and reduce profit expectations that even a very large reduction of interest rates would not stimulate private investment. In that case:

> Government investment will break the vicious circle. If you can do that for a couple of years, it will have the effect, if my diagnosis is right, of restoring business profits more nearly to normal, and if that can be achieved, then private enterprise will be revived. I believe you have first of all to do something to restore profits and then rely on private enterprise to carry the thing along.[37]

This is an important step in the Keynesian revolution. It is the first intimation that easy credit alone might not be effective even in a country not limited by the fear of gold loss. This step had been foreshadowed in *A Treatise on Money*. However, the *Treatise* suggested that we would know of the presence of the need for deficit spending only after a slump had persisted for some time in the face of vigorous measures of monetary expansion. The severity of the Depression, and the failure of Central Banks to take expansive measures on a scale commensurate with it, apparently convinced Keynes that the time had come.

This new argument applied to the United States as much as to Britain, because the collapse of prices and profits was proceeding more rapidly in the United States and because the financial system there was turning out to be very weak. By 1931 Keynes was giving a good deal of attention to the United States. On April 12, 1931, he made a radio address to the United States over the Columbia Broadcasting System network. He said that the slump might last for five years, and then delivered himself of the following observations, typical of many that alienated businessmen and endeared him to young economists:

> The spokesmen of the business world, although they are not so gay and foolish as they were a year ago, still, it seems to me, are far too optimistic and have no sound basis for their optimistic talk. They predict a business recovery six months hence and a year hence for no better reason, so far as I can discover, than that so many months are surely long enough for something to happen.

According to the *New York Times*, Keynes observed that the science of economics, banking, and finance was in a backward state and declared that those who represented themselves as experts "talk much greater rubbish than an ordinary man can ever be capable of."[38]

At the end of May, 1931, Keynes came to the United States, for the first time since 1917, to lecture at a conference at the University of Chicago on "An Economic Analysis of Unemployment."[39] His talk was largely based on *A Treatise on Money*, emphasizing the need to get interest rates down and to escape the tyranny of gold. In discussions with other economists attending the conference he was inclined to give much less weight than most of them did to increasing public works expenditure as a solution for the American problem, although he did accept that as a part of a useful program. During the discussion he said:

> I think the argument for public works in this country is much weaker than it is in Great Britain. In Great Britain I have for a long time past agitated very strongly for a public works program, and my argument has been that we are such a center of an international system that we cannot operate on the rate of interest, because if we tried to force the rate of interest down, there is too much lending, and we lose our gold. . . .
>
> In this country you haven't a problem of that kind. Here you can function as though you were a closed system, and I think all your argument hitherto has been rather based on the closed system assumption. For such a system I would use as my first method operating on the long term rate of interest. . . .
>
> I think in this country deliberate public works should be regarded much more as a tonic to change of business conditions, but the means of getting back to a state of equilibrium should be concentrated on the rate of interest.[40]

Keynes' view of the limited function of government spending in an American recovery program was reflected in a speech later during this same trip when he said that "there is nothing President Hoover can do that an earthquake could not do better."

Speaking of this period, Seymour Harris has said:

> He [Keynes] preached what has become a commonplace since he wrote: Government should spend more and tax less in depression; and spend less and tax more in boom. These simple truths were discoveries of Keynes's which had to be repeated hundreds of times before they made the required impression.[41]

Professor Jacob Viner, who was at the University of Chicago at the time, comments that:

> This formula may have been a discovery of Keynes, but I used it at least as early as the summer of 1931, and I don't think I derived it from Keynes, with whose journalistic writings I then had little acquaintance. The idea was then a commonplace in my academic surroundings of the time, and I cannot recall that any of my Chicago colleagues would have dissented, or that they needed to learn it from Keynes, or from me.[42]

While Keynes' support of expansive fiscal policy for the United States was neither original nor particularly strong in 1931, his support helped to get such ideas into circulation in an era when economists were less commonly in the public eye than they are today. However, these ideas of fiscal policy could not be put into effect in the United States at the time because of the limitations of the American financial situation—the commitment to gold, the weakness of the banks, and the inability or unwillingness of the Federal Reserve to pursue the kind of monetary expansion which, although he no longer considered it sufficient by itself, Keynes still regarded as a necessary complement to fiscal policy.

That Keynes, even though by now highly critical of American policy, *should* have understood the difficulties it faced in 1931–32 is suggested by language in his pamphlet, *The Means to Prosperity*, published in early 1933. There, after stressing the importance of increasing loan expenditure, he lists several stages in the process of achieving that. The first is to make bank credit cheap and abundant. The second is the relevant one:

> The second stage, therefore, must be reached, at which the long-term rate of interest is low for all reasonably sound borrowers. This requires a combination of maneuvers by the Government and the Central Bank in the shape of open-market operations by the Bank, of well-judged Conversion Schemes by the Treasury, and of a *restoration of financial confidence by a Budget policy approved by public opinion* and in other ways. It is at this stage that a certain dilemma exists; since it may be true, for psychological reasons, that a temporary reduction of loan-expenditure plays a necessary part in effecting the transition to a lower long-term rate of interest. Since, however, the whole object of the policy is to promote loan-expenditure, we must obviously be careful not to continue its temporary curtailment a day longer than we need.[43]

This puts the whole argument in the area of public psychology and confidence, where a President may have as much claim to expertise as an economist—which is probably little enough in either case.

KEYNES AND THE EARLY NEW DEAL

On March 4, 1933, economic policy in the United States was open to change in new directions. It did, in fact, move in several new directions. One of these was the direction in which Keynes was pointing—that is, to the attempt to bring about full employment by government spending. Probably for that reason, "New Deal" and "Keynesian" later became synonymous profanities to some people. Seymour Harris, an admirer of both Keynes and the New Deal, after some effort to describe the connection between them, concludes: "Keynes' theories and programs undoubtedly had a substantial effect, even if it is difficult to trace."[44]

The substantial effect is still difficult to trace, so difficult as to suggest that it may not be there. The New Deal and Keynes were developing along parallel tracks, but no substantial influence from Keynes on the New Deal has been found.

As we have seen, Roosevelt before his inauguration was no spender; indeed, he was scornful of spending as a solution to the unemployment problem. He did place great weight on increasing purchasing power as a way out of the Depression, and his Boston speech on that subject led Keynes to think that Roosevelt was a kindred spirit.[45] But Roosevelt's route to increasing purchasing power was not Keynes', and Keynes was later to criticize the Roosevelt route.

The idea that the New Deal was Keynesian was probably supported in the public mind by the belief that Roosevelt was surrounded by economists, a strange group of whom Keynes was the archetype and presumed leader. In fact, the early Brain Trust did not consist mainly of economists. Of the top three, Moley, Berle, and Tugwell, only the last was an economist. Tugwell favored a spending program, but only as a stopgap measure. His ideas on this subject were derived from John Hobson and Tugwell's colleague at Columbia University, Wesley Mitchell.[46] Basically, Tugwell's interest was in structural reform, not in financial expedients.

The idea of using government expenditure as one means of getting out of the Depression was commonplace in 1933 when the Roosevelt administration adopted it as part of its many-faceted program. Keynes had probably contributed, by his continuous writing and speaking on the subject, to making it commonplace. But at least in America it is impossible to detect, let alone measure, his contribution in the flood of discussion that was going on. Moreover, it is fair to say that in the early days of the New Deal none of the ideas about fiscal policy was distinctively Keynesian. This is natural, because at this time Keynes was still approaching, and had not yet published, the ideas that were later to be identified uniquely with him.

The most articulate, systematic, and thorough-going advocate of compensatory spending in an important position in the Roosevelt administration in the early days was Marriner Eccles. Tugwell later described Eccles as an "unconscious Keynesian." If this means that Eccles, without knowing it, had ideas that Keynes also had at the time, it is correct. But Eccles had not then, in the early 1930's, read anything by Keynes and never in his life read very much by him. Moreover, Eccles was not aware of deriving his views on fiscal policy from anything he ever read or heard.[47]

Keynes may indirectly have had something to do with the fact that Eccles was in Washington at all. Eccles came to the attention of Tugwell and other New Dealers through Stuart Chase, a popular writer on economics, who heard Eccles give a speech in Utah. Chase had been much impressed by Keynes—witness his 1932 book, *A New Deal*, which begins, "John Maynard Keynes tells us" and contains more references to Keynes than to any other person. Tugwell and his associates were delighted to find a *banker* with these views, and decided that he must have a place in Washington.[48]

Professional economists in staff positions in the government may be assumed to have been more familiar with Keynes' views, but there is no evidence that they were either much influenced by Keynes or very influential in fiscal policy.[49] In the view of economists of this time, before 1936, there was no distinctively Keynesian theory or policy to agree or disagree with. Economists thought of Keynes as saying, with minor modifications of language, emphasis, and application to the current situation, what they had always said, and they tended to evaluate him by the standards of the accepted doctrine of the time. The failure of his peers to recognize his *originality* bothered Keynes. This certainly helps to explain the argument and style of the *General Theory*, in which both past theory and Keynes' theory are stated in ways that emphasize—and as he himself conceded, exaggerated—the differences between them.

Before there could be Keynesian influence, Keynesian policy, and a Keynesian school, there had to be a distinctively Keynesian theory. Developing this theory was Keynes' main occupation during the early days of the New Deal. However he did have two direct contacts with American economic policy.

On December 31, 1933, the *New York Times* and a number of other newspapers in the United States carried an open letter from Keynes to President Roosevelt. Keynes distinguished between reform measures and recovery measures and urged high priority for the latter as the urgent need while warning that the reform measures, notably the NRA, impeded recovery by weakening business confidence and absorbing the energies of the administration, and probably in other ways as well. The route to recovery was through expanding loan expenditures, plus, in second place, cheap credit, in particular reduction of long-term interest rates.

The letter is not a good example of either Keynesian journalistic style or Keynesian thinking about fiscal policy at that time. Many basic terms are not defined and key points in the argument are asserted without explanation. There is no hint of the multiplier, no consideration of popular concerns about where the money is coming from, no recognition of the administration's problem of choosing between quick provision of jobs and the long-range value of projects. The letter was badly timed in relation to the government's fiscal process. The President had already initiated a big increase in spending for relief projects, and his budget message was ready for submission to Congress. The tone of the letter could not have endeared him to the President; it sounds like a letter from a school teacher to the very rich father of a very dull pupil.

The President's reaction to the letter is unknown. Senator J. Hamilton Lewis, Democrat from Illinois, defended the President, the Democratic Party, and the United States in a heavily sarcastic Senate speech against the presumption of the English theorist.[50] No other response in word or deed is known.

In June, 1934, Keynes came to the United States again, and this time had an interview with Roosevelt. During this trip Keynes was quoted as saying on several occasions that if federal recovery expenditures, then running around $300 million a month, were raised to $400 million a month, the United States would have a satisfactory recovery. Whether he told this to Roosevelt is not known. It was commonly surmised in the press, for example by Arthur Krock of the *New York Times*, that he had given the President such advice, and further that it had influenced Roosevelt's policy. After his return to England, Keynes wrote a letter to the *London Times* saying that the United States could not have a substantial recovery unless she had a large reduction in long-term interest rates and a high degree of activity in the building industry. This prompted the *Literary Digest* to publish an imaginary interview between Roosevelt and Keynes in which the economist lectured the President on the need to stimulate residential construction, as a result of which Roosevelt adopted the Federal Housing Administration program.[51]

However, later evidence suggests that this contemporary journalistic speculation greatly exaggerated the significance of the interview. Tugwell said:

> Someone remarked after he left that for the first time, after long talks with Keynes, the President knew what he was doing. But I was present at some of these interchanges, and Keynes' attitude was more that of an admiring observer than that of an instructor.[52]

It was also after these interviews that Keynes remarked to Frances Perkins that he had "supposed the President was more literate, economically speaking," and the President told her of Keynes: "He left a whole rigamorole of figures. He must be a mathematician rather than a political economist."[53]

Harrod summarizes the situation thus:

> I have been at special pains to find out whether it is true that the President was profoundly influenced by this interview and guided his policy thereafter to some extent in the light of Keynes' theories. The evidence is conflicting. The preponderating opinion among those in a good position to know is that the influence

of Keynes was not great. There need be no doubt that the President had the highest regard for Keynes; condemned by many economists in his own country, it may have pleased him to recall that this illustrious British economist was in sympathy with some of his economic experiments.[54]

The most compelling evidence, of course, is the failure of the figures of federal spending up to 1938 to reveal any Keynesian influence, and the absence of Keynesian language from Presidential talk about fiscal policy until at least two years after Keynes' visit.[55]

STEPS TOWARD THE KEYNESIAN REVOLUTION

Keynes in 1934 was engaged in a project that was to be more influential than any number of letters to the *New York Times* or interviews with Presidents. This was a severely technical book of theory addressed to his professional colleagues—*The General Theory of Employment, Interest and Money*.[56] This does not mean that it was not also a book of persuasion and propaganda. Keynes was to demonstrate once again that nothing is better persuasion or propaganda than an attractive theory. He also showed the effectiveness of the wholesale approach to changing prevailing modes of thought—that is, the approach of first converting the "intellectuals" who in turn retail the gospel to the public.

It is important in the case of the Keynesian revolution, as it was in the case of the fiscal revolution, to try to get some picture of what the revolution was against. The Keynesian revolution was in the first place a revolution against certain ways of thinking among economists, and only incidentally against the policies of governments. He was going to undermine the intellectual basis first, and expected the policies erected thereon to tumble soon after. Keynes gives his own description of the classical economics against which he is rebelling, and it is one of the prizes of his success that his picture of classical economics has come to be accepted. However, this is like accepting Lenin's account of the character and policy of Kerensky. It needs to be taken with some reserve.

Probably a fair base from which to measure the Keynesian revolution is Keynes' *A Tract on Monetary Reform*. The Keynes of 1936 was in revolt against the Keynes of 1923. The 1923 Keynes regarded himself as solidly in the tradition of his teachers, Professors Marshall and Pigou, whom he was later to take as the symbols of classical economics. Moreover, others then and later accepted it in the same way, and in the early 1930's *A Tract on Monetary Reform* was being taught in economics classes as a good modern continuation of the classical tradition.

The Keynes of 1923 did not believe that in the real world there was any effective natural tendency for the economy to stabilize at a condition of full employment. Whether in a hypothetical world that was insulated against outside disturbances there would be a tendency to reach equilibrium at full employment he did not discuss. We do not live in such a world. In the world we live in there would be fluctuations in the demand for goods which would cause instability of prices and unemployment, unless deliberate policy actions were taken to prevent them. The necessary and generally sufficient actions were monetary. It was within the power of the central bank to control the supply of money, and by doing so to offset the forces tending to cause fluctuations in the demand for goods. What these forces were he did not discuss and presumably did not consider of the first importance, as long as they could be offset by appropriate monetary policy. Neither did he pay much attention to explaining the mechanism by which variations in the supply of money affected money demand, prices and unemployment.

We have already noted two steps on Keynes' road from orthodoxy to revolt. First, in 1924 he began to point out that reliance on monetary policy alone would not be possible for a country in Britain's situation, because sufficiently easy money to achieve prosperity at home would cause an unbearable capital outflow. Therefore it was necessary to supplement monetary policy with direct government investment, or government subsidy to investment. Second, in the early days of the Depression he began to argue that after a certain point in a slump, business confidence would be so shaken that private investment would not respond to easy money. Therefore government spending was necessary to restore prosperity and in the process restore confidence, at which point private enterprise would revive. There was no hint of the possibility that once the particular conditions of the slump had been left behind, private investment might be insufficient, despite an easy-money policy, to support full employment.

Keynes' journalistic writings, little noted by economists at the time, revealed several further steps on the road to the *General Theory*.

In *The Means to Prosperity*, in early 1933, he offered another reason for the possible inadequacy of monetary policy to restore prosperity. After the experience of several years of business decline and losses, lenders would be very cautious, and this would put a floor under interest rates at which businesses could borrow, despite the efforts of the Central Bank to make money easy. Again, this was described only as a depression phenomenon, but the idea of a floor under interest rates was to play a big part in the *General Theory*.

The Means to Prosperity also contained one of Keynes' earliest uses of the multiplier. Keynes always gave credit for this idea to R. F. Kahn, who had published an article on the subject in the *Economic Journal* for June, 1931.[57] However some of Keynes' earlier articles show a fairly complete understanding of the idea. An Australian economist, Giblin, had the idea and used it in calculations in 1928–29. Although Giblin was well-known personally in British economic circles at this period, the relation of his thinking to Keynes and Kahn is not known.[58]

What the multiplier tells us is not simply that an increase of spending, say deficit spending by government, will cause an increase of total spending and total incomes that is some multiple of the initial increase. Others had seen the process by which one expenditure generates additional income for somebody, who in turn spends it and generates income for someone else, and so on. The multiplier theory explains what determines the amount of the multiplication and why, for example, it is not infinite. The size of the multiplier depends upon the size of the "leakages," the part of an addition to income that is not spent for the purchase of domestic output. These leakages would include savings out of additional income, the payment of taxes, and the purchase of imported goods. For example, if these leakages or "non-spendings" amount to one-half of additional income, the multiplier will be two. The first dollar of spending gives rise to a dollar of income, which would cause additional expenditures of fifty cents, which would give rise to another fifty cents of income and another twenty-five cents of expenditure and another twenty-five cents of income and another twelve and a half cents of spending, and so on. Adding up all these successive diminishing expenditures, we get a total approaching two dollars, or twice the initial expenditure. In general, the multiplier will be the reciprocal of the proportion of an addition to income that is not spent. If that proportion is one-third, the multiplier will be three, and if the proportion is nine-tenths, the multiplier will be 1.111, etc.

The multiplier had an important part in Keynes' developing unorthodox system for several reasons. First, it gave Keynes the complete answer to the question raised by his difference with the Treasury view. The question was, "How is a government deficit to be financed without subtracting from the savings that would otherwise go into private investment?" Keynes' answer had been that increased government spending would generate increased income from which there would be increased taxes and increased savings to finance the spending. But how did he know that the increased taxes and savings would be enough? The multiplier theory showed that it would have to be enough, because the rise of the national income would have to be just big enough to finance the expenditure. If the proportion of additional income that was paid in taxes or saved was small, the rise of national income would be large; if the proportion going to savings and taxes was large, the rise of national income would be small. In either case, the rise of the national income would be sufficient to generate enough additional taxes and savings to finance the additional spending.

The multiplier was also a step toward putting money in the background, which was to be one of the prime aspects of the Keynesian revolution. The consequences of an increase in government spending not matched by higher tax rates would depend on the proportion of additional income consumers saved, which was apparently governed by a psychological law, and the proportion they paid in taxes, which was governed by a statutory law (ignoring expenditures abroad which complicate but do not change the argument). The consequences did not depend, as had commonly been believed before, on how the deficit was financed—that is, whether or not financed by the banks with a resulting increase of the money supply. In earlier days Keynes used to say that the loyal cooperation of the central bank was needed to make a policy of deficit spending effective. Now that requirement seems to have dropped out of the picture. The multiplier idea did not prevent money from being put back in the picture. One could still say that the proportion of income saved, and also whether the multiplied effects of an increase in government deficit spending were offset by the multiplied effects of a reduction in private investment, would depend upon something about money. But the multiplier formulation does not encourage this mode of thought, and Keynes' use of the multiplier indicates how far he had travelled in the decade after *A Tract on Monetary Reform*.

Another crucial step on the road to revolution was taken, or at least revealed, in an article Keynes wrote in *The New Republic* of February 20, 1935, entitled "A Self-Adjusting Economic System?" In this article he explained that there have been two schools of thought among economists:

> On the one side were those who believed that the existing economic system is in the long run self-adjusting, though with creaks and groans and jerks, and interrupted by time-lags, outside interferences and mistakes.
>
> Those on the other side of the gulf, however, rejected the idea that the existing economic system is, in any significant sense, self-adjusting.
>
> The gulf between these two schools of thought is deeper, I believe, than most of those on either side of it realize.[59]

Keynes ranged himself with the "heretics" who believed that the system was not self-adjusting even in "the long run." This was to be the main burden of the *General Theory*, the thing that distinguished the Keynes of 1936 from the earlier Keynes and from his economically sophisticated contemporaries of the classical tradition. Earlier economists who believed that the system was in the long run self-adjusting had focussed on two different kinds of necessary adjustment. One was the adjustment of the quantity of money in existence to the quantity the community would want to hold when the national income was at a prosperity or high-employment level. If the existing quantity of money was deficient the system would tend to adjust by a decline of prices, which would increase the real value, or purchasing power, of the quantity of money. However, because of lags and interferences, the adjustment process would be accompanied by a temporary decline of production and employment. People who took this view of the necessary adjustment did not feel that they were required to sit by and wait until the system had adjusted itself. They could, and commonly did, support a policy of expanding the supply of money by government action, rather than putting the economy through the wringer; a program of deficit spending by government might be a necessary part of such a policy.

The other view of the necessary adjustment focussed on structural relations within the economy. The relations between wages and prices, or among wages and prices in different industries, or between consumption and investment were believed to get "out of line" during a boom and had to be brought back into balance during a depression before prosperity could be regained. The depression itself would, in time, bring about the needed adjustments. Moreover, there was little the government could do to assist the adjustment process. In fact, measures of general stimulation, like monetary expansion or deficit spending, would only prolong the depression by delaying needed adjustments.

The second of these viewpoints had always been alien to Keynes' thinking. It was not only that he disbelieved it. It was the kind of error that gave comfort to all the "do-nothing" forces in resisting the expansive measures Keynes proposed. However the first, or monetary, interpretation of the adjustment process was entirely consistent with what Keynes had been saying since 1923. Why he should now consider it so important to deny that the system would in the long run bring itself into monetary adjustment is something of a puzzle. Keynes had said, "In the long run we are all dead." He would not feel deterred from positive corrective action by the thought that in some "long run" of unspecified remoteness the system might come automatically into adjustment. There was nothing in the old theory of frictions, lags, and errors to say that depressions would be short. There was nothing in the new theory of possible underemployment equilibrium even in the long run to say that full employment would not in fact be the usual situation.

No policy conclusions followed from saying that unemployment might be an "equilibrium" situation rather than an incident of a long, drawn-out maladjustment. Still, the distinction was to be one of the key elements of Keynesianism. The assertion that involuntary unemployment could be an equilibrium condition which the economic system did not tend automatically to correct shocked the economics profession and gave notice that something new was being said.

THE LANGUAGE OF THE *General Theory*

As we indicated at the outset, Keynes' *General Theory* in 1936 gave us a new language for talking and thinking about economic problems, a new set of beliefs about those problems, and a new school of economists dedicated to propagating those beliefs and putting into effect their policy implications.

The basic feature of the new language is to look at economic processes in terms of the flow of incomes and expenditures, rather than in terms of relative prices or the stocks of money and other assets. It does not necessarily mean that other aspects of the economy are ignored, but it implies something about what is most important to look at in a complicated system where it is impossible to look at everything at once.

The new language tells us that to consider what determines the total volume of production and employment we should look at what determines total expenditures for goods and services. Output is not produced, and workers are not employed, unless the output is sold, which means unless expenditures are made for purchasing them. A major factor determining the volume of expenditures, although not the only one, is the incomes people earn. The incomes, in turn are determined by the expenditures, since people only earn incomes in producing things that are sold and all the proceeds of sales become income to someone. So we have a circular process in which expenditures determine income and income largely determines expenditures.

The question to be answered is at what level this circular process runs. Income and expenditures could be equal at a high level with full employment, or at a low level with much unemployment. Keynes starts by dividing the expenditures into two categories, consumption expenditures and investment expenditures, and examines what determines the level of each. It is interesting that, although Keynesian economics has been mainly applied as a guide to fiscal policy, the initial formulation did not separate out government expenditures but considered part of them to be investment and part consumption. However, soon after the *General Theory* appeared the three-way division into consumption, investment, and government became common, and we can follow that practice without doing violence to the original idea. So we can proceed by asking what determines the amounts of each of these categories of expenditure.

Government expenditures are presumably determined by government policy and therefore create no problem for the economist. He either takes them as given or, in other contexts, recommends what they should be.

Consumption expenditures are determined largely by consumers' incomes, and will be larger when consumers' incomes are larger. The relevant incomes are incomes after tax, a distinction that Keynes did not make but which must be introduced if we are going to think about fiscal policy. The Keynesian language does not require us to ignore other factors that may influence consumers' expenditures, such as the amount of money they have, the amounts of other assets they own, their expectations about future incomes and prices, and so on. However the Keynesian analysis does put the relation between consumers' expenditures and their incomes in the foreground.

Investment expenditures are determined by the prospective profitability of investment and by the rate of interest, which is the cost of raising money to invest. The prospective profitability of investment, in turn, depends in part on certain technical factors which determine how much real product certain amounts of capital can turn out. It also depends upon prospective markets for the product of the capital, which will affect how much of the product can be sold and at what prices, and upon the prospective costs of labor and materials, which will also influence the future profitability of the investment.

What determines the rate of interest? This is one key to the Keynesian revolution. His book is the *General Theory of Employment, Interest and Money*, and it is the relation between money and interest and between interest and employment that is the novelty. People who hold money, which yields no interest, have the alternative of holding other assets, such as securities. The higher the interest rates are on securities, the less money people will want to hold because the sacrifice of earnings caused by holding money will be larger. But all the money that exists must be held by someone, and interest rates must be high enough so that people do not want to hold more money than there is, and low enough so that they do want to hold all the money there is. If interest rates are so low that people want to hold more money than they have, they will sell securities in an effort to get more money, and this will drive down the prices of securities and raise interest rates until people are satisfied with the amount of money they have. There are other factors that determine how much money people want to hold. For example, people will generally want to hold more money if their incomes and the volume of business to be done rises. However, this does not contradict the proposition that interest rates must be such as to adjust people to holding the amount of money there is. In this case, if incomes rise and people want to hold more money, but the quantity of money does not rise, then interest rates must rise to reconcile people to holding the existing quantity of money at the higher levels of income.

Thus interest rates are determined by the quantity of money there is and by the amount of money people want to hold at different interest rates. The quantity of money that counts is the "real" quantity of money—that is, the purchasing power of the dollars that people have. Two hundred billion dollars of money is of much different significance in satisfying people's desire to hold money if the price index is 100 than if it is 200. If we want to explain real output, not just its money value—and it is real output not its money value that determines employment—we must look at the real value of the quantity of money.

The real value of the quantity of money depends upon the "nominal" amount of money—the number of dollars—and upon prices. The nominal amount is determined by monetary policy. The level of prices depends upon the operation of the economy and presumably rises as the level of economic activity rises toward full employment and declines as activity falls. The relationship, however, is not instantaneous or complete. Prices do not fluctuate between zero and infinity as economic activity fluctuates but vary with some stickiness. However, for example, if economic activity declines and prices fall, the nominal amount of money being assumed constant, the real amount of money rises. With larger real holdings of money, people will want to convert some of them into securities, which will raise prices of securities, reduce interest rates, stimulate investment, and in some degree cushion the decline of incomes.

These are the basic elements in the language Keynes gave us for talking about what determines the level of output and employment. We ask what is the real demand for goods and we answer that by saying:

1. What is policy about government expenditures?

2. What are the factors that determine the relation between consumers' incomes and their expenditures for consumption?

3. What are the factors that determine the prospective profitability of investment?

4. What are the factors that determine the relation between the quantity of money people want to hold and interest rates?

5. What is policy about the nominal quantity of money?

6. What are the factors that determine the relation between prices and the level of economic activity?

This language can be seen continuously at work in current discussions of economic policy. For example, the annual reports of the President's Council of Economic Advisers regularly run in these terms, with some shortcuts.

It should be emphasized that this language does not require us to say any particular thing. For example it does not require us to deny that the system will always come into adjustment at full employment, which is the point Keynes was most anxious to deny. If total expenditures are not initially enough for full employment, we might say, using this language, that unemployment will cause wages and prices to fall until the real quantity of money has risen sufficiently to reduce interest rates to the point at which investment would be sufficient to restore full employment.

The old language for which the Keynesian language is a substitute is the language of the quantity theory of money. In this language, we determine the behavior of the money value of output by the relation between the quantity of money there is and the quantity of money people want to hold. If people want to hold more money than there is they cut back on their purchases of goods, services, and securities, which reduces the money value of output until, as a consequence of lower incomes and higher interest rates, which reduce the amount of money people want to hold, and lower prices, which increase the real value of the money there is, people are reconciled to holding just the amount of money there is. With this language also it is possible to describe a variety of economic phenomena, including unemployment, with or without equilibrium. The relative value of these two languages depends on whether the demand for money is more predictable and stable than the relationships highlighted in the Keynesian language, the relation between consumers' income and their consumption expenditures, the relation between interest rates and investment, and the relation between the quantity of money and interest rates. That is, the relative value of the two languages depends upon certain matters of fact about the economy, just as the relative value of the words "horseless carriage" and "automobile" might depend upon the number of horse-drawn carriages in the country. The matters of fact upon which the usefulness of the two economic languages depends are not easy to determine, and economists are still arguing about them. However, there can be no doubt that the new language swept the economics profession and then the popularizers of economics.

Of course, Keynes was not content to give us a new language with which to say whatever we chose. He had something specific to say with that language.

KEYNESIANISM: LEVEL 1

What Keynes had to say can be taken at three different levels, or degrees of heterodoxy. The first is essentially what he had to say in 1932 and 1933, but said in the new language. The second is the full theory of 1936. The third is the 1936 theory combined with the historical vision of the *General Theory*.

The first level of Keynesianism merely says that there will sometimes be situations in which the system, with its creaks and groans, does not come into adjustment at full employment and temporarily cannot be brought into adjustment by monetary measures alone. Suppose that, starting with full employment, there is a decline in the prospective profitability of investment for whatever reason. Investment will decline, and this will have a multiplied effect on incomes and employment. Probably in the circumstances there will be some decline of wages and prices which, if the nominal money supply is unchanged, will raise the real money supply, causing a decline of interest rates and stimulating investment. However because of the stickiness of wages and prices the rise in the real money supply will be small and the decline of interest rates therefore also small. Even monetary policy to expand the money supply will not be effective in reducing interest rates, because people will expect interest rates to be high again after the slump and will prefer in the meanwhile to hold money rather than buy securities with temporarily low yields. Moreover, in the circumstances the outlook for profitable investment will be uncertain. Therefore it may be impossible for the time being to get interest rates down low enough to stimulate the amount of investment that would restore full employment. In these circumstances government spending and tax cuts to increase consumption spending will be effective in restoring full employment and may be the only way to get there.

KEYNESIANISM: LEVEL 2

However by 1936 Keynes was saying more than this. He was saying that there might be circumstances in which the economy would be permanently unable to regain full employment, barring fortunate or planned intervention from the outside. The fatal flaw was in the interest rate. Aside from all lags and expectations of recovery, it might not be possible to get the interest rate down below some floor. When the interest rate became very low it would not be sufficiently above the zero yield on money to compensate for the greater risk of holding securities as compared with holding money. Even on securities where there is no risk of default, the risk of a decline in the price of securities if interest rates should rise from a very low level is great. For example, a perpetual bond that is worth \$1,000 when interest rates are 2 percent would decline to \$667 if interest rates rose to 3 percent. At this low level of rates, the preference for holding money would become "virtually absolute in the sense that everybody prefers cash to holding a debt which yields so low a rate of interest."[60] On private securities where there is some risk of default, the minimum interest rate would be higher. Therefore, it might not be possible, even in the long run and even while flooding the economy with money, to get interest rates down low enough to evoke a volume of investment consistent with full employment. There would be a permanent need for government deficit spending or for measures to stimulate consumption, such as redistribution of income.

KEYNESIANISM: LEVEL 3

The demonstration—which of course did not go without a challenge in 1936 and later—that a situation was conceivable in which in the long run no amount of monetary expansion could bring about full employment did not necessarily mean that such a situation existed or was at all likely to emerge. That would depend upon what the productivity of capital was, how much investment was needed for full employment, and just where the interest rate floor was. Keynes himself did not think that the floor of the riskless rate of interest had ever been reached. He said: "But whilst this limiting case might become practically important in future, I know of no example of it hitherto. Indeed, owing to the unwillingness of most monetary authorities to deal boldly in debts of long term, there has not been much opportunity for a test."[61] However, his view of history suggested that this situation would inevitably be reached. As incomes grew with the growth of capital and improvement of technology, the amount of saving that would be done at full employment would steadily rise. This would mean that the amount of investment needed to sustain high employment would also steadily rise. But as capital accumulated, relative to the labor force, the profitability of further investment would fall. The rate of interest at which an adequate amount of investment would come forth would therefore decline and eventually fall below the floor of interest rates. The whole tenor of Keynes argument was that this condition would be reached soon. In fact, he ventured the guess that on certain not unlikely assumptions "a properly run community equipped with modern technical resources, of which the population is not increasing rapidly, ought to be able to bring down the marginal efficiency of capital in equilibrium approximately to zero within a single generation."[62] At this point, since interest rates could not fall to zero, full employment could only be maintained by government spending. Secular stagnation would have arrived.

It is frequently said that "We are all Keynesians now." But clearly Keynesianism comes in different degrees. We are probably all—or almost all—Keynesians now in the sense of Level 1 and there are probably few Keynesians now in the sense of Level 3. Whether there are many Keynesians who accept Level 2 is hard to tell, because Level 2 without Level 3 does not lead to any distinguishable policy positions. But within a few years of the publication of the *General Theory* in 1936 there was a widespread conversion of economists to Keynesianism at all three levels. In fact, in America we had Keynesians who were more royalist than the King.

THE KEYNESIAN SCHOOL

Professor Paul Samuelson, one of the leading American expositors of Keynes, describes the reaction of his contemporaries as graduate students of economics in 1936 when they first encountered the *General Theory*. "Bliss was it in that dawn to be alive, but to be young was very heaven!" Samuelson did not immediately share this rapture, which he describes further in reporting his initial abstention: "I must confess that my own first reaction to the *General Theory* was not at all like that of Keats on first looking into Chapman's Homer. No silent watcher, I, upon a peak in Darien."[63] It was not only in the *General Theory* that Keynes could rouse Worsdworthian or Keatsian emotions in the breasts of young economists. Another distinguished economist, Professor Kenneth Boulding, reported the effect upon him of Keynes' earlier work as follows: "I shall never forget the excitement, as an undergraduate, of reading Keynes' *Treatise on Money* in 1931. It is a clumsy, hastily written book and much of its theoretical apparatus has now been discarded. But to its youthful readers it was a peak in Darien, opening up vistas of uncharted seas—"Great [sic] was it in that dawn to be alive, and [sic] to be young was very heaven!"[64]

There is undoubtedly something about being twenty-one which predisposes to this kind of enthusiasm. Samuelson was twenty-one when the *General Theory* came out, Boulding was twenty-one when the *Treatise on Money* was published, and Wordsworth was twenty-one when he went to France and experienced the French Revolution, which later inspired the lines about the bliss of being alive in that dawn. The precocious Keats was twenty when he encountered a mediocre translation of Homer and felt as if he were standing upon a peak in Darien. The young men who encountered the new *General Theory* at that sensitive age rapidly became a school of enthusiasts who identified themselves as Keynesians, distinguished from other economists, and dedicated to propagating and implementing the faith.

Keynes' personality and life qualified him as the charismatic leader of a school. In 1936 he was the beau ideal of the modern economist. He delighted to *épater le bourgeoisie* on every occasion, and yet he was listened to in the City of London and in Wall Street. He attacked the establishment and was the confidant of Prime Ministers and Presidents. He was a university professor who made a fortune, the don who married a ballet dancer. He wrote scholarly treatises and also wrote best sellers. Perhaps above all, he was a safe, respectable radical at a time when it was essential for a young man to be a radical.

But certainly the character of the book, even more than the character of the author and the readers, explains the emergence of a new school. The book declares itself to be revolutionary, in terms which alienated the older generation and for that reason attracted the young. It was not too difficult for the young economist to grasp, especially after it had been explained in a number of brilliant articles by Professors Harrod, Meade, Hicks, and Lange,[65] but not so easy that it would immediately become common property. Most important, however, the *General Theory* filled the need for an intellectually satisfying explanation of the total level of output and employment. Many "causes" for variations or deficiencies in total output and employment were recognized before the *General Theory*. The *General Theory* consolidated all of these causes into the relations among a small number of variables—consumption, investment, income, interest rates, quantity of money, and efficiency of capital. The relations among the variables were described in ways that seemed derivable from, or at least consistent with, the kinds of behavior of individuals that economists commonly assumed and expected. Whether the variables singled out were actually the important ones, and whether the relations among them were actually as described, had not been tested by the time the Keynesian wave swept over the economics profession. But this did not detract from the aesthetic appeal of the economical and elegant theoretical system.

The initial American reviews of Keynes were mostly by the older men —Viner, Knight, Hardy, Hansen—and were mostly cool to the book.[66] The review by Hansen in *The Yale Review* for the summer of 1936 is representative:

> It is reasonably safe to predict that Keynes' new book will, so far as his theoretical apparatus is concerned, fare little better than did the "Treatise." In particular, his theory of interest will certainly be challenged. His theory of equilibrium at less than full employment is not tenable except upon the assumption of an approach

to a rigid economy in which costs are highly inflexible and supplies are mono-polistically controlled, or else one in which there are relatively limited techno-logical innovations. For when these assumptions are withdrawn, a progressive and flexible community is always busily at work raising the marginal productivity of capital and the rate of investment. It may indeed be true that, under conditions of relative stagnation of technical progress, the marginal efficiency of capital may fall below the lowest attainable rate of interest, and so prevent an adequate amount of investment. It remains to be seen whether we have, in fact, reached the state of technological stagnation. There is, at any rate, no inherent imperious law of the economic system that precludes full employment. Institutional arrangements are, however, being built up which make full employment difficult, but this is in line with accepted theory.[67]

The case of Hansen is interesting because within two and half years he had become the leader of American Keynesianism and the teacher and sponsor of many of the young members of the school. In September, 1936, he published in the *Journal of Political Economy* a longer, more technical, but not more enthusiastic review of the *General Theory*. In May, 1937, he reviewed a book by Roy Harrod, *The Trade Cycle*, which relied heavily on the Keynesian analysis, and again showed his lack of sympathy with it. At this time Hansen was a professor at the University of Minnesota. In the fall of 1937 he moved to Harvard; also in the fall of 1937 the 1937–38 recession struck. Intensive discussions were going on at Harvard—and had been before Hansen's arrival—on the meaning of the *General Theory*. Some of the graduate students and young instructors there at the time had the benefit of previous exposure to the ideas at Cambridge, England. This included R. B. Bryce, Walter S. Salant, and Lorie Tarshis. Others, notably Emile Despres and Paul Samuelson, had worked out the Keynesian system from the text, which is not easy because the book is not very systematic. In the process of these discussions, Hansen's acceptance of Keynes grew.

Hansen's analysis of the causes of the 1937 downturn, given at a meeting of the Academy of Political Science in January, 1938, was a halfway mark on his road to Keynesianism. Some of the ideas in it fit well within the analy-sis of the *General Theory*, but others do not. Hansen came all the way in his presidential address to the American Economic Association in December, 1938.[68] There he revealed his own version of the theory of secular stagna-tion. What he had said "remained to be seen" in the summer of 1936 appar-ently had already been seen.

Discussions at Cambridge, Mass. in the winter and spring of 1938 also led to the first manifesto of the young Keynesian school, *An Economic Pro-gram for American Democracy*, published in October, 1938.[69] This was signed by seven economists—Richard V. Gilbert, George H. Hildebrand, Jr., Arthur W. Stuart, Maxine Y. Sweezy, Paul M. Sweezy, Lorie Tarshis, and John D. Wilson—but several others who participated in drafting it did not feel free to sign it because of government connections or for other reasons. The *Economic Program* was Keynesian in analysis, stagnationist in diagnosis, and all-out in prescription, going beyond deficit spending to drastic measures of income redistribution for the purpose of stimulating consumption.[70]

By 1940 Keynes had very largely swept the field of the younger economists, those who were soon to be the "back-room boys" in Washington and who, when they reached the age of forty-five or so, would be ready to come into the front room when John F. Kennedy became President in 1961. By that time, however, the meaning of Keynes had greatly changed, as we shall see.

THE GENERAL THEORY IN WASHINGTON

The big fiscal decision made in Washington between the publication of the *General Theory* and the absorption of the American economy in the war was the decision to embark upon a spending program in the spring of 1938. The assimilation of the *General Theory* into American thinking and the formation of a Keynesian school came too late to be of much influence in that decision. Of course, there was in this period a considerable group of "spenders" in Washington, including Eccles and Currie at the Federal Reserve, Hopkins at WPA, and Wallace, Ezekiel, and Bean at Agriculture. Their ideas were of pre-Keynesian origin and did not respond quickly, if ever, to what was new in the *General Theory*.

Currie was probably the intellectual leader of this group, the one most capable of independent analysis in the field of Keynesian economics. Ezekiel describes him as having come closer than any other American economist to anticipating Keynes. Currie said of himself: "As early as 1930 I began to feel that the self-accelerating deflationary forces were too strong to be checked by easy money and such conventional measures and to suggest, in my classes, that the Government should embark on a large scale public works program and not try to cover the current cost by taxation, i.e. deliberately incur a deficit."[71] At Harvard, where he was then an instructor, this was regarded as heresy by his elders and impeded his promotion, one consequence of which was that in 1934, at the invitation of Viner, he came to Washington where he could be much more influential.

Currie understood that the effect of fiscal policy came from the *net* expenditures, the excess of expenditures over receipts, not just from spending, that the expenditures and receipts were important because of their effects on income flows, and that not all expenditures and receipts were of equal effect upon income flows. On the basis of these ideas, in late 1935 he, with Martin Krost, developed and carried on at the Federal Reserve a monthly calculation of the "Net Income-Producing Expenditures of the Federal Government" which was later to be heavily relied on in explaining the recession of 1937. These were all concepts similar to those of Keynes but antedated the influence of the *General Theory*. The net expenditure series had been inspired by Professor Viner at the Treasury. Currie also had several important non-Keynesian ideas in his system. He believed that a continuing constant excess of expenditures over receipts would cause a continuing rise in the national income, which is quite contrary to Keynesian doctrine.[72] He kept trying to discover whether investment was bigger or smaller than savings, a difference that the Keynesian system does not allow. Also he put much more weight on the possible dangers of price and wage increases in a recovery before full employment was achieved than Keynesians typically did.

Currie's first published reaction to the *General Theory* was clearly negative. In a talk to a symposium of the National Industrial Conference Board on "The Economic Doctrines of John Maynard Keynes," published in January, 1938, he said:

> There is a precision and definiteness to Keynes' analysis that is very attractive to anyone who is struggling to interpret current developments and finds himself floundering amid a large number of variables of unknown quantitative importance. Here, perhaps, at last is the answer to an economist's prayer—the key that will enable him to make accurate interpretations and predictions. Such expectations, I am afraid, are doomed to disappointment. Certain aspects of our big problem are illuminated here and there, but all too often we find that familiar things are being described in unfamiliar language, that concepts cannot be given statistical meaning and that precision and definiteness are being purchased at the expense of reality.[73]

At the time he was writing this, Currie was one of the most active proponents in Washington of what would now undoubtedly be called a Keynesian policy to get out of the Depression.

By end of 1938, however, Currie saw fully the utility of the Keynesian analysis as a way of talking about policies which he had advocated for many years. Summing up his relation to Keynes, Currie said twenty-five years later:

> I would be distressed if I give the impression that I am not appreciative of Keynes' great contribution. I admired him, was unquestionably influenced by his earlier writings, and later counted him as a personal friend. It was rather that

I welcome his support, as I did Hansen's, and the question of priority, or who contributed what, simply did not arise. In a memorandum of March 13, 1940 to the President, I referred to the basic analysis as Keynesian but it is possible I thought this would make it more acceptable.[74]

Another example that could be cited is Beardsley Ruml, whose role in the conversion of Roosevelt to a spending policy has been described in the preceding chapter. Many of Ruml's ideas had already been reflected in the report of the Hutchins Committee in 1934. Neither in 1938 nor later did he consider himself a Keynesian.

All of the people involved in the 1938 decision lived, as Tugwell said of Roosevelt himself, in an atmosphere of which Keynes was a part. But he was not then an important part and the *General Theory* was as yet an insignificant part. We had reached the stage in which we would not only accept a deficit in depression but would deliberately and substantially increase expenditures, and not for some limited effect tied to the specific expenditures but for the purpose of raising the general level of the economy. This stage had been reached without a significant contribution from what is now called Keynesianism.

However, things were moving rapidly in 1938. It was not only in Cambridge, Mass. that the Keynesian revolution was sweeping the field. Clarification of the *General Theory* revealed how well it suited the needs of the New Dealers. For they had to show why, after five years in power, the economy was still depressed and deficit spending was still needed. They had to answer the charge that prosperity had not been regained because the New Deal had frightened off investment. The *General Theory* gave them the answer, which pre-1936 Keynesianism did not. According to this answer, the trouble was not something the New Deal had done but was the fatal flaw in capitalism. That flaw was the inexorable tendency of private investment to fall behind full-employment saving in a technically advanced economy. The only error of the New Deal was its failure to spend enough. The manifesto of the seven Harvard-Tufts economists in October, and Hansen's address in December, 1938, were instrumental in driving these points home in Washington.

Early in 1938 there had been two contending views about strategy for getting out of the Depression—the anti-monopoly view and the spending view. Roosevelt, as we have seen, acted on the spending line. At the same time, he called for a major investigation of the concentration of economic power, which was to set the stage for anti-monopoly policy. The investigation, carried on by the Temporary National Economic Committee, turned out to be as well, one might almost say instead, a showcase for Keynesian economics. In testimony in 1939 Hansen and Currie, by then well converted, were the star witnesses. The main burden of their presentations was that private investment could no longer be relied on to achieve full employment, especially with the probable concentration of incomes in the hands of wealthy individuals and large corporations where a large fraction would be saved. The suggested remedies worked on both sides of the equation—government spending to supplement private investment and income redistribution to reduce the propensity to save.

Also in 1939 the influx of the Keynesian school to Washington positions began to be visible. Probably the leading case was in the Department of Commerce where Harry Hopkins, when he became Secretary, set up a new Division of Industrial Economics and, on the recommendation of Lauchlin Currie, named as its director, Richard V. Gilbert, one of the seven Harvard-Tufts economists. The staff Gilbert engaged were for the most part already committed to Keynes—Walter Salant, Griffith Johnson, Don Humphrey, Roderick Riley, V. L. Bassie, and others. Soon after the Budget Bureau was transferred from the Treasury to the Executive Office of the President, a Fiscal Division was created within it, with Gerhard Colm, a staunch believer in Keynesianism, as one of its two chief economists. In 1940 Hansen himself came to Washington as adviser to the Federal Reserve and to the National Resources Planning Board. And these were only the earliest and best-known of a much larger number. The growing predominance of Keynesians in the government then and later is not entirely due to conscious selection. The need for economists was rising, and a large proportion of all economists, especially of the younger ones who were available to come to Washington, thought in the way taught by the *General Theory*. Once it started, the movement was self-reinforcing. Members of the school tended to know, prefer, and recruit others.

The war deferred the translation into policy of the Keynesian ideas for dealing with the Depression that came to Washington in 1938 and 1940. To some extent these ideas were influential in deciding financial policy during the war. More important for our purposes, the school was to be influential in government thinking during the war about how to manage the post-war economy.

❧ 8 ❧

Lessons of World War II

A<small>MERICAN</small> fiscal policy came out of World War II much different than it went in. In 1939 fiscal policy, and economic policy generally, had been becalmed. After a decade of depression, and despite a rise of 7 million in employment from 1932, there were still about ten million unemployed, a situation generally recognized as intolerable and yet tolerated. There was widespread agreement that, as things stood, private investment would not be sufficiently vigorous to lift the economy to full employment and keep it there. But the country was unable to adopt either of the two remedies that it was offered. It would not commit itself to permanent deficit spending to compensate for the deficiency of private investment, as it was urged to do by the stagnationists. On the other hand it would not take those steps to encourage private investment that were recommended by conservatives. Contracyclical use of the budget to help stabilize the economy was commonly accepted, either as a systematic policy or as behavior that in a pragmatic economic and political sense was inevitable. But as long as the country could not get over the big issue about stagnation and permanent deficits it could not proceed with the development of practical steps to get the maximum benefits of contracyclical policy.

The war changed all of that radically. Full employment became a national goal in a much more imperative and operational sense than it had ever been during the Depression. The debate over secular stagnation was adjourned, and even those who regarded it as the natural state of the American economy agreed that its arrival would be delayed for some years after the war. The opposition to the works of the New Deal became more discriminating, and this in turn permitted those who generally supported the New Deal to accept the possibility that some criticism might be constructive. Once the more acrimonious issues had been laid aside, attention could turn to

169

the less ideological problems of effective stabilization policy, and some possibilities were found which gave promise of reconciling values and points of view that had formerly seemed in conflict.

All of this came about primarily as a result of conditions created coincidentally and accidentally by the war. The war created full employment, deferred the prospect of secular stagnation, provided a respite from the controversies of the New Deal, involved businessmen in the management of government economic policy, and left behind an enormous federal debt, large budgets, and pay-as-you-go taxation. By the end of the war all of the ingredients of the fiscal revolution, insofar as there has been a revolution up to 1968, were present.

Our interest here is not in the financing of the war but in the ideas which the war generated about the conduct of fiscal policy in peacetime. Therefore, the focus of our story shifts from the making of current fiscal policy decisions to the discussion in the government, in professional economic circles, in business organizations, and in the press, of "plans" for the post-war economy.

The Full-Employment Goal

That full employment was the national goal and that we would not be satisfied with a permanent army of unemployed had been said before the war by President Roosevelt and by others. But this was not understood to mean that the administration had to deliver full employment in any particular year, or even produce a program which promised to lead to full employment on any definite schedule, on pain of being thrown out of office. Even the more limited and specific goal of providing work relief for all the able-bodied unemployed was not taken literally but was met very partially and unevenly during the thirties.[1]

In 1943, Paul Samuelson wrote, "in the years prior to 1939 there were noticeable signs of dwindling interest in the problem of unemployment, which took the form of ostrich-like attempts to 'think' away the very fact of unemployment by recourse to bad arithmetic and doubtful statistical techniques. And even among professional economists there was increased emphasis on the recovery of production and income to 1929 levels."[2]

In 1939 there was no strong liberal, labor, or left opposition driving for a more effective solution to the unemployment problem. While the CIO regularly supported enlarged appropriations for relief, it was otherwise mainly occupied with representing the employed—organizing them and getting wage increases—rather than with doing anything about the unemployed. The intellectual left was preoccupied with the international situation, with its own relations to communism and the Communists, and with remote ideas about general reform of the system. There was no spontaneous movement among those persons still suffering from unemployment, and there were no popular leaders—no Huey Longs or Townsends—to compete with Roosevelt for the support of the forgotten man. The President had become not only a symbol of concern for the masses but the exclusive symbol, and what he would not do no one else would propose to do.

Concern with the shape of the postwar world and postwar America began even before the United States entered the war and rose to a high pitch as the war progressed. From the beginning, and without exception, full employment was a central feature of the society that had to be constructed in the U.S. Of course, to swear devotion to full employment as a postwar goal in 1943 was much easier than to espouse full employment as an immediate goal in 1939. The postwar promise would not have to be made good for some years; no immediate action or decision was required as a demonstration of good intent. Yet there can be no doubt that the real determination to have full employment increased enormously during the war. Political leaders, government officials, and all private parties directly concerned with influencing economic policy came to give much higher priority to full employment in their own scale of national objectives for peacetime. They also came to believe that the "people" gave it such high priority that no political party or person could hope to be successful unless identified with the achievement of this goal. No party in office could remain in office without delivering full employment. No group could expect to have its views on any aspect of economic policy taken seriously unless it was thought to be constructive on this subject.

The specification of full employment as a goal is a natural consequence of the mere fact of setting goals at all. If the problem is only what to do next—in the next six or twelve months—it is more practical to take the reduction of unemployment as a goal than the achievement of full employment. But if one starts out to describe on a blank sheet of paper the kind of American economy one wants to see at some date so indefinite that time is not a limiting factor, it is hardly possible to say anything about employment other than that it should be "full," although the precise meaning of that term may be a question.

The great weight assigned to full employment as a postwar goal certainly resulted from the achievement of full employment during the war against the background of ten years of depression. The generation that lived through

1929 to 1945 knew both how valuable full employment was and how grave was the risk of falling far below it. The high level of prosperity achieved during World War I had not made peacetime prosperity a national goal to be achieved when that war would be over, because peacetime prosperity was part of the "normalcy" to which that generation expected to return. Throughout World War II, on the contrary, the public was very pessimistic about the prospect for full employment after the war, as was shown by many polls taken during that period. Fear of what might happen combined with heightened awareness of the benefits of full employment to raise that goal to the top rank of national objectives.

One important lesson of the war was that the benefits of full employment were not confined to those persons who had previously been unemployed. Aside from the direct effects of military service, everyone, or almost everyone, was much better off than he had ever been before. Although current consumption had not increased for many and had decreased for some, incomes after tax were very much higher, even after discount for higher prices, and the prospect of incomes at wartime levels without wartime taxes was dizzying. It was not only incomes that full employment provided; it was also opportunity and mobility and freedom of many kinds. Therefore the idea spread that full employment was the important and essential means to deliver what every group wanted for itself and had been seeking by other more limited means. Full employment became the first plank in programs to assist and adjust agriculture. It became the necessary condition, even before tax reform, for reviving business profits and investment opportunities. It became the way to invigorate competition by creating conditions favorable to starting and building new enterprises. It became the surest route to raising incomes of workers, not only by assuring them employment, but also by stimulating their training and upgrading.

Full employment became the flag around which every one could rally. This permitted the subordination of other more controversial and divisive goals and policies. Finally the distinction between "recovery," in its new guise of "full employment," and "reform" became possible and acceptable. Liberals could insist on full employment without insisting that it be achieved by and with the whole panoply of income equalization, planning, and expansion of government which had characterized the ideology of the New Deal. Conservatives could support a policy for full employment without insisting that it be achieved by and with a reversal of the New Deal. Both could recognize that the preservation of full employment after the war was more important for their objectives than the choice of means to that end, within reasonable limits.

Raising full employment in the scale of common goals did much to elevate fiscal policy as the main instrument for achieving the nation's economic objectives. Fiscal policy promised to be fairly efficient in achieving the full employment goal while being, at least in some variants, neutral with respect to more divisive goals. One could be for active use of fiscal policy to promote high employment without being pro-business or anti-business, or pro-planning or anti-planning. Disputes over these other issues could continue, and did, but no one had to, or could afford to, let his insistence on these other positions stand in the way of supporting a more or less neutral policy for full employment. This characteristic of fiscal policy was shared by monetary policy, but during the war the potentialities of monetary policy were still not highly regarded. When later more weight was to be placed on monetary policy, this only served to enhance the possibility of finding an effective policy for full employment, combining monetary and fiscal instruments, without involving more controversial measures or objectives.

An early example of the acceptance by conservatives of both full employment as the most urgent goal and of fiscal policy as a primary means for achieving it was the establishment of the Committee for Economic Development by a group of leading businessmen in 1942. The committee took as its first objective, specified in its charter, the attainment of high employment. While the charter did not itself prescribe how this was to be done, the committee's research program from the beginning, and the policy statements which began to appear before the end of the war, placed great emphasis on fiscal policy. That this was the original intent is clear from the prominent position in the committee of Beardsley Ruml and Ralph Flanders, both long time supporters of an active fiscal policy.

In December, 1942, *Fortune* magazine, a leading voice of the business community, proposed that the government should commit itself to the maintenance of full employment after the war, to be achieved by government spending if necessary.

Perhaps more significant, and certainly more surprising, was the position taken by the Republican candidate, Thomas Dewey, in the 1944 Presidential election campaign. He said in his speech accepting the nomination:

> It would be a tragedy after this war if Americans returned from our armed forces and failed to find the freedom and opportunity for which they fought. This must be a land where every man and woman has a fair chance to work and get ahead. Never again must free Americans face the specter of long-continued mass unemployment. We Republicans are agreed that full employment shall be a first objective of national policy. And by full employment, I mean a real chance for every man and woman to earn a decent living.[3]

Dewey emphasized the role of government as a "necessary intervenor" to see that workers had jobs, and in his most pointed statement said:

> If at any time there are not sufficient jobs in private employment to go around, then government can and must create additional job opportunities because there must be jobs for all in this country of ours.[4]

The acceptance of full employment as *the* goal and of fiscal policy as *the* means, at least as the last resort, by liberals and inheritors of the New Deal is as significant as their acceptance by conservatives. As we have seen in earlier chapters, the assurance of full employment was only one of many ways in which the earlier New Dealers proposed to reform the old order, and fiscal policy was only one of many ways by which they hoped to accomplish the reform. Their discovery that what they and the country really wanted most of all was full employment achieved in the most direct way was important in releasing policy from the stalemate in which it had been stuck before the war. Of course, by 1940 they had achieved much reform, and had discovered that the country was not prepared for more. But their conversion was also due to the war's demonstration of the many-sided blessings of full employment itself and of the irrelevance, to say the least, of many of their programs for that goal. The new attitude of the liberals is best demonstrated by their proposal of the Full Employment Bill, which will be discussed in the next chapter.

The position of the public at large on this issue seems clear. When asked, in October, 1944, "Do you think the federal government should provide jobs for everyone able and willing to work but who cannot get a job in private employment?" the results were:[5]

It should	68%
It should not	25%
No opinion	7%

How, if at all, this view is to be reconciled with the continued preference for balanced budgets, which apparently went through the war unscathed, is hard to say.

The eminence of the full-employment goal arose out of a particular historical situation and would be affected by subsequent historical developments. The proposal of a Full Employment Act at the end of the war was at attempt to freeze and preserve for the future the firm, high determination which then existed. But that was impossible. History was moving even while the bill was being considered and continued to move after it was passed. Determination alone did not assure the maintenance of any particular degree of fullness of employment. There would be experience with various degrees, and this experience would influence what came to be regarded as possible, likely, reasonably assured, and reasonably satisfactory. The result of this has been both to reduce the goal somewhat, as something less than the maximum conceivable or even attainable was found to be satisfactory, and to reduce the preeminence of the goal, as its achievement came to be regarded as more assured. But even though it was temporary, the intense concentration on the full-employment goal in the latter days of the war left a durable mark in the form of a marriage of fiscal policy and that goal.

THE POSTPONEMENT OF SECULAR STAGNATION

Acceptance of the active use of fiscal policy was made easier by a radical change in the conception of the economic problem which occurred during the war. In 1938 and 1939 it was widely believed that the United States faced for the indefinite future a problem of persistent economic stagnation. This belief was, after all, natural. We had had nine or ten years of stagnation and had not yet emerged from it. True, there had been fluctuations during the decade, but the basic problem was believed to be the low level around which the economy fluctuated rather than the fluctuations themselves.

There were, as we have seen, two common explanations for this persistent stagnation. One was that a number of historic changes, not caused by policy, had occurred in America which depressed the tendency to invest. These changes included the slowing down of the rate of population growth, the closing of the frontier, and the exhaustion of technological opportunities for investing large amounts of capital such as had been provided by the railroads, electric power, and automobiles. The other explanation was that the policies of the New Deal had made unprofitable and excessively risky the "underlying" investment opportunities that did exist.

It was largely on the basis of the first explanation, the secular stagnation thesis, that active use of fiscal policy was being advocated in the days before the war. But there were a great many people who would not accept the fiscal prescription based on this explanation. They did not like the explanation because it denied the possibility of stimulating investment by modifying policies to which they were opposed. They could not accept the view of investment as a passive response to historical factors, which seemed to deny the dynamic role of the businessmen, in which they took pride and which "legitimized" their incomes and position in society. And they could not accept the never-ending growth of the federal debt to which the thesis seemed to point.

As the war progressed, the secular stagnation argument receded into the background. The possibility of, and need for, an active fiscal policy to deal with fluctuations rather than with stagnation came to the fore. This was a position which conservatives could accept, or at least accept more readily.

The fading of secular stagnation as *the* rationale of fiscal policy was partly the result of economic argument. It took a little while after the first promulgation of the stagnation thesis by Alvin Hansen in 1938 before rebuttals from "scientific" sources began to be heard. By 1940 and 1941, however, negative analysis was reaching a flood. It came from Schumpeter, Angell, Hardy, Simons, and many others.[6] The whole thesis was under considerable suspicion by the time George Terborgh dealt it a most damaging blow in his 1945 book, *The Bogey of Economic Maturity*.[7]

This intellectual argument was reinforced by the facts which the war itself created. Even if "secular stagnation" had been an accurate description of our historical legacy as it stood in 1939, the war was itself an historical event of great power which was changing that legacy. The decline in the birth rate was being reversed. The Federal government was making large expenditures for research and development, much of which was expected to have peacetime applications that would call forth private investment. Increased American involvement with the outside world might even take the place, economically, of the vanished frontier on this continent.

All of this was hypothetical, although probably not more so than the original argument for secular stagnation. It might not prevent the arrival of that condition forever or even for a very long time. However, two wartime developments carried more general conviction for a postwar period of moderate but uncertain length. One was the backlog of business and consumers' demand resulting from limited production of plant, equipment, housing, and consumers' durable goods during the war. The other was the enormous accumulation of government securities and bank deposits in private hands that resulted from the big wartime deficits. These two factors combined promised a high postwar demand for goods and services and consequently for labor. The demand might fluctuate, being sometimes excessive and inflationary and at other times deficient, so that there would be need for a policy to moderate fluctuations and prevent them from developing into spirals. But there was no reason to think that a fiscal program to deal with these fluctuations would require persistent deficits. On this minimum position even the stagnationists could agree, with their fingers crossed about how long it would last.

This changed view of the problem, from stagnation to fluctuations, was important in permitting the development of a national consensus on fiscal policy. In fact, the fiscal revolution up to 1968 has not implied acceptance of either the secular stagnation diagnosis or the permanent deficit prescription.

PLANNING A FISCAL POLICY FOR STABILIZATION

Once attention was turned to the problem of moderating fluctuations, a number of questions came to the fore which had only been secondary as long as the issue had seemed to be how to get out of a deep hole or how to deal with secular stagnation. In part these questions became important because offsetting fluctuations requires much more precision in timing and amounts of action that the other problems. During most of the 1930's doing too much had hardly seemed possible to the leading exponents of active policy. Thus, questions of how much to do and of the choice of instruments were not critical. Also, the active entry of conservatives into the development of new fiscal plans—once they gave up ritualistic calls for balanced budgets—introduced a new set of values to be considered. These people, of whom the CED was a leading example, wanted to use fiscal policy to maintain high employment, but they were more concerned about restraining the growth of the budget and about avoiding inflation than the earlier Keynesians had been, although the wartime inflation had by then taught everyone that inflation on a dangerous scale was a real possibility. They probably also had less confidence in the wisdom and judgment of government decisionmakers. And they retained some attachment, perhaps only sentimental, to budget balancing in some form, even if it could not survive in its traditional form. These considerations required more spelling out of just how much of what was to be done by whom than had figured in earlier discussion.

Among the questions which were thus raised were the following:

1. To what extent should the desired variations in the budget be brought about by variations of expenditures and to what extent by variations of tax revenues?

2. How should decisions be made about the time and amount of action —by forecasting and judgment, or by observance of some rule?

3. How close to zero can we hope or try to keep economic fluctuations? Or alternatively, what should be the economic targets at which policy aims?

4. Can any role be retained for the balanced-budget rule?

TAXATION AS A VARIABLE INSTRUMENT

Until the war, fiscal policy to stimulate the economy had always been *spending* policy. President Hoover, as we have seen, had increased expenditures somewhat, and the big demand for a more active policy was a demand for greater spending. Roosevelt substantially stepped up expenditures beginning in 1933, and when he had his own recession to deal with in 1938 he turned to even higher expenditures. Again in 1939 his fiscal proposal for spurring the economy was a proposal for more spending. The one administration-supported tax cut of the Depression had been the temporary reduction of one percentage point in income taxes recommended by Hoover at the end of 1929. Aside from that, the Hoover and Roosevelt regimes not only had not incorporated tax reduction in their recovery policies but had repeatedly and substantially raised taxes.

This governmental emphasis on higher spending rather than lower taxes had ample support in the attitudes of economists during the 1930's. Hundreds of economists had signed petitions in favor of big public works programs during the Hoover administration, but few had opposed the 1932 tax increase and there is no record of recommendations for a tax cut instead. When the intellectual rationale of the New Deal's fiscal policy was being developed, using the Keynesian analysis, the key phrase was deficit *spending*.

There were several reasons for this concentration on spending rather than tax cuts even by those who accepted or welcomed depression deficits. In its early days, Roosevelt's fiscal policy was largely aimed at achieving certain special effects quickly—notably the employment of people on relief. The idea that jobs might be provided for these people as the indirect consequence of general fiscal measures to stimulate the economy—which would include tax cuts—was not at first appealing to Roosevelt, who found it too roundabout a process for his taste. Moreover, even those who relied upon the general process of demand-stimulation by fiscal means, and this probably included Roosevelt in the years after 1937, were skeptical of the effectiveness of tax cuts for that purpose. A federal tax cut was regarded as providing benefits mainly for the rich. With the federal tax system as it existed before the war there was a good deal to this, at least more to it than there has been since, although even then there was a significant burden of excise taxes on average and low incomes. According to the prevailing belief of the time, the rich could not be counted upon to increase their consumption expenditures if their taxes were reduced, but would only save more. At the same time, it was thought that tax reductions would not encourage private investment, which was presumed to be quite rigidly limited by the market for consumers' goods. So, little increase in total spending was foreseen from a cut in taxes. In fact, as we have observed, some kinds of tax increase, such as the imposition of the undistributed profits tax, were expected by their proponents to increase spending.

Other reasons than the presumed ineffectiveness of tax cuts were probably at least as important. Many of the people who were most active in formulating positive fiscal policies in the late 1930's did not want only to increase spending and employment. They wanted a system in which there was full employment plus a high rate of government spending plus a large amount of income redistribution via progressive taxation. They put a high value on the spending not only as a way of providing employment but also as a source of public investment—in resource development and urban improvement, for example. And they wanted redistribution of income after tax, both because they thought it would contribute to economic stability and because they preferred more nearly equal income distribution than would result from market forces alone.

The emphasis of economists on increasing government expenditures rather than cutting taxes as a means of achieving high employment was heightened by their preoccupation with the problem of secular stagnation. Hansen, for example, did consider the possible role of variations of tax rates as a stabilizing measure, but did not regard that kind of policy as relevant for the problem that really concerned him, which was secular stagnation. If the problem of demand deficiency was going to go on forever, one could not visualize cutting taxes forever but could visualize increasing government expenditures forever.[8]

Of course there were people who did not share this preference for large government expenditures and income-redistributing taxation. They might have been expected to make the case for tax reduction as the route to recovery and full employment. To some extent they did. We have already referred to the persistent opposition of the business community to the imposition of certain taxes during the Roosevelt era and in favor of the reduction of others, including the elimination of the undistributed profits tax. This position was commonly supported by the argument that high taxes of certain kinds, specifically taxes on the profits of enterprise, interfered with recovery. But this view of tax policy as a recovery instrument was not the counterpart of the deficit spending programs of the period. In the first place it did not contemplate the creation of deficits. Proponents of tax reduction for recovery were by and large also proponents of balanced budgets, usually with the idea that lower taxes would be accompanied by lower expenditures, but sometimes with the further notion that reduction of particular crucial taxes would increase total revenues as a consequence of its effect in raising the national income. In the second place the conservative advocates of tax reduction during the thirties were not thinking of a continuous flexible program of tax rate adjustment to fluctuating economic conditions.

Thus, proposals for tax reduction during this period did not ordinarily fit within the pattern of a modern program for positive fiscal policy. They did not call for making decisions about tax rates in order to achieve a relation between total revenues and expenditures, whether deficit or surplus, that was appropriate to the varying conditions of the economy. However, it would be a mistake to think that because the tax-reduction proposals of the 1930's did not rely upon modern, Keynesian reasoning they were therefore radically different from the tax-reduction proposals made and adopted in the 1960's.

The big change between the 1930's and the 1960's is not the support of businessmen and conservatives for tax reduction, even in the presence of deficits, but the inclusion of tax variation as an equal, or even senior, partner with expenditure variation in the thinking of advocates of modern, positive fiscal policy. Some early glimpses of this we have already noted. There is Viner in 1931 saying that appropriate policy in a depression is to spend much and tax little. There is Keynes in 1933 nodding to tax reduction but passing on to talk of higher expenditures. There is the Hutchins Committee of 1934, with B. Ruml as a member, suggesting that the effectiveness of the administration's fiscal policy was limited by its exclusive concentration on expenditure increase to the neglect of tax reduction. Again there is Ruml in late 1937 with his lost suggestion of tax forgiveness as a way to halt the recession. But still, there was very little of this before the war.

The mere spelling out of the logic of deficit spending was bound to reveal that it was the deficit, not the spending, that did the trick, and therefore to suggest that the trick could be done by lower taxes as well as by higher spending. This became clear to the *New York Times* in reflecting on a statement by Marriner Eccles that the government's net contribution to national income was the excess of its expenditures over its receipts. In an editorial of December 28, 1938, the *Times* pointed out that on this theory we could just as well spend only $4 billion a year and declare a complete tax holiday. "Such a course would at least have the advantage that it would keep expenditures at a manageable level for the day when taxation was once more resumed."[9] But the *Times* was not really recommending such a policy. The *Times* of 1938 was still writing as if it regarded the balanced budget as the only reliable standard. The point about the tax holiday was apparently made only with the purpose of ridiculing the idea of deficit spending. During the course of the Temporary National Economic Committee hearings in the spring of 1939 Senator O'Mahoney made a similar observation with a similar intent.

The parallelism between expenditure changes and tax changes as influences upon the economy has been implicit in economists' thinking for years before the war. For example, the Currie-Krost calculation of "the government's net contribution" was a measurement of the excess of certain kinds of expenditures over certain kinds of revenues, and this could be increased by reducing taxes as well as by increasing expenditures. Similarly, in the early Keynesian formulations fiscal policy entered the economic system through the budget deficit, which obviously depended on taxes as well as on expenditures. Still, until the war, spending rather than taxing was the active element in fiscal policy. The theory became clearer on the importance of taxation after it was elaborated to include expenditures and taxes separately rather than only the difference between them.

Treating expenditures and taxation separately also led to recognition of two other points. On the most common assumptions a reduction of taxes would have less expansive effect than an equal increase of government expenditures for the purchase of goods and services. This was because taxpayers would increase their expenditure by only part of their tax reduction, saving the remainder. As a corollary to this, an equal increase of expenditures and revenues would be expansive, because the expansive effect of the increase in expenditures would be greater than the contractive effect of the equal tax increase.[10]

By the end of the war economists had become familiar with the idea that there were three routes to full employment: increased expenditures, reduced taxes, or increased expenditures matched with increased taxes, which was the balanced budget route.[11] The size of the deficit required to achieve any specified level of employment and economic activity would be smaller —or the size of the surplus larger—the higher the level of government expenditures was. Thus, if the problem was to stimulate the economy, that could be done without a deficit if expenditures and taxes were both high enough. This proposition was subject to numerous qualifications. Moreover, the prescription had no great appeal as policy, because the people who might have been assumed to be most interested in keeping the deficit down were also most interested in keeping taxes and expenditures down. However, analysis of the three routes was an exercise in which economists further developed their sophistication in thinking about fiscal policy.

The chief policy implication of the progress of fiscal theory during the war years was to focus economists' attention more on taxation as a variable instrument of stabilization policy. Probably the clearest and most influential exposition of this point was Professor Abba Lerner's theory of "functional finance," published in 1943, with its insistence that the function of taxation was to restrain private expenditures, and that taxes should therefore never be higher than was necessary to hold total spending to a non-inflationary rate.[12]

Aside from the advances in theory, several wartime developments did much to speed acceptance, not only by economists, of the role of revenue decisions in fiscal policy to avoid both inflation and deflation:

1. Wartime fiscal policy was almost entirely tax policy. In the early days

of the war there were demands in Congress and elsewhere for reduction of non-war spending to offset the inflationary effects of the defense program. The administration was at pains to show how much it was doing in this direction. But it soon became apparent that restraint of non-war government expenditure could only be a drop in the bucket compared to the growth of war expenditure. Even if the total non-defense expenditures, which amounted to less than $8 billion in 1939, had been eliminated, that would not have been much of an offset to the $86 billion increase in defense and war expenditure between 1939 and 1944. If we were going to have any significant effect in damping the war inflation through fiscal policy it would have to be through taxation. Economists in the government became used to the idea of trying to calculate the amount of taxes needed to eliminate inflationary pressure or reduce it to manageable proportions. The country as a whole had a significant education in the proposition that taxes were imposed, not for "revenue only," in a favorite conservative phrase, and not primarily to lop off distasteful peaks of personal income or corporate power, as some liberals had seemed to think, but to hold private incomes after tax to levels that were consistent with the stabilization of the economy. This observation had a considerable influence on ideas of how the economy might operate or be managed after the war.

2. By the time the United States became heavily involved in the war it became clear that the normal postwar federal budget, excluding expenditures that might be deliberately made for relief and recovery in a depression, would be much higher than ever before, even in relation to the enlarged national income that might be expected if there was full employment. This was most dramatically true for the immediate transition period that would follow the war while demobilization was taking place. But even for a longer period there would be high expenditures for the military establishment, for veterans, for interest, and possibly for assistance to foreign countries. This meant that the possibility of creating a deficit, if one should be necessary, by holding tax rates down and without embarking on extraordinary expenditures would be very great.[13]

3. Along with the prospect of a much higher normal level of federal expenditures and revenues after the war came the prospect of a change in federal tax structure which would make it more useful as an instrument for economic stabilization. The needed revenues could not be raised, as before the war, by reliance upon high rates of income taxes on profits and large incomes plus excises on alcoholic beverages, tobacco, and a few other items. Income tax would have to be continued on the middle incomes, although not at the high rates imposed during the war. With a large amount of income tax revenue being collected from the middle income groups there seemed

to be a reliable means of raising consumption, either temporarily or permanently, by reducing the rates of income tax either temporarily or permanently.

4. The usability of the revenue side of the budget for economic stabilization was further increased by a wartime change in the system of tax collection. In 1942 the United States adopted a system of current payment of federal income tax. A large part of the tax due on earned income would be currently withheld from pay checks. Amother large part would be paid in quarterly installments in the year in which the income was earned. Whereas formerly the tax due on the income of one year would not be paid until the following year, now most of the tax would be paid in the year in which it was earned and much of it in the very week in which it was earned. This made it possible, by a decision to change tax rates, to affect the income that individuals had left in their hands after tax very promptly, and created the opportunity for flexible adjustment of after-tax incomes to meet changing economic conditions.

5. The shift from the secular stagnation problem to the problem of fluctuations in thinking about fiscal policy directed attention to the search for measures that could be flexibly applied in either an anti-deflationary direction or an anti-inflationary direction. When this consideration became important, certain technical advantages of operating on the revenue side of the budget came to the fore. Experience during the 1930's had not been encouraging about the possibility of increasing expenditures quickly without great waste. On the tax side, if the Congress was willing, billions of dollars of after-tax income could be put into people's pockets at the stroke of a pen and there was then no reason to think that people would be slow in spending the money. Further, if a spending program meant a public works constructtion program, as it did in most formulations, the construction industry might prove too narrow a base upon which to raise the necessary expenditures. In the event of a serious depression, the amount of public-works spending required to sustain or restore the economy might be so large as to inflate construction costs and discourage private investment. There was some evidence that this had happened during the Depression. A tax reduction on a large scale would have much more widely distributed impacts and would be less likely to cause price increases. This defect of a spending program would not be significant if the need for supporting the economy was chronic, because in that case the construction industry could be built up to the necessary size. But if the problem were one of serious *instability*, the attempt to achieve stability by spending on public works might involve major destabilization of the construction industry.

These wartime developments all emphasized the possibility of using revenue variation as a major instrument of active fiscal policy, and perhaps the superiority of the revenue side over the expenditure side on technical grounds. But for many of the leading advocates of active fiscal policy, revenue variation remained a barely recognized stepsister of spending. Alvin Hansen is a leading example of those who recognized the possibility in principle of operating on the revenue side of the budget, but whose practical interest was all in raising federal expenditures. Thus, in a talk to a conference of the American Federation of Labor on postwar economic problems, in 1944, Hansen said:

> Consequently, if we are really going to tackle this problem of maintaining employment we must create a balance wheel which can offset the fluctuations in private capital outlays. That balance wheel, and in my judgment there is only one balance wheel that can act as an offset, is a compensatory fiscal program. By this I mean on the one side a flexible public investment budget that can be stepped up and increased to offset the decline in private capital outlays when it occurs. I also mean a flexible tax structure, because I believe we have reached a point where we can use a flexible tax structure which can also operate flexibly as a stabilizing tax device. I am not going to talk about the tax structure as a compensatory fiscal policy today because it would get us too far afield and I shall stick to the area that is a little simpler and easier to discuss, namely, the public investment compensatory program.[14]

He then proceeded to elaborate the need for a long-range development program of government investment.

However, a number of people concerned with postwar fiscal policy began to put tax policy rather than expenditure policy in the center of the picture. The most prolific and influential of these was Beardsley Ruml. In a nationwide radio broadcast in 1943 he briefly outlined a position that he was to reiterate many times in many different ways during the war:

> Our first goal is to get as much production and create as many jobs as we can. The best way we know of doing this is to keep private business as active as possible. Government policies should foster and encourage this at all times. But whenever private activity slackens, because of the business outlook, the policies of government should replace the purchasing power which has declined because of the falling off of private business. Thus government supports private activity and compensates for any falling below the high employment and production that we want. For this reason, such a policy is sometimes referred to as a "compensatory" fiscal policy.
>
> Assuming, then, the general desirability of government to take up the slack in private employment whenever it occurs, it is worth while to point out certain things about this "compensatory" system that are often misunderstood.

In the first place, such a policy does not mean that we will always need to have a deficit in the national budget and operate in the red all the time. In times of high production and high employment we will be able to balance the budget without difficulty. In boom times we will not only be able to balance our budget, but we will want to start paying off our national debt in substantial amounts. We will want to do this in order to provide a brake on a business system that might be entering a false and dangerous boom.

Such a policy does not mean spending for its own sake. At no time would there be any need for wasteful expenditure. When government lends or spends, it should put its money into projects that are really necessary, efficient, and productive.

I repeat that the disbursements of government are not the only way of supporting high production and high employment. Indeed they may not be the best way. Our tax policy will have a great effect on these matters. If we want to keep employment at high levels, one way to do it is to give the average man greater purchasing power by reducing taxes. Why not leave at home, for the individual to spend, the income that otherwise might have to be pumped out again in order to maintain high employment? Such reduction of taxes should be made where it will do the most good in creating demand and in encouraging private enterprise. And note particularly that under this "compensatory" policy we don't have to wait until our national budget is balanced before we start reducing taxes.

I would like to set forth one basic principle that I think should govern our tax policy in the postwar years to come.

We should set our tax rates at a figure that will enable us to balance our national budget when we have a satisfactory high level of employment and production. If we have plenty of jobs and if we are turning out lots of goods and services and our national income is high, we can handle the budget on tax rates substantially lower than they are today. We should set our goals for high production. The war, very dramatically, has shown us what we can achieve if we want to strongly enough. When our national business activity goes above these adequate levels then the same tax rates would bring us enough revenue so that we can start reducing our national debt. If activity falls below these levels we can prudently leave the tax rates where they are. Doing so will reduce the tax payments from individuals and will stimulate business activity. The idea is on the one hand to use a reduction of the national debt to check an excessive business boom and on the other hand to use government fiscal and tax policy when private business activity falls off to expand and increase activity—and thereby provide the jobs we want.[15]

Most of these ideas were repeated and elaborated in a pamphlet, which Ruml wrote with H. Christian Sonne for the National Planning Association in 1944 and which received the "general endorsement" of the Business Committee of that organization.[16] The basic Ruml position was also incorporated in the 1944 statement on taxes by CED's Research Committee, of which he was a member, in two terse sentences:

> Accordingly, the Committee deems it wise that the tax structure and the budget should be so drawn as to make possible substantial reduction of the federal debt at a high level of employment. As much debt should then be retired as is consistent with maintaining high levels of employment and production.[17]

Ruml was the main bridge between the thinking of economists on fiscal policy and the thinking of businessmen. He served this function, not by "selling" the policy views of contemporary economists to the business community, but by combining what was essential and valid in the analysis of economists as he saw it with the values of businessmen to produce a new synthesis. The general system he developed was basic not only to the postwar thinking of businessmen but also to the postwar national consensus on fiscal policy.

We shall encounter many other ingredients of the Ruml program as the story proceeds. The point here being emphasized is the weight he gave to the proper adaptation of tax rates to the level of expenditures as the main element of fiscal policy for high employment. He did not deny some role to the expenditure decisions, but with respect to the maintenance of high employment and stability that role was to be limited.

This preference for reliance upon the revenue side of the budget can be found also in the writings of a number of economists during this period. Many of these people were associated with the University of Chicago, including A. G. Hart, Lloyd Mints, Theodore O. Yntema, and Henry Simons.[18] Yntema was the research director of the Committee for Economic Development from 1942 to 1948, and during parts of this period Hart was on the committee's research staff and Simons was a consultant while Ruml was an active member of the CED's Research Committee. There was a close interaction between the Chicago economists, the CED, and Ruml in his numerous capacities.[19]

This is not to say that by the end of the war national thinking assigned to tax adjustment the major role in fiscal policy which was evident in the 1960's. It was probably still true in 1945 that "compensatory fiscal policy" or fiscal policy for high employment was commonly understood to refer to expenditure policy. Significantly, when a Full Employment Bill was introduced in the Congress in 1945, calling for all-out use of fiscal policy to achieve that objective, its proponents were still relying chiefly, if not exclusively, upon expenditure policy. But by the end of the war the alternative of a tax adjustment policy had been injected into national thinking and would assume increasing importance thereafter.

BUILT-IN FLEXIBILITY

An aspect of budgetary behavior that came to much enlarged prominence during the war was built-in flexibility. As applied to taxation, this meant the tendency for revenues to rise when employment and national income rose and for revenues to decline when employment and national income fell, if the tax rates and exemptions were not changed. This variation of revenues resulted, of course, from variation in the size of the tax base to which the tax rates applied. In the case of the federal government the tax base was largely corporate incomes, individual incomes, and sales of a variety of goods, such as alcoholic beverages and tobacco. All of these, and particularly the taxable incomes, tended to vary directly with economic conditions and even more than in proportion to the national income. Thus, if the national income fell by 10 percent, corporate profits would almost certainly fall by much more than 10 percent and individual incomes above the exemption level would also fall more than 10 percent. (Suppose a family with a $5,000 income tax exemption suffers a decline of its income by ten percent, from $10,000 to $9,000. Then its taxable income declines by 20%, from $5,000 to $4,000.)

This characteristic of the federal revenue system had been well-known for a long time. In 1931 and 1932 the automatic decline of the revenue with a decline in the national income was recognized as the main cause of the federal budget deficit. The tendency of the revenues to fluctuate with business conditions was considered by many a serious defect of the federal tax system to be cured if possible before the next depression. The finger of criticism on the ground of instability of yield was especially pointed at the capital gains tax, since capital gains on the stock market ballooned prodigiously in prosperity and turned to losses in depressions. Later, as we have seen, the relationship between the national income and the federal revenue was relied upon by the Roosevelt administration to bring about that balanced budget in prosperity it so regularly promised.

In the late 1930's a new view of this relation began to emerge. It was not only that variations in the economy had certain effects upon the revenue. The new realization was that these variations of the revenue had certain feedback effects upon the economy that tended to stabilize it. When the economy declined private incomes before tax also declined, and this caused a further decline in private expenditures and a further decline of production and incomes. But if some of the decline in private incomes before taxes was offset by a decline in taxes, private incomes after taxes would not decline so much, private expenditures would as a consequence not decline so much, and the secondary decline in production and incomes would be smaller. If private individuals and businesses cut their expenditures when their income declined, but government did not cut its expenditures when its tax revenue declined, an initial decline of income would have fewer repercussions if some of it was absorbed by a decline of tax revenue than if it all fell upon private after-tax incomes. A similar cushioning process would work in a rising economy. Some part of the additional incomes earned would be absorbed in higher taxes and would not be available for a round of increased expenditures that would cause further economic expansion.

Thus, the built-in flexibility of the revenue system was a built-in stabilizer for the economy. This was pointed out in important articles by Gerhard Colm and Fritz Lehman in 1936 and by R. F. Bretherton in 1937.[20] After Samuelson wrote the following paragraph in 1942 one may assume that the idea of built-in stabilizers was part of the standard equipment of economists:

> While it used to be considered a canon of taxation that a good tax system should produce a steady yield, i.e. the marginal propensity to tax should be almost zero or perhaps even negative, it seems likely that the economist of the future will praise income taxes precisely because they fail to meet this canon, all questions of equity aside. For a high marginal propensity to tax acts as a stabilizer on the system, against both upward and downward movements.[21]

Several developments during the war to which we have already referred increased the strength that the tax system would probably have as a built-in stabilizer after the war. Federal taxes would probably be higher, relative to national income, than they had normally been before the war, a larger proportion of them would be income taxes, and most of the individual income tax would be collected shortly after the taxable income was earned. The variation of tax rates with a variation of the national income of a certain size would be larger and prompter, and presumably therefore more stabilizing.

The built-in stabilizers raised three policy questions:

1. How to keep the stabilizing effect of the automatic variation of revenues from being offset by fiscal actions? The decline in revenues during a recession will serve to moderate the recession if the government does not try to keep its budget in balance by cutting expenditures or raising taxes. In fact, the attempt to bring the budget into balance by raising taxes in 1932 did offset much of the advantage of the automatic decline of revenue up to

that point. By the time of the war there was little chance that the effect of the built-in stabilizers would be offset by raising taxes or cutting expenditures in a depression. This was not necessarily because of any recognition that the deficit resulting from the automatic decline of revenues was beneficial. It was mainly because people likely to be in decision-making positions had learned that however much they might bemoan the deficit in a recession, the steps needed to eliminate it were politically unpopular and economically dangerous as well as unnecessary. The situation might be different in a boom, with which there was no recent experience aside from the quite special conditions of total war. If the boom should generate a budget surplus by inflating tax collections, there might be a strong temptation for the government to cut tax rates and increase expenditures. This could be done without violating the sentiment for a balanced budget, but it would under-cut the anti-inflationary effect of the built-in stabilizers. Recognition of the value of the built-in stabilizers led to the search for some rules or prin-ciples that would prevent their effect from being dissipated by unstabil-izing fiscal actions, and this search had a good deal to do with the shape of postwar fiscal plans.

2. How to strengthen the built-in stabilizing effect of the tax system? The built-in stabilizing effect of the tax system was the result of decisions about the level and structure of taxation made for a variety of reasons not including the desire to have a stabilizing effect. How would these decisions be changed if considerable weight were now given to strengthening the built-in stabilizers? If, with the existing tax system, the variation of revenue would be 20 percent of the variation in the national income, could a change in the tax system raise this figure to 25 percent or 30 percent with a conse-quent gain in economic stability? One way to do this would be to raise all tax rates and thus make total revenue higher relative to the national income. But no one proposed this, at least for the purpose of increasing built-in stability. There were however numerous suggestions for changing the char-acter of the tax system in order to make it more stabilizing. These included heavier reliance on income taxes, prompter payment of tax refunds, prompter payment of corporate profits taxes, and larger allowances for offsetting losses against past profits. While such ideas had a long life in academic discussion, they never had much practical significance. It is doubtful that any tax decision has ever been made, or even seriously considered by the government, for the sake of increasing built-in flexibility. Other considera-tions always seem much more important, especially to the taxpayers.

3. How much reliance to place upon the built-in stabilizers? This was the crucial question that divided schools of fiscal policy. At one extreme was

the view that the government could keep its tax rates and expenditure programs continuously adjusted to the needs of the economy so that the economy
would always be on target, always at full employment without inflation.
In such a world the built-in stabilizers would be of no importance; they would
never come into operation because the built-in stabilizers only work when
the economy fluctuates, and tend to dampen the fluctuations. If fiscal decisions are made with such accuracy that the economy never fluctuates, there
is neither opportunity nor need for the built-in stabilizers to work. Such
accuracy would require either highly accurate forecasts of economic conditions or very rapid and frequent adjustments of fiscal decisions to unforeseen
economic changes. At the other extreme was the view that the government
should set its tax rates relative to its expenditures on the basis of some conventional rule, like balancing the budget at high employment, and keep
them there regardless of economic conditions. In that case, there would be a
tendency for the economy to fluctuate, the built-in stabilizers would come
into play, and they would serve to moderate the fluctuations.

These extreme positions were rarely held. However, they suggest a basic
difference of approach to the problem of fiscal policy which was important
in the war and postwar discussion and which has not yet been resolved in
American policy.

THE MANAGEMENT OF COMPENSATORY POLICY

Discussion of compensatory fiscal policy in the years before the war was
vague about how to know when to do how much of what. The usual
formulation was that when unemployment "threatened" government expenditures should be increased, and when inflation "threatened" expenditures should be decreased. How the government would decide that unemployment did or did not threaten, how much unemployment was a signal
for action, how much to raise expenditures if unemployment did threaten,
what was the likelihood of these decisions being correct, and what was to be
done if the decisions were incorrect—these questions were commonly
ignored.

The first serious attempt to answer such questions came during the war.
There was general agreement, as there had been during World War I, that
taxes should be raised to restrain inflation. However, no one thought that
raising taxes enough to balance the wartime budget was either possible or
necessary. Secretary Morgenthau initially set as his goal raising two-thirds
of the cost of the war by taxation. But even this turned out to be unattainable as well as arbitrary.

There was an obvious need for better methods of determining the amount of taxation required to prevent inflation. Answering this need, or attempting to answer it, was to be the great experience in which economists learned how to give answers to fiscal questions. They entered the war with some general, qualitative notions. They came out with techniques which, however imperfect, were to be their chief reliance for a long time. This hothouse development of quantitative methods was forced by the urgent need for answers. It was greatly assisted by the increase in the number of economists in Washington during the war, by the convergence of many of them on related aspects of the stabilization problem, by the development of national income statistics which had been going on before the war and was accelerated by war planning requirements, and by the unifying framework of thought which the Keynesian theory provided. Most of the work was done in government agencies, notably in the Treasury and in the Office of Price Administration, where most of the group of economists under the direction of Richard V. Gilbert had moved from the Department of Commerce. An important contribution was also made by a team working outside the government, but in close cooperation with government experts, consisting of Carl Shoup, Milton Friedman, and Ruth Mack.

The problem essentially was to determine how much total spending—by government, business, and consumers—was consistent with reasonable price stability, what total spending would be with the existing taxes, and what increase of taxes, if any, would be required to hold total spending down to the desired rate. This problem did not have to be solved in a Keynesian way. Professor James W. Angell, for example, approached the problem on the premise that total spending would be determined by the amount of money in circulation, and that fiscal policy would affect total spending through its effect on money in circulation.[22] However, the standard approach was Keynesian in the sense that it assumed a large part of total private spending, including consumption expenditures, to be determined by income, and the main effect of taxation on spending to come through its effect on income after tax. Keynes himself had demonstrated the method for Great Britain in a pamphlet, "How to Pay for the War."[23]

The technique used was called "gap analysis." It came in a variety of forms and degrees of complexity, but the general idea can be simply illustrated.[24]

Suppose we are in 1942 and the problem is to find out how much tax increase is needed to prevent inflation in 1943. First we estimate what the value of goods and services produced in 1943 would be if there were full employment and prices remained stable at the present level. To estimate that, we look at the current value of output and adjust that for the prospective growth of the labor force, for the expected increase in output per worker, and for the increase in employment that might result from the elimination of excessive unemployment, if we start with any excess. This gives us a figure of, say, $200 billion. From this we conclude that to avoid inflation total expenditures should not exceed $200 billion. We then estimate the expenditures that can be taken as more or less given, and not influenced by the tax decision. This would include federal government expenditures, both war and nonwar, as well as state and local expenditures. In the conditions of the war this would be a large part of the total—say $70 billion. In the conditions of the war, private investment expenditures could also be taken as given in this sense—that is, they would be determined by controls of some kind. Suppose the controls and plans indicated that private investment would be $20 billion. That would leave $110 billion for private consumption. The tax problem is to take enough out of private incomes so that consumers will not try to buy more than $110 billion worth of consumers' goods and services. We look at past experience and see that ordinarily consumption expenditures equal, say, 85 percent of private incomes after tax. However, in wartime with appeals to save on patriotic grounds and some goods not being available at all, consumers' expenditures might be a smaller percentage. We estimate it at 80 percent. This means that private income after tax should be $137.5 billion, because 80 percent of that is $110 billion, or just the amount of goods and services available for consumers. Now, if $200 billion of goods and services are produced, private incomes *before* taxes will be $200 billion, because the value of everything produced is income to someone. Therefore we need $62.5 billion of taxes. If the existing taxes would yield $50 billion when total income is $200 billion, then the tax gap is $12.5 billion. We need additional taxes to yield $12.5 billion at a national income of $200 billion,

Such calculations were a standard feature of Washington economics during the war. Naturally, many people thought that this kind of analysis would be the basis of postwar fiscal policy. In fact the original proposals for the Full Employment Act included a statutory requirement for gap analysis.

However, the fact that such analyses were made during the war did not demonstrate that they could be made effectively in peacetime. The accuracy of the wartime analyses and the policy recommendations that followed from them were not tested during the war. The actual fiscal policy of the war was not the policy to which the gap analyses pointed. Congress always enacted smaller tax increases than the administration requested, and the administration's requests were not closely governed by the gap analyses. So there was no opportunity to see whether the policy suggested by this kind of analysis would have achieved the results that were sought.

Also, basing fiscal policy on such estimates implied that tax rates or expenditure programs should be changed whenever the estimates indicated that the change would bring the economy closer to the full-employment target. However, changing tax rates and expenditure programs would have a cost in reduced efficiency of government operations and increased uncertainty for taxpayers. There would be advantage in holding down the frequency of such changes.

Making Room for Budget-Balancing

This line of thinking was important in the Ruml position, which was later further developed as the CED position, that tax rates should be set to balance the budget at high employment. In a fluctuating economy, this particular relation between tax rates and expenditures would sometimes, perhaps often, be wrong, sometimes too expansive and inflationary and sometimes not expansive enough. But the relation between tax rates and expenditures dictated by forecasts of the gap would also often be wrong. In fact, one could not be sure which policy would be more frequently or more seriously wrong. One could not hope to eliminate error in fiscal policy. One could hope to avoid gross error, and also to cushion the economy against the effects of such errors as were inevitable.

Balancing the budget at high employment would guard against the grossest errors of fiscal policy, especially against the error of trying to balance the budget in a depression. It would permit the full operation of the built-in stabilizers in the budget, since if the budget balanced at high employment it would automatically run a deficit in depression and a surplus in boom. This would make for stability in the economy even if, in any particular year, tax rates high enough to balance the budget at high employment were not the best of all possible policies to follow. At the same time Ruml, and later the CED, believed that setting tax rates to balance the budget at high employment and leaving them there would make for stability of tax rates, or at least eliminate one cause for instability of tax rates, and they valued that highly.

In the minds of some people, including Ruml, there was an advantage to preserving the budget-balancing principle in some form. The idea was thought to have substantial force in the country as a symbol of sound finance. There was no point to attacking that symbol frontally, creating a great debate, and weakening confidence if it was not necessary to do that in order

to enlist the power of the budget against major economic disturbances. Re-
defining budget-balancing to mean balancing the budget at high employment was one effort to preserve the symbol while making room for a desirable flexibility in the budget. [25]

Ruml did not think he was formulating a rule forever. In several statements of his position he left room, usually rather inconspicuously, for
changing the budget-balancing rule if there should be a major change in
the economy requiring it. Also, he recognized the possibility that temporary
departures from the rule might sometimes be indicated, even though there
was no basis for modifying the rule. Nevertheless the rule denied, and was
intended to deny, the idea of continuous budgetary management in response
to continuous forecasting of changes in economic conditions.

The Two Views

The developments of the war, the opportunity provided to reflect on
the experience of the 1930's, and the further digestion of Keynes led to a
convergence of thinking on two points. The first was that the government
must take responsibility for the maintenance of full employment, however
defined—or, more commonly, not defined. The second was that active
fiscal policy must be a major instrument, perhaps the major instrument, for
discharging that responsibility. But, as we have seen, two different views of
proper and feasible fiscal policy after the war emerged among people who
shared these beliefs.

One view was that the government could and should determine its
fiscal actions by reference to continuous analysis and forecast of the amount
of action which would be just sufficient to give full employment. This view
commonly but not always implied that the fiscal action would be on the
expenditure side of the budget. The other view was that the government
should rely mainly on revenues as the chief instrument of an active fiscal
policy, should ordinarily depend upon the automatic, built-in flexibility of
revenues as a stabilizing force, and should only take further positive action
to change tax rates or, in special circumstances, to vary expenditures in case
of extreme departure from the employment goal. In this view the idea of a
balanced budget could continue as a guide to fiscal policy, but the guide
would have to be stated in a way that allowed for flexibility in the actual
relation between revenues and expenditures in accordance with economic
conditions. In the first view budget-balancing was a mere shibboleth and
had no part to play.

The difference between these views cannot be identified with the difference between Keynesian and anti-Keynesian positions. Both were described in the Keynesian language of the flow of incomes and expenditures, and both accepted the idea, which is both Keynesian and pre-Keynesian, of a compensatory fiscal policy. Neither of these views necessarily implied any position on the most distinctively Keynesian doctrine of the possibility and eventual probability of equilibrium short of full employment. As for the distinction between reliance on tax policy and expenditure policy, Keynesian analysis indicated that either could be effective, and Keynes' writings had referred to both as possible instruments although his discussion had tended to run much more in terms of decisions about government spending. The distinction between the two views was partly a question of the degree of flexibility that could practically be obtained with each instrument and partly a question of the accuracy that could reasonably be expected of the forecasts upon which policy might have to rest. There was no clearly Keynesian position on these questions. The distinction between the two views was also in part a matter of political outlook, of attitude towards the probability and consequences of a rapid secular increase of government spending.

The difference between the two views may have also reflected a difference of ambition with respect to the full-employment goal. Proponents of the more continuously and completely managed policy tended to describe their goal as full employment, whereas those who would have more generally relied on built-in flexibility within the limits of a budget balanced at high employment tended to describe their goal as high employment or the avoidance of serious unemployment. However, this choice of language does not itself determine which policy would in fact have been more successful in minimizing unemployment. That would depend upon how well the alternative policies could actually work.

One point of economic doctrine which was later to be an important difference between the two views had not yet come to the fore. That was the question of the possible contribution of monetary policy, as a supplement to fiscal policy, in economic stabilization. Monetary policy was effectively frozen during the war by the commitment of the Federal Reserve to support the prices of government securities, and wartime experience did not provide the same stimulus to the discussion of monetary policy that it provided for fiscal policy. However, the question become important later, and the people who believed that monetary policy could make a significant contribution tended then also to decide that there was little necessity for continuous recourse to fiscal variations other than those that were built-in.

Of course, it should not be inferred that the whole country, or even that part of the country that wrote and talked about fiscal policy, was divided between these two views. The most common doctrine about how to manage our finances after the war was still that we should get back to balancing the budget. Business organization's plans for the postwar world usually put this at the head of the paternoster, as did innumerable speeches by Congressmen. However, this talk had as little significance as F. D. Roosevelt's 1932 speech in Pittsburgh about balancing the budget, and probably less. The budget-balancing talk was pure ritual and does not at all detract from the national commitment which existed at the end of the war to use fiscal policy to stabilize the economy around high or full employment. The two views we have distinguished here represent the range of thinking that would be influential in determining how that commitment would be executed.

❧ 9 ❧

The Development of Consensus, 1945 to 1949

Twenty years later there are still people who think that in 1946 Congress enacted something called the "Full Employment Act." It did not. It enacted the Employment Act of 1946. The failure to pass a "Full Employment Act" is as significant as the decision to pass the Employment Act. Taken together the affirmative and negative actions reveal the central agreement upon which all postwar economic policy has been based. To keep unemployment low is accepted as a national goal of very high priority, but full employment is not accepted as an absolute goal overriding all others. The government has a responsibility to use available measures, including fiscal policy, to keep unemployment low. It is not committed either to exclusive or to residual reliance on fiscal policy, and particularly not on government spending, as the means to that end. The negative and affirmative aspects of the decision are revealed in the act, but are even clearer in its legislative history.[1]

As World War II drew toward its end, Congress was flooded with legislative proposals about reconversion and the postwar economy. Most of these dealt with such immediate necessities as contract termination and disposal of war surplus property. However, by the middle of 1944 three ideas of longer-range significance were in the legislative hopper. The first, contained in a bill by Senator Kilgore, was that a "Bureau of Programs" should be established in the Office of War Mobilization and Reconversion with responsibility for "full employment and full production planning." The second was a proposal by James Patton, president of the Farmers Union, for a national commitment to full employment as a goal. The third was a proposal devised by Russell Smith, legislative representative of the Farmers Union, to achieve Mr. Patton's goal. This called upon the government to make loans or direct expenditures whenever necessary to bring total investment, by which he

197

meant private investment plus the government deficit, up to $40 billion, an amount which some Washington economists had advised him was sufficient and necessary to yield full employment. These were the main ingredients of the original Full Employment Bill—the goal, the executive responsibility, and the means to be used, which was government spending.

Through a series of Congressional maneuvers, responsibility for preparing a bill came into the hands of Senator James Murray of Montana, chairman of the War Contracts Subcommittee of the Senate Military Affairs Committee. He turned the task over to Bertram Gross, staff director of the subcommittee, who enlisted the aid of a group, mainly economists, that Bailey describes as follows:

> They all had a burning interest in postwar employment problems, and in terms of economic philosophy, they shared in the belief that the compensatory fiscal ideas stemming from the Keynes-Hansen analysis were basically sound.[2]

The draft of a bill that emerged from this group was a chapter from an elementary economics textbook translated into legislative language. After stating that every American able and willing to work had a right to employment, which right it was the government's responsibility to guarantee by assuring full employment, the draft called upon the President to submit an annual National Production and Employment Budget. This budget would show the number of jobs required for full employment, the dollar volume of gross national product that would yield this number of jobs, and the volume of gross national product expected if no steps were taken. If there was a gap, if expected GNP was below the GNP needed for full employment, the President should submit to Congress a program for eliminating it. This program might include any policies within the jurisdiction of the federal government, but the only policy spelled out in detail was a policy of federal spending. Moreover, the bill itself authorized the appropriations needed to carry out the program.

A number of revisions in this first "expert" draft were made before its sponsors, Senators Murray, Wagner, Thomas, and O'Mahoney, introduced it in January, 1945. These revisions were intended to forestall some of the expected opposition. The policy of fostering "free competitive enterprise" was put at the head of the declaration of policy. The government's "responsibility" became the government's "policy." At one point "sufficient employment opportunities" was substituted for "full employment." There were many other revisions of similar significance. These modifications of the bill correctly anticipated the nature of the attack that would be made. However, they did not satisfy the opposition. Probably nothing the sponsors could have done at that stage would have satisfied the opposition. The main importance of the bill was its reflection of the sense of the Congress; the substantive measures it required were few. Voluntary softening of the language by the sponsors could not placate the conservatives. They had to establish that the intent of the sponsors was not the intent of the Congress. They could only do that by carrying on an argument and winning some points against the sponsors.

Introduction of the bill, S. 380, gave rise to a "great debate." This must be said with some qualifications. First, a large majority of the population apparently did not know what was going on. A public opinion poll taken in the second Congressional district of Illinois during the debate revealed that 69 percent of the respondents had not heard of the bill, 19 percent had heard but had no idea what it was, 4 percent had an idea but a wrong one, and 8 percent had the correct idea of it.[3] Second, Congress was busy, and probably few congressmen though they were debating the Magna Carta of the American economy. Third, most of what was said was meaningless or not meant and could not possibly have had any effect.

Proponents of the bill charged the opposition with being indifferent to, or actually in favor of, mass unemployment.[4] Opponents of the bill charged its sponsors with wittingly or unwittingly preparing the demise of private enterprise. But arguments at this level of generality could not affect the outcome.

There was never any real issue in the Congress about the idea that keeping unemployment low was an important national goal in the achievement of which the federal government had some responsibilities. There was never any vote in which congressmen could be clearly shown to have voted against this idea. The issues were always about specific amendments, which the supporters of the original bill described as "emasculating"—their favorite word—and opponents described as necessary for the preservation of freedom. The significance of the amendments was usually difficult to see, because the meaning of the original language was itself unclear. If no one knew what "full" employment meant, it was hard to be sure of the implications of changing "full" to "high" or "maximum."

The important debate was about amendments which were designed to reflect positions on four main issues:

The Goal: This issue had two parts. The first was whether it made sense to declare the existence of a right to a job or to employment, as the proponents of the original bill wished. On this question there was a good deal of logic-chopping, with philosophic analyses of the rights of man, the Declaration of Independence, and the Bill of Rights. But it was clear as soon as the issue was raised that, although some people had an affection for the "rights" language, no one seriously meant to endow individuals with a legally-enforceable right to jobs. What was meant was that the government had a responsibility to maintain certain general conditions with respect to total employment and unemployment. So, the second issue was how to define these conditions.

The proponents of the bill set great store by the term "full employment" as the definition of the condition to be maintained. Yet from the beginning they acknowledged that they did not really mean a condition in which everyone was at work. Opponents of the bill, naively or maliciously, interpreted the phrase as meaning that people would have to work whether they wanted to or not. The other side gave ammunition for this interpretation by specifying that full employment did not mean that housewives and students would have to be employed, as if to imply that everyone else would. The bill's authors flirted with defining "full employment" as a condition in which the number of job vacancies exceeded the number of persons unemployed. However, this was obviously unsatisfactory, since it permitted the existence of a large number of unemployed who would not be less unemployed because there also existed a large number of job vacancies for which they were unqualified or geographically remote. Inability to specify what it meant weakened the case for insisting on the particular words "full employment."

The effective opposition to these words came from people who feared they would commit the government to pursuit of a goal so absolute that it might only be achievable with inflation or price-wage controls or both. This fear reflected awareness of a problem which was to become more and more worrisome in the next twenty years but which was ignored in the drafting of the Full Employment Bill—the possibility that with a very low level of unemployment, and especially if the government were committed to maintain it, uncontrolled wage and price determination might lead to continuous inflation. This concern was expressed by many economists in comment on the bill. Professor Henry Simons, for example, recommended that instead of full employment the goal should be price stability.[5] Most businessmen testifying on the bill also objected to the words "full employment" as too ambitious. Fear that "full employment" would imply inflation if not accompanied by controls was the most reasonable explanation of the typical conservative fear that the bill would undermine free enterprise.

Critics of the original language were not, in general, able to specify their employment goal either. They wanted to express their belief that at least beyond some point further reduction of unemployment might become inconsistent with other goals over which it would not necessarily take precedence. However, it was not possible, or even attempted, to draft language that would locate that point. All that was possible was to erect a warning that Congress did not intend to commit the government in advance to every step that might reduce unemployment, but meant to retain the government's freedom to decide in particular situations how far it should go. The way to erect this warning was to defeat the words "full employment" and to join it with other objectives. There were numerous suggestions, from the CED, the NAM, and others, to substitute "high" for "full" and this was done in the House. In the conference between the Senate and the House the phrase "maximum employment, production and purchasing power" was adopted. It does not sound as if there could be anything more than "maximum," but in the context of the debate, "maximum" was clearly a less absolute goal than "full." Also, coupling employment with production and purchasing power, while probably not literally very significant, had the symbolic effect of weakening the exclusive preoccupation with employment.

Apparently there was no attempt to specify price stability as a goal, despite the frequent argument that dedication of the government to full employment carried the risk of inflation. In later years the goal of "maximum purchasing power" was sometimes interpreted as meaning price stability, perhaps because there is nothing else that it could sensibly mean. But this does not seem to have been in the thinking in 1946.

The Instrument: Although the language of the original bill invited the government to use all means at its disposal to achieve full employment, this did not weaken the suspicion of opponents that what was really intended was a commitment to deficit spending as the major instrument. This suspicion may not have been entirely justified as far as some of the Congressional sponsors of the bill were concerned. But the language of the bill gave color to the suspicion. There can hardly be any doubt that the economists who were involved in drafting the bill and working for it, and who were expected to be important in implementing it if it passed, regarded the bill as a mandate for compensatory deficit spending.[6]

Some of the opposition on this point harked back to the New Deal argument. It was claimed that if the government would only stop bothering business there would be high employment, and deficit spending would be unnecessary. Some of the opposition only wanted to get away from the implied approval of deficit spending. But there were others who, recognizing the need for positive government action, objected to the subordination of other instruments that they considered at least as good. The most important of these were tax policy and monetary policy. The need for relying on these two instruments at least equally with spending policy was emphasized in statements to the Congressional committees by Beardsley Ruml and Paul Hoffman for the CED, by Allan Sproul of the New York Federal Reserve Bank, Russell Leffingwell of J. P. Morgan Co., and by several economists including Henry Simons and Gottfried Haberler.[7]

In the end it was not possible to rule out deficit spending, to insist on the use of other measures, to to specify in what combination the various measures should be used. Once it is admitted that there are a number of useful instruments, room must be allowed for judgment in deciding on their application. Senator Taft tried to set some limit to deficit spending by providing that it would have to be accompanied by taxation "designed and calculated to prevent any net increase in the national debt" over a reasonable period of years. But still he could not resist the addition to his amendment of the words "without interfering with the goal of full employment," because to object to those words would be to admit that long-range budget-balancing might interfere with full employment. When these words were added the Taft amendment became so innocuous that the Senate passed it by a vote of 82–0.

The solution adopted was not to single out any instruments but to call upon the government to use "all its plans, functions and resources." Deficit spending was not excluded, but it was given no special place. Of course, with the omission of any reference to deficit spending, even the mild attempt to specify limits for it represented by the Taft amendment was also omitted.

Forecasting: One of the chief targets of attack on the original proposal was its requirement that the President should submit to Congress periodic forecasts of the state of employment and of the measures that would be needed to make employment full. The forecasting requirement suffered ill fortune because during the debate on the bill it became apparent that the forecasts of a great postwar depression made by many economists, in and out of government, were wildly mistaken. The argument against the forecasting provision proceeded mainly on the negative point that forecasts would be inaccurate. How the government would use its future policies to achieve desired conditions in the future without forecasting was not explained. Some elements of the rationale of an anti-forecasting or minimum-forecasting position had already begun to appear in the work of B. Ruml and his associates, as we have seen in the preceding chapter. This involved the superiority of rapid, preferably automatic, response to actual conditions as compared with the commitment of policy on the basis of forecasts. However, this line of argument was as yet in an early stage and was certainly not in the minds of most of the critics of forecasting. They wanted to eliminate the requirement of a forecast, not substitute something in its place. The act as passed calls for an annual economic report from the President, and is general enough to permit him to submit such forecasts as he wishes but not to require any forecast he does not wish to submit.

The Agency: In consideration of a bill that was so open-ended about what was to be done, attention naturally focussed on the question of who was to do it. The original proponents of the bill had contemplated that the President's responsibility for forecasting, reporting, and programming would be discharged primarily with the assistance of the Bureau of the Budget—an idea conforming to their view of the budget as the chief instrument for assuring full employment. However, in order not to arouse opposition from other parts of the administration, the draftsmen did not specify the Budget Bureau or any other agency, but simply gave all responsibility to the President. This again roused suspicion. The President would obviously need help in carrying out his new responsibilities, and critics wanted to see who was helping him. In a forceful and influential statement, George Terborgh of the Machinery and Allied Products Institute said that under the provisions of the bill:

> Both the economic analysis and the economic policy may be prepared and promoted by men unknown to the public, whose appointment has not been confirmed by Congress, and who have no formal public responsibility. This set-up invites behind-the-scenes manipulation by Presidential advisers of the moment, possessed, it may be, both by a passion for anonymity and a passion for controlling national economic policy.[8]

Some wanted to go much farther than making the President's advisers visible. They wanted to make them independent and "high level." So there were numerous proposals for independent commissions, composed of members with long terms of office and possibly therefore not appointees of the incumbent President. In some versions, the proposals called for members from business, labor, and agriculture, or contemplated merely leading citizens. The motives for such proposals were varied. There was some simple partisanship—a desire to provide a check upon a Democratic, Fair Deal President. There was some desire to subordinate politics to sound economics, and on the same reasoning that is used to justify an independent Federal Federal Reserve. To some extent the proposals reflected suspicion of economists, especially Washington economists.

However, the advocates of Presidential responsibility were too strong to be circumvented in this way. Responsibility for using *all* of the government's "plans, functions and resources" could not be given to anyone less than the President, and if he was to have responsibility for decisions he could not be required to contend with a group of advisers he had not chosen. Critics of the original plan succeeded in obtaining provision for a Council of Economic Advisers, to be outside the Budget Bureau and to be confirmed by the Senate. But the council remained the President's arm, and did not become a Supreme Court of economics.

The Employment Act did not create a new American fiscal policy. It, and the debate which preceded its enactment, confirmed the policy which existed. It recognized the expectation that federal fiscal policy should be used in an attempt to maintain high employment, but high employment is not the only goal of fiscal policy, and fiscal policy is not the only means to high employment. Confirmation of this national policy was a valuable contribution. It helped to put an end to a futile, tiresome, and largely meaningless debate between extremists and cleared the way for practical work to evolve a program.

The act's other main contribution was its provision for a Council of Economic Advisers. This greatly increased the probability that professional economists would have an important role in decisions about fiscal policy. The act did not specify that the members of the council should be professional economists, but the position of the council as a personal staff to the President, responsible for helping him draft a report on economic subjects, made it extremely likely that economists would be chosen. Presidents could have economists as advisers without an Employment Act, as Roosevelt did, and Presidents don't have to listen much to economists even with an Employment Act, as Truman didn't for some years. However, the act increased the chance of professional economic advice getting to the ear of the President. While this does not imply anything very specific about the advice a President is likely to get about fiscal policy, even its general implication is important. An economist without departmental responsibilities, and especially operating under the direction of the Employment Act, will amost certainly place more weight on the direct and indirect effects of fiscal actions on economic stability than will the President's other natural advisers in this field. The chief of these other advisers is the Secretary of the Treasury who, in the U. S. government, has primary responsibility for the management of the public debt and for the conduct of international monetary policy. These other interests tend, rightly or wrongly, to dilute the Treasury Secretary's concern with the impact of fiscal policy on overall domestic economic conditions.

The Early Role of the Council of Economic Advisers

Contrary to the fears and hopes implicit in the debate over the Employ-ment Act, the council in its early years did not turn out to be influential either in developing and spreading new ideas for the management of fiscal policy or in making fiscal decisions. There were several reasons for this. For one thing, neither Edwin Nourse, the first chairman of the council, nor Leon Keyserling, his vice-chairman and successor, was greatly interested in fiscal policy. Both were outside the mainstream of professional economic thinking of their time. Although they disagreed about almost everything else, they agreed in seeing the main economic problem not in terms of the aggregate demand for goods and services but in terms of the balance among various sectors and income shares within the economy. Their first report spoke scornfully of the idea that the economic needs of the country could be met by overall financial measures, such as fiscal policy, and emphasized the need to be concerned about the structural relations within the system.[9] Dr. Nourse gave major weight to the proper relations among business, labor, and agriculture, or among wages, profits, and farm incomes. He hoped to achieve balance by voluntary cooperation among the private sectors of the economy. Mr. Keyserling was concerned as well with the proper relations among in-dustrial sectors—in the sense of avoiding bottlenecks and surpluses—and among income groups, and supported measures of fairly specific government intervention to bring about the desired relations. In numerous statements before Congressional committees he warned against preoccupation with overall conditions, like general inflation, and with overall measures of fiscal and monetary policy. In 1949 he was one of the leading advocates of a bill which would have empowered the government to promote investment in specific industries where it calculated that private forces were not providing sufficient investment to generate balanced growth.

In a sense, the concerns of both Keyserling and Nourse were reversions to the thinking of the early New Deal with its emphasis on, or at least talk about, planning and structural balance. Certainly they were out of tune not only with prevailing ideas among economists but also with the general public mood, which was not for additional detailed government intervention. Prob-ably they were also out of tune with the needs of the country, which was suffering from excessive demand and general inflation more than from any-thing else. But in any case, these concerns reduced the attention the council gave to fiscal policy.

Moreover, the council, at least before the Korean War, did not carry much weight with President Truman. He had supported passage of a "strong"

Employment Act, but seems to have had no clear idea of what he would do with the council after he had it. He was not at home with abstract ideas or with intellectuals, even with ones who had as much practical experience as Nourse and Keyserling. His old friend, John Snyder, whom he made Secretary of the Treasury, was closer to his idea of a financial adviser. Probably the continuing differences between Nourse and Keyserling, reflected in divided counsel to him before Nourse resigned, also reduced the influence of both.

It may be a mistake to expect a body like the Council of Economic Advisers to develop plans for fiscal policy, or at least to discuss such plans publicly. Fiscal blueprints, programs, even principles unless stated in the most general of terms, imply commitments about the fiscal action the government will take in the future. Governments do not like to give such commitments. Every government has a fiscal policy, in the sense that it will react to certain conditions in certain ways. But the government may not know itself what its policy will be in new conditions until the conditions arise and is certainly unlikely to commit itself in advance. The government discovers, reveals, and establishes its fiscal policy by action in particular circumstances and sometimes by the language it uses to justify the action. When the government finds itself in a new part of the map of possible economic conditions it discovers or invents policies for that part of the map. The great Depression was a new part of the map, and in dealing with it the government established some new ideas of what the government's fiscal policy is, ideas which survived the Depression. An agency like the Council of Economic Advisers contributes to the development of fiscal policy when it participates in making decisions about new conditions facing the country. In the early years of its life the council did not participate much in making decisions, and we were operating in a fairly familiar part of the map.

THE BIG TAX CUT STRUGGLE: 1947–48

The first years of the Truman administration were an active period both in the practice of fiscal policy and in the development of ideas about it. The practice of fiscal policy was the concern of the President and the Congress and was highlighted by a two-year struggle between them over whether income taxes should be cut. The development of ideas about the practice of fiscal policy went on mainly outside the government, among economists, businessmen, and others who were trying to put some workable content into the framework of general principles of stabilization policy established by depression and war experience and the largely Keynesian interpretation of that experience. During the years up to about 1949 there was little interaction between these two processes. Most of the participants in the Washington struggle were too firmly committed politically on the subject of tax reduction to be much influenced by economic analysis from the outside. And the lessons of the struggle, of the decision, and of its consequences were mainly negative. The experience showed how far the country was, despite acceptance of certain general principles, from having an effective or even reasonably agreed upon policy for guiding fiscal decisions, and how hard it would be to achieve such a policy.

Both sides in the struggle over tax reduction took up their positions in the middle of 1946 and clung to them without deviation through the Presidential election of 1948. The Republicans, seeking to regain control of Congress after a lapse of sixteen years, attacked the Democrats as the party of high spending and high taxes and promised to reduce both sides of the budget. This seemed at the time a promise that would be easy to keep. Although spending had declined substantially from its wartime peak, and taxes had been cut when the war ended, at the time of the 1946 Congressional campaign both were still far above what almost everyone regarded as the normal peacetime level. It was a good bet that in the ordinary course of events both would come down.

Truman did not disagree with this reasoning except for the timing, which was crucial. He expected that total expenditures would decline from the $40 billion estimated for the fiscal year 1946–47 to a more normal peacetime level of around $25 billion. As they declined there would be an opportunity for tax reduction. But meanwhile he was anticipating a deficit of $1.9 billion[10] for the fiscal year, and he had no intention of cutting taxes in the face of a deficit. Mr. Truman believed in budget-balancing. As he said in his memoirs, "There is nothing sacred about the pay-as-you-go idea so far as I am concerned except that it represents the soundest principle of financing that I know."[11]

Truman's belief in budget-balancing in general was reinforced by the economic and political situation of the fall of 1946. Employment was full and the national income was high. If we couldn't reduce the debt under those conditions, when could we hope to do so? Moreover, prices had skyrocketed after the demise of price control in the middle of 1946. Price control had been killed by the Republicans in Congress, with help from a few Democrats, according to the standard version which did not ask whether it had much life expectancy anyway. The President had taken up a position as the enemy of inflation and defender of the family pocketbook. The fight against the tax cut was for Truman both a fight against inflation and a fight against the Republicans as the party of inflation.

From the time the Republicans won control of the Congress in the 1946 elections the outlines of the contest over tax reduction that would occur in the 80th Congress were clear, even though the outcome was uncertain. There was a steadfast Congressional majority for large, prompt, tax reduction. However, the majority was not at the outset big enough to override a Presidential veto. So the Republican effort to achieve tax reduction took the form of an effort to win over a relatively small number of votes from Democrats who initially were opposed. This effort fell short after Truman vetoed a tax cut bill in June, 1947, and fell short again when he vetoed another a month later. However, it finally succeeded in April, 1948, and the tax cut was accomplished.

In order to convert the necessary number of Democrats to their cause, the Republicans were willing to make considerable changes in their original plan. During the 1946 campaign, Congressman Knutson, who would be the chairman of the Ways and Means Committee in a Republican Congress, and other Republicans promised a 20 percent across-the-board income tax cut, to take effect January 1, 1947. However, it was soon discovered that the 20 percent across-the-board tax cut was highly vulnerable to the charge of unfairness, because it gave very much more tax reduction to a person who paid a lot of tax, who was inevitably a rich person, than to a poor person who paid a little tax. The bill was successively modified during 1947 and the first months of 1948 to make it more salable. The personal exemption from income tax was raised from $500 to $600, the amount of rate reduction was trimmed down, and provision was made for married couples to compute their taxes as if their combined incomes were split equally between them. All this gave a much larger share of the tax cut to the low income taxpayers than the original Knutson plan had done. Also, much of the benefit to middle and upper-income taxpayers came through a provision for income-splitting, which almost everyone regarded as a step in the direction of equity.[12] These steps helped to gain the support of a few northern Democrats. There were several southern Democrats who shared the views of their Republican colleagues about the inequities of high taxes but who were especially concerned with avoiding budget deficits. Their support of tax reduction was made easier by postponement of the effective date of the tax cut, first planned for January 1, 1947, to July 1, 1947, and finally to January 1, 1948, with income tax withholding to be cut on May 1, 1948. As a consequence there was no revenue loss in fiscal 1947 and very little in fiscal 1948. This looked like a politically unbeatable combination—a tax cut going into effect early enough to be noticed in paychecks before the election but late enough not to affect the federal budget noticeably, for the benefit of those who cared about that.

The Fiscal Dividend

The addition of enough votes to override the President's veto was also assisted by the growth of the federal revenue which resulted from the inflation. This generated enough surplus in the budget to permit some debt reduction even after tax reduction. The successive estimates of the budget for fiscal 1947 were:[13]

| | (Billions of Dollars) | | |
	Expenditures	Receipts	Deficit
Estimated January, 1946	35.9	31.5	4.3
Estimated August, 1946	41.5	39.6	1.9
Estimated January, 1947	42.5	40.3	2.2
Actual	42.5	43.3	-.8 (surplus)

The initial estimate for fiscal year 1948, made in January, 1947, was that receipts would be $38.9 billion and the surplus $1.8 billion, if the President's recommendations to continue wartime excises and eliminate the postal deficit were followed. By the time the tax cut was finally enacted in 1948 the estimate of revenues had been raised to $46.5 billion and the deficit had been converted to a surplus of $8.8 billion. Despite the increases of expenditure required by the Marshall Plan, continuing anticipated growth of revenues would yield another large surplus in fiscal 1949. Senator Millikin, chairman of the Senate Finance Committee, could tell the Senate in March, 1948, that if taxes were not cut the combined surplus for the fiscal years 1948 and 1949 would be almost $16 billion, without giving any credit for expenditure cuts Congress expected to make.

All agreed with the principle that in times of inflation, such as then prevailed, the federal government should run a surplus. In the circumstances, people who believed that the government should always run a surplus in order to reduce the debt, and people who cared very little about the size of the debt, could agree to the general principle. But the agreement in principle did not prevent the administration and the Congressional leadership from being many billions of dollars apart on the question of tax reduction—the distance between zero and the size of the tax cut which, as finally enacted, was about $5 billion. Relative to the size of the budget and the national income, the $5 billion tax cut was as large as the cut made in 1964.

There were several reasons why the principle that the government should have a surplus in periods of inflation failed to give more precise guidance on the desirability of a tax cut. In 1947 especially, and to a much smaller degree in 1948, the pro- and anti–tax-cut forces were far apart in their predictions of what expenditures would be. The Republicans had come into control of

Congress with a promise to cut expenditures as well as taxes. Soon after the session began, a joint committee of the Ways and Means Committee and Appropriations Committee of the House voted to cut the Truman budget for fiscal 1948 by $6 billion. A similar committee in the Senate endorsed a cut of $4.5 billion. How seriously the authors of these numbers took them is uncertain. There were many who were skeptical of the value of such resolutions as evidence of what Congress would do, since they were devoid of specific content. In fact, the actual expenditures for the year turned out to be close to the original Truman estimates, after allowance for certain changes in accounting during the year. But for some months in 1947, before the appropriation bills for fiscal 1948 had passed, the Republicans could talk as if the expenditure reductions they planned would permit both a tax cut and more debt reduction than the administration recommended.

ESTIMATES AS WEAPONS

A more serious basis for argument on whether or not a tax cut could be afforded was a difference in estimates of the probable revenues and therefore of the probable surplus under the existing tax laws. The differences in estimates of the revenues in turn hinged upon differences in the estimates of the national income. The 1947–48 tax discussion marked the first general recognition that differences in the estimates of the national income within a quite conservative range of what was probable would make substantial differences in the revenue estimates. Congressmen were soon manipulating the statistics of national income, personal income, and income payments with great freedom, and sometimes with great confusion.

The typical practice of the administration was to estimate the revenues on the assumption that the most recently recorded actual rate of national income would continue in the future throughout the period for which estimates were being made. It would then cling to these estimates as long as possible. Thus, in April, 1946, the President raised the revenue estimates for the year ending June 30, 1946, by $4.3 billion, but refused to revise the estimates for the next fiscal year until August.[14] Testifying before the Senate Finance Committee in April, 1947, Secretary Snyder raised the revenue estimates for the year ending June 30, 1947, enough to balance the budget for that year, but resisted efforts by the committee to get him to revise the estimates for the next year.[15]

Throughout the period the national income was rising rapidly, partly as a result of the inflation. Therefore the administration always found itself in the position of defending a revenue estimate based on the assumed continuation of a rate of national income that had already been far exceeded. This was a source of some embarrassment. Committee members would ask Secretary Snyder, in hearings on tax reduction, whether he was forecasting a recession. This was a tricky question, because part of the administration's case was that there was a continuing danger of inflation. Secretary Snyder's reply had three parts: (*a*) that he had to look at the "facts," (*b*) that it would be imprudent to count on the indefinite continuation of the all-time peak national income then being experienced, and (*c*) that the administration believed prices should and could come down without a recession, and that would lower the national income.

At his press conference on the budget in January, 1948, the President was queried about the estimates:

> QUESTION: Mr. President, is there any explanation from the Treasury why people on the Hill were so far ahead of the Treasury in estimating this terrific rise in Federal revenues?
>
> PRESIDENT: Was that true?
>
> QUESTION: Yes, sir. The Treasury was still holding, I believe, to a round $40 billion estimate up until the time of the adjournment of Congress last year.
>
> PRESIDENT: Well, I think the Treasury finally revised its estimate after the first collection period was in. That is the only way it could be revised. The other was probably a guess. The Treasury works on the figures as they are.
>
> SNYDER: They must have had a better insight into the rise in prices. (Laughter) They must have known what they were going to do to them.[16]

The Republicans did not generally base their revenue estimates on forecasts of future inflation which would raise the national income. It was sufficient for their purposes to base their estimates on continuation of the rate of national income existing when they enacted the tax reduction bill, which was substantially higher than the earlier national income on which the administration's estimates were based. This usually provided them with enough prospective revenue to make a $4 or $5 billion tax cut and still show as much surplus as the administration showed with its earlier estimates. It would have been awkward for the proponents of a tax cut to make a revenue estimate based on the forecast of more inflation, because part of their case was that a serious probability of recession existed.

Low revenue estimates did not make the administration oppose tax cuts, and high revenue estimates did not make the Republicans favor them. The truth was more nearly that the administration made low revenue estimates because it was against any tax cut, and the Republicans made higher estimates because they wanted a tax cut. However, the availability of a wide range of revenue estimates from which to select permitted each side to defend its position as consistent with the general principle that there should be a budget surplus.

How Much Surplus?

This whole argument about the estimates implied an assumption the significance of which was scarcely appreciated at the time. The assumption was that there existed a desirable size of surplus which did not depend on whether it was achieved at a higher or lower price level. Thus, if a surplus of, say, $3 billion is desirable if the national income is $200 billion, then a surplus of $3 billion is also desirable if prices are 10 percent higher and the national income is $220 billion. In this case a higher estimate of the national income, which yields a larger estimate of revenues, leaves more room for tax reduction consistent with the desired surplus. However, there is another theory on which budget policy can be based. That is that a higher national income resulting from higher prices calls for a larger budget surplus and does not, by itself, justify tax reduction. The higher prices reflect stronger inflationary pressure in the economy and require a bigger budget surplus to withstand that pressure. This is the other side of the proposition which almost everyone would have accepted by 1947, that a deficit resulting from the decline in revenues during a recession does not call for a tax increase.

Part of the increase in the national income, with consequent increase in the revenues and the surplus, was real economic growth resulting from growth of the labor force and its productivity. It could have been argued that the surplus arising from this source should, at an appropriate time, be used for tax reduction, lest the mounting surplus become a drag upon the increase of real output. But to give away in tax reduction the surplus arising from inflation would nullify the force of the budget as a built-in stabilizer of the economy. However, the administration never succeeded in making this argument, and stood essentially tongue-tied in the face of the evidence of rising revenues, which would leave, after tax reduction, as much surplus as the administration had ever budgeted for.[17]

The decision to cut taxes or not to cut taxes was a decision about how big the budget surplus should be. Neither side revealed any clear answer to this question or any clear basis for thinking about it, even aside from the complications that would arise from distinguishing among surpluses arising from inflation, surpluses arising from real growth, and surpluses arising from expenditure reduction.

In December, 1946, the Council of Economic Advisers sent President Truman a memorandum saying:

> We believe that the economic outlook for the next fiscal year is such that a
> budget surplus is urgently called for. If the Government fails to plan for a budget
> surplus under prosperous conditions it may fail to command support for a wise
> policy of deficits under adverse conditions. Economic considerations lead us to
> the conclusion that it would be most desirable to show a budget surplus of at
> least $3 to $5 billion for the next fiscal year.[18]

The economic considerations were not explained in that memo or in
any published report of the council, and in any case they did not control
the decision. The budget for fiscal 1948, submitted in January, 1947, called
for a surplus of $1.8 billion. The general position of the administration was
that the surplus that would be yielded by existing taxes over the expenditures
that the President considered necessary was the correct surplus. The position
of the Congressional leadership was of a similar kind. As long as there was
not a deficit, any surplus that would be left after they had made their promised tax cut of around $5 billion was sufficient. If they could show a surplus
at least as large as Truman had forecast, so much the better. Insofar as the
Republicans had any independent idea of the proper size of the surplus, it
was in the neighborhood of $2.5 billion. This figure came up several times
in the Congressional discussion. The National Association of Manufacturers
had recommended that there should be a surplus each year of at least $2.5
billion—although no reason was given for this particular figure. Also, the
Senate Finance Committee in 1948 heard testimony from one economist,
C. F. Roos, and he demonstrated, on essentially Keynesian reasoning, that
a surplus in excess of $2.8 billion would be deflationary.

The proponents of the tax cut were willing to do some adjustment of
the expenditure figures to make the recorded surplus look better. Thus, in
April, 1947, when the issue was how the tax cut would affect the surplus for
the next fiscal year, the Chamber of Commerce recommended:

> *Transfer to 1947*—There should be analysis of those expenditures now proposed
> for fiscal 1948, which properly can be made in fiscal 1947. Fiscal 1948 might also
> be relieved by any proper deferments of expenditure to later years or by ex-
> clusion, as charges against current receipts, of contemplated reimbursable loans
> which by statute are made public debt transactions.

Immediately after suggesting this piece of window-dressing, the chamber
went on to say, in its most righteous manner:

> *Annual balance*—There should be no temporizing with a basic policy that a
> balanced budget, with definite provision for curtailment of debt, should be the
> normal procedure. This should be the objective for each year and not some
> go-as-you please theory of functional finance.[19]

Before it passed the tax bill that finally survived the President's veto in 1948 Congress inserted in the Marshall Plan authorization a provision that $3 billion of the expenditures to be made in fiscal 1949 should be charged against the 1948 budget. This had the effect of reducing the apparent surplus in the almost-past year 1948, which had a large surplus anyway and which would not be much affected by the tax cut, and increasing the apparent surplus in the year when the tax cut would reduce the revenues the most. If it is thought that excessive attention is paid to the year-by-year budget results, such bookkeeping devices may be necessary for reasonable policy. However, the advocates of this step usually regarded themselves as devoted to balancing the budget *every* year.

CONSERVATIVES AS TAX-CUTTERS

The Congressional Republicans and the businessmen who supported the tax cut found themselves taking positions quite contrary to their popular image as it existed then and as it still existed sixteen years later. These positions taken in 1947 and 1948 are important in explaining the support given by conservatives to the 1964 tax cut, which is regarded as the crown jewel of the new, liberal economics.

In the first place, the tax-cutters of 1947 and 1948 were inevitably in the posture of belittling the importance of large, immediate debt reduction. All of the witnesses in support of the tax cut faced this issue in approximately the same way. They were for debt reduction, but for less debt reduction now and more debt reduction later, and for less now because it would permit more later. For example, Mr. H. E. Humphreys, vice-president of the U. S. Rubber Committee and chairman of the Government Finance Committee of the NAM told the Senate Finance Committee in 1947:

> We agree that the size of the debt and its management are serious matters. But we would emphasize two points in this connection.
> The first is that we shall be able to accomplish more toward the ultimate reduction of the public debt if we can maintain a high level of national income. . . . It is our contention that tax relief, now, will do more to sustain and extend the high-level prosperity which we currently have than can be accomplished by keeping tax rates high.
> The second point to be made in this connection is that we are not facing a choice between debt reduction and tax reduction. The outlook for the Federal receipts is such that we can do both.[20]

The NAM witness, this time Mr. Don Mitchell of Sylvania, Inc., returned to this theme before the Senate Finance Committee in 1948:

> We as a nation may need to moderate our views on the importance of a larger budget surplus for debt reduction at the present time. . . . At the present time, we cannot afford to maintain tax rates that anticipate an extra amount of surplus in the administrative budget for debt payment at the expense of supplying the economy with more of the lifeblood of new capital.[21]

By the time Senator Millikin presented the case for a tax cut to the Senate, on March 18, 1948, the danger of excessive debt reduction had become critical, in his opinion:

> If taxes are not reduced at all, $15,900,000,000 to $18,400,000,000 may be available for debt reduction in 1948 and 1949. In view of the current uncertainty as to economic prospects, it seems clear that debt reduction of such massive proportions would be quite apt to be excessively deflationary. It might not merely check inflation, but might produce actual catastrophic deflation.[22]

Proponents of the tax cut were led, as the preceding remarks suggest, into more concern with recession and less concern with inflation than the administration was exhibiting. This issue between the administration and the tax cutters was not entirely clear-cut. President Truman's standing as the enemy of inflation was a little tarnished by his continuous insistence on the need to raise consumers' purchasing power by a combination of higher wages and lower prices. During the Senate hearings in 1947 Senator Taft claimed that there was a contradiction between the President's demand for a budget surplus and the emphasis he placed on the need to maintain purchasing power. Senator Connally tried to help Secretary Synder by pointing out that debt reduction would put money back in the hands of the people. The Secretary of the Treasury agreed. But Senator Taft then reminded the Secretary that he always said that having a surplus was anti-inflationary.[23]

President Truman's veto message on the first 1947 tax reduction bill was also unclear about the purchasing power argument. He said:

> The argument is made that the funds added to consumer purchasing power through this tax reduction are needed to maintain employment and production at maximum levels.
>
> It is true, as I have pointed out many times, that the purchasing power of large groups of our people has been seriously reduced. We must take every step possible to remedy the disparity between prices and incomes of the rank and file of our people, so as not to put the brakes on our continued prosperity and lead us toward a recession. Tax reduction as proposed in H.R. 1 is not the proper way to remedy the current price situation and its effects upon consumers and upon prospective employment. Necessary adjustments in incomes, production, and prices should be made by wise policies and improved practices of business and labor, not by hastily invoking the fiscal powers of Government on a broad scale.[24]

The administration's policy position about prices and wages did not permit it to deny the possibility of a recession. They could only deny the wisdom of the Republican way of countering that possibility, by broad fiscal action. However, the possibility of a recession was certainly much more vivid in the minds of the tax-cutters than it was for the administration, and the need for advance action to prevent it much more urgent. Thus, the witness for the NAM in 1947, Mr. Humphreys, warned the Senate Finance Committee:

> The Council of Economic Advisers, in its first report to the President, last December, referred to the somewhat artificial character of the present prosperity and expressed the view that this prosperity could not be expected to last indefinitely. It is our contention that tax relief now, to the extent provided in H.R. 1, will be a substantial anchor to windward in the event that a business recession is brewing.
>
> It is our contention, further, that a postponement of action on this important matter until a recession is at hand would be too late. Moreover, it would be dangerous, since we should be obliged to worry along for some time through the recession until the tax reduction had developed its beneficial effects. We know, from experience, that many things can go wrong in even 1 year of depression tendencies. We consider it the wise and prudent action to be prepared in advance for such a contingency.[25]

John W. Hanes, representing the Tax Foundation, testified in the same vein. He thought that it would take eighteen to twenty-four months for the stimulating effects of a tax cut to be felt; therefore, action should come promptly. He added a special twist to the argument:

> And, Senator, I think you have to pass the bill when men's minds are not distorted. Men will not act the same way in a depression period as they will act in a more normal period. I maintain that we will hardly get a tax bill passed in time to do you good if we wait until the horse is out of the stable.[26]

In 1948 the Senate Finance Committee heard evidence on the economic outlook from a "scientific" witness, Charles F. Roos, president of the Econometric Institute. He quantified the prospect as follows:

> We have made forecasts of income and employment under the two assumptions regarding taxes: (1) If the Knutson bill is passed by the Senate and becomes law; and (2) no tax reduction materializes.
>
> In the first case, that is, the Knutson bill becomes law, we forecast that personal income, which was at an annual rate of about $209.7 billion in December, 1947, will average about 210 billion dollars during the calendar year 1948. In the second case, that is, if there is no tax reduction, personal income will average about 200 billion dollars, or $250 per family less. The wide difference is due to the collateral

effect on employment in the durable-goods industries, brought about by the sharply deflationary effect of the debt retirement at a suicidal rate.[27]

The forecast of a recession was convenient for the proponents of the tax cut. But the forecast was not fabricated for their convenience. There were numerous signs throughout 1947 and 1948 that the inflationary pressure was abating and might be followed by an economic downturn. In a peculiar way the prediction that the end of price control would also end the inflation turned out to be correct. The country ended inflation by having it. With price ceilings abolished, the inflationary pressure boosted prices sharply in the second half of 1946. The price rise in turn dampened the inflationary pressure in three ways. First there was a general expectation, based on experience after World War I as well as on contemporary analysis, that if prices went up they would come down, and the more they went up the more they were expected to come down. This led to a certain caution in purchases by consumers and businesses as prices rose. Second, the rise in prices diminished the purchasing power of the huge volume of money and government securities that the war had left in the hands of individuals and businesses, and made them less free to spend. Third, the rise of prices, as we have seen, inflated incomes, profits, and tax revenues, resulting in a large budget surplus which meant that private incomes after taxes rose less than output. After the beginning of 1947 the rate of price increase slowed down, and the pressures making for further price increases diminished. In February, 1948, a sharp break in the markets for agricultural products intensified fears of a general downturn. In November, six months after rates of income tax withholding were cut by the 1948 tax reduction, the recession of 1948–49 began. Later there was to be a common belief that the cut was timely and helped to keep the recession moderate.

While it was being debated and for months after it was enacted, the standard view of economists was that the tax cut was a mistake. "At the time nobody who analyzed the situation in terms of compensatory fiscal policy had a good word to say for the Revenue Act."[28] Later, after the recession came, the standard view was that the tax-cutters had been lucky —luckier than they deserved. Thus, reviewing the tax-cut episode, E. Cary Brown said: "The period ended with correct action taken for incorrect reasons: tax reduction to cure an inflation. Since the inflation had almost ceased to exist, this action turned out relatively satisfactorily."[29] The image of Republicans and conservatives as being unconcerned about recessions and unemployment is so strong that they are disbelieved even when they not only talk, but also act, as if they are strongly concerned. Thus one economist reviewing the period said:

When it is noted that of the seven Republican members of the Finance Committee Taft and Millikin were the farthest "Left" by most standards, it is hard to take at its face value the argument about the desirability of a tax cut to prevent a recession that might happen in the future.[30]

Whether Congress was really concerned about a coming recession is impossible to tell at this date. Certainly a majority of the Congress was for a tax cut before the recession issue arose. But we do not know whether they would have continued to maintain this position if the economy had been unequivocally inflationary, or whether in that case they would have been able to acquire the additional votes needed to override the Presidential veto. It is significant, however, that the possibility of a recession was considered by the Congress to be an argument *for* a tax cut rather than against it, even though there was general awareness that a recession would reduce the revenues.[31]

A more serious lesson of the 1947–48 experience than the extent to which the Republicans of that time knew what was later called "the new economics" is the great difficulty of managing a compensatory fiscal policy. Even if all participants in the decision had been single-mindedly devoted to the use of fiscal policy to stabilize the economy, there would have been wide disagreement about what to do in the light of the uncertainties of the economic situation. Whether the outcome in that case would have been better than the outcome of the mixed economic-political considerations that dominated the decision is hard to say. The political situation of 1947–48, with a Democratic President and a Republican Congress, was unusual and served to delay the tax cut just long enough, but not too long, so that the experience does not tell us anything about the general effects of tempering economic analysis with politics.[32] Certainly it is not evidence that the deficiencies of economic forecasting will ordinarily be repaired by politics. But the experience tended to confirm the opinion already created by the errors of earlier forecasts of a great postwar depression, that forecasting was a weak reed.

Another lesson of the experience, which required more time to appreciate, was that fiscal policy was being overburdened. Fiscal policy was expected to stabilize aggregate demand in the face of a current inflation and a prospective recession, while avoiding tax rates so high as to weaken incentives seriously and keeping budgetary pressure on expenditure decisions. This was too much to expect of fiscal policy. The reason fiscal policy had to bear this great burden was the failure even to consider the use of monetary policy as a supplement to budget policy. The government, and the country generally, were committed to continuing the wartime policy of supporting the prices of government securities at par, if necessary by having the Federal Reserve purchase them with newly-created reserves which added to the expansion power of the banks. Thus it was not possible to relieve budget decisions of some of the responsibility for restraining inflation by transferring some of that responsibility to monetary policy, which would have freed budget policy to give more weight to other objectives.

Experience with the tax cut also taught another lesson—a political lesson with important economic implications. It showed that tax reduction is politically touchy and does not always benefit the party that gives it. Presumably everyone would like to have his own taxes reduced. But everyone also wants his own tax reduction to be fair in relation to the tax reduction received by others. And if everyone is his own judge of his deserts, it is quite possible for every beneficiary of a tax reduction to feel that he was unfairly treated and to be resentful. Something like that seems to have happened, not to everyone but to a substantial number, in 1948.

An objective view in 1948 would probably have been that the Republicans were being politically astute in pushing the tax cut but economically irresponsible. Certainly there was a widespread opinion at the time that the public wanted a tax cut. For example, before voting in favor of the tax cut Senator Morse delivered a long speech explaining that he felt obliged to represent his constituents' desires in this matter, even though he doubted their wisdom. The public opinion polls showed growing support for a tax cut, although it was not overwhelming. When asked to choose between tax reduction and balancing the budget or reducing the debt the public responded as follows:

	For Tax Reduction	For Balancing Budget	For Debt Reduction	No Opinion
August 14, 1946	20%	71%		9%
November 10, 1946	41%		49%	10%
November 29, 1946				
National total	48%		44%	8%
Income tax payers only	51%		44%	5%
March, 1947	33%	53%		14%
May 30, 1947	38%		53%	9%

In January, 1948, when the poll asked about the desirability of tax reduction in view of the need to give aid to Europe and reduce the national debt, the answer was 51 percent in favor of tax reduction, 36 percent against, and 13 percent with no opinion. In September, after the tax cut was already in effect, 69 percent disagreed with the proposition that taxes had been cut too much and would have to be raised again.[33]

One interpretation of these results is that the public would rather balance the budget than reduce taxes, would rather reduce the debt than reduce taxes (but this preference was less strong), would rather reduce taxes than give aid to Europe and reduce the debt, and didn't want the tax cut taken away once it got one. However, the poll that counted was the Presidential election of November, 1948. In the campaign President Truman made much use of the argument that the Republicans had passed a rich man's tax cut, and this fit in well with the general appeal he offered. How much the tax issue contributed to his victory is impossible to tell. But the victory left considerable uncertainty about the political value of being the author of a tax reduction. This uncertainty operated later as a restraint on tax reduction, weakening both the temptation to use it when it would be economically unwise and the possibility of using it when it would be wise to do so.

The 1948 tax cut came halfway in time between the tax increase of 1932 and the tax reduction of 1964. In one sense the 1948 tax cut looks more like the 1932 tax increase than like the 1964 tax cut. In 1932 taxes were raised during a depression and in 1948 taxes were cut during an inflation, whereas the 1964 tax reduction was made during a period of excessive unemployment, if not exactly a recession or depression. Thus, both the 1932 action and the 1948 action seem to violate the modern compensatory principles applied in 1964. Yet, in a more fundamental sense the 1948 action, and certainly the 1948 talk, was much closer to 1964 than to 1932. The 1948 tax cut was accompanied by forecasts of recession. The tax cutters of 1948 may have been for tax reduction whatever the economic outlook; they were certainly not for increasing taxes in a recession. The 1948 discussion foreshadowed the 1964 idea that the budget surplus could be too big—could be a drag on economic growth. The action of 1948 as well as that of 1964 showed a willingness to subordinate immediate debt reduction to economic growth, with claims in both cases that the result would be more debt reduction in the long run. Of course, there were differences also, and we still have to tell the story of the rest of the road to 1964, but the country had clearly come a long way from 1932.

THE DEVELOPMENT OF PLANS FOR FISCAL POLICY—CED

While Congress and the President were fighting out the tax-cut issues with blunt instruments, new concepts for thinking about fiscal policy and new principles for making decisions were being developed outside the government. A leading role in this development was played by the Committee for Economic Development, an organization of businessmen of which Beardsley Ruml was a key member. Essentially the CED elaborated the ideas which Ruml had put forth during the war, stating them more precisely that he had done, spelling out their implications for objectives other than economic stability, and relating them to other economic policies, notably monetary policy and debt management.

CED's basic statement on fiscal policy, *Taxes and the Budget*, was published in November, 1947.[34] When first conceived in the fall of 1946 the statement was not intended to be about fiscal policy. It was supposed to recommend a desirable tax structure for the federal government in some future, normal peacetime year which was designated 195X to indicate that it would come at an unspecified time in the 1950s. The fiscal policy evolved from the effort to answer the apparently simple question, "How high do tax rates have to be in that year?"

One element in the answer to that question seemed clearly to be the rate of federal expenditure in 195X. Estimating this was difficult and could not be done with much confidence, but it raised no serious question of principle. However, this number alone did not tell how high tax rates would have to be. The amount of revenue required would depend not only on the expenditures but also on the surplus (or deficit) that was needed or desired. The tax rates needed to yield the required revenue would depend upon the rate of national income. So it was necessary to specify two things in addition to the rate of expenditure—the surplus and the national income.

The committee had made a beginning towards specifying these things in the 1944 statement which was quoted in the previous chapter:

> The Committee deems it wise that the tax structure and the budget should be so drawn as to make possible substantial reduction of the federal debt at a high level of employment. As much debt should then be retired as is consistent with maintaining high levels of employment and production.[35]

How much surplus this meant is a question which may be deferred for the moment. However, it clearly meant that tax rates should be set so that in a year of high employment there would be some surplus of revenues over expenditures. But what if 195X, or some other year, were not a year of high employment? Should tax rates be higher in a year of low employment and lower in a year of inflationary boom in order to yield the desired revenue? The committee rejected this idea for two reasons. First, many members were deeply impressed with the need for tax rates to be stable, so that businesses could plan their operations with confidence. Second, the idea of higher tax rates in a recession and lower tax rates in an inflationary boom

⁀eemed obviously ridiculous from the standpoint of economic stability. By 1947 no sophisticated analysis was required to show that; it was simply common sense.

At this point in its reasoning, the committee had abandoned any idea of balancing the budget annually. It was prepared to accept deficits in recessions rather than raise taxes. The question then arose whether it should go further than just holding taxes stable in a recession and accepting the deficit that would result. Should taxes be cut and expenditures increased in a recession to provide a stronger boost towards high employment? The committee also answered this question in the negative. One reason for this was again the strong concern of the businessmen with stable tax rates as a condition for business planning. But a second, and probably stronger reason, was a profound skepticism about the stabilizing effect of changes in tax rates and expenditures. All experience seemed to show that, even with substantial advance planning, expenditures could not be increased quickly and usually could not be stopped quickly without much waste. While in principle tax rates could be lowered or raised more promptly, in fact the decision-making process in a political environment was likely to make this a pretty sluggish instrument also. Therefore, if the tax and expenditure changes were to be well adapted to short and moderate economic fluctuations, accurate forecasts of such fluctuations would be needed.

The committee did not believe that forecasts of the necessary accuracy could be expected. The experience of the gross errors in forecasting postwar unemployment was still fresh in their minds. The committee was particularly skeptical about the accuracy of forecasts that would be made by government officials. Such officials were assumed always to prefer higher expenditures and lower taxes. If forecasts of unemployment and economic sluggishness would justify raising expenditures and cutting taxes, the political process was likely to generate such forecasts. (Congressional reliance upon convenient economic forecasts to justify a tax cut in 1947 seemed to be a case in point). The political forecasts would be subject not to random error but to persistant inflationary bias.

Essentially because of the forecasting problems the committee concluded that in general its policy of keeping tax rates at a level where they would yield a moderate surplus at high employment would be more stabilizing than what it called the "managed, compensatory policy."[36] Moreover, the committee believed that its policy would yield a *satisfactory* degree of stability. First, the committee judged that the economy would have a high degree of "natural" stability, resulting from the great strengthening of the financial system as compared with, say, 1929, the bulwarks being provided by unemployment compensation and farm programs and the automatic variations of tax revenues that would result from their budget policy. Second, while the committee was in general opposed to discretionary changes in budget policy, it expected and welcomed discretionary flexibility in monetary policy, which it thought would make a major contribution to stability.[37] It was willing to accept discretion in monetary policy which would not accept in budget policy because it considered monetary policy the quicker-acting instrument and therefore less dependent upon forecasting, and because it had more faith in the objectivity of the Federal Reserve than in the administration and the Congress. Third, the committee regarded the stability problem as one of preventing severe fluctuations and moderating but not eliminating lesser ones. In some discussions the CED referred to the positive benefits of small fluctuations which would weed out inefficiency on the downside and stimulate risk-taking on the upside.

However, the committee was not prepared to say that budgetary action beyond its basic policy would *never* be necessary. It recognized the possibility, at least on paper, of deflationary or inflationary forces so strong that they would overwhelm the resistance of the built-in budget stabilizers and a flexible monetary policy. In such a case an emergency change of tax rates, and possibly also of expenditure programs, would be justified. However, such conditions were expected to be rare, and it is symptomatic of the committee's thinking that it did not find the necessary conditions actually to exist at any time in the twenty years after the statement was issued.

The rationale of the CED budget policy was not entirely its expected stabilizing effects. We have already noted the heavy weight the committee gave to constancy of tax rates. Two other objectives were also important in its decisions. These were traditional conservative objectives—to exert discipline over expenditures by requiring them to be paid for by taxes, and to reduce the debt. On both scores the committee concluded and argued that the policy it recommended was superior to trying to balance the budget annually. The committee did not believe that the budget would be balanced in depressions, whatever the policy. Annual balancing in practice would only mean balancing in booms when revenue was ample and in those circumstances would permit dissipation of possible surpluses and expenditure increases without tax increases. The "frightening possibility" the committee visualized was oscillation between compensatory policy in depressions and budget-balancing in prosperity, with expenditure increases in both conditions and budget surpluses in neither. Contrary to annual balancing, the CED's policy would require that the extraordinary revenues generated by booms be retained to reduce the debt and not used for increased expenditures.

The greatest difficulty the committee met in its deliberations was the decision on the size of the surplus to be realized at high employment. The stabilizing effect of the policy did not depend upon this figure. Whatever the high employment surplus, if tax rates and expenditure programs were held constant the surplus would be larger the higher was the level of economic activity and prices, and the surplus would be smaller—or deficit larger—the lower the level of the economy. These variations in the size of the surplus that automatically accompanied variations in the level of economic activity would tend to damp economic fluctuations, and would do so regardless of the level of the surplus at high employment. Thus, if tax rates were set to yield a zero surplus at high employment and stable prices, a certain range of economic fluctuations might vary the surplus from minus $10 billion to plus $10 billion, whereas if the tax rates were set to yield a $10 billion surplus at high employment the same range of economic fluctuations would vary the surplus from approximately zero to $20 billion. The stabilizing effect would be much the same. However, the decision on the size of the high employment surplus was thought to affect the *average* level of economic activity and the average amount of debt reduction actually achieved. It tax rates were set, to take an extreme example, so that there would be a surplus of $50 billion at high employment, achievement of high employment would be difficult, if not impossible—or at least so the committee believed. Private individuals and businesses would be left after paying taxes with incomes so small that they would not buy the output that would be available for private purchase under conditions of high employment. In that case high employment would not be reached, and the big surplus would not actually be realized. At the other extreme, if tax rates were set so that there would be a deficit of $50 billion at high employment, it would—in the committee's opinion—be difficult, if not impossible, to prevent inflation.

So the problem was to choose a high-employment surplus that would be compatible with the actual achievement of high employment and price stability. In the committee's opinion, there was not only one such surplus figure. Although some surpluses might be too high, and some deficits might be too high, there was a range within which any surplus or deficit would be compatible with high employment and price stability on the average, or could be made compatible. How much surplus the economy could stand and still get high employment, or would require in order to prevent inflation, would depend upon other policies the government was following. A tax structure that would encourage private investment, expansive monetary and debt management policies, and measures to improve the flow of savings into investment would all tend to raise the size of the surplus that was compatible with high employment. Therefore the committee had a choice between bigger and smaller high employment surpluses, each choice implying something about the other policies needed to maintain high employment and price stability.

There was some difference of opinion within the committee about this choice. Some wanted a high surplus figure because debt reduction was important to them. Some wanted a low or zero surplus figure for a combination of two reasons. First, they regarded maintenance of high employment as the chief problem and did not want to put too much strain on other measures to maintain high employment in the face of a big budget surplus. Second, they were reluctant to recommend the high tax rates that would be necessary to yield a big surplus. However, the main problem was less the difference between firmly-held positions than the weakness of all positions. The American economy has not operated under normal peacetime conditions for almost twenty years, and no one could have any very reliable opinion about the effects of the size of the budget surplus in the postwar world.

In the end, the issue was resolved on essentially pragmatic and expedient grounds. The committee had decided to recommend that the budget to look at for making fiscal policy decisions should be the cash-consolidated budget, which differed from the administrative budget more commonly used in that the cash-consolidated budget included the social security and unemployment compensation trust funds. In 1947 when the committee was working on its statement, the surplus in the cash-consolidated budget appeared normally to be about $3 billion larger than the surplus in the administrative budget. Thus, if there were a cash surplus of less than $3 billion there would be a deficit in the administrative budget. The committee did not want to be exposed to the charge that, along with other heresies, it had introduced a new definition of the budget in order to conceal a recommendation for a deficit in what most people regarded as the true budget. Therefore the committee could not recommend a surplus of less than $3 billion in the cash-consolidated budget. This proved to be the figure on which the low-surplus people and the high-surplus people could agree.

The operational significance of the recommendation that taxes be set to yield a $3 billion surplus at high employment depended on the definition of "high employment." To get a $3 billion surplus with five percent of the labor force unemployed would require much higher tax rates and would exert more deflationary pressure on the the economy than to get a $3 billion surplus at, say, 3 percent unemployment. The committee defined high employment as a condition in which 96 percent of the labor force was employed and 4 percent unemployed. At the time the committee was writing, actual unemployment was less than 4 percent, but there was also substantial inflation. The committee concluded, on the basis of the slight evidence then available, that unemployment could not be much below 4 percent without inflation, and that therefore to plan to get the surplus at an unemployment rate below 4 percent would be to plan for a surplus only under conditions which it should be public policy to prevent. On the other hand, to plan for a surplus at an unemployment rate significantly above 4 percent would be to place unnecessary obstacles in the way of achieving a feasible high rate of employment.

The committee pointed out that if taxes were high enough to yield a surplus of $3 billion at unemployment of 4 percent they would yield a balanced budget at unemployment of around 6 percent. However it preferred to state its recommendation as a $3 billion surplus at 4 percent unemployment rather than as a balanced budget at 6 percent unemployment, because it wanted to show that the objective of monetary policy, debt management, and other measures should be to achieve the surplus *and* the higher level of employment.

These numbers were a shot in the dark at the time, and the committee regarded them as tentative. It pointed out that they might have to be changed in the light of experience under the plan. The basic recommendation was not these particular numbers but the general principle:

> Set tax rates to balance the budget and provide a surplus for debt retirement at an agreed high level of employment and national income. Having set these rates, leave them alone unless there is some major change in national policy or condition of national life.[38]

The important point was that the relation between revenues and expenditures as they would be at some specified rate of national income should be kept stable in the absence of major and presumably durable changes in conditions. This relation should not be changed in response to forecast short-run fluctuations of the economy, or even in response to actual fluctuations unless they were major ones. The provision for a possible change in the high-employment surplus if there should be a "major change in national policy or condition of national life" was a suggestion of B. Ruml. One possible change in the condition of national life that he envisaged was the onset of secular stagnation which would make it unwise to try to generate a budget surplus at high employment. He was not forecasting that this would occur, but wanted to leave room for the possibility. However, this was not the only conceivable change in the condition of national life which would justify a change in the standard surplus. In fact, three years after it recommended the $3 billion surplus standard, the CED shifted to recommending an even balance in the budget. It did this on the ground that with the high level of defense expenditures required after the Korean War broke out, tax rates high enough to yield a surplus would be too high for the health of the economy.

CED's 1947 statement profoundly influenced fiscal discussion, fiscal thinking, and fiscal policy in the two decades that followed it. Its influence stemmed partly from what it said, partly from who said it, and partly from the continuing effort of CED to promote understanding of the policy in the economic conditions that unfolded.

One effect of the CED statement was to drive one more nail into the coffin of the idea of balancing the budget annually. Of course, this coffin was already pretty well nailed down, and there was no likelihood that serious efforts would be made to balance the budget in a depression. Yet the idea remained the standard doctrine of the organizations that spoke for business and for many of their members, and this would be an inhibition, although perhaps not a major one, on fiscal policy. The CED statement was a repudiation of the idea by a group of leading businessmen, whose soundness might be questioned by the *Wall Street Journal* or the NAM, but not by the public at large or by most public officials. Moreover, the CED rejected annual budget balancing on conservative grounds, that is, on the grounds of its effects on debt reduction and expenditure control, as well as on the more modern standard of short-run economic stability.

This did not mean that there was no longer a conservative position on fiscal policy. It meant that the conservative position had to be based on something more than ritualistic repetition of the balanced budget formula. Preference for low expenditures and low taxes, great concern about inflation and about the balance of payments, and the desire for a budget surplus to reduce the public debt and allow more funds to flow into private investment supplied the foundations for a conservative view of fiscal policy which continues to be expressed. But this did bring the conservatives into the discussion of the same kinds of economic processes and objectives that the liberals were also talking about, although possibly with different values.

At the same time the CED statement was a challenge to the liberals and orthodox Keynesians on fiscal policy. Since the statement came from a group with some standing in the country who had learned the Keynesian analysis and who had accepted the high employment objective, they could not disregard it. The basic challenge was to the idea that fiscal policy could and must consist of annual or even more frequent adaptations of tax rates and expenditure programs to fill a forecast deflationary or inflationary gap.

The first response of the proponents of the new fiscal policy was to welcome the CED statement as a sign that the business community was moving in their direction, especially in throwing over the idea of annual budget-balancing. But they could not accept the limitations on fiscal policy implied by the CED rule. They believed that the CED rule required policy-makers to disregard a valuable piece of information—the short-run economic forecast—and that CED had underrated the actual or potential reliability of such forecasts. This was the main point of an appraisal of the CED proposal written by Walter Heller in 1957, and he was representative of many others.[39] Paul Samuelson criticized what he considered the implied assumption of the CED plan that the proper level of public spending does not depend upon the intensity of private demand and that public spending should therefore be kept stable through economic fluctuations.[40] However, even economists who would not accept the CED position in principle were led by it, as well as by experience, to pay more attention to the practical problems of managing a compensatory policy. This emphasized the need to strengthen built-in stabilizers, to seek more flexible adjustment of tax rates, and to supplement fiscal policy with monetary policy.

The CED statement did not have the same kind of effect upon "managed compensatory policy" as it did upon "annual balance policy." In fact, while the CED statement is written with evenhanded rejection of both of these alternatives, the CED had accepted a measure of managed compensation in providing for departures from its rule in deep depressions and steep inflations.[41] In a 1954 reiteration of its policy, CED moderated the rigor with which it defined these exceptional circumstances. The CED position did not, and could not, prevent governments from looking at current economic conditions and short-term forecasts in making fiscal decisions. When it subsequently applied its principles from year to year, CED did not itself eschew such a look. The main import of CED's position was that this look would often be inconclusive about what fiscal policy should be followed. Its advice was that in such circumstances it would ordinarily be reasonably safe to avoid radical change in the relation between revenues and expenditures, and preferably to aim at a balanced budget or moderate surplus at high employment. Such advice had attraction for practical policy-makers seeking to avoid major errors and burdensome responsibilities in managing a large budget in an uncertain world but wishing freedom to act when they found action necessary.

In addition to the "marriage" of compensatory fiscal policy with automatic stabilization and the synthesis of the new stabilization goal with the old budget discipline goal, CED's statement made a number of more specific contributions to postwar thinking and action.

1. CED elaborated, explained, and promoted the idea of the high-employment budget, that is, the measurement of the budget position by what the revenues and expenditures *would be* at high employment rather than by what they were under the actual economic conditions or would be under forecast economic conditions. This concept turned out to be extremely useful for thinking about fiscal policy in a system where the actual budget results depended so heavily on the state of the economy. It permitted a distinction between variations in the revenues and expenditures that resulted from variations in the state of the economy and those that resulted from changes of policy. High employment was the standard condition at which the budget position should be measured, just as sea level was the standard condition at which the boiling point of liquids should be measured. Generally speaking, a decline in the high employment surplus meant that the budget was becoming less restrictive, in the sense that if other economic conditions were stable the budget would be pushing the economy in the direction of expansion. On the other hand, a decline of the actual surplus, if the high employment surplus was constant, would not mean that the budget was becoming less restrictive, but only that the budget was responding to a decline in the economy. In fact, it would be possible for the budget to be exerting a deflationary force while the deficit was rising. This would happen if the government raised tax rates during a depression which was at the same time reducing incomes and tax revenues.

CED's 1947 statement recommended that the President's annual budget message should present estimates of revenues and expenditures as they would be at high employment. Although this was not done, CED itself made such estimates from time to time and the concept was gradually adopted by others, especially after 1960. As we shall see, the high-employment budget was an important element in the discussions leading up to the 1964 tax cut. The fact that the high-employment surplus had risen to a large figure in the early 1960s was used to show that the budget was exerting a depressive influence upon the economy, despite the presence of an actual deficit. Estimates that the tax cut would still leave the high-employment budget in balance were used to allay fears about cutting taxes in the face of a deficit.

2. The CED statement was an attempt to adapt fiscal policy to the needs of an economy that was not only somewhat unstable but also growing. "An essential condition for high employment and stable prices is reasonable stability of total demand at an adequate level—which means a steadily rising level of demand as our productive capacity grows."[42] The high employment level of national income at which the standard surplus was to be achieved was a growing national income. The condition under which

the CED policy would result in an actual surplus smaller that the standard, or an actual deficit, was a condition in which the national income was below this growing high employment level. This did not necessarily mean that the actual national income was declining. It might only mean that the actual national income was rising less rapidly than its potential. The CED policy would provide resistance to a lag of actual growth behind the potential by generating a deficit which would increase as the lag increased, whether or not the lag took the form of an absolute decline in the economy.

This view of the stabilization problem as one of stabilizing around an adequately rising trend was obvious as soon as growth was recognized to be the necessary condition for high employment. CED was not alone in making this point. For example, Leon Keyserling as chairman of the Council of Economic Advisers from 1949 to early 1953 was particularly vigorous in advocating it. But many people, particularly older businessmen whose ideas were formed during the Depression, were slow to see it, and CED's adoption helped to advance its general acceptance. This was to be important in 1962 and 1963 when stimulative measures were being proposed because the economy was far below its potential, even though it was above all previous peaks in total output and employment.

3. The CED called attention to the fact that with stable tax rates economic growth would cause rising federal revenues. Some growth of federal expenditures might also be expected as national income and population increased. In addition, the size of the standard surplus, originally set at $3 billion, should perhaps rise as the national income grew. However, this still left the prospect that a gradual reduction of tax rates would be possible, and indeed necessary if an excessive surplus was to be avoided. This idea was the core of the notion of the "fiscal dividend" which was to be much talked about in the 1960s.[43]

4. CED's 1947 statement was one of the first to recommend that the cash-consolidated budget, rather than the better-known administrative budget, should be used as the guide to budget policy, and that the country should be looking at the cash-consolidated budget when it considered whether the budget was in balance or not. CED did not invent the cash-consolidated budget. Its most important feature, the consolidation of the trust accounts with other accounts, was already incorporated in Currie's figures on income-increasing expenditures in 1935. The modern form of the cash-consolidated budget was developed by Grover Ensley at the Budget Bureau during the war, and figures on that basis were regularly shown in the budget message and in the economic report thereafter. But these figures were still only auxiliary information, and when the President, Congressmen,

and others talked about the budget surplus or deficit, they were talking about the administrative budget. CED's 1947 recommendation, and the committee's subsequent application of the recommendation to arising budgetary questions, encouraged use of the cash-consolidated budget as a guide to policy. It never succeeded in making the cash-consolidated budget *the* guide to policy. The administrative budget remained, for most purposes and occasions, the budget. But the cash-consolidated budget remained in reserve, ready to be called upon when needed. Especially when the administrative budget showed a deficit it would be convenient to refer to the cash-consolidated budget, which almost always showed a better picture, i.e., a smaller deficit or a surplus. Later, around 1960, a third budget came into use. This was the statement of federal receipts and expenditures as shown in the national income accounts. It differed from the cash budget primarily in reporting corporate profits taxes when the liability accrued rather than when payments were made to the Treasury and in excluding government loan transactions. This did not supplant the other two budgets but was used along with them.

The availability of alternative forms of the budget tended to hold before policy-makers in the government a more complete and multi-dimensional picture of what they were doing in fiscal policy, revealing their policy from several angles. At the same time, the existence of three budgets gave the administration a certain added freedom of action in making fiscal policy. The ability to choose which budget it would emphasize in presenting its policy to the public widened the range of policies from which the administration could choose without rousing public concern over a deficit. A preferred policy which showed a deficit on one account might show a surplus on another. In other cases, a preferred policy which would show a large surplus on one budget, and thereby invite tax reductions or expenditure increases which the administration did not want, would not show so large a surplus on another budget. This game of choosing the budget to look at could be played by others as well as by the administration, but the administration had the advantage, at least for a while, that its form of presentation received most publicity and tended to be accepted as "the" budget.

By 1967 the game had become so confusing and confidence in the significance of any budget figures had fallen so low that no one was gaining from it, and a new start was necessary. The President then appointed a commission to study the definition of the budget. The commission issued a report which recommended that attention be concentrated on a new budget with two main parts, combining features of the cash-consolidated budget and the national income accounts.[44] This recommendation was largely applied in the January, 1968, budget message.

5. CED's statements, beginning in 1947, helped to popularize the idea of using tax rates as the chief, although not the only, variable for adjusting the relations between revenues and expenditures. In this, CED was carrying forward the position urged by Ruml and others earlier, in opposition to the emphasis placed by the earlier Keynesians on expenditure as the key variable. CED was somewhat inhibited in urging use of the tax instrument for several reasons. First, and especially in the early days, it was strongly devoted to stability of tax rates. Second, it did not want to take positive fiscal action of any kind, either on the tax side or on the expenditure side, to counter economic fluctuations unless the fluctuations were severe. Third, the committee always had a preference for lower, rather than higher, expenditures and taxes. So if the question was how to eliminate a deficit or increase a surplus, the committee was always in favor of expenditure reduction or restraint first, and higher taxes only as a last resort. Nevertheless, CED's repeated emphasis on taxation as the variable instrument of fiscal policy contributed to the general acceptance of the idea, including its acceptance by people who were less restricted in their approach to budget policy than was CED.

6. The CED statements, especially the statement of 1948,[45] helped to establish the idea of fiscal policy and monetary policy as complementary instruments. CED regarded the stabilization problem as a problem for fiscal and monetary policy together. Its rule of fiscal policy was a prescription for the division of labor between fiscal and monetary policy. That is, the definition of what fiscal policy was to do was also a definition of what monetary policy was to do. Simply stated, given the recommended fiscal policy, monetary policy was to do everything it could to maintain high employment without inflation. The division of labor between the two policies was determined by the committee's desire for some debt reduction and by its views of the superior flexibility and political integrity of monetary policy. Monetary policy had to be sufficiently expansive to achieve high employment in the face of a surplus; it had to be sufficiently flexible to cope with economic fluctuations in the face of a budget policy which would contribute only the results of the built-in stabilizers.

The common reaction of economists to the early statements of CED was that the budget policy, while a step in advance of usual business thinking, was inadequate to the stabilization problem. This view resulted in part from failure to recognize the heavy reliance the CED position placed on monetary policy as a supplement to fiscal policy, or from unwillingness to believe that monetary policy could bear the burden. However, experience and further debate led to generally renewed appreciation of the potentialities of monetary policy and of the value of being able to combine fiscal and monetary policy in variable proportions in view of the variety of objectives to be served.

OTHER PLANS FOR FISCAL POLICY

In the two years following the publication of CED's 1947 statement several other plans for fiscal policy were proposed and contributed to the emergence of the postwar consensus. These plans all wrestled with the same problems that had concerned CED. They were all attempts to use fiscal policy for economic stabilization while recognizing that there were other objectives in addition to stabilization, that economic forecasting was imperfect, and that the flexibility of fiscal policy was limited. While their proposals differed in some respects from those of CED, they were all in the same area, as contrasted with the idea of annual budget balancing and with the idea of continuously managed fiscal compensation. They all emphasized the need in general to tie decisions to raise expenditures to decisions to raise taxes in order to exercise some discipline over spending. They all wanted to assure that the built-in stabilizers were allowed to work. They all wanted to supplement fiscal policy with monetary policy. And all, in varying degrees, wanted to limit discretionary fiscal action to deal with fluctuations.

The first of these proposals was formulated by Professor Milton Friedman of the University of Chicago in 1947 at the same time the CED plan was being developed, but independently of it, and was published in June, 1948.[46] Friedman proposed that tax rates should be set so as to balance the budget or yield a specified deficit at reasonably full employment and at a predetermined price level. Monetary policy should be so arranged, either by an automatic mechanism or by instruction to the Federal Reserve, that the money supply would increase by the amount of the actual deficit or decrease by the amount of the actual surplus. He provided no exception for discretionary fiscal action to cope with economic fluctuations, whether actual or forecast and whatever their degree of severity. The actual size of the deficit or surplus would depend upon the actual level of economic activity and so, under his monetary rule, would the rate of growth of the money supply.

Friedman's difference from CED was mainly the result of his going even farther than the committee in mistrusting discretionary policy based, as it inevitably would be, on economic forecasts. CED's willingness to cut taxes in a deep depression and raise taxes in a sharp inflation reflected a belief that in such circumstances it was safer to act as if the existing situation would otherwise continue than as if the future were completely unknown. Friedman did not accept this presumption. Moreover, unlike the CED which was willing to trust the Federal Reserve to operate flexibly on the basis of forecasts, Friedman had no more confidence in the forecasts of the monetary authority than in those of the President and the Congress. Therefore he wanted to bind monetary policy by a tight rule also. A secondary difference between CED and Friedman was that the committee regarded a budget surplus as an important objective, whereas Friedman's policy was not designed to achieve a surplus. This was necessitated by Friedman's monetary rule. CED could recommend tax rates high enough to yield a surplus at a specified level of national income and at the same time recommend a monetary policy that would bring about the specified national income and thereby make the surplus an actuality. Friedman's monetary policy was determined by the size of the surplus, and if the national income did not turn out to be high enough to yield a surplus he could not call for a more expansive monetary policy to achieve the surplus.

In 1949 a group of sixteen economists assembled by the National Planning Association formulated a plan for fiscal policy which was also similar to CED's but which opted for more discretion while Friedman had opted for none.[47] CED had distinguished between two conditions of the economy. One was a condition of high employment or moderate departures from it, when the budget should be set to yield a moderate surplus. The other condition was one of serious departure from high employment and price stability, when emergency variations of tax rates or expenditure programs would be in order. The economists' group distinguished three kinds of conditions:

1. "When the economy is prosperous and stable and there is no clear-cut reason to expect a change in any particular direction," the impact of the budget should be kept approximately stable at whatever amount of surplus or deficit there is, with taxes being raised or lowered to match increases or decreases of total expenditures. This is essentially like the CED prescription for that condition except that CED specifies that the budget position should be kept stable at a moderate surplus. The economists' formulation avoided a dilemma that has sometimes troubled the CED. If the existing budget position is not such as to yield a moderate surplus at high employment there is an awkward choice between keeping the position stable and achieving the moderate surplus. This problem would not arise if the CED policy were consistently followed, but the CED often found itself having to make recommendations when its policy had not previously been followed.

2. "If recent events and the outlook for the near future pointed, on balance, toward unemployment and deflation," a certain limited amount of discretionary budget action would be appropriate. Additional taxation otherwise called for by rising expenditures should be deferred. If future declines in expenditures are in sight, the tax reductions this would later permit should be anticipated. The reverse policy should be followed in inflation. This goes beyond CED, but only to the extent of deferring or anticipating tax changes that would be required aside from the state of the economy. It introduces

no tax changes that would not otherwise be called for but only changes their timing, presumably in the expectation that errors, if any, can later be corrected.

3. "Where there is a definite expectation, justified by events, of serious recession or inflation," emergency fiscal action with respect to taxes or expenditures or both is appropriate. This is essentially the CED position, with due allowance for possible differences in the interpretation of "serious" and "justified by events."

The economists also recommended that the fiscal policy be supplemented by appropriate monetary policy but did not spell out the meaning of that or how much they relied upon it.

The economists differed from CED mainly in identifying an intermediate case where a limited amount of discretionary action could be taken, without adding in the long run to the variability of tax rates, by anticipating or deferring tax changes that would otherwise be necessary. But they agreed with CED in their emphasis on tying expenditure decisions and tax decisions together for the sake of expenditure control, in their conservatism about reliance on forecasts, and in the limited amount of action they recommended to deal with moderate fluctuations.

In the fall of 1949 a full-dress examination of fiscal and monetary policies was made by a subcommittee of the Joint Committee on the Economic Report under the chairmanship of Senator Paul H. Douglas, formerly a professor of economics at the University of Chicago. Written statements were submitted by large numbers of government officials, bankers, businessmen, leaders of labor and agriculture, and economists. Many of these people were also heard in open meetings of the subcommittee. With respect to fiscal policy the government witnesses were noncommittal, unwilling to say anything except that they would do their best at all times in the light of emerging circumstances.

The following exchange between Congressman Wolcott and Secretary Snyder illustrates the position:

> WOLCOTT: I think we should find out from the Secretary whether the Treasury has any program to offset a recession or depression or other adjustment periods.
> SYNDER: What sort of program?
> WOLCOTT: That is what I want to know.
> SNYDER: That is a pretty broad question.
> WOLCOTT: Put it this way: Have you outlined what the Treasury should do to offset a depression?
> SNYDER: You mean in the management of the debt? Is that what you have in mind?

WOLCOTT: In all the fields over which you exercise an influence.

SNYDER: We will certainly attempt in any fashion we can to adjust our policy to the condition of the times. As for having any direct program that we are going to take a certain step at a certain time, we will have to do that in consultation with other agencies because the Treasury alone does not have a great deal of control over conditions of that sort. And, as far as the taxing is concerned, that is a matter in the hands of Congress. And that, of course, is one of the biggest factors that can be used that we are connected with—the taxing program of any given year—and that is a matter, of course, that is in the hands of Congress. We can make recommendations but the Congress makes the decisions and makes the actual tax legislation.

WOLCOTT: Would you suggest that taxes be raised in periods of depression or recession?

SNYDER: Be raised in periods of recession?

WOLCOTT: Yes; if it is necessary to balance the budget.

SNYDER: Well, I think those are matters that certainly have to be decided, taking into consideration the conditions of the times. And if raising taxes is going to drive us into a deeper period of recession, we would have to give it full consideration at that time, and consider the interests of the public.[48]

From some of the business and banking witnesses there came the last flickerings of the theology of the annually balanced budget. The only suggestions that looked like a reasonably realistic and reasonably specific program were presented by the CED and the NPA Economists Conference, supported by some other economists and a few bankers.

The subcommittee's own recommendations on fiscal policy were an amalgam of the positions taken by the CED and by the NPA Economists Conference.[49] Following closely the CED's arguments about fiscal discipline, the difficulties of forecasting, and the limited flexibility of fiscal policy, it offered a three-level recommendation:

1. "The revenue-expenditure system should be so designed that in normal periods—periods when unemployment is at or near its practical minimum, when price levels are relatively stable, and when there is no clear-cut and convincing reason to expect a change in any particular direction—then Federal revenues should not only equal expenditures but should show a small surplus to permit a slow reduction of the national debt."[50] This prescription of a small surplus is in line with the CED position.

2. As an exception to this general principle, "a planned increase of expenditures should not be offset by a planned increase of revenues if there is clear and convincing evidence that the near future will be characterized by deflation and unemployment so that an injection of a net expansionary influence would be desirable."[51] That is, an increase of taxes that would other-

wise be called for by an increase of expenditures should not be made in these circumstances. Conversely, in inflationary circumstances a decrease of taxes that might otherwise be called for by a decrease of expenditures should not be made. In this recommendation the Douglas committee accepted half of the NPA economists' suggestion for the intermediate economic conditions— deferring tax changes but not anticipating them. However, recognizing the generally cautionary position represented by the CED, the Douglas committee added this caveat: "But, because of the natural human tendency to favor tax reductions and to oppose tax increases, the presumption should be strongly in favor of abiding by the general principle."[52]

3. "Though automatic flexibility probably represents the maximum extent to which fiscal policy should be employed to combat moderate economic fluctuations, it is almost certain to be inadequate in the face of serious depression or inflation. In the event of such a serious depression or inflation, automatic flexibility should be supplemented by countercyclical changes in tax rates, expenditure programs, or both."[53] This recommendation was common to both the CED and the NPA economists.

The Douglas subcommittee had only five members, and while they agreed unanimously on the fiscal recommendations of the report, these recommendations do not have the status of a formal declaration of the sense of the Congress. Nevertheless, subsequent discussion and, even more, subsequent policy show that these recommendations, and the recommendations of the CED and of the NPA economists from which they were derived, were a reasonable representation of the national fiscal policy then and for some time later. This policy was based on three main beliefs:

1. It is necessary to cling to some form of balanced budget rule, not necessarily because of its intrinsic merits but because it is the only available anchor against a drift of the budget whose ultimate direction and distance, under the play of political forces, would be otherwise unforeseeable.

2. Short-range economic forecasting is hazardous, especially when forecasts are to be made in the political process, and policy should be based on it only with great caution.

3. Nevertheless, while these limiting considerations are recognized, fiscal policy can and should contribute to economic stability and high employment.

In line with these beliefs, when the economy is in a "normal prosperous stable" condition, the government will try to stay in the neighborhood of balance in "the" budget. The neighborhood is not a point of zero surplus, but a range from zero to a few billion dollars of surplus, and the range is further widened by the availability of three somewhat different definitions of "the" budget. When the economy is moderately away from prosperous

stable conditions, deficits, or large surpluses if the departure is on the inflationary side, should be accepted while retaining tax rates and expenditure
programs that would put the budget in the right neighborhood if the economy were prosperous and stable. This does not rule out temporary deferrals
or anticipations of some action called for by the general rule. In extreme
conditions it would be necessary and desirable to take stronger fiscal action.

While the government did not contribute to the discussion which led to
the postwar consensus, its action during the 1949 slump tended to confirm
the consensus, both negatively and positively. President Truman had campaigned for reelection in 1948 partly on the ground that the Republican
party was an engine of inflation, as illustrated by its 1948 tax cut. He promised a vigorous fight against inflation. Even though the economy turned
down in the fourth quarter of 1948, as the staff of the Council of Economic
Advisers, among others, recognized, Mr. Truman maintained his anti-inflationary posture for many months into 1949. In this he was loyally seconded
by one member of the council, Leon Keyserling. A main plank in the administration's anti-inflation program was a $4 billion tax increase, which the
President requested in his January, 1949, budget message.

At a press conference on February 10, 1949, the President was questioned
about the tax increase proposal:

> QUESTION: Mr. President, are you still hopeful of a $4 billion tax raise, in view
> of some of the developments on the Hill?
> PRESIDENT: Yes, I am. I am just as strong for it now as I was when I asked for it
> in the message.
> QUESTION: Mr. President, if we should be heading into a recession of some kind,
> would you feel that 4 billion tax increase would—as advised under those
> circumstances—be apt to be inflationary [*sic*]?
> PRESIDENT: Just as advisable then as now, for the simple reason that it doesn't
> affect the expenses of the Government, and we are trying to avoid a deficit.[54]

At the end of March the President was asked about the position of Senator
George, chairman of the Senate Finance Committee and considered one of
the leading fiscal conservatives in the Congress:

> QUESTION: Mr. President, Senator George is quoted as saying that a tax increase
> this year would be the only way to get us into a serious depression. It seems
> that some of the Senators up there—
> PRESIDENT: I do not agree at all with Senator George on that. I think he is wrong.
> I think that the fact that we have to run a deficit this year would be much
> more dangerous for the country than to levy taxes necessary to run the Gov-
> ernment.[55]

By May stories were circulating that the Council of Economic Advisers had submitted a confidential report to the President suggesting that the request for a $4 billion tax increase be scaled down unless the full figure was essential to preventing an unbalanced budget.[56] But when asked whether, in the light of this report, he felt that any change was needed in his tax proposals, the President said, apparently referring to the January budget message: "In my message to the Congress my position has been very clearly stated."[57]

At the end of June, Truman was still holding off Senator George.

QUESTION: Mr. President, Senator George said yesterday he thought you should tell the country that an increase in taxes would be unwise. Any comment?
PRESIDENT: Say that again, I didn't get it.
QUESTION: Another bill—an increase in taxes now would be unwise.
PRESIDENT: I don't think Senator George has ever been for sufficient taxes to run the Government, so that is not unusual.[58]

Finally, on July 13, 1949, in a radio and television report to the nation the President announced that because of the recession he would not ask for taxes to eliminate the deficit. He took the occasion to attack the economizers who were trying to reduce his budget. (When the President made this announcement, unemployment was 6.7 percent, about as low as it was to get during the 1949 slump except for October when employment was curtailed by a strike in the coal mines.)

Until the seventh month of the recession the President persisted in an anti-inflationary posture resulting from an appraisal of the economic outlook to which he had committed himself months before the recession began. This was not encouraging for the possibility of basing an effective fiscal policy for stability on forecasts.[59] But a passive fiscal policy, a policy of relying on the built-in response of taxes and certain expenditures—notably unemployment compensation—to a recession when it occurs, seemed to come off well. The budget surplus which had been running at an annual rate of $3.8 billion in the fourth quarter of 1948 turned into a deficit of $3.9 billion in the second quarter of 1949.[60] Almost all of this change resulted from automatic declines of revenues and increases of expenditures; it is doubtful whether any of it resulted from action directed at the recession. Although Congress was unwilling to raise taxes, it was not independently embarking upon an anti-recession fiscal policy. The fiscal response to the recession was almost entirely automatic and unsought. Whether, or how much, the shift in the budget position contributed to ending the recession and initiating recovery is hard to tell. However, the main point was the demonstration that the

United States could have a short and shallow recession accompanied, so far as fiscal policy was concerned, by only such influences as resulted from acting as if the recession did not exist.

By the end of 1949 the country had reached a consensus on fiscal policy which was a long way from traditional ideas of annual budget balance and from the early post-Keynesian ideas of compensatory finance. We would not try to balance recession budgets by raising taxes or by cutting expenditures. In recessions of some exceptional degree of severity we would do more than accept the automatically resulting deficit and take affirmative steps to enlarge the deficit. In contrast to earlier thinking about deficit spending, these steps were more likely to be on the revenue side of the budget than on the expenditure side. And we would in general look to some version of balancing the budget in prosperous conditions as a norm. We would not expect positive fiscal measures to respond to and counteract every actual or forecast departure from the high-employment target, but would accept the principle that in fiscal policy, as in many other things, striving for the best may be the enemy of achieving the good. Also in contrast to earlier "new" economics, we would give a considerable role to monetary policy as the partner of fiscal policy.

This consensus still left many questions to be answered, in general and in particular. How "prosperous" are the prosperous conditions under which the budget should be balanced? How much surplus, if any, is implied in "balancing the budget"? How exceptional must be the conditions that justify exceptional action, and how strong should the exceptional action be? But these were not questions of religion or of economic theory. They were matters of estimates about which men sharing a similar philosophy could and did disagree.

The very existence of the consensus remained to be tested. First it had to be tested in a national administration which retained at least semantic ties to budget-balancing ideology. Later it was to be tested in an administration which had a strong intellectual and temperamental affinity for more activist notions of fiscal policy than are implied in what is here described as the consensus. The consensus proved to be not the final form of American fiscal policy but a step in the transition to something else. While conceived as a combination of the best elements of budget-balancing and compensatory finance, it turned out to be a way station between the former and the latter. However, some aspects of the consensus policy did survive. One of these was the rebirth of monetary policy. The next steps in that process are described in the following chapter.

❦10❧

The Liberation of Monetary Policy

Aᴌᴌ of the early postwar stabilization plans called for the use of a flexible monetary policy to supplement fiscal policy. This was, indeed, one of their distinctive differences from the Keynesian ideas which had been reflected, for example, in the first conceptions of the Full Employment Bill. It was recognized that even if fiscal policy were wholeheartedly addressed to the problem of economic stabilization, it did not have the precision and flexibility to achieve, by itself, the desirable or possible degree of stability. The necessary forecasts would be too unreliable and the fiscal actions too slow in taking effect. Moreover, one could not realistically assume that fiscal policy would be exclusively directed to the stabilization objective. Aside from what might be called "political static" in the system, there were good reasons for trying to stick to some kind of budget-balancing rules which would exercise discipline over spending decisions, even though these might in principle be inconsistent with single-minded devotion to stability. Therefore it would be unwise to neglect the possible contribution of monetary policy to economic stability.

There were differences of view among the authors of the postwar fiscal-monetary plans about the importance of monetary policy and about the mechanism by which monetary policy worked. In Friedman's position, for example, monetary policy was the major instrument and fiscal policy was useful chiefly as a convenient means for influencing monetary conditions, whereas for others monetary policy was a significant but still definitely secondary adjunct to fiscal policy. For some the chief operative factor was the supply of money, for others it was the availability of credit, and for others it was interest rates. But there was agreement on the need for a flexible monetary policy which would have as either a cardinal feature or as a necessary by-product a certain flexibility of interest rates.

241

Several factors caused the postwar rise of monetary policy from the low esteem to which it had fallen in the thinking of economists shortly after the outbreak of the Keynesian revolution. On reconsideration of what he had actually said, some of Keynes' disciples came to realize that they had gone far beyond their mentor in downgrading the importance of money and interest rates.[1] The idea of the impotence of monetary policy had been developed in the context of depression, and some who had clung to this as a correct appraisal for depression were now prepared to see more potentialities for monetary policy in the inflationary situation of postwar America. Moreover, experience with the limitations of fiscal policy turned attention to the possibility of supplementing it in some way, the obvious candidate being monetary policy. Finally, some economists and businessmen who had not been completely persuaded by the Keynesian argument in the first place began to participate in the process of developing programs for stabilization, and their natural bent was to assign more weight to monetary policy.

But, despite the important role assigned to monetary policy in the postwar plans, monetary policy in fact was handcuffed and unable to play the part. The liberation of monetary policy was essential before the consensus on monetary-fiscal policy could be put into effect.

THE WARTIME "PEG"

What handcuffed monetary policy was the commitment of the Federal Reserve to support the prices of government securities at predetermined levels. At the end of the war, banks, insurance companies, and other financial institutions, as well as individuals and businesses, held enormous amounts of government debt, issued in the process of financing the war. When the holders of the debt wanted to make more loans, investments, and expenditures they would sell some of it, and in order to keep that from lowering the prices of the securities the Federal Reserve Banks would buy it. They bought with newly-created money which was not just money but was also the reserves of the commercial banks and so determined the amount of deposits and assets the banks could have. When the Federal Reserve was buying it was injecting reserves into the banking system which enabled the banks to expand their loans and investments, and their deposits, by several times the amount of the additional reserves. The Federal Reserve tended to be a buyer when private lending, investing, and spending were high, which commonly meant in an inflationary situation. Thus, in an inflation the Federal Reserve found itself not only unable to restrain the growth of the money supply but actually forced to create new money. The reverse happened in times of economic slack when investors preferred to hold government securities, and the Federal Reserve found itself withdrawing money from the system in order to keep the prices of government securities from rising too much.

This perverse monetary policy had been adopted in 1941 when the United States entered the war. Interest rates were then unusually low as a result of the low level of investment and high level of bank reserves during the Depression. Moreover, short-term interest rates were exceptionally low relative to long-term interest rates, because investors expected that interest rates would rise and preferred to hold short-term securities rather than longer-term which would fall in price if interest rates did rise. When we entered the war the Treasury faced the certainty of having to borrow large and rising amounts of money. If nothing were done to prevent it, interest rates would rise. Moreover, investors, knowing of the Treasury's insatiable need for funds, would hold off buying securities until interest rates rose so that interest rates would be forced up immediately. Thus the Treasury had the prospect of having to finance the war at high interest rates and moreover with rates rising in an unpredictable way so that there would be a danger of failing to sell a security if the Treasury misjudged the price at which investors would buy it. Therefore, the Federal Reserve agreed that it would support the prices of securities at a fixed pattern, standing ready to buy them if they tended to fall below the pattern.

There was also agreement that the long-term securities should be supported at prices which would yield 2 1/2 percent interest, about the rate prevailing at the time.[2] However, there was considerable disagreement between the Treasury and the Federal Reserve about the short-term rate. The Treasury wanted the short-term rate to be low, because it feared that the long-term rate could not otherwise be kept down to 2 1/2 percent. The Federal Reserve wanted a higher short-term rate, because it feared that if the pegged rate were too low it would have to do a great deal of buying to keep the market at the peg, thus pumping excessive reserves into the banking system. This difference of opinion was never resolved. The Federal Reserve agreed to support the low rates if the Treasury would take the responsibility for establishing them, which Secretary Morgenthau did. However, the level of the pegged short-term rates remained a source of tension between the Treasury and the Federal Reserve for almost ten years.

The Treasury was insistent that the Federal Reserve toe the mark. Each week the Treasury staff sent the Federal Reserve a chart showing the agreed-upon pattern of rates and the pattern of rates actually prevailing in the market to remind the Federal Reserve of its commitment. When the market was a little weak and interest rates rose close to the pegged pattern, the

Treasury would call the Federal Reserve to find out what was the matter. From its side, as the war went on the Federal Reserve became more and more concerned about the amount of money and bank reserves the policy was forcing it to create. The Federal Reserve began to urge the Treasury not to issue so much short debt, which investors would not take at the pegged rates, and which therefore flowed into the Federal Reserve banks. Also there began a long story of Federal Reserve recommendations for an increase in short-term rates, which the Treasury consistently disregarded as long as the war was on and acceded to reluctantly, slowly, and partially when the war was over.

There was obviously more to the strain between the Treasury and the Federal Reserve than a difference of opinion and interests. The Federal Reserve was an independent agency. It did not legally have to follow the wishes of the Treasury. But it had voluntarily agreed to put its immense resources at the service of the Treasury. For this it expected to be treated as a partner, possibly as a junior partner but nevertheless as a partner, in decisions about the financing of the deficits. This role the Treasury would not concede. The Federal Reserve was asked its advice about Treasury financing, but in the same way that advice was solicited from commercial bankers, insurance company executives, and bond dealers. High Federal Reserve officials were expected to meet with subordinates in the Treasury. Federal Reserve suggestions were left unanswered for weeks, and then usually rejected without serious explanation.[3]

Postwar Attitudes

As long as the war lasted the Federal Reserve could only grumble, and the issue received little attention outside the government. But when the war ended the situation began to change. It could no longer be maintained that the nation's security depended upon the assured ability of the Treasury to borrow on its own terms. Neither could it be expected that inflation would be dammed up by price and wage controls, making monetary expansion irrelevant to the behavior of the price level. The Federal Reserve felt freer to talk publicly about its problem, and others outside the government began to express concern.

By early 1946 three basic positions which were to be in contention for five years had emerged.

1. One position was that interest rates on government securities had to be allowed to rise so that private investors would be willing to hold them and the Federal Reserve would not have to buy them and in the process pump reserves into the banking system. The advocates of this position were at

first, and remained for some years, very moderate in their proposals. They did not suggest that the 2 1/2 percent rate on long-term bonds would have to be increased. In fact, during 1946 and almost all of 1947 the prices of long-term bonds were well above par and their yields in the market well below 2 1/2 percent. As long as it seemed to be assured that the prices of long-term securities would not be allowed to fall below par, holders of short-term securities yielding only 3/8 percent or 7/8 percent had a strong incentive to sell them and buy long-term securities. Thus the Federal Reserve found itself absorbing short-term securities and creating reserves, not only because investors wanted money for private loans and expenditures, but also because investors wanted to switch into longer-term government securities. Supporters of a more flexible interest rate policy urged only an increase in short-term rates. They emphasized that they were not proposing to disturb the long-term rate—perhaps for tactical reasons in order not to provoke unnecessary fears and perhaps because they shared the concern of the Treasury and others about the possible consequences of any unsettlement in the long-term bond market.

The most persistent and important proponent of allowing interest rates to rise in order to reestablish the ability of the Federal Reserve to restrain monetary expansion was the Federal Reserve Bank of New York, and particularly its president, Mr. Allan Sproul. Sproul was vice-chairman of the Federal Open Market Committee, the body within the Federal Reserve System which determined policy with respect to the purchase and sale of government securities. This position, as well as force of character, personality, and expression, made him, along with the chairman of the Open Market Committee, who was also the chairman of the Board of Governors, one of the two main determinants of the system's policy. Perhaps because his base was New York rather than Washington, Sproul was particularly jealous of the independence of the Federal Reserve—meaning its right and duty to carry out its responsibilities with the powers given to it by statute, without counting upon direct controls, or fiscal policy, or new legislation, as yet nonexistent, to relieve it of its responsibilities.

The idea of flexible—i.e., higher—interest rates was a "New York" position not only because it was held by Allan Sproul and the New York Federal Reserve Bank. It was also the position of the big New York commercial banks and insurance companies and of the head of the New York Stock Exchange. There was undoubtedly some self-interest here. Mr. Schram, head of the Stock Exchange, began to make speeches in favor of more flexible interest rates after the Federal Reserve, having been stopped from using its more general powers, raised margin requirements on purchases of stocks as

a move against inflation.[4] And being the head of a bank or insurance company creates a natural predisposition towards higher interest rates. But there
were also more general considerations involved. There was a strong aversion
to inflation, a dislike of direct controls whether over prices or over lending,
and a skepticism of the government's determination to follow anti-inflationary fiscal policies.

2. The second position on support of the government securities market
recognized the danger of uncontrollable and inflationary credit expansion
involved in the support policy but sought to avoid the credit expansion with
no, or minimum, increase of interest rates. The basic policy recommendation
which followed from this position was a new kind of reserve requirement
which would require investors to hold government securities. The problem
of credit control was to assure that the volume of government securities held
outside the Federal Reserve Banks continued to be held there and was not
sold to the Federal Reserve Banks in exchange for bank reserves. The flexible
interest rate proposal was to make it unprofitable for investors to reduce
their total holdings of government securities. The special reserve proposal
would have made it illegal for investors, or at least certain classes of investors,
to reduce their holdings. In principle, such a requirement could have been
imposed on all holders of securities; in fact, it was never seriously proposed
for any investors other than banks.

Two advantages were claimed for the special reserve plans as ways of
restricting the expansion of credit. First, they would not raise the interest
costs of the Treasury and the interest earnings of the banks as much as a
straightforward increase of market interest rates. The government could
decide what interest to pay on the part of banks' investments in government
securities that they were required to hold as special reserve. Second, the plans
could be used to insulate part of the banks' holdings of government securities
from price fluctuations in the market. Banks could be given special non-
marketable securities to hold in the special reserve in exchange for some of
the marketable securities they held, and this would reduce the danger that a
decline of security prices in the market would impair the capital of the banks.[5]
There was also some thought that with the securities reserve plan in effect a
desired degree of credit restraint could be brought about with a smaller increase of interest rates on government marketable securities than would
otherwise result. That this was really true was doubtful, as long as there were
some marketable securities held by people who were not required to hold
them. But still there was an impression that the securities reserve plan at
least did not operate through higher interest rates whereas traditional means
of credit control did—a difference that was much exaggerated.

The Federal Reserve Board in Washington proposed to Congress in 1946 that it should consider some form of supplementary reserve plan, and advocated the idea repeatedly in the next three years. For the board, advocacy of the plan had a number of advantages. The board was sensitive to the criticism that it represented bankers; the special reserve plan was a way of reestablishing credit control while restraining bank earnings. Also the board did not want to tackle the Treasury head-on. It welcomed a plan which seemed to serve the Treasury's objectives in the interest burden of the debt and the stability of securities' markets while giving the Federal Reserve some freedom to restrain monetary expansion. At least the board wanted to show the Treasury, the Congress, and the country that it had exhausted all alternatives before it resorted to higher interest rates.

Sproul objected when the board first wanted to propose the special reserve plan. He saw no reason for the Federal Reserve to tie its hands while waiting for Congress to consider legislation, which even in the end might not pass, or for the Federal Reserve to give the impression that the use of its existing powers was impossible or dangerous without new reserve legislation.[6] Partly at his insistence, while the Federal Reserve repeatedly urged Congress to consider granting it new authority over reserve requirements, it also tried to retain, or regain, its freedom to use the authority it had, even at the cost of higher interest rates.

The idea of new reserve requirements was also a favorite of economists outside the Federal Reserve system. The idea lent itself to many variations and to the exercise of much ingenuity in devising ways to kill two birds with one stone—to restrain the expansion of money and credit while safeguarding the Treasury's interest in stable securities markets and low debt charges. Even economists to whom one or the other of these birds was not very important were fascinated by the thought of inventing a device that would bring down both.

Aside from the Federal Reserve and a number of economists, there was little support for the special reserve plans. The banking community did not like them because they vested more direct control over their operations in the Federal Reserve, initially for the purpose, in part, of holding down bank earnings, and later for purposes that could not yet be foreseen. Also the Federal Reserve wanted the new requirements to apply to all banks whether members of the Federal Reserve system or not, a notion which the non-member banks, with many friends in Congress, could not tolerate. The whole idea was too complicated to rally much political support, especially in the absence of any push from the administration.

Probably the net effect of the special reserve proposals was to delay the liberation of monetary policy. Proponents of the plans were in the position of admitting that there was considerable weight in the Treasury's objections to a flexible interest rate policy, because otherwise there was no need for a special reserve plan. And the opponents of flexibility could maintain that they were not really standing in the way of anti-inflationary monetary policy because there were other ways of carrying out such a policy—admittedly complicated and unlikely to be adopted. Even though the possibility of getting additional reserve authority was not very real, it diminished the vigor of the Federal Reserve's push for more flexible use of the authority it had.

3. The third position was the Treasury's. It was simply to stand fast and not rock the boat. The Treasury's first responsibility in the management of the debt, it repeatedly said, was to maintain the credit of the United States. By this it meant to maintain stability in the markets for government securities. Any move to allow an increase of interest rates on government securities would raise questions about what the next move might be and about where the series of moves would end. Such questioning was likely to unloose an avalanche of selling. If the Federal Reserve then bought securities to support the market it would have to do much more buying and pump many more reserves into the banks than if the questions had not been allowed to arise in the first place. That would be inflationary, in the Treasury's view. If the Federal Reserve did not support the market in those conditions, there could be a catastrophic decline of securities prices, undermining the liquidity and solvency of banks and other financial institutions and precipitating a depression. The Treasury often pointed to the drop in government bond prices after World War I as a cause of the 1920–21 depression.

Moreover, even though the budget was in balance and the Treasury was no longer a net borrower, the Treasury was in the market almost continuously to borrow for the repayment of maturing debt. This refinancing would be difficult in the face of the uncertainities that would follow a breach in the pattern of security price supports. And if the refinancing had to be done at higher rates, the interest burden of the debt, already large, could easily double.

These costs and dangers, in the Treasury's view, would be assumed for no good purpose. A small rise of interest rates would not deter private spending and therefore would not restrain inflation. A large rise of interest rates would cause a depression. Between an increase too small to be useful and an increase too big to be safe there was no middle ground.

At the same time, the Treasury did not endorse the proposals of the Federal Reserve for a special reserve plan designed to safeguard the Treasury's interests while gaining more freedom for the Federal Reserve to restrain credit. Mr. Eccles was disappointed in 1947 to discover that the special reserve plan which he had devised in an effort to reconcile the objectives of the Federal Reserve and the Treasury did not have the support of the Treasury or of the rest of the administration.[7]

While the Treasury was the key advocate of the standstill policy, it had influential supporters. One of these was President Truman. He remembered the decline in government bond prices when he was a young veteran after World War I, and making sure that this was not repeated during his administration was one of the fixed points of his economic policy. The Council of Economic Advisers, especially the member who dealt most with monetary matters, Mr. John D. Clark, also supported the Treasury, mainly on the ground that monetary policy had little effect on the real world except to transfer income among the banks, the government, and the public. A number of Congressmen and Senators, notably Congressman Patman and Senator O'Mahoney, had a similar view. Most surprising, in view of the position of the big New York banks, was the support of the Treasury by the American Bankers Association and by large numbers of country bankers. For the small banks "conservatism" may have meant "caution" rather than "free markets" as it did in New York. But there may have been less ideological reasons as well. The smaller banks had larger investments, relatively, in long-term securities. For them higher interest rates would have caused losses on their existing assets whereas for the more liquid banks it would have provided opportunity to invest at higher rates. There may also have been some anti-Federal Reserve bias on the part of banks that were not members of the Federal Reserve system and resented the efforts of the board to impose special reserve requirements on them along with members.

THE TERMS OF THE STRUGGLE

The resolution of the conflict was the outcome of a test of strength and will. No device was invented to reconcile the opposing views. The special reserve plans which were intended to do that gathered no support and got nowhere. No one could be sure that they would really serve the objectives of either the Treasury or the Federal Reserve. Both the part of the banking community which favored flexibility and the part which supported the Treasury were opposed to more controls over the banks. Neither is there visible evidence of conversion or persuasion of either side in the dispute. After the event the Treasury usually accepted the moves the Federal Reserve had made in the direction of flexibility, and sometimes took credit for them, but to the end it resisted each next step. By 1951 there were more evident supporters for flexibility than there had seemed to be earlier, but these gains were from those who had taken no position until the dramatic crisis arose. Moreover, what carried the day in the end was only partly the support that could be mobilized for a flexible monetary policy; it was at least as much support for the idea of an independent monetary authority. Whether a flexible monetary policy could have won at that time against the opposition of the Treasury and the President if the Federal Reserve had not been for it, or if there had not been a tradition of Federal Reserve independence, is doubtful.

There was never any question that the Federal Reserve had legal authority to decide how many government securities it would buy, or how many it would sell, within limits so remote as not to be significant. By using this authority the Federal Reserve could bring about any degree of monetary contraction, or set any limits to the expansion, it wished. Its action in this respect would have had effects on interest rates for government securities which the Treasury would not have been able to resist. But still there was a test of power between the Federal Reserve and the Treasury. The Federal Reserve's authority is not absolute. It is a creature of Congress. The Congress can always change the organization and authority of the Federal Reserve. In any issue between the Federal Reserve on the one hand and the Treasury and the President on the other, the ultimate question of power is whether the President can credibly threaten to invoke Congress to restrain the Federal Reserve. The Federal Reserve can resist the Treasury only on issues so small that the Treasury will not take them to the President or the President will not take them to the Congress, or in circumstances where the President is not reasonably assured of Congressional support. Whether the President could count on Congressional support might depend on factors having little to do with the issue in question.

First Wrigglings on the Hook

The process by which the Federal Reserve achieved its freedom consisted of a number of small steps from 1946 through 1949, each step resisted by the Treasury but none big enough to provoke a showdown, and one dramatic showdown in 1950-51 when the Treasury was not strong enough to brave an open fight in Congress.

All of the steps by which the Federal Reserve gradually achieved an increase in short-term interest rates and some degree of flexibility between 1946 and 1949 do not have to be retraced here. Some examples will serve.

During the war the Federal Reserve had maintained a preferential rate at which it would lend to banks on the security of short-term government bills and certificates. Although probably largely of symbolic significance, because banks could get cash by selling bills or certificates in the market at pegged rates, the Federal Reserve regarded this as a limitation of its ability to control bank reserves. In the summer of 1945 the Federal Reserve proposed to abolish this preferential rate but refrained when Treasury Secretary Vinson objected to the move which, he said, "particularly if it occurred at this juncture, might be interpreted by the market as an indication that the Government had abandoned its low-interest rate policy and was veering in the direction of higher rates."[8]

In December, 1945, Mr. Eccles again raised the question of discontinuing the preferential discount rate, and after about two weeks Vinson asked that the rate be retained.[9]

In January, 1946, Mr. Vinson was reported as saying that he would not discuss interest rates until he had completed comprehensive discussions with government officials, bankers, and insurance executives.[10] During the first months of the year discussion went on within the Federal Reserve about whether the system should act on its own, ask for action by Congress, or wait for the Treasury.

Finally, in action initiated by the Federal Reserve, the preferential rate was abolished on April 24, 1946. At the same time the board issued a statement:

> The Board does not favor a higher level of interest rates on U.S. Securities than the Government is now paying. Discontinuance of the special rate will not involve any increase in the cost to the Government of carrying the public debt.[11]

Such statements were to accompany each step in the move to higher rates.

Within two months after the discontinuance of the preferential rates, urgent talk about further steps were going on in the Federal Reserve. Sproul was the leading proponent of greater flexibility and uncertainty about the short-term rates and some modest increase in their level. Eccles objected, mainly on the ground that the system would be injured by an increase in rates unless Congress and the public were for it.[12]

In June, 1946, the board in its annual report argued against higher interest rates but urged consideration for supplementary reserve requirements. The October, 1946, issue of the Federal Reserve Bulletin again called attention to the system's concern:

> Recent money market tendencies have not, however, altered basic easy credit conditions. The persisting large holdings by banks of Government securities,

particularly of short-term issues, together with Federal Reserve policy of maintaining the prevailing level of interest rates on these issues, make it possible for banks to obtain at continued low rates any funds wanted to supply the credit demands of businesses and individuals.[13]

In that same month, October, 1946, attention in the Federal Reserve turned to the issue of ending the commitment to buy Treasury bills, the shortest-term security, at a yield of 3/8 percent. Sproul favored ending the commitment.[14] In a speech on December 6, 1946, which received a good deal of attention, he urged the "defrosting" of short-term rates.[15] By February, 1947, the Federal Reserve Open Market Committee was discussing a memo to the Treasury proposing the end of the posted rate for bills. Eccles and the rest of the board proposed to assure the Treasury that the step would be taken "only with the concurrence of the Treasury." Sproul objected that Federal Reserve should not "abandon whatever independence we have." Eccles reluctantly agreed to changing the language of the memo if he could tell the Treasury orally that everything would be all right.[16]

Allowing the bill rate to rise presented one special problem. Most of the Treasury bills were already held by the Federal Reserve. An increase in the interest rates on bills would require the Treasury to pay more interest to the Federal Reserve, an incidental consequence for which the Federal Reserve had no desire and to which the Treasury would surely object. At the beginning of April Eccles reported to the Open Market Committee that he thought the Treasury might agree to a higher rate on bills if the increased earnings of the Federal Reserve banks were returned to the Treasury, and a plan was devised to accomplish that.[17]

On April 18, 1946, Sproul and Eccles met with Secretary Snyder and other Treasury officials to discuss a three-point program:

1. The Federal Reserve would arrange to return earnings to the Treasury.

2. The Federal Reserve would agree to buy bills directly from the Treasury, assuring the Treasury of a market for bills regardless of what happened to the unpegged rate.

3. The Federal Reserve would give up its commitment to buy bills from the public at a yield of 3/8 percent.

Secretary Snyder said he would call back later that day, which he did. He agreed to the first two points of the program but wanted a week to think about the third point, which was, of course, the Federal Reserve's main objective.

Points one and two of the program were publicly announced April 24. When Sproul called Snyder about the third point the Secretary said that he had been too busy to make a decision, but would answer shortly.[18]

By the time of the meeting of the Open Market Committee on June 5, 1947, no reply had yet been received from the Treasury, and discussion turned on acting independently.[19] On July 1 the committee informed the Treasury that it was prepared to act immediately to end the posted bill rate. The Treasury interposed no objection and the Federal Reserve announced the move the next day with the following statement:

> Its elimination will serve a useful purpose in restoring the bill as a market instrument and giving added flexibility to the Treasury's debt management policy.
>
> The Federal Reserve System will continue to purchase and hold Treasury bills as well as other Government securities in amounts deemed necessary in the maintenance of an orderly Government security market and the discharge of the System's responsibility with regard to the general credit situation of the country.[20]

THE SCENE SHIFTS TO CERTIFICATES

As soon as the Federal Reserve had crossed the bridge of abandoning support of the rate on Treasury bills, the question of the rate on Treasury certificates, the next shortest issue, was faced. In fact, at the same June 30 meeting at which the Open Market Committee decided to eliminate the posted rate for bills it adopted a recommendation to the Treasury to begin a gradual rise of certificate rates. This subject was to occupy and divide the Federal Reserve and the Treasury for the next three years.

The year from mid-1947 to mid-1948 was one of relatively harmonious cooperation between the Treasury and the Federal Reserve on debt management and monetary policy. The Federal Reserve pushed for higher interest rates on new issues of certificates and during the second half of 1947 the Treasury went along, not so rapidly as the Federal Reserve would have liked but still fast enough so that the Federal Reserve did not feel required to consider acting on its own. In the early part of 1948 the Treasury became more reluctant, but at that time the Federal Reserve was also being very cautious, because of signs of some slowdown in the economy, and did not push the Treasury very hard.

Nevertheless, this was still a period of tension between the Federal Reserve and the Treasury, although they were not far apart on current operations. The Treasury, in Congressional testimony, expressed its opposition to the use of traditional Federal Reserve methods of credit control as well as its disapproval of the Federal Reserve's request for new powers.[21] The Federal Reserve was annoyed by several public statements of the Secretary of the Treasury which it interpreted as an attempt to commit the system more firmly to support of the government securities market.[22] At the end of 1947 the President informed Mr. Eccles, without any prior notice, that he would not reappoint him as chairman of the Board of Governors of the Federal Reserve system. The President gave no reason at the time, and no reason has since been definitely established. Mr. Eccles later came to believe that the main factor in the decision was his long fight with the Giannini banking interest of California over bank supervisory issues unrelated to monetary policy. The Gianninis were leading Democrats and friends of Mr. Snyder.[23] However, there was also suspicion that the disagreements between Eccles and Snyder over monetary policy and debt management contributed to Mr. Eccles' demotion. If one objective had been to promote harmony on that subject, the strategy was a mistake. Mr. Eccles remained a member of the board and a leading figure inside of the Federal Reserve and out. Freed from the inhibitions of the chairmanship, and undoubtedly annoyed by his treatment, he became a much more vigorous and outspoken advocate of independence from the Treasury.[24]

In the spring of 1948 disagreement between the Treasury and the Federal Reserve over increasing certificate rates began to heat up. On April 28 and May 12 Thomas McCabe, the new chairman, and Allan Sproul held discussions with the Treasury urging an increase of rates, but the Treasury decided against them. One aspect of the situation which particularly annoyed the Federal Reserve was that some bankers who, as members of the board's Advisory Council, had recommended an increase of rates, had advised the Treasury against an increase as members of the American Bankers Association Committee on Government Borrowing.[25]

On May 20 the Open Market Committee decided to push the Treasury for an increase in short-term rates and consider later what to do if the Treasury resisted.[26] On June 23 the Executive Committee of the FOMC again decided to talk to the Treasury about higher short-term rates and to consider calling a meeting of the full committee if the Treasury remained opposed.[27] Finally on August 9 Snyder agreed to raise the rate of newly-issued certificates from 1 1/8 percent to 1 1/4 percent. But still the Federal Reserve was not happy. There was a great deal of fussing between the Treasury and the Federal Reserve over the precise combination of words to be used in their private correspondence to describe what they had agreed on. Each party wanted language which described it as taking the initiative and the other as conforming.[28]

After the August, 1948, agreement to go to the 1 1/4 percent rate on certificates, the Federal Reserve continued for about seven months to press, unsuccessfully, for another step. However, by the spring of 1949 it was evident that the economy was in a decline, demand for credit had fallen off, and interest rates were coming down. The question whether the Federal Reserve should continue to hold down interest rates in the face of a natural tendency for them to rise was temporarily adjourned.

ISSUES BENEATH THE SURFACE

The situation between 1946 and 1948 was muddy in many ways. It would have been clearer if inflation had been escalating, the money supply rising rapidly, and the Federal Reserve claiming freedom to abandon the securities markets so that it could devote itself exclusively to stopping a runaway inflation. In fact, however, while inflation was going on there was a fairly general expectation that it would soon come to an end. The money supply was rising slowly, and during most of the period the Federal Reserve was reducing its holdings of government securities, despite its commitment to support their prices.[29] The Federal Reserve would have liked to reduce its holdings of government securities somewhat more and thus reduce bank reserves and restrain the expansion of bank credit somewhat, but it never gave the impression of wanting to go very far in that direction. Certainly the Federal Reserve never gave the impression that even if it had been completely free of the Treasury it would have been willing to see a radical change in the pattern of interest rates in order to bring about monetary restraint.

Thus the current issues of monetary policy between the Treasury and the Federal Reserve always seemed to be issues of a little more or a little less. At every juncture it was always hard to tell whether the principle of a flexible monetary policy was at stake, or only the question of how to apply that principle in particular cases. Moreover, "outsiders" who were deeply concerned about restoring a flexible monetary policy could never be sure whether the Federal Reserve was against them or for them, so assiduous was the board in disavowing any but the most modest objectives and so diligent in repeating its paternosters about the need for stability in the markets for government securities. Nevertheless, the small moves that the Federal Reserve made by itself and urged upon the Treasury were part of an effort to arrive at a radically different monetary policy in which economic stabilization would be the dominant goal and stability of securities markets definitely a subordinate one. Everyone in the Federal Reserve system did not initially realize that this shift was at stake, although it became increasingly clear in the discussions within the Open Market Committee during 1948.

The interest of the Federal Reserve was not only in revising the policy goal but also in regaining freedom. It was concerned not only with what was done about monetary policy from time to time, but also with who did it, and particularly with having the Treasury recognize the right and duty of the Federal Reserve to decide. But it did not want to risk a test of its independence by exercising it vigorously. The Federal Reserve was always torn between assuring the Treasury that it would "be good" and insisting that it was being good "freely" and not because it had to. The Treasury on its side did not want to risk a test either. While it argued and delayed, it went along little by little with the Federal Reserve's desires, but still tried to use each concession as an occasion for getting the Federal Reserve committed to supporting the new situation permanently.

When the recession of 1949 ended for the time being the effort of the Federal Reserve to get interest rates raised as a matter of current stabilization policy, it was not yet clear whether the efforts of the past three years had resulted in significant movement towards either flexibility or freedom. Two developments of 1949 seemed important steps toward both.

THE FALSE ACCORD

As investment demand declined in early 1949, interest rates fell, and the market prices of government securities tended to rise. In line with its policy of stabilizing the securities markets, the initial reaction of the Federal Reserve was to sell securities and try to keep their prices down. This was the opposite of the policy the Federal Reserve would have followed if its chief concern had been to stop the recession and help bring about an upturn. It would have been buying securities in order to increase the reserves of the banks and induce them to increase their loans and investments, facilitating private investment and increasing the supply of money. Instead, in order to stabilize securities prices, it was selling government securities and taking reserves out of the banks. Moreover, the Federal Reserve was missing an opportunity to strengthen the principle of flexibility.

In the spring discussions began within the Federal Reserve and between the Federal Reserve and the Treasury about a change toward a more flexible policy. In the circumstances this meant abandoning the policy of selling securities to hold their prices down and instead increasing the supply of reserves, which would have the effect of raising the prices of securities. The Treasury was not opposed to a rise in the prices of its securities. It did not, however, want the occasion to be used for the liquidation of the previous understandings about support of government securities prices in the future. The Secretary of the Treasury preferred to change the policy for the time being quietly, since any announcement would certainly have raised the delicate question of implications for the future. The Federal Reserves on the other hand, wanted to take the opportunity to float free of its commitments to support the government securities market, but was not prepared to declare total independence.[30]

In the end, on June 28, 1949, the following rather ambiguous statement was issued by the Federal Open Market Committee:

> The Federal Open Market Committee, after consultation with the Treasury, announced today that with a view to increasing the supply of funds available in the market to meet the needs of commerce, business, and agriculture it will be the policy of the committee to direct purchases, sales, and exchanges of Government securities by the Federal Reserve banks with primary regard to the general business and credit situation. The policy of maintaining orderly conditions in the Government security market, and the confidence of investors in Government bonds will be continued. Under present conditions the maintenance of a relatively fixed pattern of rates has the undesirable effect of absorbing reserves from the market at a time when the availability of credit should be increased.[31]

The Federal Reserve took the incident seriously. Testifying about it before the Douglas subcommittee on December 3, 1949, Chairman McCabe of the Federal Reserve said:

> I regard June 28, 1949, as a most important date. It signified removal of the strait-jacket in which monetary policy had been operating for nearly a decade; that is, since the beginning of the war.[32]

But as to whether the Treasury understood what had happened in the same way, Mr. McCabe's answers to Senator Douglas revealed more hope than confidence:

> DOUGLAS: Did not that announcement or decision mean that at the time it was issued—namely, one of recession or inventory adjustment—that securities would not be sold and did it not, therefore, tend to keep down or to depress interest rates and, therefore, of course, would it not be acceptable to the Treasury? But does it follow that, because the Treasury agreed at this time that the Treasury will go along with primary regard to the general business and credit situation in other periods?
>
> If we were in a period of inflation and were to carry out this policy, it might mean—it would mean to the degree that the Federal Reserve Board exercised its powers—the sale of securities, a rise in the interest rate, and a fall in the prices of Government securities.
>
> In other words, the instance of cooperation which you chose was one which was very happy from the Treasury point of view, when there was no conflict between the two purposes in a period of depression. But would this cooperation necessarily continue in a period of inflation?

McCABE: The acid test of relationships and even of partnerships, Senator, comes when you have to meet a critical situation in the future. I am going on the assumption that this was an agreement made by men of understanding and good will and that it means what it says.

DOUGLAS: That is not a statement of policy for an indefinite period of time. I think it is somewhat indefinite in language; but certainly, whatever it means, it does not mean the two bodies are bound forever.

McCABE: To the Federal Reserve, it means flexibility.

DOUGLAS: That in periods of inflation the interest rate will be increased and, if necessary, the prices of Government securities depressed?

McCABE: That the open-market operations will be flexible—

DOUGLAS: Flexible both ways?

McCABE: And that we will conform to the economic situation with which we are confronted.

DOUGLAS: You will have flexibility both ways?

McCABE: Both ways.

DOUGLAS: Do you think the Treasury so understands it?

McCABE: That is my understanding. The Treasury understands this: That they have the final decision on fixing the rate on any refunding of Treasury obligations. We so recognize that they have the final decision and that when they announce a maturity—the refunding of a maturity—they determine the rate.[33]

However, there was no intimation in Secretary Snyder's testimony before the same committee that he recognized any milestone to have been passed.[34] By early 1950 the Treasury and the Federal Reserve were back at their old argument, the only difference being that the Federal Reserve had one more lesson in how difficult it would be to get off the peg with the friendly understanding of the Treasury. The statement of June 28, 1949, was later known as the "False Accord," but unlike the False Armistice of 1918 which preceded the true armistice by only three days, the False Accord preceded the true one by twenty months.

CONGRESSIONAL SEARCHLIGHT

The hearings of the Douglas subcommittee in December, 1949, to which we have just referred, had a more durable effect on the movement towards the liberation of monetary policy. These hearings, and the subcommittee's report, did more than anything preceding them to reveal to the public what the issues were and who stood for what. They made it clear that any attempt to bring the Federal Reserve forcibly to heel would encounter considerable resistance in the Congress, and that the resistance would have leadership and principles to which there would be a popular response.

The effectiveness of the investigation was greatly assisted by its timing and by the character of the participants. The hearings were held when the securities markets were not under downward pressure. This facilitated frank discussion. The question at issue was not whether the bond market should be supported that day. People who think themselves influential, especially central bankers, can never discuss such a question candidly, because they always fear that their remarks will set loose wild speculation. However, they could talk as a general proposition about the desirability of allowing interest rates to rise and securities prices to fall in conditions of inflation which might return in the future but were not then present. In the circumstances there were much more forceful statements of the principles involved than there could have been earlier, even though many of the witnesses were still extremely cautious.

The chairman of the subcommittee, Senator Douglas, was a liberal, northern Democrat, one of the bright stars of the 1948 class of Democratic senators which also included Lyndon Johnson, Hubert Humphrey, Estes Kefauver, Robert Kerr, Russell Long, and several others. Although he never became a "power" in the Senate, he had, especially in the early years, the interest and attention of the country. On no account could he be considered a "tool of the monied interests." The fact that he was a former professor of economics who knew his subject better than most of the other participants in the argument and could explain it with rare clarity also helped to get him an audience, especially with the press. The two most colorful and forceful witnesses were Eccles and Sproul. Eccles was still the best-known name in the Federal Reserve system, with a reputation as a New Dealer and challenger of the financial interests. Relieved of the chairmanship, he was free to reveal the intensity of the board's disagreement with the Treasury. Sproul, while less well-known in the country, was highly respected in the financial community. On the same side they made a formidable team.

The hearings did not produce any new evidence or argument about monetary policy. That any large part of the public was educated about monetary theory is unlikely. What the hearings did get across was the fact that there was a deep split between the Federal Reserve and the Treasury, that this was not a contest between the bankers and "the people," and that many leaders of business, finance, and agriculture, as well as economists and at least one liberal senator believed that the flexible policy which the Federal Reserve favored was essential to economic stability and prosperity.

The recommendation of the Douglas subcommittee was clear and strong:

As a long run matter, we favor interest rates as low as they can be without inducing inflation, for low interest rates stimulate capital investment. But we believe that the advantages of avoiding inflation are so great and that a restrictive monetary policy can contribute so much to this end that the freedom of the Federal Reserve to restrict credit and raise interest rates for general stabilization purposes should be restored even if the cost should be a significant increase in service charges on the Federal debt and a greater inconvenience to the Treasury in its sale of securities for new financing and refunding purposes.[35]

One member of the subcommittee, Congressman Patman, believed "that these proposals do not make the Federal Reserve System sufficiently responsible to the executive department."[36] The full Joint Committee on the Economic Report did not endorse the report of its subcommittee but instead decided to hold its own investigation of monetary policy and debt management. However, by the time the committee got around to this, in 1952, the issue had been settled.

A few days after the report of the Douglas subcommittee was issued, President Truman gave the Federal Reserve a hint about who was boss. At a dinner given by the chairmen and directors of the Federal Reserve Banks he said:

> I had my first experience in government fiscal matters as the presiding and executive officer of a county of 500,000 people. And the problems of that county of 500,000 people were just exactly parallel with the problems of 150 million. I had exactly the same trouble with the bankers that I have now. And I had no difficulty in convincing them, when I thought I was right and when I proved to be right, that the right thing to do was what they finally did.
>
> I appreciate very much the kind remarks that your Federal Reserve Chairman [McCabe] has made about me. I hope that his compliments and his good thoughts of me never have to be called back, because my only interest, my only interest, as President of the United States, is the welfare of the United States of America.
>
> Now gentlemen, you represent the greatest financial institution in the history of the world, except the Treasury of the United States.[37]

SKIRMISHES RESUMED

The test of who was boss did not come for another year, but already in the first half of 1950 there were indications that the balance of power had shifted. As recovery from the 1949 recession proceeded, the Federal Reserve wanted to reduce the degree of ease in the money markets. In early January the Federal Reserve urged the Treasury to raise the rate on its new issues of certificates. The Treasury was uncertain of the wisdom of this. As it later said, "The Treasury was not sure that this was desirable so soon and felt that caution was called for."[38] Nevertheless the Treasury went along. Furthermore, the Federal Reserve began selling some long-term securities from its portfolio. The Treasury also had doubts about this course, which tended to depress the prices of Treasury bonds, but it made no major fight over the issue.

One incident during this period recalls the imperiousness with which Secretary Morgenthau had earlier made the Federal Reserve toe the line. The minutes of the Open Market Committee for May 3, 1950, report that Mr. Sproul made a statement "substantially as follows":

> On April 26 Chairman McCabe received a telephone call from Secretary Snyder asking what was happening in the bill market and at the Chairman's request I called the Secretary. He said he had gotten the impression from our conversation on April 12 that we would keep the long bills at 1.17 [at a price which would yield interest at a rate of 1.17 percent per annum] and commented that they were then 1.18. I told him that we had had to buy $200 million more of bills that week, that the pressure had continued, and that we had moved our buying rate up to 1.17 which meant an open market rate of 1.18. I also pointed out that we were working under an instruction of the Federal Open Market Committee which permitted purchases within a range with an upper limit of 1.17. He referred to our previous conversations in which we assured him of the maintenance of the existing market and I told him that related to the maintenance of a 1 1/4 percent rate for one-year certificates, that this contemplated some fluctuation in the bill rate in response to market pressures, and that with the additional $100 million of bills being issued each week it was to be expected that there would be some pressure in the market.[39]

But this was not 1945 any longer, and the Treasury did not insist.

The Federal Reserve's increased feeling of independence was reflected at the same meeting of the Open Market Committee in a statement by Mr. Sproul, who may have put the situation a little more directly than some other members might have done:

> With respect to the question of Federal Reserve support, Mr. Sproul expressed the view that the question had been answered as well as it could be answered last June and that he saw no reason why the System should, and every reason why it should not, make statements about support or non-support of the Government securities market at par or any other price.[40]

Still the issue was not clearly drawn. The incompleteness of the recovery induced the Federal Reserve to great moderation in its policy of monetary restriction. Although interest rates were rising they were only retracing the steps by which they had declined during the 1949 recession and had not yet exceeded the levels reached in 1948. At a meeting on June 13 the Open Market Committee did consider some actions which might have produced a confrontation with the Treasury. Mr Sproul suggested that after July 1 the Federal Reserve should bring about a rise in short-term interest rates, raise the discount rates, and continue to sell long-term bonds.

> With respect to prices of long-term Treasury bonds, Mr. Sproul did not think the Committee was now faced with the problem of whether such securities should be allowed to fall below par but that he now felt that if that question should arise during the next few weeks they should not be supported at par.[41]

But the decision of the committee was to defer the issue.

THE STRAITJACKET ONCE MORE?

The outbreak of the Korean War on June 25, 1950, changed the situation dramatically and made further avoidance of the critical issue impossible. On the one hand it raised the prospect of large budget deficits continuing for a long time. On the other hand it immediately set in motion a big wave of buying by individuals and businesses and a rapid upsurge of prices. For the Treasury the problem was to assure its ability to finance large deficits with certainty as to the rates, which should preferably be low. For the Federal Reserve the problem was to assure its ability to carry out its responsibility to help prevent inflation by restraining the growth of money and credit. The difference was not one that could be compromised by a small step to higher interest rates. In the circumstances, with the prospect of deficits, strong inflation, and the known attitudes of the Federal Reserve, any small step would create that uncertainty which it was the Treasury's prime purpose to avoid. And the Federal Reserve could not commit itself to being satisfied with any specific small step without forswearing the flexibility which it regarded as indispensable. From the standpoint of each party, what the other was prepared to give was essentially nothing.

As earlier, the dispute over policy was exacerbated by a struggle for control. The Treasury believed that it needed and was entitled to have the ultimate authority. But for the Federal Reserve, after its recent frustrating experience, this was a concession that could not be made. Slowly and painfully it had won a measure of freedom. The question was not whether it would for a time abate the effort to get free, but whether it would voluntarily put on the straitjacket again, knowing how long it might take to regain the position it had.

The struggle opened on a low key, with discussion of technicalities concealing the main issues of which both were aware. The first strong feeler came in a letter from Snyder to McCabe on July 17, 1950. After commenting on "the confidence which has been built up in our ability and determination to maintain a stable market for Federal securities," the Secretary went on:

> I know you will agree with me that it is of the utmost importance at the present time to maintain that confidence and, in addition, to do everything possible to strengthen it. This involves, first of all, avoiding any course which would give rise to a belief that significant changes in the pattern of rates were under consideration. . . . In my view, we must take extreme care to avoid introducing any factor which would run the risk of producing unsettlement in the broad market for Federal securities represented by investors throughout the nation.

Following some elaboration of this theme, the Secretary concluded with:

> In short, every circumstance at the present time calls for steadiness and manifest strength in the Federal security market as a primary measure of economic preparedness. That is the net of the situation as I see it. And, as you will note, I am sending my thoughts on to you just as they have occurred to me, in order to let you know the course of my thinking as events unfold.[42]

The Federal Reserve did not immediately reject this clear invitation to accept the Treasury's domination once more. Instead it asked for a meeting with the Secretary, which was held on August 10. Mr. McCabe and Mr. Rouse, of the New York bank in the absence of Mr. Sproul, represented the Federal Reserve. Their report back to the Open Market Committee on August 18 revealed great irritation on both sides. The Treasury rejected the Federal Reserve's suggestion that a new long-term Treasury issue be offered for sale to investors other than banks. It referred to studies by the Treasury staff which showed that there would be no market for such a security, but was reluctant to make the studies available for examination by the Federal Reserve staff. The Secretary indicated annoyance that comments by the Federal Reserve were causing investors to sell short-term government securities in the expectation of higher rates later.

Apparently for the first time, in this meeting the threat of resort to the ultimate authority, the Congress, was raised. According to the Open Market Committee minutes, "He [Snyder] stated that he sometimes thought it might be wise to ask the Congress to put the responsibility for handling the debt in the Federal Reserve which had the money market tools, adding that, of course, he realized the Congress wouldn't do that and the Federal Reserve would not want to take that responsibility." The clear implication was that, if necessary, the Congress would confirm the authority of the Treasury to manage the debt.

After a little further discussion, the minutes report:

By this time it was clear that the Treasury had no intention now of making any new effort to absorb nonbank money or of voluntarily agreeing to a change in short-term rates. In conclusion, Chairman McCabe remarked to the Secretary that in the circumstances there was nothing further that he could say except that he would report this conversation to his committee.[43]

THE FEDERAL RESERVE TAKES A STAND

The Open Market Committee's response to the report of this conversation was defiant. As Mr. Sproul said:

> The question today is what we are going to do in our sphere of primary responsibility, not what we are going to recommend to the Treasury that it do in its primary sphere. It is not a question of the long-term bond issue or of refunding the September-October maturities, but what we are going to do about making further reserve funds available to the banking system in a dangerously inflationary situation. . . .
>
> We can't do the whole job with general credit measures but in view of our responsibility and the national program I think that general credit measures should now be used. . . . We have marched up the hill several times and then marched down again. This time I think we should act on the basis of our unwillingness to continue to supply reserves to the market by supporting the existing rate structure and should advise the Treasury that this is what we intend to do—not seek instructions. . . . It seems to me that our course is clear: we should move to an immediate adjustment of market rates toward a 1 3/8 percent basis for one year money and should advise the Treasury that this is what we propose to do. If we allow ourselves to be diverted from our main responsibility we will only expose ourselves to further delay and frustration.

There was general agreement in the committee with this bold line. Mr. Eccles said that, "it was time the System, if it expected to survive as an agency with any independence whatsoever, should exercise some independence." Then, as if pointing out where the ultimate recourse might be, he reminded the committee that three members of the Senate Banking and Currency Committee, Senators Douglas, Flanders, and Fulbright, had issued a report in support of a program of general credit restriction with which the Treasury's debt-management policies should be coordinated.

Having decided for an increase of short-term rates, whether or not the Treasury approved, the committee had two questions to face:

1. What should be done if, despite the increase of short-term rates in the market, the Treasury should nevertheless try to issue certificates at a lower rate? Should the Federal Reserve allow the Treasury borrowing to

fail? The committee agreed that in such an event the Federal Reserve would buy the Treasury offerings at the rate fixed by the Treasury and offset its purchases by selling other securities out of its own portfolio at a higher rate.

2. What should be done if prices of long-term securities should decline as a result of the rise of short-term interest rates? It was agreed that, "should the price of the longest restricted issue decline to between 100 1/2 and 100 3/4, the executive committee [of the Open Market Committee] would direct only such operations as were necessary to maintain orderly market conditions pending a meeting of the full Committee which would be called promptly to consider how far any further decline that would be brought about by market conditions would be permitted to go."[44]

The first of these contingencies was faced immediately. Indeed, on the very day of the committee's decision, August 18, the Treasury announced an issue of certificates to bear a rate of 1 1/4 percent. The Federal Reserve nevertheless persisted, by raising the discount rate and withholding support from the market, in allowing the market rate of interest on one-year securities to rise to 1 3/8 percent. As a result, private investors were unwilling to take the new Treasury issue. The Federal Reserve bought most of it and offset the effect of its purchases by selling Treasury securities out of its own portfolio at the higher rates prevailing in the markets. The operation raised a furore in financial circles. It meant that the Federal Reserve had taken over the management of the federal debt. The Federal Reserve provided money to the Treasury, but the government's borrowing from the market was done by the Federal Reserve on terms decided by the Federal Reserve.

THE SHADOW OF THE WHITE HOUSE

After this experience the struggle moved to higher ground. There was no longer any question that the Federal Reserve was independent of the Treasury with respect to short-term interest rates. In the middle of October, against the opposition of Secretary Snyder, one-year rates were allowed to rise from 1 3/8 to almost 1 1/2 percent. There were two questions left. Would the Federal Reserve permit or push the rise of interest rates to a point which threatened the maintenance of the 2 1/2 percent on long-term securities? Could the authority of the President and the Congress be effectively marshalled to resist the Federal Reserve? These two issues were closely related, because it was a breach of the 2 1/2 percent ceiling, involving a decline of the prices of government bonds below par, that was most likely to bring the President and Congress into the arena. For the President, and for many Congressmen, the affective image conjured up by the idea of abandoning support of the government securities market was $100 federal bonds selling in the $80's, as they had after World War I.

During September and October the Federal Reserve tried to reassure the Treasury of its intention to maintain the prices of long-term bonds. On September 28, McCabe and Sproul met with Snyder and "spent considerable time discussing the long-term rate and brought out that we did not want to carry the short-term rate up to a point that would affect the 2 1/2 percent rate."[45] Again on October 16, after the Federal Reserve decided on another increase of the short-term rate, McCabe wrote to Snyder. "We can assure you that these actions will not affect the maintenance of the 2 1/2 percent rate for the outstanding longest term government bonds."[46] But the Secretary was not reassured. The logic of the Federal Reserve's position, both with respect to the primacy of its responsibility for general monetary conditions and with respect to its independence of the Treasury, gave the Treasury no ground for comfort.

During the fall of 1950 the possibility of intervention by higher authority came increasingly into the picture. At the meeting with Secretary Snyder on September 28, as later reported to the Open Market Committee by Mr. McCabe:

> There was some discussion also of the relative responsibilities of the Treasury and the Federal Reserve and he [Snyder] indicated that he thought it highly desirable at some time for this whole question of responsibility to be reviewed by the proper authorities because conditions had changed so materially since action by the Congress creating the Federal Open Market Committee as now constituted. At the time of that action, he said, we did not have a public debt of anything like the present magnitude, and in view of the problems involved in the handling of the debt, he felt there should be a review of the Congressional authority and the responsibilities of the agencies should be re-defined.

When the Open Market Committee met later that same day Mr. McCabe said that,

> if the decision of the Committee was at complete variance with the views of the Secretary of the Treasury the matter would probably go to the President of the United States, that in his judgment the President would not be likely to take a position against the view of the Secretary of the Treasury, and that the System would then have to decide what its course of action should be. . . . [Mr. Sproul] felt that the question should not go to the President of the United States as he should not be called upon to decide questions of this kind, and that the members of the Board and the Federal Open Market Committee could not avoid their responsibility for making decisions.[47]

However, Mr. Sproul's opinion of the proprieties did not keep the question from going to the President. On October 25, nine days after the Federal Reserve acted to allow the certificate rate to rise close to 1 1/2 percent with the assurance to the Treasury noted above, Mr. Truman invited Mr. McCabe to meet with him and Secretary Snyder the following day. What went on at their meeting is not revealed. The minutes of the Open Market Committee meeting on October 30 only say that after Mr. McCabe explained the reasons for doing so the committee approved the following letter to Secretary Snyder:

> Since our meeting on Thursday, October 26, a meeting of the Federal Open Market Committee has been held. The Committee has been and is in complete agreement that *under present conditions* it is necessary to protect the 2 1/2 percent rate (par) on the longest term Treasury bonds now outstanding. The Committee's policies have been determined in accordance with that conclusion.
>
> For the reasons outlined in my letter of October 16, 1950, the Committee is convinced that continued flexibility in the short-term money market is essential to carrying out an effective credit policy. It believes, however, that *for the present* the market yield on Government securities on a one-year basis (now about 1 1/2 percent) may have worked as high as is necessary in the light of present economic conditions and as high as it can without having such an impact on the market for the longest term Government securities as might interfere with our policy of credit restraint. Accordingly, *for the present*, the Committee will endeavor to maintain an orderly and flexible market within a maximum of 1 1/2 percent per annum for any securities maturing within one year.
>
> If further inflationary or market forces should develop at any time in the future which would make it necessary for the Committee to reconsider these decisions, we would, of course, feel it desirable and compelling to seek your counsel. In the meantime, we should like to consult with you freely concerning our mutual problems in the light of market developments and the general credit situation.[48]

The promise was not good enough from the Treasury's standpoint. There was too much emphasis on present conditions. Moreover, the agreement to protect the 2 1/2 percent rate on the longest-term bonds was not satisfying when the bonds were selling at par plus 27/32 [$100 27/32 for a $100 bond]. This left room for the bonds to fall to par before the Federal Reserve might feel obliged to act to protect the 2 1/2 percent rate. Mr. Snyder wanted support of the market where it was. A decline from par plus 27/32 to par plus 26/32 worried him. And he wanted the assurance in an unequivocal and unreserved statement which could be proclaimed to the market. He believed that if such an assurance were given the need for support would greatly diminish. Investors would accept the fact that interest rates were not going to rise and would be content to hold the government securities they had, plus more when the Treasury had to finance a deficit.

From the standpoint of the Federal Reserve this argument was incomplete. The amount of securities they had to buy was not really the key issue, although attention tended to focus on it. Assurance that interest rates would not be allowed to rise would discourage some investors from selling their securities in order to hold cash until the interest rates did rise. But it was not these sales of securities that contributed to the inflation. These investors were only getting cash to hold, not to spend. The inflationary effect came when investors, including financial institutions, sold government securities to obtain cash to finance business purchases of inventories or machinery. This inflationary process would not be damped by the knowledge that the Federal Reserve was committed to preventing interest rates from rising. On the contrary, if a Federal Reserve commitment was interpreted as immobilizing one anti-inflationary instrument, the incentive to expansion of private spending would be increased.

The absence of any real commitment from the Federal Reserve was, of course, noticed by private observers as well as by Secretary Snyder. For example, on December 1 the *New York Herald Tribune* carried the following story on its financial page:

Flexible pegs

There is again much stirring and questioning in the money market, owing to a new series of changes in the prices at which the Federal Reserve open market committee pegs Treasury issues. Although the short rate now is fairly stable at 1 1/2 percent for one-year obligations, long bonds are being permitted to sag. Victory 2 1/2s last week were toppled from the long-sustained price of 100 26/32ds and yesterday were dropped again. The official quotation at the close was 100 23/32ds bid, but many dealers quoted them at 100 22/32ds. Coming at a time when $8,000,000,000 maturing obligations are exchangeable for 1 3/4 percent five year notes, the price uncertainty in long and intermediate maturities impresses most independent observers unfavorably. Although the Treasury and Federal Reserve were reported as seeing eye to eye on the latest refinancing, there is now open speculation as to whether the Federal Reserve is again undercutting the financing. One story is that the Federal Reserve would be glad to get rid of some of the huge aggregate of 1 1/4 percent notes picked up in the turmoil of the previous financing by means of exchange in the market for the current "rights," but that makes little sense to market specialists. The Federal Reserve, however, actually is beginning to get the rights wholesale from corporate holders who do not like the trend of the market. Moreover, it is obviously risking another huge shake-out of long holdings such as that which followed the Christmas package of downward peg adjustments some years ago.[49]

This little note helped propel the story to its denouement, because Presi-

dent Truman saw it and called Chairman McCabe at home. As McCabe
later reported this conversation to the Open Market Committee, "That
article seemed to have upset the President very much." The President said
that he hoped the Federal Reserve would "stick rigidly to the pegged rates
on the longest bonds." On December 4 the President sent McCabe a letter,
enclosing the *Herald Tribune* article, and saying, in part:

> It seems to me that this situation is a very dangerous one and that the Federal
> Reserve Board should make it perfectly clear to the Open Market Committee
> and to the New York bankers that the peg is stabilized.
>
> I hope the Board will realize its responsibilities and not allow the bottom to
> drop from under our securities. If that happens that is exactly what Mr. Stalin
> wants.

Mr. McCabe's reply informed the President that the Federal Reserve
had "faithfully" followed the support policy outlined in the letter of October
30 to Snyder, having bought well over $1 billion of government securities,
net, in the preceding seventeen days in furtherance of that policy. However,
"It is our view that moderate fluctuations in price in response to market
forces serve a useful purpose and help to maintain public confidence. . . . I
would prefer not to take up with the Open Market Committee the question
of notifying the New York bankers of a fixed peg until I have had an
opportunity fully to discuss with you the possible adverse consequences of
such an action." This discussion occurred on December 18, and McCabe
left feeling that Truman had confidence in what the Federal Reserve was
doing.[50]

If the President had confidence, which we don't know, the Treasury
did not. The Secretary was further alarmed by a full and frank exposition
of Mr. Sproul's views which Sproul presented at a meeting that he and
McCabe had with Snyder on January 3. It was never clearer that in Sproul's
opinion anti-inflationary policy, with credit limitation as one of its means,
came a long way ahead of pegging the bond market. He even suggested "a
slightly higher rate than 2 1/2 percent for long term financing,"[51] thus violating the holy of holies.

The Secretary's concern was contagious. On January 17 the President
called McCabe to the White House, saying that, "yesterday he was thinking
about the subject [government securities market] again, mentioned it to
John Snyder, and suggested that the three of us get together again." The
purpose of the meeting soon became clear. As reported later by McCabe to
the Open Market Committee, the Secretary expressed, "the strong feeling
that the sooner we let the public know that the 2 1/2 percent rate was going

to be maintained, the better." The Secretary was thinking of issuing a long bond with a 2 1/2 percent rate, which he believed could be sold if the uncertainties about Federal Reserve support could be removed. Mr. McCabe sought to avoid making any commitment, while at the same time assuring the President and the Secretary that there was nothing to be concerned about and that everything was under control.[52]

The Secretary moved quickly to assert the existence of a commitment. The next day, January 18, in a speech to the New York Board of Trade, he announced the government's financial policy:

> An increase in the 2 1/2 percent rate would, I am firmly convinced, seriously upset the existing security markets—Government, corporate and municipal.
>
> We cannot allow this to happen in a time of impending crisis, with the heavy mobilization program to finance. We cannot afford the questionable luxury of tinkering with a market as delicately balanced as the Government security market. Now is no time for experimentation.
>
> In the firm belief after long consideration, that the 2 1/2 percent long-term rate is fair and equitable to the investor, and that the market stability is essential, the Treasury Department has concluded, after a joint conference with President Truman and Chairman McCabe of the Federal Reserve Board, that the refunding and new money issues will be financed within the pattern of that rate.[53]

The bond market rose on news of the speech. Tempers in the Federal Reserve system also rose. The system had been publicly committed to a policy with which it did not agree, and to which it had not consented. On the next day, January 19, Chairman McCabe complained to the President that he had not known about the speech Secretary Snyder was to deliver in New York when they had met in Truman's office. The President said that he hadn't known about it either, and would speak to the Secretary.[54] Three days later Mr. Sproul made a delicately-worded but nonetheless clear speech disapproving the support policy.[55] On January 25 Mr. Eccles appeared before the Joint Economic Committee at the invitation of Senator Taft and attacked the support policy, which involved him in a wrangle with Senator O'Mahoney and Congressman Patman.[56] On January 29 the Federal Reserve allowed the price of the longest-term bond to decline from 100 22/32 to 100 21/32.

The Treasury had not recognized the Federal Reserve's declaration of independence of August 18, 1950. Now the Federal Reserve was not recogizing the Treasury's unilateral declaration of the Federal Reserve's commitment. Something had to be done, and the ball was in the Treasury's court. The Federal Reserve did not need the concurrence of the Treasury, but the Treasury did need the concurrence of the Federal Reserve.

In the Fiery Furnace—and Out

On January 30 the President asked the whole Open Market Committee to meet with him at the White House at 4:00 PM the next day. This was a most unusual invitation, as Mr. McCabe reminded the President's secretary. January 31, 1951, was to be one of the most momentous days in the history of the Federal Reserve. When the Open Market Committee met at the Federal Reserve building in the morning before going to the White House, Mr. McCabe and Mr. Sproul recounted their dealings and discussions with the President and Secretary Snyder during the previous two months. Mr. McCabe then said that there were three alternative positions the committee might take:

a. Undertake a commitment to support the 2 1/2 percent rate on existing and new long-term issues for the duration of the emergency;

b. Undertake a commitment to support the 2 1/2 percent rate for the time being, with the understanding that the committee could ask the secretary and the President to modify the policy if changing economic conditions required that;

c. "If the views that might be expressed by the President were diametrically opposed to those of the Committee, the members of the Committee could resign."

Mr. Sproul said that the first two of these alternatives were not acceptable. He rejected the third also, "since it would be an admission of failure or inability to carry out our statutory responsibilities, without giving the Congress an opportunity to review our performance and to express its will." He suggested a fourth alternative, which was to go to Congress for new instructions, since the Federal Reserve system could not continue on the present course which "involved either continued open conflict with the Treasury or complete abdication of the responsibility of the members of the Open Market Committee."

No one suggested any other alternatives. Apparently no one was in a mood to propose that the committee continue with its independently chosen policy, leaving to the Treasury the options of falling in line or seeking Congressional remedy. The committee tried to prepare a written statement of its position, but was unable to agree on language before the time came to leave for the White House. They went to their afternoon meeting having decided only that Mr. McCabe would speak for the committee within the framework of the letter of October 30.[57]

The President opened the meeting with a recital of the world situation. "He stated that the present emergency is the greatest this country has ever faced, including the two World Wars and all the preceding wars." He sketched the difficulty of dealing with the Russians, and described the military and political problems of the United States in Asia and Europe. "The President emphasized that we must combat Communist influence on many fronts. He said one way to do this is to maintain confidence in the Government's credit and in Government securities. . . . He recalled his wartime experience when he bought Liberty bonds out of his soldier's pay. When he returned from France and had to sell his bonds to buy clothes and other civilian things, he got only $80 or a little more for his hundred dollar bonds and later they were run up to $125." In response to some explanation by Mr. McCabe of recent events in the bond market Mr. Truman said "he would not undertake to discuss details of that kind, that he was principally concerned with maintaining the confidence of the public in Government securities as one way of presenting a unified front against Communism."

In response, Mr. McCabe stated that the Open Market Committee shared the President's concern for the maintenance of the government credit. He explained the Federal Reserve's responsibility for economic stability. Then he turned to the members of the committee and said that "the President could depend on everyone in the group to do what they could to protect the Government credit. . . . The Chairman suggested the following procedure—that we consult frequently with the Secretary of the Treasury giving him our views at all times and presenting our point of view strongly, and that by every means possible we try to reach an agreement. If this could not be accomplished, he [the chairman] would like to discuss the matter with the President. The President said this was entirely satisfactory and closed the meeting on the same note as it was opened—namely, that he wanted us to do everything possible to maintain confidence in the credit of the Government and in the Government securities market and to support the President of the United States in achieving this end."[58]

The meeting was a masterpiece of deliberate misunderstanding. Neither party said what he really meant, yet each understood what the other meant but preferred to respond as if he didn't and so left the other free to interpret the response as he wished. The President couched his request for support in language sufficiently general to permit Mr. McCabe to reply as if he thought the President only wanted assurance that the Federal Reserve would not permit financial disaster. Mr. McCabe gave this assurance, but in language so indefinite as to permit the President to interpret his response as commitment to support the Treasury's policy.

The Federal Reserve people returned to their marble palace on Constitution Avenue in some disarray, and held an ultra-secret session for which no minutes appear in the record later published. Some members were critical of the chairman for not making the Federal Reserve's position clear and for allowing the President to think that there was agreement when there was not. A key motion to support the bond market at present levels until further notice was defeated by a vote of eight to four.[59] When the committee went back on the record after the secret session it was agreed that if the long-term bonds declined the Federal Reserve would not support them.

At this point the game was all over. Summoning the Open Market Committee to the White House was the President's last trump, and while there had been some fumbling around in his office, the last trump was not enough to win. Every card he played after that was a loser, only stiffening the determination of the Federal Reserve and rallying support to their side.

TRIAL BY PRESS RELEASE

The administration was anxious to nail down its interpretation of the White House meeting. About noon the next day, February 1, the White House press secretary issued a statement that, "The Federal Reserve Board has pledged its support to President Truman to maintain the stability of Government securities as long as the emergency lasts." The announcement said that the statement was issued to quiet rumors of difference of opinion between the Treasury and the Federal Reserve Board. A little later a Treasury spokesman announced to the press that, "the White House announcement means the market for Government securities will be stabilized at present levels and that these levels will be maintained during the present emergency."[60]

In a further effort to convert evasion into commitment, the President wrote McCabe a letter which he received in the afternoon of February 1:

Dear Tom,

I want the members of the Federal Reserve Board and the members of the Federal Open Market Committee to know how deeply I appreciate their expression of full cooperation given to me yesterday in our meeting.

As I expressed to you, I am deeply concerned over the international situation and its implications upon our economic stability.

Your assurance that you would fully support the Treasury defense financing program, both as to refunding and new issues, is of vital importance to me. As I understand it, I have your assurance that the market on Government securities will be stabilized and maintained at present levels in order to assure the successful financing requirements and to establish in the minds of the people confidence concerning government credit.

I wish you would convey to all the members of your group my warm appreciation of their cooperative attitude.

Sincerely yours,

Harry Truman[61]

Mr. McCabe studied this letter carefully, alone, and the next morning
decided that his best move was to discuss it with the President and ask him
to withdraw it.[62] However, that afternoon, before McCabe had a chance to
talk with the President, the White House released the letter.

The White House and Treasury press statements of February 1, and the
release of the "Dear Tom" letter on February 2, brought forth shocked reactions from press and senatorial supporters of Federal Reserve independence
and flexible monetary policy. There was one more shock in store for them.
On February 3 Marriner Eccles, on his own responsibility and without consulting other officers of the Federal Reserve system, released to the press
copies of the official report of the January 31 meeting at the White House.
This was a violation of protocol in relation to the White House and a breach
of confidence in relation to the Federal Reserve. But Mr. Eccles believed
that the release of the "Dear Tom" letter relieved him of the inhibition
against revealing what was said in meetings with the President. And he
further believed that the independence of the Federal Reserve and the policy
for which it was fighting would be hopelessly compromised if it allowed
itself to be cornered into the commitments implied by the White House.[63]

The Eccles statement with the report of the White House meeting made
a splash on the front pages on Sunday, February 4. It now appeared that the
Federal Reserve had not given a commitment after all, but that the administration was trying to sign the Federal Reserve's name to a blank check.
Moreover, what on Friday seemed to have been decided in favor of the
Treasury, on Sunday seemed still open for decision—although the decision
had already been made on the side of an independent Federal Reserve policy,
a fact which was not to be publicly appreciated for about two months.
Support for the Federal Reserve now began to come forth in volume, notably from the Senate. The persistent Senator Douglas made a statement in
opposition to the Treasury's policy, in which he was joined by Senators
Flanders and Fulbright. Senator Taft asked the Federal Reserve to supply
him with the particulars of the dispute. The Senate Banking and Currency
Committee took no immediate position but asked Senator Robertson to
look into the matter.[64] There was, of course, also support for the Treasury
in the Senate, but the Democratic majority was thin (49 to 47) and many
Democrats would certainly join the Republicans in support of the Federal

Reserve. If the administration had thought it still had one recourse left, the Congress, reactions to the Eccles release showed it was mistaken.

THE ACCORD

At the Federal Reserve the storm had cleared the air. The members of the Open Market Committee had at last convinced themselves that they really would limit the expansion of credit, even at the cost of a rise in long-term interest rates. Having reached that determination and demonstrated it against the maximum pressure the administration could muster, they were now free to consider how to effect the transition to the new regime as smoothly as possible.

One problem was to try to reestablish a relationship of mutual confidence with the President and get him off the limb of having asked for and proclaimed a commitment which did not exist. Their move in this direction was to write the President a reply to the "Dear Tom" letter which explained their position courteously, asked for no approval, made no complaints, and said, in its key paragraph:

> In inflationary times like these our buying of Government securities does not provide confidence. It undermines confidence. The inevitable result is more and more money and cheaper and cheaper dollars. This means less and less public confidence. *Mr. President, you did not ask us in our recent meeting to commit ourselves to continue on this dangerous road.*[65]

The other problem was to let the Treasury down gradually. To this end the committee, on the same day, approved a proposal as a basis for discussion with the Treasury which involved Federal Reserve support, limited in amount and duration, and a Treasury offering of a new long-term security into which the existing long-term securities could be exchanged at an attractive interest rate. In effect, the Treasury would pay to take off the market the overhang of existing securities which threatened to depress securities prices.[66]

On February 8 Messrs. McCabe and Sproul took this proposal to the Treasury. The discussion in general was an acrimonious recital of past grievances.[67] However, the most significant feature of the meeting was that for the first time the record noted the presence of Assistant Secretary of the Treasury William McChesney Martin. Within six weeks he was to move from the edge of the stage to the center, where he remained for over seventeen years. It was almost as if Mr. Martin had been providentially delivered to heal the breach between the Treasury and the Federal Reserve. He was a Missourian, like Truman and Snyder, and had served as Assistant Secretary of the Treasury since February, 1949. He had the confidence of the Secretary. However, his work in the Treasury was not in the field of debt management, and he had not been directly involved in the bitterness of the preceding years. Indeed he was regarded as the person at the Treasury who best understood the position of the Federal Reserve, and not only because he came from a "Federal Reserve family," his father having been president of the Federal Reserve Bank of St. Louis. He also had some national reputation as a financial genius, because he had been elected president of the New York Stock Exchange at the age of thirty-two, but he had not served in that capacity long enough to acquire the "Wall Street" label.

On February 10 Secretary Snyder informed Chairman McCabe that he was about to go to the hospital for an eye operation, which would keep him out of circulation for about two weeks, and during his absence the Federal Reserve should look to Mr. Martin as its contact with the Treasury. Within a few days Martin asked to begin staff-level discussions with the Federal Reserve on the basis of the Federal Reserve's proposal of February 7. These discussions, mainly between Martin and Bartelt from the Treasury and Riefler, Thomas, and Rouse from the Federal Reserve, went on until the end of February. During this period there was a good deal of maneuvering and talking on the outside, in the executive offices, the Congress, and the press, intended to hold up the hand of one side or the other in the presumed test of strength.

On February 26, 1951, President Truman called a White House meeting of administration economic officials, with McCabe and Sproul, to discuss debt management and monetary policy. He asked the Secretary of the Treasury, the chairman of the Federal Reserve Board, the director of Economic Mobilization, and the chairman of the Council of Economic Advisers to study the relations of the Treasury and the Federal Reserve. The President hoped that "while this study is underway, no attempt will be made to change the interest rate pattern, so that stability in the Government security market will be maintained."[68] However, this was all marginal to the outcome, as the basic proposition had already been decided. After a temporary period of limited support the Federal Reserve would be free to follow a flexible policy, and the Treasury would use that temporary period to refund part of the overhang of 2 1/2 percent long-term bonds into a more attractive security. The discussion revolved around details, in the handling of which considerable ingenuity was shown, but which need not concern us here.[69]

At the end of February the discussion moved from the staff level to the Federal Reserve Board and the Open Market Committee on the one hand,

and Secretary Snyder on the other. The principals agreed, the President, in Florida, assented, apparently on the basis that if it was all right with John Snyder it was all right with him, and the Accord was announced on March 3.

The joint Treasury–Federal Reserve statement was brief:

> The Treasury and the Federal Reserve System have reached full accord with respect to debt-management and monetary policies to be pursued in furthering their common purpose to assure the successful financing of the Government's requirements and, at the same time, to minimize monetization of the public debt.[70]

The significance of the Accord was not immediately clear. Senator Douglas, for example, complained that the statement had been silent on the key point, the commitment to support the bond market.[71] The *New York Times* said that the Accord might be an armed truce.[72] On March 6, Senators Douglas, Flanders, Thye, Tobey, Fulbright, and Gillette introduced a resolution to free the Federal Reserve of obligation to support the bond market. They wanted to give the Federal Reserve "added courage" in what they thought was a continuing contest.[73]

Suspicion was enhanced when Thomas McCabe resigned as chairman of the Federal Reserve on March 9 and President Truman named William Martin to succeed him. In fact, fearing that Martin would be the Treasury's agent, Senator Douglas refrained from voting on his confirmation.

However, after the exchange of the new long-term bonds for the 2 1/2 percent bonds was completed early in April, 1951, the bond market was left without Federal Reserve support, and it became clear to everyone that the era of the peg had been definitely ended. In addition, there was to be abundant evidence that Mr. Martin was not the Treasury's tool.[74]

The Accord liberated monetary policy, for the first time in ten years, to serve primarily as an instrument of general economic stabilization and as a partner of fiscal policy in the pursuit of that goal. Other objectives remained of some importance. The Federal Reserve continued to be concerned with the orderliness of financial markets and with adapting its policy temporarily to the needs of Treasury financing. After 1958 consideration of the balance of payments with the rest of the world came increasingly to the fore in decisions about monetary policy. Nevertheless, domestic economic stability remained the chief objective of monetary policy, and monetary policy retained parity with fiscal policy as a means of achieving economic stability. We had come a long way, in practice as well as in theory, from the idea of stabilizing the economy by fiscal policy alone.

It is inconceivable that monetary policy in the United States would have remained tied forever to a fixed pattern of interest rates. Such a policy would have been too inconsistent with the true priority of national objectives to have survived indefinitely. So the dramatic events of 1950 and 1951 may be viewed as only the accidental aspects of the process by which the inevitable happened. Yet the manner in which it happened left its mark. If monetary policy had floated free of the pegs without a direct confrontation, the importance of a flexible monetary policy might never have become so clear as it did to large numbers of people, and the Federal Reserve would not have been left with so vivid a reminder of the dangers of compromising its independence.

While it is inconceivable that the peg policy could have gone on forever, it is not inconceivable that it could have gone on for a few more years. Just as, with the outbreak of the Korean War, we resumed other parts of the harness of World War II economics, such as the excess-profits tax and wage and price controls, we might have resumed a rigid peg of securities prices for the duration. On the other hand, both Eccles and Sproul said later that they regretted failing to move more vigorously earlier.

Why didn't the Federal Reserve act to achieve a greater degree of freedom earlier, in 1946–48, and why did they act in 1950–51 and succeed against the opposition of the President and the Treasury? A number of factors, economic and political, made the difference.

A fundamental change in policy did not seem important or urgent to the Federal Reserve in the earlier period, whereas it did later. The Federal Reserve sought some minor increases in short-term rates in the earlier period, and always thought that one more small adjustment would enable it to make the proper contribution of monetary policy to restraining inflation. They did not think this contribution was a major one. Being a central banker generates a certain respect for the potentialities of monetary policy, but also a certain reluctance to accept primary responsibility for achieving basic objectives by monetary means. The Federal Reserve shared the common view that the real defense against inflation lay in fiscal policy. Therefore they did not think that what they were being prevented from doing was critical. While the country was experiencing inflation in 1946–48, the expectation was common that inflation was a temporary aspect of the immediate postwar adjustment. If the Federal Reserve could ride through the transition, the tension between monetary policy for stabilization and monetary policy for supporting the securities market would then abate. Particularly, the long-term 2 1/2 percent rate might not be out of line with unsupported interest rates.

After the outbreak of the Korean War we were no longer on our way out of inflation but on our way into it for a period of unforeseeable duration. Moreover, inflation was raging in the second half of 1950 despite a budget surplus, which could be expected not to increase but to turn into a deficit. Time was no longer on the side of the Federal Reserve. Its problems would get worse, not better.

In 1946 the Federal Reserve probably overestimated the fragility of the financial system. It was a long time since there had been any flexibility in the government securities market, and no one knew where the bottom would be if the Federal Reserve abandoned support. By 1950 a series of small relaxations of support had given the Federal Reserve confidence that an unsupported market would not plummet through the floor.

The Federal Reserve also underestimated its power to act independently in the years immediately after World War II. It had acquired the habit of subordination to the Treasury during the war, and before that its experience had been with a strong President, Roosevelt, from whom Marriner Eccles never thought himself independent. Moreover, the Federal Reserve still lived under the shadow of popular suspicion of bankers which was left over from the 1929 crash.

The series of confrontations with the Treasury after 1946 demonstrated that while the Treasury would delay and complain, it was unlikely to take stronger steps to resist. Also, as the existence of the issue became known, a great deal of support in the country for the Federal Reserve came to the surface. Much of this was in the business and financial community, with the notable exception of the commercial bankers, but no popular opposition to the Federal Reserve emerged. The man in the street might have been aroused if the issue had been one of "hard money" versus "full employment," but he could not be expected to rally to the defense of the pattern of interest rates, especially since any savings bonds he owned were redeemable at fixed prices and so were unaffected by the market.

In addition, and most important, major support for the Federal Reserve appeared in the Congress. Senator Douglas was peculiarly qualified to crystallize this. However, there was considerable latent support there anyway, partly derived from the idea that the Federal Reserve was the creature of the Congress, and that while the Congress might direct it, the President and the Secretary of the Treasury should not. The administration played into the hands of this sentiment at the end by seeming to violate protocol in its treatment of the Federal Reserve. And the whole relationship was conditioned by the weak standing of the President in the country when the confrontation came. A public opinion poll in February, 1951, showed that only 26 percent of the population approved of the way Truman was handling his job as President, compared with 45 percent a year earlier and 69 percent two years earlier.

The formal, legal relationship between the Federal Reserve and the Treasury was the same in 1951 as it had been in 1946 and 1941. The actual relationship had changed drastically as a result of changes in economic and political conditions, in personalities, and in the historical background from which the parties drew their understanding of their roles. The Accord of March, 1951, was in turn to be an important part of the history conditioning behavior in the future.

⋙11⋘

Eisenhower Economics

THE Eisenhower administration was to
be a test of the revolution in fiscal policy that had occurred in the preceding
twenty years. It was the first extended period since the development of
many of the new ideas in which the economy was not dominated by hot
war or its immediate aftermath. It was the first period in which monetary
policy was free to play the role of partner to fiscal policy which the postwar
consensus prescribed for it. Moreover, and this was the main element in the
test, the country had the first Republican administration in twenty years.

In the common view of the early 1950's, the fiscal revolution was part
of a more general revolution which consisted of government's acceptance of
responsibility for the performance of the economy, especially for the maintenance of high employment. The fiscal revolution was the acceptance of
the proposition that fiscal policy could and should be a major instrument for
the discharge of this responsibility. This was an overly simple view of what
had happened. The acceptance of this responsibility of government policy
in general and of fiscal policy in particular was a less radical change from
the time of Herbert Hoover than it seemed.

Nevertheless, when the Eisenhower administration came into office the
key question was considered to be whether the Republicans would accept
the responsibility to use the powers of government, including fiscal policy,
to stabilize the economy and maintain high employment. The Democratic
campaign of 1952 had been largely a campaign against Herbert Hoover and
had been based on the proposition that the Republicans had learned nothing
and forgotten nothing in the intervening twenty years. Republican campaign
oratory had done little to correct that impression. If there had been a revolution in national fiscal policy, and not just a revolution in the thinking of

intellectuals and liberals, that would have to be demonstrated in the new Republican administration.

In fact, the Eisenhower administration did confirm the victory of the fiscal revolution. It accepted without any question the idea of governmental responsibility for the overall performance of the economy and the use of fiscal policy as a primary means for discharging that responsibility. General economic effects were the main considerations, although not the only considerations, upon which fiscal decisions were based.

The Eisenhower administration would also test whether, given the desire to manage fiscal policy in a stabilizing manner, it would be practical to do so. Would administrative rigidities, political disagreements, and objectives other than stabilization frustrate the attempt to adapt the budget to the state of the economy? The experience of the Eisenhower years showed that government fiscal action could come fairly close to the expectations of what we have called consensus policy. The administration's policy did not respond to forecasts of economic changes, or even respond promptly to changes that had occurred, but consensus policy did not require that. The expected automatic variations in the budget position, from deficit to surplus, with variations in the economy did occur, and to some degree the timing of tax cuts and expenditure increases was adjusted to economic conditions.

A third test might have been made during the Eisenhower years. Is fiscal policy an effective means of economic stabilization? Is its effect on the level of economic activity powerful? Is the rather unambitious and largely automatic prescription of consensus policy the best way to use that effect? These are difficult questions. Fiscal policy is never the only influence at work on the economy; it is always hard to disentangle its effects from the effects of other variables. To compare the consequence of policies followed with the potential consequences of policies not followed is speculative. Certainly no thorough analysis of these questions was made during the period or later. The main lessons of the experience were probably negative, but negative in a way that supported the continued attempt to use fiscal policy as a stabilizer. Casual observation did not disprove the theory that fiscal policy had an important effect on the economy and could be used to make a significant contribution to stability.

For many years some observers continued to regard the economic and fiscal policy of the Eisenhower administration as backward, prerevolutionary, or even antediluvian. Aside from political reasons, there were probably two confusions which contributed to this view. One was the confusion between fiscal talk and fiscal policy. President Eisenhower and his Treasury Secretaries did not talk the language of modern economics. In this they were no different from their predecessors and not very different from their successors. Eisenhower tended to use moralistic language about pragmatic and functional matters of federal finance. His first Treasury Secretary, George Humphrey, was most at home talking about the Federal budget as if he were giving an annual report to the stockholders of the M. A. Hanna Company. But these were superficialities. The thinking and policies of the administration were much closer than their language to the economics of their time.

A second source of misunderstanding of the Eisenhower fiscal policy was the identification of budget-balancing with old-fashioned or reactionary policy. Modern fiscal policy derived mainly from the Depression when deficits were appropriate. Willingness, and indeed eagerness, to accept deficits came to be the litmus-paper test of modernity. But there was nothing in the new ideas to suggest that balancing the budget or running a surplus was *never* the proper course. The essential point was that the desirability of balancing the budget was not given by some eternal principle but depended on economic conditions which would vary.

The Eisenhower administration's conspicuous attention to budget-balancing, sometimes interpreted as evidence that they had not learned the lessons of the previous two decades, was based upon a judgment about the economic condition of the country between 1953 and 1961. The administration believed that the underlying problem of those years, and most of the time the current and overt problem, was inflation. Given this diagnosis, a prescription of balanced budgets was consistent with, indeed required by, modern fiscal policy. The diagnosis was not unique with the administration, or even unusual at the time, and there was abundant evidence in the preceding years and in the current experience to support it. The diagnosis may have been wrong; it may have been pressed too far and too long. But this is a matter of judgment in the application of a flexible, functional policy; it raises no question about the acceptance of policy itself. When *its* diagnosis was temporarily different, the administration not only tolerated large deficits but took steps to expand them.

The story of the administration's behavior to be told in this chapter will reveal how much it was a part of the fiscal revolution. For the moment we may rely upon evidence from an unexpected source. Testifying about the report of Eisenhower's Council of Economic Advisers in January, 1955, Professor J. K. Galbraith, a leading Democratic economist, said:

> There is much that is admirable in the report of the Council this year. I think
> it has shown considerable grace and ease in getting away from the clichés of
> a balanced budget and the unspeakable evils of deficit financing. Indeed, the

Administration as a whole has shown a remarkable flexibility of mind in the speed with which it has moved away from these slogans.[1]

The distinctive character of the fiscal policy of the Eisenhower administration was not the result of any distinctive philosophy about the general objectives of fiscal policy or the methods to be used in achieving them. Rather it resulted from the particular economic and budgetary conditions they faced. The Republicans came to power after a long period in which prices had risen rapidly when they were not under direct control. Moreover, unemployment was and had been very low—less than 3 percent. At the same time, the budget, despite the exceptionally high level of economic activity, was running a large deficit. The administration's view that its basic problem was inflation was confirmed by its own experience. Its first encounter with the problem of unemployment in 1954 was short and moderate and followed by the resumption of inflation. In the circumstances, its fiscal course was to convert the high-employment deficit to a balance, then to a small surplus, and then to a large one. It moderated its move in this direction during the 1954 and 1958 recessions. But believing that the persistent problem was inflation, it responded to recessions cautiously and turned quickly to the anti-inflationary policy of budget-balancing when economic revival was in sight. There was opposition to this general line of conduct from people who wanted a more expansive policy. But in general it commanded a great deal of bipartisan support and reflected the common view of the nation's economic problem.

Tax Reduction Fifth

The big question about the economic policy of the Republican administration was how it would deal with a recession. This was, of course, the question left over from the Hoover regime. The administration faced this question within a year of its inauguration. But first there was an interlude which revealed certain attitudes of lasting significance.

With the Republican administration there came also a Republican Congress. While the fiscal policy of the administration may have been uncertain, the policy of the Republican fiscal leaders in the Congress was not. That policy, in 1953 as in 1947 and 1948, was tax reduction. In 1953 as in 1947 the first bill introduced in the Republican Congress, H.R. 1, was a bill to reduce individual income taxes across the board. Its sponsor again was the chairman of the Ways and Means Committee, this time Daniel Reed.

The supporters of a cut in the individual income tax were in a strong parliamentary and political position. The excess-profits tax which had been enacted at the outbreak of the Korean War was scheduled to expire on June 30, 1953. Individual income taxes were not scheduled to go down until December 31, 1953. To continue the excess-profits tax beyond its scheduled expiration date would require affirmative action by the Congress, which would be difficult to obtain against the opposition of the powerful chairman of the Ways and Means Committee. But to allow the excess-profits tax to expire, to the benefit of corporations, without at the same time providing tax relief for individuals would be politically embarrassing, especially for an administration which had been tagged as a businessman's administration.

The Administration itself was strongly in favor of tax reduction. It regarded no part of the tax structure as more evil than the excess-profits tax. By confronting the most successful corporations with a 77 percent tax rate, that tax violated all the administration's ideas about the incentives which made the economy thrive. Moreover, the most loyal supporters of the administration, the major business organizations such as the Chamber of Commerce of the United States and the National Association of Manufacturers, regarded the excess-profits tax as the epitome of all the evils against which they had fought for so long and, as they thought, finally successfully. To find *their* administration insisting upon the retention of that tax, the expiration of which even the Democrats had provided for, would be a cruel irony.

Supporters of a tax cut could, and did, invoke modern economic argument on their side. The Korean War was drawing to a close and a substantial reduction of military expenditures was in sight. There was concern in many quarters about a postwar recession. Throughout the first half of 1953 there was discussion in the Federal Reserve Open Market Committee about whether a shift toward monetary ease was required in order to sustain the economy.[2] The shift did not come until June, and was even then described as designed to relieve congestion in the money markets rather than as an anti-recession measure, but the case was not considered closed before that. Thus Daniel Reed was not without some grounds in maintaining that tax cuts should come before expenditure cuts to assure that jobs would be available when military employment declined. As he said, "I am following the lines of Professor Schlichter [*sic*, Sumner Slichter of Harvard] and others, who advise that these cuts should come well in advance."[3] In addition, Congressman Reed used the traditional Republican argument, which went back at least as far as Andrew Mellon, that tax reduction would stimulate the economy, raise the revenues, and help balance the budget.

The administration seems not to have been even tempted by this reasoning. Its position was clearly established at the outset and did not waver. The great domestic enemy was inflation. An essential defense against this enemy was the principle that the budget should be balanced in times of prosperity and high employment. The threat to this principle was the propensity of Congress, and some administrations, under the influence of general or specific political pressures to enact popular but unessential expenditure increases or tax reductions. If the new administration followed this course with the first tax reduction opportunity that *it* faced, immediate inflationary pressures would be intensified and, even worse, it would lose the moral basis for resisting Treasury raids in the future. The issue of the excess-profits tax was an opportunity for the new team to demonstrate its sincerity and preach a lesson to the country. As for the danger of recession, this was the kind of problematic forecast that could always be summoned up in support of loose fiscal measures.

In his state of the Union message on February 2, 1953, President Eisenhower presented his financial program:

> Our immediate task is to chart a fiscal and economic policy that can:
> 1. Reduce the planned deficits and then balance the budget, which means, among other things, reducing Federal expenditures to the safe minimum;
> 2. Meet the huge costs of our defense;
> 3. Properly handle the burden of our inheritance of debt and obligations;
> 4. Check the menace of inflation;
> 5. Work toward the earliest possible reduction of the tax burden;
> 6. Make constructive plans to encourage the initiative of our citizens.[4]

This did not close the door to tax reduction, even in 1953. But tax reduction was not at the head of the list. The main emphasis of the speech was on inflation, and the argument for budget-balancing was the argument against inflation.

A characteristically Delphic passage contained the seeds of much administration thinking of those days:

> It is axiomatic that our economy is a highly complex and sensitive mechanism. Hasty and ill-considered action of any kind could seriously upset the subtle equation that encompasses debts, obligations, expenditures, defense demands, deficits, taxes, and the general economic health of the Nation. Our goals can be clear, our start toward them can be immediate—but action must be gradual.[5]

In February this was a warning to those who were all out for immediate tax reduction. But a little later in the year it could also be read to those who were all out for a draconian policy of budget-balancing.

At his press conference on February 17, the President poured more cold water on the tax-cutting drive:

> In spite of some things that I have seen in the papers over the past 8 or 9 months, I personally have never promised reduction in taxes. Never. . . .
>
> We cannot afford to reduce taxes, reduce incomes, until we have in sight a program of expenditures that shows that the factors of income and of outgo will be balanced.[6]

This still left open a possibility. The balance of the budget did not have to be attained before taxes could be cut. Only a program that showed that the budget would be balanced had to be "in sight." But on the same day, his Secretary of the Treasury, George Humphrey, was confessing to his friends in the Cleveland Chamber of Commerce how hard it was to cut the budget:

> In this matter of cutting expenses, I just want to bring to your attention this thing that I had not appreciated as fully when I was here, just engrossed in business; that I had not appreciated nearly as fully as I do now. I had not appreciated fully how very definitely there is a direct chain of events between the foreign policy of this country and a man working for the success of a business in the city of Cleveland. . . . So when you get right down to it, somewhere from 80 to 90 percent of the budget has nothing to do with just firing employees, or reducing what you may think are wasteful expenditures, but has to do with our security. . . .[7]

By April 30 the President was ready to reveal that the budget for fiscal 1954 would not be balanced, mainly because of continued high defense and foreign aid requirements. Asked at his press conference whether it was now definite that there would not be a balanced budget for fiscal 1954, he replied: "Well, I think it would be safe to say that you can't achieve—I don't see how you can achieve complete balance in your expenditure program. I don't believe it could be done." And in answer to a question about when a balanced budget would be achieved he said: "I must say that a great deal of my waking moments are given over to that problem. And we are going to do it. Now, that's all I can say."[8]

Also on that day Eisenhower disclosed the budget outlook to Congressional leaders meeting with him at the White House. This caused a great blowup between the President and Senator Taft. The Senator was not only shocked that the budget would be unbalanced in the first Republican fiscal year since Hoover; he also predicted that if they could not deliver both a tax reduction and a balanced budget in advance of the 1954 Congressional elections, the Republicans would surely be defeated.[9] But the President had the responsibility for the national security and the domestic welfare, his Cabinet Secretaries and the Budget Bureau had been over the estimates with care, and he was not about to take "hasty and ill-considered action" to achieve even goals he valued as highly as budget-balancing and tax reduction. He held out some hope for further expenditure reduction for fiscal 1955, but would make no commitments.

In fact, the administration was unnecessarily gloomy about its budget prospects. President Truman's last budget message had estimated that with all scheduled tax reductions taking effect there would be a deficit of $9.9 billion in the administrative budget. In his own message to Congress on the budget in May, 1953, after four months in office, Eisenhower reported that the new team had been able to reduce expenditures $4.5 billion below the budget but also had found it necessary to reduce the revenue estimates by $1.2 billion. Thus the deficit had been reduced to $6.6 billion. Retention of the excess-profits tax for six months, plus postponement of the excise tax reductions scheduled for April 1, 1954, would add $1 billion to the revenue for fiscal 1954, reducing the deficit to $5.6 billion. However, the decline of expenditures was grossly underestimated. Actual expenditures for the fiscal year turned out $10 billion below the original Truman estimate, almost entirely because of an unexpectedly rapid decline of military outlays. Thus, if revenues had not been held down by the recession which began in the fall of 1953, the administrative budget would have been close to balance even with all scheduled tax cuts. As it was, the administrative budget deficit for fiscal 1954 was only $3.1 billion.[10]

Moreover, the administration did not use the cash-consolidated budget as its standard of budget-balancing, although many had recommended that it do so. Since the cash-consolidated or "cash" budget reflected the operations of the trust accounts as well as other financial transactions of the government, and the trust accounts were then in surplus, the cash-consolidated budget showed much smaller deficits than the administrative budget. The same calculations which added up to a $5.6 billion deficit in the administrative budget showed a cash budget deficit of $2.8 billion. When the year was over, the cash deficit was only $.2 billion despite the recession. The President's interim budget message of May, 1953, carried the cash budget figures but made nothing of them.[11] Answers to reporters' questions during press conferences showed that in the spring of 1953 Eisenhower did not understand what the cash budget was or its significance.[12]

On the basis of his estimate of the budgetary situation, the President offered his tax program to the Congress:

1. The excess-profits tax should be continued until January 1, 1954;

2. The 5 percent reduction of the corporate profits tax scheduled for April 1, 1954, under existing legislation should be repealed;

3. The rise in the Social Security contribution rate from 1 1/2 percent

to 2 percent on employers and employees, scheduled for January 1, 1954, should be postponed until January 1, 1955, because of a large surplus in the Social Security fund;

4. The reductions in excise taxes scheduled for April 1, 1954, should be postponed until a sounder system of excise taxation can be developed; (Presumably this implied a movement toward a broader-based, uniform system of sales taxation. Recommendations were promised for January, 1954, but were not forthcoming, then or later.)

5. The individual income tax cut scheduled for January 1, 1954, should go into effect on that date;

6. The administration would submit a program for tax reform in 1954, but the message did not indicate whether this program would involve any net revenue loss.[13]

The whole message was suffused with the argument for balancing the budget as a defense against inflation.

In view of the budget and economic picture then presented, and in view of later developments, the commitment to reduction of individual income taxes on January 1, 1954, is the outstanding point in the program. The President said that this tax reduction was made possible by economies his administration had achieved. But he still showed a deficit of $5.6 billion for fiscal 1954. He might have claimed that a balanced budget was "in sight" for fiscal 1955, when the full revenue effect of the tax cut would have been felt, but he did not, and he had been unwilling to make any such commitment to Senator Taft. Later, in his January, 1954, economic report, the President referred to this decision of May, 1953, as follows:

> Early in the year, when inflation was still a real danger, it seemed reasonable to expect that in another six or twelve months the boom might recede and that at such a time some reduction in taxes would become appropriate. In the meantime, the only proper course was to maintain taxes while seeking to curtail expenditures. The Tax Message, submitted to the Congress on May 20, 1953, therefore called for full maintenance of all taxes during 1953, but suggested that taxes might be reduced in January 1954.[14]

When this statement was made the economy was already in a recession, and the administration wanted to take credit for foresight and advance preparations. However, there was no clue in May, 1953, that the recommendation for a later tax reduction was intended to forestall or cushion a recession. True, the tax message reduced Truman's revenue estimate for fiscal 1954 by $1.2 billion because of a downward revision of the economic forecast. "The new estimate is made on the assumption that employment and business will continue at a high level, but in the interest of prudence some relaxation of the extremely high rates of activity now existing is allowed for."[15] But this reduction in the economic forecast and the resulting lowering of the revenue estimate were considered by the administration to strengthen the case against tax reduction in 1953, not for tax reduction in 1954. Also the message did not give the impression that it "suggested" that taxes "might" be reduced in January 1954; rather it recommended that tax cuts should go into effect.

The fact was that the administration had no choice. It was extremely unlikely that it could prevent tax reduction in 1954. The tax cut was provided by existing law, and no new legislation was required to put it into effect. Thus, Mr. Eisenhower did not have the weapon of the veto which Mr. Truman had used in 1947 and 1949. To stop the tax cut would have required affirmative action by Congress, which Senator Taft had said he would not support and which the Congress almost certainly would not take. The administration's only option, and its chief interest, was to prevent tax reduction in 1953. To create any doubt that the tax cuts would go into effect in 1954 would have only hardened the determination of the Congressional tax cutters in 1953.

In the weeks after the tax message, Washington was treated to one of its favorite kinds of soap opera. The administration had H.R. 1, the income tax cut bill, bottled up in the House Rules Committee, and Daniel Reed couldn't get it out. But the administration needed a bill to extend the excess-profits tax, and Reed had promised that no such bill would come out of his Ways and Means Committee. Would the administration be able to overcome the committee chairman, and what would it take to do it? As a secondary story line, what would the business organizations, torn between their hatred of the excess-profits tax and their devotion to Eisenhower, do?

Both the Chamber of Commerce and the National Association of Manufacturers had approved positions in favor of the termination of the excess-profits tax on the scheduled date, June 30, 1953. After the President's tax message, each reconsidered this position. Congressman Reed charged Secretary Humphrey with "lobbying" to get the business organizations to change their stands. The Secretary denied this, but there had been contacts between the Treasury and the organizations, and it was known that the Treasury would welcome a recount. In the chamber the vote was very close, but still in favor of the termination of the tax on June 30. In the NAM the vote of the directors was actually 84 to 46 in favor of going along with the administration on postponing the expiration, but the rules of the association required a two-thirds majority to reverse a previous position, and this was not quite forthcoming. So both of the major organizations testified against the extension of the tax. However, the force of their testimony, which would have been small anyway because the testimony was so obviously expected, was weakened by knowledge of division within the ranks.[16]

The President was distressed by the positions of the chamber and the NAM. "These business organizations, in the President's opinion, did not seem to realize that the middle-of-the-road course he was pursuing was the only one that gave them any chance of having a fair share of legitimate influence with the government. If a Republican Administration was to make a go of it, he felt, the right wing would have to make certain concessions from its traditions. Taking a practical political view, both Lodge and Benson observed that no stand taken by the Chamber or the NAM would do Eisenhower much harm."[17]

In the end the Republican Congress, only the second in twenty-three years, which had come into power on Eisenhower's coattails, could not resist him. Through a series of maneuvers the power of the House leadership and the Rules Committee was brought to bear, and a majority of the Ways and Means Committee then voted to override their chairman and send the tax extension bill to the floor for a vote. It was quickly approved by the House and the Senate and signed by the President on July 16.

The issue over which the administration made its fight with Congressman Reed was not of great immediate importance, at least in economic terms. Allowing the excess-profits tax to die on June 30 would have reduced the revenue for fiscal 1954 by at most $800 million. Even if it would have been politically necessary to accompany this reduction by advancing the date of the whole income tax reduction scheduled for January 1, 1954—and some compromise might have been possible—the further revenue loss would not have exceeded $1.5 billion. Together, this was less than the amount by which the administration announced it had cut Truman's budget, and the actual expenditure reduction turned out to be much greater. There would have been no effect on balancing the fiscal 1955 budget, which was the real goal. Moreover, as long as the cuts were known to be coming anyway, the inflationary effects of advancing their date by six months would have been small, especially in the case of the excess-profits tax, and as it turned out these effects would have been welcome when the economy began to decline soon after the extension bill was signed.

However, the struggle was important as an indication of the attitudes of the parties. On the one hand it showed again the willingness of the conservatives in Congress and in business to temporize with the idea of budget-balancing to get a tax cut of the kind they liked. On the other hand it showed

the administration's great concern with inflation—the high priority it gave
to budget-balancing as a defense against inflation and its willingness to sacrifice tax reductions, even of the kind it valued most, such as elimination of the
excess-profits tax, to an anti-inflationary fiscal policy. More than that, the
incident revealed the administration's view of its responsibility as national
leader and teacher. The administration believed that the Congress, the political parties, and the public generally had been subverted by bad practice and
false doctrine to the easy path of perpetual deficits and perpetual inflation.
The administration had a duty, it thought, to correct this error, not only by
words but also by the example of good, and especially hard, works. The
administration was determined to show the way. As George Humphrey
told the Ways and Means Committee: "I think if the Administration has the
the courage to come in here and ask you gentlemen to extend this tax it is
the firmest good-faith showing that we are determined to balance the budget
and to accomplish sound economy. . . ."[18]

The President denied the charge that he made a fetish of balancing the
budget. He knew there were times when it should not be balanced. But he
did not think those times were all the time. He believed others were making
a fetish of *not* balancing the budget, and he was devoted to eradicating that
fetish.

The Republicans Face a Recession

The Republicans were soon to have an opportunity to show whether
balancing the budget was a fetish or not. In August of 1953 the economy began
to decline. This was not unexpected. There had been a common anticipation
of a possible decline when Korean War expenditures would be cut back,
although memories of the erroneous forecasts at the end of World War II
tended to make predictors cautious.[19] In fact, production began to sag even
before government expenditures started to fall as business cut back inventories, partly in anticipation of the coming reduction in military expenditures.
There was a decline of $10 billion in federal expenditures from the second
quarter of 1953 to the second quarter of 1954.

Eisenhower's statements before he became President gave little clue to the
manner in which he would react to the problem of recession. Two not quite
identical statements during the 1952 campaign indicated how sweeping, and
at the same time vague, was his commitment then.

On October 22 he said:

> If the finest brains, the finest hearts, that we can mobilize in Washington, can
> foresee the signs of any recession and depression that would put honest hard-

working men out of work, the full power of private industry, of municipal government, of state government, of the Federal government will be mobilized to see that it does not happen. I cannot pledge you more than that.[20]

Again, a week later:

At the first sign of any approaching recession in this country, there will be instantly mobilized under the finest professional, business, labor and other leaders that we have, every resource of private industry, of local government, of state government and of Federal government to see that never again shall depression come to us.[21]

While this was intended to be reassuring, and probably was, it was unrealistic and rather frightening if taken literally. Recession or depression seemed to be viewed by the Presidential candidate as an extraordinary cataclysmic event outside the regular framework of government problems, to be met by the ad hoc mobilization of leadership and resources from all sectors of the society. In fact, forestalling or moderating recessions is one of the routine functions of government, to be handled by machinery that is constantly in place and in operation and that relies upon a limited number of continuing instruments specialized to that purpose. That is, indeed, the sense of the Employment Act of 1946, although it too contains some rather flamboyant language.

When he came into office, the President was aware of this. One of his first tasks was to assure that he had one of these "finest brains" constantly available to him at the White House to advise him on the adaptation of policy to the continuing problem of maintaining high employment. The Employment Act had provided for this in the form of the Council of Economic Advisers. At the beginning of 1953, however, the future of the council was in doubt. In a mood of disaffection with the Truman council, under Leon Keyserling, Congress had appropriated funds only through March, 1953. Congress was willing to allow the President to have an economic adviser, but whether the council would survive was uncertain. However, the main intent was to make a clean sweep of the Keyserling council staff, and once this was accomplished funds were provided for the continuation of the council, at the strong urging of the President.

Eisenhower named as chairman of his council Professor Arthur F. Burns of Columbia University and the National Bureau of Economic Research. The selection of Burns was significant in several respects. The appointment of a professor who had no previous political or business connections in an administration which seemed otherwise to believe that any corporation president could do anything, indicated recognition that economic stabilization was a serious, and largely technical, job. Burns was the first chairman of the council who was a specialist in the field of the council's main activity. Moreover, although this may not have been known when he was appointed, he was a man of force and stature who could hold his own in discussions around the Eisenhower Cabinet table.

Also, Burns well represented the element of continuity and agreement within an economics profession that seemed sharply divided between Keynesians and anti-Keynesians, and between liberals and conservatives. Burns was no Keynesian. He had been thirty-two years of age when the *General Theory* appeared, probably too old to get that "peak of Darien" feeling that some younger men experienced at the occasion. If he was anyone's disciple he was a disciple of Wesley C. Mitchell who had been an economic adviser to Herbert Hoover. One of his last writings before appointment to the chairmanship of the council was a critical analysis of Keynesian doctrine. He found it too simple and mechanical as an explanation of the economic process. It assumed as constant too many relationships that were variable, and whose variation would upset predictions based on the Keynesian reasoning. Two points in Burns' thinking were of special importance to the Eisenhower policy. First, Burns believed strongly in the continuity of the economic process, with developments at each stage of economic fluctuations largely conditioning developments in succeeding stages. Thus the seeds of the recession were in the previous recovery. One conclusion from this was that stabilizing action should be taken early in an upswing or decline, or preferably before it started; otherwise it might be safest not to act at all. Second, he placed great weight on confidence and expectations as determinants of economic activity, particularly of business investment.

At the same time, although not a Keynesian he accepted certain ideas which are often considered the hallmark of Keynesian policy. He recognized that the economy would not stabilize itself, that the government could and should act to reduce instability even though complete stability was unattainable, and that the fiscal instrument was one of the most powerful the government could use for that purpose. He did not disagree with the Keynesian view of the direction of the effects of fiscal actions—that expenditure increases and tax reductions were expansive and vice versa. But concern about the difficulties of forecasting and the lags of policy made him cautious in prescribing fiscal action.

The fiscal policy of the Eisenhower administration was not the fiscal policy of Arthur Burns alone. However, he was an important influence, and especially when the economy was sick, the administration was inclined to listen to the doctor.

The other major influence on the fiscal policy of Eisenhower's first term was George Humphrey, the Secretary of the Treasury. Humphrey too was an illustration of the extent to which there was a consensus on fiscal policy in America, an illustration all the more impressive because he came to the consensus in spite of all his instincts and intuitions. Humphrey was a business-man's businessman, not only because he was a success in business, but also because other businessmen could count on his opinions to be firmly grounded in the values they shared. No one could be more sincere and persuasive in reciting the litany of budget-balancing and sound finance at the drop of a hat. But when decisions with important economic and political consequences were to be made, he relied upon the simple pragmatism of modern eco-nomics.

Although it came near the end of his term at the Treasury, an episode which began at a press conference in January, 1957, gave a good example of the two sides of Humphrey that were always present:

> QUESTION: Mr. Secretary, you say that a tax reduction must be conditioned upon the continuation of our present prosperity. Does that mean that the Administra-tion will not cut taxes so that it can add to purchasing power to offset a recession or to prevent a threatened recession?
>
> HUMPHREY: I will contest a tax cut out of deficits as long as I am able. I will not approve, myself, of a tax cut out of a deficit. I think it would start a downward spiral that would be serious. I don't believe in this idea that you can cut taxes out of deficits, and then build up from that.
>
> QUESTION: Then you don't believe in compensatory spending?
>
> HUMPHREY: What do you mean by that?
>
> QUESTION: Increasing the level of Government spending during a period in which business generally is declining and, therefore, presumably tax receipts will be declining.
>
> HUMPHREY: No, I don't think so, Joe. I don't think you can spend yourself rich. I think we went all through that for a good many years, and we kept spending and spending and spending, and we still didn't help our employment or help our total position.[22]

When this exchange took place, in January, 1957, the Secretary was not faced with any immediate problem of recession, and his answer reflected his general principles. Even then, on second thought the administration, and Humphrey also, knew he had given the wrong answer. A week later the President was asked about Humphrey's statement:

> QUESTION: Mr. President, what comment would you care to make on Secretary Humphrey's contention that deficit spending is never justified even as a tool to ease a recession?

PRESIDENT: Well, Secretary Humphrey was giving some of his convictions about a hypothetical situation.

Now, from the very time that I first agreed to enter politics, one of the questions that has been put at me most is, "What would you do to prevent a depression of the character that we experienced in the twenties [thirties]?" My answer has always been, I would do everything that was constitutional and the Federal Government could do. I do not believe there is any cure you can prescribe in advance for that sort of thing. But I do want to point out there is no such thing in prospect at this time and, frankly, I don't believe that one of the character of the twenties [thirties] can ever occur again.

I believe the social security payments, the unemployment insurance payments, the income that comes to people who were then indigent and were selling apples and walking the streets, tends to keep up purchasing power that would ameliorate the effects of a depression that might have a pretty good start.

Now, since our economy is a delicate thing, and you might see signs of a depression coming on you would think in two or three months, you begin then to apply moderate means, and then more, and if it kept going, finally you would go into every single thing, and very quickly, that would—if the thing got serious—that would correct the situation. And there would be no limit, I think, to what should be attempted as long as it was constitutional.[23]

The Secretary had his opportunity to get back in line a few days later on the television program, "Meet the Press":

CHILDS: Mr. Secretary, the President said at his press conference that he would use any Constitutional means to cure a depression, whereas, you said that you would resign, probably, if there were a tax cut in the face of deficit spending. Doesn't this open up a pretty wide difference between you and the President?

HUMPHREY: No, I don't think so, Mr. Childs. I think that we both have the same objective. We both would do anything that we thought would be effective to prevent a depression. The only question is what and when various things are effective.

CHILDS: Do you reject the theory of so many of the professional economists that you must use government spending when business falls off? Do you think that's an unsound theory?

HUMPHREY: It all depends upon what happens to income at the same time. I think that the time, the real time, to prevent a depression is before it starts. The old adage of "an ounce of prevention is worth a pound of cure" is a very good thing to remember.

CHILDS: Would it be fair to say that your disagreement is with the Council of Economic Advisers, and perhaps with Gabriel Hauge, the President's economic right hand in the White House, because they suggest, or at least the President suggested in his economic report, that there would have to be very flexible policies in relation to economy?

HUMPHREY: I don't think that necessarily there's any disagreement anywhere. Flexible policies can be used, but, as I say, the various things that you would and might do should be used at various times. I think when you attempt to answer hypothetical questions and haven't all the facts before you it's very difficult to pick out the timing of when one method would be appropriate or another would be appropriate.[24]

A few days later, on February 4, 1957, before the Joint Economic Committee, Mr. Humphrey came more directly to the point:

FLANDERS: Since you advocate less Government spending in times of inflation, would you then advocate an increase in federal expenditures during periods of deflation?

HUMPHREY: I think I would. I would if such increases were kept in reasonable bounds; as long as they did not injure the confidence of the public, the business population. . . .[25]

This probing to find the true George Humphrey under the budget-balancing veneer should not have been necessary in 1957. His statements and actions in 1953 and 1954 had already shown considerable malleability on the subject of balancing the budget. Although, as we have seen, the administration had no choice in the spring of 1953 other than to announce that it would permit taxes to decline on December 31, it was Humphrey's public role to explain that this tax reduction was desirable, even though the budget was not in balance, in order to prevent the decline of military spending from causing a recession. Thus, in an interview on June 12, 1953, he was asked:

QUESTION: Will a substantial dollar reduction in the budget give the economy of the country a jolt?

HUMPHREY: I don't think so at all. I think what would happen is this: We have already anticipated some reductions in the $74 billion, or else we would not dare to permit this individual income tax reduction to go in January 1. We have been criticized. I have been criticized for taking the position that we ought to put in a tax reduction in January before the budget is balanced. I don't think that's correct.

I don't think we ought to wait to get our budget completely in balance before we anticipate the release of some of the money that we are expecting to save for the people themselves to spend for their own purposes. I think we have to take a gamble, that we can make some of the savings we think we can. We have to take a chance and release to the people for their own expenditures some of the money that we've been spending for them and not wait until we get it all in the bank before we give any of it to them. We are betting on ourselves, that we can make some reductions ahead of time and give the money to the people before we've demonstrated that we are going to perform.[26]

The Secretary was to repeat this theme many times in the next year. A policy of allowing tax rates to decline even though the budget would not be in balance was justified by the short-term economic conditions—if a decline of expenditures could be foreseen which would subsequently bring the budget into balance at the lower tax rates. This was not a sign of preparation to take active measures in the budget to counter a recession—which was still a small cloud on the horizon—but it was a sign of willingness to interpret the budget-balancing rule in an elastic way.

Concern about a possible recession became active within the administration in the summer of 1953, and a number of defensive measures, including fiscal measures, were considered and some preparations were made. Studies of the expansibility of public works were initiated, and agencies were instructed to develop plans for an increase of public construction if that should become desirable. But no positive anti-recession fiscal measures were taken in 1953. The unemployment rate in August, 1953, was the lowest of the entire postwar period and up to the present date. According to the figures then available the rate was only 1.9 percent in August and had risen only to 3 percent in December.[27] A large tax cut was coming automatically on January 1, 1954. The administration was preparing a major tax revision bill, incorporating some tax reduction and—it believed—substantial incentives for business investment, to be enacted in the spring of 1954. Moreover, the Federal Reserve was pursuing an expansive monetary policy. The administration saw no emergency requiring it to give up its long-range goal of expenditure reduction. Its basic strategy was to push ahead toward that goal, unless conditions turned unexpectedly bad, while counting on tax reductions and monetary ease to keep the readjustment small and brief.[28]

While the administration would not take positive action that would increase the budget deficit as long as the recession was mild, it wished to assure the country that it would act vigorously if the prospect deteriorated seriously, and it would not be deterred by fear of the deficit. A picture of his flexible attitude on balancing the budget was given by Eisenhower at a news conference on October 8, 1953:

> Balancing the budget will always remain a goal of any administration that believes as much as we do that the soundness of our money must be assured, and that the unbalanced budget has a very bad effect on it.
>
> That does not mean to say that you can pick any specific date and say, "Here, all things must give way before a balanced budget." It is a question of where the importance of a balanced budget comes in; but it must be the aim of any sound money program.[29]

His general position was spelled out further a month later in answer to a question about plans to counteract the decline in business:

> Every week the subject of my conference with Dr. Arthur Burns, whom I consider one of the ablest men in this whole field, one of the subjects is to keep me informed as to what is going on there with his plans when dealing with other parts of the Government, as to what we can do, when we should do it, and how.
>
> As you know, you get favorable and unfavorable indices about the future always at the same time, and it becomes a delicate matter of judgment. I will say this to you again: When it becomes clear that the Government has to step in, as far as I am concerned, the full power of Government, of Government credit, and of everything the Government has will move in to see that there is no widespread unemployment and we never again have a repetition of conditions that so many of you here remember when we had unemployment.[30]

This philosophy, of course, leaves open two questions. First, how bad do conditions have to get before the need for strong action is clear? Second, how well prepared is the government to take strong action promptly when it is needed?

The administration was not fully tested on either of these questions during the 1954 recession. The decline never reached the point where the administration thought that strong action was needed, so one can only say that the critical point was somewhere below the low point reached in 1954. However, discussions within the administration, and some small actions, reveal that the administration thought it might not be far from the critical point at some time in the spring of 1954. And since the critical point was never reached, the adequacy of the preparations was never tested.

1954—TO ACT OR NOT TO ACT?

If the administration had a fiscal program for the recession, its first opportunity to initiate it, or at least to announce it, came in January, 1954, with the annual budget message and economic report. By this time it was clear that the economy was receding in the transition to peace, although the administration never used the term "recession".[31] The rate of unemployment in December was still only 3 percent according to the figures then available, but it had risen from 1.8 percent in October. The economic report reflected some concern: "But it was important that the transition, if there was to be one, be carried through without shock and that the readjustment be moderate and not cumulate." "It is well to recognize, however, that an inventory readjustment can affect other types of spending and communicate itself to the stream of business and consumer spending as well."[32]

However, only by reading the budget message between the lines with the aid of imagination could one detect in it any trace of the economic conditions of January 1954. There was no suggestion that the effort to reduce expenditures had been at all tempered by the decline of the economy. "In preparing this budget the administration has directed its attention to essential activities and programs rather than to those which some might consider desirable and appropriate, at this time, for the Federal Government to undertake."[33] The phrase "at this time" sounds like a rejection of the idea of increasing certain expenditures because of the economic decline then under way.

The centerpiece of the budget, and indeed one of the main pillars of Eisenhower economic policy, was the program of tax revision to be enacted in 1954. In a sense the origins of this program went back to the debates of the late 1930's. Then some economists were beginning to argue that the American economy could never reach and maintain high employment without continuous federal budget deficits. They contended that private investment would not, on the average, be sufficient to absorb all the savings that would be made in the rich American economy when it was operating at high employment. The common answer of businessmen and conservatives was that private investment would indeed usually, although not necessarily always, be sufficient if government policies did not place obstacles in the way of earning a reasonable return on investment. The obstacle at the head of the list was heavy and discriminatory taxation of investment income. So the conservative program for achieving high employment without persistent deficits started with pro-investment tax reform.

At the end of World War II the tax burden on profits and other investment income was much higher than the New Deal had ever dreamed of. Some of this came down in 1945, but much of it was restored during the Korean War so that the demand for tax revision to encourage private investment was as strong as ever when Eisenhower came into office. Unemployment had, of course, been low during most of the postwar period despite these high taxes on investment. However, this was attributed to the pent-up demands left by the war, to frequent deficits, and to continuous inflation and threat of inflation which gave a temporary spur to investment. It was the intention of the Eisenhower administration to leave all that behind—the deficits and the inflation—and to maintain high employment without them. An essential part of its program for doing this was to relieve the tax burden on investment. It wanted primarily to permit businesses to charge off their investment expenditures more rapidly, to give businesses more opportunity to balance losses of particular years against the gains of earlier or later years, and to reduce the double taxation of dividends. These reforms would cost revenue, but they were not regarded as simply means to encourage private spending by reducing the federal tax taken out of private incomes. Rather they were ways to encourage investment by raising the prospective profitability of investment.

In the economic philosophy of the Eisenhower administration the 1954 tax reform was more than a way of promoting high employment without deficits and would have been desired even if there had been no unemployment problem. It was a means of assuring that in a prosperous economy there would be a high rate of private investment, which was regarded as critical for rapid growth of total output and of output per worker. Planning for the tax reform began as soon as the new team came to Washington and was announced in the President's message of May 20, 1953.[34] The program would have been pushed even if there had been no decline of employment in 1953, and the budget message did not mention the recession. Even the economic report, which was much more concerned with the recession than the budget message was, did not describe the tax reform as an anti-recession measure but only said that the tax reform was "timely" in view of the economic conditions. Probably the economic conditions of late 1953 and early 1954 did not much affect the size of the tax reform package. In discussions within the administration Arthur Burns concerned himself mainly with supporting those parts of the proposed package which might be most quickly effective in stimulating investment and thereby guarding against a prolongation of the decline. But this did not significantly alter the composition of the package. The tax revision measure was not a response to the recession. However, it was a reflection of the administration's concern with bringing about as quickly as possible conditions which would promote high employment and growth in 1954 and subsequently, without the need to rely upon deficits and inflation.

The tax reform package would reduce revenues by about $1.4 billion in fiscal year 1955 and leave a deficit for that year of $2.9 billion in the administrative budget, according to the President's estimates. The great value the administration saw in the tax reform is indicated by its willingness to press forward with it despite the budget deficit. However, the message pointed out that there would be a small surplus—around $100 million—in the cash budget, so that the administration's failure on the budget-balancing front was not complete.

Up to this point, that is through the time of the delivery of the budget message and the economic report in January, 1954, the administration's fiscal policy to counter the recession was to carry on despite the recession with the course that would have been followed if there had been no recession. At the same time the administration insisted that it would go farther if and when that was needed. As the economic report said:

> The Government will not hesitate to make greater use of monetary, debt management, and credit policy, including liberalized use of Federal insurance of private obligations, or to modify the tax structure, or to reduce taxes, or to expand on a large scale the construction of useful public works, or to take any other steps that may be necessary. The Government must and will be ready to deal with any contingencies that may arise.[35]

The question was, when would other steps be necessary. From January, that is from the time Congress returned to Washington, there were many who said that the time had come. The standard Democratic line was that the Republicans were trying to sweep the recession under the rug. They described the administration's program as a do-nothing policy, or worse, a "trickle-down" policy which sought to help the unemployed by the circuitous, if not insincere, policy of giving tax relief to the corporations and wealthy individuals. Senator Douglas had great fun with administration witnesses before the Joint Economic Committee over the question of the definition of the word "recession" and whether what was going on did not fit into that category. The Democratic policy alternative to the administration's program was a reduction of income taxes in the lower brackets to stimulate consumption expenditures. As a political platform this had the advantage, in addition to showing a determination to do something about the recession, of offering benefits to the low-income taxpayers who were allegedly slighted in the administration's tax program.

The administration had two positions on the continuing economic decline and the criticism that came with it—one position for public consumption and one for internal consideration. The outside position was one of calm and assurance. Much had been done, nothing more needed to be done now (whatever the date), and the government was alert and prepared to do anything more that might be needed later. The government placed great weight on confidence as a factor essential to recovery and sought not only to preserve confidence through its own utterances but also to discourage others from spreading gloom or to censure those who did so. Thus, when Walter Reuther wrote to Eisenhower suggesting that he call a national conference on unemployment, the President replied with a little sermon:

> While we must recognize and seek to deal with particular instances of economic hardship as they arise, it is essential to the achievement of greater national economic strength to maintain a steady, unshakable attitude of public confidence in the

capacity of the American economy for continued growth. All of our citizens in positions of leadership have the responsibility of placing in the proper perspective transitional periods such as we are presently passing through.[36]

The administration's own posture of alertness was spelled out a little later (February 17, 1954) at the President's press conference:

QUESTION: Mr. President, do you think the economic downturn has reached a point where consumers should get larger tax concessions than your program called for?

PRESIDENT: Well, I can't give you an affirmative answer to that one at this moment. As you know, the Economic Report states that that is a measure to bring in very quickly when you see this thing spread very definitely.

I should think that March ought to be sort of the key month. March is a month when, I am told, employment begins normally to pick up and you have a definite upturn in the curve. Now, if that isn't true, I should say then we would have a very definite warning that would call for the institution of a number of measures; possibly this tax reduction would be one of the first considered, although I can't say for certain. . . .

I would say this: for the last several weeks all of us have been alert to this day by day, trying to make certain that there is no move neglected on the part of the Government that could be helpful, to make sure that we don't have any real recession. And I will tell you this: so far as using the powers of the Government are concerned why, we are using them gradually. Now, if this thing would develop so that it looks like we are going into anything major, I wouldn't hesitate one second to use every single thing that this Government can bring to bear to stop any such catastrophe in this country.[37]

On March 15 the President addressed the nation over radio and television about his tax bill and rejected the suggestion that the tax cut should be enlarged because of economic conditions. The government would do everything necessary against a depression, but the situation didn't call for a bigger tax cut then.[38] In his press conference on March 24 and in another address on April 5 he again assured the country that much had already been done and much more was in reserve to be used if necessary, "But on the other hand, your Government does not intend to go into any slambang emergency program unless it is necessary."[39]

But the administration's internal discussions in the Cabinet reveal much more anxiety. As contrasted with the public statements, there is less confidence about where the economy is going, about the ability to appraise the developing situation, and about the ability to take appropriate action in time. Most striking was the looseness of the connection between the apparent consensus of Cabinet meetings and consequent action.[40]

On February 5 the President stressed the importance of planning so that the government would be able to start work quickly if necessary on useful public works projects and set July 1 as a tentative date for being prepared to act. Various power, flood-control, and highway projects were discussed. The President indicated that he "was ready then and there to ask Congress for supplemental appropriations for a few immediate projects if any member of the Cabinet recommended it." But no request emerged from this discussion.

On March 12, "The President was in a deadly serious mood." Unemployment was rising. "Timely action would forestall the need for drastic action." Stassen and Flemming suggested some small steps that might be taken at once. But nothing was done except to ask Burns to keep everyone alert.

One week later the Cabinet encountered one of the perennial issues of stabilization policy—how to maintain confidence. Stassen suggested that continuing confidence depended on the belief that the administration would take timely action, and that the time had come to show some action such as an increase in government purchasing. Burns agreed. But Humphrey thought confidence rested on the belief that the government would follow sound fiscal policies and not act prematurely. Also politics reared its head. The Democrats were pushing their bill to raise individual income tax exemptions, and it seemed that the bill might succeed in the Congress if economic conditions worsened. This was an additional reason, in the President's opinion, "to take immediate action to counter the decline and head off the Democrats." On the basis of this reasoning, Humphrey agreed that projects which were to be started eventually might well be started immediately. However, the problem of what to do forthwith was again referred to Burns for study.

While the administration was pondering, the Republicans in Congress, perhaps because the 1954 elections meant more to them, were acting. On March 4 the Ways and Means Committee reported a bill reducing excise taxes by about $1 billion a year. Support for the bill was spearheaded, as is usual in such cases, by the industries affected. However, part of the argument for it was that it would help stimulate employment. There was the further advantage from the Republican point of view that it somewhat diluted the Democratic charge that the administration's tax program was excessively tilted toward helping the rich. The administration did not like the bill but did not fight it. Burns later said, "We felt that the cut might not be a bad idea for countercyclical reasons." On March 31, the day he signed the bill, Eisenhower said, "We have every reason to believe that it will be a stimulating factor in our economy."[41] The excise tax cut was the largest stimulating fiscal action of 1954 which would not have been taken if there had been no recession. In its economic report of January, 1955, the administration listed the excise tax cut among steps "taken by the Government to stimulate the economy," along with the tax reform bill and monetary ease.[42]

By the end of March the administration was winding up to take some steps on its own. On March 26, "the sense of mounting urgency continued" in the Cabinet. Burns presented the results of his studies in the form of a list of actions that could be taken. "Humphrey agreed that the Administration ought to get additional measures started." A first, and minor, decision was taken to speed up work on the tanker construction program.[43] Another six weeks elapsed before a major decision was made to accelerate expenditures on programs across the board, within the limits of the expenditure estimates for fiscal 1955. That is, the estimates for the fiscal year were not to be exceeded, but the proportion of the expenditure made in the early part of the fiscal year was to be increased. By the time this decision was made signs were appearing that the decline of the economy was levelling out. However, these signs were not yet conclusive, and the timing and vigor of an upturn were still uncertain. The administration might have made a case for further delay. The fact that the Congressional election was only six months off undoubtedly helps to explain why the decision was made in May when it had not been made in the gloomier days of March. But the decision may also be regarded in part as the delayed reaction to the discussions held and studies set in motion two months earlier. In any case, the action taken did not fall within Eisenhower's category of a "slambang" program. According to the estimates of Wilfred Lewis, the effect of the May 14 decision was to raise the annual rate of federal spending by $.3 billion in the third quarter of calendar 1954, $.8 billion in the fourth quarter, and $1.7 billion in the first quarter of 1955.[44] It came too late to influence the timing of the upturn but probably contributed something to its strength.

By June the evidence that the decline had ended was fairly strong. The government took no further fiscal action aimed at the recession. The administration continued to plug for its tax reform bill, which it regarded as essential for reaching high employment and growth on the other side of the recession valley, and that was finally enacted on August 16. Thereafter the administration turned its attention to budget-balancing once again.

The recession was mild. The average unemployment rate was 5.5 percent in 1954 as compared with 5.9 percent in 1949. During the 1949 recession there had been eleven months in which unemployment exceeded 6 percent. In the 1954 recession there was one month of 6.0 percent, one month of

6.1 percent, and none higher. The administration could feel that it had passed a considerable test. The country had experienced the first Republican recession since the catastrophe of 1929 and had come through relatively unscathed. Also, the stabilizing budget policy had passed a test. The decline of the national income and rise of unemployment had reduced tax liabilities substantially and increased unemployment compensation payments. The combined effect was to make the drop in the annual rate of private incomes after tax almost $10 billion less than the drop in earned private incomes before tax. This helped to sustain consumption and business fixed investment and permitted the decline of inventories to be absorbed without setting off a downward spiral. The automatic drop of revenues and increase of unemployment compensation payments temporarily stalled the administration's drive to balance the budget. The stabilizing budget policy had warned against frustrating this automatic effect by raising taxes in a recession. The experience of 1954 demonstrated what had not been clear to everyone even in the fall of 1953—that the question about tax policy in a recession would be not whether to raise taxes but whether or how much to cut them.

The administration consistently maintained that it was willing and prepared to do more if necessary. Its failure to do more did not by itself demonstrate that it would have been unwilling or unprepared. There was certainly a legitimate basis for disagreement about whether more should have been done, which even hindsight does not resolve.[45] In January, 1955, by which time unemployment had fallen to 5 percent, some were still saying not only that more should have been done but also that more should yet be done. By 1956 and 1957 when the boom had become inflationary, there was some feeling that the recovery from the 1954 recession had been too rapid.

Still, while failure to take stronger action in the circumstances of 1954 does not prove it, there is reason to doubt that either the administration or the government then had an effective policy for fiscal measures in a more severe recession. One minor factor was the administration's attitude on the question of confidence. Confidence was believed to be the key to recovery. As we have seen, there was some difference within the administration about the best strategy for maintaining confidence. However, the generally preferred posture was that no extraordinary action was needed, but that it would be taken promptly when needed. On April 2, 1954, the President cautioned that announcements of anti-recession action should be "carefully handled to avoid a jolt to public confidence."[46] When the decision was made on May 14 to speed up 1955 expenditures, it was also decided to make no public announcement in order not to disturb confidence. This was one of the reasons for not considering action which required Congressional appropriations. The desire not to acknowledge the existence of conditions calling for extraordinary action would have been an obstacle to taking extraordinary action of a kind that could not be concealed.

There were, however, more serious obstacles. On the expenditure side of the budget there were the administrative and organizational obstacles to increasing expenditures rapidly. One of Burns' first moves in 1953 had been to initiate a program for planning useful public works that might be undertaken in a recession. The administration made many optimistic statements about the "shelf" of public works ready to go in an emergency. However, later estimates indicated that what could have been accomplished quickly was small—an increase of public construction by $200 million in the first year after the go-ahead was given.[47]

Moreover, the administration's basic view of the economic prospects was inconsistent with an increase of spending. They were convinced that after the post-Korean transition they would arrive at a fertile plateau where government expenditures would be low and the economy would prosper with a balanced budget and lower taxes. As long as they believed that, and even a sharper recession in 1954 would probably not have changed that view, they were extremely reluctant to interrupt their drive for lower expenditures and to add programs which might be difficult to trim out of the budget later. A government looking ahead to rising expenditures in the long run would have been more willing to accelerate spending during the recession.

The presence of these obstacles on the expenditure side of the budget might have pointed to the possibility of emergency action on the revenue side. The administration was looking forward to additional tax reductions, beyond those proposed and enacted in 1954, as part of its longer-range program. To anticipate some of those future tax reductions in 1954, if the recession deepened, would not interfere with the long-range plan in the same way an expenditure increase would. But there was no plan for an anti-recession speed-up of tax reduction parallel to Burns' plan for public works. Of course, public-works activity was spread all over the government, and this provided an occasion for Burns to take a coordinating role in public works policy, while tax policy was centralized in the hands of Secretary Humphrey, who felt no need to be coordinated by Burns. Humphrey was less likely to think about tax policy in anti-cyclical terms than Burns might have been. However, there was also a more important and less personal obstacle to the use of tax policy as an emergency anti-recession measure. The administration was, it is true, looking forward to future tax reductions. The tax reductions it hoped to make would be oriented to promoting growth by stimulating investment; they would include reduction in corporate profits taxes and in the rates on upper incomes, plus possibly further liberalization of depreciation and other steps to increase the after-tax return on investment.

But there was a strong sentiment in the Congress for a quite different program of tax reduction—to reduce taxes on the lower income groups by raising income tax exemptions substantially. The administration faced the danger that if it opened the door to further tax reduction it would have to accept tax reduction of a kind that it regarded as less important, and which would cost so much revenue as to defer for a long time the possibility of getting the kind of tax reduction it wanted. Thus its long-range hopes for tax reform were a bar to an anti-recession tax cut.

The prescription of stabilizing budget policy for dealing with a recession had both a negative and a positive part. The negative part was to tolerate the deficits that would come automatically with a decline of incomes and employment. The positive part was to be prepared to taken affirmative action, and to take it, if a recession became serious. The government followed the negative, or passive, part of the prescription in 1954. On a reasonable interpretation of the basic policy this was probably all it was required to do. But the administration also claimed that it was prepared to move on the second part if necessary. This, although not tested in 1954, was doubtful.

The difference of view between the administration and Congress became an even more serious bar to effective tax policy, whether for stabilization or for long-range purposes, after the Democrats gained control of the Congress in the November, 1954, elections. The two sides neutralized each other; all they could agree on was to do nothing.

In a 1954 statement, the CED urged advance preparation for the use of tax reduction as an anti-recession instrument.

> To make the present procedure more flexible, it would be helpful for the Administration to decide: (a) whether in the event of a recession (actual or forecast) it would recommend tax reduction; (b) in what kinds of situations, on the basis of what facts, it would take such action; and (c) what kind of tax reduction it would recommend. The Administration should discuss these plans with Congressional leaders and attempt to reach general agreement, by mutual adjustment.

After suggesting that ordinarily the anti-recession tax cuts should be made in the personal income tax, it suggested:

> There may be some circumstances in which anti-recession tax cuts should be made in other taxes as well as in the personal income tax. For example, if there are agreed upon tax reductions of other kinds that should and would be made within a year or two anyway, the need to stimulate the economy may be a reason for advancing the date of such reductions.[48]

But all of this advance preparation depended upon the possibility of agreement, and this possibility did not exist.

~§12§~

1955–1957: Eden with Thorns

B<small>Y</small> the fall of 1954 the administration
was expecting soon to enter the promised land. The transition from the
bad old Truman days of big spending, deficits, and inflation was nearly over.
The transition had not been without some pain; but, in the administration's
view, the pain had been kept small by confidence, flexible monetary policy,
and calm, essentially passive, fiscal policy. The economic and fiscal features of
the promised land were clear. Federal expenditures would be reduced somewhat further; they were still amost $5 billion above the $60 billion figure
upon which Eisenhower and Taft had once agreed. They could not be kept
at that low figure forever with population and the economy growing, but
when the increase of expenditures was resumed the pace would be restrained.
Restraint of expenditures combined with the growth of revenues that an
expanding economy generated would permit attainment of two major goals.
The budget could be balanced and taxes could be reduced in ways that
would release private forces for investment and economic growth. Balancing
the budget and keeping a firm rein on monetary expansion would prevent
inflation, which was important in itself, and would avoid the development
of an unbalanced boom that might lead to a slump. However, in a world
with unavoidable uncertainties the possibility of a downturn could not be
ruled out, and the government would remain alert and prepared with fiscal
and monetary measures to prevent any serious decline.

Part of this vision came true. Expansion of the economy raised revenues
and a budget surplus was achieved. But that was all. The rise of expenditures
was unexpectedly large. Taxes were not reduced. Despite the surplus inflation reappeared. The economic advance was not sustained but ended in a
recession in late 1957. And when the recession came there was no evidence
that the interval of prosperity had been used to prepare for it.

There was little disagreement during the years 1955 to 1957 on the desirability of a balanced budget or a surplus. All of the leading schools of thought—whether they called for a balanced budget all the time, a balanced budget at high employment, or a compensatory policy of fiscal restraint when there was danger of inflation—converged on this prescription. In the early part of 1955 some proponents of compensatory finance were still talking about the need for fiscal stimulation. Thus, Walter W. Heller, later to be chairman of the Council of Economic Advisers under President Kennedy, testified before the Joint Economic Committee in January, 1955, to recommend an enlarged deficit:

> Turning to the 1955 fiscal-policy question, I feel that we are now in a period when deficits are constructive. As others have pointed out to the committee, our rate of production is running some $20 billion short of our potential, maybe more. Therefore, Federal deficits are more likely to evoke a higher production response than a high price response.
>
> Now, if we do not increase our deficits (or our tax-financed expenditures, if that be the route preferred) in order to meet our pressing defense and economic development needs, both at home and abroad, I think our economy can afford the risk of further tax reduction.[1]

This was about the last recommendation for a deficit to be heard until the recession of 1957–58 began. In fact, in June, 1957, two months before that recession began, Mr. Heller testified:

> I think it would not be responsible economic policy to proceed with a tax cut at the present time in the light of both the budgetary situation and the economic situation. . . . I think I have already put myself clearly on the record for the fiscal year 1958 as saying no, there are no problems of consumption and investment that take priority over a balanced cash budget. At the same time I am concerned over the possibility of a slackening of the pace of growth and the fact that we ought to have action ready, willing, and able to go into effect promptly in that eventuality.[2]

Agreement on avoiding deficits left open the question of the size of the surplus, if any, and also the question of whether to look at the administrative budget or the cash budget. Neither of these questions was much debated during the period, and the administration never made clear any specific, consistent position on either. In January, 1955, Congressman Mills asked Arthur Burns:

> What is the objective of the President with respect to balancing the budget, and which budget, the cash budget, or the administrative budget, and so on?

To which Burns replied:

> I have been asked a question concerning the President's personal objectives as to the budget, and it is not clear to me that that is a question I should try to answer.[3]

And he did not answer, but a few minutes later he did say:

> My opinion is that Federal finances are neutral, by and large, with respect to the economy when the cash budget is in balance, and that nowadays means a deficit of 2 or 3 billion dollars in the conventional budget. . . . I feel it would be desirable to shift emphasis from the conventional budget to a cash budget.[4]

However, this was not the policy of the administration. While Secretary Humphrey and others had leaned on the cash budget when it was barely in balance and the administrative budget was still in deficit in 1954, they concentrated on the administrative budget as soon as that came close to balance.

Moreover, the administration always made very conservative—which is to say, low—estimates of receipts, which held down the prospective surplus. Actual receipts far exceeded the estimates in fiscal years 1956 and 1957, but the appearance of unexpected revenues encouraged increases in expenditures so that the actual surpluses were also small. No budgeted surplus in the administrative budget exceeded $1.8 billion and no actual surplus exceeded $1.6 billion. As a result, a smaller surplus than the administration was planning meant a deficit, which no one wanted.[5] And as long as the administration was satisfied, there was no one to argue for a larger surplus. So no debate over the size of the surplus emerged. There was national agreement on a surplus not very far from zero, as long as it was more than zero.

The estimates and outcomes for the key years, fiscal 1956 and fiscal 1957, are shown below:[6]

| | (Billions of Dollars) | | | |
| | F. Y. 1956 | | F. Y. 1957 | |
	Budget	Actual	Budget	Actual
Administrative				
Expenditures	62.4	66.5	65.9	69.4
Receipts	60.0	68.1	66.3	71.0
Surplus	−2.4	1.6	.4	1.6
Cash				
Expenditures	68.2	72.6	72.9	80.0
Receipts	68.8	77.1	75.4	82.1
Surplus	.6	4.5	2.5	2.1

The administration's strategy with respect to the surplus was closely tied to its disagreements with the Congress over both sides of the budget.

The administration faced, from its point of view, a problem with the following elements:

    a. It could foresee a growth of revenues with the growth of the economy.

    b. It recognized that certain expenditures increases were important and had priority over tax reduction, but the amount of such increases was not so large as to preclude some tax reduction out of the growing revenues.

    c. There were demands for further expenditure increases in Congress, with support from various private interests, which if granted would make tax reduction impossible. These demands were only effectively contained by a tight budgetary position in which there was no large visible surplus.

    d. There was a strong demand for reduction of taxes on the mass of taxpayers which would reduce the revenues substantially. No tax cut to promote investment could be passed which did not also satisfy this demand. Therefore no small tax cut was possible.

In these circumstances the administration had two options. It could push for tax reduction first, temporarily eliminating the surplus or even creating a deficit, in the hope that the result would be restraint of expenditures and that growth of revenues would restore the surplus. Alternatively, it could try to hold back expenditures until a sufficient surplus was reached to make a tax cut of the necessary size without unbalancing the budget or falling below the minimum desired surplus. The risk in the first course was that even after taxes had been cut expenditures would grow so fast that the surplus position would not be regained. The risk in the second course was that the sight of an emerging surplus might so whet the appetite for expenditure increases that the time for tax reduction would never come.

Which course the administration would choose was not clear at first. In 1953 the administration had been willing to commit itself to some tax reduction in anticipation of expenditure reductions and surpluses that were expected but not yet in hand or even surely in sight. They might have done that again in 1955 or in 1956. For 1955 the administration decided against tax reduction immediately but held fast to the goal for the near future. The President's January, 1955, budget message asked for retention of the corporate profits and excise tax rates that were scheduled to decline that year, but added:

> However, further tax reduction remains a firm goal of this administration, and our policy is directed to achieving both the savings in expenditures and the economic growth that will make such reductions possible.
>
> I hope that tax reductions will be so justified next year. If so, I shall recommend

a reduction in taxes to spread the relief fairly among all taxpayers in a way which will be the most effective to relieve individual tax burdens and to increase incentive for effort and investment.[7]

This did not say that a balanced budget or a surplus had to be in hand before taxes could be reduced. A month later at his press conference the President showed flexibility on this question. He vigorously opposed a Democratic move to cut everybody's taxes by $20, but when asked whether that could be interpreted to mean that "there will be no tax reduction until the budget is balanced," he replied:

> Well, I don't know that you could make such an interpretation. For example, last year we gave a tax reduction in the belief that that particular tax reduction, worked out carefully, would help in the long run to balance the budget. I believe you can anticipate savings; I believe you can anticipate certain good results from things that you do, administratively and otherwise. Certainly you want to return taxes, because I assure you, every political party likes to cut taxes; there is no question about that. So we will do it as soon as we can, and I would not say by any manner of means that the budget has to be in perfect balance before you can contemplate sincerely another tax cut.[8]

However, from that time on the administration's position became harder and harder. Tax reduction remained an important objective, but its achievement would not be allowed to endanger budget balancing—and in later formulations a surplus.

On May 31, 1955, the President was asked to comment on reports that it would be possible the following year both to cut taxes and to balance the budget. To that he replied:

> Well, of course, that would be a wonderful thing.
> I think no one has said it to me in those emphatic terms. It would be a wonderful thing to have both. But I am sure that the first thing we must do is balance the budget.[9]

By the time of the January, 1956, budget message, balancing the budget had been redefined to include some surplus in order to reduce the debt, even if only minutely:

> It is essential, in the sound management of the Government's finances, that we be mindful of our enormous national debt and of the obligation we have toward future Americans to reduce that debt whenever we can appropriately do so. Under conditions of high peacetime prosperity, such as now exist, we can never justify going further into debt to give ourselves a tax cut at the expense of our children. So, in the present state of our financial affairs, I earnestly believe that a

tax cut can be deemed justifiable only when it will not unbalance the budget, a budget which makes provision for some reduction, even though modest, in our national debt.[10]

During 1956, as the economy expanded and incomes rose, it became clear that the revenue estimates made at the beginning of the year would be far exceeded. The President was asked again and again whether the improved revenue outlook made tax reduction possible or would soon do so. The answer was always negative. The importance of having a surplus grew with the prospect of having one, so rising revenues did not bring tax reduction closer. Probably the chief reason for this was the inflation which began in the spring of 1955 and gathered momentum during 1956. In reply to a question in August, 1955, the President had denied that there was a "serious threat" of inflation,[11] but by 1956 inflation was very much on his mind. The inflation was not rapid by the usual standards of business expansion. However, the country had about twenty years of inflation behind it for which the Republicans had blamed the Roosevelt and Truman administrations. The emergence of the Republican inflation was both embarrassing and worrisome. It was not only the inflation which troubled the administration's vision of itself. It was approaching the end of the first Republican term with the federal debt larger than the one Truman had left behind.

The January, 1957, budget message again emphasized the importance of a budget surplus, primarily as a defense against inflation:

> At a time like the present when the economy is operating at a very high rate and is subject to inflationary pressures, Government clearly should seek to alleviate rather than aggravate those pressures. Government can do its part. But business and labor leaders must earnestly cooperate—or what Government can do in a free society like this will *not* prevent inflation.
>
> For the Government to do its part in the coming year, taxes must be retained at the present rates so that receipts will exceed budget expenditures and the public debt can be further reduced. The prospective budget surplus in the fiscal year 1958 will reinforce the restraining effect of present credit and monetary policies.[12]

The administration's determination to have a budget surplus prevented it from taking the risk of opening the door to tax reduction in advance of the rising revenues. But expenditures did rise to absorb the revenues. As a result the administration achieved neither any very substantial surplus nor the tax reduction it wanted. A feeling developed that an iron law was at work to make expenditures rise to keep pace with the revenues and to rule out the possibility of tax reduction.

Nevertheless, although it was not achieved in the way the administration would have preferred, the administration did achieve the balanced budget plus a little surplus that was called for in times of high employment by the stabilizing budget policy. What is striking, in terms of the requirements of stabilizing budget policy, is that little use was made of the prosperous years 1955–57 to prepare fiscal policy, especially tax reduction, to deal with a recession.

The administration's *philosophy* at first placed great emphasis on alertness and on being prepared with timely action to prevent or counter either recession of inflation. Thus, in the President's economic report of January, 1955, the list of lessons learned from the 1953–54 recession was headed by: "First, that wise and early action by Government can stave off serious difficulties later."[13]

And looking ahead to the future the same report said:

> How long the current phase of expansion will continue before new international trouble or a cyclical reversal of business occurs, or how far the expansion will carry, it is impossible to say with great assurance. The uncertainty of economic predictions requires that the Federal Government be prepared to adjust its policies promptly if economic events should not bear out current expectations.[14]

The Government's aim was "to equip ourselves with better tools for checking any recession or inflation that might develop."[15]

However, the emphasis shifted as the prosperity continued. In January, 1956, the economic report listed the ways in which the administration, with the cooperation of the Congress, had sought to discharge its responsibilities for orderly economic growth. This time flexible action had fallen out of first place in the list; instead the list read "Tenth, by acting promptly and resolutely when either recessionary or inflationary influences in the general economy became evident."[16] Still, some of the previous flavor remained:

> If our economy is to advance firmly on the narrow road that separates recession from inflation, the Federal Government must pursue monetary, fiscal, and housekeeping policies with skill and circumspection. We must be alert to changes in economic conditions and be ready to adapt our policies promptly to them.[17]

By January, 1957, the idea of readiness to take positive action to deal with a recession had disappeared from the economic report. There was some reference to always-present uncertainties of the economic outlook, including the uncertainty about the continued growth of private investment—which raised the possibility of a slowdown in the economy generally. But these uncertainties did not, as in the past, point to the need for alertness in case recession should appear. They only added to the need for preventing inflation and keeping the economy "healthy" by other means, such as promoting competition, so that there would be no recession. There was no discussion of steps to be taken if, despite these efforts, a recession occurred.

It was perhaps natural that as the administration's concern with inflation mounted, the problem of recession should fade into the background of its thinking, or at least of its public reports. But more than that was going on. The conception of how to deal with the problem was also changing. In 1953 and 1954 the administration was sensitive to the notion that the Republicans were the party of depression and that they would not act vigorously to combat a recession. They felt a need to demonstrate their willingness to act, if not precipitately at least promptly. They also felt a need to take credit for their activity before and during the recession of 1953–54, especially the tax reductions. But after the Republican recession turned out to be short and mild and was followed by a Republican prosperity, their view of the experience changed. In their new philosophy it was not the contracyclical actions of the government that had made the main difference. Rather it was the health and vigor of the private economy that had survived the recession and produced the prosperity. This strength of the private economy depended upon an atmosphere of confidence and encouragement, which the administration's policies and attitudes had nourished, but the relevant government policies were not its contracyclical policies, they felt.

This was only a superficial change in view. By 1957 it was the policy of the United States, under any administration, not only to accept a deficit in a recession but also in appropriate conditions to take positive action that would increase the deficit. The principle might be forgotten in times of prosperity, but it would be promptly recalled in a recession.

Nevertheless, forgetting or submerging the principle in times of prosperity would have consequences in a recession. That would mean failure to make the preparations with respect to expenditures or taxes which would open up the widest range of choices for action in a recession. As a result, when recession did come, the government might be prevented from acting as promptly or as powerfully as it wished, or in the form it preferred, because the means had not been prepared in advance.

The administration carried forward during the 1955–57 prosperity the program of creating a "shelf" of public works which Arthur Burns had initiated in 1953. But for reasons already mentioned in connection with the 1954 recession, this could not be the main reliance of the Eisenhower administration. The possibility of providing a stimulus to the economy quickly was too limited. And, especially given the fears and values of the Eisenhower administration, there was too much danger that recession expansion of public works or other expenditures would leave a residue of higher spending long after the recession needs had passed.

The natural reliance of the Eisenhower administration, in view of its long-term objectives, would have been expected to be tax reduction in a recession. The administration had regarded the 1954 experience as showing that tax reduction was effective, and increase of government spending was unnecessary. During 1955–1957 it had held out the hope of tax reduction but had felt obliged to defer the tax reduction because of the inflationary threat. The rapid growth of revenues in a growing economy with stable tax rates had been demonstrated, as had the tendency of the expenditures to rise in step with the revenues. A tax cut made in a recession would probably not raise the inflation problem, at least immediately. If the lower tax rates continued beyond the recession, the growth of the economy would still produce a gradual rise of revenues to meet some increase of expenditures within the limits of a balanced budget. Meanwhile, a period of stringency of revenues would tend to constrain the growth of expenditures.

However, if a timely tax reduction in a recession was to be possible some advance preparation was essential. The administration had spent most of 1953, in cooperation with the House Ways and Means Committee, working out the proposed tax revision of 1954, and even with that the act was not passed until August, 1954. That was an exceptionally complicated tax bill. The next one would probably be much simpler. Still there were important, difficult, and controversial decisions to be made before any tax bill could be presented to the Congress and enacted. The government's flexibility of action in a recession would be increased if those decisions were made, even tentatively, in advance.

The need for advance preparation for a recession tax cut was pointed out by CED in the 1954 statement quoted above on page 308. Professor Walter Heller, testifying before the Joint Economic Committee in June, 1957, while denying the need for tax reduction then, urged action to create a "shelf" of tax reductions from which the government could promptly draw in a recession.[18] However, there was no action and not even any serious discussion of the question from the government. The political division between the Republican administration and the Democratic Congress would probably have stood in the way of such advance legislation as Heller proposed and even of such informal agreement between the administration and Congressional leaders as the CED proposed. But even within the administration there was no advance plan, no strategy for relating anti-recession fiscal policy to the longer-range financial prospect and program, no decision on the conditions in which taxes should be cut, on whether the cut should be permanent or temporary, or on the form of the cut. When the recession came it became immediately apparent to everyone, including the administration, that a tax cut was one of the main things to be considered. However, all the important decisions still had to be made, under fire as it were, and there were disagreements about them even within the administration. This lack of preparation even in the form of an agreed-upon administration plan was the major consequence of the administration's temporary reversion to the idea that a healthy economy would have no instability problem.

A revealing, although perhaps exaggerated, picture of the state of the administration's thinking as the boom ended and the recession began was given in the response of the President to a press conference question October 30, 1957, about the administration's plans to deal with the darkening economic situation. The President said he was watching the signs, and then:

> So all you can do is to get the very finest brains together that you can and see exactly what is the best thing Government can do. And Government generally speaking in the financial world is confined to what the Federal Reserve Board decides to do, plus the rate of Federal spending and the taxation policies and so on.[19]

This was almost exactly five years after General Eisenhower, in his first Presidential campaign, had talked about calling in "the finest brains" in the event of a recession. Since the day of that campaign speech the administration had been through one recession, and moreover had had at its service some of the finest brains. And yet the President still talked as if he approached a recession with a blank sheet of paper on which the finest brains would be asked to write a prescription.

❧13❧

The Near-Miss of 1958

THE last stop on the road to the 1964 tax cut was 1958. It was the year taxes were almost cut but weren't. Of course, there are always many reasons for wanting tax reduction. But the reason there was widespread support for tax reduction in 1958—in the administration, in Congress, and in the business, labor, and academic communities—was the recession. The country came closer than ever before to cutting taxes for the sake of general economic expansion.

Still, taxes were not cut. There was a budget deficit, and the budget-balancing religion had something to do with the failure to cut taxes. But it was not the main reason. What prevented a tax cut in 1958 was a certain view of the long-range economic and budgetary prospect held strongly in the administration but not confined to the administration. The difference between 1958, when taxes were not cut, and 1962, when the decision for tax reduction was made, lay chiefly in this view of the long-range prospect.

According to the common view in 1958, the basic, continuing economic problem was inflation. The 1958 recession was only an interruption in the inflationary pressure, and the fact that it did not result in any decline of the price indexes was considered highly ominous. If we provided expansive and inflationary stimuli at every recession, and recessions never caused any price declines, unending inflation would be inevitable. What was believed to have been the error of 1954—when expansive policy, especially monetary policy, continued too long and strengthened the inflation of 1955–57—was recalled as a warning.

The long-range prospect was also for strongly rising federal expenditures. Federal spending had risen almost 15 percent from calendar 1955 to calendar 1957. Now a new element had entered the expenditure picture. The launching of the Russian Sputnik in the fall of 1957 had drawn attention to comparisons between the United States and the Soviet Union. The common deduction from these comparisons was an American weakness in space exploration, in missile capability, in education, and in rate of economic growth —with the further conclusion that these deficiencies had to be remedied for the sake of our security and self-esteem, even at the expense of a big expansion of government programs. This expansion, caused by what Eisenhower later called "Sputnik complexes," had already begun in 1958.

The prospect of inflation, combined with the prospect of strongly rising expenditures, created the need for high and rising revenues in order to assure a budget surplus when the economy returned to its "normal" condition. This made a tax cut during the recession dangerous. Many proposals for a tax reduction specified that the cut should be temporary. But even the authors of such plans recognized a risk that, whatever the legislation might say, the tax cut might be permanent because Congress would be sorely tempted to continue it. Moreover, some who favored an anti-recession tax cut wanted it to be permanent, believing that a temporary cut would not stimulate spending either by businesses or by consumers.

The administration continued to have tax reduction as part of its long-range program, but by 1958 this objective had become quite limited and had receded in the scale of priorities. Part of the conservative program for tax reform had been accomplished in 1954. Businessmen complained about continuation of the rate of corporate profits taxation at 52 percent. But profits had been high in 1955, 1956, and 1957, many believed that they were passing the corporate tax on in higher prices, and so their eagerness to get it reduced had diminished. Some further steps to reduce the double taxation of corporate dividends remained part of the conservative program, but the step taken in 1954 had been the object of so much attack that there was little desire to reopen the question. Action to liberalize depreciation allowances would have been appreciated but was not considered urgent. The strength of the investment boom in 1955–57 did not suggest that the tax structure was a heavy burden. There was no great temptation, therefore, to seize the opportunity of the 1958 recession to make tax reductions that might be desired in the future. On the contrary, the administration believed that a tax cut enacted quickly to stimulate the economy, especially with the Democrats in control of Congress, would concentrate mainly on reduction of taxes on lower incomes. The resulting revenue loss might defer for a long time the achievement of the particular tax reductions the administration favored for stimulating investment and growth.

Thus, unlike 1954, a tax reduction in 1958 did not fit into the administration's long-range estimates and plans. Despite this, the administration's policy was to reduce taxes if the recession became serious enough. But its view of the long-range problem made the administration reluctant to recognise the seriousness of the situation and quick to detect the emergence of signs that a tax cut would not be needed. At the first evidence of an upturn in the spring the administration, in concert with the Congressional leadership, declared that taxes would not be cut and effectively put an end to the tax cut debate.

WATCHFUL WAITING

The discussion preceding this negative conclusion went on for five months, from January through most of May, 1958. The economy began to decline in July, 1957, and the decline was sufficiently clear by October to induce the Federal Reserve to move in the direction of easing credit. However, general public attention did not focus on the recession and measures to deal with it until the beginning of 1958. By December, 1957, unemployment had risen to 5.3 percent from 4.2 percent in August. The return of Congress to Washington in January and the submission of the administration's economic report and budget message set off the debate.

From the beginning, tax reduction held the center of the stage of economic policy. It was as if almost everyone recognized that if there was to be any strong, prompt, and dramatic action, it would be a tax cut. This view was not confined to Democrats or liberals. Thus, in a TV debate on January 1, Representative Richard Simpson, ranking Republican member of the House Ways and Means Committee said: "One of the best ways of solving what may be described by some as a recession may be corrected or avoided by reducing the burden of taxes upon the American people today."[1] On January 18 Mr. Philip M. Talbott, president of the Chamber of Commerce of the U.S., recommended a $3 billion tax cut on the ground that it would help economic expansion and eventually increase the revenues and keep the budget in balance.[2]

However, both the budget message and the economic report were silent on the question of tax reduction. In fact, the January, 1958, budget message was more concerned with the possibility that rising expenditures might require a tax increase. The message said: "If the Congress follows my recommendations, I believe that we shall be able to do what is required for our defense efforts and meet the basic needs of our domestic programs without an increase in tax rates."[3]

The President gave a more extended statement of his views on taxation in answer to a question at his press conference on the budget, January 15,

1958. The questioner pointed out that the budget showed only a small surplus ($500 million) for fiscal 1959, and that some people thought the budget would not actually be balanced because of the recession. "With such a situation in prospect, would you prefer to go to deficit financing or would you prefer raising taxes to maintain a balanced budget?" There then followed this exchange:

> PRESIDENT: My own feeling would be this: A reasonable amount of expenditure, even if that did mean somewhat upsetting the precarious balance, as you called it, is better than talking about a tax bill at this time.
>
> QUESTION: . . . Did I understand you to say that you would prefer a reasonable amount of definite [deficit] spending to a tax increase?
>
> PRESIDENT: Well, I think it is almost necessary to answer that way, Mr. Arrowsmith, for this reason: We don't know exactly what is going to be happening. The first thing, the assumption is that there is going to be a good advancement in the economy. This means there is more income. That being so, you certainly don't want to be raising taxes to get some funds that are probably available or we hope will be available on the present tax basis.
>
> In the same way, we are going to have possibly some expenditures. I have heard this, at least in the papers, that they are looking toward some increased expenditures. If they do, and they seem to be necessary to everybody, they will have to be financed.
>
> If we don't have as much income as we do, then it would seem to me it would be a bad time to raise taxes, because you want the economy to have that little needle, a needle rather than a checkrein on it.
>
> So I think that some necessary expenditures, even if it means a small deficit, would be better than to start now the question of tax raising.[4]

What this seems to mean is that a deficit resulting from a shortfall of revenues due to a recession, possibly combined with some increase of expenditures, would be tolerable and indeed positively beneficial as a way to give the economy "a little needle." Even though the reference is to a "small" deficit, the principle of not raising taxes in a recession had been absorbed into the Eisenhower vernacular. No one asked him about cutting taxes.

In fact, the fiscal program presented in the administration's budget was essentially neutral with respect to the recession. Whereas there had been a surplus of $2.1 billion in the cash budget for fiscal 1957, the message estimated that the cash surplus would be $200 million in fiscal 1958 and $600 million in fiscal 1959.[5] However, the receipts estimates for both years were held down by the few months of recession that had already occurred in 1957 and by the few more months that were expected in 1958. If high employment had continued the surplus would have remained approximately at the fiscal 1957 level. The budget of January, 1958, was a "stabilizing budget policy" budget—it would show a cash surplus in the $2 to $3 million range at high employment, but would show a deficit in recession, a deficit which the administration was prepared to accept. However, the budget message did not discuss the relationship between the budget and the recession.

The economic report was scarcely more revealing about the administration's fiscal policy in the recession. Referring to the economic decline of the last quarter of 1957, the report said:

> This change in economic conditions called for adjustments in economic policies. During much of the year, the task of restraining inflationary pressures was paramount, and policies were directed to this end. In the closing months of the year, and currently, the task has been to facilitate readjustments in the economy essential to the resumption of sustainable economic growth, but to do so without reviving inflationary pressures.
>
> As we look ahead in 1958, there are grounds for expecting that the decline in business activity need not be prolonged and that economic growth can be resumed without extended interruption. The policies of Government will be directed toward helping to assure this result.[6]

The report did not specify these policies, except by reference to steps which had already been taken to make credit more readily available. In a general discussion of factors tending to make the economy more stable than it had previously been, the report mentioned the automatic stabilizing effects of unemployment compensation payments and of a tax system the yield of which varied with the national income. It did not mention the possibility of deliberate action to increase expenditures or cut taxes in a recession.

The report described the budget surplus of fiscal 1957 as having "helped moderate inflationary pressures." The small deficit forecast for fiscal 1958, entirely due to the shortfall of receipts caused by the recession, was not described as helpful in moderating tendencies to recession. (This was a deficit in the administrative budget; the cash budget showed a small, diminished surplus.)

Thus, both in the budget message and in the economic report the administration played down the role of fiscal policy in stopping the recession and restoring high employment. But the administration did not think of itself as taking a purely negative position. The administration viewed the country as being flooded with rash and hysterical demands for action which was unnecessary at the time and would endanger the future stability of the economy. Against this major menace the administration was maintaining a cool but firm defense while keeping itself prepared for strong measures against the recession if "necessary." This was, to its thinking, the economically

sound and morally requisite position, even though it was politically uncomfortable.

This attitude was mirrored in Eisenhower's memoirs later:

> Of course, political opponents rushed in with all the stereotyped criticisms and
> with dozens of patent remedies.
>
> Early in January of 1958, just as in 1954, the head of the United Steel Workers,
> David McDonald—a man whom I liked personally—once again sketched out a
> free-wheeling program of federal outlays to end the downturn with little apparent
> regard for their likely long-term economic consequences. In a later meeting with
> members of the executive committee of the AFL-CIO, we went over one sober-
> ing statistic after another. Their single suggestion was posed as a question: "Why
> don't you act now?"
>
> In reply I reminisced a bit: "You know, the same thing happened in the war.
> Whenever a crisis occurred, some interested but excitable people began screaming
> for action. And when they did, I had only one answer. 'I guess I'm just too stub-
> born to act fast until all the facts are in.' "
>
> The story broke the ice at that particular meeting. But it did not stop the calls
> for crash federal action to bail the country out of its troubles."[7]

The administration not only did not want to initiate what it regarded
as premature action against the recession. It also did not want to encourage
a preemptive move by the political opposition, and therefore did not want
to suggest that the administration considered the decision whether to cut
taxes immediately to be a close one. But still it wanted to retain the option
of acting and to assure the country that it would act if necessary. Thus, on
January 16 Treasury Secretary Anderson told the Ways and Means Committee that he could "conceive of situations" in which he would recommend
a tax cut as a cure for an economic slump. However, he said, "I believe confidently that we will have a resumption of growth," and he described continuation of existing tax rates as the "most prudent" thing to do.[8] He repeated
this position a week later on a national television program and early in
February before the Joint Economic Committee.[9]

The President described the administration's position in his own terms
on February 5 at a press conference:

> QUESTION: Is a tax cut a reserve weapon in case it [business] doesn't [turn up],
> even at the expense of a bigger deficit? How do you feel about it?
> PRESIDENT: It could be, it could be. Yes. I'd say this: If things got to the point
> where you felt that it was necessary, it would be. One thing, it would have a
> very real, great stimulus on the economy, no question about that; but on the
> other hand, this is something you can take hold of and, going too far with
> trying to fool with our economy, then you get something else started. And

you just remember, all of you here, a year ago, how we were always talking about inflation. . . .[10]

For Action, or at least Preparation

However, the administration was not to be allowed to follow its policy of watchful waiting in peace. Criticism mounted from those who thought the time for waiting had passed and from those who, more moderately, thought the waiting was not very watchful and should include more preparation. One forum for this criticism was the hearings of the Joint Economic Committee held between January 27 and February 10. Except for the administration witnesses, hardly anyone appearing before the committee was satisfied with the position taken in the economic report. By this time, of course, the witnesses had data for another month of substantial economic decline since the economic report had been prepared, and the possibility was mounting that the 1958 recession would be more serious than the recessions of 1949 and 1954. However, the difference between the administration and its critics was not primarily their appraisals of the existing economic situation and the prospect for the immediate future. The difference was mainly about the strategy for dealing with the degree of uncertainty which everyone recognized.

On this question of strategy there were two schools of thought. One was for immediate fiscal action. In part this was because members of this school did not share the administration's expectation and fear of a resumption of inflation and placed relatively greater value on the quick termination of unemployment. As J. K. Galbraith, a leading supporter of immediate action, said:

> If we gamble on things getting better by themselves, and this turns out to be wrong, the whole country will suffer for the mistake. If we assume that the present recession will continue, then, at most, we shall have been a trifle too zealous in maintaining income and employment.
>
> The administration will be accused of reacting too quickly to events. But I wouldn't suppose that even this charge would be utterly damaging.[11]

But the chief difference between the administration and those who wanted immediate fiscal action involved the long-range budget prospect. The administration believed that the country faced an inexorable and excessive trend of rising federal expenditures; it did not want to encourage that trend by taking on new expenditures as anti-recession measures, and it did not want to take any chances of weakening the revenue system that would be needed later to finance the growing expenditures. Most of those who wanted immediate fiscal action, on the other hand, believed that federal expenditure programs were inadequate and needed to be increased anyway, aside from the problem of the recession, simply because the country would be better off with stronger defense or more extensive government services. In their view, an immediate increase of expenditures which would be helpful in ending the recession and restoring prosperity did not conflict with long-range budgetary objectives but was consistent with and supported them. In fact, for some who favored immediate action the anti-recession effect was only a welcome by-product of a policy that would have been desirable anyway.

Thus, Professor Lester V. Chandler of Princeton University told the Joint Economic Committee:

> The principal change in governmental economic policy that I recommend is one whose main purpose is not at all to promote economic stability, but which will have the incidental effect of promoting recovery and perhaps even of creating inflationary pressure before the year is out.
>
> I refer to an immediate and rapid increase in our national security program. I wish to emphasize that the purpose of this step-up in our national security effort should not be to induce recovery.[12]

This view of the underlying budgetary requirements not only relieved proponents of immediate action of some of the inhibitions which the administration felt. It also pointed clearly to expenditure increase rather than tax reduction as the preferred remedy. Thus, to quote Galbraith again:

> But the most important reason for favoring an increase in civilian public outlays as the principal protective device is that we now have so many things that need doing. . . . On the urgency of innumerable civilian requirements, I need not dwell. Schools and aid to education, research support and facilities, health facilities, urban rental housing, urban redevelopment, resource development, metropolitan communications, are all deficient or lagging. It would surely be a mistake to talk of tax reduction to make jobs when so many of our schools are dirty, rundown, overcrowded, understaffed, on double shifts, or scheduled to become inadequate when the next increase in the school population hits them.[13]

Others represented in the hearings of the Joint Economic Committee basically accepted the administration's view of the long-range economic and budgetary problem. They agreed that in view of the prospect of renewed inflationary pressure and rising expenditures there were risks in taking fiscal action against the recession—either by raising expenditures or by cutting taxes. They regarded these risks as a reason for not taking strong action unless the recession reached a degree of seriousness which was not yet apparent in early February. But they were not satisfied with the administration's posture. If the policy was to wait until the whites of the recession's eyes were visible, it was all the more necessary to be prepared to fire when that moment came. Most of those who took that position believed that prompt action on a large scale could only take the form of a tax cut. But if this were the reliance, preparations should have been made to institute tax reduction quickly. And if the long-range danger of inflation was real, the problems of assuring that the tax cut could be undone at the proper time would also have to be solved in advance. But none of the necessary groundwork had been laid.

As one witness, speaking within the framework of CED policy, said:

> The report [1958 economic report] appraises the plus and minus factors in the current economic situation and concludes as follows:
> "These considerations suggest that the decline in business activity need not be prolonged, and that economic growth can be resumed without extended interruption."
> It is difficult to quarrel with this conclusion but it literally says much less than it appears to say. It literally only says that the evidence does not force us to the conclusion that the recession will be deep or long. It does not say that the evidence forces us to the conclusion that the recession will be short and mild.
> I would not object if the report expressed the view that the current recession will probably be short and mild. But any such estimate of the situation is subject to great uncertainties. What I miss is any recognition of the possibility that this estimate may be incorrect and that the situation may turn out to be more serious than we now expect.
> Recognizing the possibility of a more serious recession would inevitably lead to consideration of steps that might be necessary at some time to reverse the decline—notably an emergency tax cut. Discussions should now be going on in the Government—between the administration and the Congress—about the conditions in which such a tax cut might be desirable and the form it should take. This should not be for any action now but to pave the way for action when and if necessary. The Secretary of the Treasury has recognized that circumstances are conceivable in which an emergency tax cut might be appropriate. The Economic Report should have laid the groundwork for such action.[14]

One notable feature of the testimony before the Joint Economic Committee was that the advocates of increased spending were for action now, whereas those who preferred the tax cutting route were for deferring action by making preparations. A combination of these views became the national strategy. We would proceed immediately to raise expenditures and hold a tax reduction in reserve. However, the expenditure increases were small and the preparations for tax reduction were not substantial.

The strategy of spend now and cut taxes later—if necessary—quickly became the dominant policy during February. On February 12, President Eisenhower issued a statement on the economic situation expressing confidence and determination and listing among the administration's main anti-recession measures an increase in highway expenditures, an acceleration of defense contract awards, and a program for modernizing post offices. "In all these matters of government policy it is well to remember that with an economy as complex as ours, it is necessary not only to avoid the taking of wrong steps but confidently take the right ones. This we propose to do."[15] The next day a group of Democratic governors recommended increases of spending and improvement of unemployment compensation, with a tax cut later if other measures failed. On that same day House Speaker Rayburn said that the Democratic leadership of Congress would study tax reduction and prepare for the possibility that it would be needed. However, he did not believe that it was needed then. A few days later, on February 18, Republican Congressional leaders met at the White House to discuss the economic situation.[16] They emerged with the statement that there would probably be an upturn in the early spring and that they were opposed to a tax cut then and to what Senator Knowland called "spending orgies." But on that day it was also reported that the Senate committee chairmen, under the guidance of Majority Leader Lyndon B. Johnson, were working on the acceleration of public works expenditures.[17]

On February 27 the Joint Economic Committee issued its recommendations for anti-recession policy, stressing monetary expansion and the increase of federal expenditures. It then said:

> If monetary action, expenditure measures, and other actions, public or private, fall short in stemming recession and promoting recovery, tax reduction will be in order, but such action is not now recommended. The committee is confident that the tax-writing committees of the Congress will keep a close and continuing watch on economic and budgetary developments and will be prepared to move quickly in enacting general tax reduction if needed.[18]

That the first steps should be taken on the spending side with a decision on tax reduction held in reserve was natural. The idea of increasing expenditures during a recession, especially on public works, had a long history going back at least to the time of Herbert Hoover. It had been a key idea of the latter days of the New Deal when some of the 1958 leadership, including Majority Leader Johnson, had received their education in economic policy. Moreover, that an increase of spending, say on highways, would put people to work was "obvious," whereas the contribution of a tax cut required a little more reasoning to understand. There was, indeed, a common argument in 1958 that tax reduction would not help the unemployed since they presumably did not have taxable incomes.

Furthermore, every expenditure program, or almost every one, has behind it a group of supporters in the Congress and in the country who favor expanding it at all times, recession or not. When the recession creates an atmosphere justifying increased expenditure on national economic grounds, the supporters of particular programs gain enough allies to push some increases through. There are also always people who want tax reduction, recession or not. But the potential direct benefits from a general tax reduction, while spread very widely, are spread very thin and do not motivate the kind of effective support that expenditure programs have.

The main point is probably that the expenditure route permits certain steps to be taken and displayed without requiring any major decisions. Up to a point, which was not exceeded in 1958, all that is required is doing somewhat sooner or on a somewhat larger scale what would be done anyway. Moreover, the expenditure decisions could be made in small doses. Cutting taxes, on the other hand, required a governmental admission or assertion that the recession had reached a certain degree of seriousness, called for a large decision to be justified almost entirely on the basis of the recession, and would involve the administration and the Congress in the thorny problem of who gets the cuts.

As it turned out, increasing expenditures was only a sideshow. The annual rate of expenditures resulting from actions specifically taken to combat the recession reached a maximum of $1.1 billion in the fourth quarter of 1958,[19] whereas the tax reductions commonly discussed were in the range of $5 to $10 billion. The largest and probably most important item of antirecession expenditure was the federal program to extend unemployment compensation payments. In general, activities on the expenditure side of the budget reduced pressure for an immediate decision on strong fiscal action but did not themselves constitute such action.

DIVISION WITHIN THE ADMINISTRATION

Even in February dissenters from the strategy of putting tax reduction far down on the agenda could be found in the Congress, in the administration, and outside the government. Most of these dissenters were not in favor of an immediate tax cut but wanted more preparation and more assurance that tax reduction was high on the list of possibilities. However, there were some who wanted a tax cut at once. The leader of these in the Congress was Senator Paul H. Douglas. On February 10 he made a major address in the Senate calling for an immediate tax cut affecting both individual income taxes and excises. The cut in individual income taxes would benefit chiefly the lower income tax payers and would expire on January 1, 1959, unless renewed. Excise taxes on consumers' goods would be permanently reduced. Douglas was supported in his proposal by Senators Morse of Oregon, Carroll of Colorado, and Long of Louisiana.[20]

Part of Douglas' argument, by which he hoped to win over his Democratic colleagues, was that the administration was going to propose a tax cut itself. In that case the Democrats might well take the initiative, giving the economy a stimulus when it was timely, exerting maximum influence on the nature of the cut, and getting political credit for the move. He said:

> I think the Administration will come forward after a while with a tax bill. I do not want to prejudge it, but I rather suspect that the Administration will come forward with a tax bill which will favor the upper income groups, corporations, and so forth, with the argument that what we need is to stimulate investment.[21]

In the next few weeks evidence of administration interest in a tax cut accumulated, and the possibility arose that there would be a race between Congressional and administration tax-cutters. On February 23 Secretaries Anderson and Mitchell and Republican Senators Knowland and Ives promised that there would be a tax cut if it was needed.[22] Two days later Budget Director Brundage made a speech supporting a tax cut if the economy did not turn up by July 1. Public works, he said, were too slow, and "Taxes are too high, anyway."[23] The next day at a press conference the President denied that a tax cut would be "only a last resort measure."[24] On March 10 Vice-President Nixon said that he preferred a tax cut to spending increases and that a decision on a tax cut would depend on the movement of the business indicators in the next few weeks. Budget Director Brundage was reported as seeing a good chance of a tax cut "this year." On March 11 Labor Secretary Mitchell said that a tax cut was "ready for immediate use as an additional stimulus to the economy, and it will be used if necessary."[25]

Behind this general administration position in favor of tax cuts when necessary but not yet was a deep division. There was an important faction which was prepared to recommend a tax cut if only a little more evidence of continuing recession appeared. This faction drew its inspiration and intellectual leadership in large part from Arthur Burns who had resigned as chairman of the Council of Economic Advisers after the 1956 election but still maintained close relations with the administration leadership. In the middle of February Burns gave a talk to the Columbia University alumni in New York in which he expressed fears that the current recession would be more serious than those which had preceded it in the postwar period and urged the need for prompt action, specifically a tax cut, to stop the decline before it reached dangerous proportions. He made these same points in conversations with Nixon and Mitchell, who became the chief advocates within the administration of a tax cut.

The arguments of the tax-cutters within the administration were a combination of economics and politics. First there was Burns' point that it was dangerous to wait until the economy reached some extreme depth before acting, because by that time a self-reinforcing decline might have set in which would be very difficult to halt and reverse. Second, if the administration did not take the lead with tax cuts, the initiative would lie with the Congressional proponents of larger spending, which would be ineffective in the short run and dangerous in the long run. Third, the administration had tax reduction as a basic goal, and no better time could be found for a step in this direction than during the recession. Fourth, unless the Republicans wanted to decline to an even weaker minority position in the Congress, they had to make a strong show of anti-recession action before the 1958 elections.

The opposition was led by Treasury Secretary Anderson with the assistance of Federal Reserve Chairman Martin. Anderson's argument had two elements. First, he believed that the basic economic problem was inflation, that the problem would reappear with full force after temporary interruption of the recession, and that the country could not afford to weaken its defenses against inflation by making a tax cut the prime intent of which was to increase private purchasing power. Second, he was firmly convinced that an anti-recession tax cut, a "quickie" as it was called, would be the wrong kind of a tax cut to meet the country's permanent needs. He was devoted to the idea of tax reform to stimulate growth, which meant to him mainly reduction of tax rates on the upper incomes and on corporations. He also recognized the argument for tax reduction to forestall the pressure for higher expenditures. In the fall of 1957, before the recession became clearly visible, he was seriously considering a tax proposal to be advanced by the administration to head off both the "demagogic" kinds of tax reduction which he expected the Congress to propose and demands for higher spending.[26] With the post-Sputnik increase in expenditures this idea was shelved. It seemed to him perfectly clear that the only tax cut which he could get quickly through a Democratic Congress in the recession atmosphere would be one that would "give away" a large amount of revenue in relief for the mass of tax payers with relatively little of the "reform" that he considered important. Anderson was also inclined to skepticism about the effectiveness of tax reduction as an anti-recession instrument.

The division within the administration was not, in principle, between tax cuts now and tax cuts never. Rather, it was between tax cuts at once, or at least soon if things do not get better, and tax cuts only later and if things get much worse. But for practical purposes this was the difference between cutting taxes or not.

The decision, of course, was up to the President. And he sided with Anderson during February and March and, as it turned out, through the remainder of his Presidential term. The Anderson position had the advantage that it permitted a decision to be deferred. As long as taxes had not yet been cut they could still be cut, but once the step had been taken it could not be undone, at least for some time. Moreover, taxation was the Treasury's business, and this carried weight with Eisenhower. Anderson was a more consistent and effective barrier to action than Humphrey had been in 1954. While Humphrey had all the outward signs which made him the archetype of conservatism to newspaper writers and cartoonists, Anderson's conservatism was actually firmer. Humphrey's conservatism was instinctive and intuitive without much intellectual base; it could be moved or outflanked by argument. Moreover, Humphrey was a conservative second and a Republican first; he was willing to compromise his "principles" for the party. (Of course, when out of office this leavening element in his position diminished.) Anderson was more ideological and less political. This was attractive to Eisenhower. He liked to think of himself, and have others think of him, as taking the long view rather than the short, the hard road rather than the easy, the nonpolitical course rather than the political.

In addition, Eisenhower shared Anderson's estimate of what the long-range problem was. He was unwilling to sacrifice the continuing war against inflation for the sake of a slash against recession, and he was unwilling to jeopardize his long-range goal of tax reform for the sake of a "quickie" tax cut.

Some of his thinking, particularly about the political traps of anti-recession policy, came through in a letter to Arthur Burns:

Dear Arthur:

I trust that I am not getting stubborn in my attitude about logical federal action in this business slump, but I am bound to say that I cannot help but feel that precipitate, and therefore largely unwise, action would be the worst thing that we could now do. I realize that to be conservative in this situation—and flatly to say so—can well get me tagged as an unsympathetic, reactionary fossil. But my honest conviction is that the greatest service we can now do for our country is to oppose wild-eyed schemes of every kind. I am against vast and unwise public works programs (they would need some years to get truly under way) as well as the slash-bang kinds of tax-cutting from which the proponents want nothing so much as immediate political advantage. . . .

We shall continue to push on with the things that we believe are useful. One of these, of course, is the acceleration of public works already under way. These have to be paid for in any event; acceleration of the work will cost nothing in the long run, and the additional work will be helpful now.

Administrative actions have already been taken to support home building and we have asked for legislation to push harder on this particular matter. However, some of the bills on this subject are bad.

Tax cuts *may* have to be made, and with the general proposition made in your last two letters I completely agree. But how I pray that when and if such action is necessary, we may have some statesmen and economists in controlling [Congressional] positions.[27]

The Anderson and Eisenhower position did not rule out the possibility that the administration would recommend a tax cut if the case for it was strong. Moreover, there was known to be an active faction within the administration with a more receptive attitude. Thus, in late February and early March speculation rose about an administration proposal to cut taxes. This created an unstable situation between the administration and the Congress. The Congressional leadership, Speaker Rayburn, Majority Leader Johnson, and the chairman of the House Ways and Means Committee, Wilbur Mills, were not prepared to push a tax cut, especially without administration support. But they did not want to be in the position of holding back the membership if the administration was going to come along later and get credit for cutting taxes. On the other hand, while Eisenhower and Anderson were not about to take the initiative for cutting taxes, they did not want to be left behind if Congress was going to move. There was a danger that one side or the other would act prematurely to preempt the political advantage that the other might be seeking.

THE TRUCE

On March 12 the administration moved to slow down the race. After meeting with the President, Secretary Anderson read to the press a statement approved by Eisenhower:

No decision regarding taxes has been made. Whatever decision regarding taxes is taken will be reached only when the impact of current developments on the future course of the economy has been clarified and after consultation with Congressional leaders.[28]

The next day Anderson met with Rayburn and Mills and an agreement was made that neither the administration nor the Congressional leadership would make a move to cut taxes without consulting the other. In the course of the meeting Anderson assured Rayburn and Mills that he, not Nixon, spoke for the administration on tax policy.[29]

This agreement came immediately before the first Congressional test of tax cutting later that day. Senator Douglas proposed, as an amendment to a technical tax-revision bill, the tax cut he had suggested in his speech of February 10. He emphasized that unemployment was high and rising, and there were no signs of recovery. A tax cut, he said, was inevitable. "The question is simply when it will come, and in what form it will come." In that case, why not make the cut now and get the economic benefits sooner? The opposition was desultory, and the leadership took no part in the debate. The argument was partly procedural; so important a tax matter should have been considered in the Senate Finance Committee and preferably first in the House Ways and Means Committee. The economic arguments were that a tax cut would not help the unemployed, since they generally were not taxpayers, and that a tax cut would be inflationary. The Douglas amendment was defeated by a vote of 71 to 14 with Senators John F. Kennedy and Lyndon B. Johnson both voting against it.[30]

This heavy vote did not mean that there was strong opposition in the Congress which would prevent the enactment of a tax cut. It only represented the fact that a tax cut had no chance without the support of either the Republican leadership in the administration or the Democratic leadership in the Congress. There was no doubt that the two leaderships could have a tax cut if they agreed and little doubt that either could get a tax cut through the Congress if it took the initiative alone. In the circumstances this meant that the initiative was with the administration. The Democratic leadership of Congress had little desire to expose itself further to the constant Republican charge of "fiscal irresponsibility" in order to help bail the Republicans out of "their" recession.

The prospect of a back-bencher's initiative for a tax cut was diminished after Congress went home in April for the Easter recess. Many members returned with the impression of little demand among their constituents for a tax cut. This was not surprising. Only a small minority of the population was affected by the recession, and probably few saw much connection between cutting taxes and ending the recession. But again, this did not mean that there would have been public opposition to tax reduction if the leadership had supported it.

Even after the Anderson-Rayburn-Mills agreement of March 13 and the lopsided defeat of the Douglas Amendment on the same day, debate over a tax cut continued within the administration, and public speculation continued that an administration proposal was a good possibility. Support continued to mount from sources that the administration might have been expected to regard as sound and reliable.

On March 22 Arthur Burns made a strong speech at the University of Chicago, recommending a permanent $5 billion tax cut, and saying:

> If, on the other hand, we delay more than a very few weeks, in the hope that economic recovery will come on its own by midyear, we shall be taking the risk of having to resort later to drastic action.[31]

On March 23, the Program Committee of the Committee for Economic Development, including many pro-Eisenhower businessmen, issued a statement on anti-recession policy. They pointed out that by February the recession had already been as deep as any of the three previous postwar recessions. They warned of the danger that if the decline continued much further, even if it did not accelerate, recovery might take a long time and the consequences might be serious. Therefore they recommended that if the decline continued through March and April there should be a one-year, $7.5 billion, across-the-board reduction of individual income taxes, "unless there is unmistakable evidence of quickly forthcoming improvement." They urged that planning begin at once so that the tax cut could be made promptly if the specific conditions were met.[32]

This was the only time in its history that the CED came close to invoking the "serious recession" exception to its general rule against discretionary contracyclical fiscal actions and as close as it ever came to giving a quantitative description of a serious recession.

On April 6 the National Planning Association, consisting of representatives of business, labor, agriculture, and the economics profession, also recommended a tax reduction.[33] Two weeks later a committee set up by the Rockefeller Brothers Fund, including a number of business and professional people, recommended tax reduction.[34] A ground swell of informed opinion seemed to be developing.

Nevertheless, as March and April passed it became increasingly clear that the dominant part of the administration regarded tax reduction as economically and politically dangerous, to be undertaken only in extreme economic conditions, and that the conditions they regarded as sufficiently extreme were not appearing.

In reply to a question about the administration's policy on tax cuts, at his press conference of March 26, the President said:

> I do say that we are watching every development as closely as we know how. We try to get advice, information, counsel from every phase of our American life, and we are certainly going to do those things we think should be done; but we are not going into a tax cut or any other what we believe to be unwise program that can hurt us badly in the future. We have got to think of the years to come as well as the immediate month in which we are living.[35]

The same judiciously negative attitude was shown at the press conference a week later:

> QUESTION: Mr. President, on the question of a tax cut, some economists have argued that if a substantial tax cut were made promptly there would be little loss in total revenue because of the stimulating effect on the economy that it would have as compared with not cutting taxes. What do you think of that, sir?
> PRESIDENT: Well, of course this has been argued pro and con. Mr. Baruch yesterday said he couldn't think of anything being greater folly than a general tax cut. I believe that there are factors on each side of this business. . . . Although some of my very warmest friends, men I respect in the economic field just as deeply as I do anybody else, believe that the number one thing to do is tax cuts, others are just as much on the other side.[36]

A few days later the *New York Times* reported, in a story by Edwin L. Dale who saw Secretary Anderson frequently, that the Treasury view was firming against a tax cut for five reasons:

1. Measures already taken would increase spending and raise the deficit greatly in fiscal years 1959 and 1960.
2. The sentiment of responsible people had shifted against a tax cut.
3. A tax cut might turn the economy around too sharply.
4. A tax cut and a large deficit would be inflationary.
5. An upturn was expected in 1958 even without a tax cut.

Dale reported that Anderson "is prepared, as the lesser of evils, to accept a condition of fairly serious unemployment—even close to the present levels —all through 1958, as long as the jobless situation is showing some little improvement." Other economic advisers to the President were said to disagree with this position.[37]

BY WHAT SIGNAL?

This reflected the issue on which the decision would finally be based. What was the purpose of the tax cut, and what were the signals on which it would be made or the idea abandoned? On the one hand it was argued that the purpose of the tax cut was to stop a decline when, or before, it reached a serious point and initiate some recovery. This view could be justified on the ground that only the avoidance of serious unemployment could justify so extreme an action as cutting taxes, or on the ground that once the decline stopped, recovery to high employment would come naturally and quickly. If this was the objective, a sign that the decline was slackening and reaching a bottom would eliminate further consideration of tax reduction. On the other hand, it was argued that merely to stop the decline was not sufficient, and that the end of the decline was not necessarily the beginning of a vigorous recovery. If the object was to get the economy back to high employment quickly, signs that the decline was ending were not by themselves signs that the tax cut was unnecessary.

This latter position was the logical counterpart of the position that anti-recession action should not be based on a forecast of a coming decline or even on evidence that a mild decline was under way. When the economy was close to high employment, stimulative action based on a weak signal of coming or present recession might easily cause inflation. But when the economy was far below high employment, *inaction* based on a weak signal of approaching or present recovery could easily lead to stagnation.[38]

The dominant view in the administration, which is to say the Anderson-Eisenhower view, was that a tax cut might be justified to end a decline which threatened to cumulate, and possibly to initiate recovery, but not to assure the prompt reattainment of high employment once the decline had ended and recovery begun. This view is clear in Eisenhower's recollection of the atmosphere of the spring of 1958, recorded in his memoirs:

> As in 1954, the clouds of pessimism gradually began to roll back. Between the middle of April and the middle of May unemployment had dropped by thirty thousand, in the first reversal in the upward movement since November. By June or July the experts' charts were showing rises in industrial production, personal income, non-agricultural employment, and new home construction. The Gross National Product, in the second quarter of 1958, was on its way upward again.
> The storm was over.[39]

The storm was the economic *decline*. Once the decline had ended the storm was over, and the need for action had passed. But if the storm was regarded as excessive unemployment and its consequences, the sun was not shining. In May, when the decision not to cut taxes was made, unemployment had fallen to 7.2 percent from 7.5 percent in April, which had been the highest rate of the postwar period. But by August the rate was back up to 7.6 percent and the average rate for the last seven months of 1958 was 6.8 percent. The average unemployment rate for calendar 1959 was 5.5 percent. The President was right in thinking that the decline had come to an end in the spring of 1958. However, this did not mean that the problem of unemployment had come to an end.

Signs that the decline was nearing an end were widely recognized in April and May, but the possibility that this would not be quickly followed by recovery was also widely recognized. Eisenhower recalls this:

> Dr. Raymond J. Saulnier, Dr. Burns' successor—a distinguished economist and man of integrity with whom I consulted constantly on economic trends throughout my second term—pointed out at a Cabinet meeting on May 2, 1958, that while the downward trend had abated, it had not yet flattened. Most economists, he said, did not predict an upturn before the end of the year.[40]

This possibility that recovery, even when it came, would be slow sustained interest in tax reduction until the administration and Congressional leadership definitely put an end to the idea on May 26, 1958. Until that date some members of the administration, some Congressmen, many economists, and a few businessmen continued to push for tax reduction. At hearings held at the end of April by the Subcommittee on Fiscal Policy of the Joint Economic Committee there was a good deal of support for the position that while the end of the decline might be in sight, and there was some danger of inflation, tax reduction was still timely. Thus, Theodore O. Yntema, Vice-President of Ford Motor Company, testified:

> My own preference would be to stop the collection of withheld taxes entirely for 2 or 3 months and then go to a 50 percent forgiveness until December 31, 1958 or until the seasonally corrected index of unemployment dropped below 5 percent, whichever occurred first.
>
> It is possible that we may get a recovery before long without further fiscal action to bring it about—but this is uncertain. If we take effective action to end the depression there will, I am sure, be a swift acceleration of wage inflation. If we do more than is necessary in tax reduction, we shall have correspondingly more inflation. Moreover, once the public discovers how effective mass tax reduction is, there will be a temptation to use it whenever unemployment rises to 3 percent or 4 percent instead of when it reaches 7 percent. If we use such measures when unemployment is only 3 percent or 4 percent we shall reap the whirlwind of inflation.
>
> My own judgment is that we should use temporary tax reduction such as I have described to end this recession and at the same time face up to the problem that makes it dangerous to use such remedial measures—the problem of wage inflation.[41]

Throughout April and most of May public discussion went on as if tax reduction were still a real possibility. On April 29, Senate Majority Leader Lyndon Johnson said, "if we don't provide a cure to the recession in public works, there is no other alternative but tax revision."[42] Two days later Labor Secretary Mitchell expressed the opinion that a decision on further anti-recession moves would have to be made in thirty to sixty days, and said that he preferred a tax cut if the decision was affirmative.[43] On May 17, Senator John F. Kennedy gave the following appraisal in an interview in Madison, Wisconsin:

> I believe Congress is moving toward a cut in taxes. However, there have been advanced some strong arguments against it. For one thing it would increase our deficit by some two or three billion dollars and it looks like the deficit will be eight to ten billions without it.[44]

THE DEBATE FADES AWAY

But given the administration's view of the problem, the real possibility of tax reduction ebbed rapidly after the first signs began to appear that the rate of economic decline was diminishing, even though the decline continued. The administration began seeing those signs early in April. On the eighth of April the President issued a statement that the unemployment statistics indicated a slowing up of the decline. Thereafter, although there was as yet no need to close the door to a tax cut, the President always discussed it as a remote and unlikely possibility. Thus, at his April 9 news conference he replied to a question about a tax cut with:

> I see no figures that bring this thing to a critical point and require a decision at the moment; although I have, as you know, always admitted it's a subject that is under constant study in every conference.[45]

And as his confidence increased that the recession was not going to come to a "critical point," the President increasingly emphasized what he regarded as the long-range economic problems, notably inflation. Later in the same press conference there was this exchange:

> QUESTION: Mr. President, the additional measures that have been discussed for use, if necessary, to halt the recession would involve a very large increase in the budget deficit, easily to as much as $10 billion or even more. Do you believe this is a legitimate price to pay, if necessary, to halt the slump?
> PRESIDENT: Well, I will tell you, I think now you are beginning to talk about things that are getting rather of an emergency character, because when you get very large deficits then you have to go into deficit financing, then the

money supply gets much more plentiful, and the prices of everything, Mr. Folliard remarked awhile ago, begin to go up.

So your national income goes up, but the prices that you are going to pay—and I think the possibility of an inflation under such a practice would be very greatly increased. I don't think any of us want any real inflation.[46]

The President had been reassured in his views by a conversation on March 24 with Ludwig Erhard, the West German Minister of Economics, and he told the press about it at this conference. Erhard had a towering reputation as the sage of free-market economics who had produced the German economic miracle of postwar recovery by setting the German economy free. He told Eisenhower that whereas the Germans, because of their history, always worried about inflation, the Americans, because of their history, always worried about depression. The resulting danger was that America would overrespond to threats of recession and cause serious inflation in the long run. Further he said, in words which Eisenhower later described as "welcome relief to alarm bells I had been hearing":

I would not really worry about the American economy. Because of Sputniks and fear of other developments in the uneasy world, your recession may have psychological causes which will disappear as public apprehensions lessen. I believe with you that the federal government should not start too early to intervene directly in economic affairs but should continue to reassure the public as to its own security as well as to the basic soundness of the economy.[47]

At his press conference two weeks later on April 23 the President told the reporters that some signs had appeared which indicated that the bottom of the recession had been reached. When asked why he had been for tax reduction in 1954 but was not for it in 1958 he replied that the situation was very complex, but things were getting better. He pointed out in answer to another question that we might have higher defense costs for a long time, and that we had to look at the long-range revenue requirements and not only at a "minor emergency internally"—meaning the recession. And he raised another point that always worried him about a tax cut: "No one would know what it would look like by the time you got done."[48]

It was not only the administration that backed rapidly away from a tax cut at the first signs of the beginning of the end of the decline. On April 26 House Speaker Rayburn told his Democratic colleagues that "he would be willing to announce now his opposition to a general tax cut this season if Secretary Anderson would promise not to recommend one on behalf of the Administration." The Democratic leadership was reported to believe that a tax cut was not justified unless the economy should start a faster decline.[49]

As has been noted above, the CED had recommended that if the economic decline should continue through March and April taxes should be cut "unless there is unmistakable evidence of quickly forthcoming improvement." When Mr. Frazar B. Wilde, chairman of CED's Research and Policy Committee, testified before the Douglas Subcommittee on May 1, the decline had clearly continued through March. There was also some fragmentary evidence that the decline had continued through April. Mr. Wilde repeated the previous CED recommendation but regarded the indicators then available for April as inconclusive about the desirability of a tax cut.[50] However, when in a few weeks the statistics showed that the decline had indeed continued through April, CED did not announce that the time to cut taxes had arrived. Rather it was willing to rely upon the signs that pointed to the end of the decline as the basis for withholding action.

Early in May the Business Advisory Council met to discuss, among other things, tax reduction, including the proposals of the CED and the Rockefeller Brothers Fund. The members of the BAC, leading business executives, had close personal, political, and ideological ties with the administration. If the BAC had been strongly for a tax cut, the administration would certainly have attached weight to its views. However, as it turned out, while the group was divided, a large majority was against a tax cut.[51]

The administration could not postpone a decision much beyond the middle of May. Under the terms of legislation enacted during the Korean War and extended in 1954 and 1956, a reduction of corporate profits taxes and excise taxes was scheduled to occur automatically on June 30, 1958. If the administration wanted these taxes continued, as it did regardless of whether or not it was going to ask for an anti-recession tax cut, legislation needed to start moving through the Congress. Also, if there was going to be a Congressional effort to cut taxes this would most logically come in the form of an amendment to the tax extension bill. The administration would have to take a clear position for or against such an amendment.

In a speech on May 20 the President, while not absolutely closing the door, seemed to leave little room for tax reduction. He said that the recession was near its bottom, and then, turning to the question of tax revision:

> The timing of such [tax] changes always poses problems. During periods of high business activity and high employment there is concern with inflationary effects. In a time like the present, with its rising government expenditures, we are particularly sensitive to tax burdens, but there is likewise great concern with the future impact of increasing current deficits.[52]

On May 25 Secretary Anderson, House Speaker Rayburn, and Ways and Means Committee Chairman Mills agreed informally that there would be no tax cut at that time and probably none for the rest of the year.[53] The next day the President confirmed the agreement, writing to Rayburn and Nixon—as President of the Senate—renewing his earlier recommendation that the corporation income tax and excise taxes be continued without change. He said that he made this recommendation after consultation by the Secretary of the Treasury with Congressional leaders of both parties.[54] Senate Majority Leader Johnson indicated that he would go along with his Texas colleague, Speaker Rayburn, although reluctantly. He pointed out that tax policy was "the special prerogative of the House," and that with the close party division in the Senate "it's pretty obvious you can't pass a [tax] bill the President is not for."[55]

This ended the possibility of a tax cut in 1958. Senator Douglas did propose an amendment to the tax extension bill which could have provided a reduction of taxes on individual incomes and excises. On June 18 it was voted down in the Senate 65 to 23, the supporters this time including John F. Kennedy.[56]

THE CONSENSUS IN 1958

What we have described as the postwar consensus on fiscal policy had two main prescriptions for a recession. First, there should be no attempt to offset the deficit that would automatically result from the decline of revenues. Second, in a serious recession more positive steps should be taken, notably a temporary reduction of tax rates. The first prescription was followed in 1958, as it had been in 1949 and in 1954. Indeed, because it was deeper than the earlier postwar recessions, the 1958 decline caused a larger deficit than had been experienced earlier. There also were some relatively small expenditure increases inspired or justified by the recession. But the potentially largest step, and the one receiving the most attention—tax reduction—was not taken.

Failure to make a tax cut in 1958 resulted from, and revealed, two problems about the postwar fiscal policy consensus.

First, it had been assumed that a *temporary* tax reduction would be economically effective and politically possible. By 1958 both the economics and the politics were in question. On the economic side the view was emerging that consumers' spending would not respond, or would not respond very much, to a temporary reduction of taxes. Households receiving a tax reduction to last for only six or twelve months would not raise their level of consumption significantly but would add their tax relief to their savings. This belief received strong support from the publication in 1957 of Milton Friedman's *A Theory of the Consumption Function* which argued that consumption was much more influenced by what people thought their permanent level of income was than by the income they had available in a particular year.[57] If this was true, then a powerful stimulus to consumption during the recession could only be provided by a permanent tax reduction which would, however, have effects lasting long after the recession.

This argument about the economic effects of a temporary tax cut was not universally accepted and was probably unknown to many who participated in the tax cut debate. More generally persuasive was the political consideration. Whatever the legislation might say, it seemed doubtful that a popular tax cut enacted during a recession would be allowed to expire and taxes allowed to rise when a certain date had passed or a certain economic condition had been reached.

If a temporary tax cut was either not economically useful or not politically possible, serious attention had to be given to the long-range consequences of a permanent tax cut that might be enacted in a recession. The structure of the anti-recession tax cut became more important than it would otherwise have been, because that structure would survive. The administration's belief that the only kind of tax cut that could be quickly passed through the Democratic Congress would be a demagogic tax cut, quite contrary to the administration's long-range tax goals, made the administration extremely reluctant to embark upon any "quickie" tax cut if there was a strong probability that the "quickie" would last.

The possibility that a "temporary" tax cut would not really be temporary also greatly increased the danger that it would be inflationary. The tax reduction would persist beyond the period when it was appropriate as an anti-recession measure into a period when it was not needed but would contribute to inflation.

This aspect of the inflationary danger in anti-recession tax cuts was joined by another which had been ignored in the original formulation of consensus policy. The policy formulations of 1947–49 had assumed that recession and inflation were distinct conditions which would not exist simultaneously. Recession and inflation might alternate with each other rapidly and unpredictably. There was a danger that policy actions designed to correct one, if taken at the wrong time or in the wrong amount, might intensify the other. But in principle, if there were perfect foresight and flexibility in applying policy, there would be some scale and timing of action that would prevent either condition without causing or intensifying the other.

However, in 1958 it began to appear that we might have, and indeed were having, both recession and inflation at once. At least the index of consumers prices continued to rise throughout the recession. In April, 1958, when the unemployment rate hit 7.5 percent, the price index was 2.5 percent higher than it had been in the middle of 1957 when the recession started. The recession, in Eisenhower's words the "temporary emergency internally," seemed to be superimposed on a long-range trend of inflation which was then almost twenty years old. Moreover, the inflation appeared more difficult to stop the longer it went on because the continued record of inflation led to the expectation of further inflation and caused labor to demand wage increases which made more price increases inevitable. So the question was not simply whether to accept a little more inflation for a brief period while expansive measures were needed to reduce unemployment. The problem was that the "little more inflation" would add to the continuing inflationary trend which could be expected to reassert itself in full force when the recession had passed.

Consensus fiscal policy, like other versions of stabilizing fiscal policy, had prescribed a course of action to be followed in a period of recession unmixed with inflation, and another course to be followed in a period of inflation unmixed with recession. It had not told what to do in a recession superimposed on an inflation.

In the circumstances a choice had to be made, and the Eisenhower administration made it on the side of continuing the fight against inflation while making the minimum concessions to ending the recession. If the recession had continued longer and deeper they apparently were prepared to move more vigorously against it, primarily by tax reduction. But they would undoubtedly have been much more prepared to act if they had not had the inflationary record behind them and the inflationary danger before them.

This heavy weight given to the danger of inflation was consistent with the attitude of the administration throughout its term. But it was not peculiar to Eisenhower and Anderson in 1958. The Federal Reserve, for one, shared this view. In a rare confession of error, the board later said that it had continued expansive monetary policy too long after the 1954 recession and so contributed to the inflation of 1955–57.[58] The board was not going to repeat that mistake and turned to a policy of restraint with unusual promptness after the recession bottomed out in mid-1958. Moreover, the board, and especially its chairman, William McChesney Martin, were influential with the President in his thinking about anti-recession policy. After the President made his decision against tax reduction, Labor Secretary Mitchell told a reporter that he and Nixon had lost the tax cut fight to Anderson and the Federal Reserve Board.[59]

It is representative of the atmosphere of that spring that in April, 1958, near the bottom of the recession, the CED issued a statement, "Defense Against Inflation," describing inflation as "one of the major unsolved economic problems of our times." However, it was not only the President, bankers, and businessmen who were concerned with the problem of inflation in the midst of the recession. Testifying before the Douglas Subcommittee on April 28, Professor Paul Samuelson of MIT, one of the brightest stars of "the new economics," revealed the same concern, although he came to a different policy conclusion. He forecast a slow rise of production beginning sometime in 1958, but with unemployment remaining high and possibly rising. He then went on to say:

> Such a forecast assumes that we shall have some continuation of the "new inflation". . . . The rise in money wages, and in lesser degree in prices, will be modest and will not touch off any avalanche of inflation-consciousness among the American people.
>
> But what it will do is create dilemmas for conscientious Congressman [*sic*], and I fear that overconcern over the admitted evil of price inflation will in some measure inhibit Government fiscal and monetary policies needed to restore us on the trend of progressively growing real national income.
>
> Speaking for myself, and after much weighing of the relative evils involved, I would say that the primary concern at this time should not be with an intensification of inflation that may come tomorrow if high employment and production is restored.[60]

That inflation was going on, that its continuation was not only possible but likely, that this was a legitimate cause for concern, and that this concern was relevant to the decision about anti-recession policy—on these matters there was general agreement. Beyond that lay an area where judgments differed. How much inflation was likely? How much more would there be if vigorous steps were taken to reverse the recession and get quickly back to high employment? What would be the consequences of prolonging and increasing the inflation? Were there other ways to restrain the inflation than tolerating a slow recovery from the recession? Different judgments about such questions led to differences of view about policy in 1958. After "much weighing of the relative evils involved," the administration, unlike Professor Samuelson, concluded that inflation was the primary concern. But this was no longer a difference about the general principles of fiscal policy. The argument assumed the agreement of both sides that economic stabilization is a primary objective of fiscal policy, that this requires deficits at some times, that increasing expenditures and reducing taxes are expansionary or, depending upon the circumstances, inflationary, or both, and that variation of tax rates is in many conditions the preferred way of making fiscal adjustments for the sake of economic stability. But these general principles did not answer the question of policy for 1958.

⚜14⚜

The Drive for the Big Surplus: 1959–1960

Once the economic decline had ended, in mid-1958, and "the storm was over," as Eisenhower put it, he quickly resumed the fiscal course from which the recession had diverted him. That course was to generate a large budget surplus. In fact, the determination was stronger and the objective more ambitious than before the recession.

What was not fully recognized in 1959 and 1960 was the magnitude of the result. The government moved from a large deficit in calendar 1958 to a moderate surplus in 1960, but that was thought to be mainly the natural consequence of recovery, which raised individual and corporate incomes and therefore tax receipts, rather than the consequence of budget policy. The 1960 surplus was smaller than in 1956, the last previous year of prosperity.

Federal Budget Surplus[1]
(Billions of Dollars)
Calendar Years

	1956	1958	1960
Administrative Budget	$3.8	–$7.1	$2.0
Cash-Consolidated Budget	5.6	– 7.2	3.6
National Income Accounts	5.7	–10.2	3.5

The recovery from 1958 to 1960 was only partial, and 1960 was not a year of prosperity on a par with 1956. Whereas the unemployment rate had been 4.2 percent in 1956 and 6.8 percent in 1958, it was still 5.6 percent in 1960. Only a part of the swing from the 1958 deficit to the 1960 surplus was due to the recovery. If the economy had been operating in 1960 with as low a rate of unemployment as in 1956, the 1960 surplus would have been much larger.

A measure of the effects of budget policy, as distinguished from the automatic response of revenues and expenditures to fluctuations in the rate of economic activity, is provided by the "full-employment surplus." This is an estimate of the amount of surplus that would have been realized in any year if there had been full employment—conventionally defined as 4 percent unemployment—with the tax rates and expenditure programs then in effect, and with the estimated labor force, productivity, and price level of that year. This figure shows the surplus that would result from the actual tax and expenditure policies if the economy moved along a path of steady growth without any departures from the 4 percent unemployment rate. The full-employment surplus is the surplus the CED had recommended for use as a guide to budget policy in its 1947 statement. By this method of calculation, the surplus, according to estimates made subsequently, would have been $6.4 billion in 1956, $4.6 billion in 1958, and $14.8 billion in 1960, in the national income accounts.[2]

Thus, if the effects of variations in the rate of unemployment and economic activity are excluded, the 1960 surplus was about $8 billion larger than the 1956 surplus and $10 billion larger than the 1958 surplus. This increase in the budget surplus that would have been realized at full employment was the main fiscal achievement of the last two Eisenhower years. It was accomplished by holding a tight rein on the growth of expenditures while, with constant tax rates, the rising labor force and rising productivity were substantially increasing the potential full-employment revenues. From calendar 1958 to calendar 1960 expenditures increased by only $5 billion while full-employment revenues increased by about $15 billion.

Although the magnitude of the achievement was not immediately apparent, the growth of the surplus was not an accident. It was a high-priority objective of the administration's policy. The President spoke so often and so earnestly about balancing the budget that he was thought to be making a fetish of it. He explained his position on this in response to a question at his news conference of February 18, 1959:

> QUESTION: Mr. President, among the Lincoln Day speeches last week was one by a Republican Senator who said we should not make a fetish out of balancing the budget. There are certain conditions that he named, the reversal of the economy or increased military threat, could make deficit spending more important than a balanced budget.
>   Would you say that conditions could change this year to make you change your mind on a balanced budget?
> PRESIDENT: Well, I will say this: very manifestly, last year we didn't have a balanced budget, and we could foresee that it wasn't, and we didn't make any fetish about it. I don't know why suddenly a balanced budget is getting to be

a bad word. I think it is rather a good thing to be a bit frugal and say that we can live within our income.

I do not know what is the future, and I can't even see beyond the next day; I am not a seventh son of a seventh son.

I can say this: when the conditions allow it, and with the conditions of rising prosperity—remember, personal income in the month of January is the highest it has ever been in this country—this kind of thing opens up this great question: if we cannot live within our means as prosperity is growing and developing, when are we going to do it? And if we are going to always live under deficit spending, what is going to happen to our currency?

This question doesn't seem to me to demand any detailed answer. It is clear.

Now, on the other hand, it has sometimes seemed a little bit odd that we have to make our whole economic, in some strange way, economic cycle coincide with the time it takes the earth to get around the sun.

I sometimes wonder whether we shouldn't think of our budget balancing in terms of 5-year terms, or at least to include the length of time that we find the ordinary business cycle. Then you could have maybe a discussion on the balancing of the budget and living within your income on a little better basis. One year's budget is not the whole answer, and we didn't ask for it last year. I am asking for it this year because I think it is good for the country and I think we can do it in this kind of a period. I think we must do it.[3]

Reasons for a Surplus

While the President did not make a fetish of balancing the budget, he had a number of strongly-held objectives and beliefs which pointed in the direction of restraining expenditures and creating not only a balanced budget but a large surplus.

One of these objectives was tax reduction, and one reason for holding expenditures down was to generate sufficient surplus so that taxes could be cut without a deficit. He held out the prospect of tax reduction as the fruit of a balanced budget in a talk at the National Press Club in January, 1959:

QUESTION: Mr. President, is it correct to assume that if Congress maintains a balanced budget this year, that next year you will propose a reduction in individual income taxes?

PRESIDENT: Well, the first thing I believe we have to do is to reform our tax structure in a number of ways. . . . I would not be prepared to say that we would be recommending next year, as the first move in this field, reduction of personal income tax. I do say we must reform our tax structure so that incentives are enhanced and not damaged.

And if Congress does keep this budget balanced, I say that increases our prospect for that kind of reform, as I say, eventually a lowering of taxes all along the line.[4]

A similar picture was painted in the economic report that same month. However, as in the 1955–57 period, the objective of reducing taxes was the first to go. On July 21, 1959, the President met with a small group of newsmen and told them, among other things, that he was giving up the hope of tax reduction during his term.

> President Eisenhower has abandoned the idea of reducing taxes while he remains in the White House—a prospect he held out in a message to Congress last January.
>
> Instead he has the Treasury Department working to increase revenues without higher tax rates. He hopes that with a heavy lid on Government spending this would produce a surplus of $2,000,000,000 to $5,000,000,000 during the 1961 fiscal year, including his last six months in office.[5]

The basis of this decision, which would mean the failure of so many Republican hopes and promises, was the belief that merely balancing the budget was not enough and that some reduction of the debt was imperative. Of course, tax reduction was not ruled out forever. As the President said in his budget message in January, 1960:

> The budget recommendations for 1961 lay the groundwork for a sound and flexible fiscal policy in the years ahead. A continuance of economic prosperity in 1962 and later years can be expected to bring with it further increases in Federal revenues. If expenditures are held to the levels I am proposing for 1961, and reasonable restraint is exercised in the future, higher revenues in later years will give the next Administration and the next Congress the choice they should rightly have in deciding between reductions in the public debt and lightening of the tax burden, or both.[6]

The next administration was the Kennedy administration. It was to exercise its choice, which was at least in part the legacy of Eisenhower, on the side of tax reduction.

At the time of his decision to forego tax reduction, the President was greatly impressed with the need to reduce the interest cost of the federal debt by reducing the size of the debt. When asked to explain the reasons for his decision on taxes he said:

> Well, I think there is only this one statement to be made. I believe we should start paying off something on this big debt of ours. Already the estimates are that the interest alone on our debt for 1961, and we are already working on that budget, will be 8,700,000,000. Now when you are getting to this kind of cost

just for interest, it would look to be the part of wisdom to start getting the debt down a little bit, thereby creating the kind of confidence that will make a tax cut more justifiable.[7]

But this concern with the interest burden of the debt was transitory. The interest burden was less than 10 percent of the total budget. More important, the amounts by which anyone could conceive of reducing the debt would not have a significant effect in reducing the interest burden within the period of most people's concern. The debt was almost $300 billion. The largest surplus Eisenhower ever achieved in one year would have reduced the debt by a little over 1 percent.

Reducing the interest burden and paving the way for later tax reduction were marginal and passing reasons for the administration's great drive to achieve a budget surplus. There were three basic and continuing reasons— the connections believed to exist between a budget surplus and economic growth, the international position of the dollar, and inflation.

Grandchildren and Growth

In January, 1960, President Eisenhower began to talk about the federal debt in terms of the burden passed on to our children and grandchildren. During his state of the Union message that month he departed from his prepared text to interpolate remarks referring to the budget surplus as "reduction on our children's inherited mortgage."[8] At a press conference a few days later he mentioned "this debt that we are passing on to someone else."[9] In August he warned Congress against the "burden of debt of our grandchildren."[10] And the grandchildren argument was used on many other occasions.

In his informal talks the President never explained what the content of this argument was. And, of course, there is something to explain, since our children and grandchildren will own the debt as well as owe it, so it is not obvious in what sense they are being left a burden. However, some of the formal statements made the argument clearer. Thus, the January, 1960, budget message said that, "In times of prosperity . . . sound fiscal and economic policy requires a budget surplus to help counteract inflationary pressures, to ease conditions in capital and credit markets, and to increase the supply of savings available for the productive investment so essential to continued economic growth."[11] It is this last clause which explains what a budget surplus and debt reduction do for our grandchildren. The budget surplus is a part of the national income that is not spent for private consumption or for the provision of current services by government. Therefore, it is available, like private savings, to finance private investment. If the surplus is achieved in a way that does not reduce private savings by an equal amount, then total savings is increased by the surplus and a higher rate of total private investment will be possible. When the government uses the surplus to repay part of the federal debt, the holders of the debt acquire funds which they can use to finance private investment. The increase in private investment raises the real assets—the real productive capacity—we leave to the future, to our grandchildren. On the other hand, if the government runs a deficit it must finance the deficit by borrowing private savings, which consequently are not available for investment, and this reduces the real assets we leave our grandchildren.

This argument, on the grounds of economic growth, is the classic 19th Century argument for a budget surplus and against a budget deficit. Its revival in the latter days of the Eisenhower administration was stimulated by a greatly heightened interest in economic growth as a national objective. For a long time it had been taken for granted that the American rate of economic growth—the rate of increase of total output, or of output per capita or per worker—was not merely satisfactory but was the marvel of the world. There was real concern about assuring that our potential to produce was fully used, but increasing the rate of growth of the potential seemed a secondary objective.

In the late 1950's the country awoke to the fact, or belief, that a number of countries were growing faster than the United States. This included not only our friends—Germany, France, and Japan—but also the Soviet Union. Some of these countries had, in fact, been growing more rapidly than the United States for years, but this had been discounted at first as the process of recovery from the devastation of the war and unlikely to continue for long. However, it did continue. Moreover, the Soviet performance was called to American attention in a dramatic and exaggerated way by the launching of Sputnik and the reconsideration of the Soviet economic and technological system which that stimulated. Thus the country had before it the example of what other countries could do and the threat of what the Soviets could do.

As growth, rather than mere stability, rose in the scale of national objectives the case for a large budget surplus rose with it. This case found its way into Eisenhower's thinking in the form of the grandchildren argument.

REASSURING OUR FOREIGN FRIENDS

A second consideration strengthening Eisenhower's determination to have a large surplus was the international position of the dollar. The United States had run a deficit in its balance of payments almost continuously since the end of World War II. That is, U.S. payments to the rest of the world, including U.S. loans and investments abroad, had exceeded U.S. receipts from the rest of the world. The consequence was that foreigners acquired dollar assets, usually deposits in U.S. banks or U.S. government securities which were liabilities of the U.S., or that gold flowed out of the United States. During the first decade after the war, when the rest of the world was recovering economically and replenishing its international reserves, this seemed an appropriate thing to happen. However, as the process continued into 1958 and 1959, concern mounted at home and abroad about whether it was not going too far—about whether the U.S. reserve position was not being excessively weakened by increase of liabilities and loss of gold, and about whether the U.S. would be able to stop the drain. There was talk about loss of confidence in the dollar and about what the U.S. had to do in order to maintain confidence in the dollar. In the opinion of many bankers and other financial experts it was necessary that the U.S. should stop its inflation and its budget deficits.

This consideration impressed Eisenhower greatly. It was a matter of an external obligation which had to be met—or so it seemed. Moreover, what was at stake was connected somehow with the nation's position of leadership in the world, which was an absolute necessity, not something more or less desirable like many domestic goals.

One of Eisenhower's earliest expressions of this concern came at his March 4, 1959, news conference in answer to a question about budget-balancing:

> Well, remember, balancing the budget is not of interest merely to ourselves. Our friends, the nations with whom we trade, the nations that are increasingly using the dollar as a medium of exchange, they are interested in the knowledge that we can pay our bills.
>
> Now, we have had this very bad year from the standpoint of budgetary balance in 1957 [sic, should be 1958], when income was way down, and the expenditures, some of it due to one reason or other—one, to help increase employment, and the other brought about by sputnik complexes—caused a big gap.
>
> Now, as quickly as we can get back to a pay-as-you-go basis, the freer the world will feel about this whole affair. . . .
>
> I have used the judgment of all the advisers I can get in the whole administration to put down a balanced budget. That, to my mind, is one of the things that will keep our dollar stable, it will be one of the great influences in keeping the living costs from going up; and *above all*, it will be one of the things to inspire more confidence throughout the world in the American currency and American economy.[12]

A month later he gave a clear picture of what had frightened him.

The Secretary of the Treasury told me, when he came back from New Delhi [meeting of International Monetary Fund] a couple of months back, that he was questioned by twenty-one different governments as to our ability to pay our bills and therefore to keep the dollar as sound as it needs to be if we, America, are to be secure in our alliances, and do our part in making certain that communism will make no inroads into the free world.[13]

How much weight the international position of the dollar carried in the President's thinking about the budget was shown in his memoirs where, recalling this period, he said:

A number of respected business analysts, one of whom was Gabriel Hauge, cautioned me against the damaging effects that might result from trying to return too quickly to a balanced budget in fiscal year 1960 after the $12 billion deficit of the previous year. I was impressed by Dr. Hauge's arguments but an overriding consideration, in my mind, was the worsening situation in our balance of payments. I felt that a rapid return to a balanced budget would help reassure other nations as to America's ability to pay her debts and lessen their desire to convert their dollars into gold.[14]

The President never explained the connection between balancing the federal budget and "America's ability to pay her debts" to the rest of the world, but his references to the matter always implied that the connection was direct and close. In fact, the connection is at most indirect and loose. Balancing the budget might be some sign of the government's ability to raise enough dollars to meet its domestic obligations. But this was never in question and threw no light on America's ability to pay foreign debts which in the end had to be paid not with dollars but with gold or with goods. Of course, insofar as a balanced budget or surplus helped to restrain inflation in the United States it increased the competitiveness of American exports and so improved the balance of payments. But Eisenhower seemed to have something more—and more direct—in mind. Basically what was involved was that our creditors—mainly foreign bankers—thought that a balanced budget was a good thing; and as long as they thought that, it really was a good thing. Later the view developed that the best policy for the balance of payments was a budget deficit rather than a budget surplus. The government's borrowing to finance the deficit would make interest rates high and discourage the outflow of capital, and the inflation could be restrained by stringent monetary policy. However, this view did not become important until the Kennedy administration when it was used as an argument for a tax cut, which the administration wanted. Eisenhower's view of the connection between the budget and the balance of payments supported his view of the need for a budget surplus.

The War on Inflation Again

Considerations of growth and the balance of payments were influential in the administration's drive for a surplus. But the main, continuing argument was the argument about inflation. The President and his chief economic advisers came out of the 1958 recession more convinced than ever that inflation was *the* great problem, and that a budget surplus was the necessary condition for solving the problem, if not the solution itself.

The President's January, 1959, state of the Union message laid great stress on the battle against inflation. Eisenhower announced that he intended to balance the budget for fiscal year 1960, mainly as an anti-inflation step. He also informed the Congress that he was establishing a Cabinet Committee on Price Stability for Economic Growth, [Vice-President Nixon was later named chairman] to develop and coordinate the government's anti-inflation policies. Furthermore he would ask Congress to amend the Employment Act of 1946 to list price stability as one of the goals of national economic policy, along with "maximum employment, production, and purchasing power" already contained in the act.[15]

Preventing inflation became identified with, and the road to, all other good things. Thus, at his news conference of January 21, 1959:

> QUESTION: Mr. President, some people have said that you seem to worry a little too much about inflation, sir, and perhaps not enough about the slow rate of growth of our economy. I would like to know how you feel about that.
>
> PRESIDENT: Well I can only say this: I've got a big Cabinet Committee that has been appointed to study the subject, price stability for economic growth; and that takes the whole field, as far as I can see. The expanding economy is a thing that I believe I have talked more about than almost any individual that I know of, publicly. And the kind of concern that you speak of is really not two different problems—inflation or economic growth. I believe that economic growth in the long run cannot be soundly brought about except with stability in your price structure.[16]

The President's main concerns in fiscal policy were summed up in a speech on June 8, 1959, to a testimonial dinner of Republicans:

> At the moment we are engaged in a highly important battle for a sound dollar. This is not a fight to balance the budget as an end in itself. This is not a fight just to pinch pennies. This is a fight to keep our nation fiscally strong so that we may maintain the forces we must have for the security of ourselves and the free world. This is a fight to promote an expanding economy and domestic prosperity. This is a fight to make sure that a dollar earned today will tomorrow buy for the housewife an equal amount of groceries.[17]

THE SURPLUS AS MODERN FISCAL POLICY

The administration believed that its drive for a surplus in 1959 and 1960 was consistent with, indeed required by, a long run moderate contracyclical fiscal policy of the kind advocated by the CED, the Douglas subcommittee, and others ten years earlier. This policy called for a balanced budget or a moderate surplus at high employment, with deficits in recessions resulting from the automatic decline of revenues and the increase of unemployment compensation. We had had the deficit this policy called for in the 1958 recession—$12 billion worth—and it was now time, according to the administration, to follow the other part of the policy and have the surplus.

The President's Cabinet Committee on Price Stability for Economic Growth issued a statement on budget policy in October, 1959, which sounded much like the CED position of 1947. The statement rejected annual budget-balancing as impossible to carry out and unstabilizing if carried out. It rejected a managed compensatory policy on the ground that changes in tax rates and expenditures take so long to come into effect that they would be unstabilizing, rather than stabilizing. A third approach, which the committee favored, was:

> to rely upon the automatic tendency for tax revenues to rise and certain types of expenditure (such as unemployment benefits) to fall during periods of strong demand, and for the opposite to occur in recessions. According to this approach, spending programs and tax rates should be such as to produce a sizable surplus under conditions of strong business activity and relatively full use of economic resources, thereby checking unsustainable booms. Then in recessions the same spending programs and tax rates would automatically generate deficits, thereby stimulating recovery. This approach is consistent with the goal of a balanced budget, but the periods within which balance would be attained would correspond with cycles in American economic activity rather than with cycles in the calendar.[18]

Treasury Secretary Anderson was, of course, a member of the Cabinet Committee which issued this statement. Moreover, when he appeared before the Joint Economic Committee in February, 1960, to describe the administration's fiscal policy, he responded with an exposition of what he called the "stabilizing budget proposal" which was an almost exact statement of what CED had called the Stabilizing Budget Policy in 1947.[19] The ideas of President Eisenhower on this subject were never stated precisely, but he also had in mind a model in which there were deficits in recessions and surpluses in prosperity, in which the recession deficit made the prosperity surplus all the more necessary, and in which budget balance would be achieved over a cycle lasting longer than one year. We have already noted his remark on the irrelevance of the solar year for fiscal policy.

The administration, in pushing for a surplus in 1959 and 1960, did not regard itself as following an old-fashioned policy in defiance of modern economic knowledge. Rather it regarded itself as fighting for modern, flexible policy against the biases of the political process. The problem with contracyclical policy is that the political flesh is weak, and while it readily accepts the deficits of recessions, it does not have the stamina to generate the surpluses in prosperity. As the report of the Cabinet Committee said, referring to the moderate stabilizing policy it recommended:

> The chief practical difficulty with the third approach is the tendency, especially in times of recession, to enact new spending programs that do not automatically contract at high levels of economic activity. Policies appropriate to the third approach tend to be followed during recessions when this approach calls for deficit spending; but later, when expansion is resumed and budget surpluses are called for, the approach is abandoned and arguments of a different kind are improvised to justify continued heavy spending. Thus there is a tendency in practice for budget deficits to cumulate rather than to be balanced by later budget surpluses. The third approach offers greater practical possibilities of success than either of the two extreme approaches, but it does require a high level of economic understanding on the part of the public and resolution on the part of their elected representatives and officials.[20]

The administration was trying to provide the necessary resolution.

How Much?

However, the issue of fiscal policy in 1959 and 1960 was not only a matter of having the resolution to resist political temptations. The issue was also what was the right policy. And by 1959 and 1960 this question had gotten beyond the principle that there should be a balanced budget or a surplus in prosperity and a deficit during a recession. During the 1958 recession there had been general agreement that there should be a deficit, but the question was how much deficit at what degree of recession. So in 1959 and 1960 the question was how much surplus at what level of prosperity.

The administration never answered this quantitative question, except of course by its actions. The Cabinet Committee report talked of producing "a sizable surplus under conditions of strong business activity and relatively full use of economic resources," but it did not define "sizable" or "relatively full" or indicate which of several possible concepts of the budget it had in mind.

The administration did not distinguish much between recovery and prosperity, or between one degree of prosperity and another. From the beginning of 1959 the President talked as if we were in that condition of prosperity which, according to stabilizing policy, calls for a budget surplus. The budget surplus in hand or in prospect during 1959 and 1960 seemed moderate for a period of prosperity. These surpluses were less than had been achieved in, for example, 1955 to 1957. The fact that the 1959 and 1960 prosperity was a significantly lower level of prosperity, relative to the economy's potential, was not recognized as significant.

In January, 1959, Eisenhower sounded a note he was to repeat many times: "If we cannot live within our means during such a time of rising prosperity, the hope for fiscal integrity will fade."[21] At that time the unemployment rate was almost 6 percent.

A month later, as quoted above, in further emphasis of this point he reminded reporters that personal income in January, 1959, had been at an all-time high.[22] But with a growing labor force and productivity, and with prices rising, an all-time high of personal income was not itself a sign of prosperity. The President acknowledged that the unemployment rate was unsatisfactory, but this did not cloud his view of the situation as one of "rising prosperity" in which we should balance the budget.

By January, 1960, the economy had advanced further and unemployment had fallen almost to 5 percent. Moreover, the administration, like almost everyone else, was expecting continued economic expansion during the year. The budget program submitted in January would have yielded a surplus of $3 billion in the national income accounts with a Gross National Product of $510 billion in the calendar year 1960, and this looked fairly close to the Gross National Product that could be expected at high employment. However, estimates made shortly thereafter suggested that the GNP at high employment would have been about $20 to $30 billion above the $510 billion estimate on which the budget was based.[23] The surplus at high employment would have been much above $3 billion on the basis of those estimates.

Whether the administration's policy would have been different if it had a different and higher estimate of the surplus its programs would generate at high employment is uncertain. The administration expressed no clear idea of how big the surplus *should* be, except that it should be bigger. In the remarks interpolated in his January, 1960, state of the Union message, the President said, "Personally, I do not feel that any amount can be properly called a 'surplus' as long as the nation is in debt."[24]

The press tried unsuccessfully to find out how the President had arrived at the particular surplus figure to which his budget recommendations would lead:

> QUESTION: Can you tell us how you reached the $4.2 billion surplus for fiscal 1961?
>
> PRESIDENT: Easily; $84 billion of revenue, and $79.8 of expenditure.
>
> Now, we did it on this basis, Mr. Brandt: we took a $510 billion GNP. Already, we are accused that it is too conservative. I saw one in a financial page the other day, a guess of 524; I saw where several bankers said 514.
>
> We made ours 510; and on the basis of such a GNP and our tax rates, why, it was very simple to get a pretty accurate estimate of our expected revenues. Of course, we are hopeful that the Congress will see the wisdom of the recommendations we have made in the expenditure side, and by that means we hope to have that much to put on the debt.
>
> QUESTION: I can see how you get your 84, but how do you get the 79.8?
>
> PRESIDENT: I put that—yes, I said that in the State of the Union Message. It is the total amount of the budget.
>
> QUESTION: Is that variable?
>
> PRESIDENT: Well, look: now, let's don't pretend that anyone has got a sacrosanct judgment on something that reaches 18 months ahead. Of course, there are going to be some needs that are increased, and some that are probably decreased—hopefully. But that is our best guess at this time.
>
> A budget, after all, is not a paper that you go to jail on if you happen to be a little bit wrong. A budget is an estimate, a plan for expenditures and revenues, and you get your balances on that basis.
>
> But I do point out that it is absolutely necessary that we have savings to put on this debt that we are passing on to someone else; and possibly we seem to think it will be all right for us and them to increase it. I think the kind of alleged economist that says that the United States can afford to keep piling this debt on and on and on is not one to be very highly respected as an economist.[25]

Although the administration was unaware of how big a potential surplus at high employment was being generated, it did know, as Eisenhower's later reference to Hauge's warning indicates, that the budget was going through an exceptionally rapid shift from the large actual deficit of 1958 to the moderate actual surplus of 1960. It was unmoved by this knowledge. As long as the economy was rising, even though it was below high employment, as long as the fears of foreign bankers needed to be calmed, as long as promotion of economic growth by generating a budget surplus was urgent, and especially as long as inflation remained a present danger, the administration was unlikely to think that any surplus that would be politically attainable would be economically excessive.

The high-employment surplus for calender 1960 implicit in the administration's budget was much larger than the surplus contemplated by the CED and others when they formulated the consensus fiscal policy in 1947 to 1949. This does not necessarily imply a departure from the consensus policy. As the CED said in 1947, the initial proposals for the standard high-employment surplus were based on little information about the character and problems of the postwar economy. If the assumptions and estimates on which the initial proposals were based proved seriously unrealistic, the standard high-employment surplus figure would have to be changed. What was implicit in the administration's position was that the high-employment surplus needed to prevent inflation, to inspire confidence in the dollar, and to provide savings for adequate growth was larger than had previously been thought.

AGREEMENT ON THE SURPLUS

In the months when Eisenhower was making the decisions that led to the large surplus—in 1959 and early 1960—and even as 1960 unfolded, there was little complaint. The rigor with which the administration was holding down particular expenditure programs aroused opposition from the supporters of those programs. But there was little opposition to the policy of larger surpluses.

Of course, there were some dissenters. Testifying before the Joint Economic Committee in February, 1960, Walter Reuther, head of the United Automobile Workers, maintained that the administration was trying to balance the budget at too low a level of economic activity. One witness was strongly for tax reduction. He was Ralph Robey, speaking for the National Association of Manufacturers:

> Now, when a substantial surplus in Federal fiscal operations is finally in sight, the Economic Report intentionally ignores and omits any discussion of tax reduction. Apparently this omission was intentional for the recent budget message emphatically stated that tax reduction is not planned for this year. It is inconceivable to me how the Federal Government can fail to seize upon the very earliest opportunity of relieving its people of a very serious deterrent to economic health and growth. . . .
>
> The President recommends that the expected $4.2 billion surplus be applied to a reduction in the national debt. With the debt presently standing at $290 billion, and involving an annual interest service charge of $9.6 billion, debt reduction is a sound long-range objective. I do not believe, however, that the immediate need for tax rate reform should be sacrificed in favor of maintaining a substantial surplus in the budget for fiscal 1961. In the long run, we shall be able to reduce

the national debt substantially only if we have a flourishing and growing economy.[26]

However, these were exceptions. The support for the surplus policy from economists who subscribed to what was later called "the new economics" are especially significant. Thus, at these hearings Professor R. Aaron Gordon told the committee:

> I also favor a planning of receipts and expenditures such that, at the levels of economic activity the Administration anticipates, a budgetary surplus will ensue. Hence, I support the President's request that the corporate income tax be continued at its present rate, that the scheduled reduction in certain excises be postponed, and that postal rates be increased. Clearly this is not the time for any sort of general reduction in taxes, particularly since expenditures may well turn out to be larger than proposed in the budget message.[27]

On the same occasion Professor Richard A. Musgrave said:

> The coming budget thus represents the combined benefits of cyclical upswing and secular growth. This is a happy development in which we all may rejoice, and chances are that the resulting surplus may play a useful role in the coming year.[28]

Professor Paul Samuelson, soon to be one of President Kennedy's chief advisers, was circumspect but expressed no alarm about the Eisenhower budget policy. He disputed the view that the surplus would be deflationary—a view which he attributed to Wall Street traders—and warned that the fact of a surplus should not be an invitation to tax reduction or to borderline government expenditures. However, he also said:

> If unemployment were the only consideration, the desirability of preserving a sizable budget surplus in fiscal 1961 would be very much less than I indicated in my remarks.
>
> It is to the degree that you deliberately hope to rely on a sizable level of excess unemployment in the economy to counteract inflationary pressures and our "unfavorable balance" of international payments that you will be eager to push toward surpluses as high as or higher than those recommended by the President for a 1960 gross national product of $510 billion.[29]

After hearing these witnesses, the Joint Economic Committee—both the Democratic majority and the Republican minority—supported the administration's proposal for a large budget surplus in fiscal 1961.

THE FISCAL-MONETARY MIX

In part, agreement with the policy of a large surplus reflected a sharing of the administration's concern with inflation and the balance of payments.

But for many of the economists and for the majority of the Joint Economic Committee it reflected much more a sharing of the interest in rapid growth, combined with an important turn in the economic theory of fiscal policy which had been occurring in the 1950's.

Early American Keynesian theory of fiscal policy, as taught in the 1940's, led to the conclusion that at any time there was one unique size of deficit or surplus that was consistent with full employment. The argument ran as follows: If there is to be full employment, the amount that is saved when there is full employment must either be invested privately or borrowed and spent by the government. If the amount of private investment plus the government deficit spending is less than the saving that would be made at full employment, it will be impossible to have full employment because total spending will be insufficient to buy the full-employment output. The amount of saving that would be done at full employment is determined by a psychological law, by the distribution of income, and possibly by other factors which, while they may change from time to time, are not readily changed by public policy. Similarly, the amount of private investment that would be made at full employment is determined by technological conditions and other given factors. Thus, there is at any time a full-employment amount of saving and a full-employment amount of investment which the government must accept as given. If there is to be full employment, the government deficit must equal the excess of the full-employment saving over the full-employment investment. If the full-employment investment exceeds the full-employment saving, a government surplus equal to the difference is needed to prevent inflation. There is at any time one, and only one, size of surplus or deficit appropriate to achieving full employment and preventing inflation.

The theory as stated by Keynes was less rigid that this. Specifically, he left room for the possibility that the amount of full-employment investment could be influenced by monetary policy. At least in some circumstances, a larger stock of money would cause lower interest rates and this would cause higher private investment that if the money stock had been smaller; if so, the larger stock of money would require a smaller budget deficit to close the gap. However, Keynes visualized conditions in which this would not work because interest rates were at a floor below which they would not fall. His American disciples took this as the general condition and added another—that even if interest rates could be reduced by monetary policy, investment would not respond, being determined mainly by technical conditions of production. Thus, throughout the war and for a few years thereafter standard American Keynesian economics operated with the assumption that there was one given size of surplus or deficit appropriate to full employment and that its size could not be influenced by monetary policy. The function of monetary policy was to keep interest rates at the floor in order to hold down the interest burden of the public debt.[30]

This position became increasingly difficult to maintain after the war, as we have seen in chapter 10. The connection between monetary behavior and inflation in the United States and abroad in the post-war years was evidence of the importance of money. There was a flow of analysis and evidence from economists who had never accepted the Keynesian argument wholeheartedly, notably Professor Milton Friedman.[31] The Keynesians themselves reconsidered the logic of their position in a world far removed from the special conditions of the Depression. Interest rates obviously were not lying at the floor and there were variations in investment which seemed to be related to variations in monetary conditions.

An early and important recognition of the change by a leading American Keynesian came in 1951. In that year Professor Samuelson said:

> But in any case we are all agreed that over the long run, monetary policy has considerable leverage in helping to determine the mix of high-employment national product between consumption and investment goods of different categories, and that *fiscal policy need not take as ultimate data quantitatively predetermined deflationary or inflationary gaps.*[32]

The implication of this for Keynesian fiscal policy was profound. It meant that there was not a single deficit or surplus consistent with high employment. Monetary policy could influence the rate of private investment significantly and thereby influence the amount of deficit or surplus needed to achieve full employment. Full employment could be achieved with any one of a number of combinations or mixes of fiscal and monetary policy— with various combinations of monetary expansion and fiscal expansion.

If this is true it raises the question of the basis for choosing among the different mixes of policy that are consistent with full employment. One possibility might be to try to keep taxes down in order to avoid their distorting and incentive-weakening effects, and therefore to choose a mix with a large deficit and tight money. Another possibility would be to adapt the mix to the requirements of the balance of payments, choosing the mix which yields higher interest rates when it is desired to discourage capital outflow and the mix which yields lower interest rates when it is desired to encourage capital outflow.

In the second half of the 1950's, with the rising concern about economic growth, attention focussed on selecting the mix that would promote it:

Samuelson told the Joint Economic Committee in 1955, "With proper fiscal and monetary policies, our economy can have full employment and whatever rate of capital formation and growth it wants."[33]

If the community wanted a higher rate of growth it could choose a mix of easy money and large budget surpluses, the easy money to stimulate investment and the budget surpluses to provide the savings that would finance the investment and prevent inflation. In the late 1950's it was assumed that the community did want a higher rate of growth, so the analysis led directly to that prescription. This mix had two other qualities which appealed to many people. First, it offered a justification for a policy of easy money and low interest rates, a policy which has always had a good deal of support—including that of Congressman Patman, a leading member of the Joint Economic Committee during this period. It also provided a counter to the more conservative argument that the way to get growth was to reduce the taxes on corporations and on upper-bracket individuals in order to increase savings and incentives to investment. Samuelson used the mix analysis for this purpose in his 1955 testimony, assuring the committee that the proper mix would permit the country to have not only full employment and rapid growth but also whatever degree of income redistribution through the tax system it wished.[34]

In the last years of the Eisenhower administration the Joint Economic Committee became the leading advocate of a big surplus-easy money combination of policies. This was one of the main outcomes of its large study of "Employment, Growth and Price Levels" conducted during 1959.[35] In its 1960 report the committee said: "In the interests of a higher rate of economic growth, we must place greater reliance on fiscal policy. This includes larger budget surpluses in prosperous periods than we have had."[36]

Thus the Democratic majority of the Joint Economic Committee came to a position like Eisenhower's on the budget surplus, and for one of the reasons which influenced him—the desire to stimulate growth. However, they also wanted to increase the rate of expansion of demand in order to get to high employment faster.

So while they did not regard the administration's proposed surplus as large, or even adequate from the standpoint of desirable growth, they would recommend a larger surplus only if accompanied by a more expansive monetary policy.

> The proposed surplus, when translated into terms of Federal Government payments to and receipts from the public, amounts to a little more than $2 billion in calendar 1960, or about one-half of 1 percent of expected gross national product. For fiscal 1961, the estimated cash surplus is $5.9 billion, slightly more than 1

percent of the likely gross national product for the fiscal year. These are low ratios of surplus to the gross national product by postwar standards.

Since the levels of income upon which these budget estimates are based are less than full employment levels, it is perhaps just as well, assuming the President's program were to be accepted, that no larger surplus be achieved, unless there were assurance that materially easier monetary and credit conditions would be provided by action of the Federal Reserve System.[37]

THE FULL-EMPLOYMENT SURPLUS AS ECONOMIC DRAG

The general agreement on the policy of a large surplus which existed at the beginning of 1960 began to erode shortly thereafter. There were two reasons for this:

1. The sluggishness of the economy, which suggested that the recovery might end before high employment had been regained.

2. New and more realistic estimates of what the surplus would be at high employment in 1960, which showed that the high-employment surplus had increased not only in comparison with 1958 and 1959 but also in comparison with 1955–57. Whereas only a year earlier the common estimate had been that the budget was becoming less restrictive, the situation was seen to have changed significantly in 1960.

The combination of these two facts led to the view that the economy needed more stimulation and that there was room, within a reasonable definition of "budget-balancing," for tax reductions or expenditure increases to provide it.

One of the earliest estimates of the high-employment surplus in 1960, probably the earliest public estimate, was made by David Lusher of the staff of the Council of Economic Advisers. In a speech in May he presented an estimate of $6.5 billion as the high-employment surplus in 1960.[38] The speech did not draw policy conclusions for 1960 from this estimate. However, within the council Lusher was pointing out that the enlarged surplus was contributing to the sluggishness of the economy, and he urged that the surplus should be reduced.

Similar estimates of the high-employment surplus were made in the summer of 1960 by the staff of the Committee for Economic Development, which was used to looking at fiscal policy as measured by the high-employment surplus. Professor Charles L. Schultze, working on the CED staff that summer on leave from Indiana University, wrote a memorandum to a CED committee saying:

The fact that existing budget policies imply a $6–$7 billion surplus at full utilization of resources should be a major consideration in framing both monetary and fiscal policies. We wish a combination of fiscal and monetary policies, which, (among other goals) would balance aggregate demand and aggregate supply at full employment levels of income. To use extreme examples, a budget which *would* yield a $20 billion surplus at full employment will insure that we will never reach that income level; similarly a budget which would yield a $20 billion deficit at full employment income level will certainly insure that we overshoot the mark in an inflationary direction.[39]

In a paper written at about the same time for President Eisenhower's Commission on National Goals, two members of the CED staff, Herbert Stein and Edward F. Denison, pointed out that, in contrast to the view which had been common a year earlier, the path to growth lay through reduction of the surplus:

> As of this writing, in the autumn of 1960, the relevant conditions are these: We have not been at high employment for three years and show no signs of an imminent approach to high employment. Investment is running below the rate of saving that would come forth at high employment. With present tax and expenditure programs, high employment would give the federal budget a cash surplus in excess of $6 billion.
>
> In these conditions it would be desirable, if a decision is made to promote growth by the savings-investment route, to start with the stimulation of investment. This would call for: (1) accelerating the rate of growth of the money supply; (2) reducing the taxes that bear most heavily on property incomes in order to increase private investment; (3) increasing public investments that will meet the test of productivity.[40]

In December, 1960, Schultze, now back at Indiana University, gave new estimates and the most vigorous public statement of the new look at fiscal policy in testimony before the Joint Economic Committee:

> In other words, existing tax rates are such, that in combination with expenditures, they would yield an $11 to $12 billion surplus if the economy were operating at full employment.
>
> Because of this relationship between tax rates and expenditures, during a period in which private demands have not been particularly vigorous, the economy has not been able to reach full employment. . . . Because we have not attained full employment levels of income, the actual level of tax receipts and the actual budget surplus has not reached this $11 billion level.
>
> The moral of this is that if the Government aims at an overly large full employment surplus, it will achieve neither full employment nor the surplus it aims at.

Schultze took note of the previous discussion of the fiscal-monetary mix which had suggested that the way to get growth and high employment was to increase the budget surplus and the rate of growth of the money supply:

> It is, of course, true that the size of the surplus consistent with full employment will depend on the nature of monetary policy. In fact, one of the chief conclusions of this committee's recent study of employment, growth, and the price level was that economic growth could be fostered by changing the "mix" of stabilization policy toward greater reliance on budget surpluses and less on monetary restraints. With this general objective I have no quarrel. But I would insist that under current conditions, the $11 to $12 billion budget surplus implicit in existing tax rates and expenditure programs is too large to be consistent with full employment, even if monetary policy had been substantially easier than has actually been the case.[41]

A somewhat different view of the relationship between the large budget surplus and monetary policy was presented to the Joint Economic Committee by CED's Research Director, Herbert Stein, in February, 1961. This was that while sufficient monetary expansion might have offset the depressing effect of the large surplus, such monetary expansion would have aggravated the balance-of-payments problem:

> The attempt to achieve high employment in the face of a budget that would yield very large surpluses at high employment requires rapid monetary expansion to offset the depressing effect of the budget. This means low interest rates, and, unless other countries are following a similar policy, this is likely to cause an outflow of capital and balance-of-payments difficulties.
>
> In fact, during 1960 we did get an easing of monetary policy. This was not sufficient to maintain high employment, but it did contribute to the decline of U.S. interest rates, to the outflow of short-term capital and to the balance-of-payments deficit.[42]

No Concessions for Mr. Nixon

These arguments based on the size of the full-employment surplus came late and had no strong influence behind them. They could not have been expected to influence President Eisenhower's policy during his last year in office. However, there had been an earlier suggestion from a more important source, Vice-President Nixon.

In February of 1960 Arthur Burns came to the opinion, correct as it turned out, that the economy was heading for another decline. He urged upon Mr. Nixon the need for expansive fiscal action including some relaxation on the expenditure side and tax reduction.

Nixon tried, through the Cabinet Committee on Price Stability for °

Economic Growth, of which he was chairman, and in other ways to get the administration to take fiscal action to stimulate the economy. However, neither the weakness of the economy nor the imminence of the Presidential election would now divert the administration from its drive for a large surplus as the necessary condition for defeating inflation, strengthening confidence in the dollar, and promoting economic growth.[43]

In August, after a recess for the Presidential nominating conventions, Congress reconvened for a short session. In an opening message the President warned the members of Congress of the dangerous consequences of increasing expenditures above his budget recommendations and stressed "the need of avoiding further deficit spending and of making, in years of prosperity, savings to be applied either to debt reduction or to tax reform. . . . I shall not be a party to reckless spending schemes which would increase the burden of debt of our grandchildren, by resuming, in prosperous times, the practice of deficit financing. I shall not fail to resist inflationary pressures by whatever means are available to me."[44]

By this time unemployment was rising again, and after having receded to 5.1 percent in the first quarter of 1960, climbed to 5.6 percent. In January, 1961, when the unemployment rate was 6.7 percent, Eisenhower delivered his last budget message:

> A surplus in good times, as provided in this budget, helps make up the deficits which inevitably occur during periods of recession. To ignore these principles is to undermine our strength as a nation through deficits, unmanageable debt, and the resulting inflation and cheapening of our currency.[45]

Was it a Mistake?

Later the fiscal policy of the last three Eisenhower years came to be regarded as a great mistake, the main fiscal policy mistake of the twenty years between the end of World War II and the acceleration of the Vietnam War in 1965. Some regarded the mistake as the failure to cut taxes in the spring of 1958 during the recession.[46] Others regarded the mistake as the failure to cut taxes or increase expenditures in 1960 to reduce the large full-employment surplus.

The reason for considering this policy a mistake was, of course, the failure of the economy to recover completely from the 1958 recession. Although Eisenhower had thought "the storm was over" in the spring of 1958, it was to be seven years—not until 1965—before unemployment was again as low as it had been in 1957, before the 1957–58 recession began. If taxes had been cut in 1958 the recovery might have brought the economy back to high employment instead of losing force and subsiding early in 1960 before high employment was reached. Failing that, a tax cut early in 1960 might have prevented the recession that started in that year or cut it short so that the first half of the 1960's would have been years of high prosperity instead of years with unemployment rates ranging from 5 percent to 7 percent. Moreover, it is argued, the administration's zealous crusade against inflation was unnecessary. The index of wholesale prices was level from 1958 to 1964 and the index of consumers' prices rose by only a little over 1 percent a year during the same period.

When he came to write his memoirs of this period, in 1965, Eisenhower recognized the criticism that had been made of his tight fiscal policy. Characteristically, he thought that the complaints against him included the deficit that was finally realized in 1961:

> Later some economists challenged these policies. In swinging too rapidly from deficit to surplus, they argued, the administration has demonstrated a wholly needless concern about inflation; by refusing to reduce taxes, we had failed, they averred, to assure the continuance of the economy's upswing out of the trough of the 1958 recession and, instead, had induced a slowing down in the economy which had contributed to the $4 billion deficit in 1961.

His reply to this criticism was expressed in terms of the need to stop inflation:

> Critics overlooked the inflationary psychology which prevailed during the mid-fifties and which I thought it necessary to defeat. In 1957, for example, consumer prices were rising at an unacceptably high annual rate of 3.2 percent. Ten years of this could devalue the current dollar more than 30 percent while if the rate accelerated, we would have had an entirely intolerable situation on our hands. . . .
>
> The administration believed that if wages and prices could *increase* during a recession, we could get into real inflationary trouble in time of prosperity. Monetary and fiscal policy had to be so fashioned as to forestall such a result and to reestablish confidence in the dollar. . . .
>
> As we looked backward from the spring of 1960, we enjoyed a moment of satisfaction. . . . Now evidence was appearing that that inflationary thrust, powerful as it was, had been blunted.
>
> The anti-inflation battle is never-ending, though I fear that in 1959 the public was apathetic, at least uninformed, regarding this issue. This attitude caused me to recall a laconic comment of Winston Churchill when someone asked him during World War II what the allies were fighting for: "If we stop," he replied, "you will find out."[47]

Whether the fiscal policy of 1958–60 was a mistake is still impossible to say. The answer depends upon the answer to a number of difficult questions.

1. Would a more expansive fiscal policy have strengthened the recovery after 1958 and prevented the recession which began in 1960, or were these developments so rigidly determined by the slow growth of the money supply during this period that they could not have been changed by fiscal policy?[48]

2. Even if the economy could have been invigorated by a different fiscal policy with a smaller shift in the direction of a budget surplus, would that have been the best way to achieve the result? As we have seen, many economists thought that a policy of a large budget surplus combined with rapid monetary expansion was the right mix for the country in 1959 and 1960. This was the position taken by the Democratic Party and John F. Kennedy during the 1960 election campaign.

3. If the fiscal policy was responsible for the sluggishness of the economy, was that a bad thing? Professor Samuelson later called the policy of this period an "investment in sadism."[49] That is, it was a policy of inflicting certain short-run costs in an effort to achieve some long-range benefits. The costs were slow recovery and high unemployment. The benefit sought was to wring the inflationary psychology and expectations out of the system in the hope of making it possible thereafter to have full employment without inflation. Whether this was a good investment depends partly on a matter of fact—how much was paid in unemployment for how much restraint of inflation, and for how long? And it is partly a matter of values—how much restraint of inflation is worth how much unemployment?

We shall not try to answer these questions here. However, one thing is clear. If there was a mistake in fiscal policy it did not result from failure of the administration to accept the responsibility for the general state of the economy or to accept the modern view of the way in which the government's fiscal policy affects the economy. Neither did it result in any large degree from devotion to the balanced-budget ideology. President Eisenhower liked the budget-balancing language more, and used it more, than his successors. But a preference for a balanced budget for its own sake would not have dominated his decisions if other considerations had not also pointed to the desirability of a large surplus. If fiscal policy was inadequate from the standpoint of full employment it was because more aggressive devotion of fiscal policy to the objective of full employment was considered to entail too high a price in other objectives—eventually getting tax revision of the right kind, checking the lone-range growth of federal spending, promoting economic growth, supporting international confidence in the dollar, and fighting inflation.

Eisenhower's Gift to Kennedy

Whether or not the 1958–60 fiscal policy was a mistake economically, it was certainly a great irony politically. For one of the chief victims of President's Eisenhower's determination to have a large budget surplus was probably Mr. Nixon and the Republican Party. Reflecting later on the 1960 Presidential campaign, Nixon said that two developments occurred before the conventions "which were to have far more effect on the election than all our carefully considered strategy decisions put together." One was the shooting down of the U-2 reconnaissance plane over the Soviet Union. The other was the failure of the administration to respond to Nixon's request, prompted by Burns' advice and forecast, for an expansive economic policy. Nixon wrote ruefully:

> Unfortunately, Arthur Burns turned out to be a good prophet. The bottom of the 1960 dip did come in October and the economy started to move up again in November—after it was too late to affect the election returns. In October, usually a month of rising employment, the jobless rolls increased by 452,000. All the speeches, television broadcasts, and precinct work in the world could not counteract that one hard fact.[50]

Perhaps unemployment would have been rising before the election even if Nixon's advice had been followed. But Nixon, who had wanted to cut taxes in 1958 and wanted to fight the recession in 1960, would at least have been able to conduct his campaign in the role of an activist for high employment, rather than as a spokesman for complacence and conservatism. Since the 1960 election was very close, even that might have made a difference.

The Eisenhower fiscal policy not only made a contribution, possibly decisive, to the election of a Democratic successor, it also made a contribution to the economic program that Democratic administration would follow when in office.

The Eisenhower administration finally succeeded in making room for tax reduction in the form of a budget that would yield a large surplus at high employment. They did not use the opportunity, partly because they did not recognize the size of the surplus, but mainly because they wanted to keep a large surplus. The Kennedy administration was slow to use the opportunity at first, but finally they saw and used the chance to make a big tax cut while keeping the budget balanced in the significant sense that it would be balanced at high employment. So it was not the Republicans, who prided themselves on being the party of low taxes, but the Democrats who installed a tax credit for business investment, gave business its long-desired acceleration of depreciation charges, reduced the corporate profits tax, and cut income taxes across the board.

The Eisenhower administration also bequeathed to its successor an economy in which unemployment was high and prices had been fairly stable for about three years. This gave the new administration substantial room for expansion before an acute conflict between high employment and price stability would be encountered.

Finally, the Eisenhower administration left behind it a fiscal record which included a deficit of $12.5 billion in one year, fiscal 1959. This was a standard upon which his successor could rely, since obviously a deficit less than Eisenhower ran could not be "unsound" or "fiscally irresponsible."

Thus, the austerity of the Eisenhower administration left the Kennedy administration able to practice the happy side of a modern fiscal policy—to cut taxes and increase expenditures, stimulating employment and economic growth, without transgressing conventional limits of fiscal soundness or re-awakening the dragon of inflation.

❧ 15 ❧

Tax Cut in Camelot: The Stage Is Set

O_N John F. Kennedy's Inauguration
Day in January, 1961, the stage was set for the act which, more than any
other, came to symbolize the fiscal revolution. The play had been written,
a receptive or at least permissive audience was in its seats, and the actors in
the wings. However, the action was not to begin immediately.

The stage setting was the longest, most serious period of unemployment
since the war. It was almost three and a half years since unemployment had
been near the conventional 4 percent measure of high employment. After
an abortive recovery from the 1958 recession, unemployment had risen again
and was nearing 7 percent on Inauguration Day. Moreover, the recent
experience led to the fear that the next recovery, when it came, would also
stop short of high employment. Two other items were prominent in the
scene. First, tax rates were so high relative to expenditures that they would
yield a large surplus at high employment. There was room to cut taxes or
raise expenditures and still retain the expectation that the budget would be
in balance when high employment was regained. Second, the balance-of-
payments deficit was believed to require high interest rates in the United
States to curb the flow of United States funds to the rest of the world. This
meant that the 1960 Democratic campaign formula of easy money with
budget surpluses could not be relied upon the achieve high employment
because that was a formula for low interest rates. The main, if not exclusive,
reliance for economic stimulation would have to be placed on fiscal policy.

There were several possible routes to the conclusion that tax reduction
was the appropriate act to be performed on this stage. On conventional
"functional finance" principles, the principles to be found in the textbooks
of 1961, when unemployment was high the budget deficit should be increased. On the more cautious principles of CED, the 1949 Douglas Sub-

committee, and others of the postwar consensus, a large full-employment surplus should be reduced to more moderate size in the absence of strong evidence of inflationary danger. And even if fiscal policy was not to be used to manage the level of economic activity, a balance-of-payments deficit might call for a reduction of taxes relative to expenditures in order to raise interest rates and curb the flow of dollars abroad. This idea was commonly advanced in European financial circles. Certainly the combination of excessive unemployment, a large high-employment surplus, and a balance-of-payments deficit wrote the script for expansive fiscal policy. And most of the informed audience would have agreed that if the play was to be a success the main act would have to be tax reduction. Moreover, there were, as always, many who wanted their taxes reduced.

How the country would receive this act—tax reduction—was more in question but should not have been. That part of the labor movement which expressed opinions on national economic policy, as distinguished from labor policy, had been for fiscal expansion for years. A considerable sector of the business and financial community had come to accept compensatory fiscal policy, if not in totally uninhibited form then in the form of balancing the budget at high employment or some version of cyclical balancing. Even among those who had not come that far, the desire for tax reduction was so great that they were prepared to swallow its unorthodox fiscal trimmings. Much of the Republican national leadership—outside the Congress—accepted the role of expansionist tax reduction, and while they would not cheer a Democratic administration for doing it, they would not make a great issue of it either. We have seen Mr. Nixon's opinions earlier.

Of course there would be opposition, especially in the Congress. Much of the opposition would be partisan and ritualistic and would require a partisan and ritualistic response. Given their standing in Congress, the opponents could delay the outcome. But they could not prevent it or punish those who produced it. In the postwar period there had been several cases in which Congress had tried, successfully and unsuccessfully, to cut taxes against the opposition of the President. There were no cases of Congressional resistance to tax reduction proposed by the administration.

The players who were to perform the tax reduction were President Kennedy and his advisers. We shall turn to them in a moment. But first it must be made clear that while the setting, the script, and the audience were prepared, the performance was not easy or inevitable. In 1492 it was known that the earth was round. Columbus had neither made it round nor discovered its shape. Others had made long ocean voyages before him, and some, it would appear, had been to America. But it was not inevitable that Columbus should go to American in 1492, and the fact that the times were ripe does not detract from the performance. Decisions still had to be made, and they required courage.

The Kennedy administration could not be sure that the conditions called for a tax cut according to their own guidebook. By early 1961 the appraisal of the economic situation as one of persistent sluggishness, and not merely transitory recession, was a common one. But this was an economic forecast like many others, and it could be wrong. If it were wrong a large cut might only open the way for the return of inflation. The idea that the balance-of-payments deficit called for reducing taxes rather than balancing the budget was also common. But there was an opposing view that the first essential was to reassure our foreign creditors by pursuing a "sound" fiscal policy.

Moreover, aside from its appraisal of the economic situation, the administration was not sure that tax-cutting was the role they had been chosen to play. Kennedy, in his inaugural address, had called upon the nation for sacrifice, and this seemed to him inconsistent with tax reduction. In other and perhaps less romantic terms, the administration had promised to improve the nation's educational system, to provide better medical care for the aged, to rebuild the cities, and to do many other things that would cost money. It had promised to accelerate growth, and the prevailing view was that more growth required budget surpluses. There was a long-standing Democratic interest in tax reform to close loopholes. All of these seemed incompatible with tax reduction. To start on the tax-reduction road might keep the administration from reaching more important goals.

Probably most important, the administration could not be sure of the political consequences of cutting taxes when the budget was in deficit. "Fiscal responsibility," symbolized by a balanced budget, had been a commonly used term in the 1960 election campaign as in previous campaigns for thirty years. The fact that "fiscal responsibility" was considered to be the property of the Republicans had not prevented the Democrats from winning six of the last eight Presidential elections and thirteen of the last fifteen Congressional elections. Perhaps the public's affection for budget-balancing did not run very deep. But it was something for a President, especially a Democrat, to think about.

By 1961, thirty years of experience, analysis, and discussion had made a tax reduction in the conditions then prevailing not only an available course but a probable course. But the action still had to be taken, and knowing that it could and should be done was different from doing it.

THE PRE-INAUGURATION KENNEDY

The most important thing about Kennedy's ideas on fiscal policy before he became President is that they were lightly held. Kennedy has been called the first modern economist in the American Presidency. This may have been true in 1963, but it was not true on Inauguration Day. At that time Kennedy's fiscal thinking was conventional. He believed in budget-balancing. While he was aware of circumstances in which the budget could not or should not be balanced, he preferred a balanced budget, being in this respect like most other people but unlike modern economists. But if he brought into the White House no very sophisticated or systematic ideas about compensatory fical policy, neither did he bring with him any deep intellectual or emotional commitment to the old ideas. This was partly a matter of his youth. He was not the first Keynesian President on Inauguration Day, but he was the first who was not a pre-Keynesian—the first who had passed the majority of his life in the post-Keynesian world where the old orthodoxy was giving way to the new. This characteristic he shared with his contemporaries. But he had in addition special characteristics which helped prepare him to accept the new economics he did not yet know. The son of an extremely wealthy, urban, Catholic family was unlikely to confuse personal budget-balancing with financial acumen or financial acumen with moral virtue. Moreover, there was in his home enough familiarity with the banking and financial community to reveal that its financial precepts were not necessarily Holy Writ.[1] His one course in economics at Harvard had been modern, i.e. post-Keynesian, and while it left no affirmative impression on him it did nothing to inhibit him from later looking at fiscal policy in a functional way.

Men of an earlier generation or different background, like Eisenhower, could be taught not to make a fetish of balancing the budget, and with strong advice and in clear situations they would make fiscal decisions that violated the traditional rules of sound finance. But they could never get over a feeling of discomfort about this, and when there was any reasonable economic case for doing so they would lean toward balancing the budget. Moreover, their spontaneous talk, free of speech-writers, would have a much more conventional cast than their actions. Whatever their course, they would prefer to sail under the traditional colors, not simply as a political stratagem, but because they found those colors more congenial.

Such a person in a position of responsibility would probably have recommended a tax reduction if confronted with the problems of 1961-63. But a person like Kennedy, with less firm attachment to the older ideas, would come to the tax cut more surely and quickly.

Kennedy was also free of older ideas of a different kind—in this case traditional, liberal, Democratic ideas. He was not shocked by the fact that some people were very wealthy, or even by the fact that some of them managed through various tax loopholes to escape paying very much tax. He was not likely to let a functional fiscal policy for economic expansion get permanently entangled with anti-rich and anti-corporation reformism, thereby alienating the people whose testimony to the soundness of his policy he needed. Unlike Roosevelt, he would not make his program of recovery carry too much burden of reform.[2]

Kennedy's record as a congressman showed no firm ideas about national fiscal policy and little interest in the subject. When Senator Douglas made his first effort in 1958 to enact an anti-recession tax cut, Senator Kennedy voted against it. A few months later, partly on the advice of Professor Seymour Harris of Harvard, he voted for Douglas' second tax cut proposal— which also failed.[3] Later in his term Kennedy obtained appointment to the Joint Economic Committee, the Congress' great seminar on fiscal policy, but he did not attend its meetings.

Kennedy campaigned in 1960 as a fiscal conservative. He did not match Roosevelt's 1932 Pittsburgh speech in which the Democratic candidate attempted to take the mantle of sound finance away from Herbert Hoover, but at least he was careful not to arouse conservative sensibilities. In a debate during the West Virginia primary campaign, on May 4, 1960, Senator Humphrey came out for raising income tax exemptions from $600 to $800 per person. Kennedy replied that he couldn't go around the country urging increased expenditure programs and also say that he was for reducing income taxes that year. "And I don't think, therefore, that at the present time until the economy is moved up, I think it's going to be impossible to reduce income taxes."[4] This exchange prompted Arthur Krock to say, in the *New York Times*, "To those who have carefully noted the public records of the Senators there could have been no surprise in yesterday's evidence that Kennedy is more of a fiscal conservative and is less special-group minded than Humphrey."[5]

The Democratic platform on which Kennedy ran was expansive in monetary policy and restrained in fiscal policy:

> We Democrats believe that our economy can and must grow at an average rate of 5 percent annually, almost twice as fast as our average rate since 1953. We pledge ourselves to policies that will achieve this goal without inflation.
>
> As the first step in speeding economic growth, a Democratic President will put an end to the present high-interest, tight-money policy.

Among the ways to assure that the goal would be achieved without inflation was "budget surpluses in times of high employment."[6]

The campaign discussions on both sides were marked by confusion between the problem of growth, meaning the problem of the rate at which the *potential* output of the economy rises, and the problem of full employment, meaning the problem of keeping actual output close to its potential. The Democrats seemed to be promising not only to get actual output up to its potential but also to make the potential rise more rapidly than its historical average. That is what the 5 percent goal meant.[7] But the statistics they used to demonstrate the poor performance of the Eisenhower administration indicated failure to keep output at its potential level, and the remedies they proposed also related mainly to this problem.

In any case, neither the platform nor Kennedy's campaign speeches suggested that Eisenhower's fiscal policy had been too restrictive, in the sense of having too large surpluses, or that the Democrats would behave differently in that respect. Their main fiscal promise was that they were going to spend more. But this spending had its intellectual rationale in Galbraith rather than in Keynes. That is, it was spending which would divert a larger part of the national output to public purposes from private purposes, not spending which would be undertaken to compensate for a deficiency in private demand and to bring about full employment. Its motivation was not that private spending was inadequate in amount, but that much of it was unworthy in quality.

Both the platform and Kennedy were firm in declaring an intention to finance the enlarged government expenditures within the limits of a balanced budget. After pointing to the needs for larger public programs, the platform said, "We believe moreover, that except in periods of recession or national emergency, these needs can be met with a balanced budget, with no increase in present tax rates, and with some surplus for the gradual reduction of our national debt."[8] However, the Democrats said that they were prepared to raise taxes if necessary.

Kennedy was even more cautious about the conditions in which a deficit might be justified. They were not merely a "national emergency" but a "grave national emergency" and not merely a "recession" but a "serious recession." However, he held out no promise of debt reduction—at least not in 1961, 1962, or 1963.[9]

The idea of reducing taxes in a recession came up in the October 7 television debate between the candidates. Mr. Nixon was asked his opinion about what to do in a recession. He mentioned credit expansion as the first move, and then said:

> In addition to that, if we do get into a recessionary period we should move on the part of the economy which is represented by the private sector—and I mean stimulate that part of the economy that can create jobs—the private sector of the economy. This means through tax reform and if necessary tax cuts that will stimulate more jobs.

Asked the same question, Kennedy took the opportunity to give his standard talk against hard money and then turned to fiscal policy:

> If we move into a recession in '61 then I would agree that we have to put more money into the economy, and it can be done by either of the two methods discussed. One is by a program such as aid to education, the other would be to make a judgment of what's the more effective tax program to stimulate our economy.[10]

Kennedy's most developed formulation of a fiscal policy was presented near the end of the campaign, on October 30, in a statement about the international position of the dollar. This statement was intended to assure foreign holders of dollars that the election of Kennedy would not lead to a depreciation of the currency, and also to assure the American business and financial community on the same point. He said:

> First, we are pledged to maintain a balanced budget except in times of national emergency or severe recession. Furthermore, we will seek to maintain a budget surplus in times of prosperity as a brake on inflationary forces. Through the vigorous use of fiscal policies to help control inflation we will be able to lessen reliance on restrictive monetary policies which hamper growth.
>
> Wherever we are certain that tax revision—including accelerated depreciation —will stimulate investment in new plant and equipment, without damage to our principles of equity, we will proceed with such revision.
>
> We will also carefully examine our entire tax structure in order to close loopholes which are unnecessarily depriving the Government of needed tax revenue, and in order to develop tax policies which will stimulate growth.[11]

In a few words, the Kennedy economics of 1960 was increased expenditures for defense and for public services, financed within a budget which would be balanced in prosperity out of the growing yield of the existing tax system plus higher taxes if necessary, and monetary expansion to keep the economy operating close to its rising potential.

Platforms and campaign speeches are notoriously poor indicators of what a candidate thinks or will do if elected. The 1960 program might have been just an election tactic—easy money for the populists, balanced budgets for the conservatives, and more public benefits for everyone. But there is no reason to doubt the sincerity of his belief in the budget-balancing part of the program. And indeed, it would have been most surprising if he had thought anything different in 1960, because the program happened to be not only the old conventional wisdom of Democratic politicians but also the new conventional wisdom of the Democratic intellectuals. For several years the Joint Economic Committee, on the advice of leading economists, had been promoting the idea of easier money to stimulate the economy, coupled with a budget surplus to prevent inflation and add to the savings available to finance investment and thereby accelerate growth.[12] And the idea that the country badly needed more government spending had been given a new rationale in Galbraith's *The Affluent Society*, one of the most influential economics books of the postwar period.[13]

Some of these ideas were already, during the campaign, in the process of changing. First, it was coming to be realized that the budget already had a very large implicit surplus—would yield a large surplus at high employment —so that there was no need to drive for more fiscal restraint. Second, the persistence of the balance-of-payments problem was suggesting that the easy-money part of the fiscal-monetary program was not timely. Third, the thought was spreading that we were not simply going through another recession but were in a period of persistent stagnation, so that the problem of getting our potential output converted into actual output took precedence over the problem of choosing between public and private uses of the output. This appraisal of the situation was to be important when Kennedy took office, but it came too late to influence Kennedy before the election.

SUPPORTING PLAYERS—THE KENNEDY ECONOMISTS

Kennedy's economists did not dictate either his ideas or his actions in the field of fiscal policy. Nevertheless, he was more influenced by professional economists than his predecessors had been. In part this was simply the continuation of a rising trend of influence which dated back to Roosevelt and his Brain Trust and ran through the Truman-Keyserling and Eisenhower-Burns relationships. But while the trend of economists' influence was rising anyway, it made a leap upward with the Kennedy administration. Kennedy was especially prepared to accept new ideas. Moreover, he had, for a President, an unusual interest in abstract thinking; he read a great deal, enjoyed the company of intellectuals, and was for these reasons open to education by economists.

The economists in turn had exceptional qualities. They were, for one thing, extremely self-confident. Of course, anyone who becomes an adviser to a President is likely to be self-confident, but there are degrees of this. The Kennedy economists were, in the main, of that generation which had been most moved intellectually and emotionally by Keynes' *General Theory*. They were neither so old as to have learned it grudgingly and with qualifications nor so young as to have first met it as an already well-established doctrine. They had enlisted as foot soldiers in the Keynesian army at the beginning and risen through the ranks to become marshals. The Keynesian movement swept economics. Although the meaning of Keynesianism as a doctrine had changed substantially, the esprit de corps of the school remained. Now its leaders were coming victoriously to Washington to practice what they had been teaching. They had no reason to doubt that they knew what to do.

This self-confidence helped to make them persuasive with the President. They did not regard their role, however, as merely advising the President. Their role was to bring about the policies they regarded as correct, as long as the issue had not been foreclosed by a decision of the President. They were assiduous in mobilizing support for their views, inside and outside the government, in order to increase the likelihood that the President's decision would be their decision. Once the President's decision was made they were equally vigorous in trying to sell it to the country. In these efforts they were assisted by the presence of like-minded economists in other government agencies, on the staffs of Congressional committees, and to some extent in the press and in organizations of labor and business.

Of course, a President may be influenced by his advisers, but he also chooses his advisers. There is, thus, always some uncertainty about how far the advisers are to be regarded as exerting an independent influence. One of Kennedy's most important advisers, Paul A. Samuelson, put the question this way:

> The leaders of this world may seem to be led around through the nose by their economist advisers. But who is pulling and who is pushing? And note this: he who picks his own doctor from an array of competing doctors is in a real sense his own doctor. The Prince often gets to hear what he wants to hear.[14]

The key words here are "array of competing doctors." As far as ideas on fiscal policy are concerned Kennedy did not choose from an array of competing doctors; he chose from an array of doctors whose ideas were basically the same. If he had chosen six American economists at random the odds were high that he would have obtained five with the ideas on fiscal policy which his advisers actually had, because those ideas were shared by almost all economists in 1960. As Heller later said: "Thus the rationale of the 1964 tax-cut proposal came straight out of the country's postwar economics textbooks."[15] His economic advisers were eminent expositors of the standard economics of their time. They had done much to make it the standard economics. For example, the man who might be regarded as their intellectual leader, Paul Samuelson, was also the author of the most popular economics textbook of the postwar period. Kennedy did not choose them to advocate and practice a particular brand of fiscal policy upon which he had already determined. He chose them as representative of the economics of his time, and having done that he exposed his policy to influence by the economics of that time.

In the fall of 1958 Senator Kennedy began to expand his staff in preparation for the race for the 1960 nomination. Sorensen writes:

> At the same time, with the help of Professor Earl Latham of Amherst College and a graduate student in Cambridge, I initiated at the Senator's request and in his name an informal committee to tap the ideas and information of scholars and thinkers in Massachusetts and elsewhere. Drawn primarily from the Harvard and Massachusetts Institute of Technology faculties, with a smattering of names from other schools and professions, the members of our "Academic Advisory Committee" held their first organizational meeting with me at the Hotel Commander in Cambridge on December 3, 1958.[16]

The economists in this group who later became advisers on fiscal policy to President Kennedy were J. K. Galbraith and Seymour Harris of Harvard, Paul Samuelson of MIT, and James Tobin of Yale.

What was expected from this committee was more than information and ideas.

> No announcement was made at the time about the committee's formation, but its very existence, when known, helped recruit Kennedy supporters in the liberal intellectual "community" who had leaned to Stevenson or Humphrey. This was in part its purpose, for the liberal intellectuals, with few delegates but many prestigious and articulate voices, could be a formidable foe, as Barkley and Kefauver had learned. Suspicious of Kennedy's father, religion and supposed McCarthy history, they were in these pre-1960 days held in the Stevenson camp by Eleanor Roosevelt and others. Kennedy's "academic advisers" formed an important beachhead on this front.[17]

The Kennedy economists, like most American economists of 1960, believed that the chief economic problem of the country was to achieve and maintain high and rapidly rising total output. That is, the problem was full employment and economic growth. The keys to the management of that problem were fiscal policy and monetary policy, with fiscal policy being the senior partner in the combination. Full employment—or economic stabilization—and economic growth were the main objectives and guides of fiscal policy; budget-balancing was an irrelevancy. The economy was not in need of any basic structural reform of the character of the NRA, French planning, or nationalization of industry. In general, the free market worked well and should not be tampered with, but particular issues of government intervention in the market had to be considered on their merits and without prejudice. Steps to make the distribution of income more nearly equal were good, but they were not the urgent need and not the main road to improving the economic condition of the mass of the population, and they had to be evaluated with due regard for their effects on economic growth.

This set of ideas, which not only justified the big tax cut but also made it the centerpiece of Kennedy's entire economic policy, was the standard economics of 1960. It was Keynesian but much modified from the American Keynesianism of 1946. What Milton Friedman said in 1966 was already true in 1960: "We are all Keynesians now and nobody is any longer a Keynesian."[18] What had produced this change was the agreement by all parties that both monetary policy and fiscal policy could affect total spending and the level of total money income. In a previous chapter we have shown how monetary policy had been reincorporated into Keynesian thinking. Once this happened the distinction between Keynesians and non-Keynesians ceased to be significant.

Within this general consensus of economists there were, of course, differences of emphasis and of degree. Three points distinguished the Kennedy economists from the Eisenhower economists and from a probably small minority of other economists in the 1960's.

1. The Kennedy economists were less concerned with the problem of inflation than the Eisenhower economists, to say nothing of Eisenhower himself. Samuelson had foreseen this in 1956 in discussing the economics of Eisenhower:

> I should like to put forward the hypothesis that the relatively minor economic differences between the Republicans and Democrats during 1953–56 has been in the nature of a lucky accident. For reasons that will not necessarily be relevant in the future, *we have been able since 1951 to have a very high degree of prosperity and also to have stable prices.* The drop in farm and other staple prices made this possible.
>
> In the future the dilemma between very high employment and stable prices is likely to reassert itself with increasing force. Then it will be found that the Republicans do differ from the Democrats in the greater weight that they will give to the goal of maintaining an honest dollar in comparison with the clashing goal of keeping unemployment extremely low.
>
> In this clash of ideologies, social welfare functions and not scientific economic principles must play the decisive role.[19]

Samuelson stated the choice in a Democratic way. There is also a scientific problem involved in calculating how much additional unemployment, and for how long, would result from "maintaining an honest dollar." Some who would opt for avoiding inflation would say that in the long run such a policy would cost little, if any, additional unemployment. Nevertheless, it was undoubtedly true that the Kennedy economists attached less value to the avoidance of inflation than the Eisenhower economists did.

2. The Kennedy economists were willing to supplement general fiscal-monetary policy with other measures to loosen the constraints under which these general policies operated in achieving high employment. Specifically, they were prepared to "intervene in the market" to a degree which more conservative economists would not have accepted. If confronted with the dilemma that high employment could not be achieved without inflation, they would not be content to choose one horn or the other of the dilemma. They would want to try to remove the dilemma and alter the terms of choice — in this case by government action to influence the decisions of individuals, businesses, and labor unions in setting wages and prices. If they found that monetary expansion was limited by the need to keep U.S. interest rates high enough so that money would not flow abroad, they would wish to remove that inhibition also, by selective measures to alter the pattern of interest rates, by placing a tax on lending abroad, or by pressure on U.S. lenders.

This willingness to operate directly upon the market should not be exaggerated. In comparison with standard European or Japanese practices, the interventions the Kennedy economists were prepared to recommend were small. But they were prepared to go further than the Eisenhower economists. As Walter Heller later said:

> It is hard to study the modern economics of relative prices, resource allocation, and distribution without developing a healthy respect for the market mechanisms. . . . But I do not carry respect to the point of reverence.[20]

3. The Kennedy economists had a high degree of confidence in their ability to forecast economic fluctuations accurately and to adapt fiscal and monetary policy continuously on the basis of these forecasts to achieve economic stability within a narrow range. As we have seen, lack of such confidence was a major element in the preference of CED and others in the earlier postwar period for a largely passive fiscal policy aimed at minimizing the risk of gross errors but not at trying to counter forecast fluctuations unless they were big or foreseen with unusual clarity. Walter Heller's main writing on fiscal policy before he became chairman of the Council of Economic Advisers under Kennedy was an argument against this position. His view then, in 1957, was stated mildly:

> No conclusive evidence is available to prove that forecasting techniques are now a thoroughly reliable basis for discretionary stabilization policy. But many new or improved forecasts of important segments of the economy, such as plant and equipment outlays, are now available. The Council of Economic Advisers

does not hesitate to invoke "prospective economic conditions" as a basis for discretionary judgments to hold the line on federal taxes. Qualified observers judge our short-term forecasting record as having operated "not too unsuccessfully" in recent years. Guarded optimism as to the future of economic forecasting seems justified.[21]

After his experience on the Council of Economic Advisers Heller believed that his "guarded optimism" about forecasting had been confirmed:

> In part, this shift from a more passive to a more active policy has been made possible by steady advances in fact-gathering, forecasting techniques, and business practice. Our statistical net is now spread wider and brings in its catch faster. Forecasting has the benefit of not only more refined, computer-assisted methods but of improved surveys of consumer and investment intentions.[22]

The Kennedy economists did not come to Washington in January, 1961, with a plan for a large permanent tax cut in their briefcases. This became their program only a year and a half later and was their reaction to the developments, including the frustrations, of the intervening months. But it was the reaction of men who because of the attitudes we have just described were committed to expansionist policies. They were not afraid of overdoing things because they were not very worried about inflation; they were willing if necessary to intervene in the market to control the consequences of inflation if it should come; and they had great confidence in their ability to foresee how much expansionary policy would be enough but not too much.

The effort to stimulate the economy by fiscal policy, culminating in the 1964 tax cut, was smaller and later than the Kennedy economists would have liked. But the fiscal stimulus would almost certainly have been smaller and later without them. Moreover, while the tax cut was being considered, and after it was adopted, they were the chief interpreters of its significance. If the tax cut was a lesson for the future, it was a lesson first seen through their eyes.

❧16❧

The Decision to Cut Taxes

ALTHOUGH the stage was set for it, tax reduction was not the act the Kennedy administration intended to perform when it entered the scene in January, 1961. Reduction of taxes did not fit well into the administration's longer-range economic plans. Moreover, the administration feared the political consequences of the direct confrontation with the budget-balancing principle which would probably be provoked by the suggestion of tax reduction. The economic situation of 1961 and early 1962, despite an excessive rate of unemployment, did not seem so serious as to require the administration to sacrifice its longer-range objectives and risk a dangerous Congressional struggle in order to get strong expansive fiscal action.

These conditions would change by the middle of 1962. The prospect would emerge that economic conditions would deteriorate, and that the Kennedy administration would be held responsible. The administration's preferred route to economic expansion through increasing government expenditures would seem to be blocked by opposition to the spending programs themselves. And it would become clear that much of the opposition to expansive fiscal policy, including budget deficits, would turn into support if the deficits were created by tax reduction rather than by expenditure increases. When these things happened the decision to cut taxes was made.

PROSPERITY MAY BE JUST AROUND THE CORNER

When the Kennedy administration came into office the rate of unemployment was about 6.7 percent as compared with 5.3 percent in January, 1960. A basic element in the economic thinking of the administration was that the country suffered from something more fundamental than one more economic recession. At his first press conference, when his selection as chairman of the Council of Economic Advisers was announced, Walter Heller emphasized that the problem was not just recession but also years of slack.[1] The same point was made by Professor Paul Samuelson in the report, in January before the inauguration, of a task force which Kennedy had appointed: "More fraught with significance for public policy than the recession itself is the vital fact that it has been superimposed upon an economy which, in the last few years, has been sluggish and tired."[2]

This diagnosis runs through the Kennedy statements of 1961. In his state of the Union message on January 30 he said, "The present state of our economy is disturbing. We take office in the wake of seven months of recession, three and one-half years of slack, seven years of diminished economic growth, and nine years of falling farm income."[3]

One implication of this diagnosis was that the economy was running substantially below its potential when the Kennedy administration came into office, even though the recession had so far been brief and mild. The Council of Economic Advisers estimated that the actual rate of production, as measured by GNP, was about $50 billion below the annual rate that would be achievable at full employment at the beginning of 1961.[4]

The diagnosis also had several important policy implications. It meant that merely to end the recession and initiate a recovery was an inadequate goal. The danger that recovery would not spontaneously carry the economy all the way up to full employment, or would not do so in a reasonable period, was exceptionally great. Therefore, the need for expansive measures would not end with the beginning of recovery, and the size of expansive action which could be safely risked was increased.

But while the administration accepted this diagnosis and its policy implications on paper, it was reluctant to act upon them. It preferred to wait and see if things would not turn up by themselves. Even Professor Samuelson's report was tentative in its recommendations for expansive measures. Although the problem was described in long-range terms, the President was advised to wait a few months to see how much recovery might come before committing himself to strong action. The President's own economic message on February 2, 1961, followed a similar pattern. It took a grave view of the situation and pledged maximum effort in dealing with it, but its immediate recommendations were mild and conventional. The President promised new recovery proposals if needed in seventy-five days—which meant again a policy of waiting and seeing if something would turn up.[5]

The promise of new proposals if needed in seventy-five days "reflected pressure from within the Administration, from liberal Congressmen and from organized labor" for massive public works programs and emergency tax cuts. According to Sorensen, "By late Spring he [Kennedy] was convinced that the recovery would continue without either, and that the Congress would pass neither."[6] The new proposals never came.

On its own economic diagnosis the belief that "the recovery would continue" should not have relieved the administration of the need to take strong stimulative measures. But still the administration did not find strong measures imperative. The achievement of full employment was, of course, desirable. Its prompt achievement, or its achievement at any specified rate, was not urgent. What was urgent was that the administration should not be responsible for unemployment and should be able to demonstrate successful efforts to reduce it. These conditions could be met in 1961 and early 1962 without action so radical as tax reduction. The unemployment which existed when the Kennedy administration came into office was Eisenhower's unemployment, and the recovery, with its accompanying small decline of unemployment which began in the spring, was Kennedy's. The Republicans sometimes complained that the recovery had started too soon after the inauguration to be creditable to Kennedy policies. However, this was a fine point. For the time being, the low level of the economy was charged to Eisenhower, and the rising trend was credited to Kennedy.

This policy of waiting was not entirely satisfactory to Kennedy's economists who wanted full employment to be approached more rapidly and who were not sure it would be achieved at all without stronger measures. But for the time being this policy met the political necessities.

MAINTAINING THE REVENUE STRUCTURE

It was the administration's policy to promote recovery by means that were otherwise acceptable and consistent with its plans. The urgency of speeding recovery was not so great as to require the administration to adopt measures that did not conform to its longer-range posture.

This long-range posture did not include lower taxes. The Kennedy administration's initial picture of the development of the American economy included a substantial continuing increase in federal spending as a major element. Part of this increase in spending was to repair what it regarded as a deterioration of America's military and political strength in the world and would involve a step-up in defense outlays and in foreign aid. In addition, the administration had a list of domestic programs for which it wanted to increase spending. These included federal aid to education, urban renewal, regional economic development, manpower training, and the provision of medical care for the aged.

Another element in the administration's long-range view was a budget surplus to be achieved at high employment as a means of promoting economic growth. As commonly put by the Kennedy economists, the budget surplus would permit monetary policy to be easy without causing inflation. This would keep interest rates down, encourage investment, and thereby assist economic growth. This idea had been central Kennedy doctrine during the 1960 campaign and had its antecedents in the reports of the Joint Economic Committee and in the writings of Paul Samuelson.

In 1961 the possibility of pursuing the easy-money part of this growth plan was limited by the U.S. balance-of-payments position. However, this might not be true for very long. Meanwhile, and in addition, something might be done to encourage private investment by modifying the tax structure.

This long-range picture pointed to the steps that could be consistently taken in a short time to get the economy up to full employment. These steps included increased government spending, easier money and credit insofar as the situation would allow, and tax revision to encourage investment. It did not include general tax reduction. If the goal was to raise federal expenditures and yet be able to generate a budget surplus at high employment, tax reduction was ruled out however much it might contribute to solving the immediate recovery and employment problem.

The influence of these longer-range considerations in limiting short-run policies for high employment is seen in the report which Paul Samuelson submitted to President-elect Kennedy in January, 1961. His first line of measures to promote recovery did not include tax reduction but consisted entirely of expenditure increases that were considered to be of permanent value plus such monetary ease as might be consistent with the balance-of-payments position. Only if developments in the early part of 1961 "begin to suggest" that economic conditions would worsen—not just stay at their present depressed level—so that unemployment would rise toward and perhaps beyond 7 1/2 percent, would a temporary tax cut "then deserve consideration." "At this time it would be urgently important to make sure that any tax cut was clearly a temporary one. With the continued international uncertainty and with new public programs coming up in the years ahead, sound finance may require maintenance of our present tax structure and any weakening of it in order to fight a recession might be tragic."[7]

Walter Heller, as chairman of the Council of Economic Advisers, also emphasized the long-range value of preserving the revenue-raising power of the existing tax system. Testifying before the Joint Economic Committee on March 6, 1961, he said:

> The revenue-raising power of the existing Federal tax system can be an important asset in achieving the levels of investment needed for rapid advance in productive capacity. First, the potential high-employment surplus can be used, as discussed above, to finance the desirable Government programs which contribute to the buildup of human capital. Second, it can indirectly increase incentives for private investment by facilitating a policy of relative monetary ease, as noted in the preceding section. Third, it can be placed at the disposal of the economy for investment purposes by the process of debt retirement. When the Federal Government retires debt it, in effect, exchanges cash for an asset which had been a store of wealth for the owners of the debt. These owners then seek other assets to hold, primarily the debt and equity securities of business firms and the bonds of State and local governments. In other words, the debt retirement process channels savings into uses which facilitate investment for economic growth.
>
> In addition, the tax system can be used to provide specific financial incentives for investment. In his economic message, the President announced that we would propose a modification of the income tax law to favor investment in plant and equipment. This can be done in such a way as to yield strong incentive effects per dollar of revenue loss. Accompanying measures would restore the revenue loss and improve the fairness of the tax system.[8]

The administration's long-range objectives and problems did not necessarily preclude *temporary* tax reduction in 1961. But the idea of a temporary tax reduction did not fit comfortably into the picture of an economy suffering from a low-grade secular stagnation. Moreover, there was no assurance that a "temporary" tax reduction would actually be temporary; in fact there was considerable doubt about the ability of the government to take the tax reduction back once it had been given to the taxpayer. Temporary tax reduction remained on the administration's agenda of things to consider. But it was to be considered only in an emergency—which meant an economic decline, not merely failure to grow at a sufficiently rapid rate. This kind of emergency did not occur in 1961.

A Program for High Employment Without Tax Reduction

Tax reduction having been ruled out, the government was left with three instruments for achieving high employment—monetary expansion, tax reform, and expenditure increase. Although monetary expansion had been a key element of the Democratic program in 1960 and earlier, the administration was reconciled in 1961 to the fact that the balance-of-payments deficit would not permit as much monetary expansion as it would otherwise have wished. Moreover, monetary policy was under the control of the Federal Reserve, and the administration was cautious not to appear to be intruding in that field. When asked at a press conference in February whether he had any intention to expand the authority of the Presidency with respect to domestic interest rates, Kennedy said that he did not. He would like to see short-term rates high enough to attract gold and long-term rates low enough to stimulate growth, "But this is a matter under the control, of course, directly of the Federal Reserve Board, with the Treasury having, of course, a direct interest in it."[9] Nevertheless, although little was expected of monetary policy, and there was little the administration could do about it directly, there was a considerable monetary expansion in 1961. The supply of money, excluding time deposits, increased by about 3 percent, whereas there had been no increase in 1959 and 1960 taken together. Money plus time deposits increased by 6.6 percent, as against less than 2 percent per annum in the preceding two years.

The second part of the program for economic expansion, revision of the tax system without revenue loss, failed of enactment in 1961. The administration presented a package of tax revisions with three main parts.

1. A tax credit (reduction of tax) equal to 8 percent of business investment in excess of depreciation allowances.

2. Taxation of income earned by U.S. corporations abroad but not repatriated.

3. Withholding of income tax on interest and dividends at the source.

The tax credit was intended to stimulate investment. The provision that the credit should be given only for investment expenditures in excess of depreciation allowances was an attempt to confine the credit to investment that would not otherwise have been made and thus get the maximum incentive effect per dollar of revenue loss. The other proposals were intended to regain the revenue lost from the tax credit.

All parts of the tax reform program immediately encountered strong opposition in the Congress and in the business community. Businesses with investments abroad claimed that the increased taxation of foreign income would, in a short period, hurt rather than help the United States balance of payments, because the investment would earn foreign funds. Corporations and financial institutions maintained that the withholding of tax on interest and dividends would impose intolerable costs on them, and they stirred up a storm of objection from small shareholders and depositors. Businesses, which would have been the immediate beneficiary of the investment credit, also objected to that part of the package. In general, business preferred provision for speeding up depreciation, which would have had effects similar to the tax credit but which had some advantages from the standpoint of business. The depreciation reform had more appearance of giving business its just deserts than did the tax credit, which looked like a handout to business.

There was no opposition, at least from conservative quarters, to the revenue-losing part of the package on the ground that the budget had to be balanced. In fact, the conservative opposition to the revenue-gaining part of the package was much stronger than to the revenue-losing part of it. In 1962 the Congress finally enacted the revenue-losing part, the tax credit, revised to make it more acceptable to business, but only a shadow of the revenue-raising part was passed.

Tax reform in 1961 being blocked by Congressional and taxpayer opposition, and monetary policy being out of its hands and also believed to be limited by the balance of payments, the administration was left with increasing government expenditures as its route to recovery and growth. This was the route that it would have preferred to travel and had most confidence in anyway—even if the other routes had also been open. The recovery program described in the President's economic message on February 2, 1961, consisted largely of expenditure-increasing steps. These were spelled out in March in two messages revising the budget for fiscal year 1962 as originally submitted by President Eisenhower. The net of these revisions was to increase spending in fiscal 1962 by about $3 billion over the Eisenhower estimates. There was no further request to increase spending, and no evidence of any intention to do so for fiscal 1962, until the intensification of the Soviet threat to Berlin. Then, in a report to the nation on July 25 on the Berlin crisis, Kennedy announced that he was asking for an increase in the defense budget which would raise fiscal 1962 spending by an additional $3 billion. He had seriously considered and, indeed, tentatively decided upon a $3 billion tax increase to accompany this expenditure increase but was dissuaded by the arguments of his economic advisers that a tax increase would obstruct the recovery then in progress.[10]

The initial program, before the Berlin crisis, was too small to satisfy Kennedy's economic advisers. As Samuelson later said:

> In brief, the first Kennedy program was a modest one: designed to help bring the recession to a speedy end, it was not large enough to lead to so rapid a recovery as would be wanted by those anxious to bring unemployment substantially down from its 7 percent rate and anxious to speed up America's real growth rate.[11]

Even the program as expanded in response to the Berlin crisis did not meet the goals of the economic advisers. Again we have the evidence of Samuelson: "The resulting program of expansion has been something less than all that could be desired by academic perfectionists (the caste to which I happen to belong)."[12] And the recovery did sputter in ths spring of 1962, well short of full employment.

We have already suggested that Kennedy's goals were less ambitious than those of his economic advisers and that he would be more satisfied than they with a continuous, visible recovery initiated under his regime, even if the attainment of full employment was only gradual. Still, there is no reason to doubt that he would have preferred a more rapid recovery if it could have been achieved by means consistent with his other objectives. His decision not to recommend a tax increase to finance the increased defense expenditures after the Berlin crisis shows his willingness to inject more stimulus into the economy if the means were acceptable. Moreover, it is clear that the President's spending proposals were not limited by the lack of spending programs the expansion of which he thought would be desirable for their own sake, aside from their effects on recovery.

THE OPPOSITION

All witnesses who were close to President Kennedy agree that the spending program was limited by the fear of opposition, that this opposition was conservative and especially concentrated in the Congress, in the Republican Party, and in the business community, that the opposition was basically ideological, and that the ideology focused on the need to balance the budget. Thus, Sorensen described Kennedy's attitude as follows:

> Nevertheless his [Kennedy's] political judgment told him that a period of gradual re-education would be required before the country and Congress, accustomed to nearly sixteen years of White House homilies on the wickedness of government deficits, would approve of an administration deliberately and severely unbalancing the Budget.[13]

Samuelson appraised the situation similarly:

> Had President Kennedy come out boldly for the sizeable deficit which objective economic analysis called for, he would have run into severe opposition in the divided Congress; and by becoming tarred with the asinine label of an "irresponsible spender," the President might have put all his new programs in jeopardy.[14]

There was a great deal of opposition in Congress to many of the Kennedy programs for increased spending in 1961. Although in fact total spending and total non-defense spending in fiscal year 1962 turned out as large as Kennedy recommended, the Congress did not follow the Kennedy recommendations in many of the fields where the administration would have looked for still larger expenditure increases—including aid to education, medical care, and urban redevelopment. Thus it is probably true that to have sent up larger requests in these fields would have been vain and self-defeating.

However, this is not to say that the opposition to spending was primarily on budget-balancing grounds or that, insofar as it was, the desire for a balanced budget was pure ideology or traditionalism. The opponents of Kennedy's spending programs, or at least many of them, had more affection for the idea of a balanced budget than Kennedy did, but this was not the main basis of their opposition. They objected to the particular spending programs aside from their effects on the deficit, just as Kennedy wanted those programs for reasons other than their contribution to the deficit and to economic recovery. They did not like federal aid to education, and what they called "socialized medicine," and federal intervention in the business of the states and localities; and they would not have liked them if the budget had been balanced, or if there had been a surplus. While Kennedy had seriously considered asking for a tax increase to finance the increased military spending after the Berlin crisis, no one criticized him for failure to do so or advanced an independent recommendation that taxes be raised in order to hold down the budget deficit. The request for additional defense spending provoked some discussion of fiscal policy in the Congress. The main point of this discussion was that the need for additional defense spending made it more imperative than ever to cut domestic welfare spending. Failure to cut these domestic programs would cause higher deficits or higher taxes, which were considered equally objectionable.

In addition to disliking the particular expenditure programs the administration preferred, the opposition had a strong preference for lower taxes. President Kennedy wanted to hold on to the existing tax structure because he expected and desired a rise of expenditures which would make the revenue yield of that structure necessary. The opposition wanted to hold down spending in the hope that expenditure restraint would bring a day when the revenue yield of the existing tax structure would be unnecessary, and taxes could be cut.

Both the administration and the opponents of its spending programs believed that there was a considerable budget-balancing sentiment in the country. The administration tried to show that it was not violating that sentiment. In his first state of the Union message, after describing the budget plans left behind by Eisenhower, Kennedy said: "Within that framework, barring the development of urgent national defense needs or a worsening of the economy, it is my current intention to advocate a program of expenditures which, including revenues from a stimulation of the economy, will not of and by themselves unbalance the earlier Budget."[15] When he asked for additional defense spending in July, 1961, during the Berlin crisis, the President promised that he would submit a balanced budget in January, 1962, for the fiscal year 1963.[16] The administration hoped by such statements to pick up a little immediate support at no more cost than the possibility of minor embarrassment later. Similarly, it was natural for opponents of the Kennedy spending programs to invoke the traditional budget-balancing slogans, hoping thereby to pick up some support they might otherwise miss. This did not mean permanent opposition by them to deficits without regard to the means by which they were created and the surrounding conditions.

In addition to dislike of particular government programs, hope for later tax reduction, and traditional budget-balancing ideology, there was a fourth reason for opposition to increased government spending in 1961. This was disagreement with the administration's diagnosis of the economic situation and the prescription of general fiscal stimulus that went with it. There were several elements in this disagreement. After the spring the economy was recovering, and it was possible that the economy would quickly regain its potential without more fiscal stimulus. The danger of renewed inflation had to be watched carefully, especially in view of the balance-of-payments deficit. Concern for the international position of the dollar was also believed by many to require a cautious fiscal policy in order to preserve the confidence of foreign holders of dollars. This view had some influence within the administration as well as outside. At the first meeting of the Kennedy Cabinet, in January, 1961. Treasury Secretary Dillon warned against too large a deficit which would frighten the foreign financial community.[17] Some who accepted the proposition that there was a problem with the level of employment, which might not be solved by the recovery then in process, did not accept the view that what the situation required was a still larger stimulus to total demand. They maintained that the problem was structural—that the unemployed had the wrong skills, or no skills, or were in the wrong places, or were too young, or were otherwise unsuited for the jobs that were available or that might be made available by fiscal expansion. Finally there were those who believed that the sluggishness of the economy since 1957 had been due to the poor prospects for profitable private investment, which had to be corrected by specific measures, notably tax reform, rather than by injection of more general purchasing power into the economy.

The opposition which deterred Kennedy from proposing more fiscal expansion in 1961 would fade and turn into support when the administration proposed fiscal stimulation in the *form* that was acceptable—general tax reduction—and when economic developments made the need for stimulation seem clearer. The administration, for its part, would turn to general tax reduction when it began to appear that the opposition would restrain the growth of federal spending and that the spontaneous course of the economy was not strongly upward but might decline, so that the administration felt a great need for expansive policy in an acceptable form, even if it could not get it in its own preferred form. These changes in economic conditions and in political strategy occurred in 1962 and led up to the tax reduction proposal by the middle of the year.

THE PROCESS OF EDUCATION

Meanwhile, pending the economic and political developments that would permit strong, expansive fiscal measures to be taken, the Council of Economic Advisers was prepared to participate in the process of education, or reeducation, that the administration believed necessary. How much this educational effort contributed to the decision to cut taxes is hard to say. As long as the President had not espoused vigorous fiscal stimulation the council was restrained in advocating it and even in presenting analysis which had as an inescapable conclusion the need for stronger measures. During the period up to the middle of 1962 the President was the chief student in the council's economic seminar. After the President and, in an effective sense, the country had decided to reduce taxes the council's exposition of the underlying rationale became louder and clearer. While the public education probably had some influence on the decision to cut taxes, its main effect was on the way people interpreted that decision after it had been made and on the way they thought about fiscal policy subsequently.

The education that was required and provided was not about deficits. By 1961 the country did not need to be educated about the utility, or at least legitimacy, of deficits in recessions. On the other hand, the country did not accept the propriety of deficits as a permanent way of life, and the education did not persuade them to do so and was not intended to persuade them. Insofar as there were ideological or intellectual obstacles to strong fiscal action they were these:

1. Strong fiscal action, including deficits, is called for in a recession, but the economy is not in a recession.

2. If the economy is in a condition of persistent stagnation or failure to reach full employment, deficit financing is an unacceptable solution because

the deficits would also have to be persistent, and deficits are unacceptable as a permanent policy.

3. If the economy is in a condition of persistent stagnation there must be something wrong, and that should be corrected rather than being compensated for by the artificial device of fiscal stimulation.

The first of these points was attacked by means of the concept and measurement of the "gap," meaning the deficiency of total output below the output the economy would produce when operating at full employment. The thing to look at, the council argued, was not only whether total output was rising or falling or even whether it was at record highs, but also whether and by how much total output was below its potential, because that was the true measure of the avoidable loss of output.[18] This idea was, of course, the obvious implication of taking full employment as a goal. If unemployment is to be kept low, with the population and labor force rising, the number of persons employed must also rise from year to year. And with output per worker rising as it does in the United States, total output must rise faster than employment. Therefore the goal of high employment means a goal of rising output, and failure to meet the employment goal will appear in failure to keep total output at its rising potential. Several estimates of potential output and of the gap were made during the 1950's, notably by the staff of the Joint Economic Committee under James W. Knowles.[19]

Basically, the gap is another way of looking at the same phenomenon of under-utilization of our productive resources that is shown by unemployment. A gap will only appear when unemployment is above the rate considered to be full employment in the calculation of the output potential; if the output potential is calculated on the assumption of 4 percent unemployment there will be an output gap only when unemployment is more than 4 percent.[20] If one does not accept the 4 percent unemployment rate as a goal, he will not accept the gap calculated on the basis of that rate as relevant.

However, the gap estimates do add something to the picture presented by the unemployment figures. There is often an inclination to say that although unemployment may be excessive, production is high, meaning higher than last year or even higher than ever before, so that the economic situation must be regarded as at worst mixed. In fact this view was common in the second half of 1961 and much of 1962. What the gap estimates say in this situation is that production is not really high by the relevant standard, which is comparison with potential output. Also, the output gap expressed in billions of dollars may add to the weight of the unemployment figures expressed in percentages; at least to some people, to know that the economy is falling $50 billion below its potential annual output is a stronger indication that something is wrong than the unemployment percentage itself.[21]

The council estimated that in the first quarter of 1961 the output gap was running at the rate of about $50 billion of gross national product a year, or about 10 percent of the actual GNP. Moreover, the council's estimates showed that there had been a gap since 1955, although its size, of course, had varied from time to time. Even during the 1955–67 boom there had been a small gap according to their estimates. There had been a substantial gap at the high point of the recovery from 1958 to 1960. Thus the American economy had a long way to go, in the spring of 1961, to achieve its potential output, and the record of the preceding years indicated that the ending of a recession did not assure closing the gap. On the basis of this analysis of the situation the council emphasized that the need for action would not end with the beginning of recovery.

But if the economy is suffering from persistent slack, will not the effort to correct it by fiscal stimulation involve persistent deficits? The question is reminiscent of the discussion of the late 1930's when the analysis of the American stagnationists raised the prospect of the need for perpetual deficits. The answer of the stagnationists of the 1930's was that if the situation required permanent deficits there was nothing wrong with that. The "new economists" of 1961 did not take that position. Although they did not concede any merit to balancing the budget, either in the long run or in the short, aside from particular economic circumstances which might happen to call for a balanced budget, they launched no frontal attack on the budget-balancing idea. Rather they suggested that the issue was not a real one in the early 1960's because their analysis and prescription did not involve persistent deficits.

The main ingredient of this argument was the concept of the full-employment surplus as the significant measure of the budget position. This idea, of course, had a long history going back to the CED 1947 statement and to the earlier writing of Beardsley Ruml.[22] The full-employment surplus is the excess of the receipts that would be collected from the existing tax rates when the economy is operating at full employment over the expenditures that existing government programs would call for at the same full employment conditions. Much of the analysis by which economists concluded in 1960 that fiscal policy had become too restrictive used estimates based on the full-employment surplus.[23]

The full-employment surplus idea had a special value for advocates of fiscal expansion in 1961 because the full-employment surplus then was large. A substantial increase of expenditures or reduction of taxes would still leave the full-employment budget in balance. Even if the advocates of fiscal expansion did not think budget-balancing was important, there were still those in the country who did. It was convenient to be able to show them that on the basis of a certain significant definition there was a large surplus and room for expansive measures without creating a deficit.

In its March, 1961, statement to the Joint Economic Committee the council said:

> Were the economy to operate at full employment levels in 1961, and at comparable rates in the first 6 months of 1962, it is estimated that Federal revenues in fiscal 1962 would be $92 billion. This would exceed the expenditures estimated in the Budget Message of January 16, 1961, by $11 billion and the revenues by $9 1/2 billion. Moreover, if the economy grows at 3 1/2 percent per year, the present Federal tax structure will increase budget receipts by $3 to $3 1/2 billion per year. The revenues of a fully operating economy would finance the Federal programs needed to accelerate the growth of productive capacity and meet national priorities at home and abroad, while leaving room for substantial retirements of Federal debt from budget surplus.[24]

The idea of the full-employment surplus and the fact that it was so large contributed to the credibility of a third item in the fiscal lexicon of the Kennedy economists. This was the idea of the "fiscal drag."

Even though it might be conceded that the economy was suffering from persistent inability to get up to full employment, and even though there was room for expansive fiscal measures without creating a deficit—at least in the full-employment budget—a question would remain. Why try to deal with the problem by reducing taxes relative to expenditures? Why not get to the causes of the problem and solve them, rather than paper them over with compensatory fiscal policy? This kind of question was raised especially by businessmen and other conservatives who had a definite view of what the basic causes of the economic slack were. They pointed out that the main lag in the economy since the fall of 1957 had been a lag in private investment. While this was said to have a variety of causes, the one on which attention focused, probably because of the belief that it would be easier to correct than the others, was the high rate of taxation on the return from investment. Reduction of such taxes, it was argued, would contribute to both high employment and more rapid growth. Moreover, this correction of the underlying problem would not require a step toward lower surpluses in the budget, or toward deficits, because the reduction of the taxes bearing on investment could be offset by raising other taxes or by cutting expenditures.

The argument on this point in 1961 and 1962 had its antecedents in the 1930's. The basic position of the business community then was that recovery was impeded by government policies which repressed private investment, including tax policies, and that removal of these impediments would restore prosperity without continuous "artificial" fiscal stimulus. By and large, Franklin Roosevelt had rejected this argument. The Kennedy administration did not entirely reject it. In fact, this was the rationale of the administration's tax reform proposal of 1961, which sought to encourage private investment without any net loss of federal revenue.

However, the Kennedy administration, and most of all its economists, did not believe that this kind of policy was likely to be sufficient. They wanted to open the door for net expenditure increases and tax reductions. And they did not accept the view that fiscal stimulation was artificial and failed to deal with the basic causes of the persistent lag in the economy. On the contrary, they maintained that the fiscal position of the federal government itself was a basic cause of the economic problem, and that reducing taxes relative to expenditures was indeed a way of dealing with a basic cause and not just compensating for some deficiency in the private economy. The tendency of the tax structure to extract larger and larger amounts from private income as the economy approached high employment was a drag on expansion keeping private demand from rising enough to generate full employment. The fiscal prescription was not to intervene in, or compensate, the private economy but to remove or relax a restraint which the federal sector was imposing upon the expansion of the private economy. The Kennedy administration almost always described its fiscal policy in this way.

The concept of fiscal drag directs attention to part of what is actually a more complicated picture. The federal fiscal position is one of many factors which, taken together, determine the level of economic activity. As the council itself pointed out, if private investment demand is very strong, even a very large surplus will not prevent full employment from being achieved. All one can say then is that the budget position is too restrictive given the state of private investment. In that case there is no more reason to speak of a fiscal drag than of a private investment drag.

The idea that there was something wrong on the fiscal side—that there was specifically a fiscal drag—was appealing because there was a large full-employment surplus. Logically, even a budget with a full-employment deficit can be a drag in the sense that a still larger deficit might be necessary or helpful for getting to full employment. But it would surely have been more difficult to get across the impression that the budget was a drag if it wasn't also true that the budget would have had a large surplus if full-employment had been achieved.

Moreover, that there should be a fiscal drag was made to seem entirely natural and expectable by the council's exposition. It was pointed out that in a growing economy, with constant tax rates levied on incomes and sales which would also be growing, the government's revenues would be steadily increasing. Unless expenditures of government rose at an equal rate, the government's subtractions from private incomes by taxes would exceed the government's additions through its expenditures by an ever increasing amount, and this would constitute a drag upon the growth of the economy. Prevention of this drag required positive policy and action—the declaration of fiscal dividends in the form of higher expenditures or lower taxes. Therefore, one did not have to ask how the fiscal drag happened to befall the Amerian economy. There was a continuous tendency for the drag to emerge unless it was forestalled by adequate fiscal dividends. In the later years of the Eisenhower administration the fiscal dividends had not been adequate; expenditures rose slowly while taxes were not reduced, so that the full-employment surplus became large.

The tendency for revenues to rise with the growth of the economy was, of course, obvious and had been pointed out much earlier along with the kinds of fiscal action that it would require or permit. For example, the CED had made the point in its 1947 statement, although CED had regarded it as creating an opportunity rather than a problem.[25] Many economists in the postwar period had made projections of the economy which showed that unless taxes were reduced or expenditures increased substantially there would emerge within a few years a surplus which they thought inconsistent with full employment. However, the Kennedy administration gave these ideas publicity they had not received before.

The idea of the fiscal drag was more firmly established in Kennedy's own thinking than any of the other fiscal concepts of his advisers. Thus, discussing the economic outlook at a press conference in June, 1961, he said:

> Now we had a recession in '54, we had a recession in '58, we had a recession in '60. The '60 recession came right on the heels of the '58 recession. Two of the reasons why it may have contributed—it was the movement from a $12 billion deficit in '58–59 to a prospective $4 billion surplus, which was a change of more than $16 billion in the total receipts of the Government, which did have a re-straining influence on the recovery.[26]

At a press conference a month later he repeated that the "tax structure is so strong that it contributed to strangling the recovery after the '58 recession."[27]

In October, 1961, when asked whether he would raise taxes to balance the budget, he replied:

> We don't want to—which I think is one of the difficulties—the recovery of

'58 which was aborted in 1960, so that we don't want to provide a tax structure which already is very heavy—and brings in tremendous receipts at full employment—we don't want it to result in waste of resources and manpower. So that's the judgment we must make.[28]

During 1961 the administration espoused and repeatedly expounded a philosophy designed to reconcile a policy of fiscal expansion with what it believed were the ideas prevalent in the country. The economy was described as suffering from a persistent inability to reach full employment, which was caused in part by the drag which fiscal policy itself exerted. The remedy was to remove or reduce this drag, and since there was already a large surplus in the budget at full employment, the reduction of the drag did not require the generation of a deficit. These ideas were all well within the framework of the consensus on fiscal policy that had been reached in the late 1940's. Essentially they called, as that policy had done, for adjusting the budget so that it would balance or yield a moderate surplus at high employment. Extraordinary action was required to achieve that position because the budget had been allowed to get far away from it in 1960 when an unusually large full-employment surplus was generated. What was proposed did not fall within the category later described as "fine tuning"—the temporary adjustment of fiscal policy to small actual or forecast deviations of the economy from some goal. Rather the analysis called for a reduction of the full-employment budget surplus which was expected to be permanent, or at least not expected to be reversed, and the need for which was independent of the current or forecast cyclical phase of the economy.

Thus the administration was continuing an educational process which had been going on for many years to explain how fiscal policy could contribute to full employment and price stability without a commitment to permanent deficits or to continuous tinkering with taxes and expenditures in response to highly fallible forecasts of economic fluctuations. The elements in the theory—the gap, the full-employment surplus, and the fiscal drag—were not new, but their use by the Council of Economic Advisers and by the President himself gave them a currency they had not achieved before. Of course, it would be an exaggeration to think that these ideas ever became part of the lexicon of the man in the street. Congressional debates show that few congressmen have found these concepts congenial or useful. The main effect of increased exposure of the man in the street or the congressman to sophisticated discussion of fiscal policy is probably negative. It does not furnish him with a set of new ideas he can use but weakens his confidence in the ideas he previously held, and in the people he previously regarded as authorities, and makes him less resistant to the recommendations of other authorities. The main conclusion the average reader reaches is that the subject is really much more difficult that he thought.

Comments by Congressman Richard Bolling at the hearings of the Joint Economic Committee on the January, 1962, economic report illustrate the reactions:

> Mr. Heller, on page 77 of the report, you have a very interesting discussion of the budget. I find that in talking with my constituents there seems to be a tremendous amount of oversimplification in the public mind, at least, in dealing with this problem. I want to compliment you on that section of the report because it brings out very clearly that there are a variety of budgets and that the budget is a great deal more than the symbol it has become in, let's say, political terms. I have been extremely disturbed by the general public's acceptance of the notion that there is something almost sanctified in a balanced budget, and I have also been very much disturbed by the general view that our public debt is in a dangerous situation.
>
> My own view is that the budget basically involves a very complicated set of tools and that the public debt is no great threat to our economy at its present level.[29]

JUNE IN JANUARY?

When President Kennedy submitted his first budget message in January, 1962, the whole edifice of New Frontier fiscal policy seemed to have melted in the rising sun of economic recovery. Despite the idea that fiscal drag was keeping the economy from attaining full employment, the budget was predicated on the assumption that unemployment would decline to 4 percent by mid-1963.[30] This recovery was to be achieved without any reduction of the fiscal drag. The budget for fiscal 1963 was to be balanced. There was to be a surplus of $463 million in the administrative budget, and a surplus of $4.4 billion in the national income accounts budget—the budget that the Kennedy economists considered much more significant than the traditional administrative budget. Moreover, the surplus in the national income accounts budget would be achieved in fiscal 1963 even though that year as a whole would be substantially below full employment, since full employment would be achieved only at its end. For fiscal 1963 the full-employment surplus would be about $8 billion. The full-employment surplus would be rising from the first half of calendar 1962 through the second half of that year and the first half of calendar 1963.[31] Thus, the recovery would have to continue in the face of an increasing fiscal drag.

This abandonment of all of the implications of the New Frontier fiscal theories was in part the result of the commitment Kennedy had made when he recommended an increase in defense spending in July, 1961, without a tax increase. He had said then that he would submit a balanced budget for fiscal 1963 and would recommend a tax increase if necessary to achieve it. The expansionists in the administration had considered this a necessary, and small, price to pay to avoid a tax increase in the middle of 1961. As Sorensen later said about the budget-balancing promise:

> While this committed us to a restricted Budget effort the following year, that was far better than a tax increase in the midst of recovery, for we were determined to find fair means or foul of making that Budget look balanced and dropping all thought of new taxes.[32]

As Heller later described the President's attitude in the fall of 1961:

> But eventually the President found that he had to "paper over" a deficit in order to move ahead on his expenditure programs and get what we hoped would be a sufficiently stimulative budget. One day in October [1961] he recalled with some admiration Roosevelt's and Eisenhower's abilities to talk balanced budgets even in the face of repeated deficits. Increasingly he was trying to find ways of reconciling sensible economic policy with popular values that, however mistaken, could not be transformed overnight.[33]

One way in which the deficit was papered over was to inflate the revenue estimates by assuming a pace of recovery in 1962 and 1963 which many observers at the time thought, correctly as it turned out, was improbably high. However, the move toward a balanced budget was not entirely on paper, and the reason for it was not entirely the promise given in July and the need to conform to popular values. Within the administration enthusiasm for expansive fiscal policy waned as the economy expanded. Recovery proceeded in the second half of 1961 more rapidly than the council had anticipated. Despite the revival of production during the year, the rate of unemployment had varied only from 6.8 percent to 6.9 percent from February to October. Then, however, it fell dramatically to 6.1 percent in November and December. After Labor Day the stock market was showing signs of anticipating a boom. Worries about inflation reappeared. At the same time the U.S. balance-of-payments position was worsening again after some improvement in the first half of 1961.

In this atmosphere, budgetary restraint seemed to some within the administration to be not only satisfaction of a prior commitment but also the best prescription for the economy. On October 26, 1961, the President issued a statement to Cabinet officers and agency heads asking for frugality in spending for fiscal 1962 and 1963, mainly out of concern for the economic situation. He pointed out that for several reasons, including good weather which increased crops and therefore agricultural price support payments, the estimated deficit for fiscal 1962 had risen.

> There is general agreement that under the present conditions of high unemployment and recession-reduced tax receipts, a deficit is normally to be expected. It is important to make sure that the deficit is kept within reasonable limits and reflects only essential expenditures.
>
> There is no evidence that the currently-estimated deficit presents serious risks to the domestic price level or the U.S. balance of payments. Moreover, considering the economic effect of the budget on a month-by-month basis, as contrasted to the annual totals, the current impact of Government operations is expected to change early in calendar 1962 from a net stimulative to a net restraining influence on the economy.
>
> While the recent rises in the estimates of expenditures and the deficit, therefore, are compatible with the sound fiscal and budget policies we have been following, they are further grounds for insistence on economy in executing Government programs. This is the reason I have asked each of you to follow a most careful and frugal policy with respect to commitments and expenditures under the 1962 budget as enacted by the Congress.
>
> Let me add a word about the 1963 budget. *In view of the prospective gains in the economy*, it is my intention to propose a balanced budget for that year, barring extraordinary and unforeseen defense requirements.[34]

The Council of Economic Advisers was less susceptible than most to the growing optimism. "Sorensen, seeing the three Council members . . . in somewhat solemn conclave at the White House Staff Mess one day, called out, 'There they are, contemplating the dangers of an upturn'!"[35] The dangers of an upturn were precisely what the council had been warning against in their discussion of the gap. They had said that as long as unemployment was high and the output gap large, an upturn would not mean that the need to stimulate the economy had passed. But as the upturn continued the administration chose to take the risks on the side of fiscal restraint.

The administration felt the need to justify this policy to those who expected, from all that had been said, a more determined drive for expansion. The budget message explained:

> . . . the Federal Government is expected to operate in 1963 with some surplus. This is the policy which seems appropriate at the present time. The economy is moving strongly forward, with employment and incomes rising. The prospects are favorable for further rises in the coming year in private expenditures, both consumption and investment. To plan a deficit under such circumstances would

increase the risk of inflationary pressures, damaging alike to our domestic economy and to our international balance of payments.[36]

The annual report of the Council of Economic Advisers acknowledged that the full-employment surplus would be rising. "But it [the full-employment surplus] remains considerably below the level of 1960. Fiscal policy will be less restrictive than it was in the late stages of the last recovery."[37]

In recognition of the possible inadequacy of his fiscal program from the standpoint of full recovery, the President asked for authority to make a temporary tax cut in a recession, authority to accelerate public-works spending if unemployment rose by specified amounts, and strengthening of the unemployment compensation system. There was no chance that Congress would delegate the tax-cutting authority to the President in 1962, and in any case the whole back-up program would be operative only in the event that the economy turned down again, not if the expansion continued at a rate insufficient to produce full employment.

Also in January, 1962, the President made an appeal to business and labor to observe certain guideposts of price and wage behavior in order to help maintain price stability. One motivation behind this policy was to clear the way for future expansive policy by negating the argument that expansive measures would be inflationary and therefore dangerous for the domestic economy and for the balance of payments.

Although the administration economists defended the decisions which had been made, they barely concealed their concern at the risks. Senator Douglas asked Budget Director David Bell: "If we could consider these issues on their merits, without regard to the idols of the marketplace, and if we were concerned about the volume of unemployment, might not this be too restrictive a budget in terms of the high rate of unemployment which exists?"

Bell replied:

> It has been my experience, in the past few months, in talking with a large number of the economists who specialize in these problems, of differing political ideas, that this is the question they ask. Their question is: Is the budget surplus calculated this way too much? Is it too high? Is this going to contribute to pinching out the economic recovery?
>
> For the reasons I gave in my earlier statement, we are persuaded that this is not the case. However, I personally would feel that if one had to lean in one direction or the other, in judging the economic impact of this budget, it certainly leans a little bit that way, rather than being too expansionary.[38]

Fear that the budget had shifted too far in a restrictive direction was expressed by Theodore O. Yntema, testifying on behalf of the Committee for Economic Development before the Joint Economic Committee on February 7, 1962:

> It is worth noting that the administration's budget is estimated by the Council of Economic Advisers to have a high employment surplus running at the rate of $10 billion a year in the first half of calendar 1963. This is higher, even in relation to the size of the economy, than in any previous period of high employment since the unusual conditions of 1948.
>
> Moreover this surplus would be accompanied by higher interest rates than at any earlier time in the postwar period. It may be that the Council has overestimated what the GNP and national income would be at high employment, in which case the size of the high employment surplus implicit in the budget is also overestimated. It is possible, too, that the Council may be overestimating the tax yields and underestimating the expenditures that will occur at high employment GNP.
>
> But if the Council's estimates are correct the question of whether the contemplated budget and monetary policy will permit us to get and keep high employment needs further examination.[39]

The majority of the Joint Economic Committee, in its report, raised the same question: "As we pointed out a year ago, we are seriously concerned lest our revenue system be capable of generating too large a Federal surplus at high employment, in which case employment high enough to produce any surplus will likely not be achieved."[40]

But such misgivings had no effect as long as the trend of the economy was strongly upward.

How far the country was in early 1962 from cutting taxes as a means of stimulating the economy was shown in remarks of the President at a press conference on February 21:

> QUESTION: Would you tell us what the prospects are for an income tax cut within the next few years?
>
> PRESIDENT: . . . obviously our present tax structure brings in, in good times, a tremendous revenue and if we do not have a recession and our present tax structure remains we would be in a position, obviously, where a tax reduction in a few years or a period of time might be possible. The fact of the matter is that if we had not had the Berlin crisis, which required a $3.5 billion additional expenditure last summer at the time when we were considering our tax reform bill, it might have been possible to make changes in some of the categories. That was denied to us.
>
> Therefore, for the present time there is not a chance of tax reduction. The key will be whether we can have continued prosperity, and I therefore urge again that the Congress consider very carefully the proposals that we've made which we hope can keep the economy moving ahead.[41]

OPENING THE DOOR TO TAX REDUCTION

Three and a half months later there was more than a chance of tax reduction. Tax reduction had become inevitable. On June 7 at a press conference the President announced:

> A comprehensive tax reform bill which in no way overlaps the pending tax credit and loophole-closing bill offered a year ago will be offered for action by the next Congress, making effective as of January 1 of next year an across-the-board reduction in personal and corporate income tax rates which will not be wholly offset by other reforms—in other words, a net tax reduction.

He also kept open the possibility of a tax cut before January 1, 1963, saying:

> Of course, this is our best judgment at this time . . . if new circumstances brought a new situation, then we would have to make other judgments.[42]

What happened between the press conference of February 21 when Kennedy said there was "not a chance" and the press conference of June 7 when he promised "net tax reduction" in 1963 and possibly earlier was a change in economic conditions and prospects. The change in the underlying conditions was not dramatic. The unemployment rate, which had fallen from 6.7 percent in October, 1961, to 5.5 percent in March, 1962, levelled out and stayed there during the remainder of the second quarter, and indeed during the remainder of the year, standing at 5.6 percent in December. The rise in total output continued in the second quarter, but at a slower rate than in the previous year, and was less than the Council of Economic Advisers had forecast. The gap of actual output below potential increased slightly.

This rather minor lull in the pace of recovery was accompanied by one highly dramatic event. The stock market, which had been falling since March, on May 28 dropped "sickeningly," to recall Morgenthau's word of 1938. This in turn was related, at least in widespread public thinking, to a noisy public confrontation between the President and the steel industry over an increase in the price of steel.

Even when the stock market crash is added to the picture, the developments do not seem large enough by themselves to explain so prompt and eventually so strong a response. Although there were warnings of more trouble ahead, these by themselves were not so certain or so serious as to precipitate action. All that Kennedy's economists could tell him on June 6, the day before he announced that he would propose net tax reduction, was that "for the first time the prudent odds for a so-called 'Kennedy recession' . . . have ceased to be negligible."[43]

What made the difference was the fact that the pause in the economy and the worries about the future came after five years of economic slack in which the preceding recovery had stopped well short of full employment. The decision taken in June, 1962, to cut taxes was not a prompt response to a minor change and uncertain forecasts of further changes in the economy. It was a delayed response to a chronic condition after hopes of a spontaneous recovery were dimmed.

The need for action was heightened by the coincidence of the dispute with the steel companies and the stock market crash. The steel episode had left hostility on both sides—in business and in the administration—and a public picture of a degree of hostility between the two that probably exaggerated the facts. The stock market collapse was widely interpreted as being due to the lack of confidence of business in the administration. Even if this was not the cause of the decline in the market, the decline in the market certainly caused business unhappiness with the state of affairs. If there was to be a recession it would be a Kennedy recession not only in the sense that it began during his tenure in office but also in the sense that he was believed to have created it by laying violent hands on business.

On May 29, the day after the sharp decline in the stock market, President Kennedy met with Dillon, Heller, Martin, and others to consider what should be done to restore confidence and bolster the economy. Three possibilities were on the agenda. First, the President could address the nation on radio and television. This was rejected as probably being more alarming than reassuring. Second, the Federal Reserve might reduce margin requirements. It was agreed that this was not a fundamental solution and also that it was open to interpretation as a sign of alarm. The third was a prompt income tax cut. The Council of Economic Advisers wanted this unless the economy improved. Secretary Dillon opposed it unless the economy deteriorated. The President deferred a decision.[44]

The next week was a period of argument within the administration about the wisdom of tax reduction in relation to the domestic economic situation, in relation to foreign confidence and the international balance of payments, and in relation to domestic politics. It was also a period of testing the atmosphere outside the administration. Probably the main conclusion of the testing was that the way was clear. The President was known to be considering a tax reduction in violation of the budget-balancing taboo, and there was no storm of budget-balancing reaction. In fact there was evidence of support, or at least acquiescence, from some quarters usually believed to be strong-holds of budget-balancing.

The *Washington Post* reported on June 2:

> White House aides noted that during the stock market dives, the business com-munity was stressing that the remedy lies in tax cuts. Few businessmen were heard uttering cries like "Balance the Budget."
>
> This sentiment, it was said, has impressed Mr. Kennedy.[45]

A speech by Secretary Dillon on June 4, before a meeting of financial writers, acknowledged the existence of support outside the administration for tax reduction and provided a further test of the strength of that sup-port. He said:

> There has been growing talk in recent weeks of the desirability of income tax reductions as a stimulus to the economy. I, for one, am glad to hear such talk. To me, it portends a sympathetic reception to the overall income tax reform on which we have been working since last year, and which was first promised by the President in his tax reform message a year ago last April. This tax reform program will be ready for congressional action next January and we plan to submit its general outlines before the close of the present session. It will not be a hasty, ill-considered reaction to the gyrations of the stock market. Rather, it will be a fundamental restructuring of our income tax system, designed to pro-mote the maximum of long-term economic growth.
>
> Over the past year, I have frequently stated that the central element in this reform would be a proposal to readjust the rate structure of the income tax. I had not thought it necessary to spell out the fact that readjustment necessarily meant readjustment downward. But in case there is any misunderstanding, let me make clear that this is just what it means—a top-to-bottom reduction in the rates of income tax. Naturally, any reduction will cost the Government revenue, and will bring with it the need to broaden the base of our tax structure so as to offset the reductions in whole or in part.[46]

Although Dillon said that the tax reduction would be offset "in whole or in part," this was generally understood to be acceptance of net tax reduc-tion but not immediate tax reduction. The Democratic Congressional leader-ship applauded Secretary Dillon's tax cutting suggestions. Perhaps unaware that the country was about to embark on a new fiscal adventure, House Speaker McCormack said simply, "Congress is always receptive to this kind of proposal."[47]

On the day after Dillon's speech Henry Ford II indicated that he would not object to another deficit. Also, "A little bit of inflation is not going to hurt us," he said.[48]

When President Kennedy made his commitment to tax reduction at the June 7 press conference, he was, as Sorensen said, "seeking to give the nation more cause for confidence after the drop in the market and the pause in the economy, and seeking to answer *public pressures for a tax cut that summer*."[49] If the administration was entering into unexplored territory of economic policy, it was not entering it alone.

The President's June 7 statement did not specify the size of the net tax cut he would recommend. The figure commonly considered at the time was $3 billion. A tax reduction of that size would not have been in substance a radical departure of fiscal policy for an economy where federal revenues were normally growing by about $6 billion a year, and expenditures commonly grew as much. Still, even a reduction of $3 billion would have been symbolically significant. The tax cut would be made "in cold blood." Expenditure increases always have their reasons—to defend the country, improve the roads, care for the destitute of West Virginia, and so on. Such increases are regularly justified and made with the general economic state of the nation a secondary consideration. But a prime reason for the tax reduction would be economic stimulation.

However, once the President announced that he would propose across-the-board reduction of individual and corporate income taxes, a large net cut was inevitable. This was a matter of political arithmetic. The highest rate of individual income tax was than 91 percent. To make a cut in this rate which would have any value in strengthening business confidence and unleashing incentives would require reduction at least to 70 percent. Such a reduction in the top rate by itself would not cost much revenue. Reducing to 50 percent all the rates then in excess of that figure would cost about $500 million in annual revenue. But, of course, it was politically unthinkable to reduce the top bracket rates without reducing rates in the middle and especially the lower rates in approximately equal proportion. And since there were so many people in the middle and low brackets, even a small cut in their taxes would cost many billions. A reduction of one percentage point in the rate applied to the lowest income bracket would reduce the revenue by $1.2 billion. Moreover, the President had promised that the cut would extend also to corporate profits tax, and the logic of strengthening the economy and promoting growth required that it should. The corporate rate was 52 percent. Any reduction that did not get the rate down below 50 percent would have been economically insignificant and psychologically absurd. To reduce the rate to, say, 48 percent would cost about $2 billion. Therefore, once a start was made down the road of rate reduction it was hard to stop short of about $10 billion.

The only possibility of holding the net tax cut to the neighborhood of $3 billion was to accompany the rate reduction with major revenue-raising "reforms" or "loophole-closings." This was, indeed, the Treasury's intention. But each of these reforms would be unpopular with someone. The loopholes were not in the tax law by accident; someone had wanted them and the Congress had agreed. Once the President had proposed and promised rate reduction, and described it as terribly important, where would be the compulsion on Congress to enact the reforms? It could only be in the sentiment for balancing the budget. But this sentiment was not strong enough for the task. Therefore the administration, having opened the door, was led unavoidably to large net tax reduction.

Neither in June nor later was there any serious consideration of increasing federal expenditures. In 1961 this had been Kennedy's preferred route to economic expansion. In the summer of 1962 he still believed that there were unmet social needs much more important than the private needs that would be satisfied by tax reduction.[50] Still, in 1962 there was little debate over the relative merits of increasing spending or reducing taxes, except for some representations on the side of spending from J. K. Galbraith and from heads of spending departments.

If what was required was an immediate stimulus to the economy, tax reduction had a mechanical superiority over expenditure increase. If everyone agreed, tax reduction could put income into private hands in a matter of days and increase private expenditures substantially in a short period, whereas even if everyone agreed on increasing government expenditures the lag there would be much longer. But tax cutting remained the chosen route after attention had shifted from action immediately, in the summer of 1962, to action later, following January 1, 1963. The first reason for this was clearly that Congress would not approve a large increase of spending, except in a defense emergency, or at best would not approve it without a considerable fight. Congress in 1962 was already resisting many Kennedy proposals for higher spending. The second reason was that the situation was interpreted as requiring some move to strengthen business confidence, and what business wanted was tax reduction, not more spending.

In many ways 1962 was like 1937–38, except that this time the responses came more quickly and in answer to smaller signals. In 1962 as in 1937 there had been a premature move toward budget-balancing, accompanied by some monetary tightening. There had been a slowdown in the economy followed by a sharp slump in the stock market. In both cases there was a crisis of confidence between the administration and business. In both cases there was a conciliatory move by the administration. But at that point the paths diverged. Roosevelt made a concession to the traditional symbol of virtue—the balanced budget. But as a gesture to business this was ineffective, partly because Roosevelt couldn't deliver the balanced budget, but mainly because that wasn't what business really wanted. Kennedy offered what business had wanted in 1937–38 and still wanted in 1962—tax reduction.

THE BASIS FOR AGREEMENT

The Kennedy administration had felt itself inhibited in the pursuit of an expansive fiscal policy in 1961 by what it believed to be the budget-balancing ideology of the conservatives in the country, especially in the Congress. Why did it nevertheless embark on that course in 1962? One reason was that although economic conditions were actually better than in 1961, the economic outlook was worse, especially from the standpoint of the administration. Whereas the economy had been clearly rising in 1961, although at a low level, in 1962 there was danger of a decline which would be, moreover, a Kennedy recession. This danger increased the administration's willingness to take the risks of proposing a program which would expose it to the charge of fiscal irresponsibility. The danger of another recession, or of a long drawn-out failure to regain prosperity, was also much clearer to the rest of the country, including its conservative elements, and this might be expected to soften opposition to expansive measures.

However, an important additional reason which freed the administration in 1962 was the growing realization that the budget-balancing ideology was not an immovable barrier to fiscal stimulation. Of course the argument would be made, and some would be affected by it, but it would not stand in the way if other conditions were favorable. This was illustrated after the stock market drop in May when businessmen and other conservatives began to call for measures to restore confidence and invigorate the economy. As we have seen, the demand then was not for balancing the budget but for cutting taxes.

It is a fair generalization, subject to few exceptions, that conservatives, especially businessmen, not only want tax reduction, like almost everyone else, but place it higher on their agenda than almost anyone else. Except in wartime, tax reduction has been at or near the top of the list of recommendations in almost every statement of the national business organizations, such as the National Association of Manufacturers, the United States Chamber of Commerce, and the Committee for Economic Development. These recommendations emphasized reduction of particular taxes, notably the individual income tax rates in the upper brackets and the rates of corporate profits tax. But the proposed reductions were not confined to those taxes, and no one thought they could be.

Of course, these recommendations for tax reduction were usually coupled with recommendations that the budget should be balanced. The people who were most anxious for tax reduction would have preferred a balanced budget. But if it was necessary in order to achieve the tax reduction, they were prepared to accept a deficit, at least if it did not exceed a certain size and duration. The Congressional conservatives with business support had put through a tax reduction in 1938 although there was a deficit. They had fought for tax reduction in 1947 even though, on the official estimates, that would have caused a deficit in the next fiscal year. They had tried to reduce taxes in 1953 despite the deficit in hand and in prospect.

By 1962 the commandment to balance the budget was a paper tiger. The country had been through too many deficits without obvious ill effects to be shocked or frightened by more. Although Sorensen and Samuelson thought that the Eisenhower homilies had restored the budget-balancing fetish, his actions had spoken louder, and his $12.4 billion deficit of fiscal 1958 had set a new standard of orthodoxy by which his successors could, and did, measure themselves. And while few other than professional economists had any understanding of modern fiscal theory, there was a much wider appreciation that the whole subject had become very complicated, and that any general proposition about it was subject to many exceptions.

But still, in 1962 no one could be quite sure that the tiger was only paper, and that is what made Kennedy's decision to recommend tax reduction a major event in the history of fiscal policy. Aside from economists and a few other intellectuals, no public figure was prepared to omit obeisance to the idea of balancing the budget in some form. Everyone believed that others cared about it, and everyone wanted to identify himself with the idea and use it. This was particularly true of conservatives. They were fearful of the rising trend of expenditures and wanted to restrain it. They were also fearful of inflation, if not immediately then in the long run. They sought to preserve and appeal to what they believed was the budget-balancing sentiment in the country to achieve these two goals. They considered themselves weak politically and believed that if the restraint of the budget-balancing idea was further relaxed the result of the new freedom in fiscal policy would not be lower taxes but higher expenditures and more inflation. So they perpetuated the dogmatic invocation of budget-balancing and the uncertainty about what the country really wanted.

Although businessmen wanted tax reduction, and many were prepared to pay for it by increasing the deficit if that should be necessary, none said so before the President's decision. Their reluctance to say this is shown by the behavior of the CED whose general doctrine should have made them best prepared to take the step. The high-employment surplus in 1961 was higher than CED had ever said was necessary. Certainly the CED wanted tax reduction. Nothing would have been more consistent than to recommend that taxes be cut and as a consequence the high-employment surplus reduced. However, in the circumstances of 1961 and 1962, reducing the high-employment surplus would have meant increasing at least temporarily the actual deficit then in existence. Four times between May, 1961, and January, 1962, the CED walked up to the line of recommending that the high-employment surplus be reduced and that the actual deficit be increased, but it did not quite cross the line.

In a statement issued in May, 1961, the committee said: "However, in our current position greater stress should be placed upon possible adverse balance of payments effects of a combination of tax rates and expenditure programs that would yield a large surplus under conditions of high employment."[51]

The argument was that a large high-employment surplus held interest rates down and encouraged capital outflow. However, the statement did not specify the implications of this for 1961.

In the same month Mr. Howard C. Petersen, testifying on behalf of CED during the Ways and Means Committee's hearings on the 1961 tax revision bill, was more specific but quite tentative.

> The time may have at last arrived when we not only can stand but also require a permanent tax reduction. There have been several estimates that the existing tax system would, under conditions of high employment, yield a very large budget surplus, a surplus possibly so large as to endanger the attainment of high employment. . . . Certainly we take very seriously the possibility—and I emphasize that at the present stage of our study, I can only speak of a possibility—that a permanent tax reduction is required. Moreover, if it is desirable thorough consideration should be given to doing it now. There may be no reason to defer for a year the benefits of tax reduction, in the form of accelerated recovery and higher employment. In fact, this may be the time when we most need those benefits.[52]

Mr. Petersen promised to send the Ways and Means Committee a more definite statement on the subject from CED soon, but the statement was never sent. His reference was to a statement on fiscal and monetary policy for high employment on which the committee was then working. The analysis underlying the statement suggested that the large high-employment surplus had at least contributed to the economic slowdown of 1960, and the most obvious conclusion was that the high-employment surplus should be reduced. However, the committee did not come unequivocally to this conclusion. After much discussion a statement was issued which said:

> We cannot now tell with confidence what the relation between receipts and expenditures would be in calendar 1962 or fiscal 1963 under existing expenditure programs and tax rates at high employment. Much more information will be available on this point when the President submits his budget in January 1963. At that time the government should decide what is the high employment surplus at which it will normally aim. If the budget reveals the existence of a high employment surplus exceeding this target, our recommendation would call for a reduction of the surplus, preferably by tax reduction.[53]

Finally, T. O. Yntema, chairman of the CED Research and Policy Committee, made the statement to the Joint Economic Committee, which we have already quoted, raising the question whether the high-employment surplus might not be too large.

However reluctant they were to take the lead in saying that tax reduction within limits was more important than budget-balancing, the business community would be quick to follow after Kennedy took the lead. Of course, business was not the most direct opposition with which Kennedy would have to contend. The problem was how Congress would react to the idea of cutting taxes in the face of a deficit. But many conservative congressmen had the same scale of priorities as the businessmen. Indeed, the proportion of ritual observance in Congressional talk about budget-balancing was probably larger than in business organization talk. And even if they did not come to that conclusion on their own, there were few congressmen who would believe that the tax cut was morally, economically, and politically unsound if respectable leaders of business and finance said it was not.

The tax reduction became possible, and indeed inevitable, when two conditions existed simultaneously:

1. The administration wanted expansive fiscal action enough to subordinate its preference for expenditure increases and choose tax reduction as the route.

2. The conservatives saw the opportunity to get the tax reduction, which was what they wanted most, if they would forgo insistence on budget-balancing.

These two conditions existed in the summer of 1962 and produced agreement on the course of action—tax reduction. Behind this agreement on what to do lay a disagreement on how it would work and therefore on the reasons for doing it. One view was that the action which would stimulate the economy was a *reduction of taxes relative to expenditures, which involved an increase in the deficit.* The other view was that what would stimulate the economy was the reduction of tax rates; an increase in the deficit was a price that might have to be paid to get the tax reduction, but the effective action was the *tax reduction, not the increase in the deficit.*

Emphasis on the need to increase the deficit rested on the theory that the initial means by which tax reduction would stimulate the economy was increasing the flow of income. The reduction of taxes would leave more income in the hands of individuals and businesses to spend. The resulting increased private expenditure would stimulate the economy. However, if the reduction were matched by an equal reduction of government spending there would be no stimulating effect, because the gain in private after-tax income resulting from the tax reduction would be offset by the loss in private before-tax income resulting from the cut in government spending. Taxpayers would pay less, but on the other hand government suppliers and their employees would earn less. Indeed, the usual argument was that an equal reduction of taxes and government purchases would depress the economy because some of the additional income left in private hands by cutting taxes would not be spent.

The idea that cutting taxes would have a stimulating effect without an increase of the deficit rested on the theory that tax reduction would strengthen incentives to invest and to develop new products and thereby increase private expenditures and production even without a prior increase of income. This theory did not necessarily deny that a cut in government spending was by itself deflationary, but it did imply that a matching cut in taxes would have a more than offsetting effect, so that the net result would be a stimulus to the economy.

These two views were not mutually exclusive. One could believe that both processes were at work and that a tax reduction would be beneficial both if matched by an increased deficit and if matched by lower expenditures, up to some point. Both views were represented within the administration, with Council Chairman Heller tending to emphasize the effects of increasing private after-tax incomes and Secretary Dillon emphasizing the incentive effects. President Kennedy's exposition of the philosophy of the tax cut usually made both points. And while conservatives, especially the business spokesmen, tended to emphasize the incentive effects as distinguished from the income effects, this did not keep some of them from agreeing that an increase in the deficit, at least if temporary, was desirable.

What was important in 1962 was that, despite differences in analysis and perhaps in ultimate objectives, almost everyone could agree on the action to be taken. A large reduction in taxes, matched in part by restraint of expenditure increases and in part by an increase of the deficit, would satisfy the main interests. There would be differences of opinion about the proportions between restraining expenditures and increasing the deficit to pay for the tax cut. However, this was a matter of degree which could be negotiated, and while the negotiation might delay, it need not prevent the enactment of the tax cut.

THE APPEARANCE OF AGREEMENT

As we have already noted, while the underlying basis for agreement on tax reduction already existed, President Kennedy could not be sure of the extent of this agreement on June 7, 1962, when he made his commitment to tax reduction. However, during the months after this announcement the agreement became much clearer, and this contributed to the President's determination, which was not at first assured, to make a large cut of taxes the highest priority item on his legislative agenda for 1963. In the fall of 1962, according to Sorensen, "the President remained unenthusiastic, if not skeptical, about tax reduction. He still thought in terms of tax reform more than a tax cut for 1963. He was committed to no figure. He barely mentioned it in the mid-term campaign. . . . The President did not become fully enthusiastic until December, and it was the effect of one of his own speeches that helped convert him. The speech, designed to unveil the basic tax and budget outlines, was delivered to a conservative gathering of mostly Republican businessmen, the Economic Club of New York." After a favorable reception to his tax program from this conservative group, "The President's own enthusiasm grew."[54]

The favorable response given the speech to the Economic Club of New York confirmed earlier strong indications of support for tax reduction from the business community. One of the first of these had come from the Chamber of Commerce of the United States on June 29, 1962. Mr. Ladd Plumley, speaking for the chamber's committee on taxation, recommended an immediate tax reduction of about $8 billion and said:

> The Committee is not unmindful of the immediate impact of the rate reduction on the unbalance of the budget; but the Committee is convinced that the best hope and prospect for future balanced budgets and fiscal sanity lies in removing these tax deterrents to economic growth. . . . The tax cut must be substantial. Half way measures are futile. Further, all is not lost for with higher taxable income much is recouped. It is to be remembered that recessions cost money too. The

1957–58 recession resulted in a deficit of $12.5 billion. If successful this could be, by far, the least costly way to combat this problem.[55]

From this source this was, to some, shocking doctrine. Senator Harry F. Byrd accused the chamber of "fiscal irresponsibility," and an exchange of letters between him and Mr. Plumley followed. However, the chamber stood its ground. Mr. Plumley said: "To await the day when spending is cut, as propitious for reducing tax rates, may be to wait in vain."[56]

In November support for large tax reduction came from the President's Advisory Committee on Labor-Management Policy. This committee was the closest thing the United States had to an official voice of business, labor, and the "public." Its membership at the time included Henry Ford II, Thomas Watson, Jr., Joseph L. Block, George Meany, Walter Reuther, Arthur F. Burns, Clark Kerr, and others. The committee reported its views as follows:

> The main tool for promoting our economic objectives in 1963 should be a prompt and significant reduction in income tax rates.
>
> A majority of the Committee favors a reduction of about $10 billion early in 1963. Some members, however, would prefer to have specific legislation enacted which would provide that any such reduction be spaced over a two-to-three-year period. A few favor limiting tax reduction to $4,000,000,000 to $5,000,000,000 during the next year.
>
> It is important to note that a reduction in tax rates will not entail an equivalent decline in collections. Indeed, over the longer run, it may well generate increased tax revenues. But it should be recognized that in the near future, the significant tax reduction we recommend is likely to mean appreciable deficits in the Federal administrative budget.
>
> The built-in character of most Federal outlays militates against either a rapid expansion or absolute cut-back in expenditures for purposes of economic policy. Some Committee members feel, however, that expanding Federal expenditure programs can make a contribution to stimulating the economy. Other members feel that special efforts should be made to hold down Federal expenditures.[57]

While this statement reveals some disagreement about the size and timing of the cut, a majority of the committee recommended a larger cut for 1963 than the administration later proposed. News reports indicated that the divisions of opinion about the size of the immediate tax cut did not run along the line between business and labor.

The most thorough exposition of a business attitude to tax reduction was a statement released by the Committee for Economic Development on December 14, 1962, the morning of the day on which President Kennedy addressed the Economic Club of New York.[58] The CED recommended a tax reduction of $11 billion in two parts. One part—$6 billion—would be enacted immediately upon Congress' return to Washington to take effect on January 1, 1963. The other part—$5 billion—would be enacted when and if it became clear that expenditures for fiscal 1964 would be held at the level of fiscal 1963. The committee estimated that for fiscal 1963 the high-employment surplus with existing tax rates was about $6 billion. The $6 billion tax reduction would therefore leave the budget just in balance at high employment. It also estimated that revenues were rising by about $5 billion a year, so if expenditures could be kept from rising for one year another $5 billion of tax reduction would be consistent with keeping the high-employment budget in balance.[59] Thus the committee was recommending tax reduction of $11 billion to reduce the high-employment surplus by $6 billion and leave the high-employment budget in balance. The committee expressed the hope that tax reduction would stimulate investment sufficiently to make achievement of high employment consistent with running a surplus at high employment; however, at best this would take time and for the present it was better to eliminate the high-employment surplus. This, of course, meant that there would be an actual deficit until high employment was regained.

CED stressed the importance of reducing the rate of corporate profits tax in order to encourage private investment and recommended a rate cut from 52 percent to 42 percent. However, it recognized that the response of private investment to tax reduction would not be immediate and also that the size of the response was uncertain. Partly for these reasons it recommended that there should also be a general reduction of individual income taxes, which it was believed would have a quicker and surer effect upon the economy. The committee warned against trying to combine rate reduction with revenue-raising reforms, which would certainly delay enactment of the tax cut. In the committee's opinion, tax reduction was the best tax reform.

The CED statement released on the morning of December 14 clearly represented the conservative compromise. The hearts of the CED members belonged to reduction of the corporate profits tax and of the upper-bracket individual income taxes, coupled with restraint of federal spending. But they knew that for political reasons, and perhaps also for good economic reasons, the package would also have to include reduction of income taxes across the board and increased deficits, and they were willing to accept that.

The Kennedy speech delivered to the Economic Club of New York on the evening of December 14 clearly revealed the liberal compromise. While referring to the effect of tax reduction in increasing available incomes, he stressed its effect in strengthening investment incentives, which encouraged his hearers to expect favorable treatment of corporate profits and higher individual incomes in the tax bill. He promised reduction of non-defense spending of the federal government, emphasized his own interest in balancing the budget, and held out the vision of tax reduction as the surest route to budget-balancing.[60] The speech was well received both by the audience present that evening and by the press the next day. This reception, as we have noted above, impressed Kennedy as to both the economic importance and the political charms of the tax reduction program.

McKinley, Hoover, Keynes, and Heller

After his Economic Club speech Kennedy called Heller to say, "I gave them straight Keynes and Heller, and they loved it."[61] But while agreeing that they had loved it, Sorensen had a different view of what it had been. He later said of the speech. "It sounded like Hoover, but it was actually Heller."[62] Heller also accepted this view. He cited the Economic Club speech and Sorensen's comment on it as evidence for a more general proposition: "In the search for consensus on responsible use of fiscal and monetary powers to achieve growth and stability, both Presidents [Kennedy and Johnson] recognized that it was necessary to make concessions to popular economic ideology and precepts. Their responsibilities as national leaders did not permit them to wait until the economic intelligence gap had been closed. So they drew on what Norton Long calls "the great psychological assets of sailing under the familiar colors."[63]

But the Economic Club speech was not a case of the administration selling the conservatives liberal Keynes-and-Heller doctrine, either "straight" or "under the familiar colors," presumably the colors of Herbert Hoover. That Kennedy, Sorensen, and Heller thought it was reflected their belief that their main issue with the conservatives related to budget-balancing and Keynesianism. They thought that by using Hoover-like language about incentives, the burden of taxes, and economy in government they had persuaded the opposition to relax its resistance to expansive fiscal policy. But by 1962 this was not the issue, at least not with the conservatives of the business community to be found in the Economic Club of New York. The issue was tax reduction, particularly reduction of those taxes which affected the return from investment most directly, and expenditure restraint as a means to future tax reduction. In these terms Kennedy's audience at the Economic Club was getting not only some congenial language but also some real benefits.

Professor (at that time Ambassador) J. K. Galbraith did not think the issue was the old one of deficits and Keynesianism. It will be recalled from

Chapter 11 that in 1955 Galbraith recognized how far the Eisenhower administration had gone in accepting Keynesian economics, and that Walter Heller thought Galbraith exaggerated. For Galbraith the issue was the level and rate of growth of public spending, and he identified the liberal Democratic position with high spending. From that standpoint, he called the Economic Club speech "the most Republican speech since McKinley."[64]

Galbraith may have gone too far; Mellon might have been a better reference than McKinley. But certainly there was a great deal of conservative philosophy—of Mellon and Hoover—in the Economic Club speech as there was in the tax reduction policy itself. There was also a good deal of newer doctrine in it—of the flexible use of fiscal policy to achieve high employment. It was this marriage that produced the tax cut.

ꞔ17ꞕ

Enacting the Tax Cut of 1964

THE tax reduction promised by President Kennedy on June 7, 1962, was signed into law by President Johnson on February 26, 1964. At no time was the enactment of a large tax cut seriously in doubt. The delay resulted from the need to resolve a number of other issues, especially about the tax reforms that would be included in the tax revision package and about the federal expenditure levels that would accompany the tax cut. The delay, the discussion that went on during it, and the outcome all reveal the complexity of the considerations that entered into the decision. These considerations were not only the "new economics" of full employment and the old Puritan ethic of balancing the budget, but also the old Mellon philosophy of reducing taxes to stimulate economic growth, the ageless divisions of opinion about the scale of government activity and expenditures, the desire of taxpayers for tax reduction, and the desire of politicians to obtain credit as donors of tax reduction.

A "QUICKIE" TAX CUT?

For about two months in the summer of 1962 there seemed to be a possibility that tax reduction would take effect very soon, well before the January 1, 1963, date for which the President had promised it. In fact, the President's own statement of June 7, 1962, indicated that under some circumstances he would ask for an immediate tax cut. However, those circumstances never came.

The tax reduction that Kennedy and his advisers considered on May 29, the day after the stock-market crash, was a "quickie." As applied to tax reduction the word "quickie" of course means that the reduction should be enacted and put into effect quickly. It also often has the implication that the tax cut will be temporary. In the summer of 1962 there was confusion about whether the quickie under discussion was to be temporary or not. According to Sorensen, the quickie that was considered in the White House on May 29 was to be temporary. "It was to apply to both individuals and corporations, and last one year or even less."[1] Heller describes the 1962 "quickie tax cut" idea a little differently—"a temporary cut in 1962 to serve as the first installment of the basic tax reduction required to remove fiscal drag."[2] This suggests that while there was to be permanent tax reduction, the quickie proposed for 1962 might not necessarily be part of it. By 1962 a quick, temporary tax cut was the traditional means for dealing with a recession, if an idea can become traditional without ever having been tried. President Kennedy had asked Congress to give him authority to make a temporary tax cut in a recession, and although Congress showed no sign of giving it this influenced the picture of what a quickie cut meant. Professor Samuelson told the President in July that a majority of economists inside and outside the government believed a temporary emergency tax cut was needed to prevent a recession.[3]

But there was nothing in the administration's thinking in 1962 to suggest that tax reduction should be temporary. The problem, as Kennedy and the Council of Economic Advisers had said repeatedly, was that taxes were too high relative to expenditures and that the excess grew too rapidly as the economy grew. If tax reduction was the remedy at all, the reduction would have to be permanent. In fact, there would have to be repeated tax reductions unless the rate of increase of government spending was accelerated. Still, the idea persisted that what was under consideration in the summer of 1962 was a temporary tax cut. This confusion tended to weaken enthusiasm for immediate tax reduction. Those who sought the incentive-creating effects of tax reduction on investment had little interest in a temporary tax cut. If businessmen were to be induced to invest more by the promise that they would be allowed to retain a larger share of the profits after tax, a tax reduction that would expire before most of the profits from the investment had been earned would not be effective.

However, the main issue was whether there should be a quick tax cut, whether permanent or not. A great deal of support for this idea arose in June and July. Secretary Hodges, Senators Humphrey, Javits, Keating, and Case, many congressmen, the AFL-CIO, the U.S. Chamber of Commerce, *The New York Times*, *The Washington Post*, and innumerable economists were all on that side. Dire consequences were predicted if taxes were not cut quickly. Walter Lippmann's opinions were typical of many. "Tax reduction is something which we must have if we are to avoid very serious consequences not only to business and employment and to our standard of life but also to our position in the world." The Congressional committees would take a year to agree on tax reform. "But tax reduction cannot wait a year. All the indications are that if tax reduction to reflate the economy is put off until next year the trouble will be so serious that much more drastic measures will be needed." The tax cut had to be substantial; otherwise it would "discredit the medicine without preventing the disease." Lippmann said that a conservative estimate was that the tax cut should be at least $10 billion.[4]

As we have seen, President Kennedy's June 7 promise that taxes would be reduced in 1963 was intended in part to respond to public pressures for an immediate tax cut. But if the administration was willing to commit itself to a tax reduction taking effect at the beginning of 1963, there was no economic reason for not making the cut immediately, say on July 1, 1962. Still, the President was reluctant to recommend tax reduction in 1962 and finally closed off discussion of the question with a television and radio address to the nation on August 13. This was not because he doubted that tax reduction in 1962 would be a good thing. He did think a tax cut would be useful. Why then did he not recommend it?

In his address of August 13 the President said:

> Timing is of the essence, and in the absence of a clear and present danger to the American economy today I believe the American people are willing to bear the burdens of freedom and progress, to face the facts of fiscal responsibility and to share my view that proposing an emergency tax cut tonight, *a cut which could not now be either justified or enacted*, would needlessly undermine confidence at home and abroad.[5]

Sorensen later explained the significance of this sentence:

> The operative words, which are italicized, satisfied both sides within the ranks of his advisers. Those opposed to the temporary tax cut agreed with his judgment that it could not be justified, and those favoring it accepted his judgment that it could not be enacted.[6]

Both Kennedy's words and Sorensen's explanation of them raise the question of what Kennedy himself thought. One view of the issue of 1962 is Heller's:

> Yet there was many a thorn among the roses in the summer of 1962. Logic called for immediate fiscal action to overcome persistent economic slack and, more urgently, to deal with the unexpected slowdown of recovery in mid-1962. But political barriers did not succumb readily to the force of economic logic. Kennedy was persuaded that he could not get swift action from a Congress still

bound in large part by the very mythology he had attacked at Yale. So our hopes for a "quickie tax cut"—a temporary cut in 1962 to serve as the first installment of the basic tax reduction required to remove fiscal drag—had to give way to his commitment to act in 1963.[7]

Sorensen, however, does not draw so dramatic a contrast between Kennedy, economics, and logic on the one hand and Congress, politics, and mythology on the other. He asks the question and gives his own answer:

> Did Kennedy really want a quickie tax cut in 1962 which the Congress prevented him from obtaining? Its advocates thought so. The press said so. But, having taken part in all the meetings, my own judgment is that he, too, was unconvinced that a temporary cut at that time was essential, as distinguished from merely being helpful, in the absence of that overwhelming evidence that was required to get the bill through. "We want to be convinced," he told a news conference questioner, "that the course of action we are advocating is essential before we advocate it."[8]

In the summer of 1962, as we have seen in the previous chapter, the President and the Congress, liberals and conservatives, were all in favor of tax reduction. Moreover, the various parties were willing to concede enough —with respect to the character of the tax changes and with respect to the accompanying expenditure policy, which also meant deficit policy—to make agreement on tax reduction possible. However, to test out the interests and power of parties and discover the terms of an acceptable tax reduction would take time. It actually took a year, from January, 1963, until January, 1964. Even with the widespread agreement on tax reduction which existed in the summer of 1962, this agreement on the specific form of action could not have been reached quickly without much more compulsion to speed than existed at the time.

Advocates of a quick tax cut in a recession had always recognized that the cut would have to be of a simple and apparently neutral character, such as an across-the-board income tax reduction, if enactment of the cut was not to be excessively delayed by argument about who should get the benefits of the tax reduction. This was probably the only kind of tax reduction that could have been quickly enacted in the summer of 1962, if for no other reason, because of the practical difficulties of considering and reaching agreement on anything more complicated. But many of the key people whose approval was necessary were unwilling to settle for anything like that in order to get tax reduction promptly, even though they were for tax reduction.

Within the administration itself there was no agreement on the kind of tax reduction they would ask for if they were to ask for quick action. The shelf of tax reduction ideas which Walter Heller had recommended in 1957 did not exist in 1962. Rather there was an attic full of tax reduction and tax reform ideas from which the administration had not yet made a selection. The Kennedy Treasury had been building up a program of tax reforms, including revenue-raising, loophole-closing measures, which it intended to present to Congress at the first opportunity. The Treasury's plan was to submit its tax reforms in a package which would also include rate reduction in the hope that the popularity of the rate reduction would carry through the less popular reforms. The Treasury was unwilling to give up this plan and recommend a simple rate reduction in 1962 to obtain quick action against the recession.

There was in the Congress a similar unwillingness to subordinate tax reform to quick tax reduction. The desire of Mr. Wilbur Mills, chairman of the House Ways and Means Committee, was most important. What kinds of tax reforms Mr. Mills wanted never became clear; it became apparent in 1963 that his and the Treasury's wishes were not the same. In any case, he was not prepared to defer and possibly lose the chance for a thorough review of the tax structure in order to push through a quickie. This is the almost inevitable view of the chairman of the Ways and Means Committee. Quick tax action generally means an opportunity for Congress to vote yes or no on an administration proposal, and this downgrades the power of the committee chairman. Furthermore, even if the administration and Mr. Mills had come to terms on omitting tax reform or on adopting an agreed program of tax reform, there was another group, mainly in the Senate, who probably would not have agreed. These were the liberals, like Senators Douglas and Gore, who wanted a much more radical package of tax revisions than Dillon and Mills would have been likely to accept; and while they could not get their way they could cause a considerable delay. On the other hand, while the business community was generally in favor of a prompt and simple tax reduction, there was some fear among them that too much emphasis on promptness might require too much simplicity. Specifically, they feared that if a tax reduction was made under extreme time pressure it could only consist of a flat reduction of the individual income tax, in which case their objectives of reducing the corporate profits tax and very substantially reducing the upper-bracket individual income tax rates would be lost.[9]

In addition to the question of the character of the tax reduction there was another issue which would have had to be subordinated if quick action was to be taken. That was the issue of expenditure policy. Many of the supporters of tax reduction also wanted to slow down the rate of growth of federal spending. This did not necessarily require that the slowdown of spending be equal in amount to the tax reduction, but it required some concessions on the expenditure side of the budget. Moreover, President Kennedy was willing to make some concessions on that side to get the tax reduction through. But the economizers wanted to withhold their support of tax reduction as long as possible in order to force the President to trim the expenditures, and the President wanted to resist as long as possible in the hope of forcing the economizers to vote on tax reduction, which in the end they could hardly vote against. Each side needed time to test how far it could go.

If the economic situation had been critical and generally recognized as such, these obstacles to speed might have been overcome. But the situation was not that critical, or at least—which is more important—the President and the Congressional leadership did not think it was. As Sorensen said, the President did not think that a quick tax cut was "essential, as distinguished from being merely helpful."

The situation was complicated by the imminence of the Congressional elections in November, 1962. The administration could not expect quick action on taxes unless it claimed, or at least conceded, that the economy was in serious straits—an uncomfortable admission to make just before an election, especially when enough time has passed to prevent placing all the blame on the preceding administration. If the administration requested quick tax reduction and Congress failed to act before the election, the picture would be even worse because the administration would have conceded the bad shape of the economy and demonstrated its inability to get a Democratic Congress to take the measures it considered necessary. Moreover, Congress also did not want to get into the hornet's nest of deciding who got how much tax reduction only a few months before election. And if Congress adjourned without passing the tax bill the whole effort would have been for nothing, and the legislative process would have to start over again in 1963.[10]

Kennedy was looking, during the summer of 1962, for a sign that the economic situation was so urgent as to require him to push for a quickie despite all the disadvantages. The sign never came. After a number of meetings in early July with economists, businessmen, and Congressional leaders it was announced that a decision would be deferred until August when the economic statistics for July would be available. This was like Eisenhower in 1958 waiting for the March figures, and, as in Eisenhower's case, the figures when they came were not so dramatic as to overcome an aversion to quick action.

Kennedy was also looking that summer for a sign on the political front. Was there enough demand in the country for quick action so that he could

not afford to delay, or more realistically, was there enough support in the
Congress and in the country to put across an acceptable tax cut quickly and
without an embarrassing fight? The key here was Congressman Mills, chairman of the Ways and Means Committee; the administration could get
nowhere without him. Mills wanted to test opinion and sentiment and called
a series of closed hearings beginning on July 26 at which about forty witnesses
appeared. A large proportion of the witnesses were from business and finance,
although some labor people and unattached economists also appeared. While
the hearings were not published, the views of enough witnesses became
known to make the general burden of the evidence clear. That was that
taxes should be cut, and although a few of the witnesses favored immediate action, the more common opinion was that there was no emergency
requiring enactment of the tax cut before the beginning of 1963. The hearings did not overcome Mr. Mills' objections to a quickie. Also in the latter
part of July Senator Humphrey polled the Democratic membership of the
Senate and discovered that only a bare majority favored an immediate tax
cut. Humphrey himself was for it and believed that Kennedy's leadership
could get it through the Congress.[11] However that was not Kennedy's
question, and Humphrey's evidence strengthened the fear that quick action
could only be obtained with a fight, if at all.

On the basis of this review of the economic and political situation, the
President abandoned the idea of a quickie tax cut and announced that decision in his address of August 13. The state of national policy on this subject
was about what it had been in 1958. The possible value of an emergency tax
cut in a recession was widely recognized. At the same time the cut was believed to entail serious risks, especially with respect to the future shape of the
tax structure. Therefore the tax cut would not be undertaken unless the
immediate economic situation was grave. Neither the conditions of 1958
nor the conditions of 1962 met the test.

SHAPING THE ADMINISTRATION'S TAX CUT PACKAGE

Once the question of a quickie tax cut had been answered in the negative, the administration and the country could get down to the business of
considering the tax proposals to be made early in 1963 as promised by the
President. We have already referred to the fact that the President himself did
not pay a great deal of attention to taxation during the fall of 1962, apparently not foreseeing the significance which historians—mainly members of
his staff—would later find in the tax cut. Of course there were distractions,
such as the Cuban missile crisis and the November Congressional elections.

Kennedy's campaign speeches before the elections did not highlight the tax issue or give a very clear idea of what the issue was. His most extended reference to taxation during the campaign was made in a speech in Cincinnati on October 5 when he said:

> We go back in January to write a new tax bill. Is that tax bill going to be a bill which takes care of a few people, or are we going to write a tax bill which will give this economy sufficient stimulus to move it ahead and not have a recession in 1963? That's why this campaign is important, and that's why we're here to-night.[12]

However, while the President was not yet personally involved, the Treasury, the Council of Economic Advisers, and the Budget Bureau were actively engaged in preparing the tax package for submission in January. At the same time, all the people outside of government who hoped to influence tax policy were developing their positions, trying to affect the decisions made within the administration and getting ready to react to whatever the administration finally proposed.

By this time, whether or not there would be a tax cut was no longer an issue. There were four questions to be answered:

1. How big should the net tax cut be—how much revenue reduction after allowing for the effect of revenue-increasing reforms?

2. What should be the composition of the tax reduction and reform package—how much cut in corporate tax rates, how much cut in individual rates in different brackets, which structural reforms?

3. How big should the net change in the fiscal position—the deficit or surplus—be? This adds to the question of the size of the net tax cut the question of the size of the expenditure increase.

4. How should the tax and expenditure changes be scheduled?

The answers to these questions depended upon a number of interrelated economic and political considerations. The tax cut had to be large enough to provide some benefits for all of the groups whose support would be necessary to get the cut enacted and to offset the distaste of some taxpayers for the kinds of reforms the Treasury wanted. The tax cut and the net change in the fiscal position should be large enough to give the economy a substantial boost toward full employment but not large enough to raise a serious danger of inflation. The net change in the fiscal position should not be so large, or apparently so permanent, as to rouse or justify strong opposition on budget-balancing grounds. The expenditure policy should reconcile interests for and against particular programs as well as concerns about the long-range trend of federal expenditures in total.

While in the end there had to be a simultaneous solution to all the questions in terms of all the considerations, a fairly general consensus on the size of the net tax cut was reached first, and the other decisions were accommodated to that. As soon as the President opened the door to tax reduction in June of 1962, claims for tax relief began to emerge from many quarters. There were two main kinds of suggestions—the investment-oriented proposals mainly originating from business and the consumption-oriented proposals mainly originating from labor. The investment-oriented proposals emphasized cutting the corporate profits tax and the upper-bracket individual income taxes. Since the bases of these taxes were relatively small, significant cuts could be made in the rates without much loss of revenue. But everyone knew there was not the slightest chance of achieving such tax reductions unless they were balanced with reductions for the lower-bracket taxpayers. The balanced programs turned out to be much more expensive than the particular tax revisions which were their apparent main object. Thus the U.S. Chamber of Commerce statement of June, 1962, argued almost entirely for the advantages of reducing corporate and upper-bracket individual income taxes.[13] The proposals it made for these parts of the tax structure would have reduced the revenue by less than $3 billion a year. However the total package recommended by the chamber, including major cuts in lower-bracket individual income taxes, was variously estimated to cost from $7.5 to $9.5 billion. Similarly the program of the CED had as its centerpiece a ten-point cut in the rate of corporate profits tax, which would have cost about $5 billion, but its total program would have reduced the revenues by $11 billion.[14]

The labor organizations felt no need on economic, political, or other grounds for a balanced tax package including concessions for corporations and upper-bracket individuals. Their tax proposals were concentrated about as exclusively as was technically feasible on relief for lower-income individuals.[15] However the numbers of people and amounts of income and tax in the lower brackets were so large that any show of generosity there would cost a great deal of revenue.

Such calculations and considerations led to convergence, in the fall of 1962, on $10 billion as the size of a tax cut within which the main taxpaying parties would be reasonably confident of a favorable outcome. Labor and business would each still feel that it had not obtained a fair share of tax reduction, but satisfaction with the absolute amount would outweigh dissatisfaction with the share. The clearest evidence of this convergence was the recommendation of a $10 billion tax cut by the President's Advisory Committee on Labor-Management Policy which included business, labor, and public members, on November 19.[16]

Within the administration also, this kind of bargaining consideration—this calculation of the size and character of tax reduction that would satisfy the main parties—was influential. The President's speech of August 13 had promised that he would recommend an across-the-board cut of income tax rates, both individual and corporate. By September this was understood within the government to mean as a first approximation something like reduction of the corporate rate from 52 percent to 47 percent and reduction of individual income tax rates from the existing 20 to 91 percent schedule to a 15 to 65 percent schedule.[17] So the administration also was thinking of rate reduction amounting to around $10 billion.

However, this did not settle the issue. Unlike the business and labor groups, the Treasury was interested in a list of revenue-raising reforms which could be extended to almost any desired size and thus hold down the net tax reduction in any desired degree. The decision on a fairly large across-the-board rate reduction did not necessarily imply for the Treasury a net tax cut as big as $10 billion. And the Treasury was not initially enthusiastic about a large net cut. After all, as recently as March, 1962, the Secretary of the Treasury had said:

> Those who reject our concept of tax reform to be achieved largely through a broadening of the tax base and urge instead massive reduction in tax rates, without any provision for compensating revenue—are simply refusing to recognize that such a course would leave us no alternative but withdrawal from our world commitments and neglect of our pressing needs at home—a course that would be entirely unacceptable.[18]

As late as June the Secretary was still considering the possibility that the revenue loss from rate reduction would be wholly offset by revenue gains from reforms. Around the time the President, in his statement of June 7, was committing the administration to net tax reduction, newspaper guesses of what the administration had in mind came to a net tax cut of $2 or $3 billion.[19] In the discussions within the administration the Treasury did not become the committed advocate of any particular figure for the size of the net tax cut. Its main interest was in the reform package and in the amount of net tax reduction necessary to "sweeten" the reforms and get them through the Congress. However, the general influence of the Treasury was in the direction of keeping the net tax cut small.

Inside the administration the main proponent of a net cut around $10 billion was the Council of Economic Advisers. The council arrived at this figure by a calculation of the amount of net tax reduction that was necessary to get the economy promptly up to full employment. At the end of 1962 the council estimated that total production was running about $30 billion below its potential and that a tax cut of about $10 billion, reducing the full-employment surplus by that amount, would approximately close the gap. The council's calculations assumed that government spending would be rising at about the same rate as the natural increase of revenues resulting from economic growth, so that if there were no tax cut the full-employment surplus would be stable.

Walter Heller later described this element in the council's thinking:

> On the basis of observed stable relationships between disposable income and consumption, together with not-so-stable investment relationships, the Administration spelled out how the proposed cut would multiply itself into an increment of GNP that could "close or nearly close, the gap between potential and actual output . . ."[20]

Heller's quotation about closing the gap is from his own testimony before the Joint Economic Committee on January 28, 1963. In fact, while that testimony did spell out the process by which the tax cut was expected to multiply itself into an increment of GNP, it was vague and tentative about the numbers involved.[21] The general argument would have been consistent with a tax cut much larger or much smaller than the one the administration was proposing. This failure to spell out more precisely the quantitative model from which the council predicted the consequences of the tax reduction may have been due to the failure of the President to recommend the tax program which the council derived from its quantitative analysis. However, within the administration in the fall of 1962 the council was arguing strongly for a net tax cut in the neighborhood of $10 billion on the basis of an estimate that about $10 billion was the necessary amount for getting up to full employment.

The council supported the $10 billion cut on another basis also, that such a cut would leave the full-employment budget approximately in balance. Thus Heller said later: "The tax cut was also designed to bring the high-employment surplus—which had been reduced to $6 1/2 billion in 1962 but grew to over $11 billion [by the end of 1963] while Congress was debating the tax cut—down to, or close to, zero."[22] In previous use of the full-employment surplus the council had described it as an approximate index of the degree of restrictiveness or expansiveness of the budget, without any implication that it was good for the surplus to be zero. However, in the fall of 1962 the council, in discussions within the administration, did use the fact that a $10 billion tax cut would still leave the full-employment budget balanced as an argument in favor of it.[23]

Later, when the time came to explain and defend the tax reduction program of the administration, the council did not rely on the fact that it would leave the full-employment budget in balance. The January, 1963, economic report, unlike that of a year earlier, presented no estimates of the full-employment surplus. Mr. Heller did not mention the concept in his testimony before the Joint Economic Committee until he was asked about it by Congressman Curtis, at which point he said that there would still be a small full-employment surplus at the end of 1964 if the tax program were adopted.

In any case, the council's economic calculations were a major influence in the administration's decision to recommend a net tax cut of about $10 billion. The council's economic calculations and the bargaining calculations being made outside the government reinforced each other. The fact that many private groups had come out for a tax cut of around $10 billion enabled the council to say not only that $10 billion fit into its models, but also that $10 billion was the figure the private sector had come to expect and would support. At the same time, knowledge that the council was pushing for a $10 billion cut encouraged those outside to develop programs up to that size.

Acceptance of approximately $10 billion as the proper size of the net tax cut left problems about the timing of the tax cut and about the expenditure program to go with it. Both inside the administration and out these were partly budget-balancing questions. Many of the conservatives outside the administration who urged a prompt $10 billion tax cut accepted and used the argument that tax reduction would in the end increase the revenues and bring the time of budget-balancing closer. They also accepted the fact that the process would involve an increase in the deficit in the interim. They were, however, concerned about the size of this interim increase of the deficit. Moreover they were strongly in favor of restraint of expenditures, partly because of opposition to specific expenditure programs and partly because they hoped for more tax reduction later. In fact, one of their main reasons for supporting a large tax cut was to limit and forestall the growth of expenditures. Their proposal, therefore, was to accompany the tax cut with restraint of expenditures below the levels to which they would otherwise be growing.

Within the administration also there was concern with the size of the interim increase of the deficit that would result from the tax cut. In part, at least in the Treasury, the reasons for this were economic. Secretary Dillon later explained the decision to spread the tax cut over three years by saying that to do it more quickly would risk inflation at home and endanger the stability of the dollar abroad.[24] Heller also later defended the program against the criticism that it should have been bigger or quicker by referring to possible inflationary consequences of overstimulating the economy. However, it is clear that he did not regard the program recommended by the administration as coming close to the limit of economic safety.[25]

In fact, the administration's decision about the timing of the tax cut and about the expenditure policy that should accompany it was made by Kennedy and made essentially on political grounds. The tax cut had to be part of a package that could get through Congress and that would not unnecessarily and excessively expose the President to the much-feared charge of fiscal irresponsibility. As a standard of what that meant the views of Congressman Wilbur Mills were most important. Being chairman of the Ways and Means Committee, he was the most powerful man in the Congress on tax matters. More than that, he both represented and led conservative thinking in the Congress and in the country. The Treasury had consulted him in the fall of 1962—Undersecretary Fowler had gone to Arkansas to visit him—and the administration tried to adapt its program to his wishes. The most extensive publication of Mr. Mills' views appeared in an interview in *U.S. News and World Report* in December. This interview was widely interpreted as being extremely negative on tax reduction, and the President was asked about this at his news conference of December 12.

> QUESTION: Mr. President, has the opposition expressed by Chairman Wilbur Mills of the Ways and Means Committee changed the administration's position on tax cuts that it has proposed for next year?
>
> PRESIDENT: Well, I think that Mr. Mills' interview should be read in entirety. And if you read the entire article, it does not suggest that the administration, under some circumstances, and Mr. Mills may be so far apart. In fact, I'm going to see Congressman Mills today.[26]

Read carefully in its entirety, the interview did reveal the conditions on which agreement with Mr. Mills might be possible. The tax cut should not be a quickie intended to take effect on January 1, 1963. It should not be made "without regard" to the deficit. It should not be justified by the current economic situation "alone." There must be evidence of better control of rises in expenditures and preferably some reduction, but not necessarily a reduction as big as the tax reduction. The tax rate cut should be balanced in part by revenue-raising reforms.[27]

The President tried to meet these conditions, not only because they were Wilbur Mills' but also because they were believed to have much support in the country. The President insisted that his tax and budget program should meet three tests.[28] Total expenditures for fiscal 1964 should not exceed $100 billion, lest transgressing that figure should give color to the belief that the budget was out of control. Total spending, excluding expenditures for defense, space, and interest, should decline between 1963 and 1964, the nearest the administration could come to "some reduction" in expenditures and a token of intention to keep expenditures under restraint so that with growth of the economy the budget would come into balance. Finally, the budget for fiscal 1964 should have a deficit smaller than the $12.4 billion deficit Eisenhower had in fiscal 1959. This was considered to be a talisman against charges of fiscal irresponsibility, any Eisenhower deficit being, by association, prudent. In subsequent explanations of his program Kennedy returned again and again to the idea that he was going to incur a smaller deficit in his positive effort to sustain economic growth than Eisenhower incurred as a consequence of failure to avoid a recession.

Even with expenditures held below $100 billion—the budget figure was $98.8 billion—there was only one way to reconcile the $10 billion tax cut with the Eisenhower-deficit standard of fiscal prudence. This was to put the cut into effect in stages so that only a small part of the revenue loss would be felt in fiscal 1964 and the full effect not until 1966. By that time it was hoped, the economy would have expanded sufficiently to yield a balanced budget, or at least a much smaller deficit, with the full tax reduction in force. Congressman Mills' condition that part of the revenue loss from rate reduction should be offset by tax reforms had of course been part of the administration's plan from the outset. The program submitted by the President in January, 1963, called for $13.6 billion gross of revenue reduction, mainly from rate reduction, and $3.4 billion of revenue increase from reforms. The decision to include a major package of reforms also took care of another of Mills' conditions—that the tax bill should not be a quickie to go into effect on January 1, 1963. The administration's proposal was that the first step of tax reduction should occur on July 1, 1963.

The administration wanted to keep the interim deficit below some conventional limit—the size of the maximum Eisenhower deficit—and was willing to defer some of the tax cut until the beginning of 1964 and some until the beginning of 1965 in order to do that. In this the administration differed from the typical position of business which wanted to make the whole tax cut promptly and limit the interim deficit by more restraint of expenditures. In the end the program included some of each—more postponement of tax reduction than business wanted and more reduction or postponement of expenditures than the administration initially included in its plans.

The administration's proposals to make the tax cut effective in steps extending until January 1, 1965, and hold down the growth of expenditures were major departures from the program the Kennedy economists derived from their economic analysis. They meant that instead of a sharp reduction in the full employment surplus approximately to zero early in 1963 there would be a gradual reduction that would not eliminate the surplus until the beginning of 1965. In fact the first step of tax reduction was delayed until January 1, 1964, and expenditures were more severely restricted than had been initially contemplated. As a result the full-employment surplus rose through 1963 and at the end of 1963 was as high as when Kennedy took office. Even in the first half of calendar 1965, when the 1964 tax cut was fully in effect, the full-employment surplus was at an annual rate in excess of $7 billion as compared with $9 billion in the second half of 1962 before the tax bill was introduced. The full-employment surplus was finally reduced to zero in the second half of 1965 by a cut of excise taxes and by an upsurge of federal spending, partly associated with the Vietnam War.

THE ISSUES

The President announced and explained his tax program in four messages in January, 1963—the state of the Union message, the budget message, the economic report, and a special message on taxation. The emphasis was no longer, as it had been in the summer of 1962, on the danger of an imminent economic decline. The economy was rising and the object of the tax program was to insure and accelerate continuation of the rise. This would be done by removing the drag caused by an excessively burdensome wartime tax structure which both siphoned off purchasing power and stifled incentives to invest and produce. Tax reduction would promote the expansion of production, employment, and incomes, thereby raising the revenues despite the reduction of the tax rates. It was the best and probably the only route to a balanced budget.

The immediate reaction indicated clearly the lines which the debate and the bargaining were to take in the next year. Everyone was for the rate reductions. There was much opposition to the revenue-raising reforms and little support for them. There were many protests about failure to prevent expenditures from rising when tax reduction was so badly needed.

From the beginning there was little doubt that a substantial tax cut would be enacted, although the timing and the fate of the reforms were in doubt. Before any of the President's messages, *Business Week* reported, "Whether the tax bill gets through Congress this year at all—or takes two years to pass—is still a large question. Mills (Chairman of Ways and Means Committee) himself is on record as doubting that action can come soon enough to make cuts effective before Jan. 1, 1964."[29] After the budget message, which revealed the spacing of the tax cut over three fiscal years and the slight reduction in the budget—excluding defense, space programs, and interest—

House Speaker McCormack and Senate Republican Leader Dirksen were reported as thinking that the President could get a tax package through Congress in 1963 if he fought for it.[30] After the tax message the *New York Times* found that there was widespread agreement on cuts in tax rates and predicted that while there would be a debate on spending it would not have much effect.[31] James Reston, in the *New York Times*, summed up the prospect tersely: "No doubt the President will get his tax cut in the end, for conservatives and liberals tend to like money more than they like theories."[32]

Still it was to be a year before the tax bill was enacted. The delay was caused by two issues: What reforms should accompany the tax reduction? What expenditure totals should accompany tax reduction? Neither of these was an issue between the new economics and the old, or between budget-balancing and high employment, or even between different sizes of deficits.

TAX REFORM VS. TAX REDUCTION

A short summary of the administration's tax proposal was 66 pages long, and 62 of those pages were devoted to tax reform as distinguished from rate reduction. Consideration and drafting of the reform sections of the bill would obviously take a long time. Most of the hundreds of witnesses who testified before the Ways and Means Committee were concerned primarily with the reform aspects of the bill. The committee bill, when submitted to the House, was 304 pages long and only 7 of those pages dealt with rate reduction.

The administration had of course known that inclusion of so large a tax reform package would delay action on the tax bill and possibly delay it so long as to prevent any tax reduction from taking effect in calendar 1963. However, the strength of the opposition to the reforms had not been anticipated. According to *Business Week*, "Kennedy aides admit they completely misjudged public and Congressional reaction—particularly the backlash against reforms that would cut the deductions itemized by middle- and upper-income taxpayers."[33] This opposition not only increased the delay but also strengthened the probability that after the delay the Treasury would still not get the reforms it wanted.

This situation immediately raised the possibility of abandoning the reforms in order to obtain quicker action on the tax reduction. President Kennedy was asked about this at his news conference on January 24, the day of his tax message:

> QUESTION: Mr. President, would you accept a revision and a tax cut which did not embody these reforms either this year or in some agreement?
> PRESIDENT: Well, I think it would be too early to make a judgment. I would

think it would be unwise to carry out our total tax reduction package, which would then be $13 1/2 billion, unless we picked up revenue some other place, or reduced the amount of the cuts. So my judgment is that the package is the best approach. I'm hopeful that Congress will hold on to both. I put as the first priority, however, action this year, so we'll just have to wait and see whether both can be done this year. In any case we should be able to make progress, come what may, on the first step of the three-stage reduction, and I think it's physically possible to do both the reform and the revision this year and I think that is Chairman Mills' idea too.[34]

Early in February the President's Labor-Management Committee called at the White House to tell him that they didn't like the tax package. "The cuts are too small this year to give the economy any real stimulus, and they are complicated by the reform proposals, the group said. The committee is standing on last fall's recommendation of a $10 billion tax cut with no strings attached."[35]

For a time it appeared that the President might be willing to give up the reforms in the interest of quick action to reduce taxes. After a speech to a conference sponsored by the American Bankers Association on February 25 he was asked:

Mr. President, I believe you said that you did not predict a recession in 1963, and you say that without a tax cut we are liable to have a recession. Now, with a tax cut, tied so closely to tax reform, isn't it possible that the tax reform angle might delay this to the point where the tax cut stimulus might be lost?

In reply the President explained the rationale of the package of tax reductions combined with tax reforms, but most attention was paid to the following part of his remarks:

But I quite agree that what we need is the bill this year, and nothing should stand in its way. Our feeling is that the best bill that can be gotten will be the one we recommended. But I would say the first priority is a bill. . . . Whatever is necessary to get that bill, I would support.[36]

This statement was widely interpreted as an invitation to Congress to enact tax reductions without tax reform. However the Treasury was not prepared to concede the failure of its reform program. Moreover, Congressman Mills was also believed to insist on a reform element in the package. At his news conference on March 6 the President took the opportunity to rectify the impression he had given.

QUESTION: Mr. President, is it fair to assume from the language you used before the American Bankers symposium that, if necessary, if all else fails in Congress, you would accept a $13 1/2 billion tax cut without any reforms at all?

PRESIDENT: No, that isn't what I said. The program which we have sent up is
the fairest and most equitable program, and the most fiscally responsible program. It provides for a combination of tax reduction and tax reform, and I
think that a good many of the reforms make more equitable the tax reductions,
make more equitable the burdens which the great mass of our taxpayers carry.

So that I think that the best program is the one we sent up which provides
for $13 1/2 billion in tax reduction and $3 1/4 billion revenue in tax reform.
I think that's the best combination. What we will do will depend of course on
what kind of a bill the Congress enacts, but my judgment is that they will
enact a tax reduction bill which will include important elements of the reforms
that we sent up.[37]

When the administration, partly because of Mr. Mills' wishes, committed
itself to continuing the struggle for tax reform, it also committed itself to
retention of the existing taxes without reduction for all of 1963 at least.
Whether the proposal for tax cuts to take effect on July 1, 1963, could have
been enacted without the complicated and controversial reforms is uncertain
but it was impossible with them. Outside groups continued to press for quick
action. This was notably true of the Business Committee for Tax Reduction
in 1963, an organization of business leaders formed to lobby for a prompt
tax cut.[38] However, by the spring of 1963 the practical question was whether
the tax cut could be enacted in that calendar year to take effect on January 1,
1964.

Pressure on Congress to act swiftly on the whole package, including the
reforms, was weakened by the unexpected strength of the economy. Although the President, in proposing the tax program in January, had maintained that it was not aimed at an imminent recession, he soon thereafter
began to stress the danger of recession in the hope of speeding action. However, by April the economy appeared to be expanding faster than the administration had expected, and the administration had to contend with the
argument that the urgency of action had diminished.

On April 19, the President was asked: "In view of the marked and welcome improvement in our economy's performance recently, do you still regard a substantial tax reduction as essential?" To which he replied: "I don't
see anything in the economy that would make the tax bill unnecessary."[39]

Other officers of the administration tried to strengthen this answer. In a
speech before the Chamber of Commerce of the United States on April 30,
Secretary Dillon said: "A tax cut when the economy is reasonably buoyant
would be far more effective in carrying us toward full employment than a
tax cut when the economy is merely limping along."[40] In May Walter Heller
used a space-age metaphor to explain that the expanding economy and im-

proved prospects "offer a solid launching-pad" for the tax cut.[41] However the argument was not impressive. A tax cut might be more effective in a buoyant economy than in a limping one, but whether the effect was as necessary was a different question. In any case it was impossible to generate a belief in Congress that speed was essential for economic reasons.

In the end almost all of the reforms were eliminated from the tax bill as enacted. The chief significance of the reform proposals, from the standpoint of the history of fiscal policy, was to assure delay in the enactment of the tax cut. It showed the impossibility of making fiscal policy decisions single-mindedly in terms of short-term effects on the overall level of economic activity when those decisions also have important other effects, in this case on the tax structure.

Once the administration had proposed its reforms, much of the opposition to them came from conservative and especially business circles. This was not opposition based on budget-balancing ideology. The reforms were revenue-raising measures, and opposition to them had the effect of opposing steps intended in part to hold down the size of the deficit. Moreover, the business groups recommended against including the reforms in the package in the first place and urged their early abandonment in the hope that without them the tax reductions could be enacted and go into effect earlier. The conservatives were not less concerned about the size of the deficit or more anxious for a quick stimulus to the economy than the administration was. The conservatives were willing to subordinate their traditional view about the deficit in order to avoid tax reforms which they didn't like and get tax cuts which they did like. The administration was willing to subordinate its interest in quick reduction of taxes to spur the economy in order to fight for certain reforms that it wanted—although it didn't get them.[42]

EXPENDITURE CONTROL AND TAX REDUCTION

It was September 10 when the tax bill was through the Ways and Means Committee and introduced in the House. By then the issue of tax reform had been settled; there would be little of it. Part of the question of timing had also been settled; there would be no tax cut before January 1, 1964. Two questions remained: What level of expenditures would accompany the tax cut, and could the Congress and the President agree on the expenditure policy in time to permit the tax cuts to go into effect on January 1?

From the time of the President's budget and tax messages in January, 1963, much of the opposition had focused on the spending program. No one could be against tax reduction itself. But it was possible to be against tax reduction unless something were done about expenditures, and many were. The prescription of expenditure policy necessary to justify tax reduction took several forms. One was that taxes should not be cut unless expenditures were reduced enough to balance the budget—meaning the actual budget, not the high-employment budget. While a number of people, including former President Truman, took this position, it was generally recognized as a prescription for indefinite postponement of tax reduction since it would require extremely large expenditure cuts. A second stopping point, that expenditures should be reduced by the amount of tax reduction, was also beyond serious discussion if a tax reduction as large as $10 billion was contemplated. A more moderate suggestion was that there should be at least *some* expenditure reduction. Republicans pointed out that although they had cut taxes in 1954 in the face of a deficit, expenditures were then declining. In the end, however, the specific expenditure proposal around which debate and negotiation revolved was even less ambitious. It was that expenditures should be kept from rising for one year.

In its statement of December, 1962, the CED had recommended a tax cut of $11 billion to take effect early in 1963 contingent upon the adoption of a budget which would hold fiscal 1964 expenditures to the level of fiscal 1963. If this were not done the tax cut was to be held to $6 billion. The Business Committee for Tax Reduction in 1963 also recommended that fiscal 1964 expenditures should be held to the fiscal 1963 level. However, by the time the tax bill reached the House floor in September talk about such an expenditure policy for fiscal 1964 was already too late. Moreover the tax cut under consideration was to take effect on January 1, 1964, rather than early in 1963. Therefore the levelling out of expenditures had to be postponed a year, and the proposal became essentially to make the tax cut contingent on holding fiscal 1965 expenditures at the fiscal 1964 level. Specifically, expenditures in fiscal 1963 had been $92.6 billion, and by September fiscal 1964 was estimated at $98 billion and fiscal 1965 at $102 billion. The Republican proposal debated in the House was to make the tax cut contingent on holding estimated expenditures for 1964 to $97 billion and 1965 to $98 billion.

There were several motives behind the drive for expenditure control as a condition of tax reduction. The move had possible political benefits for the Republicans in the House who sponsored the amendment which would have hinged the tax cut on the limitation of spending. The tax cut was very popular. They could not oppose it and did not want to leave the Democrats in sole possession of the credit for it. If their expenditure-limit amendment was rejected and the tax cut passed, the Republicans could say that they also had been for a tax cut but had tried to make it part of a sound fiscal package. If their expenditure-limit amendment was adopted and the expenditure program was made to conform to it, they could claim credit for having forced through a "meaningful" tax cut—as the Republican congressmen referred to tax reduction accompanied by expenditure restraint. In the unlikely event that the expenditure limit prevented the tax cut from taking effect, the President could be blamed for failing to make the adjustments in his budget which would have permitted tax reduction. This was all a normal political procedure such as the Democrats had followed in the 80th Congress when the Republicans were the champions of tax reduction. In fact, in 1963 the Republicans quoted some of the sound-finance sermons which the Democrats had uttered fifteen years earlier in opposing the tax cut pushed through by the Republicans in 1948.

However there were principles and objectives involved in addition to political tactics. In part the effort to restrain expenditures had traditional budget-balancing motivations. The report on the tax bill by the minority of the Ways and Means Committee contained all the clichés of the budget-balancing doctrine. A tax cut on borrowed money was "morally wrong," a "fraud," "fiscally wrong," a " 'time bomb' for inflation," and so on. But this concern for a balanced budget was not made of stern stuff. The Republicans did not propose to make the tax cut contingent on such severe restraint of spending as to create any real danger that the tax cut would not take effect. They proposed to hold fiscal 1965 expenditures $4 billion below the administration's estimate—as the price for making a tax cut of $11 billion. If their suggestion had been adopted there would still, according to current estimates, have been a deficit of $5 billion in fiscal 1965. No one was so devoted to balancing the budget as to suggest that the tax cut should be smaller than $11 billion.[43] No one even suggested that the cut should be phased out over a longer period. In fact the business organizations that were arguing for expenditure restraint were also arguing for putting the tax cut into effect earlier than the administration had proposed, which would have increased the deficit.

A more deeply felt and widely shared reason for wanting to hold down federal expenditures was the desire to restrain the expansion of federal activity, particularly in the new directions where the Kennedy administration was pointing, and to retain the option of further tax reduction later. Between fiscal 1955 and fiscal 1963, federal revenues had increased by $26 billion—over 40 percent. And yet, until 1963 the time had never seemed appropriate for tax reduction, because expenditures had risen a little more—$28 billion. There seemed to be an irresistible pressure which forced expenditures up as fast as the revenues increased, or a little faster. Many feared that the process would be resumed after the tax cut went into effect. The intense desire of the administration for tax reduction provided the economizers with a lever to force the administration to cut spending. Thus the issue was only partly about budget-balancing—about the relationship between revenues and expenditures. The issue was also, and mainly, about the level of both. The effort was to slow down the growth of both expenditures and revenues, as compared with their past rate and with what was believed to be the intention of the administration.

The idea of balancing the tax reduction in whole or in part by reduction of expenditures—below the President's proposals, not below actual past rates of expenditures—provoked some discussion of the economics of the tax reduction. The discussion was carried on mainly by economists who presented their views to Congressional committees and to other "amateurs" but who did not confront each other with rigorous analysis or quantitative evidence. The contribution to economic knowledge was small, except as evidence of how far the "science" had come from the earlier post-Keynesian confidence in its knowledge. The influence on policy was probably also small, as almost everyone could find some respectable economic rationale for his views.

The question was whether tax reduction matched by expenditure reduction would yield the results sought from the tax reduction. The answer to this, of course, depended on the results sought. Much of the argument proceeded on the assumption that the objective was to increase total demand. The basic position of the administration was that reduction of expenditures would offset, or almost offset, or more than offset—the formulation varied —the demand-stimulating effect of the tax reduction. Thus Senator Douglas inquired of Walter Heller:

> DOUGLAS: Many people are saying that they would favor a tax cut only if it were compensated for by an equal cut in expenditures.
>
> The question I would like to ask is this: If this were done, would it not take away much of the stimulative effect upon which you count?
>
> HELLER: Senator, it would take away almost all of the stimulative effect. It is fair to say, however, that in talking about a tax cut, one looks at two aspects of the drag that taxes exert on the economy.
>
> One is the drag on purchasing power, on income, on consumption, and investment demand.
>
> The other is the drag on incentives. It is perfectly true, if you had paired reductions in expenditures, and in taxes, you would still gain something on the incentive side, though you would more than offset it on the demand side.[44]

In response to a similar question from Senator Proxmire, Heller said:

HELLER: I would say that every dollar of expenditure cut that is made without a corresponding increase in the tax cut would be an offset to the stimulus that the tax cut offers to total demand. As I stated earlier in responding to questions from Senator Douglas, you would still have some effect on incentives by reducing the taxes in any event.

But as far as the overall impact on the demand for the products of industry and agriculture, and for services—as far as that demand is concerned—the pairing of tax cuts and expenditure cuts in effect simply wipes it out and makes it self-defeating.

PROXMIRE: What you are asking for, then, is an increased deficit rather than a tax cut, and it makes very little difference if we spend more or reduce taxes, but on the other hand, increased Government spending would provide a greater multiplier effect and, therefore, that would tend to balance the increase in incentives you would have.

HELLER: I would restate it this way: It isn't the deficit we seek. What we seek is an increase in the total demand in the economy, a removal, as it were, of the fiscal drag on spending in the economy. The President has pointed out—

PROXMIRE: I understand that, but in order to achieve that, you say no matter whether we do it through the tax route or the spending route, we will have to achieve a bigger deficit in order to promote greater demand, stimulate the economy.

HELLER: Under current circumstances, the net effect is going to be the achievement of a bigger deficit, as you either increase spending or cut taxes.[45]

The acknowledgement of the incentive effect introduced a camel of considerable size into the Keynesian tent. The standard argument had been that the way in which tax reduction affected spending was through the increase it caused in the after-tax incomes of individuals and businesses, who could be expected to spend part, but not all or more than all, of their in-increased available incomes. As long as that was the only mechanism at work, it could be shown by a simple logical exercise that tax reduction matched by an equal expenditure reduction would depress total spending. The increased expenditure by taxpayers of less than 100 percent of their increased after-tax income would not match the decreased expenditures of the government. Thus, suppose that taxpayers spend 80 percent of their after-tax income. Then a tax reduction of $10 billion would increase their spending by $8 billion, whereas an equal cut of government spending would be a reduction of $10 billion immediately. Both the $8 billion increase and the $10 billion decrease in initial spending would be multiplied as a consequence of subsequent earning and spending, but the result would always be a net reduction of spending. However, the picture is changed if the effect of cutting tax rates is not only to increase after-tax incomes but also to increase incentives to spend out of income, for example by increasing the profitability of investment. Suppose that before the tax cut the available incomes of individuals and businesses amounted to $400 billion, out of which they spent 80 percent or $320 billion. Then a tax cut is enacted which increases their available incomes by $10 billion and the proportion of the total they spend from 80 percent to 82 percent. Their spending will then rise from $320 billion to $336.2 billion (82 percent of $410 billion) for a total increase of $16.2 billion. This would more than offset the effects of a $10 billion cut in government spending.

Once the incentive effects were acknowledged in principle, the results of a balanced cut of taxes and expenditures depended on their size. On this there was no hard evidence. Mr. Heller's analysis tended to belittle these effects, but no discussable estimates were ever presented. In fact, the subject had to be treated with caution because the President's exposition of the case for tax reduction placed considerable weight on the incentive effects.

The incentive argument did not mean that a tax cut with expenditure reduction would be as stimulating as a tax cut without expenditure reduction. But it held open the possibility that the stimulating effect of a balanced reduction might be substantial.

This kind of case for a balanced reduction was implicit in the position commonly taken by business organizations but was not clearly stated by them. Probably its most explicit use was in the testimony of Professor Arthur Burns before the Joint Economic Committee.

PROXMIRE: Dr. Burns, it is very refreshing to get testimony which contradicts the overwhelming support for the administration's viewpoint which previous witnesses have professed. I think you have analyzed this most impressively and I am happy to hear a renowned economist who feels that we can achieve our economic goals without increasing our deficit.

I would like to press you on that particular point because it seems to me that that is the crux of your difference with the many people who have testified before who are also very capable.

Isn't it true, Dr. Burns, that if we maintain the—if we, say, adopt the President's tax cut recommendations generally, but maintain spending at the present level, that is, at the 1963 level, which is $4 1/2 billion less than the President recommended that the impact on the economy would not be as stimulative, would not provoke growth to the extent that the administration's proposal would?

I am hopeful that your answer is going to be that it would be at least as stimulative, but I am not so sure from your remarks that I have yet gotten the documentation to refute other arguments.

BURNS: Senator, let us make the assumption that the Government adopts a fiscal policy with a view to stimulating the economy and that this fiscal policy involves incurring deliberately a budget deficit of some size.

Let us say that the planned budget deficit is $10 billion. This deficit can be realized in different ways.

Plan A, let us say, involves increasing Federal expenditures by $10 billion. Plan B involves, let us say, increasing expenditures by $5 billion, and also cutting taxes by $5 billion.

Plan C involves, let us say, a cut in taxes of $10 billion.

Now let us contrast these three plans.

The theory which is now fashionable among economists is that the first of these plans would be most stimulative. The reasoning is that if the Government undertakes to increase the deficit by spending $10 billion, that much purchasing power will be promptly added to the economy. Those who take this viewpoint will go on to argue that if, on the other hand, taxes are cut by $10 billion, a portion of that sum will be saved by individuals or by business firms. In other words, the deficit of $10 billion created through a tax reduction will lead to an increase in the community's spending of something less than $10 billion.

It follows that plan A is the most stimulative on this line of thinking, that plan B is somewhat less stimulative, and that plan C is still less stimulative.

I disagree with this theory. The difficulty with it is that the theory lays exclusive stress on the direct flow of dollars to individuals or businesses, on the cash flow effect. The theory ignores entirely the effect on the thinking of individuals and business firms about their future and therefore misses what may be most important about a tax reduction. The reason why I think that plan C, to return to my example, is more stimulative than plan A is that under plan C individuals and businessmen will begin thinking very differently about the future. They will be in a position not merely to use the larger cash income which is at their disposal, but they may well be in a mood also to dip into their accumulated assets and to use their credit.

Now, the important objective of fiscal policy at a time like the present should be to stimulate individuals to use their brains, their energy, their disposable income, and also their assets and even their borrowing power in the interest of enlarging their economic activities and through that the Nation's economy. Plan C especially when so designed as to stimulate investment, will do this.

My theory, therefore, Senator, is different from the theory that has now become so familiar.[46]

The significance of this statement was not elaborated. It seemed only to say that a $10 billion tax reduction would be more stimulating than a $10 billion expenditure increase. But if that were true, it would also probably be true that a $10 billion tax cut coupled with a $10 billion expenditure reduction would have a net stimulating effect. Professor Burns obviously thought that the net effect would be substantial, but he presented no more evidence for that opinion than Mr. Heller had presented for his contrary view.

Professor Burns had another string to his bow. The incentive effects of different kinds of taxes would differ. Therefore the net effect of tax and expenditure reduction would depend upon the kinds of taxes that were reduced. A balanced reduction of taxes and expenditures might be more stimulating than tax reduction alone if the kinds of tax reductions included in the balanced package were more stimulating. Burns suggested more concentration of reduction on the corporate profits tax and upper-bracket income tax than the administration had proposed, with the thought that this would permit the desired amount of stimulation to be achieved with less deficit. Again, the results would depend not on general principles but on the magnitudes involved, and no one knew what they were.

In addition to the incentive effect of tax reduction there was another camel in the Keynesian tent. That was monetary policy. Could the desired expansion of total demand be achieved by more monetary expansion with less increase in government spending and the budget deficit than the administration proposed? The argument that it could was presented to the Joint Economic Committee by Dr. George Terborgh of the Machinery and Allied Products Institute[47] and by Professor Allan H. Meltzer of the Carnegie Institute of Technology.[48] Terborgh showed that the relationship between changes in the deficit and changes in economic activity in the past had been very loose and argued that the administration's confidence in the stimulating effects of fiscal policy was unfounded. He, and more extensively Meltzer, showed that there had been a close relationship between changes in the supply of money and changes in economic activity. Both claimed that the desired expansion of the economy could be obtained by increasing the rate of growth of the money supply with little if any increase in the budget deficit.

The Council of Economic Advisers did not contest this in principle, as indeed they could not since the idea of the fiscal-monetary mix had become standard doctrine. In their January, 1963, report they said, in a discussion of ways to finance the budget deficit:

> At one logical extreme—which of course no one seriously contemplates—
> the Federal Reserve could buy Treasury securities and increase the quantity of
> bank reserves in an amount equal to the deficit. In this way, the reserve base of
> the banking system would be increased by virtually the entire amount of the
> deficit, paving the way for a multiple expansion of bank deposits and bank credit.
> This is the most liquid and most expansionary way of increasing the debt of the
> Federal Government.[49]

If financing the whole proposed deficit in this way would have been too expansionary to contemplate, there presumably was some smaller deficit that could be financed in this way with just the right expansionary results. The council's argument against this was that it would reduce interest rates and thereby worsen the U.S. balance of payments by increasing the flow of capital out of the United States. In public discussion however the administration did not rely heavily on the proposition that its spending and deficit policy was for the purpose of raising or keeping up interest rates and thus defending the balance of payments. To rest the case on high employment and economic growth was much more appealing. Terborgh and Meltzer maintained that the existing degree of monetary restraint could not be explained or justified by balance-of-payments requirements. The difference of opinion hinged again on estimates of the quantities involved and also on appraisal of alternative ways of dealing with the balance-of-payments problem. On these issues there was never any resolution or even serious confrontation.

The discussion about whether balancing tax reduction, in whole or in part, with expenditure reduction would defeat the purpose of tax reduction assumed that the purpose was to stimulate the economy up to or toward high employment by increasing total demand. Everyone did not accept that as the only or main goal. Some were mainly interested in raising private investment to increase growth, or in holding down the expansion of government, or simply in permitting taxpayers to enjoy a larger share of the incomes they earned. For them the reduction of spending did not obstruct achievement of the main goal and might indeed be essential to it.

The arguments of economists about the consequences for aggregate demand of expenditure reduction had little reflection in the Congressional debate. The opposition cited the Heller analysis to show that the administration really wanted a bigger deficit. The administration and the Democratic leaders in the House did not find it necessary or desirable to defend the Heller position. And since they did not, the Republicans had no need for the counterarguments about incentives and monetary policy. Some of them would not have accepted the case for monetary expansion any more than they accepted the case for deficits, except as an unfortunately necessary consequence of what they really wanted—which was tax reduction.[50] With respect to the modern economics of fiscal and monetary policy, the Congressional debates show more skepticism and indifference than conviction and conversion.

The specific proposal offered by the Republicans in the House, which would have made the tax cut contingent on the President's submitting a budget in January, 1964, which showed fiscal 1964 expenditures below $97 billion and fiscal 1965 below $98 billion, was defeated by a vote of 226 to

199. However the sentiment behind it had wide support. President Kennedy had made concessions to this sentiment in his original proposals by holding estimated fiscal 1964 expenditures below $100 billion and by stretching out the tax cut in order to minimize the fiscal 1964 deficit. He made further concessions in a letter to Wilbur Mills as the House debate was about to open:

> First, our long-range goal remains a balanced budget in the balanced full em-
> ployment economy. It is clear that this goal cannot be achieved without a substan-
> tial tax reduction and the greater national income it will produce.
>
> Second, tax reduction must also, therefore, be accompanied by the exercise of
> an even tighter rein on Government expenditures, limiting outlays to those ex-
> penditures which meet strict criteria of national need.
>
> Third, consistent with these policies, as the tax cut becomes fully effective and
> the economy climbs toward full employment, a substantial part of the increased
> tax revenues will be applied toward a reduction in the transitional deficits which
> accompany the initial cut in tax rates.
>
> Fourth, assuming enactment of the tax program incorporated in your commit-
> tee's bill with a consequent loss of revenue of $5 billion more in fiscal 1965 than
> in fiscal 1964, I nevertheless expect—in strict accordance with the above policies,
> and in the absence of any unforeseen slowdown in the economy or any serious
> international contingency in the next 5 months—to be able to submit next January
> a budget for fiscal 1965 involving an estimated deficit of less than the $9.2 billion
> forecast for fiscal 1964 by the Secretary of the Treasury in your executive sessions
> last week.[51]

However the specific commitment contained in this statement was small and was directed only to the size of next year's deficit. Those who were concerned about the trend of expenditures were little impressed by a promise to limit outlays to "those expenditures which meet [Kennedy's] strict criteria of national need." A more forceful expression of the hopes and expectations which for many justified or rationalized support of the tax cut was presented in Congressman Mills' speech introducing the bill in the House:

> We have a choice to make today which in any event transcends the question
> of the immediate level of spending and deficits. I believe it is quite clear with the
> slow growth rate, unemployment, and unused plant capacity that we have facing
> us today, and can expect in still greater volume tomorrow if our growth rate
> is not increased, the country is going to demand some kind of action to meet
> these problems.
>
> I am convinced that there are two roads the Government can follow toward
> the achievement of this larger and more prosperous economy. I believe we are
> at the fork of these two roads today. One is the tax reduction road. The other
> is the road of Government expenditure increases.
>
> Many believe that we can spend our way to prosperity. On the other hand, I

am firmly convinced that if Congress adopts a tax reduction and revision bill of the type which is before this body today, we can also achieve this more prosperous economy by loosening the constraints which the present Federal tax system imposes on our free enterprise system. These tax reductions will bring about a higher level of economic activity, fuller use of our manpower, more intensive and prosperous use of our plant and equipment, and with the increases in wages, salaries, profits, consumption and investment, there will be increases in Federal tax revenues.

Although it may be possible to achieve the prosperity we desire by either of the two routes I have outlined to you, nevertheless there is a big difference—a vital difference—between them. The route of Government expenditure increase achieves this higher level of economic activity with larger and larger shares of that activity initiating in the Government—with more labor and more capital being used directly by the Government and with the Government's activities determining in larger and larger part the use of labor and capital in the private sector of the economy. This road leads to big Government, especially big Central Government. My own view, and I believe the view of all of us, is that we should to the full extent possible call upon the private sector of our economy to give us the needed growth. . . . The route I prefer is the tax reduction road which gives us a higher level of economic activity and a bigger and more prosperous and more efficient economy with a larger and larger share of the enlarged activity initiating in the private sector of the economy . . .

The greatest psychological factor that we can create to control spending is the denial of additional revenues to the Treasury of the United States. If you think this administration, or if you think you as an individual Member of Congress, can continue after this tax reduction to advocate and vote for everything that you may have advocated and voted for before tax reduction to stimulate this economy, my guess is you are going to find your constituency and the American people leaving you.

I would think, Mr. Chairman, that those who may doubt would want to think further with respect to the position they put themselves in if they vote for the motion to recommit or if they vote against this bill. This is truly a turning point in economic policy. I plead with you to be a part in making it possible. Let us get away from the mistakes of the past. Let us get on this new road.[52]

Mr. Mills made the usual respectful references to balancing the budget, but the turning point in economic policy did not have to do with budget-balancing. The proper relation between revenues and expenditures might be a balanced budget or it might be something else, but whatever it was the proper relation could be achieved either by higher expenditures and revenues or by lower expenditures and revenues. Mr. Mills called upon the House to choose the road of lower expenditures and revenues, and he assured the House that the tax cut was the way to declare and implement that choice.

The tax bill was passed by the House on September 25 without any provision requiring the limitation of expenditures. There was one more hurdle to jump—the Senate, or more particularly the Senate Finance Committee, or even more particularly Senator Harry F. Byrd. During thirty years in the Senate, Byrd had achieved a national reputation in the role of champion of economy and sound finance. He could be expected to continue to play that role and was in an excellent position to do so. Eight months had elapsed between President Kennedy's tax message and House action on the tax bill. For Byrd to require four months to bring the bill to a vote in the Senate would not be unreasonable. By that time the administration would have had to submit its budget for fiscal 1965. If the expenditure figures were not satisfactory to Senator Byrd, he would then have an issue on which to delay action further. The economizers would be assisted in their delaying tactics by the fact that a number of liberals in the Senate were disenchanted with the tax bill, because as passed by the House it omitted reform provisions that they considered important. While the result might not be defeat of the tax cut, it might be postponement of its effective date until 1965. Thus Senator Byrd was well placed to put pressure on the administration to hold down the 1965 budget.

The administration tried in vain to get action out of Byrd before the end of 1963. The situation was reported in *Newsweek* as follows:

> On the eve of the House's tax vote, he [Dillon] paid Byrd a side-door visit to explore ways of speeding Finance Committee action on the bill.
>
> Byrd shook his head: there would have to be ten days of briefings by staff experts, four weeks of testimony from at least 60 witnesses, submission of more than twenty amendments by Tennessee's Sen. Albert Gore (who considers the bill a rich man's measure), and two weeks to write a Senate version. But before this schedule runs into December, Byrd noted, the civil-rights bill is likely to reach the Senate floor. The resulting filibuster would not only block access to the floor but disrupt the work of all the Senate's committees.
>
> Byrd suggested a deal. If Dillon would wait until January and the President submitted a reduced budget he would "personally guarantee" the tax cut would be passed and made retroactive to the first of the year. Dillon turned down the idea. He argued that delay might bring on a recession and that withholding of taxes would not be feasible on a retroactive basis.[53]

But while Dillon could reject the deal, he had no way to make Byrd move. The Senator was equally resistant to the appeals of businessmen who, while expressing a fervent desire for expenditure reduction, wanted tax reduction more—and quicker. On November 4 Mr. Stuart Saunders, chairman of the board of the Pennsylvania Railroad, and Mr. Henry Ford II, cochairmen of the Business Committee for Tax Reduction in 1963, appeared before the Senate Finance Committee to urge action before the end of the year which would make the tax cut effective January 1, 1964. Senator Byrd quizzed them skeptically:

> BYRD: What great harm would be done, if this bill were not enacted until after the budget is submitted in January, and we find out whether there will be reductions in expenditures?
>
> SAUNDERS: Well, I think that is a very plausible suggestion.
>
> On the other hand, I think it is fraught with danger, and I think it is unnecessary. In the first place, I do not believe that the budget, whatever budget the President sends up, should be controlling on whether this tax cut should go forward or not. I, of course, am very hopeful that the budget next year will be no higher than fiscal 1964. But even if it is $1 billion or something higher, I think the Congress of the United States has the responsibility to cut it back, and I would hope you would do it, or even cut it more than that.
>
> Moreover, as you well know, after the first of the year you are flooded with all sorts of messages and proposals. Congress traditionally never passes or passes few, if any, bills in the early part of the year.
>
> Being an election year, I do not know what might happen to this tax bill; and you are also going to get into a great debate, I am afraid, over the question of retroactivity, when the effective date should be. All in all we think this is a good bill. It is going to help our economy, and if it is a good bill, why postpone the day? Why don't we take action now?[54]

Further discussion of this subject only revealed that the captains of industry cared more for tax reduction and less for expenditure reduction than Senator Byrd.

After the assassination of President Kennedy on November 22, President Lyndon Johnson took over the task of getting the tax bill enacted.[55] In his first address to the Congress on November 27 Johnson said:

> No act of ours could more fittingly continue the work of President Kennedy than the early passage of the tax bill for which he fought all this long year. This is a bill designed to increase our national income and Federal revenues, and to provide insurance against recession.[56]

However, Johnson did not expect Senator Byrd to rush through the tax bill as a memorial to John F. Kennedy, and he did know what the condition was for assured passage. Two days before the address to Congress he had made that clear at a meeting with officers of the Treasury, the Council of Economic Advisers, and the Budget Bureau. Heller was urging a budget of $101.5 billion for fiscal 1965, which would have been an exceptionally small increase over the $98 billion then estimated for fiscal 1964. Dillon wanted to get the fiscal 1965 figure still lower in order to assure passage of the tax bill by the Senate. Johnson agreed with Dillon. "We won't even get it to the Senate floor unless we tell Congress that the new budget will be about one hundred billion dollars." Later, turning to Heller: " 'If you don't get this budget down around 100 billion dollars,' Johnson went on, 'you won't pee one drop' (nervous laughter)."[57]

In fact, Johnson kept well below the $100 billion figure. His budget for fiscal 1965 was $97.9 billion—even below the $98 billion which the House Republicans had wanted to make the necessary condition for tax reduction. While some "foul" means were used to make the budget look as small as possible, there was also real restraint. When the year was over actual expenditures were $96.5 billion—or $1.4 billion below the budget. Moreover, budget measurements less easy to manipulate than the administrative budget to which these figures refer also show that fiscal 1965 was a year of marked slowdown in the rate of expenditure growth. The slowdown was temporary, as Johnson had suggested it might be during his November 25 conference on the budget. " 'Once you have the tax cut,' Johnson added, 'you can do what you want just like Eisenhower did. Eisenhower talked economy and then spent,' Johnson said wryly."[58] But for 1965 there was a real cut.

The new budget figures were published on January 21 and had been shown privately to Senator Byrd before that date. On January 28 the Senate Finance Committee reported out the tax bill. The Senate passed the bill on February 7, differences between the House and the Senate were ironed out by February 26, and the bill was signed into law by President Johnson that same day.

$$\approx\!\! 18 \!\!\approx$$

Epilogue

B Y the time the tax cut of 1964 was enacted, budget-balancing had ceased to have an important influence on fiscal decisions and compensatory finance had taken its place as standard doctrine and major, though by no means exclusive, determinant of action. This change was confirmed by experience in the years that followed.

During the discussion of the tax cut there were repeated respectful references to budget-balancing as a goal, by the President and his economic advisers as well as by conservatives. However the references were ritualistic. No decisions followed from them. This was true not only of the old-fashioned idea that the budget should always be balanced, which obviously had carried no weight for years. It was true also of more elastic concepts of budget-balancing such as the idea that the hypothetical full-employment budget should be balanced, or the somewhat different idea that the actual budget should come into balance when high employment was reached. Both of these ideas, especially the latter, appeared in the discussion, but neither was used in the end as a test of the propriety of the fiscal decision that was made. They were arguments to convince others if possible, but they were not guides to policy.

After the tax cut the Johnson administration continued to talk about achieving a balanced budget in a balanced full-employment economy. When full-employment was reached at the end of 1965 this goal disappeared from the discussion. The circumstances were difficult; with rising expenditures for the Vietnam War, extraordinary measures would have been required to balance the budget. What was significant was that the fiscal decision was argued with hardly any reference to balancing the budget. One of the few exceptions was President Johnson. During 1967 when he was trying to win support for a tax increase, the President would sometimes urge the necessity of holding down the budget deficit, as if that were another argument in addition to the arguments about economic effects like inflation. But there was no response to this attempt to revive the Puritan ethic. The failure of Congress to raise taxes was assessed as a violation of the principles of compensatory finance, not as a violation of the doctrine of the balanced budget.

For years economists had regarded the budget-balancing dogma as the main obstacle to rational decisions about fiscal policy. They had looked forward to the day when, the budget-balancing doctrine having been laid to rest, compensatory policy would take its place and decisions would be based on a calculation—presumably made by economists—of the tax and expenditure policies that would yield "economic stability," meaning high employment and stable prices or the best compromise between those goals. When the day came in 1964 the ambition was achieved only partially and loosely. But still a significant step was made.

Ever since Roosevelt's spending program of 1938 it had been accepted policy to take strong expansive fiscal action in a situation of serious unemployment. Between 1938 and 1962 the extent of departure from prosperity and high employment necessary to trigger such action had substantially declined. Whether the reaction mechanism had become more sensitive between the Eisenhower years and the Kennedy years is difficult to say. The unemployment rate in 1962 when Kennedy decided to act was about the same as in 1954 and significantly lower than in 1958 when Eisenhower had decided not to act. But if other aspects of the economic problem are taken into consideration, the case for action was clearer in 1962 then in either of the earlier years. The average rate of unemployment in 1954 and the four preceding years was four percent, in 1958 and the four preceding years it was five percent, and in 1962 and the four preceding years it was six percent. The five year period 1958–62 had a higher rate of unemployment than any other period of five consecutive years since the war. On the other hand, the price rise in the years preceding 1962 was much smaller than in the years preceding 1954 and 1958. Thus Kennedy in 1962 looked back on a more serious record of unemployment and a less serious record of inflation than Eisenhower had in 1954 or 1958. But whatever may have been the difference between Eisenhower and Kennedy, the country was prepared to take strong action on a much weaker signal of unemployment in 1962 then in 1938.

Of course nothing was less in need of a new theory to explain it than support of tax reduction by the Congress and the tax-paying public. There is no case, at least in the past fifty years, in which the President recommended a tax reduction which Congress failed to pass. The typical situation has been that the President has asked Congress for more taxes than it wanted to give, and the Congress has pushed for tax reductions the President did not want. What tax reduction required was not conversion of the Congress and the country but conversion of the President.

Still, the 1964 tax cut would not have come at that time and in that amount without the idea that fiscal policy should be used to achieve full employment and economic stability. Moreover, the action taken in 1964 helped to increase the weight that would be given to that idea later in fiscal decisions. However varied were the motives leading to support of the tax cut, its chief proponents described it in terms of compensatory finance and hailed its passage as a triumph for that way of thinking. The country had done what "the economists" wanted, even if not for their reasons. There were no evident ill effects. On the contrary the economy continued to expand, and there were plausible although not unquestionable claims that this was due to the tax cut. The probability that future decisions would be heavily influenced by the principles of compensatory finance was surely increased by the tax cut.

This probability was to be tested soon in different and more difficult circumstances. After the mid-1965 upsurge of defense spending for the Vietnam War the inflationary pressures in the economy became strong. By the beginning of 1966 a number of "new economists," including President Kennedy's chief economist Walter Heller, were calling for a tax increase on the basis of the same method of analysis which they had used to call for a tax cut in 1962. The administration's response to this call in 1966 was minor. But by the beginning of 1967 the administration had reached the point of recommending a tax increase to restrain inflation. However Congress was extremely reluctant and did not approve the tax increase until the summer of 1968. Also, Congress insisted that the tax increase of 1968, like the tax reduction of 1964, be accompanied by expenditure cuts.

For those who looked upon the fiscal problem as basically the economic stabilization problem, the unwillingness of Congress to raise taxes in 1967 was inconsistent with its willingness to cut taxes in 1964. But that was not the only way to look at the problem. Those who, following Congressman Mills, voted for tax reduction as a way of expressing their desire for a smaller government with lower taxes and expenditures were consistent in 1967–68 when they resisted tax increases and insisted on expenditure cuts.

The Congressional position in 1967–68 was not necessarily rejection of compensatory finance. It could mean that compensatory finance was not everything and that other considerations had to be taken into account. It could also reflect doubt about the forecasts that led to the prescription of a tax increase. But more fundamental questions were also being asked. One was whether forecasts, not only the forecasts of 1965–67 but forecasts in general, were good enough to justify frequent adaptations of fiscal policy, especially changes of tax rates, in response to them. Another was whether, in view of the rising emphasis being placed on the role of monetary policy, the contribution of fiscal policy to economic stabilization was either so great or so indispensable as to justify making stability its primary goal.

The experience of 1966–68 confirmed the evidence of 1962–64 that fiscal decisions would not be dominated by considerations of compensatory finance exclusively. Moreover, the questions raised about fiscal policy during the Vietnam War made the future direction of fiscal policy less certain than it had seemed earlier. The next steps might not be toward more flexible, fine-tuned adaptation of fiscal policy to short-term changes in the economic situation and outlook. They might instead be toward a division of labor between fiscal and monetary policy which would require less frequent adjustment of tax and expenditure decisions. Nevertheless, the 1966–68 experience did not alter the fact that by the 1960's compensatory finance had become the standard doctrine of fiscal policy to which action would approximate.

How It Happened

Both budget-balancing and compensatory finance were in the picture of fiscal policy doctrines in 1929 at the beginning of the great depression. Budget-balancing was clearly the dominant partner. Compensatory finance was represented by the idea of the contracyclical management of government public works expenditure. This was a respectable idea not only among academic economists but also among national leaders, including most particularly Herbert Hoover. However it was a minor idea the implications of which had not been perceived intellectually and which the country was not psychologically or administratively prepared to implement on any significant scale. On the other hand, budget-balancing was never a compelling rule during the time covered by this study. In the forty years from fiscal 1930 through fiscal 1969 there were only seven balanced budgets, and only one of those came before 1947.

Throughout the period after 1929 at least, the force of the budget-balancing idea was based on the belief that other people believed in it. The idea that the public has a strong feeling about balancing the budget has been an influence upon Presidents as recent as John F. Kennedy. The conviction of the American people on this score has probably always been exaggerated by politicians. When polled, the public always shows a large preference for budget-balancing, but this is rarely a subject that ranks high on the public's list of concerns or for which they are willing to sacrifice much. The American people in polls of opinion vote heavily for the big, traditional, conservative generalizations but do not translate this ideology into votes on particular issues and candidates.[1] The balanced budget doctrine is a good example of those conservative flags which are more often saluted than followed.

The belief that businessmen had a strong devotion to budget-balancing was especially important. Businessmen make large economic decisions about the management of their cash and their investments. If failure on the part of government to behave in a budget-balancing way causes them to lose confidence, their decisions may be influenced in a direction that is bad for the whole economy. Concern with the business-confidence aspects of budget policy was important to Hoover and Roosevelt. It was also shared by more sophisticated observers including J. M. Keynes.

Certainly the utterances of business leaders gave politicians and economists every reason to think that the business community regarded budget-balancing as very important. In part this was because businessmen really did consider it important. But there was also a strong element of circularity. Businessmen are always reluctant to disagree publicly with what they believe are the views of other businessmen, and this was particularly true in the 1930's when the business community felt itself besieged by hostile forces. Moreover, the business leadership thought, as the politicians did, that there was a strong budget-balancing sentiment in the country, and they wanted to use that for beating an administration whose other policies, including both high spending and high taxes, they disliked more than deficit finance but found less easy to attack publicly.

In addition to voters and businessmen there was a third group whose alleged belief in budget-balancing influenced policy. These were foreign holders of U.S. dollars. President Hoover's fear that if the budget remained in substantial deficit French and other foreign bankers would demand gold for their dollars, with disastrous effects on the U.S. banking system, was a major element in his decision to ask for a tax increase in 1931. A similar idea returned to the scene, but with much less force, in the late 1950's and the 1960's.

What was it that these groups, who were believed to worry about the deficit, were believed to be worried about? There was the fear that continued deficits would impair the "national credit." This was sometimes described as national bankruptcy, but in more prosaic versions it meant a serious decline in the prices of government securities and an increase in the interest rates which would have to be paid on new issues. There was fear that deficits would cause inflation, and there was concern about the interest burden of a rising debt.

The inhibition of fiscal policy by budget-balancing doctrine was greatly relaxed by changes in monetary conditions which occurred mainly in 1933. However the main cause of the disappearance of budget-balancing as a serious limitation on fiscal policy was the continued experience of large budget deficits without serious consequences. Presidents Hoover and Roosevelt ran large deficits in the extreme circumstances of the Depression, and there were enormous deficits during the war. No one was struck by lightning. The country did not "go bankrupt," whatever that meant. Interest rates fell to, and remained at, low levels. President Roosevelt apparently did not suffer at the polls as a result of his deficits. If business lost confidence during the Depression as a result of deficits, this was not easily separated out from all the other possible causes of loss of confidence, and in any case the loss did not seem to survive the war. True there had been a big wartime inflation, but this was only evidence that an enormous deficit might be too big. At the end of the war the federal debt was almost $300 billion. This point having been reached, even pessimists found it unconvincing to predict that a further rise would be calamitous. Relative to the existing size of the debt, the increases that were at issue in possible peacetime deficits were insignificant.

By the end of the war the country was used to large deficits and a large debt. Appeals to the budget-balancing principle not only generated little response but were recognized as generating little response. The process of habituation continued in the postwar period, notable with the $12.4 billion deficit run in 1958–59 by President Eisenhower which the economic and political system accepted calmly. President Kennedy and his advisers in 1961 and 1962 still thought there was a budget-balancing faction to be reckoned with, but when they finally decided to take the plunge to deliberate deficit creation they found that the opposition they feared was a shadow.

Merely to get rid of the idea that budget-balancing is a cardinal virtue does not automatically establish the rule of compensatory finance. Budget policy might be guided by other principles, or by no principle at all. But in fact, the mere weakening of budget-balancing went a long way toward introducing compensatory policy. Government revenues would tend to fall and expenditures to rise relative to their normal level or trend when unemployment increased. In the absence of a budget-balancing rule there would be no reason to try to offset these variations in revenues and expenditures by raising tax rates in a recession and reducing them in prosperity; in fact, concern with the convenience of taxpayers would argue strongly against changing tax rates in that way. The result would be compensatory behavior of the budget—that is, contracyclical variations of deficits and surpluses— without compensatory theory or compensatory policy.

This kind of by-product compensation roughly describes the fiscal policy of the Roosevelt administration up to 1938, except that the record was marred by tax increases. It also helps to explain the acceptance after the war by CED and others of policies which heavily emphasized built-in stabilizers. No great enthusiasm for compensatory policy was necessary to reach the conclusion that the attempt to offset the automatic cyclical variations in the budget was foolish—once the budget-balancing idea had lost its grip. If these automatic variations were stabilizing, so much the better. After the war, when federal taxation was high relative to the national income and consisted overwhelmingly of taxes on income, these variations were large. They have constituted an important part of all stabilizing fiscal response to economic conditions.

Although it was in practical effect a large part of the fiscal revolution, this willingness to accept automatic variations in the budget position was not all of the revolution. The revolution also included the belief that fiscal decisions, not merely passive acceptance of what would happen anyway but active decisions, should be governed by the attempt to stabilize the economy and that these fiscal decisions should be the primary reliance for keeping the economy at a high but non-inflationary rate of operation.

The Depression and the war were the major, and probably sufficient, factors raising economic stabilization to the head of the list of objectives by which fiscal policy should be guided. The severity and duration of the Depression were an irrefutable argument for doing something. Every politician, economist, and businessman who went through the Depression at an impressionable age would rate high employment as a primary objective of policy for the rest of his life. This attitude was underscored by the experience of the war which showed in what profound and pervasive ways full employment would affect the society. The result was that during the thirties and early forties it became inescapable to look at all policies—not just fiscal policies—in terms of their possible contribution to full employment and economic stability.

The critical commitment to a policy of managing the overall performance of the economy by fiscal and monetary policy was made by President Roosevelt in 1938 and confirmed in the course of national discussion over the next ten years. Roosevelt's choice of the fiscal-monetary path of enlarged spending and monetary expansion in 1938 was essentially a conservative choice involving the least disruption of the existing economic system and the least political struggle. The general public acceptance of this choice, once it had been made, assured that this would be the chosen path in the future.

This final movement of fiscal-monetary policy to the center of the stage after almost nine years of depression was not the result of any marked shift in the content of economic science since 1929. It only carried out what had been conventional thinking much earlier. The Keynesian revolution came too late to have much effect on the 1938 decision. It did however dominate discussion of fiscal policy for the next ten years. Keynes provided economists with a more satisfying theory on which to base the argument for a fiscal solution of stabilization problems than they had previously had. His work mobilized economists in a crusade for active fiscal policy. At the same time, the standard interpretations of Keynesian theory for American conditions antagonized many people in business and in economics. While they might have been prepared to accept an important role for fiscal policy, they could not accept the idea of secular stagnation with the consequent implication of perpetually rising deficits to be achieved by even more rapidly rising expenditures, the emphasis on redistributive taxation, the denial of the role of incentives in investment decisions, the rejection of any role for monetary policy except to get interest rates as close to zero as possible, and the neglect of all political and operational problems.

Conservative opposition to these features of American Keynesianism and conservative counterproposals, together with changes in economic conditions brought or revealed by the war, produced a new version of fiscal and monetary policy by 1950 on which there was substantial consensus and from which much of early American Keynesianism had been purged. Secular stagnation was abandoned or indefinitely postponed. With federal spending necessarily high relative to the national income it became clear that any desired amount of fiscal stimulation could be generated by tax reduction. The possibilities of affecting total consumption by redistributive taxation were found to be small. The possibilities of affecting the rate of investment by the character of taxation were recognized. Monetary policy was reintroduced as an important, flexible, two-way instrument. As a restraint on the political tendency to approve expenditures without counting the costs adequately, a version of budget-balancing was proposed which would ordinarily require expenditure decisions to be accompanied by taxing decisions but would not prevent variations in the deficit or surplus as economic conditions fluctuated. Deliberate fiscal actions to stimulate or restrain the economy were to be confined to clear and serious cases in order to reduce the risks of errors of timing and amount.

This postwar consensus was the third step in the fiscal revolution, the first having been the relaxation of monetary constraints in 1933 and the second Roosevelt's choice of the fiscal and monetary path when confronted with the 1938 recession. The postwar consensus regularized compensatory policy and incorporated it into standard, generally acceptable thinking. On the one hand it was conservative recognition that compensatory fiscal behavior was to be an ordinary feature of policy, not something reserved for emergencies so grave as to be qualitatively different from the rest of history. True, the consensus formulations relied upon the built-in stabilizers for ordinary circumstances and confined deliberate fiscal action to serious situations. But this was not an issue of principle. There was no way to define a "serious" situation, and the recommendation amounted only to a warning to adapt actions to circumstances, a warning which governments would interpret in the light of their own ambitions and self-confidence.

On the other hand the postwar consensus removed those features of early Keynesianism which had been most controversial and objectionable— its leanings toward big government and egalitarian policy and its skepticism about the function of profits and interest in the economic system. It helped to resolve the differences between Keynesians and anti-Keynesians which had obstructed agreement on policy. In the process it also helped to make "Keynesian" a term synonomous with "modern" or "scientific" but not otherwise related to ideas originating with J. M. Keynes. Thus Randolph Churchill, writing in 1967, could describe as "almost Keynesian" a speech given by his father Winston in 1908 when Keynes was still a young bureaucrat in the India Office.[2]

From this point, around 1950, the further elevation of compensatory finance to standard doctrine and major, but not sole, influence in fiscal decisions was mainly the product of further habituation. The contribution of the Eisenhower administration to this process was especially important in confirming the fact that Republicans as well as Democrats, conservatives as well as liberals, would henceforth discuss and make fiscal policy decisions with major attention to their expected effects on the overall behavior of the economy.

Issues remained of course. What was the desired behavior of the economy and what fiscal actions would help most to achieve it were matters of debate. But there was no debate over the proposition that these were in principle the most relevant considerations, although the government for various reasons might be at times unwilling or unable to follow the prescription derived from these considerations.

The general acceptance of compensatory finance as the basic principle of fiscal policy did not rest on any conclusive scientific demonstration that a policy of compensatory finance had worked or would work. The scientific issues were still unsettled in the mid-1960's when the history related here ends.

As far as the public at large was concerned, the underpinnings of compensatory finance were slight. Probably most important was the belief, mainly derived from the Depression, that something had to be done, and had to be done by the government, about unemployment. The idea that a compensatory fiscal policy was a proper way of doing that, which did not imply that fiscal policy was the only way, was simply conformity to what "all" informed, responsible people thought.

The acceptance of the idea by leaders of opinion, in government, business, labor, the press, and the intellectual community, had somewhat more basis. First, there was the accumulating experience of behaving in a compensatory way, starting no later than Roosevelt's 1938 spending program and including the automatic deficits of postwar recessions plus some steps in the direction of active use of fiscal policy for stabilization. This was influential even apart from any evidence of its success, because it made compensatory action the normal thing to do. But it was also a fact that the automatic or intended responses of the budget position to the economic situation seemed to have caused no harm. More than that, the economy performed much better in the postwar years when the compensatory idea was gaining influence than it had in the 1930's, and there were few who retained any clear view of what the economy had been like before the 1930's.

The economic theory underlying the compensatory policy had a directness which made it believable to non-economists. Nothing could be more obvious than that if the government employed more people total employment would rise or that if the government bought more goods more goods would be produced. Only slightly less obvious was the proposition that if taxes were reduced people would have more income to spend and would spend more, buying more output and employing more workers.

Still, endorsement of the compensatory ideas by a large proportion of all economists contributed to their general acceptance. Insofar as scientific evidence entered into the common acceptance of compensatory fiscal policy, it entered through its influence on the thinking of economists. But in fact the enthusiastic endorsement by economists of the idea that fiscal policy should be mainly governed by the economic stability objective and should be the main instrument for achieving that objective was based largely on a plausible and attractive theory for which the initial evidence was slight and about which subsequent investigation has tended to raise more questions.

To say that compensatory fiscal policy works implies two different things. First it implies that fiscal actions have powerful effects on the total national income, from which other effects on production, employment, and prices are expected. Second it implies that under a compensatory policy the timing and size of fiscal actions will be so managed as to keep the national income closer to the desired path than it would be with some other fiscal policy.

That fiscal actions should have some effect on the national income is not sufficient to justify a compensatory fiscal policy. These effects should be large —large enough to justify some sacrifice of other objectives of fiscal policy for the sake of the gain in economic stability. To use fiscal policy for compensatory purposes may involve more frequent tax changes than taxpayers would like, more frequent changes in the rates of government spending than are consistent with maximum efficiency, loss of the expenditure discipline that would result from adherence to the rule that expenditures should be matched by taxes, and possibly diversion of attention from more efficient ways of stabilizing the economy. To make economic stabilization the main guide to fiscal policy and fiscal policy the main instrument of stabilization implies that the effects of fiscal action are strong.

The Keynesian theory, upon which most modern economic thinking about fiscal policy rests, could not by itself show that the effects were strong. While the theory made explicit room for the possibility that fiscal policy would have strong effects, whether the effects were actually strong would depend upon certain quantities in the economic system which could not be deduced from the theory. These quantities would have to be observed in the world.

If the effects of fiscal action had been very strong they might have shown up directly in history. It might have appeared that whenever fiscal action was taken in an expansive direction the economy actually expanded in a significant degree simultaneously or after some regular period. But in fact no such regularity exists. A common criticism of compensatory fiscal policy was that the large deficits of the Depression did not end the Depression. The answer given in support of the power of fiscal action was a demonstration that in fact the expansive fiscal action taken during the Depression was small, which leaves open the question whether the effect would have been large if the action had been large. There are many other historical episodes which, at least, fail to reveal the power of fiscal action. The 1948 tax cut was followed by a recession. Most of the Korean War inflation occurred while the budget surplus was rising, and the inflation abated when the surplus turned into a large deficit. The 1954 recession, which occurred with a rising full-employment surplus, was milder than the 1957–58 recession which coincided with a falling full-employment surplus.

Of course there are also cases which conform to the normal expectation. The huge deficits of World War II were accompanied by movement of the economy from depression to full employment and inflation.[3] Eisenhower's drive for a budget surplus in 1959–60 was followed by a slowdown in the economy. Strong expansion of the economy went on after the 1964 tax cut. There was a rapid inflation when deficits rose with the Vietnam War.

More generally, systematic comparison of the movement of the budget position and the movement of the economy in the same or succeeding periods show no systematic relationship even in direction.[4] But this is inconclusive evidence. There are always many things going on in the economy, and these may swamp the effects of fiscal action. The fiscal action may still be important in affecting the economy, even though it is not always or often on a big enough scale to dominate the economy. All that can be said is that the directly visible historical evidence does not reveal the power of fiscal policy, which may nevertheless be present.

The evidence upon which economists have based their confidence in the power of fiscal policy has not consisted mainly of direct observation of fiscal policy. Rather it has consisted of certain observations about the nature of the economy which, if correct, would strongly imply the power of fiscal policy. Two propositions were particularly important. The first was that the amount of income currently being earned has a relatively large effect on spending. The second was that the amount of money people have—as distinct from their flow of income—has a relatively small effect on spending. If the first was true, an increase of government spending by generating income would cause a large increase in private spending and so would have a large multiplier. If the second was true, the rise of total spending and income resulting from the government expenditure would be only a little restrained by the failure of the amount of money to rise. It would also mean that an increase in the amount of money would not increase spending much and would not be an adequate substitute for the government expenditure as a means of stimulating the economy.

In the early years after the publication of Keynes' *General Theory*, in 1936, both of these propositions were empirically investigated. Comparison of the historical record of incomes and consumption, the largest element in total spending, suggested a close relationship between them which was interpreted as confirming the first of these propositions. The second proposition, about money, was tested indirectly. In the belief that the quantity of money would affect spending only through its effects on interest rates, businessmen and others were asked what effect a change of interest rates would have on their investment spending. Such surveys generally found the opinion that the effects would be small. Taken together these investigations confirmed Keynes' hunches from which the importance of fiscal policy had been deduced.

However, since about 1945 the net effect of study has been progressively to reduce certainty about these questions. Further analysis of the determinants of consumption has shown the importance of factors other than current income.[5] Even more clearly, accumulating experience and study have increased the weight given to monetary factors in the determination of income and expenditures.[6] How far these trends of thinking will legitimately go is uncertain. Differences of opinion among experts remain.[7] However it was clear in 1968 that the confidence in the power of fiscal policy common among economists in 1948, by which time the confidence was firmly established, went beyond the evidence available to them in 1948, even though it was still possible that future study would validate their view.

Whether fiscal policy works or not depends not only on how powerful it is but also on how well it is applied. Even from the point of view of stabilization, a policy of trying to determine fiscal action in terms of the best estimates of the changing requirements for economic stability may turn out to be inferior to a fiscal policy which follows other guides. Whether it is or not will depend on the accuracy with which responsible people estimate the future course of the economy and prescribe compensatory measures when indicated, and also upon the fidelity with which policy-makers follow these prescriptions. It will also depend upon the nature of the policy which is a possible alternative to compensatory policy.

To judge compensatory policy in these terms is extremely difficult. In a rough way, with many assumptions, past policy can be assessed. If assumptions are made about what the goals were and about the magnitude and timing of the effects of fiscal actions, the effects of past policy can be compared with the effects of alternative specified policies. For example,the comparison might be with a policy of keeping the full-employment surplus constant at zero. Analysis of this kind would probably suggest that the balanced full-employment budget policy would have given superior results.[8] However such a paper experiment would not answer the relevant question. If the full-employment balanced budget had been national policy, there would undoubtedly have been departures from strict adherence to it which would have made it in fact less effective than would seem from the assumption of precise conformity to it. On the other hand, whether past policy was actually compensatory policy may be questioned. At least it is always possible to say that the compensatory policy proposed for the future, with the advantage of past experience, will be much better than anything done in the past.

The point here is not to establish whether a fully compensatory policy would be more or less stabilizing in practice than a policy of adherence to some other rule, recognizing the looseness with which any policy will actually be executed. The point here is that the country moved to a compensatory policy without a scientific answer to this question. Shortly after World War II, when economists' forecasts of the postwar depression had proved radically wrong, there was a considerable interest in rules which would protect the economy from the translation of such errors into policy. CED's stabilizing budget policy rule was a leading example. However, this was a passing phase, and not because the rules proved inferior or unnecessary. There was no way to obtain adherence to the rules. However much a President and his economic advisers might agree that a simple rule would have prescribed better policy than their predecessors had followed, they could not believe that of themselves. Even the authors of the rules wanted to use their "best judgment" rather than follow the rules when they were confronted with specific situations. There had been some hope that the budget-balancing sentiment in the country would require the government to adhere to a rule if it was specified in a way which made it look like budget-balancing. But by 1964, if not much earlier, the budget-balancing sentiment was clearly too weak to enforce anything, and in any case it was not going to rise in support of a pale reflection of the balanced budget.

Recognition of this fact was the fourth step in the fiscal revolution. Fiscal policy was liberated not only from the old fashioned notion of budget-balancing but also from all other rules, such as balance at high employment, balance over the business cycle, or balance of tax and expenditure changes. There was no longer any general rule to inhibit the continuous and complete adaptation of fiscal decisions to the estimated requirements of economic stability at high employment. This did not mean that such adaptation would in fact govern fiscal decisions. Compensatory finance would still have to contend with and adapt itself to the other interests that decision-makers have in taxes and expenditures, as was demonstrated by the failure to raise taxes in 1966 and 1967.

The evolution of policy to this stage was mainly the expression of forces set in motion by the Depression of the 1930's. Whether future steps will be in the same direction is uncertain. The argument for still more complete and precise determination of fiscal policy by compensatory goals and calculations continues. At the same time, intellectual criticism of the analytical and empirical underpinnings of this argument is probably more intense than at any time in the previous twenty years. The history related here suggests that the outcome is unlikely to be determined by the weight of scientific evidence. Despite the preeminence of compensatory finance as the standard doctrine there is still substantial looseness in the adaptation of policy to it. What we do will influence future doctrine as much as present doctrine will influence future practice.

Notes

Chapter 2 (pages 6–38)

1. President's Conference on Unemployment, Herbert Hoover, Chairman, Committee on Recent Economic Changes, *Recent Economic Changes in the United States* (New York: McGraw Hill Book Co., 1929), p. 867.

2. In November, 1920, he said in an address as president of the Federation of American Engineering Societies: "This regulation [of public utilities, etc.] is, itself, also proof of the abandonment of the unrestricted capitalism of Adam Smith." (Herbert Hoover, "A Plea for Cooperation," *American Federationist*, 28[1921]:36.)

3. Arch W. Shaw File, Hoover Institution on War, Revolution, and Peace, Stanford University, Stanford, California.

4. *International Labor Review*, March, 1922, p.359.

5. Herbert Hoover, *The Memoirs of Herbert Hoover* (New York: Macmillan Co., 1952), 3:30–31.

6. Walter Lippmann, *Interpretations, 1931–1932* (New York: Macmillan Co., 1932), p. 87.

7. Herbert C. Hoover, *The State Papers and Other Public Writings of Herbert Hoover*, ed. William Starr Myers (Garden City, N.Y.: Doubleday, Doran & Co., 1934), 1:241.

8. Lawrence R. Klein, *The Keynesian Revolution* (New York: Macmillan Co., 1947), p. 31.

9. "A reform of taxation such as a reduction of the high surtaxes increases the taxable income through stimulation of business and productive investment so that what apparently would be a loss is later made up. Still it is well not to cut revenue beyond the reasonable requirements of the Government. . . . It has been the experience of the Treasury that every time there has been a material reduction in surtaxes it has stimulated business and brought about an increase in taxable income which has made up a great part, if not all, of the loss of revenue from the higher incomes. . . . A reduction in the lower brackets in itself means no increase in taxable income. A man with a $5,000 salary does not carry funds in nonproductive investments and a reduction of his taxes does not therefore create additional taxable income." (U.S., Congress, House, Hearings before the Committee on Ways and Means, *Revenue Revision*, 69th Cong., 1st sess. 1925, pp. 2, 5.)

10. William T. Foster and Waddell Catchings, "Mr. Hoover's Plan: What It Is and What It Is Not—The New Attack on Poverty," *Review of Reviews*, April, 1929, p. 77. Foster and Catchings' evaluation of the Hoover plan is symptomatic of current (1929) attitudes toward the times and the President: "The Plan is not philanthropy. It is business, guided by measurements instead of by hunches. It is economics for an age of science—economics worthy of the new President."

11. E. Jay Howenstine, Jr., "Public Works Policy in the Twenties," *Social Research*, 13(1946):500.

12. Paul H. Douglas and Aaron Director, *The Problem of Unemployment* (New York: Macmillan Co., 1931), pp. 210–11.

13. Hoover, *Memoirs*, 2:46.

14. Hoover, *State Papers*, 1:33.

15. A sample of Hoover's method, at least in his later, more irritable phase, is given in the notes of his friend, James H. MacLafferty. On July 27, 1932, Hoover had a secret meeting with leading bankers of the country. He told them that if they didn't perform their functions as bankers so that conditions would speedily improve, he would see to it that the Federal Reserve acted in their stead. They would have to make commodity prices advance. There was stubborn resistance from the bankers, and Hoover threatened to go to the country. MacLafferty observed, "H.H. does not intend to go down with this depression except after the hardest kind of fight." (MacLafferty File, Hoover Institution on War, Revolution, and Peace, Stanford University, Stanford, California.)

16. Lippmann, *Interpretations, 1931–1932*, pp. 67–68.

17. Hoover, *State Papers*, 1:133.

18. *Ibid.*, pp. 133–34.

19. *Ibid.*, pp. 145–46.

20. Hoover, *Memoirs*, 3:43, 57.

21. Mr. Hoover's sense of carrying out a plan previously determined is suggested in a speech to the U.S. Chamber of Commerce on May 1, 1930, where he referred to the previous government studies of unemployment and said: "In remedial measures we have followed the recommendation of seven years ago as to the acceleration of construction work, the most practicable remedy for unemployment." (Hoover, *State Papers*, 1:295.)

22. Dated December 2 and submitted to Congress December 4 (*Ibid.*, p. 167).

23. *Ibid.*, p. 179.

24. Receipts for the fiscal year 1930 depended on corporate and individual incomes in calendar years 1928 and 1929, whereas receipts for fiscal year 1931 depended on incomes in calendar years 1929 and 1930. Roughly, the receipts estimates assumed that taxable incomes in 1930 would be as high as in 1928.

25. The Administration was working on plans to accelerate its expenditures for public works within existing appropriations, but found no need to discuss that in the budget message, since the acceleration would not affect the fiscal year appropriation or expenditure totals. Moreover, total federal construction expenditures were running at the rate of $150 million a year. Possible acceleration of this during the remaining six months of fiscal 1930 could not have added much to the year's totals as shown in the budget. As for the next fiscal year, the Administration was not yet ready to commit itself to an enlarged program.

26. The standard presentation of the budget totals at the time included as expenditure a certain amount of debt reduction required by the sinking fund statute. On this basis, which is the basis used by the President in talking about the surplus, the excess of receipts was $185 million in 1929, estimated at $145 million in 1930, and estimated at $42 million in 1931, after the proposed tax cut.

27. Hoover, *State Papers*, 1:189–90.

28. *Ibid.*, p. 201.

29. *Ibid.*, pp. 345–47.

30. *Ibid.*, p. 266.

31. *Ibid.*, p. 359.

32. Hoover, *Memoirs*, 2:58.

33. Erving P. Hayes, *Activities of the President's Emergency Committee for Employment (October 17, 1930–August 19, 1931)* (Concord N. H.: Rumford Press, 1936), p. 43.

34. "The Financial Situation," *Commercial and Financial Chronicle*, 131 (1930):2419.

35. Louis Bean, *Memoir* (MS in Oral History Collection, Columbia University Libraries, New York City), p. 94.

36. U.S. Department of Commerce, Office of Business Economics, *The National Income and Product Accounts of the United States, 1929–1965*. These figures are total government construction as estimated in the national income accounts in 1966. (Washington: U.S. Department of Commerce, 1966) p. 80.

37. Hoover, *State Papers*, 1:459.

38. These are the figures as the budget was regarded at the time, including statutory debt reduction as an expenditure. If that expenditure had been excluded there would have been a surplus of receipts throughout—an actual surplus of about $700 million in fiscal 1930 and estimated surpluses of $250 million in fiscal 1931 and $500 million in fiscal 1932.

39. Edward E. Hunt File, Hoover Institution on War, Revolution, and Peace, Stanford University, Stanford, California.

40. Arthur M. Schlesinger, Jr., *The Age of Roosevelt*, 3 vols. (Boston: Houghton Mifflin Co., 1957–60), vol. 3, *The Politics of Upheaval* (1960), p. 10.

41. E. Cary Brown, "Fiscal Policy in the 'Thirties': A Reappraisal," *American Economic Review*, 46 (December, 1956):857.

42. Hoover, *State Papers*, 1:456–57.

43. In an editorial on May 27, 1931, the *New York Times* said: "There is no mystery concerning the reasons which kept Secretary Mellon from being definite [about additional taxes]. They are the same reasons which are brought out in our Washington correspondence and elsewhere, and which lead to the belief that no new taxes will be voted by Congress in the next session. Probably none will be recommended by the President. Should they be, the chances are that his own party would not favor enacting them before the Presidential election. That political event is already laying a paralyzing hand upon governmental activities.

"This judgment of the case, in its political aspects, goes well with the intimation that the Administration will urge the desirability of studying the whole question of revenue and expenditure and taxation until a year from next December—that is, until after the Presidential election. Before it, nothing must be done to embarrass Republican campaign orators. . . . It would never do to shock the Republican leaders by asking them to adopt and proclaim a practical way of raising by new taxes the money which the Government is sure to need within the next twelve months. 'Men and brethren,' they would say, 'do you want to hand the Presidency to the Democrats on a gold platter?' " (*New York Times*, May 27, 1931.)

Hoover believed that budget balancing and economy were good political issues, as Roosevelt did in 1932. MacLafferty reports, for example, that in April, 1932, Hoover hoped, for political reasons, that Congress would pass the bonus bill so that he could veto it. But Hoover, because he was President and because he had Mellon and Mills in his corner, was better able than any likely opponent to define what budget balancing meant and what was par for the budget-balancing course. So he could hardly lose on that issue. The President was better able to persuade people that the budget was balanced when it was not than that they were employed and prosperous when they were not.

44. *New York Times*, March 29, 1931.

45. *Ibid.*

46. *Ibid.*, April 1, 1931.

47. *Ibid.*, May 22, 1931.

48. T.R.B., "Washington Notes," *New Republic*, June 10, 1931, p. 97.

49. *New York Times*, June 30, 1931.

50. On September 8 Hoover wrote Eugene Meyer, Governor of the Federal Reserve Board, a nagging, threatening letter, pointing out that the deposits of banks that

had suspended since the Depression began amounted to $1.5 billion and that there must be some good assets in those banks. He said that the banking community must organize to make loans on those assets, to repay the depositors. Hoover reminded Meyer that he had mentioned this to him on several earlier occasions. (Letter in Hoover file, Hoover Institution on War, Revolution, and Peace, Stanford University, Stanford, California.)

51. Hoover, *Memoirs*, 3:85, 90

52. Hoover, *State Papers*, 2:46–48.

53. U.S., Treasury Department, *Annual Report of Secretary of the Treasury on the State of the Finances*, 1932, pp. 254–55.

54. The atmosphere of the time is suggested by the notes of George L. Harrison on the meetings of the Federal Reserve Bank of New York:

"Oct. 5, 1931: Mr. Mitchell said that a good part of our present troubles are in the nature of an international run on this country, and expressed the opinion that that is not surprising in view of the unbalanced budget of our government.

"Oct. 15, 1931: Mr. Harrison had asked representatives of the Bank of France whether there was anything we could do to allay fears concerning this country's position. They said we should act 'in as natural a manner as possible.' They expressed the opinion that any unusual action such as Hoover's proposal of a National Credit Corporation raised doubts in Europe—the corporation was viewed as involving inflationary tendencies.

"Jan. 7, 1932: The Treasury could not meet its immediate needs unless discount rates are adjusted so that banks can borrow from the Federal Reserve at a profit on government securities. If we are to deviate from straight and narrow central bank theory because of the terrible economic situation, the government must do all it can to improve the situation—we require an authoritative pronouncement of its intentions with respect to borrowing between now and July 1 and a commitment to operate on a balanced budget beginning July 1, 1932.

"Jan. 21, 1932: European alarm has been fed by reports coming from the United States of increasing governmental budgetary difficulties." (*George Leslie Harrison Papers on the Federal Reserve System: Discussion Notes* [MS in Columbia University Libraries].)

55. Milton Friedman and Anna Jacobson Schwartz, *A Monetary History of the United States, 1867–1960* (Princeton: Princeton University Press, 1963), pp. 395–406.

56. U.S., Congress, Senate, *Congressional Record*, 72nd Cong., 1st sess., 1932, Vol. 75, pt. 10, p. 10314.

57. Jacob Viner, *Balanced Deflation, Inflation or More Depression* (Minneapolis: University of Minnesota, 1933) pp. 24–25.

58. *Ibid.*, pp. 26–27.

59. He goes on to say: "Had it not been for this campaign of fear, however, it would have been sound policy on the part of the Federal government deliberately to permit a deficit to accumulate during the depression years, to be liquidated during prosperity years from the higher productivity of the tax system and from increases in tax rates when they would do no harm. The outstanding though unintentional achievement of the Hoover Administration in counteracting the depression has in fact been its deficits of the last two years, and it was only its own alleged fears as to the ill effects of these deficits, and the panic which the big business world professed to foresee if these deficits should recur, which have made this method of depression finance seriously risky. Had the government and the business magnates retained their mental balance, there would have been less cause to fear net ill effects during a depression than during the war from even a ten billion bollar deficit." (*Ibid.*, pp. 18–19.)

60. Some flavor of the reality that President Hoover saw in the fall of 1931 is suggested by the following account of a discussion between Hoover and French Premier Laval around October 23, as reported in the notes of James H. MacLafferty:

"Hoover told Lavall [*sic*] that he wanted France to withdraw her gold from this country because as it is now the gold France has in this country now is just a threat against financial stability because France can withdraw it any time she chooses and might choose to do so at a very inopportune time and so bring great embarrassment. Hoover cited that a high official of the Bank of France had expressed the opinion that America could not pay her debts if she were called on to do so and that this had caused a run on America which for a time bid fair to cause panic.

"Lavall [*sic*] sought to reassure Hoover but Hoover stuck to his guns and when Lavall [*sic*] asked what France could do Hoover told him France could buy bills that would assure American bankers that they were safe for a specified time anyway. This Lavall [*sic*] agreed France would do and this they did do. And then the run on gold now in the United States stopped and things began to look better. Hoover told Lavall [*sic*] that all this had caused greatly increased hoardings that threatened disaster in the United States and that it must be stopped or in another week we would see an awful panic." (Memo, November 7, 1931, MacLafferty File, Hoover Institution.)

France was at that time the largest holder of foreign short-term balances in the United States. It appears that the increase of discount rates in the United States in the fall of 1931 was motivated in part by the desire to demonstrate to France the determination of the United States to stay on the gold standard, although there is even now some uncertainty about whether an explicit agreement was made with France on this point. "Balancing the budget" was then as now, though probably to a lesser extent now, a key sign of a country's intention to defend its currency. On several occasions in the spring of 1932 declines in the value of the dollar relative to foreign currencies were explained by American and European financial circles as being due to uncertainty about whether Congress would pass the tax-raising bill and balance the budget.

61. John Maynard Keynes, *The General Theory of Employment, Interest and Money* (New York: Harcourt, Brace and Co., 1936), pp. 119–20.

Chapter 3 (pages 39–54)

1. Elliott Roosevelt, ed., *F.D.R. His Personal Letters*, 4 vols. (New York: Duell, Sloan and Pearce, 1950), 3:342.

2. On February 11, 1932, Hoover told his friend MacLafferty about calling in the Congressional leaders and informing them of the need for legislation permitting the Federal Reserve Banks to lend on any sound asset. Senator Carter Glass said that the proposed measure "would make William Jennings Bryan turn over in his grave because of his delight." Glass said that "he had never even dreamed of anything as revolutionary."

"The President then told me [MacLafferty] that the measure he is now proposing makes the Reconstruction Finance Corporation seem conservative. He said also that he had told the Congressional leaders that if they did not do what he wanted them to do it would likely mean that the country would have to abandon the gold standard within thirty days." (MacLafferty File, Hoover Institution of War, Revolution, and Peace, Stanford University, Stanford, California.)

3. At a meeting of the Federal Reserve Board and the Open Market Policy Conference on April 12, 1932, Mills had said: "For a great central banking system to stand by with a 70% gold reserve without taking active steps in such a situation was almost inconceivable and almost unforgiveable. The resources of the System should be put to work on a scale commensurate with the existing emergency." (Quoted in Milton Friedman and Anna J. Schwartz, *A Monetary History of the United States, 1867–1960* [Princeton: Princeton University Press, 1963] p. 385.)

4. The National Bureau of Economic Research places the beginning of the recovery in March, 1933.

5. Raymond Moley, *After Seven Years* (New York: Harper and Bros., 1939), pp. 158–61.

6. Franklin D. Roosevelt, *The Public Papers and Addresses of Franklin D. Roosevelt*, (New York: Random House, 1938), 2:120–21.

7. Roosevelt, *Public Papers*, 3:46–47.

8. Schlesinger, *The Age of Roosevelt*, 3 vols. (Boston: Houghton Mifflin, 1957–60) vol. 3, *The Politics of Upheaval* (1960), p. 263.

9. James MacGregor Burns, *Roosevelt: The Lion and the Fox* (New York: Harcourt, Brace and Co., 1956), p. 323.

10. Schlesinger, *Age of Roosevelt*, vol. 1, *The Crisis of the Old Order, 1919–1933* (1957), p. 414.

11. Johnson called this his "muscleinny" memo. It is reprinted in Hugh S. Johnson, *The Blue Eagle from Egg to Earth* (Garden City, N. Y.: Doubleday, Doran and Co., 1935), pp. 123–32.

12. Daniel L. Fusfeld, *The Economic Thought of Franklin D. Roosevelt and the Origins of the New Deal* (New York: Columbia University Press, 1956), p. 203.

13. Schlesinger, *Crisis of the Old Order*, p. 451 (italics added).

14. "Pierre Jay to Franklin D. Roosevelt, Jan. 26, 1933," "Franklin D. Roosevelt to Pierre Jay, Feb. 1, 1933," F. D. Roosevelt Library, Hyde Park, New York.

15. Roosevelt, *Public Papers*, 2: p. 49.

16. *Ibid.*, p. 51. In his notes on this message, written when his papers were being prepared for publication in 1937, Roosevelt said, "One of the most important factors in the decreased public confidence of these early days was the continued lack of balance of the normal budget during the preceding three years." (*Ibid.*, p. 51, n.) But neither the analysis nor the assurance of the March, 1933, message used the word "normal" or gave any hint that something less than the total budget was intended.

17. National City Bank of New York, *Monthly Letter*, April, 1933, p. 53.

18. Marriner S. Eccles, *Beckoning Frontiers* (New York: Alfred A. Knopf, 1951), pp. 117, 118, 122.

19. Apparently Roosevelt did not even know what had happened. According to Tugwell: "It was something of a shock for him [FDR] to learn, for instance, that just when he was pressing the Congress to make a large appropriation for public works, he had brought to an arbitrary stop all those works that had been going on under the old Hoover program. A stop order put before him by Douglas, and signed without realization of its effect, had paralyzed such public building as there was." (Rexford Guy Tugwell, *The Democratic Roosevelt: A Biography of Franklin D. Roosevelt* [Garden City, N. Y.: Doubleday, Doran and Co., 1957], p. 319.)

20. Roosevelt, *Public Papers*, 2:202–03.

21. *Ibid.*, p. 296.

22. Roosevelt, *Public Papers*, 1:853.

23. Member bank reserve balances increased from $2,509 million at the end of 1932 to $2,709 million at the end of 1933, while Reserve Bank credit increased by about $500 million. From the end of 1933 to the end of 1937 member bank reserve balances rose $4.3 billion, almost all as a result of gold inflow.

24. Roosevelt, *Public Papers*, 1:625.

25. Moley, *After Seven Years*, p. 173, n.8.

26. Frances Perkins, *The Roosevelt I Knew* (New York: The Viking Press, 1946), p. 152.

27. Johnson, *Blue Eagle*, pp. 163–64.

28. In several memos to Johnson in late 1932 and early 1933 Sachs emphasized

the importance of measures to stimulate public and private investment and expressed his reservations about the NRA kind of policy, on both economic and political grounds. Also, in the Spring of 1933 Sachs and R. F. Kahn made computations of the "multiplier" of federal expenditures, and concluded that every dollar of federal spending would indirectly generate $2.57 of total spending on goods and services. (Charles F. Roos, *NRA Economic Planning* [Bloomington, Ind.: The Principia Press Inc., 1937], pp. 417–18, 520–36.) Kahn, an English economist, had published in the *Economic Journal* in 1931 his famous article to which Keynes attributed the multiplier theory. This injection of the multiplier idea into the stream of Washington thinking in 1933 did not take, and it had to be done over later.

29. Johnson, *Blue Eagle*, pp. 196–97.

30. "On May 10 he convened a White House meeting of the leaders of groups working on recovery programs.

"For two hours the discussion ranged through a score of proposals. Finally the President remarked that the group seemed basically divided between a large public works program and government-industry codes. Why not do both? someone spoke up. 'I think you're right', the President said quickly, and he designated several present to 'lock themselves into a room' until they reached agreement." (Burns, *Lion and the Fox*, p. 180.)

31. Roosevelt. *Public Papers*, 2:140–41.

32. Harold L. Ickes, *The Secret Diary of L. Ickes*, 3 vols. (New York: Simon and Schuster, 1953–54), vol. 1, *The First Thousand Days, 1933–1936*, p. 28.

33. Moley, *After Seven Years*, p. 173, n. 8.

34. Roosevelt, *Public Papers*, 2: 202–03.

Chapter 4 (pages 55–73)

1. Frances Perkins, *The Roosevelt I Knew* (New York: The Viking Press, 1941), pp. 202–203.

2. Harold L. Ickes, *The Secret Diary of Harold L. Ickes*, 3 vols. (New York: Simon and Schuster, 1953–54), vol. 1, *The First Thousand Days, 1933–1936*, p. 62.

3. Arthur M. Schlesinger, Jr., *The Age of Roosevelt*, 3 vols. (Boston: Houghton Mifflin Co., 1957–60), vol. 2, *The Coming of the New Deal* (1958), p. 287.

4. Marriner S. Eccles, *Beckoning Frontiers* (New York: Alfred A. Knopf, 1951), p. 131.

5. Ickes, *First Thousand Days*, p. 438.

6. John Morton Blum, *From the Morgenthau Diaries*, 3 vols. to date, vol. 1, *Years of Crisis, 1928–1938* (Boston: Houghton Mifflin Co., 1959), p. 250.

7. Franklin D. Roosevelt, *The Public Papers and Addresses of Franklin D. Roosevelt*, (New York: Random House, 1938), 4:187.

8. *Ibid.*, p. 189.

9. *Ibid.*, p. 401.

10. *Ibid.*, 5:21 (italics added).

11. John H. Williams, "The Implications of Fiscal Policy for Monetary Policy and the Banking System," *American Economic Review*, 32, no. 1, supplement (March, 1942): 239.

12. *New York Times*, January 11, 1935.

13. Roosevelt, *Public Papers*, 4:260.

14. Quoted in James MacGregor Burns, *Roosevelt: The Lion and the Fox* (New York: Harcourt, Brace and Co., 1956), p. 197.

15. Blum, *Years of Crisis*, p. 230.

16. *Ibid.*, pp. 274–75; Roosevelt, *Public Papers*, 5:408.

17. Roosevelt, *Public Papers*, 5:19–20.

18. Arthur Krock, *Memoir* (MS in Oral History Collection, Columbia University Libraries, New York City).

19. Hadley Cantril, ed. *Public Opinion, 1935–1946* (Princeton: Princeton University Press, 1951) p. 678.

20. *Ibid.*, p. 58.

21. *Ibid.*, p. 58.

22. Roosevelt, *Public Papers*, 3:16–24. The summary figures presented on the January 3, 1934, budget message were:

	Fiscal Years (Millions of Dollars)		
	1933	1934	1935
Receipts (Including processing tax)	2,080	3,260	3,975
Expenditures (excluding debt retirement)	4,681	10,569	5,961
General	3,404	2,531	2,487
Agricultural Adjustment	—	515	751
Emergency	1,277	7,523	2,723
Deficit	2,601	7,309	1,986

23. Blum, *Years of Crisis*, 1:238.

24. Roosevelt, *Public Papers*, 4:34. The summary figures presented in the January, 1935, budget message were:

	Fiscal Years (Millions of Dollars)		
	1934	1935	1936
Total receipts (including processing taxes)	3,116	3,712	3,992
Total expenditures (excluding debt retirement)	6,745	8,008	7,884
Regular	2,462	2,748	3,302
Agricultural Adjustment	290	788	472
Recovery and Relief	3,993	4,472	4,110
Deficit	3,629	4,296	3,892

25. Ickes, *First Thousand Days*, pp. 487–88.

26. Roosevelt, *Public Papers*, 5:20–21.

27. *Ibid.*, p. 33.

28. Blum, *Years of Crisis*, 1:266.

29. Roosevelt, *Public Papers*, 5:129.

30. *Ibid.*

31. Ickes, *First Thousand Days*, pp. 666–67.

32. Roosevelt, *Public Papers*, 5:595.

33. *Ibid.*, pp. 660–62.

34. *Ibid.*, p. 497.

Chapter 5 (pages 74–90)

1. Franklin D. Roosevelt, *The Public Papers and Addresses of Franklin D. Roosevelt*, (New York: Random House, 1938) 4:476.

2. *The Guaranty Survey*, Jan. 29, 1934, p. 1. (New York: Guaranty Trust Co. 1934).

3. "Grenville Clark to Franklin D. Roosevelt, Sept. 14, 1934," F. D. Roosevelt Library, Hyde Park, New York.

4. Raymond Moley, *After Seven Years* (New York: Harper and Bros., 1939), pp. 296–98; Rexford G. Tugwell, *The Democratic Roosevelt* (Garden City, N.Y.: Doubleday & Co. 1957), pp. 380–81.

5. Harold L. Ickes, *The Secret Diary of Harold L. Ickes*, 3 vols. (New York: Simon and Schuster, 1953–54), vol. 1, *The First Thousand Days, 1933–1936*, p. 217.

6. *New York Times*, Jan. 8, 1935.

7. Moley, *After Seven Years*, p. 300.

8. Walter Lippmann, *Interpretations, 1933–1935* (New York: Macmillan Co., 1935), p. 205. In the same article Lippmann detected certain basic principles implied in the President's messages; the first of which was: "It is the duty of the government to provide the unemployed with the opportunity to work. That is to say, there is a right to work." This is more interesting as prophecy than as reporting of what the President said or did in 1935.

9. Arthur M. Schlesinger, Jr. *The Age of Roosevelt*, 3 vols. (Boston: Houghton Mifflin, 1957–60), vol. 3, *The Politics of Upheaval* (1960), p. 213.

10. Moley, *After Seven Years*, p. 300.

11. Lippmann, *Interpretations, 1933–1935*, p. 207.

12. Schlesinger, *Politics of Upheaval*, p. 270.

13. *New York Times*, May 2, 1935.

14. *New York Times*, May 5, 1935.

15. Roosevelt, *Public Papers*, 4:163.

16. Ickes, *First Thousand Days*, p. 363.

17. See chapter 2, pp. 9-10 and fn. 9.

18. John Morton Blum, *From the Morgenthau Diaries*, 3 vols. to date, vol. 1, *Years of Crisis, 1928–1938* (Boston: Houghton Mifflin, 1959), p. 301. Morgenthau's testimony in support of the tax proposals before the House Ways and Means Committee (July 8, 1935) did place more emphasis on the revenue-raising aspect of the recommendation: "The Treasury's first concern is with the adequacy of the national revenue. There are many times of emergency when the Treasury must finance expenditures in excess of income by borrowings which increase the public debt. But the national welfare demands that, when such emergency has passed, sufficient income be raised both to meet current expenditures and to make substantial reductions in the debt. The time has come to move in this direction. It would, of course, be unwise to impose tax burdens which would retard recovery. But it would be equally unwise not to call on sources of revenue which would reduce our borrowings and later reduce the national debt without interfering with recovery." (U.S. Cong. House Ways and Means Committee, *Proposed Taxation of Individual and Corporate Incomes, Hearings* 74th Cong. 1st Sess. 1935, p. 5.) The Secretary proposed that the additional revenues provided by increased taxation should be ear-marked to reduce borrowing and debt and should not be available to finance increased expenditure. The President in his message had suggested this treatment only for the revenue yielded by the proposed federal inheritance taxes. Morgenthau stubbornly refused requests from Republican members of the Ways and Means Committee that he tell them how much additional revenue they would have to raise to put the federal finances in good order. The Democratic leadership of the committee praised the Secretary's reticence as proper recognition of the powers and responsibilities of the Congress.

19. Dean Acheson, *Morning and Noon* (Boston: Houghton Mifflin Co., 1965), p. 167. Recalling his experience with FDR in 1933, Dean Acheson later said: "As time went on, they [the President's advisers] became aware that he would not permit anyone, including Huey Long, to occupy a position to the left of him—not that he proposed to operate from the position but to preclude anyone else from doing so."

20. William E. Leuchtenburg, *Franklin D. Roosevelt and the New Deal 1932–1940* (New York: Harper and Row, 1963), p. 152.

21. On July 27, 1936, Ickes made the following entry in his diary: "Sunday morning Harry F. Guggenheim, former Minister to Cuba and son of Simon Guggenheim, came over to see Cissy [Patterson]. He had been out to the notification ceremonies at

Topeka and was quite enthusiastic not only about Landon but about his acceptance speech. He is the only man I have yet met of either party who has had even faint praise for the acceptance speech. I asked him, as I had asked others the night before, what were the specifications to support the charge that Roosevelt was antagonistic to business. My discussion with Guggenheim clarified the whole thing in my mind. It became clear that, exactly as I had said in my speech at the University of Virginia, the fundamental political issue today is taxation. Roosevelt, according to these very rich people, is penalizing business and tearing it down because he has increased the income tax rates in the higher brackets and because he is taxing surpluses in corporation treasuries. This was the only reaction that I could get to my insistent questions asking what Roosevelt had done or proposed to do that was inimical to business." (Ickes, *First Thousand Days*, pp. 651–52.)

22. The Business Advisory Council was a little clearer. In a report to the President on August 8, 1935, the council said: "We believe the Federal budget should be balanced at the earliest possible moment. We recognize, however, that so long as millions of our people are without normal employment, extraordinary expenditures by the Federal Government will continue. While it might be theoretically possible, despite such extraordinary expenditures, immediately to balance the budget, it would entail the enactment of extreme tax measures. . . . The price of a balanced budget may be too high, therefore, for the country to pay at this time."

The council objected to the tax bill as not suited to the revenue requirements of the time. (Business Advisory Council to President Roosevelt, Aug. 8, 1935, [MS in F. D. Roosevelt Library, Hyde Park, New York.])

23. Both Howard's letter and Roosevelt's reply are in Roosevelt, *Public Papers*, 4:353–57.

24. Roosevelt, *Public Papers*, 4:392.

25. Blum, *Years of Crisis*, pp. 305–06.

26. Marriner S. Eccles, *Beckoning Frontiers* (New York: Alfred A. Knopf, 1951), p. 256.

27. Columbia University Commission, *Economic Reconstruction* (New York: Columbia University Press, 1934), p. 239.

28. Commission of Inquiry into National Policy in International Economic Relations, *International Economic Relations* (Minneapolis: University of Minnesota Press, 1934), pp. 92–93 (italics added).

Chapter 6 (pages 91–130)

1. On March 9, 1937, FDR, reviewing the recovery program, was to say: "Today we are only part-way through that program—and recovery is speeding up to a point where the dangers of 1929 are again becoming possible, not this week or month perhaps, but within a year or two." (Franklin D. Roosevelt, *The Public Papers and Addresses of Franklin D. Roosevelt* [New York: Macmillan Co., 1941], 1937 vol., p. 123.) This was said in the context of an explanation of his program to reorganize the Supreme Court and was intended to emphasize the dangers of the Court's obstructionism. However, it suggests the kind of appraisal of the economic situation that was plausible at the time.

2. Roosevelt, *Public Papers*, 5:162.

3. Harry L. Hopkins, *Spending to Save* (New York: W. N. Norton, 1936), p. 180.

4. John Morton Blum, *From the Morgenthau Diaries*, 3 vols. to date, vol. 1, *Years of Crisis, 1928–1938* (Boston: Houghton Mifflin Co., 1959), p. 280.

5. *Ibid.*, p. 281.

6. Roosevelt, *Public Papers*, 5:646–54.

7. Roosevelt, *Public Papers*, 1937 vol., pp. 140–43.

8. For a complete account see Milton Friedman and Anna Jacobson Schwartz,

A Monetary History of the United States, 1867–1960 (Princeton: Princeton University Press, 1963), pp. 511–34.

9. Marriner S. Eccles, *Beckoning Frontiers* (New York: Alfred A. Knopf, 1951), p. 289.

10. U. S. Federal Open Market Committee, *Minutes, 1937* (Washington: Board of Governors of the Federal Reserve System, 1964), pp. 8–15.

11. *Ibid.*, pp. 32, 55 (italics added).

12. Morgenthau reports that Eccles was converted to budget-balancing after FDR gave him a lecture on the subject early in April. (Blum, *Years of Crisis*, p. 282.) This is hard to reconcile with Eccles' statements quoted in the preceding paragraph which are from the minutes of the Federal Open Market Committee for March 13 and 15.

13. Harold L. Ickes, *The Secret Diary of Harold L. Ickes*, 3 vols. (New York: Simon and Schuster, 1953–54), vol. 2, *The Inside Struggle, 1936–1939*, p. 144.

14. Roosevelt, *Public Papers*, 1937 vol., p. 164.

15. *Ibid.*, p. 165.

16. *Ibid.*, p. 446.

17. U.S. Department of Commerce, Office of Business Economics, *The National Income and Product Accounts of the United States, 1929–1965* (Washington: U.S. Department of Commerce, 1966), pp. 52, 58.

18. In May, 1937, Lauchlin Currie, in the Federal Reserve, pointed out that the net government contribution to expenditures was being reduced too rapidly, but, as he wrote later, he "took a too complacent attitude toward the possibility of a recession." (Lauchlin Currie, Unpublished memoir. [Made available by Dr. Currie]).

19. Roosevelt, *Public Papers*, 5:164.

20. Roosevelt, *Public Papers*, 1937 vol., p. 30.

21. When Eccles called it the "second" Roosevelt recession the President was offended and startled. Mrs. Roosevelt reminded him of the short recession in the fall of 1933. (Eccles, *Beckoning Frontiers*, pp. 126–27.)

22. Roosevelt, *Public Papers*, 1937 vol., pp. 474–75.

23. *Ibid.*, 1938 vol., pp. 33–34.

24. *Ibid.*, 1937 vol., p. 475.

25. Currie, Unpublished memoir.

26. Jesse H. Jones with Edward Angly, *Fifty Billion Dollars: My Thirteen Years with the RFC, 1932–1945* (New York: Macmillan Co., 1951), pp. 266–69.

27. Currie, Unpublished memoir.

28. Roosevelt, *Public Papers*, 1937, vol., p. 493.

29. *Ibid.*, 1938 vol., pp. 14–30.

30. This letter is the source of Keynes' famous discourse on the psychology of businessmen: "Businessmen have a different set of delusions from politicians; and need, therefore, different handling. They are, however, much milder than politicians, at the same time allured and terrified by the glare of publicity, easily persuaded to be 'patriots,' perplexed, bemused, indeed terrified, yet only too anxious to take a cheerful view, vain perhaps but very unsure of themselves, pathetically responsive to a kind word. You could do anything you liked with them, if you would treat them (even the big ones), not as wolves and tigers, but as domestic animals by nature, even though they have been badly brought up and not trained as you would wish. It is a mistake to think that they are more *immoral* than politicians. If you work them into the surly, obstinate, terrified mood, of which domestic animals, wrongly handled, are so capable, the nation's burdens will not get carried to market; and in the end public opinion will veer their way." (Quoted in Blum, *Years of Crisis*, p. 404.)

31. Ickes, *Inside Struggle*, p. 317.

32. Blum, *Years of Crisis*, p. 404.

33. "J. M. Keynes to F. D. Roosevelt, March 25, 1938," F. D. Roosevelt Library, Hyde Park, New York.

34. Roosevelt, *Public Papers*, 1938 vol., p. 97.

35. Ruml Papers, University of Chicago Library, Chicago, Ill.

36. John Garner said about Morgenthau's threat to resign: "He won't. His father wouldn't let him." (Quoted in Ellis W. Hawley, *The New Deal and the Problem of Monopoly*, [Princeton: Princeton University Press, 1966], p. 410.)

37. Roosevelt, *Public Papers*, 1938 vol., pp. 221–48.

38. *Ibid.*, p. 222.

39. *Ibid.*, p. 243.

40. *New York Times*, April 15, 1938.

41. Friedman and Schwartz, *Monetary History*, pp. 511–34.

42. National Association of Manufacturers, *A Study of Depressions* (New York: National Association of Manufacturers, 1938) p. 23.

43. Roosevelt, *Public Papers*, 1939 vol., p. 36–53.

44. Fortune Poll. See Hadley Cantril, ed., *Public Opinion, 1935–1946* (Princeton: Princeton University Press, 1951), p. 59.

45. Currie was a leading exponent of this idea, which seems to have been in his mind in November 1937 when he proposed that the fiscal year 1939 budget should be "technically balanced." (Currie, Unpublished memoir.)

46. Blum, *Years of Crisis*, p. 450.

47. The old age program, the railroad retirement program, and the unemployment compensation program were each treated differently and the treatment changed from time to time, but the net effect was as indicated in the text.

48. Beginning in 1935 Lauchlin Currie and Martin Krost at the Federal Reserve Board regularly calculated a statement of federal finance, which they called "Net Income Creating Expenditures of the Federal Government," and which made this and other adjustments. The resulting figures were widely used in economic analysis, both inside the government and out, but they never acquired any official status.

49. Roosevelt, *Public Papers*, 1939 vol., p. 43.

50. *Ibid.*, pp. 46–47.

51. *Ibid.*, pp. 36–37.

52. Roosevelt told Eccles that he was going to "steal" Currie and reconciled Eccles to the loss by saying: "I'm sure you will realize that it isn't such a bad thing after all as far as the Board and you are concerned. You, of course, see the advantages at once of having a friend in court who can represent and speak for your point of view." (Eccles, *Beckoning Frontiers*, p. 333.)

53. Currie, Unpublished memoir.

54. Roosevelt, *Public Papers*, 1938 vol., p. 602.

Chapter 7 (pages 131–68)

1. Quoted in Roy F. Harrod, *The Life of John Maynard Keynes* (London: Macmillan & Co. Ltd., 1951) p. 462.

2. Joseph A. Schumpeter, "John Maynard Keynes, 1883–1946," *American Economic Review*, 36 (1946):515.

3. The flavor of these portraits is suggested by the following sentences on Wilson:
"If only the President had not been so conscientious, if only he had not concealed from himself what he had been doing, even at the last moment he was in a position to have recovered lost ground and to have achieved some very considerable successes. But the President was set. His arms and legs had been spliced by the surgeons to a certain posture, and they must be broken again before they could be altered. To his horror,

Mr. Lloyd George, desiring at the last moment all the moderation he dared, discovered that he could not in five days persuade the President of error in what it had taken five months to prove to him to be just and right. After all, it was harder to debamboozle this old Presbyterian than it had been to bamboozle him; for the former involved his belief in and respect for himself.

"Thus in the last act the President stood for stubbornness and a refusal of conciliations." (John M. Keynes, *The Economic Consequences of the Peace* [New York: Harcourt, Brace and Howe, 1920], pp. 54–55.)

4. *Ibid.*, p. 274.

5. Robert Lekachman, *The Age of Keynes* (New York: Random House, 1966), p. 32.

6. In *The Economic Consequences of the Peace* Keynes described in part the successful operation of the European economy in the prewar half century as follows: "Europe was so organized socially and politically as to secure the maximum accumulation of capital. . . . The immense accumulations of fixed capital which, to the great benefit of mankind, were built up during the half-century before the War, could never have come about in a Society where wealth was divided equitably. . . . If only the cake were not cut but was allowed to grow in the geometrical proportion predicted by Malthus of population, but not less true of compound interest, perhaps a day might come when there would be at last enough to go round, and when posterity would enter into the enjoyment of *our* labors.

"There were two pitfalls in this prospect: lest, population still outstripping accumulation, our self-denials promote not happiness but numbers; and lest the cake be after all consumed, prematurely, in war, the consumer of all such hopes."

But it was not only war that threatened to cut the rate of saving and capital accumulation. Social and psychological changes that would reduce the ability and willingness of the rich to save were real postwar possibilities. As Keynes said, "It was not natural for a population, of whom so few enjoyed the comforts of life, to accumulate so hugely." (Keynes, *Economic Consequences*, pp. 16–19.)

7. Harrod, *Life of Keynes*, p. 350.

8. Keynes said: "My exposition follows the general lines of Prof. Pigou (*Quarterly Journal of Economics*, Nov. 1917) and of Dr. Marshall (*Money, Credit and Commerce*, I, xiv) rather than the more familiar analysis of Prof. Irving Fisher. Instead of starting with the amount of cash held by the public, Prof. Fisher begins with the volume of business transacted by means of money and the frequency with which each unit of money changes hands. It comes to the same thing in the end and it is easy to pass from the above formula to Prof. Fisher's; but the above method of approach seems less artificial than Prof. Fisher's and nearer to the observed facts." (John M. Keynes, *A Tract on Monetary Reform* [London: Macmillan & Co. Ltd., 1923], p. 78, fn. 1.) Marshall and Pigous were the archetypes of British classical economics against which Keynes later felt himself to be in rebellion.

9. "Unemployment, the precarious life of the worker, the disappointment of expectations, the sudden loss of savings, the excessive windfalls to individuals, the speculator, the profiteer—all proceed in large measure from the instability of the standard of value." (Keynes, *Tract on Monetary Reform*, p. v.)

10. Keynes, *Tract on Monetary Reform*, pp. 155–56. See note 9 above for Keynes' list of the "evils" of price instability.

11. The situation and the proposals in Britain in the 1920's were similar to those in the United States in the early 1960's. The United States was suffering from excessive unemployment and balance of payments deficits. It was widely believed that monetary policy could not be made more expansive in the effort to reduce unemployment without causing an outflow of funds and deterioration of the balance of payments. Therefore,

it was suggested that reliance should be placed on expansive fiscal policy, notably the 1964 tax reduction, to raise employment while continuing a tight monetary policy for the sake of the balance of payments. This was called a shift in the "monetary-fiscal mix." The 1924 Keynesian antecedent was not recalled at the later date.

12. Some insight into the order of causation of the fiscal revolution is provided by the following paragraph from Lekachman's generally idolatrous account of The Age of Keynes. The Robertson mentioned is Prof. D. H. Robertson, who published an important study, *Banking Policy and the Price Level*, in January, 1926, which moved in the direction Keynes later followed.

"Public works were not a novel proposal. Lloyd George in 1924 preached public works as the remedy for unemployment to a national audience which ignored his message. What was important in Robertson's analysis [January, 1926] was the giant step taken toward the full-dress demonstration in the *General Theory* [Keynes' work of January, 1936] that economic analysis, properly understood, reinforced the common sense of the alert politician in demanding that the community undertake substantial private [sic—probably should be 'public'] investment in circumstances where private investment manifestly was failing to do its job. That politicians felt the truth before economists proved it was not unique in the history of political economy. Between them Robertson and Keynes finally brought their profession up to the level of political instinct." (Lekachman, *Age of Keynes*, p. 69.)

Since Keynes saw the value of public works at about the same time that Lloyd George saw it, one might also say that it took him twelve years to bring his own theory up to the level of his own instinct. In any case, if the idea appealed to the common sense of alert politicians already, what is the contribution to policy made by bringing the economics profession up to their level, even if there may be a contribution to the economics profession in doing so? And how are we to reconcile that order of events with Keynes' dictum, of which economists are so proud, that, "Practical men, who believe themselves to be quite exempt from any intellectual influences, are usually the slaves of some defunct economist." Perhaps one contribution of economists is to legitimize the ideas of practical men by underpinning them with attractive theories so as thereby to permit their translation into action in a world that is not entirely practical.

13. David Lloyd George, "The Statesman's Task," *Nation and Athenaeum*, April 12, 1924, p. 40.

14. J. M. Keynes, "Does Unemployment need a Drastic Remedy," *Nation and Athenaeum*, May 24, 1924, pp. 235–36.

15. J. M. Keynes, "A Drastic Remedy for Unemployment: Reply to Critics," *Nation and Athenaeum*, June 7, 1924, p. 312.

16. J. M. Keynes, "Foreign Investment and National Advantage," *Nation and Athenaeum*, August 9, 1924, p. 587.

17. That this was the Treasury view, and not the view of British economics, was insisted by Keynes. Speaking of the Treasury he said: "That they are ill-acquainted with the literature of the subject is confirmed by their apparent belief that what they are talking is orthodoxy; whereas this is simply not the case. Not one of the leading economists of the country, who has published his view or with whose opinions I am otherwise familiar, would endorse the general character of their argument." (*Nation and Athenaeum*, May 18, 1929, p. 227.)

The Treasury view is a particular application of "Say's Law," an old economic principle which says that supply creates its own demand and that there cannot be a general deficiency of demand. This is the same as saying that all income that is saved is automatically invested and constitutes a demand for goods. Since Keynes and his followers, after he published the *General Theory*, maintained that one of his main original contributions was the refutation of Say's Law, his statement in 1929 that no leading

British economist subscribed to the Treasury view suggests a certain lapse of memory later.

18. John M. Keynes and Hubert D. Henderson, *Can Lloyd George Do It?* (London: The Nation and Athenaeum, 1929), p. 34, reprinted in John M. Keynes, *Essays in Persuasion* (Harcourt, Brace and Co., 1932), p. 121. In fact, Keynes misquoted Churchill. What Churchill actually said was that the Conservative government had spent £400 million on development work from "a desire to induce a speedier return to prosperity and to diminish unemployment," but "for the purpose of curing unemployment the results have certainly been disappointing. They are, in fact, so meagre as to lend considerable colour to the orthodox Treasury doctrine which has steadfastly held that . . ." and the rest was as Keynes quoted it. In fact, the *Nation and Athenaeum* said, editorially: " 'Considerable colour to the Treasury doctrine!' That is not the same as saying that you think it right. And Mr. Churchill hestitates to say that it is right. 'Our own practice,' he observes, 'does not entitle me to do so.' " This was in April, 1929. A month later Chancellor Churchill was still hestitating to endorse the Treasury view. The government issued a White Paper entitled "Memoranda on Certain Proposals Relating to Unemployment," all of the memoranda but one being signed by responsible ministers. The one exception was the Treasury memorandum, which was not signed by Churchill but was issued on the responsibility of the Treasury staff.

19. Keynes gave a more "modern Keynesian" version of where the money would come from in his *Nation and Athenaeum* article of May 18, 1929, on "The Treasury Contribution to the White Paper." There he listed five sources which would supply the finance for an increase in government spending without an increase in tax rates: (1) cut in foreign investment; (2) cut in the dole; (3) increase in government revenues resulting from increase in national income, (4) increase in profits, part of which will be saved; and (5) increase in wage payments, part of which will be saved. What is "modern Keynesian" about this is that all of the financing comes out of the flow of income, taxes, and saving, and none of it "out of" creation of credit, although the creation of credit may be a necessary condition for the increased income flows out of which the expenditure is to be financed.

20. Keynes, *Essays in Persuasion*, pp. 125–26. Keynes does not refer here to the possible adverse effect on the balance of payments, and on the gold flow, resulting from the increase of domestic income and employment. Presumably the argument is that a given increase of domestic income and employment will cause less gold outflow if it is accompanied by government investment than if it is not.

21. John M. Keynes, *A Treatise on Money*, 2 vols. (New York: Harcourt, Brace and Co., 1930), 2:376. Keynes explained that since he had written so much about the application of this policy to Great Britain in 1929–30 he did not have to say much about that in *A Treatise on Money*. However, this does not explain why he did not have more to say about the subject in general, if he thought that the British conditions of the 1920's were likely to be met at other times and places. Harrod says: "This was a treatise on money and banking policy and not, therefore, the proper place for a full discussion of Public Works and the direct Government stimulation of capital outlay . . ." (Harrod, *Life of Keynes*, p. 413.) Still, that Keynes should have said so little about fiscal policy in so big and far-ranging a book shows what a small place it then had in Keynes' system of thought. Surely, no modern Keynesian could write so much on this subject without saying much more about fiscal policy.

22. Keynes, *Treatise on Money*, 2:373–74.

23. *Ibid.*, p. 387.

24. Keynes, *Essays in Persuasion*, p. ix.

25. Speaking of Keynes' attack on the gold standard in *A Tract on Monetary Reform* (1923), Harrod says: ". . . in spite of the book, Britain and most other countries returned

to the Gold Standard shortly afterwards, and the matter appeared to be closed. However, the book caused a controversy which was sufficiently lively to be remembered for some years; the leading politicians and bankers took notice; the seeds of doubt had been sown among a wide public. For a year or two Keynes' view was in eclipse. But within a decade it had won the allegiance of at least half the world. Affection for the Gold Standard may yet revive. If it does not, the historian will record that Keynes, almost single-handed, killed that most ancient and venerable institution." (Harrod, *Life of Keynes*, pp. 339–40.)

However, it would be more pertinent to say that within a decade half of the world had run out of gold than that half the world had come to Keynes' view of the gold standard. And by the 1960's, although "affection" for the gold standard may not have revived, except possibly in France, most of the features of the gold standard which worried Keynes had returned, as was evidenced by the contortions Britain went through in an effort to defend the exchange value of the pound. Keynes had not killed the gold standard, either single-handed or with help, although it must be said that he made a noble effort.

26. Keynes, *Tract on Monetary Reform*, pp. 197–98.

27. Fisher recognized many predecessors, notably the American economist and astronomer, Simon Newcomb, who had made a proposal for monetary stabilization in an article published in 1879. (Simon Newcomb, "The Standard of Value," *North American Review*, 120 [1879]:223–27.)

28. See above, p. 481, fn. 8.

29. Keynes in *A Treatise on Money* said that he then (1930) had more sympathy with the reservations expressed by the Federal Reserve people than he had felt earlier but nevertheless believed they went entirely too far in belittling their potential accomplishments in economic stabilization. (Keynes, *Treatise on Money*, 2:339–52.)

30. *New York Times*, August 24, 1923.

31. *New York Times*, August 13, 1924.

32. *New York Times*, January 27, 1926.

33. *New York Times*, April 10, 1926. The *Times*' dislike of Keynes was not confined to his economics. They didn't like his manners either. In one editorial they complained that his attitude towards foreigners came near echoing Samuel Johnson's observation: "So far as I can see, foreigners are mostly fools."

34. For example, a popular textbook of the 1920's, Garver and Hansen, *Principles of Economics*, covered the subject in its 1928 edition in these words: "Another proposal for stabilization would require all governmental units, and especially the Federal government, to plan the building of public works over a long period of time in such a manner that these undertakings could be pushed forward vigorously as soon as a decline in trade begins to appear. It is especially desirable that these public works should be financed out of additional bank loans so that the monetary purchasing power of the community may be increased." (Frank B. Garver and Alvin H. Hansen, *Principles of Economics* [Boston: Ginn and Co., 1928], p. 399.)

35. We have noted Keynes' assertion that no leading British economist agreed with the Treasury view (see above, fn. 17). He could probably have made the same statement about American economists. For example, one of the best American economics texts of the 1920's, Fred M. Taylor's *Principles of Economics*, clearly states and affirms Say's Law that the supply of goods constitutes the demand for goods, that there can be no general deficiency of demand, and that any particular increase of expenditures must be at the expense of some other expenditures. But Taylor then went on to point out that "Say's Law is a Long-Run Principle." The process of exchange has two parts—goods for money and money for goods. "It follows from the facts just brought out that it is possible for us to *postpone* for a long period, even *indefinitely*, the second part of the opera-

tion, thus cutting down for the time being the general demand for goods, though we have not cut down the amount of production. . . . If now, under such a condition of things, the public authorities step in and undertake a large program of road-making or building construction or harbor improvements, this will really mean a considerable increase in total demand and so an increase in general prosperity.*"

"*It may even be the beginning of a general revival of business."
(Fred M. Taylor, *Principles of Economics* [New York: The Ronald Press Co., 1925], pp. 196–203.)

36. Later, in 1936, Ogden Mills seems to have discovered the Treasury view. In his book of that year, *Liberalism Fights On*, he said that government borrowing on "too large a scale" sucks off funds that would otherwise be available for private investment. If it were claimed that the funds would not be privately used, this would only be, in his opinion, because the deficit had made business frightened of future taxes or inflation. This was said in criticism of Roosevelt's deficits. It was not said about his own deficits when he was Mr. Hoover's Secretary of the Treasury. (Ogden L. Mills, *Liberalism Fights On* [New York: Macmillan Co., 1936], pp. 136–37.)

37. Quoted in Harrod, *Life of Keynes*, p. 417, from Keynes' 1930 testimony before the British Committee on Finance and Industry (Macmillan Committee) of which Keynes was a member.

38. *New York Times*, April 13, 1931.

39. Quincy Wright, ed., *Unemployment as a World Problem* (Chicago: University of Chicago Press, 1931), pp. 1–42.

40. University of Chicago, Norman Wait Harris Foundation, *Minutes of Conference on Unemployment as a World Problem*, mimeographed, Univ. of Chicago Library, Chicago, Ill.), p. 303.

41. Seymour E. Harris, *John Maynard Keynes: Economist and Policy Maker* (New York: Charles Scribners' Sons, 1955), p. 149.

42. Jacob Viner, "Comments on my 1936 Review of Keynes' *General Theory*," in Robert Lekachman, ed., *Keynes' General Theory after Three Decades* (New York: St. Martin's Press, 1964), p. 263.

43. John M. Keynes, *The Means to Prosperity* (London: Macmillan & Co. Ltd., 1933), pp. 20–21 (italics added).

44. Seymour E. Harris, ed., *The New Economics* (New York: Alfred A. Knopf, 1948), p. 18.

45. According to Tugwell, "John Maynard Keynes, over in England, cocked an ear when he read this speech or an excerpt from it, in the *Times*. He was not fond of America and he had no great respect for Americans; he paid little attention to theorists among them; but this sounded like the doctrine for which he stood. He made a note to watch this man if he became President." (Rexford G. Tugwell, *The Democratic Roosevelt* [Garden City, N. Y.: Doubleday and Co., 1957], p. 251.)

46. Hobson was an English economist (1858–1940) whom Keynes later credited with having foreseen some aspects of his *General Theory*. Mitchell we have already encountered as an economist in whom Herbert Hoover had confidence.

47. Eccles presents his views as being the outgrowth of his experience as a banker during the early days of the Depression. In conversation with the author he gave two reasons for his arriving at an "unorthodox" position when other bankers did not. First, as a country banker he felt the pressure of the crisis earlier and more severely than the bankers in New York, Chicago, and other money centers. The other reason was that he had never been to college and therefore did not have any orthodox economics to unlearn.

48. In the fall of 1933, before Eccles took a position in the government, Tugwell arranged for him to meet with the "spenders" in Washington, in the hope that he could

give them arguments to use in the debates then going on within the government. The "spenders" were Tugwell, Ezekiel, Wallace, Hopkins, Jerome Frank, Dern, and others. Eccles observed: "With the exception of Ezekiel and Tugwell, I doubt whether any of the men in my room had ever heard of John Maynard Keynes, the English economist who had frequently been referred to as the economic philosopher of the New Deal." (Marriner S. Eccles, *Beckoning Frontiers* [New York: Alfred A. Knopf, 1951], p. 131.)

49. This becomes clear if we call the roll of economists in important Washington positions in 1933–36. We have already given Viner's appraisal of Keynes' influence, and Viner was Morgenthau's chief economic adviser at the Treasury. At the Federal Reserve, Lauchlin Currie had arrived at the idea of compensatory spending independently, as had Eccles, and his initial reaction to Keynes' *General Theory* was negative. At Agriculture, then a leading source of economic ideas, Ezekiel was not inclined to place much reliance on fiscal policy and did not absorb "modern Keynesianism" until about 1939, according to his memoir in the Columbia University Libraries' Oral History Collection, and Gardiner Means never was a Keynesian of either the pre-1936 or post-1936 variety.

50. U. S., Congress, Senate, *Congressional Record*, 73rd Cong., 2nd sess., vol. 78, pt. 1, 1934, p. 188.

51. W. M. H. "At the Observation Post," *The Literary Digest*, August 25, 1934, p. 11.

52. Rexford G. Tugwell, *The Democratic Roosevelt: a Biography of Franklin D. Roosevelt* (Garden City, New York: Doubleday & Co., 1957) p. 375.

53. Frances Perkins, *The Roosevelt I Knew* (New York: The Viking Press, 1946), pp. 225–26.

54. Harrod, *Life of Keynes*, p. 449. That Roosevelt later turned a letter from Keynes over to Morgenthau for reply, knowing that there was no one in the administration less sympathetic to Keynes' argument, does not suggest the highest regard for Keynes.

It was during this trip that Keynes acted out his new economics for Calvin Hoover, economics professor at Duke University, then on leave to work at the Department of Agriculture. Hoover called on Keynes at his room in the Mayflower Hotel before they went out to dinner. Using Keynes' bathroom to wash up, Hoover was careful to take one towel from the pile of clean ones without disturbing the others. Entering after him, Keynes swept several of the clean towels to the floor and told Hoover, "I am convinced that I have served the economy of the U.S.A. better by stimulating employment through mussing up these towels than you have by your carefulness in avoiding waste." (Calvin B. Hoover, *Memoirs of Capitalism, Communism and Nazism* [Durham: Duke University Press, 1965], p. 173.)

55. It has become a cardinal point with latter-day American Keynesians that Roosevelt was *not* influenced by Keynes as early as 1934. How otherwise would they explain the duration of the Depression? For example, Edwin L. Dale, writing in the *New York Times* in 1966 said: "If President Franklin Roosevelt had received the message, the great Depression would probably have been over in a year or two instead of lasting nearly half a generation." (*New York Times*, September 18, 1966.)

56. John M. Keynes, *The General Theory of Employment, Interest and Money* (New York: Harcourt, Brace and Co., 1936).

57. R. F. Kahn, "The Relation of Home Investment to Unemployment," *Economic Journal*, June, 1931, 173–98. Kahn came to the United States and gave a paper to the December, 1932, meetings of the American Statistical Association which rested largely on the multiplier concept. He also worked with Alexander Sachs in the NRA in 1933 estimating the multiplier for the United States.

58. P. H. Karmer, "Giblin and the Multiplier," in Douglas Copland, ed., *Giblin The Scholar and the Man* (Melbourne: F. W. Cheshire, 1960), pp. 164–65.

59. John M. Keynes, "A Self-Adjusting Economic System," *New Republic*, 82:35–37, Feb. 20, 1935.

60. Keynes, *General Theory*, p. 207.

61. *Ibid.*

62. *Ibid.*, p. 220.

63. Paul A. Samuelson, "The General Theory," in Harris, *New Economics*, pp. 145–46.

64. Kenneth Boulding, "Economics—The Taming of Mammon," in Lynn T. White, ed., *Frontiers of Knowledge in the Study of Man* (New York: Harper and Brothers, 1956), p. 133.

65. R. F. Harrod, "Mr. Keynes and Traditional Theory," *Econometrica*, January, 1937, pp. 74–86; J. E. Meade, "A Simplified Model of Mr. Keynes' System," *Review of Economic Studies*, February, 1937, pp. 98–107; J. R. Hicks, "Mr. Keynes and the Classics: A Suggested Interpretation," *Econometrica*, April, 1937, pp. 147–59; O. Lange, "The Rate of Interest and the Optimum Propensity to Consume," *Economica*, February, 1938, pp. 12–32.

66. The *New York Times* did not review the book, and it generally passed unnoticed in the daily press. The *Springfield* [Mass.] *Republican* carried a favorable review by Professor Walter B. Smith of Williams College. The "liberal" *New Republic* did not inform its readers that the revolution had come. Their review, by Horace Taylor, said: "Mr. Keynes undoubtedly will write other books as correctives to this one. In his present study he apparently has taken a step toward the positive position he will finally come to occupy in economic theory. But since it is presented in a highly abstruse and mathematical fashion, 'The General Theory of Employment' probably will not add directly to his popular prestige." (*New Republic*, April 29, 1936.)

67. *The Yale Review*, Summer, 1936, p.62.

68. A. H. Hansen, "Economic Progress and Declining Population Growth," *American Economic Review*, 29 (1939):1–15.

69. Richard V. Gilbert *et al.*, *An Economic Program for American Democracy* (New York: The Vanguard Press, 1938).

70. On February 2, 1939, James Roosevelt telegraphed FDR at the White House: "What is the name of the little book you told me was such a swell story for this business? Much Love, Jimmy" FDR replied: "Title of book 'An Economic Program for American Democracy' by seven Harvard Tufts economists. Father" The notes to FDR's personal letters, edited by Elliott Roosevelt, explain that FDR had discussed with James Roosevelt, who was working for Samuel Goldwyn at the time, the possibility of an educational film on the program and purposes of the New Deal and had suggested this book as the best dramatic material for picturization of the economic philosophy of his administration. According to the note, the book, "which reflected the Keynesian approach to full employment, was a bible of the New Dealers." (Elliott Roosevelt, ed., *F.D.R. His Personal Letters*, 4 vols. [New York: Duell, Sloan and Pearce, 1950], 4:857–58.)

71. Lauchlin Currie, Unpublished memoir. (Made available by Dr. Currie)

72. One of the earliest applications of strict Keynesian logic to economic policy in the United States is on this point. (Walter S. Salant, "A Note on the Effects of a Changing Deficit," *Quarterly Journal of Economics*, 53 [1939]:298–304.)

73. Lauchlin Currie, "Some Theoretical and Practical Implications of J. M. Keynes' General Theory," in National Industrial Conference Board, *The Economic Doctrines of John Maynard Keynes* (New York: NICB, 1938), p. 15.

74. Currie, Unpublished memoir.

Chapter 8 (pages 169–96)

1. Donald S. Howard, *The WPA and Federal Relief Policy* (New York: Russell Sage Foundation, 1943), esp. pp. 561–66.

2. Paul A. Samuelson, "Full Employment after the War," in Seymour E. Harris, ed., *Postwar Economic Problems* (New York: McGraw-Hill, 1943), p. 27.

3. *New York Times*, June 29, 1944.

4. *New York Times*, September 22, 1944.

5. Elmo Roper, *You and Your Leaders* (New York: William Morris and Co., 1957), p. 56.

6. Joseph A. Schumpeter, *Business Cycles*, 2 vols. (New York: McGraw-Hill, 1939), 2:1032–50; James W. Angell, *Investment and Business Cycles* (New York: McGraw-Hill, 1941), pp. 257–89; Charles O. Hardy, "Fiscal Policy and National Income," *American Economic Review*, 32 (1942):103–10; Henry C. Simons, "Hansen on Fiscal Policy," *Journal of Political Economy*, 50 (1942):161–96, reprinted in Henry C. Simons, *Economic Policy for a Free Society* (Chicago: University of Chicago Press, 1948), pp. 184–219.

7. George W. Terborgh, *The Bogey of Economic Maturity* (Chicago: Machinery and Allied Products Institute, 1945).

8. The prewar stagnationists were concerned with questions of the tax structure, mainly from the standpoint of how a given amount of tax revenue could be raised with the least restraint upon private spending. This was a search for ways to reduce the necessary deficit, not for ways to reduce the necessary expenditure. The idea was that if we relied upon kinds of taxes that did not reduce private spending very much we could afford to raise more taxes in total and wouldn't have to run such big deficits. A typical expression was by J. K. Galbraith: "Theoretically a tax system could be imagined which would tap that income, the non-expenditure of which chokes off an upward movement in employment. This, I believe, amounts to little more than saying that taxation could be much better designed than at present to promote employment." (John K. Galbraith, "Fiscal Policy and the Employment-Investment Controversy," *Harvard Business Review* 18 [1939]:30.) What Galbraith could imagine was taxing certain income more in order to promote employment, not taxing less in total.

9. *New York Times*, December 28, 1938.

10. The idea that an equal increase of receipts and expenditures was expansive was contained in an unpublished memorandum by William A. Salant in June, 1942. (MS in possession of Walter S. Salant, Washington, D.C.). Early published discussions of the subject were Henry Wallich, "Income-Generating Effects of a Balanced Budget," *Quarterly Journal of Economics*, 59(1944):78–91; Trygve Haavelmo, "Multiplier Effects of a Balanced Budget," *Econometrica*, 13(1945):311–18.

11. See William H. Beveridge, *Full Employment in a Free Society* (New York: W. W. Norton & Co., 1945), pp. 142–46, and appendix C by Nicholas Kaldor, pp. 345–49; Richard A. Musgrave, "Alternative Budget Policies for Full Employment," *American Economic Review*, 35(1945):387–400.

12. Abba P. Lerner, "Functional Finance and the Federal Debt," *Social Research*, 10(1943):38–51.

13. One of the early discussions of tax reduction as an economic stimulus, while sympathetic to the idea, pointed out that its effectiveness was limited by the amount of taxes paid and it could not therefore be relied upon without the accompaniment of expenditure increases. (Kenyon Poole, "Tax Remission as a Means of Influencing Cyclical Fluctuations," *Quarterly Journal of Economics*, 53[1939]:261–74.) The postwar budget prospects greatly reduced the force of this kind of reservation.

14. American Federation of Labor, *Post-War Program* (Washington: American Federation of Labor, 1944), p. 20.

15. Beardsley Ruml, "Financing Post-War Prosperity—Controlling Booms and Depressions," delivered over NBC radio network, reprinted in *Vital Speeches*, November 15, 1943, pp. 95–96.

16. Beardsley Ruml and H. C. Sonne, *Fiscal and Monetary Policy* (Washington, D.C.: National Planning Association, 1944).

17. Committee for Economic Development, Research Committee, *A Postwar Federal Tax Plan for High Employment* (New York: Committee for Economic Development, 1944), p. 24. This was as far as the committee would go in 1944. However, when the committee later spelled out the meaning of these two sentences, it found that it had committed itself to a comprehensive and far-reaching fiscal program.

18. Thus Simons, in his review of Hansen in 1942, said: "The argument of this chapter is evidently designed to support the view, common among Keynesians, that attention should be focused on spending adjustments and not upon taxes. This again involves, if it does not candidly represent, a collectivist bias in stabilization proposals which, I think, is justified no more by Hansen's argument than by the usual ignoring of the question. Stabilization in principle admits of action on both sides of the budget. and, on its face, calls for rather equal reliance on spending and on taxing adjustments Indeed, political considerations argue, I believe, for allowing to tax adjustments more than an equal share, for it seems much less difficult to maintain real political flexibility in revenues than in expenditures. (Pressure groups are a greater obstacle to expenditure reductions than to tax increases.) Moreover, as already suggested, to make spending the only variable—whether for currency issue or for debt expansion—requires, with increasing income, a continuous, rapid expansion of governmental activities which, even if desirable, ought not to proceed merely as an incident of stabilization." (Simons, "Hansen on Fiscal Policy," in *Economic Policy*, p. 210.)

19. In 1944 Ruml was one of four judges in a national contest for plans for postwar employment. The winning plan, discussing the need to generate budget surpluses or deficits for economic stabilization, said: "The deficit should be created by a combination of increased expenditures and reduced taxes; the surplus should be created by the converse methods. It is important to recognize the role of adjusting taxes in this process. Government spending should be confined to functions in which government operation is efficient and clearly preferable to private operation. This is a large sphere—including health and education—but it is not indefinitely expansible." (Herbert Stein, "A Plan for Postwar Employment," in *The Winning Plans in the Pabst Postwar Employment Awards* [Milwaukee, Wis.: Pabst Brewing Co., 1944] p. 8.) The author of this essay had been a student of Simons, Mints, and Yntema at the University of Chicago and later joined the staff of the CED.

20. Gerhard Colm and Fritz Lehman, "Public Spending and Recovery in the United States," *Social Research*, 3(1936):129–66; R. F. Bretherton, "The Sensitivity of Taxes to Fluctuations of Trade," *Econometrica*, 1937, pp. 171–83.

21. Paul A. Samuelson, "Fiscal Policy and Income Determination," *Quarterly Journal of Economics*, 56(1942):582.

22. James W. Angell, "Taxation, Inflation and the Defense Program," *Review of Economic Statistics*, May, 1941, 78–82.

23. John M. Keynes, *How to Pay for the War* (New York: Harcourt, Brace and Co., 1940). When Keynes visited Washington in June, 1941, on behalf of the British government, he was surprised at the extent to which the Washington economists had absorbed his thinking and the sophistication with which they applied it. At the same time he was critical of some of the procedures used, for reasons which suggested that he was still more classical than his Washington followers. (John M. Keynes to Walter S. Salant, July 9, 1941, July 24, 1941, July 27, 1941 [In Possession of W. S. Salant, Washington, D.C.]).

24. See Carl Shoup, Milton Friedman, and Ruth P. Mack, *Taxing to Prevent Inflation; Techniques for Estimating Revenue Requirements* (New York: Columbia University Press, 1943).

25. At the same time, Ruml was averse to any further glorification of the symbol and warned against saying that budget-balancing was essential to the avoidance of inflation or national bankruptcy.

Chapter 9 (pages 197–240)

1. This history is admirably told in Stephen K. Bailey, *Congress Makes a Law* (New York: Columbia University Press, 1950) upon which we rely heavily here, although with some differences of interpretation.

2. *Ibid.*, p. 45.

3. *Ibid.*, pp. 180–81.

4. This charge was continued beyond the heat of battle in "scientific" discussion. See Sidney S. Alexander, "Opposition to Deficit Spending for the Prevention of Unemployment," in *Income, Employment and Public Policy: Essays in Honor of Alvin Hansen* (New York: W. W. Norton, 1948), pp. 177–78. Alexander maintained that the businessmen opposing the bill wanted a reserve army of unemployed.

5. U. S., Congress, Senate, Banking and Currency Committee, *Hearings on Full Employment Act of 1945*, 79th Cong., 1st sess., 1945, pp. 1210–12.

6. On the basis of an interview with Alvin Hansen, Bailey says that it was certainly Hansen's view that "everything in the original bill except the spending provisions was window dressing." (Bailey, *Congress Makes a Law*, pp. 47–48.)

7. U.S., Congress, Senate, Banking and Currency Committee, *Hearings on Full Employment Act of 1945*, 79th Cong., 1st sess., 1945, pp. 393–400, 705–19, 1219–21, 1210–12, 1092–93.

8. U. S., Congress, House, Committee on Expenditures in the Executive Departments, *Hearings on Full Employment Act of 1945*, 79th Cong., 1st sess., 1945, p. 612.

9. U. S., Council of Economic Advisers, *First Annual Report to the President* (Washington, D.C.: Government Printing Office, 1946).

10. This was the estimate for fiscal year 1947 made in August, 1946.

11. Harry S. Truman, *Years of Trial and Hope*, in *Memoirs by Harry S. Truman*, 2 vols. (Garden City, N.Y.: Doubleday & Co., 1956), 2:41. Truman also said in his memoirs: "I think that the virtue of a 'balanced budget' can at times be exaggerated. Andrew Jackson paid off the national debt entirely, and the budget was balanced when the unprecedented panic of 1837 struck. Even the depression following the crash of 1929 overtook a government which was operating in the black." (Truman, *Memoirs*, 2:40.) However, this can be interpreted to mean that while a balanced budget is a good thing it is not always enough to keep the country out of trouble.

12. Married taxpayers in the "community property states," mainly states of Spanish settlement, were already able to compute their federal taxes as if their combined incomes were equally divided between husband and wife. Income-splitting put married couples in all other states on a par with them.

13. U.S., Bureau of the Budget, *The Budget of the U.S. Government, Fiscal Year 1947* (Washington: Government Printing Office, 1946) p. lix, *Fiscal Year 1948* (Washington: GPO, 1947) p. M63, *Fiscal Year 1949* (Washington: GPO, 1948) p. A2; *Public Papers of the Presidents, Harry S. Truman, 1946* (Washington, D.C.: Government Printing Office, 1962), p. 392.

14. Truman, *Public Papers, 1946*, p. 191.

15. U.S., Congress, Senate, Committee on Finance, *Hearings on Individual Income Tax Reduction*, 80th Cong., 1st sess., 1947, pp. 40–66.

16. *Public Papers of the Presidents, Harry S. Truman, 1948* (Washington, D.C.: Government Printing Office, 1964), p. 16.

17. There were some glimmerings of this argument during the debate. Something of it was implicit in the question that Senator George asked Secretary Snyder in the course of the 1947 hearings: "As I understand it, the position of the Treasury is substantially this: That the dependable basis upon which you can reduce taxes is a reduction of your expenditure budget, rather than the more hazardous basis of possible rises in your national income." Snyder replied: "I quite agree with you." (Senate, Committee on Finance, *Hearings*, 1947, p. 52.)

But this interchange was subject to other interpretations and the clue was not followed. In the summer of 1948, after the tax cut had been enacted, Truman said that "it is hardly sound fiscal policy to rely on inflation as a method of balancing the Budget," but this was too late, and in any case was a comment about relying on future inflation, not about responding to past inflation. (*Public Papers, Harry S. Truman, 1948*, p. 442.)

One witness before the Senate Finance Committee in 1948 who did see the issue clearly was J. Cameron Thomson, president of the Northwest Bancorporation, who testified on behalf of the Committee for Economic Development. He estimated that there would be a surplus of $10 billion in the cash budget for the calendar year 1948 and recommended as a general policy that there should be a $3 billion surplus at high employment. However, he calculated that $3 billion of the 1948 surplus was due to inflation since early 1947 and said that the surplus from that source should not be used for tax reduction. Therefore, he recommended a tax cut of about $4 billion, not all of which should take effect immediately. (U.S., Congress, Senate, Committee on Finance, *Hearings on Reduction of Individual Income Taxes*, 80th Cong., 2nd sess., 1948, pp. 563–73.)

18. Edwin G. Nourse, *Economics in the Public Service* (New York: Harcourt Brace and Co., 1953), p. 138, fn. 12.

19. Senate, Committee on Finance, *Hearings*, 1947, p. 318.

20. *Ibid.*, p. 199.

21. Senate, Committee on Finance, *Hearings*, 1948, p. 233.

22. U.S., Congress, Senate, *Congressional Record*, 80th Cong., 2nd sess., 1948, p. 3038.

23. Senate, Committee on Finance, *Hearings*, 1947, pp. 87–88.

24. *Public Papers of the Presidents, Harry S. Truman, 1947* (Washington, D.C.: Government Printing Office, 1962), p. 280.

25. Senate, Committee on Finance, *Hearings*, 1947, pp. 198–99.

26. *Ibid.*, p. 171.

27. Senate, Committee on Finance, *Hearings*, 1948, p. 145.

28. A. E. Holmans, *United States Fiscal Policy, 1945–1959* (London: Oxford University Press, 1961), p. 99.

29. E. Cary Brown, "Federal Fiscal Policy in the Postwar Period," in R. E. Freeman, ed., *Postwar Economic Trends in the United States* (New York: Harper and Bros., 1960), p. 155.

30. Holmans, *United States Fiscal Policy*, pp. 66–67.

31. Senator Millikin's position was clear. If there was going to be inflation there would be plenty of revenue and we could afford a tax cut, but if there was going to be a recession we would need a tax cut even though there would not be plenty of revenue. (Senate, Committee on Finance, *Hearings*, 1947, p. 57.)

32. How the outcome would have differed if the administration had controlled the Congress is uncertain. The President might in that case have been less opposed to a tax cut, and the cut might have come sooner.

33. 1946 polls from Hadley Cantril, ed., *Public Opinion, 1935–1946* (Princeton: Princeton University Press, 1951), pp. 59–60, 323. 1947 and 1948 polls from *Public Opinion Quarterly*, 11:283, 477 and 12:175, 781–82.

34. Committee for Economic Development, Research and Policy Committee,

Taxes and the Budget: A Program for Prosperity in a Free Economy (New York: Committee for Economic Development, 1947).

35. Committee for Economic Development, Research Committee, *A Postwar Federal Tax Plan for High Employment* (New York: Committee for Economic Development, 1944), p. 24.

36. The committee called its policy the "stabilizing budget policy," in distinction from the "annually-balanced budget policy" and the "managed compensatory policy." The terms were carefully chosen and illustrate the common practice of describing one's own policy by its aims while other people's policies are described by their means.

37. In its 1947 statement the committee talked about "debt management policy," not about monetary policy, as the supplement to budget policy. This was partly a reflection of the preoccupations of 1947, when the problem of monetary policy was the problem of debt management because the possibility of conducting a flexible monetary policy was severely limited by the policy of supporting the prices of government securities. It was also a reflection of a "hobby" of Mr. Ruml's, who believed that a considerable effect upon the stability of the economy could be achieved by varying the packaging and selling of government securities. Later statements by the CED, beginning in 1948, used more conventional language and concepts of monetary policy.

38. Committee for Economic Development, *Taxes and the Budget*, p. 22.

39. Walter W. Heller, "CED's Stabilizing Budget Policy after Ten Years," *American Economic Review*, 47(1957):634–51.

40. Paul A. Samuelson, "Principles and Rules in Modern Fiscal Policy: A Neo-Classical Reformulation," in *Money Trade and Economic Growth: Essays in Honor of John H. Williams* (New York: Macmillan Co., 1951), pp. 157–76. In fact, the CED did not argue that the optimum rate of public spending did not depend upon fluctuation in private demand; its position was that for political and administrative reasons a better approximation of the optimum would be obtained if in the ordinary case no effort was made to adjust actual public spending to short-run fluctuations in the optimum.

41. When J. Cameron Thomson described CED's policy before a subcommittee of the Joint Economic Committee in 1949, Senator Douglas said that CED had really effected a partial marriage between automatic stabilization and managed compensation. Senator Ralph Flanders, who had been the first chairman of CED's Research Committee, thought the arrangement might be better described as a trial marriage. (U.S., Congress, Joint Committee on the Economic Report, Subcommittee on Monetary, Credit and Fiscal Policies, *Hearings on Monetary, Credit and Fiscal Policies*, 81st Cong., 1st sess., 1949, p. 276.)

42. Committee for Economic Development, *Taxes and the Budget*, p. 10.

43. In 1947 CED recommended that the fiscal dividend should not be declared annually but should be accumulated and paid in the form of tax rate reduction at less frequent intervals, such as every five years, to avoid the unsettling effects of annual rate changes. This shows how much weight the committee placed on stability of tax rates. (Committee for Economic Development, *Taxes and the Budget*, p. 24.)

44. U.S. President's Commission on Budget Concepts, *Report* (Washington, D.C.: Government Printing Office, 1967).

45. Committee for Economic Development, Research and Policy Committee, *Monetary and Fiscal Policy for Greater Economic Stability* (New York: Committee for Economic Development, 1948).

46. Milton Friedman, "A Monetary and Fiscal Framework for Economic Stability," *American Economic Review*, 38(1948):245–64.

47. NPA Conference of University Economists, "Federal Expenditure and Revenue Policy for Economic Stability," in U.S., Congress, Joint Committee on the Economic Report, *Money, Credit and Fiscal Policies, A Collection of Statements*, 81st Cong., 1st sess., 1949, pp. 435–40.

48. Joint Committee on the Economic Report, Subcommittee on Monetary, Credit and Fiscal Policies, *Hearings*, 1949, pp. 414–15.

49. U.S., Congress, Joint Committee on the Economic Report, Subcommittee on Monetary, Credit and Fiscal Policies, *Report*, 81st Cong., 2nd sess., 1950.

50. *Ibid.*, p. 15.

51. *Ibid.*, p. 16.

52. *Ibid.*

53. *Ibid.*

54. *Public Papers of the Presidents, Harry S. Truman, 1949* (Washington, D.C.: Government Printing Office, 1964), p. 133.

55. *Ibid.*, p. 192.

56. *New York Times*, May 13, 1949.

57. *Truman, Public Papers*, 1949, p. 247.

58. *Ibid.*, p. 343.

59. Some staff people in the government did see the economic picture more promptly, but the question about economic forecasting is a question about the forecasts on which decision-makers will act.

60. These are figures on the national income accounts basis as shown in Wilfred Lewis, Jr., *Federal Fiscal Policy in the Postwar Recessions* (Washington, D.C.: The Brookings Institution, 1962), p. 128. Subsequent revisions reduced the size of the shift from surplus to deficit, but did not change the basic point that there was a substantial shift hardly any of which was due to active fiscal policy to combat the recession.

Chapter 10 (pages 241–80)

1. Keynes himself was aware of this. A few months before Keynes' death John H. Williams had a conversation with him which he later reported as follows: "He [Keynes] complained that the easy money policy was being pushed too far, both in England and here, and emphasized interest as an element of income, and its basic importance in the structure and functioning of private capitalism. He was amused by my remark that it was time to write another book because the all-out easy money policy was being preached in his name, and replied that he did think he ought to keep one jump ahead." (John H. Williams, "An Appraisal of Keynesian Economics," *American Economic Review*, 38, no. 2 [1948]:287–88, fn. 33.)

2. President Sproul of the New York Federal Reserve bank and some others would have preferred a 3 percent rate, but everyone involved accepted the proposition that the rate could not be higher than existed in the markets at the time. In his authoritative account, Henry Murphy, who was in the Treasury during the war, gives the following reasons for the 2 1/2 percent rate: "First, it was the rate which had been established by the 'natural' forces of the market—i.e. the large volume of excess reserves—just prior to the entrance of the United States into the war. . . . Second, it was a simple rate—an 'even' rate, and not a 'hat size' as 2 3/8 percent or 2 5/8 per cent would have been. Third, it was one-half per cent lower than the rate which had been established in England and consequently met the requirement of 'keeping up with the Joneses' and even going them one better. . . . Fourth, it was reasonably in line with the interest rates then being paid on the long-term liabilities of financial institutions. . . . Fifth, any rate higher than 2 1/2 percent would have resulted in interest receivers 'profiting' from the war [as compared with their previous position]." (Henry C. Murphy, *The National Debt in War and Transition* [New York: McGraw-Hill, 1950], p. 26.)

3. In March, 1944, the Federal Open Market Committee adopted a resolution asking the Treasury to seek advice from the Federal Reserve through the chairman and vice-chairman of the committee, rather than from the individual members. They also asked that they be permitted to meet with the Secretary and Undersecretary alone, after

the Treasury had obtained advice on financing from all other sources. The Treasury objected to this proposal, but procedure was somewhat more satisfactory to the Federal Reserve after it was made. (U.S., Federal Open Market Committee, *Minutes 1944* [Washington, D.C.: Board of Governors of the Federal Reserve System, 1964], pp. 28–36, 65–67 [hereafter cited as FOMC *Minutes*].)

4. *New York Times*, February 6, 1946; March 31, 1946; April 2, 1946.

5. This danger was more talked about than real, because bank holdings of government securities are not valued at their market prices.

6. FOMC *Minutes*, 1946, p. 8.

7. Marriner S. Eccles, *Beckoning Frontiers* (New York: Alfred A. Knopf, 1951), pp. 429–33.

8. *Ibid.*, p. 423.

9. Interchange of December 1945 reported in letter of Fred M. Vinson to Marriner S. Eccles, March 28, 1946, quoted in U.S., Congress, Joint Committee on the Economic Report, *Monetary Policy and the Management of the Public Debt: Replies to Questions, Part 1*, 82nd Cong., 2nd sess., 1952, p. 57.

10. *New York Times*, January 17, 1946.

11. *Federal Reserve Bulletin*, May, 1946, p. 462.

12. FOMC *Minutes*, 1946, pp. 55–66.

13. *Federal Reserve Bulletin*, October, 1946, p. 1097.

14. FOMC *Minutes*, 1946, pp. 101–02.

15. *New York Times*, December 7, 1946.

16. FOMC *Minutes*, 1947, pp. 38–41.

17. FOMC *Minutes*, 1947, pp. 69–70.

18. FOMC *Minutes*, 1947, pp. 83–84.

19. FOMC *Minutes*, 1947, pp. 104–05.

20. *Federal Reserve Bulletin*, July, 1947, pp. 776–77.

21. U.S., Congress, Joint Committee on the Economic Report, *Hearings on Anti-Inflation Program as Recommended in the President's Message of November 17, 1947*, 80th Cong., 1st sess., 1947, pp. 245–47.

22. FOMC *Minutes*, 1948, pp. 50–51.

23. Eccles, *Beckoning Frontiers*, pp. 245–47.

24. When President Truman informed Eccles that he would not reappoint him as chairman he asked him to accept the vice-chairmanship, to which Eccles agreed. However, after a lapse of several months in which the appointment as vice-chairman was not forthcoming, Eccles asked the President to remove his name from consideration for that post.

25. FOMC *Minutes*, 1948, pp. 81, 95–97.

26. FOMC *Minutes*, 1948, p. 102.

27. FOMC *Minutes*, 1948, p. 119.

28. FOMC *Minutes*, 1948, pp. 122–32.

29. The Treasury claimed that its policy of using its surplus as well as the large cash balances with which it ended the war to repay short-term debts of the kind largely held by the Federal Reserve Banks and the commercial banks was responsible for the decline in Federal Reserve Bank and commercial bank holdings of government securities and for the slow growth of the money supply. In fact, the Treasury policy had only a secondary and minor effect. As long as the Federal Reserve stood ready to buy government securities at a fixed pattern of interest rates, the amount the Federal Reserve held was determined by the willingness of others to hold government securities at the fixed rates. The Federal Reserve held whatever the public, including the commercial banks, did not. The distribution of the securities held outside of the Federal Reserve banks between banks and other investors was also determined by the pattern of rates, and not

by Treasury policy. Which is not to say that the budget surplus which permitted some debt reduction was unimportant, but that the Treasury's decisions about which part of the debt to reduce were unimportant.

30. FOMC *Minutes*, 1949, pp. 81–91.

31. *Federal Reserve Bulletin*, July, 1949, p. 776.

32. U.S., Congress, Joint Committee on the Economic Report, Subcommittee on Monetary, Credit and Fiscal Policies, *Hearings*, 81st Cong., 1st sess., 1949, p. 471.

33. *Ibid.*, pp. 493–94.

34. *Ibid.*, pp. 387–418.

35. U.S., Congress, Joint Committee on the Economic Report, Subcommittee on Monetary, Credit and Fiscal Policies, *Report*, 81st Cong., 2nd sess., 1950, p. 17.

36. *Ibid.*, p. 1, fn. 1.

37. *Public Papers of the Presidents, Harry S. Truman, 1950* (Washington, D.C.: Government Printing Office, 1957), pp. 113–14.

38. U.S., Congress, Joint Committee on the Economic Report, *Monetary Policies and the Management of the Public Debt: Replies to Questions, Part 1*, 82nd Cong., 2nd sess., 1952, p. 65.

39. FOMC *Minutes*, 1950, p. 71.

40. *Ibid.*, p. 74.

41. *Ibid.*, p. 91.

42. *Ibid.*, pp. 119, 121.

43. *Ibid.*, pp. 130–32.

44. *Ibid.*, pp. 135–51.

45. *Ibid.*, p. 176.

46. *Ibid.*, p. 209.

47. *Ibid.*, pp. 176–78.

48. *Ibid.*, p. 211 (italics added).

49. *New York Herald Tribune*, December 1, 1950.

50. FOMC *Minutes*, 1951, pp. 9–12.

51. *Ibid.*, 1951, p. 6.

52. *Ibid.*, 1951, pp. 12–14.

53. U.S., Treasury, *Annual Report of the Secretary of the Treasury on the State of the Finances for the Fiscal Year Ended June 30, 1951* (Washington, D.C.: Government Printing Office, 1952), p. 616.

54. FOMC *Minutes*, 1951, p. 14.

55. *New York Times*, January 23, 1951.

56. FOMC *Minutes*, 1951, pp. 15–19.

57. *Ibid.*

58. This account of the meeting is from the confidential report written later in the day by Governor Evans of the Federal Reserve Board and approved by all members of the Open Market Committee. It was published soon after, as we shall see, without any denials from any source. (FOMC *Minutes*, 1951, pp. 24–27.)

59. Miss Doris Fleeson, a Washington newspaper columnist, spoke to some members of the board on February 4 and obtained a story of the secret session which was published on February 5. (*The Evening Star* [Washington, D.C.], February 5, 1951.) This story was discussed at a meeting of the Open Market Committee on February 6 with emphasis on the impropriety of the "leak" but with no implication that the story was incorrect. (FOMC *Minutes*, 1951, pp. 39–41.)

60. FOMC *Minutes*, 1951, p. 27.

61. *Ibid.*, p. 36.

62. *Ibid.*

63. Eccles, *Beckoning Frontiers*, pp. 490–98.

64. *New York Times,* February 6, 1951.
65. FOMC *Minutes,* 1951, p. 60 (italics added).
66. *Ibid.,* pp. 63–64.
67. *Ibid.,* pp. 67–70.
68. Allan Sproul, "The 'Accord'—A Landmark in the First Fifty Years of the Federal Reserve System," *Federal Reserve Bank of New York Monthly Review,* November, 1964, p. 232.
69. FOMC *Minutes,* 1951, pp. 113–33, 138–63, 183–92.
70. *Federal Reserve Bulletin,* March, 1951, p. 267.
71. *New York Times,* March 4, 1951.
72. *Ibid.*
73. *Ibid.,* March 7, 1951.
74. Mr. McCabe's efforts as chairman to serve as a bridge between the Federal Reserve and the Treasury in a period when their relationship was in hot dispute made him the focus of the irritation of both sides. His departure contributed to the establishment of a new relationship in which a man without that background could take a less ambivalent position.

Chapter 11 (pages 281–308)

1. U.S., Congress, Joint Committee on the Economic Report, *January 1955 Economic Report of the President, Hearings,* 84th Cong., 1st sess., 1955, p. 326.
2. U.S., Federal Open Market Committee, *Minutes* (Washington, D.C.), 1953, pp. 43–53, 109–15, 127–35, 162–75.
3. U.S., Congress, House, Committee on Ways and Means, *Excess Profits Tax Extension Hearings,* 83rd Cong., 1st sess., 1953, p. 37.
4. *Public Papers of the Presidents of the United States, Dwight D. Eisenhower, 1953* (Washington, D.C.: Government Printing Office, 1960), p. 19.
5. *Ibid.,* p. 21.
6. *Ibid.,* pp. 47, 48.
7. George M. Humphrey, *The Basic Papers of George M. Humphrey, 1953–1957,* ed. Nathaniel R. Howard (Cleveland: The Western Reserve Historical Society, 1965), p. 41.
8. Eisenhower, *Public Papers, 1953,* pp. 246, 249.
9. Robert J. Donovan, *Eisenhower: The Inside Story* (New York: Harper & Bros., 1956), pp. 108–09.
10. U.S., Bureau of the Budget, *The Budget of the U.S. Government for the Fiscal Year Ending June 30, 1954* (Washington, D.C.: Government Printing Office, 1953), p. M6; Eisenhower, *Public Papers, 1953,* pp. 319–20; U.S., Bureau of the Budget, *The Budget of the U.S. Government for the Fiscal Year Ending June 30, 1956* (Washington, D.C.: Government Printing Office, 1955), p. M4.
11. Eisenhower, *Public Papers, 1953,* p. 321.
12. *Ibid.,* pp. 114–15, 251.
13. *Ibid.,* pp. 322–25.
14. U.S., President, *January 1954 Economic Report of the President* (Washington, D.C.: Government Printing Office, 1954), p. 52.
15. Eisenhower, *Public Papers, 1953,* pp. 320–21.
16. The CED was the only general business organization to testify in favor of the extension. Mr. Reed was suspicious of this and inquired about the position taken by individual members of the committee. His suspicions were partly prompted by the fact that Mr. Marion B. Folsom, Undersecretary of the Treasury, was a former chairman of CED. However, in a statement approved in March and issued on April 7, before the Treasury began its campaign for extension of the excess-profits tax, CED's Research

and Policy Committee had recommended that the tax be retained for six months unless the administration's estimates showed a balanced cash budget for fiscal 1954. (Committee for Economic Development, Research and Policy Committee, *Tax and Expenditure Policy for 1953* [New York:Committee for Economic Development, 1953]).

17. Donovan, *Eisenhower: The Inside Story*, p. 61. Lodge and Benson were administration officials present at the June 5 Cabinet meeting when Eisenhower discussed the matter.

18. Humphrey, *Papers*, p. 71.

19. In January, 1953, a small delegation from the Committee for Economic Development called on Eisenhower to give him a memorandum of their views on the economic problems he might have to face. The memo said that, "it is of extreme importance to begin preparations now against the possibility of a depression." Eisenhower had been a trustee of CED, and there was some tendency in the press to try to deduce Eisenhower's view from the positions taken by CED. However, Eisenhower had not been active in the work of the committee, and while there was a certain similarity of outlook between Eisenhower and many other trustees of CED it was unwise to assume agreement on any specific point.

20. *New York Times*, October 23, 1952.

21. *New York Times*, October 30, 1952.

22. Humphrey, *Papers*, pp. 248–49.

23. *Public Papers of the Presidents of the United States, Dwight D. Eisenhower, 1957* (Washington, D.C.: Government Printing Office, 1958), pp. 85–86.

24. Humphrey, *Papers*, p. 255.

25. *Ibid.*, p. 264.

26. *Ibid.*, p. 83, reprinted from *U.S. News and World Report*, June 12, 1953.

27. Later estimates give the following unemployment rates:

	Aug. 1953	Dec. 1953
Not seasonally adjusted	2.4%	4.2%
Seasonally adjusted	2.7	4.5

(U.S., Department of Labor, Bureau of Labor Statistics, *Employment and Earnings*, March 1967, pp. 10, 21.)

28. The one fiscal action of 1953 which the administration later took credit for as an anti-recession measure was a speech by Secretary Humphrey to the American Bankers Association on September 22 saying that the tax reductions scheduled for January 1 would go through. Later there was discussion of whether this was really an action or whether the administration was entitled to any credit for it, since the cut was provided for by law, Congress was not in session, and it would hardly have been possible to prevent the tax cut, which the administration had promised in May, 1953, anyway. However, there does seem to have been a good deal of uncertainty, probably unjustified and partly the result of loose statements by the administration itself, and Humphrey's speech put this uncertainty to rest.

The President's message in May had referred to plans for reforming the excise tax system. This was commonly interpreted as implying some kind of sales tax, and several business organizations took the idea seriously enough to begin offering recommendations on the form of the tax. On September 20, 1953 the *New York Times* said:

"For months the Eisenhower Administration has been weighing the financial advantages against the political disadvantages of imposing a sales tax. A 5 percent tax on all commodities except food and medicines would produce an estimated $5 billion a year. The Administration needs the money badly. It is already committed to the expiration next year of post-Korean tax increases which will mean a loss of about $5 billion a year. So it must either cut the budget so hard that the defense program would suffer, or else find new revenue."

Although by 1953 a recession assured that government would not defer tax reductions that were otherwise planned, this was not yet understood by the public. Thus, A. H. Raskin in the *New York Times* of September 13, 1953, said: "If unemployment does become a threat, the Administration may have to scrap its plans for tax reduction and a balanced budget in favor of a large-scale public works program."

The administration itself contributed to the uncertainty. When asked on September 16 whether the tax cuts would go through, Secretary Humphrey replied weakly, "I do feel sincerely that the President's program of letting the excess profits tax die as well as making effective the reduction in personal income taxes on January 1 should be allowed to go through on schedule." (Humphrey, *Papers*, p. 114.)

More attention was paid to a sentence in a speech by President Eisenhower on September 21 reviewing the world situation. There he said: "There is no sacrifice—no labor, no tax, no service—too hard for us to bear to support a logical and necessary defense of our freedom." (Eisenhower, *Public Papers, 1953*, p. 598.) This set off a flurry of speculation about the President's intent. Was he breaking the news that he might after all ask for postponement of the scheduled tax reductions, or for the imposition of a new tax? It is clear in retrospect that the President was making a timeless statement with no particular relevance to 1953, but that was not clear on September 21.

It was against this background that Humphrey made his September 22 speech. According to Burns, the secretary was reluctant to give an irrevocable commitment, but he was persuaded that the economic situation required it. He said: "As I promised at the time, the excess profits tax will expire on December 31st, and there will be no request for renewal. At the same time an average of 10 percent reduction in individual income taxes is scheduled to go into effect, and it will become effective. Many further adjustments in taxes are now under consideration by the Ways & Means Committee and the Treasury for submission to the next Congress." (Humphrey, *Papers*, p. 125.) He also assured his listeners "that this Government is dedicated to the maintenance of a high level of employment and production, and it will pursue policies to foster that end. . . . " (*Ibid.*, p. 126.)

The Secretary received an ovation from the bankers. In part this was a tribute to him personally and to the argument he made in his speech for "sound money." But his assurance that taxes would go down despite the prospective deficit did not sour the bankers' reception of him. The press treated the speech as news and as an important step in the administration's attack on the economic slowdown. The story was given a two column headline on page 1 of the *New York Times* of September 23.

29. Eisenhower, *Public Papers, 1953*, p. 647.

30. *Ibid.*, p. 785.

31. At a news conference on February 3, the President was asked: "Mr. President, several top Republicans have suggested that there is something unethical, almost un-American, about using this word 'recession' in connection with the present business conditions. What could you say about that?"

The President replied in part: "I suppose we have receded from something, because not everything is at its peak today, so you have to use the word as you see fit." (*Public Papers of the Presidents of the United States, Dwight D. Eisenhower, 1954* [Washington, D.C.: Government Printing Office, 1960], p. 231.)

32. *January 1954 Economic Report of the President*, pp. 20, 22.

33. Eisenhower, *Public Papers, 1954*, p. 81.

34. See above, pp. 288–89.

35. *January 1954 Economic Report of the President*, p. 113. This formula, "The Government will not hesitate," appears so often in official statements—and not only of the Eisenhower administration—and the sequel is so consistent as to justify the warning that the phrase should be interpreted to mean "The Government will hesitate a long time."

36. Eisenhower, *Public Papers, 1954*, p. 235. The President's reply was dated February 1, 1954.

37. *Ibid.*, pp. 276, 274.

38. *Ibid.*, p. 317.

39. *Ibid.*, pp. 340, 341, 380.

40. The following references to discussions in Cabinet meetings are based on Donovan, *Eisenhower: The Inside Story*.

41. Eisenhower, *Public Papers*, 1954, p. 365.

42. U. S., President, *January 1955 Economic Report of the President* (Washington, D.C.: Government Printing Office, 1955), p. 20.

43. Donovan, *Eisenhower, The Inside Story*, p. 217.

44. Wilfred Lewis, Jr., *Federal Fiscal Policy in the Postwar Recessions* (Washington, D.C.: The Brookings Institution, 1962), p. 184.

45. A March, 1954, statement by the Committee for Economic Development, Research and Policy Committee, *Defense Against Recession* (New York: Committee for Economic Development, 1954), indicates what one of the originators of the stabilizing budget policy interpreted it to mean at that time. In 1947 the committee had described the economic condition calling for deliberate contracyclical budgetary action as "an economic crisis of great magnitude—either severe depression or major inflation." In 1954 this language was softened considerably and became "more serious situations— either for an existing recession of some severity or for a recession that is forecast with a high degree of certainty." This language had been written some months before it was released and without the recession of 1954 in mind. When it released the statement in March, the committee considered whether its policy called for extraordinary action then and decided that the situation did not fall within even the milder terms of its new position.

46. Donovan, *Eisenhower: The Inside Story*, p. 218.

47. Lewis, *Federal Fiscal Policy*, p. 164.

48. Committee for Economic Development, *Defense Against Recession*, pp. 33–34.

Chapter 12 (pages 309–18)

1. U. S., Congress, Joint Committee on the Economic Report, *January 1955 Economic Report of the President: Hearings*, 84th Cong., 1st sess., 1955, p. 329. Mr. Heller took the occasion to disagree with the assessment of the Eisenhower administration by Professor Galbraith quoted on page 283. Heller said: "I would like to start by taking a little exception to Mr. Galbraith's comments that Keynesian economics has been embraced by the present administration, if that is in effect what he is saying. Although the administration has incurred continual deficits, they have done so with evident distaste. This distate is certainly not as strong in the Council of Economic Advisers, whose excellent and beautifully written statement acknowledges the need for deficits at times, as it is in the Treasury Department, where the distaste seems to be both strong and persistent."

2. U. S., Congress, Joint Economic Committee, Subcommittee on Fiscal Policy, *Fiscal Policy Implications of the Economic Outlook and Budget Developments: Hearings*, 85th Cong., 1st sess., 1957, p. 136.

3. Joint Committee on the Economic Report, *January 1955 Hearings*, pp. 24–26.

4. *Ibid.*, p. 33.

5. But see, Committee for Economic Development, Program Committee, *Tax Policy in 1956* (New York: Committee for Economic Development, 1956), p. 5. The committee held that it was sufficient to plan for a balance in the cash budget and that there would therefore probably be room for tax reduction in 1956. (The committee

had by that time revised its 1947 position to call for an even balance in the cash budget at high employment rather than a $3 billion surplus.) This was a recommendation against too large a surplus and against excessive reliance on a surplus as a defense against inflation. As it turned out, even though expenditures increased by $7.4 billion from fiscal 1956 to fiscal 1957, there was a cash surplus of $4.5 billion in fiscal 1956 and $2.0 billion in fiscal 1957. On the basis of CED's principles there was room for a tax cut, especially since a reduction of the revenues might have restrained the growth of expenditures.

6. *The Budget of the U.S. Government for the Fiscal Year Ending June 30, 1956* (Washington, D.C.: Government Printing Office, 1955), pp. M4, 1133; *The Budget of the U.S. Government for the Fiscal Year Ending June 30, 1957* (Washington, D.C.: Government Printing Office, 1956), pp. M4, 1085; *The Budget of the U.S. Government for the Fiscal Year Ending June 30, 1958* (Washington, D.C.: Government Printing Office, 1957), pp. M4, 1067; *The Budget of the U.S. Government for the Fiscal Year Ending June 30, 1959* (Washington, D.C.: Government Printing Office, 1958), pp. M4, 879.

7. *Public Papers of the Presidents of the United States, Dwight D. Eisenhower, 1955* (Washington, D.C.: Government Printing Office, 1959), pp. 98–99.

8. *Ibid.*, p. 288.

9. *Ibid.*, p. 548.

10. *Public Papers of the Presidents of the United States, Dwight D. Eisenhower, 1956* (Washington, D.C.: Government Printing Office, 1958), p. 90.

11. Eisenhower, *Public Papers, 1955,* pp. 766–67.

12. *Public Papers of the Presidents of the United States, Dwight D. Eisenhower, 1957* (Washington, D.C.: Government Printing Office, 1958), p. 40.

13. U.S., President, *January 1955 Economic Report of the President,* (Washington, D.C.: Government Printing Office, 1955), p. 22.

14. *Ibid.*, pp. 24–25.

15. *Ibid.*, p. 66.

16. U.S., President, *January 1956 Economic Report of the President* (Washington, D.C.: Government Printing Office, 1956), p. 8.

17. *Ibid.*, pp. 11–12.

18. Joint Economic Committee, *Fiscal Policy, Hearings,* (1957) pp. 108–09.

19. Eisenhower, *Public Papers, 1957,* pp. 782–83.

Chapter 13 (pages 319–45)

1. *New York Times,* January 2, 1958.

2. *New York Times,* January 19, 1958.

3. *Public Papers of the Presidents of the United States, Dwight D. Eisenhower, 1958* (Washington, D.C.: Government Printing Office, 1959), p. 22.

4. *Ibid.*, pp. 90, 96–97.

5. *Ibid.*, p. 24.

6. U.S., President, *January 1958 Economic Report of the President,* (Washington, D.C.: Government Printing Office, 1958), p. III.

7. Dwight David Eisenhower, *Waging Peace, 1956–61* (Garden City, N. Y.: Doubleday & Company, Inc., 1965), pp. 305–06.

8. U.S., Congress, House, Committee on Ways and Means, *General Revenue Revision: Hearings,* 85th Cong., 2nd sess., 1958, pp. 1102, 1116.

9. U.S., Congress, Joint Economic Committee, *January 1958 Economic Report of the President: Hearings,* 85th Cong., 2nd sess., 1958, p. 418.

10. Eisenhower, *Public Papers, 1958,* p. 147.

11. Joint Economic Committee, *January 1958 Hearings,* p. 460.

12. *Ibid.*, p. 457.

13. *Ibid.*, p. 464. Dr. Galbraith was again generous in recognizing the administration's acceptance of "the new economics":

"Principal reliance in contending with recession will have to be on fiscal measures —on increased public outlays for civilian purposes and on tax reduction. Both have the now well-known effect of adding to the demand for goods and services and thus raising the rate of output and employment. Both accept the fact that a deficit is to be preferred to unnecessary unemployment. Incidentally, I think we are entitled to take satisfaction in the bipartisan agreement that now exists on the latter point. Those who first argued this case in detail—Prof. Alvin Hansen and notably the late Lord Keynes—were subject to no small amount of criticism and calumny. Now that they have President Eisenhower as their admitted disciple they can be regarded as admirably vindicated. We may hope that the President, who is a generous man, will one day give public recognition to his economic mentors."

At the same time that Galbraith was recognizing the Keynesian in Eisenhower he was revealing the Victorian in Galbraith, for he gave as his own view: "We can't have a deficit in both depression and boom. Life is not yet that wonderful."

14. Joint Economic Committee, *January 1958 Hearings* (testimony of Herbert Stein), p. 277.

15. Eisenhower, *Public Papers, 1958*, p. 152.

16. President Eisenhower was not present at the White House. The administration was represented by Secretaries Anderson (Treasury), Weeks (Commerce), and Mitchell (Labor), and Messrs. Saulnier (chairman of the Council of Economic Advisers), Hauge, and Adams (Presidential assistants).

17. *New York Times*, February 14, 1958; February 19, 1958.

18. U.S., Congress, Joint Economic Committee, *Report on January 1958 Economic Report of the President,* 85th Cong., 2nd sess., 1958, p. 2.

19. Wilfred Lewis, Jr., *Federal Fiscal Policy in the Postwar Recessions* (Washington, D.C.: The Brookings Institution, 1962), p. 232.

20. U.S., Congress, Senate, *Congressional Record*, 85th Cong., 2nd sess., 1958, vol. 104, pt. 2, pp. 1949–58.

21. *Ibid.*, p. 1953.

22. *New York Times*, February 24, 1958.

23. *New York Times*, February 26, 1958.

24. Eisenhower, *Public Papers, 1958*, p. 188.

25. *New York Times*, March 12, 1958.

26. In September, 1957, he set up a private committee of businessmen under the chairmanship of Thomas B. McCabe, formerly chairman of the Federal Reserve, to advise him on a tax program which might be proposed in 1958.

27. Eisenhower, *Waging Peace*, pp. 309–10.

28. *New York Times*, March 13, 1958.

29. *New York Times*, March 14, 1958.

30. U.S., Congress, Senate, *Congressional Record*, 85th Cong., 2nd sess., 1958, vol. 104, pt. 4, pp. 4274–4302.

31. *New York Times*, March 23, 1958.

32. Committee for Economic Development, Program Committee, *Anti-Recession Policy for 1958* (New York: Committee for Economic Development, 1958).

33. *New York Times*, April 7, 1958.

34. Rockefeller Brothers Fund, Special Studies Project, *The Challenge to America: Its Economic and Social Aspects* (Garden City, N.Y.: Doubleday & Company, Inc., 1958), pp. 10–11.

35. Eisenhower, *Public Papers, 1958*, pp. 234–35.

36. *Ibid.*, p. 264. Baruch had testified before the Senate Finance Committee on April 1 and told them that inflation was the great danger, that any action increasing the federal debt would spur inflation and weaken the federal credit, and that any increased spending should be matched by new taxes.

37. *New York Times*, April 6, 1958.

38. This was approximately what was said by the CED in its March, 1958, statement:

"We do not wish to fire our heaviest anti-depression artillery each time business activity slackens, simply because we fear future economic collapse. A practice of doing so in periods such as we are in today would make inflation unavoidable, and also impair the flexibility that our economy requires to adapt to changing patterns of market demand. But in a serious situation we do not want to temporize and delay because of successive forecasts that an upturn is just ahead. When the existing situation is clear, we want vigorous action by the Federal Government to help restore high employment and production, and we need the confident action of the business community based on knowledge of our longer-term growth. It is always possible to find scraps of information, seasonal movements, and signs and portents to rationalize optimism and pessimism as to near-term future events. But they provide no basis for national policy."

The existing situation (i.e., February data) did not call for strong action, but a further decline of two months would, and in that case action should not be deterred by weak forecasts and signs of recovery. The purpose of the tax cut was not merely to stop the decline but to "Provide a stimulus that would provide the basis for quickly eliminating the larger part of the gap between actual and potential production."

However, the statement was not quite ironclad. Action was to be taken if the economy declined for two more months "unless there is unmistakable evidence of quickly forthcoming improvement." This left room for judgment about how unmistakable the evidence was and how quick and large the coming improvement had to be. This judgment was later exercised to permit CED in the end to withhold a recommendation that taxes should be cut. (Committee for Economic Development, *Anti-Recession Policy*, pp. 9, 16, 20.)

39. Eisenhower, *Waging Peace*, p. 310.

40. *Ibid.*

41. U.S., Congress, Joint Economic Committee, Subcommittee on Fiscal Policy, *Fiscal Policy Implications of the Current Economic Outlook: Hearings*, 85th Cong., 2nd sess., 1958, p. 73.

42. *New York Times*, April 30, 1958.

43. *New York Times*, May 2, 1958.

44. *New York Times*, May 18, 1958.

45. Eisenhower, *Public Papers, 1958*, p. 294.

46. *Ibid.*,p. 304.

47. Eisenhower, *Waging Peace*, p. 308.

48. Eisenhower, *Public Papers, 1958*, pp. 344–45, 338.

49. *New York Times*, April 27, 1958.

50. U.S., Congress, Joint Economic Committee, Subcommittee on Fiscal Policy, *Fiscal Policy Implications of the Current Economic Outlook*, 85th Cong., 2nd sess., 1958, p. 162.

51. *New York Times*, May 9, 1958.

52. Eisenhower, *Public Papers, 1958*, p. 415.

53. *New York Times*, May 26, 1958.

54. Eisenhower, *Public Papers, 1958*, p. 424.

55. *New York Times*, May 28, 1958.

56. U.S., Congress, *Congressional Record*, 85th Cong., 2nd sess., 1958, pp. 11570–98.

57. Milton Friedman, *A Theory of the Consumption Function* (Princeton: Princeton University Press, 1957).

58. In August, 1957, Federal Reserve Chairman Martin said: "And I think in retrospect that one of the errors we made was that, in 1954, when the adjustments that were being made by the market were culminating and the base was being laid for the recovery that we had, we got a little bit enthusiastic about increasing the money supply, and we lowered our discount rate in February of 1954 from 2 to 1 3/4 percent; and then we lowered it again to 1 1/2 percent in April of that year. And we were then fomenting a psychology of expansion rather than letting the natural forces take their play, and I am inclined to think, in retrospect, that we were permitting a validation at that time of a price level which probably was not warranted, and that we therefore laid the seeds for some of our later difficulties." (U.S., Congress, Senate, Committee on Finance, *Investigation of the Financial Condition of the United States: Hearings*, 85th Cong., 1st sess., 1957, pt. 3:1305.)

59. *New York Times*, June 14, 1958.

60. Joint Economic Committee, *Fiscal Policy Implications* (1958), p. 30.

Chapter 14 (pages 346–71)

1. U.S., President, *January 1967 Economic Report of the President*, pp. 284–86.

2. Estimates of Research Department, Federal Reserve Bank, St. Louis, Mo. For method, see the Bank's *Review*, June, 1967, pp. 6–14. Figures presented here are from the Bank's *Monthly Budget Trends*, November 7, 1967.

3. *Public Papers of the Presidents of the United States, Dwight D. Eisenhower, 1959* (Washington, D.C.: Government Printing Office, 1960), pp. 196–97.

4. *Ibid.*, pp. 20–21.

5. *New York Times,*, July 22, 1959.

6. *Public Papers of the Presidents of the United States, Dwight D. Eisenhower, 1960–61* (Washington, D.C.: Government Printing Office, 1961), p. 40.

7. Eisenhower, *Public Papers, 1959*, p. 542.

8. Eisenhower, *Public Papers, 1960–61*, p. 13.

9. *Ibid.*, p. 30.

10. *Ibid.*, p. 618.

11. *Ibid.*, p. 40.

12. Eisenhower, *Public Papers, 1959*, pp. 234–35 (italics added).

13. *Ibid.*, p. 334. (speech to National Association of Manufacturers, April 23, 1959).

14. Dwight David Eisenhower, *Waging Peace, 1956–61* (Garden City, N.Y.: Doubleday & Company, Inc., 1965), p. 460. On December 12, 1958, Dr. Hauge had written President Eisenhower, in part, as follows: "To sum up these comments I would say this: a *balanced budget* for FY 1960 must be a *credible budget* if it is to help rather than hurt confidence in the management of federal finances. There are many competent analysts of revenue and expenditure trends outside the Government today whose evaluation of budget figures have great weight in the financial and business community. Our budget estimates, on both the revenue and expenditure side, have rather proved badly off over the years. With the huge error in the budget picture that has developed since January, there is heavy skepticism about these figures. They should be as realistic as possible if they are to build confidence in our fiscal policy. I realize the political advantage in putting on the defensive anyone who proposes to break a balanced budget. But such a balanced budget must strike informed people as reasonable in the first place. I personally believe that, if you find that restoring the balance takes two years, such a proposal could be sold as a reasonable and attainable goal both here and abroad. Direction may well be as important as speed in this case." (Gabriel Hauge to Dwight D. Eisenhower, December 12, 1958 [In files of Dr. Hauge, New York City]).

15. Eisenhower, *Public Papers, 1959*, pp. 12–14.

16. *Ibid.*, p. 125.

17. *Ibid.*, pp. 446–47.

18. The President's Cabinet Committee on Price Stability for Economic Growth, *Managing Our Money, Our Budget, and Our Debt, October 25, 1959* (Washington, D.C.: Government Printing Office, 1959), pp. 5–6.

19. U.S., Congress, Joint Economic Committee, *January 1960 Economic Report of the President: Hearings*, 86th Cong., 2d sess., 1960, p. 455. "We should, in my opinion, follow some variation of the stabilizing budget proposal, in which budget policy, year in and year out, would be geared to the attainment of a surplus under conditions of strong economic activity and relatively complete use of labor and other resources. On this basis, the automatic decline in revenues and increase in expenditures during a recession—reflecting in part the operation of the so-called built-in stabilizers—would generate a moderate budget deficit. In prosperous periods, tax receipts would automatically rise and certain types of spending would contract, producing a budget surplus.

"Over a period of a complete business cycle, a surplus for debt retirement would be achieved, but without the disrupting effects of necessarily trying to balance the budget in recession. While intentional variations in tax rates and spending for cyclical purposes would thus be kept to a minimum, conditions might well arise in which such variations would be desirable.

"The budget submitted by the President for fiscal year 1961 is fully consistent with this approach; about 5 per cent of Federal revenues are earmarked as a surplus for debt retirement. If economic conditions were to change drastically and recession were to set in—a contingency which does not seem likely but is of course possible—the surplus would automatically be converted into a moderate deficit as tax revenues decreased and certain types of expenditures rose."

The policy as described here, and as described by CED, does not necessarily imply that there would be a balanced budget or a surplus over a complete business cycle. That would depend on the relative duration and magnitude of the recession and prosperity within the cycle.

20. President's Cabinet Committee, *Managing Our Money*, p. 6.

21. Eisenhower, *Public Papers, 1959*, p. 12 (state of the Union message, January 9, 1959).

22. See page 348.

23. U.S., Congress, Joint Economic Committee, *Report on the January 1960 Economic Report of the President*, 86th Cong., 2nd sess., 1960, p. 5.

24. Eisenhower, *Public Papers, 1960–61*, p. 13.

25. *Ibid.*, pp. 29–30.

26. U.S., Congress, Joint Economic Committee, *January 1960 Economic Report of the President: Hearings*, 86th Cong., 2d sess., 1960, pp. 345, 348.

27. *Ibid.*, p. 404.

28. *Ibid.*, p. 239.

29. *Ibid.*, p. 409.

30. See, for example, Paul A. Samuelson, "The Effect of Interest Rate Increases on the Banking System," *American Economic Review*, 35, no. 1 (March 1945): 16–27. Arguing against increases in interest rates in 1945 Samuelson said: "They imply *enormous*, unneeded, unnecessary, undesirable and arbitrary gifts to certain investors at the expense of the Treasury. In addition, their long-run harmful effects greatly outweigh, in my opinion, the doubtful minor benefits in controlling a hypothetical situation, which can in any case be better handled in other ways, even within the framework of banking policy. I shall not dwell here on the considerations which make it seem likely that the post-war epoch will witness even lower rates than the present."

31. See for example Milton Friedman, "Comments on Monetary Policy," *Review of Economics and Statistics*, 33, no. 3 (1951):186–91. This article contains an early, clear statement of the idea of the fiscal-monetary mix: "Monetary and fiscal measures are substitutes within a wide range. A large budget surplus would mean that *relatively* easy money would be consistent with no (or any given degree of) inflation. A balanced budget would require tighter money to prevent inflation; a budget deficit, still tighter money."

32. Paul A. Samuelson, "Principles and Rules in Modern Fiscal Policy: A Neo-Classical Reformulation," in *Money, Trade and Economic Growth: Essays in Honor of John Henry Williams* (New York: Macmillan Co., 1951), pp. 173–74 (italics added).

33. U.S., Congress, Joint Committee on the Economic Report, *Federal Tax Policy for Economic Growth and Stability*, 84th Cong., 1st sess., 1955, p. 233.

34. *Ibid.*

35. U.S., Congress, Joint Economic Committee, *Staff Report on Employment, Growth and Price Levels*, 86th Cong., 1st sess., 1959.
"Federal fiscal policy has tended to become less restrictive with respect to the expansion of total demand." (p. 255)
"Federal fiscal policy should aim at substantially greater surpluses for any given level of desired restraint on demand than have been realized during the post-Korean period." (p. 269)

36. Joint Economic Committee, *Report on the January 1960 Report*, pp. 9–10.

37. *Ibid.*,

38. David W. Lusher, "Some Key Economic Variables in the 1960's," in *Planning and Forecasting in the Defense Industries*, ed. J. A. Stockfisch (Belmont, Calif.: Wadsworth Publishing Co., 1962).

39. Charles L. Schultze, "Lessons of Postwar Recessions," September 23, 1960, p. 50 (unpublished MS in files of Committee for Economic Development, Washington).

40. Herbert Stein and Edward F. Denison, "High Employment and Economic Growth," in *Goals for Americans* (Englewood, N. J.: Prentice-Hall, 1960), p. 184.

41. U.S., Congress, Joint Economic Committee, *Current Economic Situation and Short-Run Outlook: Hearings*, 86th Cong., 2d sess., December 1960, pp. 121–22.

42. U.S., Congress, Joint Economic Committee, *January 1961 Economic Report of the President and the Economic Situation and Outlook: Hearings*, 87th Cong., 1st sess., 1961, p. 213.

43. As Nixon later described the reasons for rejecting his suggestions:
"The matter was thoroughly discussed by the Cabinet but, for two reasons, Burns' recommendation that immediate action be taken along the lines he had suggested did not prevail. First, several of the Administration's economic experts who attended the meeting did not share his bearish prognosis of the economic prospects. Second, even assuming his predictions might be right, there was strong sentiment against using the spending and credit powers of the Federal Government to affect the economy, unless and until conditions clearly indicated a major recession in prospect." (Richard M. Nixon, *Six Crises* [Garden City, N.Y.: Doubleday & Company, Inc., 1962], p. 310) This "strong sentiment against using the spending and credit powers of the Federal Government to affect the economy" must be interpreted as meaning to *stimulate* the economy, since the administration left no doubt that it was trying to use its fiscal and monetary powers to stop inflation, defend the international position of the dollar, and encourage long-range growth.

44. Eisenhower, *Public Papers, 1960–61*, p. 618.

45. *Ibid.*, p. 935.

46. Thus Professor Paul McCracken, who was a member of the Council of Economic Advisers during those years, has said: "The 1964 tax reduction and the subsequent

return to full employment in 1965 was all the more impressive against the back-drop of the unwise decision in 1958 against tax reduction. This and the glacial pace of monetary expansion caused the subsequent failure of the economy to re-gain full employment in 1960. That was a bad decision and it was my own view at the time that it was a bad decision. It is one of the two major bungles of fiscal policy in the postwar period (the other being the January 1966 under-estimate of defense spending)." (Paul McCracken, "An Elder Statesman Looks at the New Economics," *Michigan Business Review*, 19, no. 4[1967]:15.)

    47. Eisenhower, *Waging Peace*, pp. 460, 461, 462.

    48. For a description of monetary policy in 1958–60 see Milton Friedman and Anna J. Schwartz, *A Monetary History of the United States 1867–1960* (Princeton: Princeton University Press, 1963), pp. 618–20.

    49. Paul A. Samuelson in Arthur F. Burns and Paul A. Samuelson, *Full Employment, Guideposts and Economic Stability* (Washington, D.C.: American Enterprise Institute for Public Policy Research, 1967), p. 87. "Second, I also want to agree that the Kennedy-Johnson America of the 1960's did derive considerable benefit from this investment in sadism by the second Eisenhower Administration. I don't mean merely to joke, but President Kennedy's predecessor made him look good. I think that this was true because of Eisenhower's inactivism and errors of omission. But also he created conditions which were helpful to the long expansion which we have had in the 1960's and which perhaps we still are having."

    50. Nixon, *Six Crises*, pp. 309–11.

Chapter 15 (pages 372–84)

    1. His father, Joseph Kennedy, had been chairman of the Securities and Exchange Commission in the New Deal days. In 1936 the elder Kennedy wrote a little book, *I'm for Roosevelt* (Clifton, N.J.: Reynal, 1936) which was of interest to a later generation for the statement that he wrote as the father of nine children who had no political ambitions for himself or his family.

    2. This attitude was expressed in a conversation between Kennedy and Andre Malraux in May 1962. " 'In the nineteenth century,' Malraux said, 'the ostensible issue within the European states was the monarchy vs. the republic. But the real issue was capitalism vs. the proletariat. In the twentieth century the ostensible issue is capitalism vs. the proletariat. But the world has moved on. What is the real issue now?' 'The real issue today,' Kennedy replied, 'was the management of industrial society—a problem,' he said, 'not of ideology but of administration.' " (Arthur M. Schlesinger, Jr., *A Thousand Days: John F. Kennedy in the White House* [Boston: Houghton Mifflin Co., 1965], p. 644.)

    3. Seymour E. Harris, *Economics of the Kennedy Years* (New York: Harper & Row, 1964), p. xi.

    4. *New York Times*, May 5, 1960.

    5. *Ibid.*, May 6, 1960.

    6. *Ibid.*, July 13, 1960.

    7. Kennedy himself was uncertain in 1960 about the feasibility of the 5 percent growth rate goal and about how to achieve it if it could be achieved at all. ". . . he quizzed every economist he met in the hope of finding out how to bring the expansion rate up to 5 percent. In August 1960 he summoned Galbraith, Seymour Harris, Archibald Cox, Paul Samuelson of the Massachusetts Institute of Technology and Richard Lester of Princeton to a seminar on the boat off Hyannis Port in an effort to learn the secret. They did their best, but there was no philosopher's stone." (Schlesinger, *A Thousand Days*, pp. 625–26.)

8. *New York Times*, July 13, 1960.

9. Television debate with Richard Nixon, September 26, 1960, reported in *New York Times*, September 27, 1960.

10. *New York Times*, October 8, 1960.

11. *New York Times*, October 31, 1960.

12. See chapter 14, p. 363.

13. John K. Galbraith, *The Affluent Society* (Boston: Houghton Mifflin, 1958).

14. Paul A. Samuelson, "Economics and the History of Ideas," *American Economic Review*, 52, no. 1(1962):17.

15. Walter W. Heller, *New Dimensions of Political Economy* (Cambridge: Harvard University Press, 1966), p. 72.

16. Theodore C. Sorensen, *Kennedy* (New York: Harper & Row, 1965), p. 117.

17. Sorensen, *Kennedy*, p. 118.

18. Friedman was quoted in *Time* (December 31, 1965, p. 65) as having said: "We are all Keynesians now. . . . " In a subsequent letter to the editor of *Time* Friedman pointed out that he had also said, . . . "nobody is any longer a Keynesian." (*Time* [February 4, 1966]:13).

19. Paul A. Samuelson, "The Economics of Eisenhower," *Review of Economics and Statistics*, 38, no. 4(1956):373.

20. Heller, *New Dimensions*, p. 8.

21. Walter W. Heller, "CED's Stabilizing Budget Policy after Ten Years," *American Economic Review*, 47, no. 5(1957):644.

22. Heller, *New Dimensions*, p. 69.

Chapter 16 (pages 385–421)

1. *New York Times*, December 24, 1960.

2. Paul A. Samuelson, "Economic Frontiers," in *The Collected Scientific Papers of Paul A. Samuelson*, 2 vols. (Cambridge: The MIT Press, 1966), 2:1479.

3. *Public Papers of the Presidents of the United States, John F. Kennedy, 1961* (Washington, D.C.: Government Printing Office, 1962), p. 19.

4. U.S., Congress, Joint Economic Committee, *January 1961 Economic Report of the President and the Economic Situation and Outlook: Hearings*, 87th Cong., 1st sess., 1961, p. 329 (testimony of Walter W. Heller).

5. *Kennedy, Public Papers, 1961*, pp. 40–53.

6. Theodore C. Sorensen, *Kennedy* (New York: Harper & Row, 1965), p. 398.

7. Samuelson, "Economic Frontiers," in *Collected Papers*, 2:1490–91.

8. Joint Economic Committee, *January 1961 Hearings*, pp. 364–65.

9. Kennedy, *Public Papers, 1961*, p. 71.

10. Walter W. Heller, *New Dimensions of Political Economy* (Cambridge: Harvard University Press, 1966), p. 32.

11. Paul A. Samuelson, "Economic Policy for 1962," *Review of Economics and Statistics*, 44, no. 1(1962):4.

12. Samuelson, "Economic Policy for 1962," p. 5.

13. Sorensen, *Kennedy*, p. 413.

14. Samuelson, "Economic Policy for 1962," pp. 3–4. Samuelson shares Sorensen's view that in some earlier period Congress had been more sophisticated but had retrogressed under the influence of the administration. In the Samuelson version the retrogression occurred during the Eisenhower administration only, but Sorensen's reference to "nearly sixteen years," quoted above, suggests that it began earlier.

15. *Kennedy, Public Papers, 1961*, p. 22.

16. *Ibid.*, p. 537.

17. Sorensen, *Kennedy*, pp. 407–08.

18. For discussions of the gap by the Council of Economic Advisers see Joint Economic Committee, *January 1961 Hearings*, pp. 321–29, and annual reports of the council in 1962 and 1963.

19. U.S., Congress, Joint Economic Committee, *Potential Economic Growth of the United States During the Next Decade*, 83rd Cong., 2nd sess., 1954; and *The Potential Economic Growth of the United States*, 86th Cong., 2nd sess., 1960.

20. There are some exceptions to this in the actual gap calculations; that is, there can be periods when there is an output gap even though unemployment is 4 percent. This is because the estimates of potential output assume that the size of the labor force and output per worker will be on their long-term trend when unemployment is 4 percent, and this is not always the case.

21. The proportionate deficiency of output is usually larger than the proportionate deficiency in employment, because low employment is likely to cause the labor force and average productivity both to be below their trends. The Council of Economic Advisers estimated that one percentage point deficiency in the employment rate would ordinarily be associated with a three percentage point deficiency of actual below potential output. This three-to-one relationship became known as "Okun's Law," after Dr. Arthur Okun who joined the staff of the Council of Economic Advisers in 1961 and later became a member and then chairman of the council. (Joint Economic Committee, *January 1961 Hearings*, pp. 373–77.)

22. See above, p. 229.

23. See above, pp. 264–66.

24. Joint Economic Committee, *January 1961 Hearings*, p. 331.

25. See above, p. 230.

26. *Kennedy, Public Papers, 1961*, p. 482.

27. *Ibid.*, p. 516.

28. *Ibid.*, p. 663.

29. U.S., Congress, Joint Economic Committee, *January 1962 Economic Report of the President: Hearings*, 87th Cong., 2nd sess., 1962, p. 17.

30. In fact, that rate was not achieved until the end of 1965, after the Vietnam War buildup was under way.

31. U.S., President, *January 1962 Economic Report of the President and Annual Report of the Council of Economic Advisers* (Washington, D.C.: Government Printing Office, 1962), p. 82.

32. Sorensen, *Kennedy*, p. 400.

33. Heller, *New Dimensions*, pp. 32–33.

34. *Kennedy, Public Papers, 1961*, pp. 684–85 (italics added).

35. Heller, *New Dimensions*, pp. 31–32.

36. *Public Papers of the Presidents of the United States, John F. Kennedy, 1962* (Washington, D.C.: Government Printing Office, 1963), p. 27.

37. *January 1962 Economic Report*, p. 84.

38. U.S., Congress, Joint Economic Committee, *January 1962 Economic Report of the President: Hearings*, 87th Cong., 2nd sess., 1962, p. 128.

39. Joint Economic Committee, *January 1962 Economic Report*, p. 657.

40. U.S., Congress, Joint Economic Committee, *Report on the 1962 Economic Report of the President*, 87th Cong., 2nd sess., 1962, p. 38.

41. *Kennedy, Public Papers, 1962*, p. 157.

42. *Ibid.*, pp. 457–58.

43. Sorensen, *Kennedy*, p. 424.

44. *Ibid.*, pp. 423–424.

45. *The Washington Post*, June 2, 1962.

46. Douglas Dillon, "Address to New York Financial Writers Association," June 4, 1962, in U.S., Congress, Senate, *Congressional Record*, 87th Cong., 2nd sess., Vol. 108, pt. 8, p. 10299.

47. *New York Times*, June 6, 1962.

48. *Ibid.*,

49. Sorensen, *Kennedy*, p. 428, (italics added).

50. Arthur M. Schlesinger, Jr., who was a special assistant to President Kennedy, reports Kennedy's view at this time as he saw it: "As between stimulus through social spending or through tax cuts, the President, I believe, political conditions permitting, would have preferred the policy which would enable him to meet the nation's public needs . . . 'You know, I like spending money,' he once told Heller. 'What I want from you are good programs by which money can be spent effectively.' . . . But political conditions, in his judgment, did not permit further social spending; they even cast doubt upon a tax cut." (Arthur M. Schlesinger, Jr., *A Thousand Days: John F. Kennedy in the White House* [Boston: Houghton Mifflin Co., 1965], pp. 649–650.)

51. Committee for Economic Development, Research and Policy Committee, *The International Position of the Dollar* (New York: Committee for Economic Development, 1961), p. 64.

52. U.S., Congress, House, Committee on Ways and Means, *President's 1961 Tax Recommendations: Hearings*, 87th Cong., 1st sess., 1961, pp. 1181–82.

53. Committee for Economic Development, Research and Policy Committee, *Fiscal and Monetary Policy for High Employment* (New York: Committee for Economic Development, 1962), pp. 31–32.

54. Sorensen, *Kennedy*, pp. 429–30.

55. Chamber of Commerce of the United States, *News Service*, release of June 29, 1962, mimeographed.

56. *Ibid.*, July 6, 1962.

57. *New York Times*, November 20, 1962.

58. Committee for Economic Development, Research and Policy Committee, *Reducing Tax Rates for Production and Growth* (New York: Committee for Economic Development, 1962).

59. The estimate of the high-employment surplus and the estimate of the normal rate of revenue growth were both lower than the Council of Economic Advisers was using at the same time.

60. *Kennedy, Public Papers, 1962*, pp. 875–87.

61. Heller, *New Dimensions*, p. 35.

62. Sorensen, *Kennedy*, p. 430.

63. Heller, *New Dimensions*, p. 39.

64. Sorensen, *Kennedy*, p. 430.

Chapter 17 (pages 422–53)

1. Theodore C. Sorensen, *Kennedy* (New York: Harper & Row, 1965), p. 424.

2. Walter W. Heller, *New Dimensions in Political Economy* (Cambridge: Harvard University Press, 1966), p. 33.

3. Sorensen, *Kennedy*, p. 424.

4. *Washington Post*, July 19, 1962.

5. *Public Papers of the Presidents of the United States, John F. Kennedy, 1962* (Washington, D.C.: Government Printing Office, 1963), pp. 616–17 (italics added).

6. Sorensen, *Kennedy*, p. 427.

7. Heller, *New Dimensions*, p. 33. The reference to Yale is to a speech the President

delivered on June 11, 1962, in which he attacked the ideas that deficits were inevitably inflationary, that the size of government was growing at an excessive rate, and that the burden of the debt was increasing dangerously.

8. Sorensen, *Kennedy*, p. 426.

9. On the other hand business was accused of pushing for a quick, permanent tax cut, including reduction of rates on corporations and upper-bracket individual incomes, in order to preclude the possibility of a more deliberate reform later which would presumably tax the rich more heavily. See testimony of Stanley H. Ruttenberg, Director, Department of Research, AFL-CIO in U.S., Congress, Joint Economic Committee, *State of the Economy and Policies for Full Employment*, 87th Cong., 2nd sess, 1962, p. 344.

10. For contemporary appraisals of the politics of the tax cut see Richard H. Rovere, "Letter From Washington," *New Yorker*, August 25, 1962, pp. 101–07; Bernard P. Nossiter, "The Day Taxes Weren't Cut," *Reporter*, September 13, 1962, pp. 25–28.

11. *Washington Post*, July 20, 1962.

12. *Kennedy, Public Papers, 1962*, pp. 736–37.

13. Chamber of Commerce of the United States, *News Service*, release of June 29, 1962, mimeographed.

14. Committee for Economic Development, Research and Policy Committee, *Reducing Tax Rates for Production and Growth* (New York: Committee for Economic Development, 1962).

15. See testimony of Stanley Ruttenberg in U.S., Congress, Joint Economic Committee, *State of the Economy and Policies for Full Employment: Hearings*, 87th Cong., 2nd sess., 1962, pp. 344–45; testimony of Walter Reuther in U.S., Congress, Joint Economic Committee, *January 1963 Economic Report of the President: Hearings*, 88th Cong., 1st sess., 1963, pp. 659–61.

16. *New York Times*, November 20, 1962.

17. Edward S. Flash, Jr., *Economic Advice and Presidential Leadership* (New York: Columbia University Press, 1965), p. 250.

18. Douglas Dillon, "Address before the Tax Executives Institute," March 19, 1962, in *Annual Report of the Secretary of the Treasury for the Fiscal Year ended June 30, 1962* (Washington, D.C.: Government Printing Office, 1963), p. 308.

19. *New York Times*, June 6, 1962; *Washington Post*, June 8, 1962.

20. Heller, *New Dimensions*, p. 72.

21. Joint Economic Committee, *January 1963 Hearings*, p. 8.

The argument assumed that the tax cut would have a substantial effect on investment, but no estimate of its size was presented. Later, testifying before the Senate Finance Committee on November 12, 1963, Heller gave an estimate of the incentive effect but with no explanation of its derivation. (U.S., Congress, Senate, Committee on Finance, *Revenue Act of 1963: Hearings*, 88th Cong., 1st sess., 1963, p. 1583.)

22. Heller, *New Dimensions*, p. 72.

23. Flash, *Economic Advice*, pp. 253–69 relates some of the discussions within the administration as later reported by economists who participated in them.

24. *New York Times*, January 28, 1963.

25. January, 1963, press conference on the economic report, quoted in Hobart Rowan, *The Free Enterprisers* (New York: G. P. Putnam's Sons, 1964), p. 236; also Heller testimony in Joint Economic Committee, *January 1963 Hearings*, pp. 38–39.

26. *Kennedy, Public Papers, 1962*, p. 868.

27. "Why a Tax Cut is Unlikely in '63," *U.S. News & World Report*, December 17, 1962, pp. 42–43.

28. Sorensen, *Kennedy*, p. 429.

29. *Business Week*, January 5, 1963, p. 16.

30. *Ibid.*, January 19, 1963, p. 24.

31. *New York Times*, January 28, 1963.

32. *Ibid.*, January 23, 1963.

33. *Business Week*, February 9, 1963, p. 24.

34. *Public Papers of the Presidents of the United States, John F. Kennedy, 1963* (Washington, D.C.: Government Printing Office, 1964), p. 96.

35. *Business Week*, February 9, 1963, p. 24.

36. *Kennedy, Public Papers, 1963*, pp. 216–17.

37. *Ibid.*, pp. 236–37.

38. Formation of the Business Committee for Tax Reduction in 1963 was suggested by Treasury Undersecretary Fowler after the President's January tax message. Its leadership consisted mainly of businessmen who had favored tax reduction before the President's message. They were men of unquestionable financial soundness—the presidents or board chairmen of the Ford Motor Co., the Pennsylvania Railroad, the Connecticut General Life Insurance Co., the American Can Co., etc. The committee had about 3,000 members, spent about $150,000, and issued 24 press releases. Its members made the views of the committee known to individual congressmen and senators by mail, telephone, and personal visit. Aside from the administration, the Business Committee was the most effective lobby in support of large and prompt tax reduction.

39. *Kennedy, Public Papers, 1963*, p. 332.

40. *New York Times*, May 1, 1963.

41. *Ibid.*, May 21, 1963.

42. As finally enacted the bill contained 24 percent of the revenue-raising reforms originally recommended by the administration and 59 percent of the revenue-losing reforms in the individual income tax (Joseph A. Pechman, "Individual Income Tax Provisions of the Revenue Act of 1964," [*Journal of Finance*, vol. 20] May 1965 p. 256.)

43. Arthur Burns suggested that if expenditures could not be substantially held down the income tax cut might be accompanied by the imposition of a federal sales tax or other indirect tax. (Joint Economic Committee, *January 1963 Hearings*, p. 494.)

44. Joint Economic Committee, *January 1963 Hearings*, p. 46.

45. *Ibid.*, p. 55.

46. *Ibid.*, pp. 494–95.

47. *Ibid.*, pp. 773–85.

48. *Ibid.*, pp. 595–601.

49. U.S., Council of Economic Advisers, *Annual Report* (Washington, D.C.: Government Printing Office, 1963), p. 54.

50. Congressman Thomas Curtis showed great interest in the monetary, or as he called it, "debt management," aspects of the tax cut. His position was that if the deficit were financed by borrowing outside the banking system it would not be expansionary, but if it were financed by borrowing from the banking system it would be inflationary. Therefore, tax reduction that increased the deficit would either fail of its expansive purpose or cause inflation. For an exposition of Congressman Curtis' views on this subject see his speech on the tax bill, U.S., Congress, House, *Congressional Record*, 88th Cong., 1st sess., 1963, vol. 109, pt. 13, p. 17911.

51. *Ibid.*, p. 17907.

52. *Ibid.*, pp. 17908–9.

53. *Newsweek*, October 7, 1963, p. 31.

54. U.S., Congress, Senate, Committee on Finance, *Revenue Act of 1963: Hearings*, 88th Cong., 1st sess., 1963, pp. 1231–32.

55. At the time of the assassination, Secretaries Dillon, Hodges, Wirtz, Freeman, and Udall and Economic Council Chairman Heller were in a plane over the Pacific enroute to Japan. When the news was received the plane returned to the United States. On the trip back, according to Manchester, the conversation turned to Johnson's quali-

ties and policies: "No one could say much for LBJ's grasp of economics. They weren't even sure he understood the Keynesian theory behind the proposed tax cut." (William Manchester, *The Death of a President* [New York: Harper & Row, 1967], p. 360.) However an understanding of Keynesian theory was not necessary to support the tax cut, and whether or not he understood Keynesian theory Lyndon Johnson supported the tax cut.

56. *Public Papers of the Presidents of the United States, Lyndon B. Johnson, 1963–1964* (Washington, D.C.: Government Printing Office, 1965), bk. 1, pp. 9–10.

57. Rowland Evans and Robert Novak, *Lyndon B. Johnson: The Exercise of Power* (New York: The New American Library, 1966), pp. 370–72.

58. Evans and Novak; *Lyndon B. Johnson*, p. 372. Evans and Novak do not think that Johnson's budget restraint was necessary to the passage of the tax bill. However the administration had so much to gain—in eliminating uncertainty, bitterness, and delay in the passage of the tax bill—that a strong effort to hold down the budget for fiscal 1965 was inevitable. President Kennedy had been pointing in the same direction before his death.

Chapter 18 (pages 454–68)

1. See Lloyd A. Free and Hadley Cantril, *The Political Beliefs of Americans* (New Brunswick: Rutgers University Press, 1967).

2. "Firstly, he [Winston Churchill] saw 'the lack of any central organisation of industry, or any general and concerted control either of ordinary government work, or of any extraordinary relief works.' He felt it should be possible for 'some authority in some Government Office' to 'exert a powerful influence over the general distribution of government contracts,' after foretelling 'the whole situation in advance.' He adopted an almost Keynesian position, when he advocated the need to have 'in permanent existence certain recognized industries of a useful, but uncompetitive character, like afforestation, managed by public departments and capable of being expanded or contracted according to the needs of the labour market, just as easily as you can pull out the stops or work the pedals of an organ.' This would at least limit, if not eradicate, unemployment." (Randolph S. Churchill, *Winston S. Churchill: Young Statesman 1901–1914* in *Winston S. Churchill*, 2 vols. to date, [Boston: Houghton Mifflin Co., 1967], 2:293.)

3. Twenty years after the war this was still regarded as major evidence of the potency of fiscal policy. It was the only evidence cited by Samuelson in his textbook. "The war years have shown fiscal policy to be a powerful weapon." (Paul A. Samuelson, *Economics: An Introductory Analysis*, 6th ed. [New York: McGraw Hill, 1964], p. 347.) The 5th edition, in 1961, had said: "The war years have shown fiscal policy to be a very powerful weapon." (*Ibid.*, 5th ed., p. 386).

4. Norman B. Ture, "Discussion," in *Fiscal Policy and Business Capital Formation* (Washington, D.C.: American Enterprise Institute for Public Policy Research, 1967), p. 202. "Perhaps the least demanding test the full-employment surplus thesis should be asked to pass is that changes in the rate of change of gross national product should be of opposite sign to changes in the full-employment surplus. Beginning with the first quarter of 1948 and continuing through the last quarter of 1966, the signs of the respective changes [are] the same—therefore wrong—in 37 of the 74 quarterly observations." Ture shows similar negative results if changes in the surplus are related to changes in the growth of GNP two, three, or four quarters later.

5. See Harry G. Johnson, "The *General Theory* after Twenty-Five Years," *American Economic Review*, 51, no. 2 (May 1961):11: "The statistical estimation of the consumption function offered itself as an important exercise for the emerging discipline of econometrics; and an early analysis of time-series and cross-section data seemed abundantly to

confirm the hypothesis that consumption is a stable function of income. Alas for the consumption function, it dismally failed the test of forecasting postwar unemployment. This failure, together with the paradox disclosed by Kuznets' data on the long-run constancy of the savings ratio, prompted a rapid independent development of the theory of the consumption function, and led to substantive modifications of Keynesian income theory."

6. In 1967 Professor Paul Samuelson recalled some of the early studies which "demonstrated" the unimportance of money and concluded: "Well, that was the 1939 view. Unfortunately, some people get frozen into what they learned in their youth, and those views still prevail in some circles. Still, those fellows are dying out in this country." (Paul A. Samuelson, "Money, Interest Rates and Economic Activity: Their Interrelationship in a Market Economy," in *Money, Interest Rates and Economic Activity* [New York: The American Bankers Association, 1967], p. 41.)

7. For an indication of the extent of differences of opinion and the difficulty of resolving them see articles by Ando and Modigliani, DePrano and Mayer, Friedman and Meiselman, in *American Economic Review*, 55(September, 1965).

8. Thus, according to Professor Otto Eckstein, "Nevertheless, CED policy would have worked tolerably well in the last 15 years, probably better than actual policy a good part of the time. And that is not a small recommendation." (Otto Eckstein, *Public Finance* [Englewood Cliffs, N.J.: Prentice-Hall, 1964], p. 98.)

Index